THE WESLEYAN EDITION OF THE
WORKS OF HENRY FIELDING

———

THE JACOBITE'S JOURNAL
AND RELATED WRITINGS

HENRY FIELDING

The Jacobite's Journal and Related Writings

EDITED BY

W. B. COLEY

WESLEYAN UNIVERSITY PRESS

1975

First American Edition
Library of Congress Catalog Card Number: 73–17030

ISBN 0 8195 4072 2

Printed in Great Britain
at the University Press, Oxford
by Vivian Ridler
Printer to the University

IN MEMORIAM

B. L. C.

1892–1961

PREFACE

THE Wesleyan edition of the works of Henry Fielding has as its primary aims a fuller definition of the canon and the establishment of a reliable text according to modern bibliographical standards. Accordingly, the editors' duty is to supply the reader with whatever is relevant to the immediate context and essential meaning of their respective texts. They will not, in this place at least, attempt interpretations or 'readings' of their texts. In short, the Wesleyan Fielding is a textual, not a critical, edition.

The principles underlying the text of the present volume and the detailed procedures which were followed in establishing that text are set forth by Professor Bowers in his essay immediately following the General Introduction. Because the text of this volume has had to be more conservatively handled than certain other Fielding texts, the interested reader is invited to read Professor Bowers's essay in the *Joseph Andrews* volume for a sense of how the bibliographical principles of the Wesleyan edition affect the handling of more sophisticated problems.

The present volume provides a useful first example of how the edition as a whole attempts to combine chronological with generic coverage wherever possible. As the largest item in the volume, *The Jacobite's Journal* has both a real and a titular prominence. Were the plan of the edition strictly and solely chronological, *The Jacobite's Journal* would be grouped with, say, Fielding's contributions to his sister's *Familiar Letters between the Principal Characters in David Simple* (1747). Such a grouping, though it would preserve chronology, would obscure the generic clustering so characteristic of Fielding's output. Instead the *Journal* is here grouped with Fielding's other political writings occasioned by the ministerial changes of 1747-8.

Roughly three-quarters of the present volume has never been published since the originals of Fielding's own lifetime. Arthur Murphy, whose 1762 edition tyrannized Fielding studies for so many years, prints only two of the 49 numbers of *The Jacobite's Journal* and neither of the two political pamphlets. The so-called Henley edition (1903), which is the edition most frequently relied on by modern scholars, follows Murphy in its selection of only two numbers of the *Journal* and adds the *Proper Answer* but not the *Dialogue*. Henley's text is of no help to the modern bibliographer, however, and since Henley provides not a single explanatory note, it can fairly be said that there has never been an annotated edition of any of the material in the present volume. For these reasons, as well as for the reason that this material is extraordinarily topical in nature, both the Introduction and the explanatory notes are full.

As *The Jacobite's Journal* progresses, there are signs either that Fielding's own hand grew careless or that other hands were helping. Since the present editor is unable to resolve the question of authorship, he includes, upon advice, all 49 numbers of the original, even those which consist mostly of reprintings from other authors.

As perhaps only those who have done scholarly editing can know, projects of this kind are the result of many years' work and much assistance. The years one can only lament. The assistance, on the other hand, is gratifying testimony to the unselfish nature of scholarship. My debts are many. My own university has been generous with both financial support and periodic release time. The opportunities afforded by such support were enlarged by grants-in-aid from the American Philosophical Society and the American Council of Learned Societies. The latter also appointed me a research fellow in 1963–4.

Because the material of this volume is ephemeral and unusually dispersed, I have had occasion to draw upon the resources and courtesy of many institutions, in America and abroad. I wish especially to thank the staffs of the British Museum, the Bodleian Library, the National Library of Scotland, the Warburg Institute, the John Rylands Library, and the Public Record Office (London); those of the New York Public Library, the Huntington Library, and the William Andrews Clark Memorial Library; and those of Wesleyan, Yale, and Harvard Universities.

I have also been the beneficiary of many unrecorded individual kindnesses. Those of us who were in on the edition from the start know the crucial role played by my colleague Richard L. Greene, who, though no Fielding scholar himself, got us the support of those who were, thereby assuring the unique publishers' co-operation which the edition currently enjoys. Before his death Charles B. Woods, possibly the most knowledgeable Fielding person of us all, proffered kindness and learning in equal amounts; his loss has affected the edition personally and professionally. The working editors and the advisory editors of the edition have been helpful in many ways. Martin C. Battestin, James L. Clifford, Louis A. Landa, Henry K. Miller, and James M. Osborn read portions of the manuscript at various stages, as did Hugh Amory, who in addition gave me the benefit of his expertise in eighteenth-century law. In moments of bibliographical despair I sought calming counsel of Allen Hazen. William B. Todd took the trouble to enlarge on his published views of the printing vagaries of the *Dialogue*. My friend J. B. Trapp, librarian of the Warburg Institute, helped me greatly in matters having to do with the attribution of the woodcut at the head of the early numbers of *The Jacobite's Journal*. Without the privilege of working in Mr. Wilmarth S. Lewis's great collection at Farmington, I should doubtless have missed, among other things, the way in which Fielding's trail crossed that of Horace Walpole when they were both writing what amounted to political journalism. For assistance in the collations and in the assembling of textual appendixes I am indebted to Keith Reierstad, whose accuracy and eminent good sense saved me from many blunders as the project neared completion.

For one's maiden voyage in bibliographical waters one could hardly hope for a better guide than Fredson Bowers. Not only did he establish the principles which the editors of this edition will follow, but he also elucidated these principles to those who, like myself, were encountering them for the first time. His patience in going over my painfully marked-up copy must be seen to be appreciated. Whatever rigour the handling of the present text possesses is owing to his precept and his example. Whatever falls short of his high standard is of course my fault.

During long projects like this one the editor requires personal as well as professional sustenance. The Dedication of the volume alludes to my principal debt, an inexpressible one in every way. My own family has been patient and supportive beyond my legitimate expectations. I wish I had not tested them so much.

W. B. C.

LIST OF CONTENTS

ABBREVIATIONS

Apology	*An Apology for the Conduct of a late celebrated second-rate Minister.* London, 1747.
Baker	*A Catalogue of the Entire and Valuable Library and Books of the Late Henry Fielding, Esq; ... sold by Auction by Samuel Baker.* [London, 1755].
CGJ	*The Covent-Garden Journal,* by Sir Alexander Drawcansir, Knt. Censor of Great Britain. London, 4 January–25 November 1752.
Coxe, *Pelham*	William Coxe. *Memoirs of the Administration of the Right Honourable Henry Pelham.* 2 vols., London, 1829.
Cross	Wilbur L. Cross. *The History of Henry Fielding.* 3 vols., New Haven, Conn., 1918.
DA	*The Daily Advertiser.* London, 1731– .
Dialogue	*A Dialogue between a Gentleman from London, Agent for two Court Candidates, and an Honest Alderman of the Country Party.* London, 17 47.
Dudden	F. Homes Dudden. *Henry Fielding, his Life, Works, and Times.* 2 vols., Oxford, 1952.
EHR	*The English Historical Review.*
GA	*The General Advertiser.* London, 1744– .
GEP	*The General Evening Post.* London, 1733– .
GM	*The Gentleman's Magazine.* London, 1731– .
Hansard	*The Parliamentary History of England, from the Earliest Period to the Year 1803.* Vols. xiii [1743–47] and xiv [1747–53], London, 1812, 1813.
Henley	*The Complete Works of Henry Fielding, Esq. With an Essay on the Life, Genius and Achievement of the Author,* by *William Ernest Henley, LL.D.* 16 vols., London, 1903.
JEGP	*Journal of English and Germanic Philology.*
JJ	*The Jacobite's Journal,* by John Trott-Plaid, Esq. London, 5 December 1747–5 November 1748.
Joseph Andrews	Henry Fielding. *Joseph Andrews,* ed. Martin C. Battestin. Oxford and Middletown, Conn., 1967.
Journals of . . . Commons	*Journals of the House of Commons.*
LEP	*The London Evening-Post.* London, 1727– .
Lodge, *Studies*	Sir Richard Lodge. *Studies in Eighteenth-Century Diplomacy, 1740–1748.* London, 1930.

Loeb	The Loeb Classical Library.
London Stage	*The London Stage, 1660–1800.* Part 3 [*1729–47*], ed. Arthur H. Scouten. 2 vols., Carbondale, Ill., 1961. Part 4 [*1747–76*], ed. George Winchester Stone, Jr. 3 vols., Carbondale, Ill., 1962.
Miscellanies (1743)	*Miscellanies, by Henry Fielding Esq; Volume One,* ed. Henry Knight Miller. Oxford and Middletown, Conn., 1972.
MLN	*Modern Language Notes.*
MLR	*Modern Language Review.*
MP	*Modern Philology.*
N&Q	*Notes and Queries.*
OE	*Old England; or, The Broadbottom Journal.* London, [*1743–47*], 1747– .
OED	*Oxford English Dictionary.*
Plomer, *Dictionary*	*A Dictionary of the Printers and Booksellers . . . in England, Scotland and Ireland from 1726 to 1775,* ed. H. R. Plomer *et al.* Oxford, 1932.
PQ	*Philological Quarterly.*
Proper Answer	*A Proper Answer to a Late Scurrilous Libel.* London, 1747.
SB	*Studies in Bibliography.*
Statutes at Large	*The Statutes at Large, from Magna Charta to . . . 1761,* ed. Danby Pickering. Cambridge, 1762– .
Stephens, *Catalogue*	*Catalogue of Prints and Drawings in the British Museum.* Division I (*Political and Personal Satires*), ed. Frederic G. Stephens. Vol. iii, part i, London, 1877.
TP	*The True Patriot: and The History of Our Own Times.* London, 12 November 1745–17 June 1746.
Yale Walpole	*The Yale Edition of Horace Walpole's Correspondence,* ed. W. S. Lewis. New Haven, Conn., 1937– .

GENERAL INTRODUCTION

I. BIOGRAPHICAL CONTEXT

THE writings included in the present volume represent what might be called the final phase of Fielding's *political* journalism, and the short period which covers their composition and publication marks an important transition in Fielding's personal career. During the years 1747 and 1748 he published the last of the writings by which he was enabled to end a decade of political hackwork with an appointment as a Justice of the Peace for Westminster.[1] If lacking in prestige and far short of what he might reasonably have expected—Cross conjectures, plausibly enough, that Fielding wished to end his career on the King's Bench like his cousins the Goulds[2]—the appointment was at least more stable than political journalism and made very different demands on its occupant. After he took up his magistracy, late in 1748,[3] Fielding's tendentious writings became of another sort altogether. Perhaps no less designed to draw him to the attention of the politicians, but in both text and tone far more public minded and non-partisan, they are in the main documents of sociology or law.

In 1747, however, *Tom Jones* was still unfinished, the long courtship of the politicians still unfruitful, the traditionally presumed financial worries presumably still unresolved. Regrettably we know very few of the facts. It has often been said of Fielding that we know less about him than about any other eighteenth-century writer of comparable importance, and certainly the biographical details of this period of his life are dismayingly scarce or contradictory. There were, we can conjecture, two more or less unsatisfactory sources of regular income available to him: barrister's fees and political hackwork. Of the two, oddly enough, less is known at present about the former,

---

[1] For the intricacies of this reward see W. B. Coley, 'Fielding's Two Appointments to the Magistracy', *MP*, lxiii (1965), 144–9.

[2] Cross, ii. 96.

[3] He seems to have been holding court by 2 November 1748, three days before the date of the last issue of the *JJ*. See Archibald Bolling Shepperson, 'Additions and Corrections to Facts about Fielding', *MP*, li (1954), 217.

B

and much of what is known is anecdotal, malicious to a degree, and unreliable. No one has been able to say for certain that Fielding was still travelling the Western Circuit as late as 1747 and 1748. Arthur Murphy, his earliest biographer, speaks of 'repeated shocks of illness' and 'frequent intermissions' of his subject's attendance at the bar 'from this time' (after the publication of *Joseph Andrews*),[1] but Murphy does not supply precise dates or supporting evidence. The closest student of Fielding's legal career postulates that Fielding did not attend the spring assizes in 1748. *The Jacobite's Journal* ran a mistaken obituary notice about his cousin Henry Gould, then on the circuit himself, and had Fielding also been on the circuit, so the argument runs, the obituary, which originated with another paper, would not have been allowed to stand in *The Jacobite's Journal*.[2] This is typical of the sort of reasoning to which the biographers are driven by the lack of firm evidence. In the present instance it would be at least equally logical to argue that the appearance of the mistaken obituary notice indicated Fielding's absence from London, and hence his absence from a position of careful control over the contents of his paper. All an editor can now say is that until the Western Circuit archives unlock their secrets (if any),[3] we must remain in relative ignorance concerning the extent of Fielding's activity as a barrister.

There are, of course, a few records and anecdotes pertaining to the period covered by the present volume. Fragmentary for the most part, they speak, however ambiguously, more to the question of his finances than to the question of his exact legal obligations. Legal records show, for example, an adverse judgment of £400 by the King's Bench against Fielding and his friend James Harris, author of 'Hermes', both of whom had pledged their lands and chattels as surety in a case of defaulted debt involving Arthur Collier, a fellow townsman from the Salisbury days and friend of the family.[4] For technical reasons an execution for the entire amount was taken out against Fielding in June 1746, the month

---

[1] 'Essay on the Life and Genius of Henry Fielding, Esq;' in *Works* (London, 1762), i. 38, 37.

[2] B. M. Jones, *Henry Fielding, Novelist and Magistrate* (London, 1933), pp. 99–100.

[3] Herbert Du Parcq, Foreword to B. M. Jones, *Henry Fielding, Novelist and Magistrate*, p. 7, speaks of the absence of records about Fielding in the archives of the Western Circuit.

[4] J. Paul de Castro, 'Fielding and the Collier Family', *N&Q*, 12th Ser. ii (5 Aug. 1916), 104–6.

in which he stopped publishing *The True Patriot*, and Cross suggests that there may have been a causal relationship between the two events.[1] Once again the clinching evidence is lacking. We do not know how much of the total obligation Fielding actually did pay, though he did record his hatred of Collier in a letter written in the last year of his life.[2] It is possible to argue that the court's acceptance of Fielding as surety for such an amount bespoke a certain degree of financial substance. Even the charming anecdote about his putting off the tax collector with the remark that 'Friendship has called for the money and had it;—let the collector call again' is deeply compromised by the records of his regular payment of taxes during this period on the second largest house in Old Boswell Court.[3] *The Annual Register* for 1762 tells another anecdote, a 'tradition' among the lawyers on the Western Circuit, which touches briefly on both his legal activities and his finances. According to this tradition, after he had waited on the judges for two or three years without much success, Fielding published proposals for a new law book and circulated them around the country, thereby markedly increasing his practice, which, 'thus suddenly increased, almost as suddenly declined'.[4] Cross conjectured that the anecdote in *The Annual Register* had confused the proposals for a law book with proposals referring to publication of the *Miscellanies* in 1743.[5] We know now that such was not the case. Advertisements for the law book have recently been discovered among the newspapers of 1745, and there is gossip, malicious, to be sure, of a projected law book in the Opposition journal *Old England*, during 1748 and 1749.[6] But even this evidence does not permit any very strong assertion about the precise details of Fielding's professional life in 1747 and 1748.

[1] ii. 44.

[2] Letter to John Fielding [n.d., n.p.], presumably from Lisbon in August–September 1754; cited by Cross, iii. 57. Unpublished letters from Fielding to Harris, in the Malmesbury papers, may yield further information about both the Collier litigation and Fielding's financial obligations during this period.

[3] *GM*, lvi (1786), 659–60, and John Nichols, *Literary Anecdotes of the Eighteenth Century* (London, 1812), iii. 383–4.

[4] 'Some Account of the late Henry Fielding, Esq;' in 'Characters', *Annual Register . . . for the Year 1762*, 6th ed. (London, 1805), p. 18 n.

[5] ii. 2.

[6] See William B. Coley, 'Henry Fielding's "Lost" Law Book', *MLN*, lxxvi (1961), 408–13.

Doubtless the traditional image of him as professionally frustrated and financially embarrassed is more or less true. Nevertheless, it seems equally true that the nature and significance of the kinds of writing which are included in the present volume cannot be properly explained in the old terms of the pressures of poverty. Much as some readers will wish that the author of *Tom Jones* had not stooped so low as to write anti-Catholic passages in the pamphlets or the political 'smears' in *The Jacobite's Journal*, it will not do to exaggerate the extent to which maintaining a bare subsistence *forced* him into these things. The Augustan man of letters, especially if he had no private income, was caught in what seems, retrospectively at least, like a difficult situation— halfway between the traditional relation of poet and patron, on the one hand, and the more modern relation of writer and 'audience', on the other. The effect of this literary precondition on the nature and kinds of work produced during its tenure needs to be studied much more fully than it has been.[1] There is evidence—perhaps Fielding's various pronouncements about political inconstancy in writers are part of that evidence—that Augustans were much less apologetic about it, perhaps much less depressed by it, than are modern students of the period. In Fielding's case, at any rate, the hypothesis of compelling financial need may actually becloud the issue. Furthermore, it is not yet fully proved. All the editor—as opposed to the biographer—of Fielding can do is to insist on the priority of the texts and the circumstances of their composition and publication, wherever these are known.

2. *A DIALOGUE BETWEEN A GENTLEMAN FROM LONDON ...*

The first text reproduced in the present volume is that of *A Dialogue between a Gentleman from London ... and an Honest Alderman of the Country Party*. Published on or about 23 June 1747,[2] it is the first of Fielding's political writings after the demise of *The True Patriot* in June 1746. The year's hiatus is not quite so striking or so significant as it appears to be. Presumably the masterwork, *Tom Jones*, was going on apace,[3] and also inter-

---

[1] See William K. Wimsatt, Jr., Introduction, *Alexander Pope: Selected Poetry and Prose* (Rinehart Editions 46, New York, 1951), xvi–xxi.

[2] *GA* of Tuesday 23 June 1747.

[3] Cross, ii. 100, and Dudden, ii. 585, accept the traditional dating of the commencement

venient were at least two minor works—*Ovid's Art of Love Paraphrased* and the contributions to Sarah Fielding's *Familiar Letters*[1]—which, although basically non-political in character and hence outside the scope of the present volume, do contain enough political references to show that Fielding was not so completely neglectful of his opportunities *vis-à-vis* the politicians as the year's hiatus might suggest. The Preface of the first edition of *Ovid's Art of Love Paraphrased* states that what inclined its author to publish in February 1747 a work begun 'many Years ago, though altered in some Places', was 'that Passage so justly applicable to the Glorious Duke of Cumberland, which cannot fail of pleasing every good Briton'.[2] Cumberland had recently been appointed commander-in-chief of the Allied forces in the Netherlands, and there was in many quarters a certain expectation that the imminent campaign would go well for the hero of Fontenoy and Culloden.[3] Though fulsome by modern standards, by those of his contemporaries the passage referring to Cumberland was merely conventional panegyric.[4] Placed as it was within a broader context of praise for the House of Hanover, it cannot fairly be interpreted as unusually political or partisan. On the other hand, the fact of judicious *alteration* of the text and the somewhat ostentatious way in which attention is called to this fact by the Preface do suggest a self-conscious awareness of the opportunities. Rather more surprising are the traces of political concern in his contributions to his sister's *Familiar Letters*, which appeared after several delays in April 1747.[5] The bulk of the *Familiar Letters* is totally lacking in either topicality or specific political reference, which intensifies by contrast the effect of Fielding's often bitter mixture of panegyric and complaint. His

of composition in the summer of 1746, shortly after Fielding terminated *The True Patriot*; Martin C. Battestin, co-editor of the novel for the Wesleyan edition, argues a date earlier than the Jacobite uprising, possibly as early as the winter of 1744–5.

[1] *Ovid's Art of Love Paraphrased* appeared during February 1747; *GM*, xvii (1747), 108. *Familiar Letters between the Principal Characters in David Simple* appeared on 10 April 1747; *St. James's Evening Post* of 7–9 April 1747. A third intervenient work, *The Female Husband*, which was published on or about 12 November 1746, is totally non-political.

[2] Preface, p. iii. See also the review of *The Lover's Assistant, or New Art of Love* (1760), ed. Claude E. Jones, in *PQ*, xli (1962), 587–8.

[3] Cumberland had been appointed by the terms of The Hague Convention of 12 January 1747 N.S.; *Journals of . . . Commons*, xxv. 251–6.

[4] *Ovid's Art of Love Paraphrased*, pp. 23, 25.

[5] Cross, ii. 46.

Preface is a critical document of some importance, and goes only a little out of its way to praise Lyttelton, 'that inimitable Writer' and a 'master of Style, as of every other Excellence'.[1] The major adumbrations of his concern with politics and patronage occur in 'Letter XL: Valentine to David Simple':

> The Administration of our public Affairs is, in my Opinion, at present in the Hands of the very Men, whom you, and every honest Person would wish to be intrusted with it. Amongst those, tho' there is no absolute Prime Minister, yet there is one, whose Genius must always make him the Superior in every Society, as he hath joined to the most penetrating Wit, the clearest Judgment both in Men and Things, and the profoundest Knowledge of them, of any Man, whom, perhaps the World ever saw. . . . What but a Genius of the highest kind could have preserved *Ireland* in a perfect State of Tranquility and Obedience during the late Troubles! Or what could have restored this Nation from that drooping and languid Fit of Despair, which so lately appeared in every honest Countenance, to those chearful Expectations, which the present Prospect of Things affords us?[2]

This passage, and some of its sentiments at least, will be met with again in the more tendentious pages of *The Jacobite's Journal*. In the *Familiar Letters*, however, we get a clearer sense of the strain on the man of letters from the way in which the compliment to Chesterfield modulates quickly to an almost contradictory note of complaint: 'for I think I may affirm with Truth, that there is no one Patron of true Genius, nor the least Encouragement left for it in this Kingdom'.[3] In other words, for all of Chesterfield's alleged genius in the world of affairs, the world of letters finds 'Wit and Genius being in a Manner deposed, and Impostors advanced in their Place'.[4] In its way, of course, the complaint is as conventional as the panegyric which precedes it. Both are based on the Augustan supposition of a reciprocity between affairs and letters. But behind this particular complaint there may lie a personal appeal for patronage. Curious echoes of such an appeal seem to occur in 'Letter XLI',[5] and in view of the considerable patronage accorded the *Familiar Letters* by its patient subscribers,[6] Fielding must be taken to refer more to his personal situation. If

---

[1] *Familiar Letters*, i, pp. x–xi.

[2] Ibid., ii. 295–6. The compliments are paid to Chesterfield, who had been Lord Lieutenant of Ireland (1745–6) before becoming Secretary of State for the Northern Department in October 1746.

[3] Ibid., ii. 297.   [4] Ibid., ii. 303.   [5] Ibid., ii. 306–24.

[6] Cross, ii. 47, puts the figure of subscribers at more than 500.

this be so, perhaps his later and presumably deliberate neglect of Chesterfield was founded on the awareness that the latter, for whatever reason, was no longer interested in furthering Fielding's fortunes.[1] In the absence of any 'Patron of true Genius' and of 'the least Encouragement left for it in this Kingdom' the writer in the throes of *Tom Jones* may have found it expedient in 1747 to turn once again to political journalism.

Politically speaking, the year 1747 might be said to have begun with a formal declaration, by the Prince of Wales, of a new Opposition party.[2] To the politically sophisticated the declaration may not have come altogether as a surprise. Premonitions that some sort of Opposition alignment was afoot between the Prince and the Earl of Bath (Pulteney) were communicated by Philip Yorke to his brother in a letter dated 23 December 1746.[3] The Prince's reversion—he had been prominent in the Opposition of Walpole's last years—to a position of declared hostility to the Administration was in fact perfectly characteristic of eighteenth-century politics. An heir to the throne who supported the existing ministry was the exception rather than the rule, and any declarations of allegiance by him would always be suspect.[4]

Nevertheless, when the new Opposition first made itself public, there seems to have been a certain amount of shock in the response. On 22 January 1747 the Prince's adherents forced a close division (184 to 143) over a motion to investigate the state of the Navy debt by a committee of the whole House.[5] The small size of the majority, Walpole wrote to Horace Mann, 'frightened the ministry like a bomb', and Mann, far away in Florence, confessed himself much alarmed at the possible consequences.[6] Although it was generally acknowledged, even by sympathetic observers,[7]

---

[1] For Fielding's increasing neglect of Chesterfield see below, pp. xlix–l, lxiii.

[2] Walpole to Mann, 27 January 1747 (*Yale Walpole*, xix. 360). Walpole had earlier written to Mann that 'the Prince waits for an opportunity of erecting his standard', and suggested that the Bridport by-election later in December might furnish that opportunity; *Yale Walpole*, xix. 342.

[3] B.M. Add. MS. 35363, f. 143: Philip Yorke to Joseph Yorke, 23 December 1746, as cited by John B. Owen, *The Rise of the Pelhams* (London, 1957), p. 311.

[4] Owen, *Rise of the Pelhams*, p. 311.

[5] *Journals of . . . Commons*, xxv. 256.

[6] Walpole to Mann, 27 January 1747, and Mann to Walpole, 7 March 1747 N.S. (*Yale Walpole*, xix. 360, 372).

[7] Walpole to Mann, 27 January 1747 (*Yale Walpole*, xix. 360): 'This new party wants nothing but heads.'

that the new Opposition lacked real leadership in the Commons, the Administration seems to have been apprehensive of the effects such a party might have on the House.[1] And there were good grounds for apprehension.

In the first place, the war with France had dragged on, confusedly and inconclusively, for more than a year and a half. Although tentative peace negotiations were under way at Breda, the Administration itself was by no means united on foreign policy. On the question of an early peace Newcastle, who with Hardwicke led what might be called the belligerent wing of the government, differed so radically from Pelham, who counted costs, that for a time late in 1746 the two brothers seem to have communicated with each other only through the medium of Newcastle's secretary.[2] In addition, the early optimism about the 1747 campaign in Flanders had dissipated before a steady series of French successes and of failures among the Allies to supply the manpower they had promised. Faced with imminent invasion, Zeeland, the second most important of the United Provinces, threw out its republican government for seeming too responsive to French pressures for a separate peace, and proclaimed William IV of Orange as Stadtholder, an action which was emulated by the principal cities of the other provinces. In England the sudden elevation of the Prince of Orange, who was George II's son-in-law, seemed an event of great promise. Newcastle thought it would lead to a separate peace with Spain. British diplomats counted on the Dutch finally to declare war against France and to commit themselves more vigorously to the war effort. There was even some hope of Dutch support for the retention of Cape Breton Island by England, easily the most incendiary of the popular issues.[3]

Unhappily for the Pelham ministry none of these things came to pass. Furthermore, there were grounds for apprehension in other theatres as well. The victories of the Allied forces in Italy during 1746 had done much to take the edge off English disappointment concerning the disasters in the Netherlands. Newcastle saw in the Italian successes good reason for throwing

---

[1] See below, p. xxv.

[2] B.M. Add. MS. 32709, ff. 9–12: Pelham to Andrew Stone, 4 October 1746, as cited by Owen, *Rise of the Pelhams*, p. 311 n.

[3] Lodge, *Studies*, pp. 248–50.

his energies into a plan to invade France through Provence and to seize the French naval base at Toulon, thereby presumably assuring absolute British naval supremacy in the Mediterranean, and perhaps even compelling France to detach some troops from the armies facing Cumberland in the Low Countries.[1] After some initial diplomatic and military successes the unexpected insurrection of Genoa in December 1746 cut off the army in Provence from direct land communication with Italy, and disaffection rapidly paralysed the Austrian and Sardinian allies. By 1747 the invasion of Provence, of which so much had been expected in certain quarters, was in effect a dead letter. In May 1747 the ministers of France and Spain patched up their differences sufficiently to propose that the peace conference be moved from Breda, which was in danger of French attack, to some more suitable town, for example, Aix-la-Chapelle. At that moment, however, none of the major participants really desired a prolongation, whatever the site, and so matters were suffered to rest until the results of the year's military action should move one side or the other to call for a resumption of talks.[2]

All these events—or at least their domestic repercussions—figure in the background of Fielding's *Dialogue*. But that background also comprises a number of events a good deal closer to home. As Newcastle wrote to Cumberland on 17 March 1747, the new Opposition seemed not yet to have consolidated its strength, but 'unfortunate publick events, or private disappointments, and personal views, may render that opposition formidable, which at present is far from being so.'[3] The Marquis de Tabuerniga, Newcastle's private intelligence agent, had succeeded in penetrating Leicester House circles, from which he reported on 27 April that important persons were joining the new Opposition party, some of them secretly. On 5 May he wrote to Newcastle that the Prince of Wales counted on 225 M.P.s, not counting Tories, who at this time were not wanted. The Prince's master strategy included the acquisition of some Scottish members,[4] a fact which calls attention to, though it by no means explains, the rise in professed apprehension concerning the Jacobites. In some

[1] Lodge, *Studies*, p. 198.   [2] Lodge, *Studies*, pp. 253-8.
[3] B.M. Add. MS. 32710, f. 361, cited by Owen, *Rise of the Pelhams*, p. 312 n.
[4] B.M. Add. MS. 32808, ff. 126, 167, and Sir George Young, *Poor Fred* (London, 1937), p. 201; cited in *Yale Walpole*, xix. 360 n., 412 n.

quarters uncertainty as to the whereabouts and activities of the
Young Pretender encouraged rumours that France and Spain had
secretly agreed to concert in an invasionary expedition on his
behalf, in hopes of forcing England to withdraw some of her
troops in Flanders for defence of the homeland.[1] Horace Mann,
whose post in Florence, far from the domestic scene and in the
midst of Continental Jacobitism, may account for his alarmist
tendencies, reported fears that the alleged severity with which the
rebel lords had been treated in 1746 would provoke greater
numbers to rise in the event of another invasion than had done so
in the Forty-Five.[2] Whether such views were sufficiently wide-
spread in England to be a political factor is doubtful. Horace
Walpole, who at the time of the rebel trials in 1746 had written
that 'now [unlike 1715] the city and the generality are very angry
that so many rebels have been pardoned',[3] dismissed Mann's
alarmism and, in doing so, probably represented the majority of
his countrymen.[4]

But if the threat of a Jacobite invasion under the Young
Pretender could not be taken very seriously, other Scottish
matters were. One of the most perplexing difficulties arising out
of the Union with Scotland (1707) was the difference in the administration of justice in the two countries. In England the
administration of justice was regulated by the supreme authority
of the Crown, whereas in Scotland it belonged in part, by right,
custom, or even purchase, to certain great feudal families, who
were thus able to exert what seemed to many an excessive legal
power over their vassals.[5] After the Forty-Five, as after 1715,
there was considerable talk of abolishing these heritable jurisdictions, as they were called, so that the power of the feudal lords,
many of whom had been deeply involved in the rebellion, could
not be used to force their vassals into similar actions. Under the
direction of Hardwicke, the Lord Chancellor, the intended legal
reform was first entrusted to the Scottish Lords of Sessions, who
reported back that since the heritable jurisdictions were secured,

[1] Mann to Walpole, 21 March 1747 N.S. (*Yale Walpole*, xix. 377–8; see also xix. 368, 376).

[2] Mann to Walpole, 25 April 1747 N.S. (*Yale Walpole*, xix. 392–3).

[3] Walpole to Mann, 12 August 1746 (*Yale Walpole*, xix. 296).

[4] However, the press continued to carry dispatches implying preparations for a French
invasion of Ireland on the Pretender's behalf; e.g., *DA* of 12 January 1747.

[5] Coxe, *Pelham*, i. 351; N. Tindall, Book XXVIII, sect. iii (*sub* 1747), *History of England*,
iv (London, 1789), 267.

by the articles of the Union, as rights of property, their appropriation without compensation would be illegal.[1] The inclusion of compensation payments made the Bill a money bill, and money bills had to originate in the Commons.[2] Accordingly, on 7 April 1747 a 'Bill for taking away and abolishing the heritable Jurisdictions in . . . *Scotland*' was presented to the House by the Attorney-General. After considerable discussion and frequent amendment, the Bill passed the Commons on 4 June, was reported out by the Lords on 12 June, and received the royal assent on 17 June.[3]

To judge from the printed debates and contemporary comments, the Bill was the most controversial of the entire session. Indeed, in April, according to Horace Walpole, the Administration was 'trembling at home, with fear of losing the Scotch bills for humbling the Highland chiefs'.[4] As its treatment in Fielding's *Dialogue* suggests, the Bill touched a number of sensitive spots. When he presented the original Bill from the Lords of Sessions, Hardwicke stated that his reasons for supporting it had nothing to do with the recent rebellion, the supposed disaffection among the Scots, or the supposed unfitness of the present proprietors of the jurisdictions.[5] This seems to have been the Administration position—the printed speeches of the proponents of the Bill all carefully refer to the rebellion, only to dismiss it as a genuine reason[6]—but in all likelihood the themes of unnecessary revenge and excessive punishment were prominent in the minds of many of the participants. Like Fielding's 'Alderman', opponents of the Bill argued that it was a breach of the articles of Union, particularly of the nineteenth and twentieth; that it would do away with rights and privileges which were in no way dangerous or inconvenient; and that it would produce disaffection among many of the first families of England as well as of Scotland.[7]

But concern for the sensibilities of Scotsmen, and legalism in the matter of the articles of Union, however emotional they may have been as issues, do not account for the strong controversy provoked by the Bill. A far more powerful issue, one which

[1] Hansard, xiv. 1–16.
[2] *GM*, xvii (1747), 102.
[3] *Journals of . . . Commons*, xxv. 349, 359, 386, 399, 402, 407.
[4] Walpole to Mann, 10 April 1747 (*Yale Walpole*, xix. 388–9).
[5] Hansard, xiv. 19–20.
[6] Hansard, xiv. 27–9, 43–51 n.
[7] Hansard, xiv. 30–43.

subsumed all the others and stirred up (though for different reasons) Tory and non-Tory Opposition alike, was that of the concentration of executive power. The printed speeches against the Bill emphasize that its passage would further increase the executive power of the Crown, and hence further decrease the 'liberty' of the people.[1] To the Tories, one of whose most stable characteristics was a reflexive dislike of central, as opposed to local, administration, the Bill was clearly vexatious, eliciting the kind of anti-monarchical response which Fielding's *Dialogue* cunningly describes as Jacobitism upon republican principles.[2] For its part, the non-Tory majority in the Prince of Wales's new alignment hoped to revive the old antagonism between George II and the Pelhams by harping on the theme that the King was the 'captive' of his unscrupulous ministers and must somehow be restored to the people.[3] By giving the ministry the ultimate power to appoint local sheriffs, the Bill seemed also to insure that the ministry would be able to control the local electorate through these sheriffs, who were said to have more power over the people within their jurisdictions than did their counterparts in England. At stake, according to the printed debates, were the forty-five M.P.s for Scotland.[4] If the Pelham ministry were to be unseated at a future election, the Opposition would have to block or neutralize legislation which might subject the Scottish members to undue Administration control.

For students of Fielding's political writings by no means the least interesting thing about the Bill for abolishing the heritable jurisdictions is that on its second reading George Lyttelton, Fielding's friend and political mentor, made an important speech in its favour. Horace Walpole, politically no admirer of Lyttelton, called it 'the finest oration imaginable',[5] an opinion which was more or less universal.[6] The approbation of this speech by Lyttelton's contemporaries is relevant here because it seems to have

---

[1] Hansard, xiv. 37–8.

[2] See below, p. 8.

[3] Tabuerniga to Newcastle, 27 April 1747 (B.M. Add. MS. 32808, f. 126), cited in *Yale Walpole*, xix. 360 n. See also xix. 412.

[4] Hansard, xiv. 35–7. It was an Opposition commonplace.

[5] *Letters of Horace Walpole*, ed. Toynbee, ii (Oxford, 1903), 272. Walpole dates Lyttelton's speech 16 April 1747.

[6] See Rose Mary Davis, *The Good Lord Lyttelton* (Bethlehem, Pa., 1939), pp. 192–3.

assured his preservation of it in manuscript,[1] thereby permitting a useful comparison with the arguments about the Bill in Fielding's *Dialogue*, which takes essentially the same position and utilizes essentially the same arguments for it.[2]

The general issue of Jacobitism was considerably stimulated by two other popularly related events of the spring. The trials of the rebel lords in 1746 were doubtless too faint in the public memory to have been an effective election issue a year later,[3] but the trial and subsequent execution of Simon Fraser, 11th Baron Lovat, in March–April 1747 furnished an excuse to revive the issue.[4] Lovat, with an impeccable record of Jacobitism dating back to the seventeenth century, was the stuff of which legends are made. He captured the public's imagination, if not its sympathy, by the colour and force of his personality and by the composure with which he faced his execution. But, except for some parliamentary soul-searching about the way the legalities had been handled,[5] there does not seem to have been any great resentment of the trial or its verdict. The larger issue of Administration clemency (or brutality) lingered on in altered forms, however, as in the claims of certain segments of the Opposition that the remedial legislation affecting the Highlands was at bottom motivated only by a spirit of vengefulness on the part of the English.[6] And it could also be revived in the service of the issue of Jacobitism *per se*, as is evidenced by the way politicians of both sides managed to relate Lovat's trial to another event of the same period.

On 19 March 1747, which curiously enough was the last day of Lovat's trial, a Tory faction calling itself 'The Independent Electors of the City and Liberty of Westminster' held its anniversary feast at Vintner's Hall.[7] First organized in 1741 for the purpose of supporting Opposition candidates in the Westminster

---

[1] It is one of only four that he preserved; Davis, p. 191. Hansard, xiv. 43–51, claims to reprint the speech 'from his own copy'.

[2] Particularly in the supposed threat to the 18th article of the Union; cf. Hansard, xiv. 45–6 and *Dialogue*, below, pp. 50–1. Most supporters of the Bill emphasized the 19th article instead. Lyttelton may well have helped Fielding with the *Dialogue*.

[3] Evidently Fielding did not think so, for their trials seem to be included in his general reference to the legal proceedings against the rebels, *Dialogue*, pp. 15–16.

[4] Lovat's trial lasted seven days: 9–11, 13, 16, 18–19 March 1747; *Journals of . . . Commons*, xxv. 314–15, 317–18, 320–1. Lovat was executed on 9 April.

[5] Having to do with the Lords' refusal to permit Lovat's counsel to examine and cross-examine witnesses; *Journals of the House of Lords*, xxvii. 19, and *Yale Walpole*, xix. 396 n.

[6] See, for example, Hansard, xiv. 36–7.   [7] *DA* of 20 March 1747; *GM*, xvii (1747), 150.

elections of that year, the Independent Electors 'agreed to meet monthly to commemorate the noble struggle they . . . made to assert their privileges'.¹ These meetings were customarily held on the first Friday of each month. The anniversary feast, on the other hand, seems to have been a movable feast, which raises the question whether it was planned to coincide with Lovat's trial. In any case, the 1747 feast at Vintner's Hall took place in an aura of bad feeling. According to the newspaper accounts, the Independents drank a number of neo-Jacobite toasts, and severely beat one John Williams, keeper of the White Horse Inn in Piccadilly, who was observed to be making memoranda of the proceedings.² A complaint on Williams's behalf, made to the Commons on 24 March, stated that the occasion of the assault upon him was 'a publick Assertion made by some Persons . . . that *Fraser*, said by them to be One of the principal Witnesses against the Lord *Lovat*, was in his [Williams's] custody'.³ This connection between the Independents' feast and Lovat's trial was reinforced by the Commons' action ordering an investigating committee, to be made up of the 'managers' of the impeachment proceedings against Lovat.⁴ Lyttelton was one of the 'managers', and hence on the committee, where, according to Horace Walpole, he was plagued to death by Lord Doneraile, comptroller to the Prince of Wales, with inquiries as to the behaviour of the Opposition in 1743.⁵ The committee failed to produce a report, but echoes of the affair persisted, at least in the political literature preceding the elections. In June Fielding apparently thought the public memory of it was strong enough to justify an allusion to 'Williams' as the sort of person the 'Alderman' did not want eavesdropping while he and the 'Gentleman' discussed politics.⁶

So much for the general background of Fielding's *Dialogue*, which is nothing more or less than an electioneering pamphlet, its immediate 'occasion' being the parliamentary elections of June–July 1747. Under the septennial arrangements then in force new elections were not mandatory until the summer of 1748. However, at the end of the session, on 17 June 1747, Parliament was

---

¹ *DA* of 5 June 1741; *Yale Walpole*, xix. 388.
² *DA* of 23 March 1747; *GM*, xvii (1747), 150.
³ *Journals of . . . Commons*, xxv. 326.
⁴ Ibid.
⁵ Walpole to Mann, 10 April 1747 (*Yale Walpole*, xix. 388).
⁶ *Dialogue*, p. 7.

first prorogued and then, on the following day, dissolved by royal proclamation,[1] apparently on the advice of Hardwicke and Newcastle and against the wishes of Henry Pelham.[2] The case for a premature dissolution rested mainly on the supposed un-readiness of the Prince of Wales's Opposition party, which, in Newcastle's words, was 'yet unsupported, unconnected, and not in high reputation'.[3] To be sure, many other reasons were put forward by both sides, as Fielding's *Dialogue* indicates. England's allies were alleged to be reluctant to negotiate in good faith with a parliament that had only a year to go. Foreign policy required unequivocal signs of domestic solidarity. In addition, there was some feeling that the advantages of the successful crushing of the Forty-Five might be lost or seriously dissipated if the elections were deferred until 1748. Like Fielding's 'Alderman' the dis-gruntled electors claimed that the Administration had some 'very bad Measures now on the Tapis' and preferred to risk an election before they came to a head.[4] It was even suggested that the ministry was contemplating so pusillanimous a peace treaty that it required a hand-picked parliament to approve the treaty, and thus remove any threat of impeachment such as might have been made by a parliament selected according to the customary procedures.[5]

These and other reasons notwithstanding, the decisive argu-ment clearly lay in the ministerial expectations of 'stealing a Parliament by Surprize'.[6] Just when the intention to hold pre-mature elections first became known is not certain. Cross, un-aware of the June 23 advertisement of the *Dialogue* in the *General Advertiser*,[7] was none the less troubled by the implication that

---

[1] *Journals of . . . Commons*, xxv. 409, 412.

[2] Tabuerniga to Newcastle, 4 June 1747 (B.M. Add. MS. 32808, f. 263), cited in *Yale Walpole*, xix. 412 n. But cf. Owen, *Rise of the Pelhams*, p. 312, who states, without sup-porting evidence, that the two brothers were in agreement about dissolving Parliament at this juncture.

[3] B.M. Add. MS. 32710, f. 361, cited by Owen, *Rise of the Pelhams*, p. 312.

[4] *Dialogue*, p. 55.

[5] *A Letter from a Travelling Tutor, to a Noble Young Lord . . . containing Good Advice to the Independent Electors of Great-Britain* (London, 1747), pp. 22–4. This pamphlet pro-vides an interesting comparison with Fielding's *Dialogue*.

[6] *Dialogue*, p. 55, where it is so described by the 'Alderman' and denied by the 'Gentle-man'.

[7] Cross, ii. 58, citing *GM*, xvii (1747), 300, dates the *Dialogue* from June, without giving any specific date. The *GA* advertisement of Tuesday 23 June reads 'This Day at Noon will be Published . . .'. Further advertisements appeared in the *GA* through Saturday 27 June.

Fielding had turned out a work of more than ninety pages between June 18 and the end of the month. Fielding, he states, must have been 'in the secret',[1] which is possibly true, but by no means necessarily true. The 'secret' was let out in the public press some time during the first week of June.[2] Fielding may have known the 'secret' before it became public—perhaps he was told by Lyttelton, who seems to have influenced the *Dialogue* in other ways—but we no longer need the hypothesis of privileged information to account for rapid publication, and there is no evidence for such an hypothesis.

Internal evidence does not permit any certainty as to the date of composition, but at least it does not contradict the date suggested by external evidence. Always excepting the presumption of new elections, a presumption made by the informed public during the first week in June, the latest datable allusion in the *Dialogue* is to the so-called 'Scotch bills', that is, the Bill for abolishing the heritable jurisdictions and the Bill 'for taking away the Tenure of Ward-holding in *Scotland*'.[3] When the 'Alderman' alludes to the former of these as 'the late Bill',[4] can we be sure he means that the Bill has already achieved passage and is now in fact an Act? Or does he mean merely that the Bill was introduced and discussed *lately*? If we take the former meaning as the more likely, then the earliest time at which one could afford to talk of the heritable jurisdictions Bill as passed, or even as good as passed, was about June 4, the date when the Commons defeated a motion to defer consideration of the amendments for two months.[5] As for the

---

[1] Cross, ii. 58.

[2] *GM*, xvii (1747), 265–7, reprints from the *London Courant* of 6 June 1747 a piece entitled 'Reasons why we should acquiesce in the *Dissolution* of the Parliament'; and pp. 275–6 reprint from the *Westminster Journal* of June 6 a piece entitled 'Topics of Self-Enquiry for Electors, and Candidates before Voting'. On June 4 the Prince of Wales may have signalized his final, unhappy awareness of the 'secret' by offering terms to the Tories, who had hitherto been excluded from his party; B.M. Add. MS. 35870, ff. 129–30, cited by Owen, *Rise of the Pelhams*, p. 312. However, rumours of an impending election had been circulated by the Opposition press since early May. See, for example, *LEP* of 30 April–2 May 1747.

[3] For the former, see above, pp. xxvi–xxviii. The second Bill sought to do away with the feudal right of the clan chiefs to claim military service as a condition of tenancy. Presented to Commons on 30 April, it too received the royal assent on 17 June; *Journals of . . . Commons*, xxv. 371, 376, 392–4, 404.

[4] *Dialogue*, p. 50.

[5] *Journals of . . . Commons*, xxv. 402. The Commons then voted to send the Bill back to the Lords with certain minor amendments. Although ultimate approval by the two bodies

Bill's taking away the tenure of ward-holding, it was being, in Walpole's words, 'whittled . . . down' by emendations as late as 16 June, the penultimate day of the session.[1] All this suggests that the last sixth of the *Dialogue*, roughly speaking, is not likely to have been written before 4–16 June, and in all likelihood was written later. A kind of confirmation for a late date of composition comes from the printing history of the *Dialogue*. The manuscript ledgers of William Strahan, the printer, record, apparently in conjunction with other printing costs of the *Dialogue*, the expenditure of an unspecified amount 'For Drinkmoney to the Men'.[2] This unusual expense was in general allowed only when the pressmen were required to work overtime in the interests of haste.[3] Further evidence of haste in the printing of the *Dialogue* appears on the last leaf of the pamphlet, where two separate lists of errata have been entered in such a manner as to produce a total of five variant states.[4] The nature of these variants is such that we may infer printing by half-sheet imposition, a method economical not only of type but also of time. If the bibliographer is corrrect in his assumption that the list of errata originated outside the printing shop,[5] the impression of hasty production might well be extended to include the preparation of the manuscript copy itself. On the whole, then, the available evidence favours a date of composition not greatly in advance of publication on 23 June 1747.

It does not seem to have been noticed previously that, although certainly applicable to the 1747 elections in general, the *Dialogue* was written with a particular local election in mind. Most of the advertisements for it bear the legend, 'Earnestly address'd to the Electors of Great Britain, particularly to the glorious Independent

---

may have seemed certain at this point, the Lords in fact did not signify acceptance of the Amendments until 12 June, at which time all that remained was the royal assent of 17 June. See above, pp. xxvii, n. 3.

[1] Walpole to Mann, 10 April 1747 (*Yale Walpole*, xix. 389); *Journals of . . . Commons*, xxv. 406.

[2] 'The Strahan Papers', B.M. Add. MS. 48800, f. 58ᵛ. For Strahan, the printer of a number of Fielding's works, see below, pp. liii–liv.

[3] J. Paul de Castro, 'The Printing of Fielding's Works', *The Library*, 4th Ser. i (1921), 261; William B. Todd, 'Three Notes on Fielding', *Papers of the Bibliographical Society of America*, xlvii (1953), 71.

[4] Todd, 'Three Notes on Fielding', p. 72, describes four variants and offers a conjectural account of their genesis. A fifth state, unknown to Todd, is noted in the Textual Appendix below, pp. 437–8.

[5] Todd, 'Three Notes on Fielding', p. 72.

Electors of Westminster',[1] and certain details of the *Dialogue* are strikingly relevant to the Westminster election. The nervousness of the 'Alderman' lest his politics should be overheard by a 'Williams' requires a reader to supply the background of the March 19 feast at Vintner's Hall. The name 'Toastum' inevitably recalls the Independents' reputation for drinking disloyal or ambiguous toasts, which was made so much of by the contemporary press.[2] 'Leadenhead' is called 'Sir Thomas', surely a name common enough to be harmless, but it happens also to have been the name of the Independent candidate, Sir Thomas Clarges (1688–1759), later, if not then, a Justice of the Peace from Aston, Herts.[3] Clarges was one of the stewards elected for the coming year by the Independent Electors of Westminster at their anniversary feast on 19 March.[4] Like 'Leadenhead', he was a 'notorious Jacobite', though it cannot now be ascertained if contemporaries thought him 'as notorious a Blockhead'.[5]

The contemporary advertisements and the possibility of such personal references notwithstanding, it seems clear that neither the characters nor the 'situation' of the *Dialogue* were intended to reflect very exactly the facts of the Westminster election, as can be demonstrated by the case of 'Mr. *Toastum*', the running-mate of 'Sir *Thomas Leadenhead*'. In the Westminster elections Sir Thomas Clarges's first running-mate was Sir John Philipps, Welsh M.P. and leading Tory spokesman in the Commons.[6] 'Mr. *Toastum*', on the other hand, is obviously no baronet, 'calls himself a Whig',[7] and seems designed to represent the general

---

[1] The legend appears in an advertisement in the second number of *The Jacobite's Journal* (12 December 1747), which may imply that it had Fielding's approval.

[2] *GM*, xvii (1747), 150. 'Toastum' and 'Leadenhead' are the two 'country' (i.e. Opposition) candidates to whom the 'Alderman' has pledged his support.

[3] *GM*, xxix (1759), 94, and *Yale Walpole*, ix. 134 n. It could also have been applied to the other Opposition candidate, Sir Thomas Dyke, but see below, note 6.

[4] *GM*, xvii (1747), 150.

[5] *Dialogue*, p. 59.

[6] Clarges and Philipps announced their candidacies by advertisement on 15 June 1747, but on 24 June Philipps advertised his decision to withdraw, on the plea of ill health, and the next day the name of Sir Thomas Dyke was substituted. The substitution of Dyke was too late to be reflected in the *Dialogue*, so that any personal references therein would be to Philipps (*c.* 1701–64), M.P. for Carmarthen (1741–7), Petersfield (1754–61), and Pembrokeshire (1761–4); a Lord of Trade and Plantations (1744–5). See *GA* of 23, 24 June 1747; Stephens, *Catalogue*, 647; Owen, *Rise of the Pelhams*, p. 335; *Yale Walpole*, ix. 69.

[7] *Dialogue*, p. 6. He is also called, p. 59, 'a Person of known profligate Principles', but

category of independent or Opposition Whig, a category of some prominence in the Prince of Wales's plans. Whatever the nature of its relationship to the Westminster elections, the *Dialogue* addresses itself to larger party considerations.[1] Further support for this view may be found in the printing history of the pamphlet. According to the Strahan ledgers, in June the printer charged the account of Andrew Millar £12. 12s. 0d. 'For printing Dialogue between a Gentleman & Alderman Six Sheets No. 3500 @ £2:2 –p Sheet'.[2] A first printing of 3,500 copies is a large one—indeed, it is the largest recorded by Strahan for any Fielding pamphlet of the period[3]—and raises the possibility of political subsidy in the distribution. In July Strahan's ledgers record that Millar was charged for a reprinting of 1,000 copies,[4] which indicates that, subsidized or not, the *Dialogue* had good distribution and was thought useful for other elections later in that month.

3. *A PROPER ANSWER...*

In the six-month interval between the *Dialogue* (23 June) and Fielding's next pamphlet, *A Proper Answer* (24 December) the general political climate showed some interesting changes. The voting trends established by the Westminster election were, it turned out, virtually those followed by the country at large. Despite its last-minute alliance with the Tories, the Prince of

---

this may refer to his political principles, not to his private morality; cf. p. 6. No application to Philipps has been discovered.

[1] That it had broader aims may be inferred from the locale of a letter from an anonymous 'Freeholder of Middlesex', printed in *GA* of 29 June 1747. The letter is of further interest because it suggests that the ironical subtitle of the *Dialogue* may have been designed to attract the attention of readers disaffected with the Administration. The letter reads in part as follows: 'I am one, among many others, who have been deceived by the Title of a Pamphlet which is lately published, called, *A Dialogue between a Gentleman* . . . But if this Pamphlet deceived me in its Title, it has undeceived me in many Points . . . For my Part, I am not ashamed to own I have been led astray like the Alderman; like him I am convinced . . .' I owe the latter point and the citation to Martin C. Battestin.

[2] B.M. Add. MS. 48800, f. 58ᵛ. It is not clear why Strahan charged Millar for works bearing the Cooper imprint, not his own. Perhaps some private arrangement existed between Millar and Mrs. Cooper with respect to Fielding's pamphlet writings.

[3] *A Serious Address to the People of Great Britain*, which was published on or about 3 October 1745, during the emergency of the Forty-Five, comes closest to it, with a first printing of 3,000 copies; B.M. Add. MS. 48800, f. 38ᵛ.

[4] B.M. Add. MS. 48800, f. 58ᵛ. The fact that the *Dialogue* was advertised once again in December 1747 suggests that there may have been remainders from the reprinting.

Wales's Opposition party signally failed to repeat its successes of 1741—when its strength in Scotland and Cornwall had supplied the final leverage against Walpole—and showed distinct signs of insufficient preparation. The Duke of Argyll kept Scotland in line for the Administration, whereas Thomas Pitt, the Prince's election manager, simply could not deliver Cornwall in the face of enormous expenditures of Administration money.[1] Elsewhere perhaps the bitterest conflict was in Staffordshire, a county with traditional Jacobite sympathies, where the Tories actively expressed resentment at the conversion of certain of their leaders to the Administration side. The bitter campaign at Lichfield was rumoured to have cost £30,000,[2] and at the county town of Stafford Lord Chetwynd removed himself from an election marked by riots which demolished his brother's house.[3] Although Fielding was to make frequent use of the Staffordshire and Lichfield disturbances as evidence of increased Jacobitism in England, and of the need to unite behind the ministry, in other parts of the country elections seem to have been normally restrained. Indeed the final results must have given the Administration good reason to congratulate itself for having anticipated the septennial arrangements by a year. Generally accepted figures indicate the Administration won 341 seats to the Opposition's 216, a very comfortable majority of 125.[4] Electorally speaking, at least, the Pelham ministry had achieved a stability unmatched since the early days of 1739.

But if domestic affairs belied the urgency of charges that a significant element was disaffected with the Administration, foreign affairs were another matter. In the Italian theatre the failure of the Allies to take Genoa produced an even more profound stalemate there and made it clear to all participants that the decisive issue of the war had to be fought, if anywhere, on other fields. In the Netherlands, however, the Allied position was hardly more favourable to great resolutions. To be sure, on 3 May 1747 Anson and Warren had dealt a devastating blow off Cape

---

[1] Owen, *Rise of the Pelhams*, p. 314.

[2] Charles Yorke to Joseph Yorke, 6 August 1747 (B.M. Add. MS. 35385, f. 72), cited by Owen, *Rise of the Pelhams*, p. 316 n.

[3] W. Chetwynd to Andrew Stone, 15 July 1747 (B.M. Add. MS. 32712, f. 117), cited by Owen, *Rise of the Pelhams*, p. 316 n.

[4] B.M. Add. MS. 33002, ff. 440–6, cited by Owen, *Rise of the Pelhams*, p. 317. See also A. N. Newman, 'Leicester House Politics, 1748–1751', *EHR*, cci (1961), 579 and note.

Finisterre to the French armed ships and their East India fleet, thereby seriously affecting the course of affairs in both Canada and India.[1] This victory, the first truly decisive naval action in seven years of war, caused a drop of over ten per cent in the French stock market, but in England, at least among persons responsible for policy decisions, it met with a mixed reception. Inextricably committed, by treaty as well as by royal inclination, to land warfare on the Continent, the ministry at moments found itself embarrassed by the Opposition clamour that the only sane policy for England was to withdraw from her military operations in the Netherlands, even if it meant violating agreements, and to restrict operations to the area of her traditional supremacy, the sea.[2] Popularly welcome though it was, the Finisterre victory in a sense placed added burdens on an Administration already in disagreement as to the urgency of an early peace.

Though hailed by some as a moral victory and a promise of better things to come, Cumberland's defeat at Laffeldt (Var) on 2 July N.S. struck the pacific wing of the ministry as further evidence of the futility of holding out for a more advantageous situation, given the demonstrable unreliability of England's allies, the Dutch and the Austrians.[3] After Laffeldt even Cumberland, who had initially shared Newcastle's optimism about the 1747 campaign, privately declared himself for peace.[4] When Marshal Saxe proposed that he and Cumberland bypass the customary diplomatic channels and treat for peace directly with one another, the effect on the English ministers at home was remarkable.[5] To be sure, France had made peaceful overtures before, but always through the agency of Holland. Furthermore, Saxe's direct invitation to Cumberland was flattering to the Duke and hence conciliative of his father, George II. Pelham, Chesterfield, and the pacific wing were certain that peace lay within reach and that Cumberland should lose no time in arranging for the

---

[1] H. W. Richmond, *The Navy in the War of 1739–48* (Cambridge, 1920), iii. 86–94.

[2] Hints of this old dispute among advocates of a naval war and advocates of a land war appear in all the writings included in the present volume; see, for example, pp. 36, 74, 182.

[3] Lodge, *Studies*, pp. 260, 270. The French losses were in excess of 9,000, the English just under 6,000; *Oesterreichischer Erbfolge-Krieg*, ix. 628, 627.

[4] B.M. Add. MS. 32712 f. 1, cited by Lodge, *Studies*, p. 267. Cumberland did not remain pacific for long, and by autumn was once again Newcastle's ally in belligerency.

[5] The account of the Saxe-Ligonier overtures is based on Lodge, *Studies*, pp. 268–70.

first preliminaries. 'We talk of nothing but peace,' wrote Horace Walpole in July, adding significantly, 'I hope we shall not make as bad an one, as we have made a war, though one is the natural consequence of the other.'[1]

This last, of course, had always been Newcastle's point. Before the designation of the Stadtholder and certain other events of the spring and early summer, Newcastle had taken the strong line that peace, though very desirable, could only be made tolerable from a position of greater strength than the Allies occupied at the time. After Laffeldt and the French peace overtures, however, he took the slightly different line that France would stand to gain more by breaking up England's alliances—Saxe's first overtures specifically excluded all allies—than by the most advantageous terms of peace, and that therefore England would be better off risking even a worse peace provided it kept her alliances intact. The modern view is that if Newcastle had abandoned his stiffer posture, peace preliminaries might well have been settled in the autumn of 1747 instead of in April 1748. But he did not. Instead, by considerable acrimonious manœuvring he kept negotiations prolongedly non-committal until the overtures hardened into ultimata and he could persuade reluctant colleagues that preparations must be taken for a new campaign. Parliament granted what seemed like the incredible sum of eleven millions for the coming year.[2] The military convention under draft at The Hague promised, on paper, an army of more than 190,000 in the Netherlands alone.[3] And by December 1747 a veteran observer of foreign policy, old Horatio Walpole, could accuse Newcastle of having ousted Granville (Carteret) from office only to follow Granville's policy of aggressive diplomacy.[4]

With the national attitude towards renewed war effort at best ambivalent, there appeared on or about 30 November 1747 a highly incendiary antiministerial pamphlet entitled *An Apology*

---

[1] *Yale Walpole*, xix. 430–1.

[2] For a summary of the supply for 1748 see Coxe, *Pelham*, i. 381.

[3] For the terms of The Hague Convention concluded on 26 January 1748 N.S., see *Journals of . . . Commons*, xxv. 489–91. Sandwich, who signed for England, estimated that the new army might reach 198,000, 'the greatest force the Allies ever brought together'; B.M. Add. MS. 32811, ff. 54–55, cited in *Yale Walpole*, xix. 455 n.

[4] Walpole to Newcastle, 28 December 1747 (B.M. Add. MS. 32713, f. 608), cited by Lodge, *Studies*, p. 303 n. Horatio Walpole (1678–1757), brother of Sir Robert Walpole and uncle to Horace Walpole, had been ambassador to France (1724–8) and to The Hague (1733–40).

for the Conduct of a late celebrated second-rate Minister.[1] In terms of the attention it received and the controversy it stirred up, the *Apology* was one of the most effective Opposition writings of its immediate time. The reasons are not far to seek. To begin with, the 'Preface' claimed that the manuscript of the *Apology* was found among the papers of the late Thomas Winnington (1696–1746), protegé of Sir Robert Walpole, sometime junior commissioner of the treasury (1736–42) and, at his death on 23 April 1746, Paymaster-General of the Forces and 'one of his majesty's most honourable privy council'.[2] Born of a Tory family—his father had been solicitor-general under Charles II—Winnington as M.P. faithfully supported Walpole's brand of Whiggism, yet managed to keep his feet politically under the two ministries which followed Walpole's demise, thus making his career a useful 'type' for satirists of political opportunism. Winnington also achieved notoriety in death. Having contracted inflammatory rheumatism, he put himself under the care of Dr. Thomas Thompson (d. 1763), a well-known quack and, curiously enough, later Fielding's family doctor,[3] whose vigorous course of treatment, in Horace Walpole's bitter words, 'madly or wickedly . . . murdered' his patient,[4] and immediately evoked charges of malpractice and unorthodox procedures. Although the controversy surrounding the manner of his death had doubtless subsided by December 1747,[5] it could not have been without its usefulness to the author of the *Apology*. In the *Apology* Winnington is made to say that he wrote the piece to justify his parliamentary conduct and to clear his reputation from the charges of political inconstancy.[6] According to the pamphlet, as a young man he made

---

[1] *GA* of 30 November and *Whitehall Evening-Post* of 28 November–1 December 1747; also *GM*, xvii (1747), 596.

[2] *GM*, xvi (1746), 222; *Yale Walpole*, xix. 249. A public denial, over the names of H. Fox, William Bromley, and John Ingram, executors of Winnington's estate, claimed that no such manuscript was found among Winnington's papers, and offered a reward of £250 for the discovery of the true author of the *Apology*. See *Whitehall Evening-Post* of 19–21 January 1748; *GM*, xviii (1748), 56; and *GA* of 20–1 January 1748.

[3] Cross, ii. 247–8.

[4] Walpole to Mann, 25 April 1746 (*Yale Walpole*, xix. 250).

[5] Cross, ii. 72, without citing his evidence, speaks of the gossip still surrounding Winnington's death as late as December 1747. The present editor has not discovered any such evidence.

[6] *Apology*, p. 10. In the following resumé of the *Apology* all statements about historical figures are to be understood as originating in that pamphlet.

a careful study of the motives, the justice, and even the necessity of the Revolution of 1688, and concluded that even those persons most responsible for it did not intend so radical a change as in fact came to pass.[1] Accordingly, Winnington embarked on a lifelong scheme to restore the 'old Constitution' by whatsoever means seemed most effective. In pursuance of this scheme he received important tutelage from Robert Harley (1st Earl of Oxford), Charles Spencer (3rd Earl of Sunderland) and, most particularly, Sir Robert Walpole, all of whom, like 'most if not all the chief Ministers, since the Revolution, have had their Eye on the *old Constitution*'.[2] But if the chief ministers were all working to the same end, their means were often very different. The 1st Earl Stanhope, for example, outwardly a staunch Hanoverian Whig, is said by the *Apology* to have schemed to put so much power in the hands of George I that the latter would be bound to misuse it, thereby permitting a republic to rise from the ruins of monarchy and, ultimately, the 'old Constitution' from the 'Confusion of the Popular'.[3] But of all the schemes Winnington encountered, Walpole's was the simplest: 'to drain away the Riches of the Nation, and waste and enervate their Strength, so as that in Length of Time, they would come of themselves, to a Sense of their Condition, and be ready to exchange it for a better'.[4]

Originally in opposition, Winnington 'came over' to Walpole out of a conviction that in politics, as in religion, courts and ministers thrive by opposition. To his new convert Walpole stated that the major principle of his foreign policy was to support treaties and alliances which perplexed and weakened the position of Hanover. Winnington himself came to disagree with this principle because he saw that the attempts to enlarge the Electoral power in Germany in fact weakened the Hanoverian interest by intensifying the jealousy of Prussia, which considered itself excluded from leadership of the Protestant elements of Germany.[5] Walpole and Winnington also disagreed about the final effects of an English alliance with the House of Orange. The master took the view that such an alliance would so strengthen the Hanoverian interest that 'the Patriot Scheme' of restoring the 'old Constitu-

---

[1] *Apology*, pp. 16–17.   [2] *Apology*, p. 25.   [3] *Apology*, p. 26.
[4] *Apology*, p. 28.
[5] *Apology*, p. 36. It was an Opposition commonplace to argue that Newcastle had merely taken over Carteret's policy of favouring Austria at the expense of Prussia.

tion' could not be realized. The pupil, on the other hand, argued that the alliance would further alienate Prussia, as well as the Dutch republicans and France, the two latter having already considered a peace negotiation which excluded England.[1] It is on the more general topic of war or peace, however, that Winnington and his mentor have, for 1747 at least, their most apposite disagreement. Winnington argued that if England conducted a successful war, the irritation of the Bourbon powers would be increased, to the eventual discomfiture of the House of Hanover. Walpole agreed that such would likely be the result of a successful war. However, if the war were *un*successful, he thought that France would prefer to have the present Hanoverian ministry continue because the latter was doing such a good job of ruining England with taxes, increases in the national debt, and the like. By contrast the Patriot scheme of a return to the 'old Constitution' would be disagreeable to France because it would make for a stronger, sounder England.[2] Feeling as he did that under its present degenerate leadership England could never win the war, Walpole always opted for peace as more likely to introduce the conditions necessary for a return to the 'old Constitution'. He complained to Winnington that the Prince of Wales's Opposition party obstructed his every measure and, unknown to its leader, had imbibed the spirit of 1641 to the point of restoring, not the 'old Constitution', but a commonwealth. Winnington took the different view that the commonwealth scheme, 'which I knew to be that of his Opponents and many of his Abettors', would finally help the Patriot scheme, not hinder it, as it is easy to build 'in the Confusion of the Popular'.[3]

To a modern reader the unremitting irony of the *Apology* may be too cynical, too inclusive, to be effective. All those mentioned in the pamphlet—Tories, Whigs, Granvilleans, Hanoverians, Jacobites, kings, queens, ministers—are said to have the same duplicitous ends in view. Indeed, the condemnation is so sweeping that at times it seems directed more against faction and politics of any and all kinds than against merely the Pelhamite coalition.[4] Amusing though it may have been to some to observe the Administration's favourite 'smear' of Jacobitism turned back upon it, the broadly anti-political bias of the *Apology* also served

[1] *Apology*, p. 37.   [2] *Apology*, pp. 43–5.   [3] *Apology*, pp. 47–8.
[4] Something like this evaluation is made in *The Patriot Analized* (1748), pp. 5–7.

a much more serious purpose, one consistent with an important
Opposition objective. Frustrated by the need to avoid attacking
the King himself too directly, the Prince of Wales's party attempted to make much of the supposed fact—just possibly a
true fact early in 1746,[1] but certainly not true in December 1747
—that George II was the captive of his ministers and that his
captivity was significant because it marked the shift of political
power away from the locus favoured by the Opposition, in the king
and the people, toward the locus favoured by most Whigs, in the
placemen and 'professional' parliamentarians. One of the major
objectives of the *Apology*, therefore, was to associate these politicians, as represented by their principal ministers, with an atmosphere of self-seeking inconsistency and disregard for the public
weal.

There were of course other, more particular charges pendent to
the sweeping anti-politics of the *Apology*. A clue to their identification may be found in the relative unanimity with which contemporary reviewers picked them out for rebuttal. The rather
detailed review in *The Gentleman's Magazine*, for example,
itemized some of the more sensational charges made by the
Apology: that Harley had intended, though secretly, to indulge
Queen Anne's inclinations towards the 'old Constitution'; that
Godolphin, Marlborough, Sunderland, Stanhope, Walpole, as
well as the present ministry, were all Jacobites at bottom; that
George I's dislike of England had led him to consider abdication,
but not in favour of his own son, whom he hated; that France
really preferred the present, ruinous Hanoverian regime to anything the Stuart pretenders might set up. The review then quotes
at some length passages dealing with two very sensitive points,
the ruinous effects of prolonging the war and the falling off in
public morals as evidenced also in the decline of the church and
the clergy.[2]

Of these two points, the former was politically the more

---

[1] On 10–11 February 1746 the Pelhamites in the Administration, unwilling to put up any
longer with George II's obvious preference for Granville (Carteret) and Bath (Pulteney),
resigned in a body. When his favourites were unable to muster an alternative ministry, the
King was compelled to ask the Pelhams to resume their duties. The fiasco of the so-called
'forty-eight-hour ministry' gave a certain credibility to the Opposition charge that George
II was indeed a 'King in Toils'; Owen, *Rise of the Pelhams*, pp. 294–7, 299. Modern
historians are by no means agreed that George II was so dependent on his ministers.

[2] *GM*, xvii (1747), 574–5.

pressing. Ever since the 1747 elections had unequivocally established its stability at home, the Pelham administration had been able to concentrate its attention on the touchy question of how to conduct the war, clearly the most important public issue, indeed perhaps the only important public issue facing the Administration at this time. Just how important it was may be judged from the prominence given it by the Opposition press, which was not above reproving the pacific wing of the Administration in one breath and the bellicose wing in the next, according to whichever seemed about to dominate foreign policy. Although there is evidence that in November 1747 the Prince of Wales's party privately concurred in Newcastle's decision to prolong the war until a more favourable situation had been achieved,[1] the Opposition author of the *Apology* wrote one of his most lurid and effective passages on the depressing consequences of that decision.[2] Then there was the ancillary issue of whether the war should have been fought mainly on land or mainly at sea. Here at least the author of the *Apology* squares his position with that frequently taken by his party, by implying that the cost of supporting great land forces abroad and of playing paymaster to a lot of pusillanimous allies was what was ruining England financially.

In the spiritual realm, meanwhile, a general falling-off in morals could easily be postulated and then blamed on the politicians, who were assumed to have been responsible for weakening those traditional guardians of public morality, the church and the clergy, so as to be better able to shape and warp the people to their own political ends. Such a charge was an old one, of course, full of Tory and High-Church resonances from the past, and capable of incorporating an entire spectrum of issues. In the *Apology*, however, the charge is modulated from the conventional Tory expression of it, updated, as it were, to suggest that the best way to judge the true nature of the drift in ministerial politics is to take a long look at the alterations in traditional piety which are its necessary accompaniment.[3] The more practical implications of this charge are perhaps best seen in the way the *Apology* handles the case of Chesterfield. The friend of Voltaire and Montesquieu is praised—and the praise is all the more striking in a context of

---

[1] Walpole to Mann, 24 November 1747 (*Yale Walpole*, xix. 449).

[2] *Apology*, pp. 49–50. This passage is cited, in part, by *GM*, xvii (1747), 574, and Fielding's *Proper Answer*, below, p. 73. [3] *Apology*, pp. 39–40.

deliberate dispraise for other statesmen—for his fire, his wit, his oratory, indeed for his intellectual virtues. But the clear implication is that these virtues are in the service of a very strong dislike of the church and of the clergy, a dislike very different from that maintained by the author of the pamphlet, who accuses the contemporary clergy of failing to stand up for the people against the will of the politicians. Chesterfield's dislike of the church, on the contrary, is more that of a freethinker, of an atheist perhaps, and the *Apology* rather pointedly overemphasizes his connection with the Administration scheme to bring in a commonwealth.[1] Once again the 'apologist' has reversed a favourite ministerial charge. To adapt the language of Fielding's *Dialogue*, Chesterfield was a Pelhamite upon republican principles.[2]

But there is no need to quote, anachronistically, from the *Dialogue* in this connection. Among several replies specifically elicited by the *Apology* was one by Fielding himself, *A Proper Answer to a Late Scurrilous Libel, entitled 'An Apology for the Conduct of a late celebrated Second-rate Minister'*, published on or about 24 December 1747 by Mrs. Cooper, at one shilling.[3] Apparently Fielding's pamphlet underwent a last-minute change of title, for without exception the pre-publication advertisements[4] —and a number of post-publication ones as well—give the title as *A Full Answer*. In its review of the work *The Gentleman's Magazine* cites the title as *A Proper Answer*, but in the 'Register of Books' in the same issue, a register apparently drawn up on the basis of booksellers' or publishers' notices, not on the basis of actual copies received, the title is given as *A Full Answer*.[5] Since no copy bearing that title has ever been identified and since all contemporary discussions of the published work itself use the title *A Proper Answer*,[6] it seems safe to say that a change of title, not a variant impression, is the reason for the discrepancy.

[1] *Apology*, pp. 38–42.   [2] Cf. *Dialogue*, below, p. 8.

[3] See, for example, *GA* of 23–4 December; *GEP* of 19–22 December; *JJ* no. 3 of 19 December; *Whitehall Evening-Post* of 19–22, 22–4 December; and *LEP* of 22–4, 24–6 December 1747, where the advertisement in both cases reads, 'Next Thursday will be publish'd', indicating a December 31 publication date. However, this discrepancy appears to have been the result of a failure to make the necessary adjustments of the original advertising copy, in which Thursday 23 December was meant.

[4] Including, interestingly enough, the one in *JJ* no. 3 of 19 December 1747.

[5] *GM*, xvii (1747), 574, 596.

[6] See, for example, *The Patriot Analized*, p. 63. *GM*, xviii (1748), 96 lists this pamphlet among the February 1748 books. *GA* of 18 February 1748 gives that date of publication.

Like the *Dialogue*, the *Proper Answer* was published anonymously. There was, however, little serious attempt to conceal its authorship. All known states of the title page carry the legend, 'By the Author of the *Jacobite's Journal*'.¹ And it did not take long for contemporary reviewers to make the attribution by name. The review in the *GM* begins: 'This Answer is written by Mr. Fielding. . . .'² A strongly hostile pamphlet, entitled *The Patriot Analized*, described the author of the *Proper Answer* first as 'one of our scribbling Champions', referring to Fielding's well-known tenure on the journal of that name, and then as 'Mr. F—g', wielder of 'the Pen that writ *Pasquin*, *Joseph Andrews*, and the *Champion*'.³ In addition, *The Patriot Analized* presses some interesting charges. One of the speakers in the pamphlet is made to say of Fielding that 'little Notice is to be taken of one who, according to the *Comment*, wrote round the whole Compass of Parties', to which another speaker replies, 'And of Religions too'.⁴ The supposed inferiority of the *Proper Answer* is then charged to Fielding's lack of heart for the business: 'Had he not approved of the *Apology* in his Heart, you would have seen him mince and hash it so as to make half the Town weep and the other laugh.' As to the reason Fielding lacks heart for the business, *The Patriot Analized* asserts it to be the same reason he undertook *The Jacobite's Journal*, namely, the power of necessity: 'If a Man that wants Bread, can establish a Paper by the P—t Off—e taking off *Two Thousand* every week, is he not more excusable than a Man of Fortune, who votes against his Conscience and the Interest of his Country, for a Place or Pension?'⁵ To the objection that it was possibly Fielding's 'wavering Principles' which had brought him to the necessity of writing for bread, another speaker poses the question of authorship: 'What would you say, if the *Apology* had been wrote by the Answerer himself?'⁶ The pamphlet concludes

¹ This much of an attribution was made even before publication by the advertisement in *GA* of 23 December.
² *GM*, xvii (1747), 575.   ³ pp. 28, 37.
⁴ p. 29. The 'Comment' referred to is *A Free Comment on the Late Mr. W—G—N's Apology for his Conduct* (London, 1748), p. 48 of which accused Fielding of travelling 'round the whole Circle of Parties and Ministers'. Its title-page date notwithstanding, there were publication notices of *A Free Comment* at least as early as 21 December 1747. See *GA* for that date.
⁵ p. 37. The reference to the Post Office's providing free distribution for 2,000 copies per week is a reference to the *JJ*. See also below, pp. liv–lv.
⁶ p. 38. Presumably a hit at Fielding's alleged amphibiousness in politics.

its discussion of Fielding by reiterating the charge that the inferiority of his *Proper Answer* is owing to his being of the same persuasion as the 'apologist' and hence 'unwilling to efface any Impressions such a Work as the *Apology* might have made on the Mind of the Subjects'.[1]

This last charge is witty, but undemonstrable, an extension of the central ironic strategy used in the *Apology* itself. Writers, like the ministers who hire them, most often appear to reprehend policies with which they are secretly in sympathy. The fact remains, however, that the *Proper Answer* is an inferior performance, even by the standards of topical journalism. With good reason, it is defensive about its scope[2] (it frankly omits all discussion of Walpole's foreign policy, a subject to which the *Apology* devotes considerable space) as well as about its structure (toward the end of the *Proper Answer* there is considerable and admitted repetition of earlier points).[3] Compared to that of Fielding's *Dialogue*, for example, the argument of the *Proper Answer* seems unsustained and unsystematic. For present purposes these essentially 'aesthetic' considerations are relevant only in that they provoke speculation about how the pamphlet was composed. Such inferiority as the *Proper Answer* manifests may have been due to a certain haste[4] (it appeared at most a little more than three weeks after the *Apology*) or to a crowded schedule of writing (it was composed during the time Fielding was getting *The Jacobite's Journal* off the ground).[5] However, inasmuch as the *Dialogue*, a somewhat longer work, was apparently composed in a shorter time, perhaps a combination of the two factors is more likely.

On the other hand, *The Patriot Analized* may have been partly correct in attributing the inferiority of the *Proper Answer* to the ambiguity of Fielding's attitude toward consistency in politics.

---

[1] p. 38. Cross, ii. 75–6, extracts the relevant quotations from *The Patriot Analized*.

[2] 'Advertisement' of the *Proper Answer*, below, p. 63: 'All that Part [the charge that the revolution of 1688 was not intended to be so sweeping as it in fact turned out to be] therefore is waved, as well as what relates to foreign Politicks, during the Administration of the late Earl of Orford. . . .'

[3] *Proper Answer*, below, p. 82: 'I am sensible that I have, in this Pamphlet, repeated the same Thing more than once'.

[4] There is no firm evidence that the *Proper Answer*, like the *Dialogue*, was printed in a hurry, but the setting of a number of pages in the first impression suggests a certain lack of care, which may or may not have been the result of haste.

[5] The first number of the *JJ* appeared on 5 December 1747.

One must be careful, of course, not to condemn Fielding by standards not generally in force in his time. A 'foolish consistency' in politics at least was no more a hobgoblin of Georgian statesmen than it was of statesmen from many other periods. Perhaps less. However, the formation of the 'Broad-Bottom' ministry, composed as the latter was of many strange bedfellows, including some who had been violently prominent in the late Opposition to Walpole, raised the question in a more practical form. Even by the standards of contemporaries, the behaviour of the Opposition immediately after Walpole's fall from power was egregiously inconsistent, as Fielding's *The Opposition: A Vision* (1741) somewhat plaintively attests.[1] Inasmuch as the Prince of Wales, by 1737 and after, the nominal leader of the Opposition in its successful phase, was still (and unsuccessfully) opposed ten years later—and opposed, furthermore, to many of his colleagues in the earlier Opposition—it was natural that the writers of his party made an issue of political inconstancy. To this issue Fielding seems to have been remarkably sensitive. In both of what might be called his 'ministerial' periodicals, *The True Patriot* and *The Jacobite's Journal*, he published defences of the right to change one's political notions, and it is something of an object lesson in the pressures at work on the Augustan man of letters to compare the positions taken in these two journals, not only with those taken in *The Opposition* and in the political essays in *The Champion*, but also with each other. *The True Patriot*, for example, professes to wish to avoid the stigma of party journalism, 'to skreen the Author', in the words of one of the essays, 'from the Scandal of being the Tool of a Ministry'. Such dislike of faction does not mean that the journalist must be completely apolitical: 'I am engaged in no Party, nor in the Support of any, unless of such as are truely and sincerely attached to the true Interest of their Country.' Undue adherence to party, what some have traditionally called party loyalty, is in fact nothing more than 'Obstinacy'. Since the proper end of individual political action is the good of the country as a whole, and since the choice of party is only a means to that end, 'He who *adheres* to his *Cause* has no Reason of being ashamed of *leaving* his *Party*'. On the contrary, 'we shall find, that both the

---

[1] For differing readings of this ambiguous pamphlet, see Martin C. Battestin, 'Fielding's Changing Politics and *Joseph Andrews*', *PQ*, xxxix (1960), 39–40, 44–7; and W. B. Coley, 'Henry Fielding and the Two Walpoles', *PQ*, xlv (1966), 157–78.

greatest and the honestest Men that have ever flourished in this Nation have frequently changed their Parties'.[1]

But what carried conviction during the black days of the Forty-Five does not seem to have done so two or three years later. The later and more abject corollary of such high-minded, almost Bolingbrokean metafactionalism may be found in *The Jacobite's Journal* no. 17.[2] 'Why', asks Fielding in that essay, 'is he, whose Livelihood is in his Pen, a greater Monster in using it to serve himself, than he who uses his Tongue to the same Purpose?'[3] This analogy between the pen of the journalist and the tongue of the pseudo-patriot is at worst disingenuous, at best disillusioned. Elsewhere in the essay the dominant tone seems to be one of profound disaffection with the nature of politics: 'In a Time therefore of profound Tranquility, and when the Consequence, at the worst, can probably be no greater than the Change of a Ministry, I do not think a Writer, whose only Livelihood is his Pen, to deserve a very flagitious Character, if, when one Set of Men deny him Encouragement, he seeks it from another, at their Expence'.[4] It is not often that Fielding allows himself publicly to be so indifferent to the fate of ministries, even in irony. That he does allow himself to be so here, in a way confirms the position taken by *The Patriot Analized*, namely, that Fielding was not at his most comfortable when writing about the issue of political inconstancy.

Whatever his private feelings about administrations and politics in general, in the *Proper Answer* Fielding does not allow himself the luxury of neglecting to court the individual minister who wielded real power, Henry Pelham. Although the *Apology* handles him but briefly, in the *Proper Answer* Pelham is the only living minister singled out for expanded mention.[5] Fielding's panegyric of him is in the form of a defence against two charges levelled at Pelham by the *Apology*: that he was Walpole's 'creature'

---

[1] Of the preceding five quotations the first two are from *TP* no. 14 of 28 January–4 February 1746, and the last three are from 'The Present History of Great Britain' in *TP* no. 25 of 15–22 April 1746.

[2] Where Bolingbroke and his adherents saw the destruction of political parties as a necessary precondition of his idea of a Patriot King, the Pelhamites saw the destruction of political parties as a necessary precondition of *parliamentary* coalitions like the 'Broad-Bottom' ministry.

[3] *JJ* no. 17 of 26 March 1748, below, p. 214.

[4] See below, p. 215.   [5] See below, pp. 84–5.

and had merely succeeded to the latter's influence; and that he did not possess the necessary qualities to be a principal minister.[1] The charge of Walpoleism may account, at least in part, for what seems like Fielding's 'soft' attitude toward Walpole in the *Proper Answer*.[2] The fact of the matter is that Walpole and Pelham had been closely associated. If Fielding could not bring himself to offer a defence of Walpole's foreign policies, he was at least aware of the virtues of tactful silence. The charge that Pelham lacked sufficient 'head' was a commonplace of Opposition satire, which often made it part of an invidious comparison of Pelham with Newcastle in hopes of exploiting the differences between the 'two Brothers'. In his *Proper Answer* Fielding uses this charge as an 'occasion' for extolling Pelham's ministerial qualities and for asserting his primacy among the leaders of the coalition.[3] Although by December 1747 Pelham had pretty well consolidated his position as *de facto* principal of the coalition,[4] the increasing importance of foreign policy matters, which were clearly Newcastle's responsibility, seemed to some to eclipse Pelham's leadership and allowed the Opposition to play on the remote possibility that fraternal jealousy might be fruitfully increased. By calling attention to Pelham's primacy and by omitting all reference to Newcastle, who is also attacked in the *Apology*,[5] Fielding is putting himself down as not simply a ministry man, but a Pelham man. The failure, if it may be called that, to make any mention of Newcastle, even when such mention might be appropriate, is not limited to the *Proper Answer*. Throughout the entire run of *The Jacobite's Journal*, for example, there are almost no editorial references to Newcastle, whereas both Pelham and Hardwicke, the Lord Chancellor, are frequently praised.

Further evidence of the extent to which Fielding had committed himself to the ministry in general and to Pelham in particular may be seen in the failure to come to the defence of Chesterfield, whom the *Apology* anatomized in greater detail than it did any other living minister.[6] That the failure to mention

---

[1] *Apology*, pp. 32–3.

[2] See below, pp. 63, 73–4.

[3] See below, pp. 84–5. Cf. Fielding's description of the ministry in the *Familiar Letters*, above, p. xxii.

[4] Owen, *Rise of the Pelhams*, p. 318.

[5] p. 33.

[6] See esp. pp. 38–42.

Chesterfield, even after great provocation, was probably not an oversight is suggested by the fact that when the latter suddenly resigned the seals as secretary of state in February 1748,[1] his withdrawal from the Pelham ministry was neither lamented nor editorially noticed anywhere in *The Jacobite's Journal*, although the appointment of his successor, Fielding's 'princely' benefactor, the Duke of Bedford, was both noticed and applauded.[2] Yet it was Chesterfield whom Fielding could single out as recently as the *Familiar Letters* (1747) for the superiority of his 'Genius', the penetration of his wit, the charity of his judgment, and the profundity of his knowledge.[3] If the fulsomeness of the original passage can be said to contain the barest suggestion of a wish that Chesterfield might assume a dominant role in the ministry, by the time of the *Proper Answer*, eight months later, such a wish must also be said to have evaporated. Whatever the reasons—and surely one of them was Chesterfield's gradual withdrawal from active politics—the orbits of Fielding and his sometime patron were drawing apart.

Although there is every evidence that the *Proper Answer* was written with the Pelham ministry expressly in mind, there is no real evidence that the pamphlet was in any way subsidized by the ministry. The Strahan ledgers record a modest first printing of 500 copies in December 1747.[4] This is the smallest first printing of any Fielding pamphlet, except the *Dialogue between the Devil, the Pope, and the Pretender* (1745), for which the Strahan ledgers provide a record.[5] Its small size militates against the view that any ministerial subsidy was involved, although the Strahan ledgers do record a 'Second Edition' of 500 copies in January

---

[1] On 6 February 1748 he resigned as secretary of state for the Northern Department after a steady deterioration in his relationship with Newcastle.

[2] Among the 'Domestic News' items in *JJ* no. 12 of 20 February 1748. Newcastle took the opportunity to switch to the Northern Department. Bedford took the Southern, 'To the great Joy of all who wish well to the true Interest of their Country'.

[3] See above, p. xxii and note 2. The date of composition of Fielding's 'letter' (XL) is not known, but the final compliment to Chesterfield appears to refer to his statesmanship after he became secretary of state in the autumn of 1746.

[4] B.M. Add. MS. 48800, f. 58ᵛ.

[5] For the *Dialogue* of 1745 they record a first and only impression of 500 copies in October 1745. By comparison, *A Serious Address to the People of Great Britain* (1745) had a first impression of 3,000 copies and a second of 1,000; *The History of the Present Rebellion* (1745) had a first and only impression of 1,000 copies; and the *Dialogue* of 1747 a first impression of 3,500 and a second of 1,000. The non-political *Female Husband* (1746) had a first and only impression of 1,000 copies. See B.M. Add. MS. 48800, ff. 38ᵛ and 58ᵛ.

1748.¹ To judge from contemporary advertisements, which announce a 'Second Edition' as early as 2 January 1748,² not much time elapsed between the first impression (on or about 24 December 1747) and the so-called 'Second Edition', perhaps as little as eight or nine days. Were it not for the evidence of the Strahan ledgers that the two impressions were in fact extremely modest, one might have assumed a greater popularity for the *Proper Answer* than seems to have been the case. The title-page assertion of a 'Second Edition' is misleading. Eighteenth-century printers were in the habit of supplying only enough copies to meet estimated needs and then reimpressing, from standing type, if continuing demand required.³ Frequently these reimpressions were given adjusted title-pages with the legend 'Second Edition' on them, even when neither revision nor resetting was involved.⁴ Such is the case with the so-called 'Second Edition' of the *Proper Answer*, which is not truly an *edition* at all. Its differing set of press figures supports the implication of the Strahan entry, namely, that there was a reimpression from standing type, not merely a retitling of remainders from the first impression. The implication of great popular demand suggested by the use of the term 'Second Edition' does not seem to have had much effect on the sales of the *Proper Answer*. The Strahan ledgers do not list any additional impression beside the two modest ones already mentioned. There was, to be sure, a Dublin edition in duodecimo, which was apparently set up from an uncorrected copy of one of the two London impressions and not from MS.⁵ In the absence of any printer's records for the Dublin edition it is impossible to determine whether the Irish reception accorded the *Proper Answer* was better or worse than its

---

¹ B.M. Add. MS. 48800, f. 58ᵛ.

² See, for example, *JJ* no. 5 of 2 January 1748, and *GA* of the same date. The advertisement is repeated in *JJ* no. 6 and no. 7.

³ See William B. Todd, 'Recurrent Printing', *SB*, xii (1959), 189, and Arthur Friedman, 'The Problem of Indifferent Readings in the Eighteenth Century, with a Solution from *The Deserted Village*', *SB*, xiii (1960), 146.

⁴ Andrew Millar, under whose account Strahan lists the charges for printing the *Proper Answer*, told his friend David Hume, 'I said I considered yr Works as Classicks, that I never numbered ye Editions as I did in Books We wished to puff'; *Letters of David Hume*, ed. J. Y. T. Greig (Oxford, 1932), ii. 354.

⁵ Unremarked by Cross, Dudden, and the biographers, there are two copies of the Dublin edition at Yale and one at the Huntington Library. A 12mo in sixes, it collates: title page [A¹], 'Advertisement' [A²], text, pp. 5–27 A³–B⁶, C² [verso blank].

English reception. On the whole, the pamphlet does not seem to have been among Fielding's most successful political pieces.

4. *THE JACOBITE'S JOURNAL*

On Saturday 5 December 1747 appeared the first number of *The Jacobite's Journal*,[1] chronologically the third of Fielding's four essay periodicals.[2] Bearing the legend '*By* John Trott-Plaid, *Esq*' on its title-page, *The Jacobite's Journal* was a four-page weekly selling for twopence a copy.[3] Its format is more or less conventional, resembling in many ways Fielding's earlier periodicals, especially *The True Patriot* of 1745–6. The front page is devoted to editorial matter, either a lead essay or letters to the editor or both. Next come the departments of 'Foreign Affairs' and 'Domestic News', which consist of dispatches from abroad and 'straight' news items, both reprinted from other papers. To this 'news' portion of *The Jacobite's Journal* in many numbers are appended departments with titles like 'Credenda' and 'Gallimatia', made up of reprints, with short, satirical commentary, of some of the more egregious items from other papers, usually those in Opposition.[4] The remainder of *The Jacobite's Journal* is devoted to advertisements, mainly of books. The first twelve numbers carry a 'curious Frontispiece' engraved in wood and traditionally associated with Hogarth.[5] In his essay

[1] The dateline of the Yale copy of the first number reads 'Saturday, December 6, 1747'. But 6 December 1747 in fact fell on a Sunday. The B.M. copy reads 'December 5, 1747'. A correction at some point during the press run is indicated.

[2] The others, in order, are *The Champion* (1739–41), *The True Patriot* (1745–6) and *The Covent-Garden Journal* (1752).

[3] The price was given in the pre-publication advertisements, e.g. in the *Whitehall Evening-Post* of 26–8 November 1747.

[4] The satirical commentaries, with the items that occasioned them, are reprinted in Appendix VI, below, pp. 443–84. Even before he set up special departments for commenting on the news, Fielding permitted the intrusion of commentary in both 'Foreign Affairs' and 'Domestic News'.

[5] The quoted phrase is that of the pre-publication advertisements, e.g. in *The London Courant* of 4 December 1747. For the traditional association of the woodcut with Hogarth, see Horace Walpole, *Anecdotes of Painting in England* (Strawberry Hill, 1762–71; 1780), iv. 82; J. Nichols, *Biographical Anecdotes of William Hogarth* (London, 1781), p. 109; Samuel Ireland, *Graphic Illustrations of Hogarth* (London, 1833), p. 225; Stephens, *Catalogue*, pp. 672–3. The drawing from which the woodcut seems to have been derived is extant; A. P. Oppé, *The Drawings of William Hogarth* (New York, 1948), pp. 20, 45, and Plate no. 40; Frederick Antal, *Hogarth and His Place in European Art* (London, 1962), Plate no. 114. It seems probable that the drawing, not the woodcut, should be the basis of the association with Hogarth, but for a case against any Hogarth association, see W. B. Coley, 'Hogarth,

'explaining' why he dropped the frontispiece,[1] Fielding cites lack of room and the 'gross misunderstanding' of it by the public. Most commentators on the woodcut have argued that its faint execution, leading to premature wear, was responsible for the decision to drop it from the paper.[2] Samuel Ireland, however, offers another reason: 'From the strength of the impression before us, that does not appear to be the case: it may possibly have been discontinued from some political ill tendency.'[3] In view of Fielding's marked uncertainty about the success of his ironical posturing as a Jacobite, Ireland's hypothesis may possibly be the correct one. There is evidence that contemporaries did mistake the journal's irony.[4]

The colophon of the first number of *The Jacobite's Journal* reads in part as follows: 'LONDON: Printed by W. Strahan, in *Wine-Office-Court, Fleetstreet*; and Sold by M. Cooper, in *Pater-Noster-Row*, and G. Woodfall, at *Charing-Cross.*' After the first number the colophon omits Strahan's name and adds those of 'C. Corbett, in *Fleet-street*; Mrs. Nutt, at the *Royal-Exchange'.*[5] Mrs. Nutt's involvement seems to have been short-lived, however, for her name appears in the colophons only of the second and third numbers. Thereafter only Cooper, Corbett and Woodfall are listed. In publishing *The Jacobite's Journal* Fielding was working

Fielding, and the Dating of the *March to Finchley', Journal of the Warburg and Courtauld Institutes*, xxx (1967), 317–26.

[1] *JJ* no. 13 of 27 February 1748, below, pp. 172–8.

[2] For example, J. Nichols, *Biographical Anecdotes*, 2nd ed. (London, 1782), p. 234; John Nichols and George Steevens, *Genuine Works of William Hogarth* (London, 1810), ii. 189; Stephens, *Catalogue*, item no. 2893, pp. 672–3.

[3] *Graphic Illustrations*, i. 148. Cf. Fielding's remarks in *JJ* no. 13 with those in no. 17, below, pp. 172–8, 210–16.

[4] Fielding implies as much in *JJ* no. 17, below, p. 211. In the print of his *March to Finchley* (1750) Hogarth has the 'Jacobite' newsvendor selling copies of *The Jacobite's Journal* and James Ralph's Opposition weekly, *The Remembrancer*. Two contemporary 'readings' of Hogarth's print mistook the irony of Fielding's title and described the news-vendor as against the government because she sold 'Opposition' papers. See *The Midwife, or, the Old Woman's Magazine*, i (London, [n.d.]), no. iv, pp. 182–5; and *The Student, or The Oxford and Cambridge Monthly Miscellany*, ii (Oxford, 1751), no. v, p. 163, where the letter containing the reference bears the date 20 January 1750.

[5] For William Strahan, printer of a number of Fielding's works, see Plomer, *Dictionary*, pp. 239–40; for George Woodfall, son of Henry Woodfall, the printer of *Joseph Andrews*, see Plomer, p. 269, and John Nichols, *Literary Anecdotes*, i. 300; for Charles Corbett (1710–52), publisher of plays, political pamphlets, and children's books, see Plomer, pp. 61–2; for Mrs. Nutt, see Plomer, pp. 183–5. Apparently she was Sarah Nutt, a pamphlet-seller active in the Royal Exchange from about 1735, and perhaps the widow of Edward Nutt, for whom see below, p. liv, n. 2.

wholly with booksellers who appear to have had earlier dealings with him. In addition to publishing many of his pamphlets, Mrs. Cooper had been the principal publisher of *The True Patriot*, the colophon of the nineteenth number of which lists Woodfall as participating in the distribution. Earlier in 1747 Woodfall had been one of the booksellers involved in *Ovid's Art of Love Paraphrased*.[1] Charles Corbett, of *'Addison's Head'*, against *St. Dunstan's Church* in *Fleet-street'*, published Fielding's *Of True Greatness* (1741) and *The Vernoniad* (1741), and an 'E. Nutt, at the *Royal-Exchange'*[2] participated in the publication of *The Crisis: A Sermon* (1741), a work often attributed to Fielding.[3] The fact that Strahan was the printer of at least the first number of *The Jacobite's Journal* would lead one to expect some data concerning its printing history in the Strahan ledgers. However, no such data appear to have been recorded there. What this means is not clear. It seems unlikely that Strahan printed no number except the first. As a Scot, he perhaps had reasons for not wishing to publicize his connection with a title implying Jacobitism. During this period Strahan charged Millar's account for printing Fielding pamphlets bearing Mrs. Cooper's imprint, which supports the hypothesis of some sort of private arrangement between Millar and Mrs. Cooper. Perhaps the omission from Millar's account of any charges for *The Jacobite's Journal* should be taken to mean that in this case Mrs. Cooper had made extraordinary arrangements, possibly involving disbursements by the Administration.[4] In the absence of hard data about press runs, circulation figures, and distribution, one is forced to record the opinion professed by a number of hostile contemporaries that 2,000 copies of each number were taken off by the government and given free distribution throughout England and Ireland by the Post Office.[5]

---

[1] The imprint of this rare item, apparently first published in February 1747, reads in part as follows: 'Printed for M. Cooper, in *Pater-Noster-Row*; A. Dodd, without *Temple-Bar*; and G. Woodfall, at *Charing-Cross*.'

[2] Presumably Edward Nutt, husband of Sarah Nutt, but see Plomer, *Dictionary*, pp. 183–5, for the difficulties of identifying the relationships of this family.

[3] For example, John Nichols, *Literary Anecdotes*, viii (London, 1814), 446, and Henry Knight Miller, *Essays on Fielding's 'Miscellanies'* (Princeton, N.J., 1961), p. 191 n.

[4] See below, pp. lxxv–lxxvii.

[5] For example, *The Patriot Analized* (1748), p. 37; *OE* of 12 November 1748; *Westminster Journal* of 13 February 1748. On the mechanics of Post-Office distribution see Laurence Hanson, *Government and the Press, 1695–1763* (Oxford, 1936), pp. 109–11, and K. L. Ellis, *The Post Office in the Eighteenth Century* (London, 1958), Ch. V.

Unfortunately, the *Calendar of Treasury Books and Papers* for this period has not yet been published;[1] the detailed breakdown of secret service expenditures during the Pelham administration does not appear to have survived;[2] and lists of recipients of the Post Office secret service money apparently do not cover 1747–8.[3] Nor is there even the kind of quasi-official evidence that emerged from the parliamentary investigations of Walpole's latter days. There is, however, incontrovertible evidence that Pelham spent a good deal less on secret service generally than Walpole had,[4] and whereas the latter had at times as many as eight or nine papers 'supporting' his administration, in 1747–8 'the only paper to give ungrudging support to the ministry' was *The Jacobite's Journal*.[5] Whether Fielding got any direct, regular subsidy from the Pelhams for it remains an open question.

It is not known when Fielding first projected *The Jacobite's Journal* or what, precisely, were the circumstances which prompted him to undertake the paper at this particular time. The earliest identifiable references to *The Jacobite's Journal* are the advertisements, late in November 1747, of its imminent publication;[6] all other references to it seem to postdate its appearance. Fielding's farewell essay speaks of the 'Strange Spirit of Jacobitism . . . at the latter End of the Year 1747' and of the design of his journal to remedy 'this dangerous, epidemical Madness' by ridicule.[7] And there is some evidence that the Administration itself was alarmed (or professed to be alarmed) by the state of affairs at that time.[8] But whether the impetus to publish *The*

---

[1] There is, of course, no guarantee that the *Calendar* would have records pertaining to the salaries paid to journalists. The *Calendar* for 1742–5 does not record many such payments.

[2] Apparently the secret service accounts kept by John Roberts for Pelham were burned by George II; Lewis Namier, *The Structure of Politics at the Accession of George III*, 2nd ed. (London, 1957), pp. 173, 175, 177.

[3] Namier, *Structure*, p. 194, identifies lists of recipients of the Post-Office secret service money only for 1742 and 1745. See also Ellis, *The Post Office in the Eighteenth Century*, p. 136.

[4] See 'An Accompt shewing the Monies issued for . . . secret service . . . from Midsummer 1727 to Midsummer 1760', Liverpool Papers, B.M. Add. MS. 38337, f. 44, cited by Namier, *Structure*, p. 195; cf. also *Calendar of Treasury Books and Papers, 1742–1745*, ed. William A. Shaw (London, 1903), p. viii.

[5] Laurence Hanson, *Government and the Press*, pp. 109, 119.

[6] For example, in *LEP*, *Whitehall Evening-Post*, and *General Evening Post*, of 26–8 November 1747.   [7] *JJ* no. 49 of 5 December 1748, below, p. 424.

[8] Pelham wrote Cumberland on 8 September 1747 that a 'lurking Jacobite spirit begins

Jacobite's Journal came from the Administration, perhaps through the agency of Fielding's friend Lyttelton, or from Fielding, perhaps with an eye to ingratiating himself further with the men who dispensed positions, is not known. One plausible assumption might be that the project of a pro-ministerial journal was actively considered sometime after the new Parliament first convened on 10 November 1747.

As a 'model' for *The Jacobite's Journal* Fielding had, of course, his own earlier efforts in political journalism, to say nothing of those of a great many contemporary practitioners. To judge from his own acknowledgements, however, he liked to think of himself as in the tradition of Addison and Steele, those exemplars of a supposedly more detached and 'patriotic' posture with respect to political issues. In *The Jacobite's Journal* there is a surprising number of indebtednesses—large and small, explicit and implicit—to Addison's *Freeholder* (1715–16),[1] which like *The Jacobite's Journal* was published during a period of nervousness about Jacobite activity and about a prospective invasion from France. For a journalist whose assumed premises included that of a 'crisis' in the country's affairs, there were numerous strategies of a useful nature to be found in *The Freeholder*. Exactly what considerations prompted Fielding's decision to depart from his 'model' by choosing so dangerously ironical a title as *The Jacobite's Journal*, it is difficult to specify. Perhaps two should be suggested here. The first has to do with the affinity between irony and the Augustan literary mind. The second has to do with the editorial decision, perhaps arrived at after consultation with Lyttelton and the politicians, to follow a common political stratagem of the day, that is, to stigmatize the Opposition with the label 'Jacobite'.[2] For his ironical *persona* (John Trott-Plaid, *Esq*) Fielding may well have drawn on the 'John Trot' *persona* of Nicholas Amhurst's *The Craftsman* (1726–47),[3] a 'country' party journal whose

to shew itself'; Coxe, *Pelham*, i. 375. Pelham was angling for recall of some of the British troops abroad, and may have deliberately exaggerated the danger at home.

[1] The entire leader of *JJ* no. 36 is a reprint of *Freeholder* no. 28 (26 March 1716). Cf. *TP* no. 2 (12 November 1745), and Miriam Austin Locke (ed.), *The True Patriot* (University of Alabama Press, 1964), p. 158: 'Fielding was particularly indebted to the earlier periodical [*The Freeholder*] in the writing of the *True Patriot*.'

[2] For grudging testimony of its effectiveness in the June 1747 elections see Walpole to Mann, 3 July 1747 (*Yale Walpole*, xix. 425).

[3] See, for example, *The Country Journal: or, The Craftsman* of 4 January 1729. A 'John Trott' is the signatory of a letter attacking Fielding in *The Daily Gazetteer* of 5 November

leading contributors in the anti-Walpole days were Bolingbroke and Pulteney (Bath), the latter apparently still active in 1747 helping the Prince of Wales's Opposition in the Parliamentary elections.[1]

As his exemplars Addison and Steele had done—and as he himself did in his two earlier periodicals—Fielding in *The Jacobite's Journal* pays considerable attention to literature and morals, most often indeed to the relationship between the two in a social, not a theoretical, context. Although *The Jacobite's Journal* is primarily political in emphasis, for the more particular consideration of literary and ethical matters Fielding belatedly added another department to those with which his journal began publication. Entitled the 'Court of Criticism' and derived ultimately from 'our most dear Predecessor *Isaac Bickerstaff*, Esq; of facetious Memory',[2] the new department had as its professed concern 'all Matters any wise concerning the Republic of Literature, and for the due Correction and Punishment of all Abuses committed therein', especially the scurrilous and defamatory journalism which did not come under the statutes of 'any Laws now in Being'.[3] From its first appearance in no. 7 to its final appearance in no. 33, the 'Court' appears in almost every number. Of the total of just under two dozen, almost every one except the acknowledged reprintings from other works seems to have been by Fielding himself. Therefore, the abandonment of the 'Court' in mid-July 1748, almost four months before the termination of *The Jacobite's Journal*, indicates a real slackening of Fielding's involvement with his paper.

In his announcement of his intention to resurrect the 'Court' Fielding implied that it would have two principal functions: to

1740. See also *Spectator* no. 296 (8 February 1712), and, for the ultimate source, Etherege's *The Man of Mode* (1676), III. iii, where the name is that of the 'one damn'd English blockhead' among Sir Fopling Flutter's foreign servants. Fielding himself seems to have been the inspiration of a satirical print entitled 'Jaco-Independo-Rebello-Plaido', which attacks the Independent Electors of Westminster for allegedly Jacobite behaviour prior to the June 1747 elections, and carries the inscription line 'I Trott Plaid Junr. Inv^r.' See Stephens, *Catalogue*, p. 643. The print bears the dateline 13 February 1747, which the topical allusions indicate is Old Style (i.e. 1748).

[1] See Coxe, *Pelham*, ii. 50–1; Archibald S. Foord, *His Majesty's Opposition, 1714–1830* (Oxford, 1964), pp. 262–3.

[2] The quotation is from *JJ* no. 6 of 9 January 1748, below, p. 128. 'Isaac Bickerstaff' was the principal *persona* of *The Tatler*.

[3] *JJ* no. 6, below, p. 128.

censure the abusive and to commend the meritorious. In no. 29 he distinguishes the 'Court of Censure' and the 'Court of Recommendation'.[1] As might be expected from the generic title, the censorious is more pronounced than the commendatory. Indeed, the announcement of intention describes the 'Court' as if the latter were in part an attack on a conspiracy of Grubstreet writers who were trying to mislead the public 'to the great Prejudice of the Reputation of Men of the best and most solemn Characters, and . . . to the utmost Abuse, Disgrace, and Discouragement of Literature, and, lastly, to the great Scandal of this Nation'.[2] In addition to remarks on a number of political ephemeræ the 'Court' censures in some detail Thomas Carte's *General History of England*, the scurrilities of 'Porcupinus Pelagius', Horace Walpole's three 'Letters to the Whigs', the libellous mimicries staged by Samuel Foote, the bad grammar and 'soft' attitudes of certain Oxford administrators, and the low standards of contemporary writers. What was not announced, of course, and what is therefore perhaps more surprising, is the personal basis of much of the censure. The attack on Horace Walpole, for example, is really a defence of Fielding's close friend and mentor, Lyttelton,[3] whom Walpole had accused of political inconstancy and designs on the liberty of the press, both of them issues to which Fielding elsewhere shows himself extremely sensitive. The attack on Foote was largely retaliatory in nature. Foote had made Fielding the subject of one of his notorious mimicries,[4] and John Rich, Fielding's former competitor and in 1747–8 manager at Covent Garden, not only allowed Foote, who was a member of his company, to maintain a separate troupe for the purpose of giving his mimicries, but also occasionally loaned him the Covent Garden stage on which to exhibit them.[5] Finally, what seems like

[1] Of 18 June 1748; see below, p. 313.

[2] *JJ* no. 6, below, p. 128.

[3] See *JJ* no. 18 of 2 April 1748, below, p. 217. There is no evidence that Fielding knew Walpole to be the author of the three 'Letters to the Whigs'. See W. B. Coley, 'Henry Fielding and the Two Walpoles', *PQ*, xlv (1966), 170–7.

[4] See *JJ* no. 22 of 30 April 1748, below, p. 262. For evidence that it may have had its commercial aspect as well see below, p. lix, n. 9.

[5] For example, on 11, 13, 14, 16, 18 November 1747 and thereafter; *London Stage*, part 4, i. 14–16. Later in the season, for the performance of his 'Collection of Pictures', Foote played at the New (or Little) Theatre in the Haymarket. In the 'Court of Criticism' of *JJ* no. 10 (6 February 1748) Rich is specifically censured for allowing his Covent Garden stage to be so used.

the undue attention paid to the writings and identity of 'Porcupinus Pelagius' must be attributed in part to the latter's attacks on
Fielding, as well as to the more general and objective issue of
factional journalism.[1]

The 'Court of Recommendation' provides some of the pleasan-
ter moments of *The Jacobite's Journal*, but even here the personal
element is by no means lacking. Fielding's praise of that in-
tellectually important work, the Abbé Banier's *Mythology and
Fables of the Ancients Explained*,[2] is both a compliment to its
reviewer's wit and intelligence and a clue to the possibility of
euhemerist influence on his thinking. It must be noted, however,
that Millar was the book's publisher, and in *The Jacobite's Journal*
Fielding at times seems to go out of his way to 'puff' books published by Millar and Cooper, both of whom were substantial
advertisers in the paper.[3] Also in the 'Court' are many indications
of a warm and continuing interest in the theatre, particularly the
Drury Lane, which was in its first full season under the joint
management of James Lacy and Fielding's friend, David
Garrick. The 'Court' provides Fielding with a convenient forum
in which to defend Garrick against charges of mismanagement or
mistaken policies,[4] to compliment many old friends in the Drury
Lane company by 'puffing' their benefit nights in his paper and
giving them incidental praise,[5] to pronounce in favour of the new
'natural' style of acting which Garrick was in the process of
establishing,[6] and to give judgment on specific plays like *Miss in
Her Teens* (as a vehicle for Mrs. Clive)[7] or an even more controversial play by another friend, Edward Moore's *The Foundling*.[8]
Among the Opposition papers there was malicious gossip to the
effect that Fielding was somehow actively and, in view of his
pretensions as a ministerial journalist and imminent justice of the
peace, indecently involved in the theatre at this time.[9] Such a

[1] See, for example, *JJ* no. 11 of 13 February and *JJ* no. 15 of 12 March 1748, below,
pp. 160, 197.

[2] In the 'Court' of *JJ* no. 9 (30 January 1748). Banier's work is handled in even greater
detail in the lead essays of *JJ* no. 6 and no. 12.

[3] The reference to Banier's *Mythology* in the 'Court' of *JJ* no. 9 takes note of the fact
that the work had already been advertised in the paper.

[4] See *JJ* no. 10 of 6 February 1748, below, p. 152–4.

[5] For example, that of 'Billy' Mills in *JJ* no. 21 of 23 April 1748, below, p. 254.

[6] *JJ* no. 10, below, p. 153.　　　　　　[7] *JJ* nos. 9 and 10, below, pp. 147, 152.

[8] *JJ* no. 16 of 19 March 1748, below, pp. 207–9.

[9] For example, *OE* of 9 July and 27 August 1748. For evidence that Fielding was in fact

charge doubtless drew added strength from his frequent attendance at plays, as well as from the fact that in 1747–8 he was still very much a performed playwright, with a total of 7 plays staged by the two major companies alone.¹ He was also a practising novelist, of course, with *Tom Jones* nearing completion and a fourth edition of *Joseph Andrews* to be published with authorial revisions.² So it is not altogether surprising that shortly after its publication the first part of Richardson's *Clarissa* is noticed in *The Jacobite's Journal*. It is noticed twice in fact: in the leader of no. 5 and in the 'Court' of no. 14. Furthermore, both notices are favourable—unambiguously and even ostentatiously so, drawing attention to their defence of the novel against what they claim is a flurry of adverse criticism. Although they no longer occasion the surprise they once did,³ these notices of *Clarissa* still seem to indicate a change in Fielding's attitude toward Richardson the novelist. Only a short time earlier, in the Introduction he contributed to his sister's *Familiar Letters* (April 1747), Fielding had rather tactlessly denied that 'the epistolary Style is in general the most proper to a Novelist, or that it hath been used by the best Writers of this Kind'.⁴ Inasmuch as the author of *Pamela* was both a particular friend of Sarah Fielding's and a subscriber to her *Familiar Letters*, such remarks about the epistolary style may well have seemed gratuitous. Whether owing to sisterly intervention or to Fielding's own genuine admiration for *Clarissa*, remarks of that kind are missing from *The Jacobite's Journal*. However, personal concerns quite clearly play a role in the 'Court' notices of two lesser literary accomplishments. To the 'Court' must go credit for the first published critical analysis of James Thomson's

operating a puppet theatre under the pseudonym of 'Madame de la Nash' in March, April, and May 1748, see Martin C. Battestin, 'Fielding and "Master Punch" in Panton Street', *PQ*, xlv (1966), 191–208.

¹ Between them Drury Lane and Covent Garden put on *The Author's Farce*, *The Debauchees*, *The Intriguing Chambermaid*, *The Lottery*, *The Miser*, *The Mock Doctor*, and *The Virgin Unmasked*; see *London Stage*, part 4, i. 9–54.

² The fourth edition of *Joseph Andrews*, with brief revisions by Fielding, appeared on or about 29 October 1748; it was apparently in press by June. See General Introduction, p. xxxiv, of the Wesleyan edition.

³ Since the discovery of a friendly letter from Fielding to Richardson, dated *c.* 15 October 1748, and praising the fifth volume of *Clarissa*; see E. L. McAdam, Jr., 'A New Letter from Fielding', *Yale Review*, xxxviii (1948), 300–10. For the *JJ* notices see below, pp. 118–20, 187–9.

⁴ *Familiar Letters* (1747), I. ix.

Castle of Indolence,[1] an analysis which may have owed its appearance to an association with Lyttelton, 'almost the only Patron which the Muses at present can boast among the Great'.[2] Lyttelton, who in 1748 was badgering Pelham to give Thomson a pension to replace the one withdrawn by the Prince of Wales,[3] is the subject of a highly complimentary portrait in *The Castle of Indolence*, a fact which is carefully singled out for attention in Fielding's review of the poem.[4] Finally, association with Lyttelton is surely in large part responsible for the partisan review given by the 'Court' to Edward Moore's *Trial of Selim the Persian*, an ironic verse defence of Lyttelton against charges of apostasy in politics.[5]

As regards his broader editorial position Fielding laid claim to a disinterested, almost transcendent patriotism, alike above personalities and party. Replying to charges that his journal was simply a vehicle for Administration propaganda, he asserted that he wrote in defence of the House of Hanover, 'the present Royal Establishment', and that 'so very little of that kind [Administration propaganda] hath been made the Subject of this Paper, that those who will call it Ministerial, must acknowledge, that to defend the King and the present Administration, are one and the same Thing.'[6] Public acceptance of this last sly equation was of course just what *The Jacobite's Journal* was designed to effect. In its more common form the equation read: to oppose the Pelham coalition is to oppose king and country. This blatant, but commonplace political strategy irritated Horace Walpole among others, and he called it the metamorphosing of private foes into public enemies.[7] If it could be changed to read 'metamorphosing private

---

[1] Alan Dugald McKillop (ed.), *James Thomson: 'The Castle of Indolence' and Other Poems* (Lawrence, Kansas, 1961), Introduction, p. 56.

[2] The quotation is from *JJ* no. 33 of 16 July 1748, below, p. 346.

[3] Chesterfield to David Mallet, 9 March 1748, *Letters of . . . Chesterfield*, ed. Bonamy Dobrée (London, 1932), iii. 1119. Chesterfield wrote that Pelham 'had been exceedingly pressed by Lyttelton in favour of Thomson'. In 1737 Thomson had been given a pension of £100 per annum by the Prince of Wales for his writings on behalf of the Opposition; see Rose Mary Davis, *The Good Lord Lyttelton*, pp. 59–62.

[4] See *JJ* no. 27 of 4 June 1748, below, p. 301. Thomson's compliment to Lyttelton is in stanzas lxv–lxvi of Canto I. Fielding and Thomson may have become acquainted about 1737, perhaps through the agency of Lyttelton, when both were writing on behalf of the Opposition.

[5] *JJ* no. 33 of 16 July 1748, below, p. 345. On Lyttelton's relations with Moore, see Rose Mary Davis, *The Good Lord Lyttelton*, pp. 200–1, 223–4.

[6] *JJ* no. 20 of 16 April 1748, below, p. 237.

[7] *A Second and Third Letter to the Whigs* (1748), p. 75.

friends into public saviours', Walpole's remark might well be applied to the rhetorical strategy of *The Jacobite's Journal*. Not that Fielding fails to acknowledge the corporate responsibility which the coalition worked hard to build up: 'We have an Administration not consisting of one absolute Prime Minister, supported only by his Tools and Dependents, and obnoxious to the Great Men in the Nation: but an Administration composed really of all the Great Men, whose Abilities of any Kind make them worthy of any Place in it'.[1] It is simply that certain members of the Administration—Hardwicke, Pelham, Lyttelton, and, to a degree, Bedford—come in for special consideration, and that these particular members happened to have figured or to be about to figure importantly in Fielding's personal career. Hardwicke, for example, 'that great and admirable Person who is at the Head of the Law' and 'the noble Person who at present so illustriously presides in Westminster Hall',[2] was titular head of the profession in which Fielding had elected to try his living. Furthermore, by the time of *The Jacobite's Journal* the Chancellor seems already to have prepared the way for Fielding's entry into the judiciary,[3] albeit at a lower level than the latter may have hoped. Pelham, 'one of the best and worthiest Men in this Nation' and 'one of the greatest Men now alive',[4] although not by any means a Walpole, was more or less winning acceptance as the principal minister of the coalition and was therefore in a position to bestow upon faithful writers like Fielding the sort of pension or place which Lyttelton was urging him to give James Thomson or Gilbert West. Lyttelton himself, 'whose Character is very dear to all who have the Honour of his Acquaintance',[5] may have held only a junior position in the Treasury, but if Opposition gossip is to be trusted, he seems to have been performing, without portfolio and perhaps even without direct commission, the duties of a sort of press lord on behalf of the Administration. In any event, as the cases of Thomson and West indicate, Lyttelton was an active intermediary between Pelham and writers seeking governmental recognition for services rendered. Finally the Duke of Bedford,

---

[1] *JJ* no. 4 of 26 December 1747, below, pp. 113–14.

[2] *JJ* no. 15 of 12 March 1748, and no. 11 of 13 February 1748, below, pp. 199, 161.

[3] See Archibald Bolling Shepperson, 'Additions and Corrections to Facts about Fielding', *MP*, li (1954), 218.

[4] *JJ* no. 43 of 24 September 1748, and no. 31 of 2 July 1748, below, pp. 398, 325.

[5] *JJ* no. 18 of 2 April 1748, below, p. 217.

'a Nobleman of the highest Rank and Dignity, and eminent for
the most exalted public as well as private Virtues',[1] figured
prominently in one of Fielding's favourite 'occasions' for satirizing
Jacobite activity, namely, the Lichfield race-meeting disturbances.
According to contemporary testimony, the Duke, to whose
'princely Benefactions' Fielding had been introduced by Lyttelton, was publicly horsewhipped by a dancing-master named Toll,
to the great delectation of Opposition writers and cartoonists.[2]
There was nothing necessarily venal, of course, about Fielding's
frequent editorial praise of these 'Great Men', but that praise does
somewhat vitiate his claim to be conducting a regnal, not a
ministerial, paper. Not only was *The Jacobite's Journal* a ministerial
paper; it was also, and perhaps more precisely, a paper supporting a certain wing of the ministry, the Pelham or, as it could be
called in view of its attitude toward the management of foreign
affairs in 1747–8, the pacific wing of the ministry.[3] The surprising omission of editorial praise of Newcastle and Chesterfield,
for example, goes a long way toward suggesting the nature and
extent of Fielding's personal affiliations while he was editing *The
Jacobite's Journal.*

On broader political issues, however, Fielding manages a less
personal, if hardly less 'ministerial', posture. We have seen how he
gave as his reason for undertaking *The Jacobite's Journal* the progress of a spirit of Jacobitism, a 'dangerous epidemical Madness
at so critical a Season'.[4] Such a presumption of national crisis
follows naturally and easily from the politically convenient presumption that all who oppose the ministry are in effect Jacobites,
for the latter were associated in the popular mind with acute
disloyalty, and acute disloyalty requires some sense of crisis.
Clear evidence that the season was in fact 'critical' is hard to come
by. Fielding speaks frequently of 'all those Tokens of Disaffection which we have lately heard of; and . . . all those Outrages
and Riots which have been so scandalously committed in more
Parts than one of this Kingdom'.[5] A survey of the contemporary
press indicates that his account is exaggerated. Party disturbances

[1] *JJ* no. 28 of 11 June 1748, below, p. 307.
[2] See, for example, *GM*, xviii (1748), 378, and *JJ* no. 28 of 11 June 1748, below, p. 307,
n. 1. For the 'princely Benefactions' of the Duke of Bedford see the Dedication to *Tom
Jones.*   [3] See below, pp. lxxi–lxxiv.
[4] See above, p. lv, and *JJ* no. 49 of 5 November 1748, below, p. 424.
[5] *JJ* no. 37 of 13 August 1748, below, p. 368.

at the Lichfield races in August 1747, perhaps echoes of the Staffordshire election riots in July 1747, undergraduate Jacobitism at Oxford in February 1748—these are the 'Tokens of Disaffection' to which Fielding returns again and again with expressions of outrage and apprehension scarcely justified by the facts. Pelham, as we know, wrote Cumberland in September 1747 that he had heard Jacobite activity was on the increase.[1] But Pelham was strongly pacific and nervous lest domestic troop garrisons be reduced too far for an effective defence of the homeland, and the published news reports do not really support his fears.

Nor is there more substantial proof of Fielding's corollary presumption that those who opposed the administration were political Jacobites. Indeed he uses much the same evidence to 'prove' the existence of political Jacobitism that he used to prove the 'critical' season in English affairs—Lichfield, Staffordshire, Oxford. Political writers tended to discover or deny the existence of Jacobitism according to their political prejudices. Samuel Squire, whose *Historical Essay upon the Ballance of Civil Power in England* (1748) provided material for one of the early leaders in *The Jacobite's Journal*,[2] wrote that the administration had 'no internal Dangers to fear for your darling Constitution, but from Tories and Republicans'.[3] The 'Alderman' of Fielding's *Dialogue*, 'a Jacobite upon republican Principles', is told by the 'Gentleman' that 'the Republican doth indeed serve the Purpose of the *Jacobite*, as the Atheist doth that of the Papist . . . while the one assists in undermining our Government, and the other in undermining our Religion, the Schemes of Slavery and Popery are in Fact carried on.'[4] The woodcut frontispiece of *The Jacobite's Journal* represents, in Fielding's ironic formula, 'that notable and mysterious Union of *French* Interest, Popery, Jacobitism, and Republicanism; by a Coalition of all which Parties this Nation is to be redeemed from the deplorable State of Slavery under which

---

[1] Coxe, *Pelham*, i. 375: 'Many insolences and petty riots have broken out; and those who, in open rebellion, thought it best not to appear, begin now to pull off the mask.'

[2] See *JJ* no. 7 of 16 January 1748, below, pp. 130–3. Samuel Squire (1713–66), Archdeacon of Bath and chaplain to the Duke of Newcastle, later (1760) Dean of Bristol and Bishop of St. David's (1761), contributed also to the literature on Thomas Carte's *General History of England*; see *JJ* no. 9 of 30 January 1748, below, p. 145, n. 2.

[3] *Historical Essay upon the Ballance of Power* (London, 1748), xxv–xxvi.

[4] *Dialogue*, below, pp. 57–8.

it at present labours'.[1] Tories there were, of course, and after the June 1747 elections they were represented in Parliament by approximately 120 members.[2] Although it now appears that the Pelhams were not very successful at converting Tories to the Administration,[3] their failure cannot be taken to mean that any great percentage of Tories were Jacobites. Indeed, after the admitted failure of the Forty-Five to recruit significant numbers of English for its cause it was difficult to maintain seriously that Jacobitism, at least in any acceptable sense of the term, was still a significant political force. This does not mean that Tory Jacobitism was a dead issue in politics. Bolingbroke and other Tory spokesmen had insisted that modern Toryism was no longer Jacobite, whatever the tendency of its antecedents, and that it was patently unfair to attribute to mid-century Tories such antiquated and anachronistic principles as indefeasible hereditary right and passive obedience.[4] But the Tories did have an ancient history of Jacobite associations, and Administration Whigs were careful not to let the voting public forget this fact. What has been called the 'perpetual reproach' of Jacobitism was successfully played off against the Opposition in the 1747 elections,[5] and it seems to have been Fielding's clear intention to try to keep the reproach alive during the first year of the new parliament.

The republicans, the other domestic 'party' in 'that notable and mysterious Union' emblematized by the frontispiece of *The Jacobite's Journal*, certainly had no status as a political party in any customary sense of that term, and there is considerable doubt that in mid-century England there was anything even resembling genuine republican sentiment.[6] In politics 'republican' was mostly a cant term, applied loosely and irresponsibly, not to latter-day Harringtonians, but to any and all persons who were thought to desire a more extensive limitation of kingly prerogative than was currently the case. Oddly enough, both sides found

---

[1] *JJ* no. 13 of 27 February 1748, below, p. 173.

[2] A. N. Newman, 'Leicester House Politics, 1748–1751', *EHR*, cci (1961), 579.

[3] Owen, *Rise of the Pelhams*, pp. 257–8, 312–14; cf. Keith Grahame Feiling, *The Second Tory Party, 1714–1832* (London, 1938), p. 44.

[4] As Fielding does, satirically, in *JJ* no. 3 and elsewhere; see below, pp. 104–6.

[5] The quoted phrase is from Feiling, *Second Tory Party*, p. 22. For Walpole's view that Jacobitism had been an issue in the 1747 elections see *Yale Walpole*, xix. 425.

[6] See J. M. Robertson, *Bolingbroke and Walpole* (London, 1919), p. 132; cf. Caroline Robbins, *The Eighteenth-Century Commonwealthman* (Cambridge, Mass., 1961), Ch. VIII.

the term useful. The Winningtonian *Apology*, for example, attempts several times to link republicanism and modern whiggism by virtue of a supposedly shared aim of restoring the 'old Constitution'.[1] Similar charges were levelled against the Tories, who were said to have cultivated republican sentiments in parts of the electorate out of a desire to damage the Hanoverian dynasty so that the Stuarts might be recalled. Fielding embodies this charge in an inverted form, so to speak, in the character of the 'Alderman' who is 'a *Jacobite upon republican Principles*'.[2] In *The Jacobite's Journal* the republicans and the Jacobites are represented as the extremes which lead to the same end. Desiring, though for different reasons, the destruction of the Hanoverian king, they are the poles—Jacobin and Jacobite, one might say—between which steers the true Whig, who, as 'a Ballancer, a Mediator', is against 'an over-bearing, a domineering, an unconstitutional Power, in whatever Hands it may chance to be lodged'.[3]

Fielding's editorial use of the Oxford disturbances to 'prove' the 'Strange Spirit of Jacobitism' illustrates the coming together of two other topics of considerable interest to him in *The Jacobite's Journal*: the supposed political unreliability of the educational system, and the uncertain place of the Church in the political scheme of things. Although the journal also treats these two topics separately, their convergence, so to speak, in the Oxford episode emphasizes the ultimately political basis of Fielding's concern with an episode which bore all the earmarks of a student prank. Under the Chancellorship of Ormonde's brother, Lord Arran,[4] Oxford had retained an aura of emotional Jacobitism. On Cardinal York's birthday some 'young scholars of the university' loudly proclaimed their disaffection for the king ('God damn King George') in what amounted, according to the official Oxford statement, to 'a notorious insult on his majesty's crown and government'.[5] The latter came down hard on two of the undergraduates;[6] the Privy Council, under prodding from

---

[1] See above, p. xl.   [2] *Dialogue*, below, p. 8.

[3] Samuel Squire, *Historical Essay*, p. xxx, quoted in *JJ* no. 7 of 16 January 1748, below, pp. 133, 132.

[4] Charles Butler (1671–1758), cr. (1693) Earl of Arran; Chancellor of Oxford, 1715–58.

[5] See *GM*, xviii (1748), 214; Feiling, *Second Tory Party*, p. 49; and below, p. 212.

[6] They were fined, sentenced to two years in prison, and made to pay security for seven years' good behaviour; *Yale Walpole*, xx. 6 n.

Bedford and Gower, attempted to bring to trial the Vice-Chancellor, John Purnell;[1] and late in 1748 the Administration informally broached a scheme whereby the power of nominating the Chancellor of Oxford would be vested in the king, so that on the death of Arran the post might be conferred upon Cumberland instead of another 'Jacobite'.[2] Neither Purnell's trial nor the Administration scheme came to anything, but these reverberations show that Fielding was by no means merely naive in taking seriously the original episode. Furthermore, Oxford, if the major, was not the sole focus of Fielding's attack on tendencies in education. Cambridge, presumably by virtue of its preferred place in the ministerial affections,[3] is not handled roughly in *The Jacobite's Journal*, but Fielding does broaden his attack to include the schools, those 'Seminaries half-reformed from Popery'.[4] His phrase indicates the connection he wished to draw between the high incidence of clerically trained among the schoolteachers and other persons in a position to shape opinion, and the possibility that such persons would nurture their charges on a diet of Jacobite principles. That he wished particularly to implicate the clergy seems clear from the fictional illustrations he provides. We are told, for example, of a town in which the Jacobites have managed to dismiss the old schoolmaster, who was a Whig, and to replace him with 'a good and firm Jacobite . . . for this you know is our chief Aim in all public Schools'. The Jacobite schoolmaster, the Reverend Mr. Robert Artful, 'our good and learned Divine', instructs a potential office-holder in how to take the required oaths without meaning them and without feeling perjured. He has done so himself, and 'I take care to bring up all my pupils in that Way of thinking.'[5] In another essay Fielding

---

[1] Walpole to Mann, 26 December 1748 (*Yale Walpole*, xx. 18). Purnell (*c.* 1708–64), Warden of New College (1740–64), was Vice-Chancellor 1747–50. The charge against him was that he failed to act, according to his duty, as a magistrate and Justice of the Peace.

[2] 'Horace Walpole's Short Notes', *Yale Walpole*, xiii. 22–3. See also Walpole to Mann, 26 December 1748 (ibid., xx. 18).

[3] Newcastle, who had been High Steward, succeeded the Duke of Somerset in December 1748 after much political manœuvring; D. A. Winstanley, *The University of Cambridge in the Eighteenth Century* (Cambridge, 1922), pp. 38–57. 'Cambridge', Newcastle wrote to the Bishop of London in January 1749, 'is as meritorious as the other is justly to be censured'; B.M. Add. MS. 32718, cited by Feiling, *Second Tory Party*, p. 49. Cf. *JJ* no. 27 of 4 June 1748, below, pp. 299–300.

[4] *JJ* no. 23 of 7 May 1748, below, p. 271.

[5] *JJ* no. 21 of 23 April 1748, below, p. 247.

creates a 'grave Clergyman from *Oxford*' who comes to board with a family named Supple and succeeds in converting parents and children alike to Jacobitism, before reporting them to the government as a sacrifice for a promised preferment.[1] Such emphasis on the role of clergymen in disseminating Jacobite principles contrasts sharply with the attempts elsewhere in *The Jacobite's Journal* to conciliate the clergy by applauding their 'loyal' performances, by documenting their fundamental incompatibility with the tenets of Jacobitism, and by recommending various schemes for the relief of their relicts and poor.[2] In a sense, the sharpness of the contrast indicates how seriously Whig politicians took the clergy and education as instruments of the polity. Fielding could hardly have mixed praise and blame of the clergy in so striking a way if he had not presumed two things about them: that they were important in shaping public opinion by various means, and that a number of them were of Opposition sympathies. Since coming into extended power in 1714 the Whigs had cultivated the established clergy as a helpful political instrument, and had done so chiefly by means of the system of ecclesiastical patronage.[3] But if the bishops and their immediate dependents were mostly Whig by 1748, many country parsons and reverend schoolteachers obviously were not. The influence of the latter, especially upon education, could hardly have been diminished by the fact that of the two universities one had a reputation for Jacobitism and both discriminated against Dissenters,[4] who from a Whig point of view provided a loyal and useful counterbalance to Tory effectiveness. When Fielding suggests a tightening-up of the laws regarding education, particularly in the matter of examining prospective teachers,[5] he may just possibly have been echoing a sentiment from somewhere within the ministry itself.

---

[1] *JJ* no. 34 of 23 July 1748, below, pp. 350–4.

[2] See esp. *JJ* no. 17 ('Court of Criticism'), nos. 16, 21, and 31, below, pp.216, 201, 250, and 328.

[3] Basil Williams, *The Whig Supremacy*, 2nd ed. (Oxford, 1962), pp. 78–82.

[4] Oxford did not admit Dissenters as undergraduates; at Cambridge they could matriculate and pass the examination, but could not proceed to degrees; Olive M. Griffiths, *Religion and Learning* (Cambridge, 1935), pp.33–4, cited by Williams, *The Whig Supremacy*, p. 69.

[5] See *JJ* no. 22 of 30 April 1748, below, p. 260; and cf. *JJ* no. 27 of 4 June 1748, below, p. 297.

Another issue of considerable prominence in *The Jacobite's Journal* is the liberty of the press. A hardy perennial among political issues, it became controversial as a result of Lord Lovat's trial in March 1747. Despite the prohibition against reporting the proceedings of either house, both *The Gentleman's Magazine* and *The London Magazine* reported Lovat's trial before the Lords, including the speeches of the Lord Chancellor on that occasion. Cave and Astley, the respective printers, were summoned to the bar of the Lords, taken into custody for breach of privilege, and later released after expressions of contrition and the payment of heavy fines.[1] The arrest of Cave and Astley started a rash of Opposition speculation, very likely designed to embarrass the Administration, about the future of the liberty of the press. In June 1747, in time for the parliamentary elections, there appeared an anonymous pamphlet entitled *A Letter to the Tories*,[2] which invited the Tories to join the coalition and thereby avoid the stigma of Jacobitism. The *Letter* further suggested that a government made up of Whigs and loyal Tories 'might, without any Danger, exert with Spirit and Vigour the full Power of legal Government, check and even suppress the infamous Licence of the Press (unknown to all other Ages and Nations, and destructive of all Civil Society)'.[3] The *Letter* was widely attributed to Lyttelton—perhaps as part of the attack on him for deserting the Opposition[4]—and its remarks about suppressing the liberty of the press were given wide coverage in the papers. 'The Fool No. 162', for example, speaks of the Administration's 'projecting a Scheme to stop the Press',[5] and *The London Evening-Post* of 30 July–1 August 1747, professing to believe that the Pelhams were 'slily meditating to subvert' the same liberty, reports an imminent 'Meeting of Merchants and Liverymen at the Crown Tavern behind the Royal Exchange, to . . . oppose every Attack made upon the *Liberty of the Press*'. On 28 November 1747 *Old England* published the first of a series of six papers on the same topic, in which it noted that 'a Person, vested with great Power, is said some time since, to have declared that the Liberty of the

---

[1] Hansard, xiv. 57–61; Coxe, *Pelham*, i. 354–5.
[2] See *JJ* no. 18 of 2 April 1748, below, p. 218.
[3] *Letter to the Tories* (London, 1747), p. 17.
[4] Hanson, *Government and the Press*, p. 14.
[5] In *The Daily Gazetteer* of 17 July 1747.

Press shall not survive the next Sessions of Parliament.'[1] Elsewhere in the same issue it was suggested, rather portentously, that
the daily papers print nothing so incendiary that it might bring
on the censorship.

Such hits at the ministry were part of a much broader attack on
the supposedly repressive nature of the over-all policies of the
Pelhams.[2] After the riots at the Lichfield races in September
the Opposition papers hinted at punitive legislation to come: 'The
Sowers of Sedition having made themselves so *formidable* in
the L—tch—d and Tothill-Field-Races, 'tis said a *Law* will be
apply'd for to *enforce* those already made against *riotous Assem-
blies*.'[3] Earlier in 1747, during the debates over the heritable
jurisdictions bills, there had been considerable Opposition
grumbling about the supposed harshness of the government in
general and Hardwicke in particular.[4] When the Lords unanimously passed a bill suspending Habeas Corpus for a second
time and sent it to the Commons, it was violently opposed by the
Tories and the Jacobitical associates of Sir John Hynde Cotton on
the stated grounds that as the rebellion had now been thoroughly
suppressed, there was no reason further to delimit the liberties of
the subjects.[5] Inasmuch as evidence that the issue of coercive
legislation was still touchy in 1747–8 can be found scattered
through Fielding's political writings of the period, it seems odd
to discover him apparently supporting just such legislation in a
number of areas: education, censorship of the stage, and censorship of the press.[6] His enemies accused him of being an informer
against the press, under the direction of Lyttelton, the paymaster,
by which they apparently meant that his function was to display

[1] The identity of the 'Person, vested with great Power' is not certain. In the light of
other remarks to the same effect he may have been Lyttelton, who, despite his relatively
junior commission in the Treasury, seems to have been considered a ministerial power by
the Opposition press. See references to the alleged withdrawal of the liberty of the press
in *LEP* of 11–14 July and 13–15 August, and in *OE* of 10 October 1747.

[2] On the apparent sensitivity of the Administration to this charge see Fielding's *Dialogue*,
below, pp. 15–17, and *Proper Answer*, pp. 81–3.

[3] *LEP* of 24–6 September 1747.

[4] Hansard, xiv. 51–7.

[5] Coxe, *Pelham*, i. 348–9. On the suspension of *Habeas Corpus* see *Dialogue*, below, p. 16.

[6] See the lead essay and the 'Court of Criticism' of *JJ* no. 22 (30 April 1748), and the
'Court of Criticism' of *JJ* no. 15 (12 March 1748), below, pp. 256–61, 261–6, 197–200.
In none of these cases does Fielding positively advocate restrictive legislation. His strategy
is rather to make out a brief for such legislation and then to praise the Administration for
not intending any.

the supposed scurrilities of the Opposition press in such a way as to prepare for eventual suppressive legislation.[1] When in the course of an attack on 'Porcupinus Pelagius', a particularly active anti-ministerial writer, Fielding annotated a passage from Horace by reference to a Roman law which imposed the death penalty upon the composers of libels, an Opposition paper commented: 'As the known pension'd Scribler for the M—try, the Author of *The Jacobite Journal* has this Day openly thrown off the Mask, and declar'd himself an Advocate for taking away the *Liberty of the Press*, Mankind can no longer doubt the Designs of his Patrons.'[2] Fielding had immediately professed himself opposed to any such limitation of the press, but, he added, 'I am likewise an Enemy to the Abuse of this Liberty: and it is from this Abuse alone it can ever be destroyed.'[3] To Opposition writers seeking either grounds for linking Fielding with the ministry or genuine hints as to ministerial policies with respect to the press, his somewhat weak disclaimer must have seemed convenient.

A final editorial issue of some importance in *The Jacobite's Journal* is that of peace. In one of its later attacks on Fielding *The London Evening-Post* claimed to have acquired a misplaced letter to him from 'Selim Slim' (Lyttelton) in which the latter assigned his 'creature' editor to celebrate the peace, the trustworthiness of French diplomacy, and the unimportance of retaining Cape Breton.[4] Waiving the question of Lyttelton's responsibility (if any) in the matter, one can note that *The Jacobite's Journal* editorializes from time to time on the Administration's peace policies,[5] and does so in a way which shows that the paper was more a ministerial than a regnal organ. Peace was of course the single most important issue facing the new parliament. The 1747 campaigns had not gone well, and the fall of Bergen-op-Zoom late in the year seemed to many people to presage the complete overrunning of the Low Countries by the French and possibly the threat of an invasion of England itself. As a result of Newcastle's predominance in foreign affairs, military conventions were being entered into by the Allies at the same time that English diplomats were preparing themselves, without great enthusiasm,

---

[1] See, for example, *OE* of 5 March, 2 April, and 24 September 1748.
[2] *JJ* no. 15 of 12 March 1748, below, p. 198; *LEP* of 12–15 March 1748.
[3] *JJ* no. 15, below, p. 199. [4] *LEP* of 13–15 September 1748.
[5] See esp. nos. 10, 24, 35, 43, 47, and 48.

to arrange for the preliminaries of Aix-la-Chapelle.[1] The logic
of politics obviously does not exclude the simultaneous pursuit of
war and peace, but in fact the Administration was deeply divided
over the emphasis to be given the two. Among the cabinet
members Newcastle for a long time stood nearly alone in opposing a precipitate peace, although he did have the support of
George II and, latterly, Cumberland,[2] which led the Opposition
press to insinuate that the diplomacy was being conducted
according to Hanoverian, not British, interests. If *The Jacobite's
Journal* devotes more space to domestic crises than to military
failures, more time to propounding the pacific thesis than to
attacking the policy of belligerency, perhaps its editor was aware,
like the Administration itself, of the danger of uselessly affronting
the King and of once more driving a wedge between him and the
Pelhams. It is possible, nonetheless, to trace in Fielding's political
writings of this period the increasing disaffection of the Pelham
wing with the way Newcastle kept prolonging the war. In the
Dialogue and, to a lesser degree, in the *Proper Answer* Fielding
attempts to defend the prolongation of the war on somewhat
tenuous grounds of national self-interest. But the *Dialogue* was
written before the depressing evidence of the 1747 campaign
was in, and the *Proper Answer*, written only a couple of months
after Newcastle had definitively made his point, already seems to
be saying that the Administration really did want peace but was
frustrated by a combination of factors, including the increasing
needs of self-defence. In *The Jacobite's Journal* the attitude
definitely stiffens. After first lauding the Pelham ministry for
having brought the country safely through the Forty-Five,
Fielding comes out strongly, if indirectly, against any further
prolongation of the war. He bluntly asks the ministers 'why they
do not put an immediate End to this ruinous War?' France has
been willing to offer honourable peace, and, if the war continues,
will almost certainly add Holland to her dominions, which is
hardly an encouragement to offering better terms than she now

---

[1] The St. Petersburg Convention was signed on 19 November 1747, that of The Hague
on 26 January 1748; *Journals of . . . Commons*, xxv. 486; Lodge, *Studies*, pp. 305–10.

[2] Lodge, *Studies*, p. 313. During the summer of 1747 Cumberland had entertained
pacific notions, but the French refusal to agree to unconditional abandonment of the
Stuart cause more than offset the effects of the peace overtures made by Marshall Saxe. For
the earlier disagreement between Pelham and Newcastle on the issue of immediate peace see
Owen, *Rise of the Pelhams*, pp. 311–12.

does. To his blunt, rhetorical question Fielding then gives a blunt, rhetorical answer: the ministers refuse to make peace 'for fear, lest a Set of Incendiaries should endeavour by misrepresenting their Measures, to enflame the People against their Preservers, and to make them as angry with those who put a final End to this War, as they were formerly taught to be with the Administration which declined the Beginning it'.[1] With this answer, which in the end he refuses to accept, Fielding brings together two favourite topics—the reluctance of the diplomatic wing to make an early peace, and the obstructionist activity of the Opposition press. The latter he credits with a slanderous, almost crippling power, but he encourages the Administration to be bold and to seek peace regardless, since failure in the ensuing military campaign will only strengthen its enemies. *Jacobite's Journal* no. 10, which dates, ironically, from the very day when Chesterfield, a member of the pacific wing, resigned the seals as Secretary of State,[2] is for all its obliqueness quite a strongly prescriptive piece. It comes at least as close as any other essay in the journal to presuming to instruct the ministry in the performance of its duty, and on the basis of its publication alone the journal must be characterized as a Pelham, not a Newcastle, supporter. Whether no. 10 was considered incautious or simply premature, the next extended editorial consideration given by *The Jacobite's Journal* to the peace negotiations does not occur until mid May, almost a month after the preliminaries were signed.[3] The delay cannot fully be explained in terms of the lag between the signing of the preliminaries and the disclosure of their exact terms to the public. After the terms were made public, the main task of a ministerial journalist was to condition the public to accept the unpleasing implications of some of them. Part of his task might also have been to neutralize the kind of incendiary journalism which Fielding had earlier called a deterrent to the Administration's desire for peace. At any rate, shortly after his essay on the text 'Blessed are the Peace-Makers', Fielding commences a series on the nature of slander in political writing and its effects on the general public.[4] As for direct editorializing on the theme of peace, there is not so much of that

---

[1] *JJ* no. 10 of 6 February 1748, below, p. 151.

[2] Chesterfield resigned on 6 February 1748; *Letters*, ed. Dobrée, iii. 1096.

[3] See *JJ* no. 24 of 14 May 1748, below, pp. 273–8. The preliminaries of Aix-la-Chapelle were signed 30 April N.S.　　　[4] See *JJ* nos. 26, 28, 29, and, to a lesser extent, no. 31.

as might have been expected. Indeed, one Opposition paper professed to know that the Administration was dissatisfied with Fielding precisely because he had not paid sufficient attention to that theme.[1] In mitigation, if any be needed, of Fielding's silence on the subject during the summer months it should be noted that from the preliminaries to the definitive treaty, negotiations were tedious and often uncertain. In October, however, after peace had been made almost mandatory by the sudden withdrawal of Austrian forces from the Netherlands,[2] Fielding did pay more attention to the subject, broadening his treatment of it to include further discussion of public ingratitude toward ministries and the bad influence of incendiary journalism.[3] Once the major belligerents had signed the definitive treaty and the reaction of the English public had been gauged to be without political danger to the Administration,[4] the latter had in effect got over its last major hurdle. Thus, whatever may have been the competing pressures of Fielding's personal affairs—he had already begun his duties as magistrate by 2 November 1748—the achievement of peace and the assurance of public complacency concerning it may have indicated to all those associated with *The Jacobite's Journal* that it was a good time to bring the paper to a close.

If in return for his editorial labours on behalf of the Pelhams Fielding was rewarded with a magistracy, it should also be recorded that he was paid in very different coin by the Opposition press. In *Jacobite's Journal* no. 20, an essay of considerable importance for his emotional biography, Fielding remarks that 'when I first undertook to defend the present Royal Establishment, I very little apprehended that I should, by that Means, subject myself to public Abuse'.[5] Any Augustan man of letters who took up even a part-time career in political journalism could expect to be slandered and attacked as soon as his identity was known or even guessed.[6] Just what else Fielding truly expected,

---

[1] *LEP* of 13–15 September 1748; cf. *OE* of 12 November 1748.

[2] Coxe, *Pelham*, ii. 35–6; Lodge, *Studies*, p. 404.

[3] See *JJ* nos. 43, 45, 46, 47 and 48.

[4] England, France, and the Dutch signed at Aix-la-Chapelle on 18 October N.S.; Spain acceded on 20 October and Austria on 23 October N.S.; Lodge, *Studies*, p. 407. From the English point of view, perhaps the most sensitive provision was the secret article stipulating that the hostages for the return of Cape Breton had to be peers of the realm.

[5] 16 April 1748, below, p. 235.

[6] The contentious character of even non-partisan journalism may be illustrated, in Fielding's case, by the 'paper war' which gathered around his *Covent-Garden Journal*

with a record like his, it seems difficult to say. As the author of such anti-ministerial plays as *Pasquin* (1736) and *The Historical Register* (1737) he had first earned the right to be vilified by the substantial Walpole press; his baptism by fire came when he was running *The Champion* (1739–41) in those last turbid days of the Opposition to Walpole. By his own admission, however, the heaviest 'Load of Scandal' fell upon him during his tenure as editor of *The Jacobite's Journal*. For one thing, he was better known than he had been in the days of *The Champion*: more had happened to him and more was known about his private affairs. In addition, he had 'converted' to the Administration and consequently found himself taking positions which were at considerable variance from those he had taken when in Opposition. On balance, a survey of contemporary sources upholds his implied claim that never before had he been so roughly handled by the hostile press.

Perhaps the first charge levied against Fielding as editor of *The Jacobite's Journal* was that his paper was not only a ministerial organ, but was also subsidized by the ministry and its editor paid a weekly salary for his efforts. *The London Evening-Post*, which along with *Old England* and, to a lesser degree, *The Westminster Journal* published most of the abuse against Fielding, provides an early sample of this charge: 'his [Pelham's] *mottled turn-coat Zany*, Harry Pickle, *alias* John Trot-Plaid has Leave from the Doctor [Pelham] to vent *his own Drugs, Carriage-free*, in every Part of the Kingdom, in order, as much as possible, to *poison the Constitutions* of his Majesty's Subjects against the said Doctor's next Perambulation.'[1] More details as to alleged conditions of work are provided by *Old England* in an essay published one week after the demise of *The Jacobite's Journal*:

This *Drawcansir* [Fielding] was immediately put upon the *honourable* List of *weekly* Pensioners, with an Advance of one Week's Pay in Hand, by Way of *Entrance*: while future Payments were to attend the Event of the Labours of the Week, under your [Lyttelton's] *cautionary* Care and special Direction; as it seems something had transpired from among his old Friends, the Booksellers, of his Inattention to Performance of Covenants, after the Consideration received.[2]

(1752), an essentially non-political periodical; see *The Covent-Garden Journal*, ed. Gerard Edward Jensen (New Haven, Conn., 1915), Introduction, pp. 29–98.

[1] *LEP* of 4–6 February 1748; reprinted in *Westminster Journal* of 13 February 1748.

[2] *OE* of 12 November 1748. The reference to broken covenants may refer to something that happened on *The Champion*. *OE* of 5 August 1749 claims that Fielding wrote 'Libels'

According to this same essay, the ministerial subsidy of *The Jacobite's Journal* included both purchase and distribution: 'As a further Encouragement to him and his Printer, it was stipulated that no less than 2000 of his weekly Performances should be taken off their Hands, and distributed by the Clerks of the *General-Post-Office*, through *Great-Britain* and *Ireland* gratis.'[1] The result, according to the same source, is that 'hardly a Country Alehouse can be found that is not honour'd with the *Humours* of your Hireling.'[2] Elsewhere it is stated that Lyttelton and his friends had procured Fielding 'much better Pay, by way of weekly Stipend, than he had when he wrote for them in the Opposition'.[3]

The charge that Fielding was a ministerial tool, 'a *pension'd Hackney* to a Third Rate *M——r*',[4] who wielded 'the Hireling Pen of a dirty *Drawcansir*, set up for the Coalition at a weekly Allowance',[5] was frequently associated with the charge that he was a political turncoat. One of the earliest clear references to his activity on *The Jacobite's Journal* occurs in a set of satirical predictions for April 1748: 'The first *Saturday* in this Month John Trot-Plaid, Esq; being disgusted that his New Masters have not rewarded him according to his great Merit, once more suddenly changes his Party, and within a Fortnight after libels all the Ministry round.'[6] A similar charge is made by one of the Winningtonian pamphlets: 'What had he [Fielding] to do with ridiculing any Party, who had travell'd round the whole Circle of Parties and Ministers, ever since he could brandish a Pen?'[7] The man most frequently held responsible for recruiting Fielding for the Pelhams was Lyttelton: 'Slim, *rank Apostate*, rais'd for P——m's *Ends*; / The Price—to *slander* all his *former Friends*: / *Obsequious Tool* himself:—how *mean* is Trott, / Who tails his

for *The Champion* at 'the humble Price of 5*s.* each, and a Sunday's Dinner; and at last took a small pecuniary Gratuity to betray his Paymasters and the Paper'. G. M. Godden, *Henry Fielding*, pp. 138–9, quotes from the manuscript minutes of the meetings of the *Champion* stockholders to the effect that on 1 March 1742 there had been a transfer to James Ralph of Fielding's 'Two Sixteenth Shares' of the paper, because the latter 'had withdrawn himself from that Service for above Twelve Months past and refused his Assistance . . .'.

[1] *OE* of 12 November 1748; also *OE* of 5 March 1748.
[2] Cf. *LEP* of 13–15 September 1748; also *JJ* no. 49 of 5 November 1748, below, p. 425.
[3] *OE* of 23 April 1748.
[4] *LEP* of 13–15 December 1748.   [5] *OE* of 11 June 1748.
[6] *Westminster Journal* of 16 January 1748.
[7] *A Free Comment on the late Mr. W——G——N's Apology for his Conduct* (1748), p. 48, à propos of the *JJ*. See also *LEP* of 16–19 January, 16–18 February, 15–17 March, and *OE* of 12 March 1748.

Hireling in this *Under-Plot?*[1] Lyttelton's choice of Fielding was
said by at least one Opposition paper to have depended on the old
school tie: 'for I doubt his [Fielding's] having had the Honour
to be your School-Fellow, was the most prevailing Motive to his
being employed'.[2] In his alleged capacity as Lyttelton's tool
Fielding was variously described as an expert 'in the Law of
Informing-Evidence against the Press', 'a kind of Brother Quill,
who has been translated from *Grubstreet* into the Verge of the
Court, to write, as it were, against me ['Argus Centoculi', editor
of *Old England*], for a small weekly Subsistence', an 'informer
Extraordinary', with the assigned task of 'stigmatizing every
Opposer of his Paymasters, with the Brand of Jacobitism' or of
'humorizing Disaffection out of the Land'.[3] His qualifications
for this sort of work were satirically derived from his supposed
defects in other fields, notably law and letters. Attacks on
Fielding's legal career were of course not new; they first appeared
within months of his being called to the bar on 20 June 1740.[4] At
that time Fielding was still editing *The Champion*, and the Walpole
press was mainly content to satirize his 'double Application to
Law and Politicks' without speculating overmuch about the
quality of his work as a lawyer.[5] Eight years later, however, there
was more to go on, and Fielding's failure to achieve eminence in
his profession seems to have encouraged attacks on his legal
competence.[6] As the time drew near for him to assume his
magisterial duties, Opposition writers, who must have known or
guessed the nature of his appointment as a Westminster magistrate,[7] began to harp on the impropriety of appointing a person

---

[1] *LEP* of 28–30 July 1748; also *OE* of 9 and 23 April and 12 November 1748; *LEP* of
13–15 September 1748.

[2] *OE* of 12 November 1748; *LEP* of 13–15 September and 5–8 November, and *OE* of
12 November, claimed to see a rupture in Fielding's relations with Lyttelton and the
Administration.

[3] *OE* of 23 April, 24 September (*bis*), 12 November 1748, and 27 May 1749.

[4] For example, *The Daily Gazetteer* of 17 October and 5 and 12 November 1740.

[5] *Daily Gazetteer* of 12 November 1740; see also William B. Coley, 'The "Remarkable
Queries" in the *Champion*', *PQ*, xli (1962), 433–4.

[6] For example, *LEP* of 7–9 April; *OE* of 2, 23, and 30 April, and 3 September 1748.
Fielding appears to have been sensitive on the point: 'they have followed me, with uncommon Inveteracy, into a Profession, in which they have very roundly asserted, that I
have neither Business nor Knowledge'; *JJ* no. 20 of 16 April 1748, below, p. 235.

[7] See *LEP* of 22–25 October 1748. The fiat appointing him magistrate for Westminster
is dated 30 July 1748; G. M. Godden, *Henry Fielding*, p. 175 n. But see W. B. Coley,
'Fielding's Two Appointments to the Magistracy', *MP*, lxiii (1954), 144–9.

with such a penchant for the 'low' in both life and letters.[1]
Calling attention to what it professed to consider the scurrility
of *The Jacobite's Journal*, *Old England* posed a rhetorical question:
'But what, Sir, could you expect from a Person, who set out so
meanly with *Merry-Andrew* Tricks and *Pickle-Herring* Wit, and
ever noted for Vulgarisms and Homeliness of Expressions in
every Scene of Life?'[2] In particular, his plays and the two novels,
Jonathan Wild and *Joseph Andrews*, were adduced as examples of
his preoccupation with the 'low': 'Some Plays he wrote, / Sans Wit
or Plot, / Adventures of Inferiors! / Which, with his Lives / Of
Rogues and *Thieves*, / Supply the Town's Posteriors.'[3] Or, as
another paper had it, '*Low Humour*, like *his own*, he once express't, / In Footman, Country Wench, and Country Priest.'[4]

   The enormous contempt—'more . . . than Mr. *Pope*, who had
great Merit and no less Pride in the Character of a Writer, hath
thought proper to bestow on the lowest Scribbler of his Time'[5]—
professed by Fielding's enemies for his literary gifts must have
been galling to him. But of that heavy 'Load of Scandal' he said
had been cast upon him as a result of his labours on *The Jacobite's
Journal* surely the most galling must have been the imputations
of a 'low' personal life. By his own account, Opposition writers
blackened his name 'with every kind of Reproach; pursued me
into private Life, *even to my boyish Years*; where they have given
me almost every Vice in Human Nature'.[6] At their simplest such
attacks on his private life were no more than mere name-calling,
as in an acrostic poem based on his editorial *persona*:

T	signifies *Tyburn*, Tomt—dman, and Trot;
R	Reprobate Royster, Rogue, Rope with a Knot;
O	Owl in an Ivy-Bush, Oaf, Odious, Old-Nick;
T	Turncoat, a Tavern, Trap, Trust upon Tick;
P	Profligate Poet, pox'd Pensioner, Prog;
L	Lyar, a Lawyer, a Lubbard, a Log;

---

[1] For example, *OE* of 12 November 1748, which purports to quote Fielding to the effect
that he became a lawyer 'without ever looking into *Cooke* [sic] upon *Littleton*, or any other
Law Book whatsoever', and as saying 'I have only read a few Plays, and wrote some
Pamphlets during my State of Probation, which qualified me very essentially for the
Gown.'   [2] *OE* of 12 November 1748.

[3] *OE* of 26 November 1748. Cf. *LEP* of 9–12 January and 16–18 February 1748.

[4] *LEP* of 28–30 July 1748. *OE* of 5 March 1748 also accuses Fielding of ridiculing 'all
the inferior Clergy in the dry, unnatural Character of Parson Adams'.

[5] *JJ* no. 20 of 16 April 1748, below, p. 235-6.

[6] *JJ* no. 20, below, p. 235.

A Author Atheistic, Arrest and Assault;
I Jacobite-Journal, *Informer*, a Jolt;
D Dog-in-a-Doublet, Dunce, Dunstable, Dolt.[1]

More sophisticated scurrility put words into his mouth in a kind of capsule autobiography:

> Hunted after Fortunes, and lived on Kept-Mistresses for a while; scored deep at the Taverns, borrow'd Money of my Landlords and their Drawers; burrough'd in privileg'd Places among the Flatcaps of the Town, stood Bully for them, and p*x'd them all round; abused my Benefactors in the Administration of public Affairs, of religious Dispensations, of Justice, and of the Stage; hackney'd for Booksellers and News-Papers; lampoon'd the Virtuous, wrote the Adventures of *Footmen*, and the Lives of *Thief-Catchers*; crampt the Stage, debas'd the Press, and *brought it into Jeopardy*; bilk'd every Lodging for Ten Years together, and every Alehouse and Chandler's Shop in every Neighbourhood; Defrauded and revil'd all my Acquaintance, and being quite out of Cash, Credit and Character, as well as out of Charity with all Mankind, haunted by Duns and Bumbailiffs, hallow'd, hooted at and chased from every Side and by every Voice, I escap'd with whole Bones indeed, but d—bly mangled into these Purlieus of Safety, where no venomous Creatures dare enter.[2]

His dependence upon the politicians was put in the worst possible light, as in an iconographic essay apparently alluding to his relationship with John Russell, fourth Duke of Bedford. This essay reported that a new quadrilateral pillar was to be erected near Covent Garden with an obscene image of 'Trott-Plaid' crouching naked, buttocks toward the church, brazen face toward the playhouse, genitalia shaded by the foliage, so to speak, of *The Jacobite's Journal*, right hand gripping a lodestone with which to force out of the Treasury 'Two Pieces and a Half of Gold Weekly'.[3] There were also particular attacks on his family relationships. After describing Fielding as 'the Judge *Bargown'd* out in his Seat, with a rueful Face, a hanging Look, and a Bacco-protuberating under Lip', Horace Walpole related some playhouse gossip about the journalist's taking his wife to the theatre on his poet's privilege and being refused admission by the

---

[1] *LEP* of 17–19 March 1748. In *JJ* no. 20, below, p. 238, Fielding says he has 'been more than once called' a Tom T—dman.

[2] *OE* of 5 March 1748. On Fielding's alleged fondness for drink see also *LEP* of 9–11 June and 27–29 September 1748.

[3] *OE* of 9 July 1748, in a letter signed 'Russeli'.

Boxkeeper, who in addition insisted that Fielding's wife was really only his maid and, by implication, not suitable to be admitted into the company of ladies.[1] Walpole's brutal anecdote—it belongs fittingly with his more famous one of 'the blind man, three Irishmen, and a whore',[2] which it does not exactly mitigate—must have cut deep. On 27 November 1747 Fielding had married one Mary Daniel, in fact his deceased wife's maid and, later, his own housekeeper.[3] Whatever the other, more rapturous reasons for this marriage,[4] the Twickenham parish registers record the principal reason, the birth prior to 25 February 1748 of their first child.[5] Although Fielding was to describe her later as 'a faithful Friend, an amiable Companion, and a tender Nurse',[6] his marriage to Mary Daniel seems to have upset some of his friends and to have given aid and comfort to more enemies than Walpole.[7] An anonymous poetaster saw in it a useful point of comparison between Fielding and his father, General Edmund Fielding:

> When erst the Sire resided near the Fleet,
> In Want of something, like the Son, to eat,
> For Fifty Pounds in Hand, prime Fortune! paid,
> Before the Priest he led his Servant Maid.
> *Curse on the Scoundrel* for the Deed he's done,
> *How I'm disgrac'd*! cried out his pious Son.
> . . . Another Way did operate the Curse,
> In its own Kind; *for better and for worse*,
> The Kitchen Maid is coupl'd with the 'Squire,
> Who copy'd that for which he curs'd his Sire.
> . . . This Diff-rence only 'twixt the Sire and Son,
> The first had Money but the other none.[8]

It would be interesting to know where the poetaster, whoever he was, got his information, for he seems here to be alluding to

---

[1] *OE* of 23 April 1748. For details of this Fielding–Walpole association see W. B. Coley, 'Henry Fielding and the Two Walpoles', *PQ*, xlv (1966), 171–7.

[2] Walpole to George Montagu, 18 May 1748; *Yale Walpole*, ix. 84. The 'blind man' was Fielding's half-brother, John Fielding, and the 'whore' was Mary Daniel, the second Mrs. Fielding.   [3] Cross, ii. 60–2.

[4] Lady Mary Wortley Montagu, *Letters and Works*, 3rd ed. (London, 1861), ii. 283, speaks of Fielding's 'natural spirits', which 'gave him rapture with his cook-maid'.

[5] Cross, ii. 61. The date given is that of baptism.

[6] *The Journal of a Voyage to Lisbon* (London, 1755), *sub* 'Saturday, July 13'.

[7] Cross, ii. 61–2, records some of the best-known reactions.

[8] *OE* of 24 September 1748.

Fielding family matters dating back at least twenty-five years.[1] Fielding's father, Edmund Fielding, in addition to being a gambler of sorts, was a marrying man, with three, possibly four, wives.[2] But the marriage which best fits the conditions given by the poetaster was the second, to Anne Rapha, 'Widow and Italian a Person of the Roman Catholick Profession who has severall children of her own and one who kept an eating house in London . . . and now has two daughters in a Monastery beyond Sea'.[3] This pregnant account of the second Mrs. Fielding was deposed by Lady Gould, mother of the first Mrs. Fielding, then deceased, and an interested party in litigation concerning her daughter's estate, the proceeds of which Edmund Fielding was accused of diverting from their rightful beneficiaries, Henry Fielding and his siblings.[4] Edmund Fielding denied that his new wife was Italian and that she had ever kept an eating-house, but in the Chancery proceedings considerable emphasis seems to have been placed on her supposedly inferior station and on her religion, which would account for the 'Kitchen Maid' and the 'Priest' of the poem. To relish the son's 'How I'm disgrac'd!' one needs to know not only that Edmund Fielding married beneath his station, but also that Henry Fielding, with his fondness for 'Esq.', and a certain magisterial confidence of attitude, struck contemporaries as considering himself a cut higher socially than the circumstances of his life and occupation would appear to have permitted.[5] Hence, in part at least, the brutal relish of Walpole, Smollett, and others for the fact of his marriage to his 'Maid' and his appointment to an inferior level of the judiciary.

It seems impossible to tell what effect, if any, the 'Load of Scandal', the pursuit 'into private Life, *even to my boyish Years*',[6] had on the decision to terminate *The Jacobite's Journal*, the forty-ninth and final number of which appeared on 5 November 1748. Other reasons seem to have been stronger. Perhaps, as his concluding essay states, the signing of the definitive treaty at

---

[1] Curiously, *OE* of 1 October 1748 claims to have private material for a biography of Fielding and offers it to those undertaking such a project.

[2] J. Paul de Castro, 'Fieldingiana', *N & Q*, 12th Ser. iii (Nov. 1917), 465, and xi (26 Aug. 1922), 178; and see Cross, i. 40.

[3] From *Fielding* v. *Fielding*, Chancery Proceedings (1714–58), Division Sewall, Bundle 259, no. 37, as cited in Godden, *Henry Fielding*, p. 12.

[4] Cross, i. 28–40.   [5] See, for example, *LEP* of 22–25 October 1748.

[6] The phrases are from *JJ* no. 20, below, p. 235.

Aix-la-Chapelle removed the last trace of Administration anxiety about the threat of an Opposition,[1] and hence removed also the motive for continuing to subsidize or encourage an Administration periodical. Perhaps the decline which Opposition writers professed to see in the later numbers of *The Jacobite's Journal* reflected a weariness of political journalism on Fielding's part.[2] Perhaps, as the Opposition press also suggested, there was some sort of falling out between Fielding and his 'Paymasters' owing to some failure as a ministerial propagandist.[3] Perhaps, too, the time had come for him to insist on some more substantial reward than the standard 'Two Pieces and a Half of Gold Weekly',[4] even though that reward were, as he himself remarked at the end of his life, some of 'the dirtiest money upon earth'.[5] Whatever the reason or reasons, *The Jacobite's Journal* ceased publication shortly after its editor had begun work as a Westminster justice, never again to undertake sustained political writing.[6] Some idea of the solemnity of his 'passing', so to speak, as well as of the general tone of mid-century journalism, may be had from the 'Epitaph' supplied by *Old England*:

> Beneath *this Stone,*
> *Lies* Trotplaid John,
> *His Length of Chin and Nose;*
> *His crazy Brain*
> Unhum'rous *Vein*
> *In Verse and eke in Prose*
> . . .
>
> But ah, alack!
> He broke his Back,
> When Politics he tried:
> For like a ———
> He play'd his Part,
> Crack'd loudly, stunk, and died.[7]

W. B. Coley

---

[1] *JJ* no. 49, below, p. 426.

[2] See, for example, *LEP* of 5–8 November 1748, which speaks (after the fact, to be sure) of five weeks of '*gradual* and *visible Decay*'.

[3] See, for example, *OE* of 12 November 1748, and *LEP* of 13–15 September 1748.

[4] The quoted phrase is from the 'Russeli' letter in *OE* of 9 July 1748; see above, p. lxxix, n. 3.

[5] Introduction to *The Journal of a Voyage to Lisbon* (1755), p. 26.

[6] Unless he was the 'Paul Wronghead, of the *Fleet*, Esq;' *persona* of the *Covent-Garden Journal* of 1749. *OE* of 9 and 16 December 1749 accused Fielding of writing the former paper 'for the Service of the Faction'; see 'Fielding and the Two "Covent-Garden Journals" ', *MLR*, lvii (1962), 386–7, which rejects the attribution.

[7] *OE* of 26 November 1748.

TEXTUAL INTRODUCTION

THIS edition offers a critical unmodernized text of *A Dialogue between a Gentleman from London . . . and an Honest Alderman*, *A Proper Answer*, and *The Jacobite's Journal*. The text is critical in that it has been established by the application of analytical criticism to the evidence of the various early documentary forms in which the materials appeared. It is unmodernized in that every effort has been made to present the text in as close a form to Fielding's own inscription and subsequent revision as the surviving documents permit, subject to normal editorial regulation.

I. THE COPY-TEXT AND ITS TREATMENT

No manuscript is known for any of the material in the present volume; nor is any formal assignment of copyright from Fielding to the publisher extant which would permit us to assert flatly the authoritative nature of the manuscripts which were sent to the press. In the case of the two pamphlets, however, the evidence of the Strahan ledgers demonstrates that he printed pamphlets with these titles, and so we may properly infer that the earliest impression at least was set from holograph. No known record of the printing of *The Jacobite's Journal* survives, but the presumption is surely strong that a periodical would have been set from holograph.

With the probable exception of *A Dialogue* there is no evidence that Fielding ever revised any of the texts in the present volume. We cannot tell, indeed, whether he read proof on them: if he did so, he left no clear trace of the fact. Contemporary political ephemeræ of the sort represented by Fielding's two pamphlets do not in general show much sign of careful supervision by their authors. In the case of his periodical Fielding is not likely to have had time to revise or perhaps even to read proof consistently, assuming that he would have been concerned.

A Dialogue presents a special and instructive case. It exists in five states (*a–e*), which are described bibliographically in Appendix IV. States *b–e* give clear indication that somebody outside the printing house, probably Fielding himself, requested changes to be made in the *a* text as already printed. In states *b–d* these changes are called out by means of one or two errata lists variously placed. In state *e* the errata are partially incorporated into the text, which seems to have been reset to a considerable degree. Moreover, state *e* introduces a number of variants, both substantive and accidental, found in no earlier state and not called for by either of the errata lists. What slight evidence there is suggests that the resetting of *e* may have been from a marked copy of *a* and almost certainly not from any manuscript.

For an unmodernized edition such as the Wesleyan Fielding the most authentic form of what are known as the 'accidentals' of a text—the spelling, punctuation, capitalization, word-division, and such typographical matters as the use of italicized words—can be identified only in the document which lies nearest to the lost holograph, that is, in the first edition, the one printing which was set direct from manuscript. An editor will understand that the first edition by no means represents a diplomatic reprint of the manuscript and that in most respects the accidentals are a mixture of the author's and the compositors'. But whatever the relative impurity, the first edition stands nearest to the author's own characteristics and represents the only authority that has been preserved for the texture in which his words were originally clothed. For these reasons the editor has adopted state *a* of *A Dialogue* as his copy-text. Although state *e* does represent a clearly revised state, its revisions are technically no witness to the possible features of the manuscript.

In the absence of evidence that Fielding supplied much more than the original holograph, the treatment of the texts in the present volume has been essentially conservative. Changes— even those which seemed desirable as restoring Fielding's general stylistic habits—have been made cautiously, in part because on the evidence of the copy-texts, at least, Fielding's journalistic practice seems less conformable or consistent than that of his prose fiction. Furthermore, the printing-house styling in the copy-texts themselves is by no means consistent.

With few exceptions, all accidental as well as all substantive alterations have been recorded in the textual apparatus so that the interested reader may reconstruct the copy-texts in detail as well as the substantive variations from them. In a few purely formal matters, however, the following editorial changes have been made silently. (1) Typographical errors such as turned letters or wrong fount are not recorded, and (2) the heading capitals and small capitals which in the originals begin each pamphlet as well as each number of the journal and some of the separate departments within the journal, have been ignored. (3) Throughout, necessary opening or closing quotation marks have been supplied silently, as have closing parentheses. Moreover, running quotation marks in the left margin have been omitted and quotations have been indicated according to the modern custom. This necessary modernizing of an eighteenth-century text for a modern critical edition extends also to the silent removal of closing quotation marks at the end of a paragraph when the quotation, in fact, continues without interruption in the next paragraph, marked as usual by opening quotation marks. (4) Single quotes have been normalized to double, as is the common practice of the copy-texts, wherever quotation is primary and direct. (5) When the apostrophe and roman 's' follow an italicized name, the roman is retained only when it indicates the contraction for 'is' but is silently normalized to italic when the possessive case is required. (6) The fount of punctuation is normalized without regard for the variable practice of the original. Pointing within an italic passage is italicized; but pointing following an italicized word that is succeeded by roman text is silently placed in roman when it is syntactically related to the roman text. (7) The ampersand and other standard abbreviations (*e.g.*, *viz.*, *i.e.*, *vid.*) have been placed in the fount opposite to that of the matter to which they pertain. (8) Speech assignments, wherever contracted, have been silently expanded. (9) Final periods have been additionally supplied between true independent sentences where Fielding's printer originally used only the long dash; periods thus supplied have been placed after the last word of the sentence and before the long dash, as is the common practice of the copy-text where both sorts of punctuation are present. (10) The highly variable and unsystematic treatment in the different texts of the long dash, principally in connection with Latin quotations, has been normalized. When such a quotation with its conventional following dash is itself a complete sentence and would be concluded in standard editions by a period, then the editor places the period before the dash. When the quotation itself is not syntactically complete, in headings or when used within Fielding's own prose which continues with the same sentence following the quotation, only the dash appears and any irrelevant periods are silently omitted. Finally, when such a syntactically incomplete quotation ends a Fielding sentence, the period is placed after the dash, silently, without regard for the copy-text positioning. (11) The conventional form of address which opens letters to the editor is normalized to italic and conventional capitalization (*Sir*). (12) In the mottoes and in Latin and Greek quotations generally the ampersand is silently expanded to *et*; the contracted suffix *-q* is expanded to *-que*; titles have been expanded and italicized; authors' names have been expanded; the period customarily used after the author's name has been changed to a comma where there is following matter; designations of such things as book, epistle, and verse have been englished and expanded; pronunciation marks have been removed; and in the case of Greek diphthongs modern lettering has been adopted.

A few procedures for dealing with the text may be mentioned although they involve matters that are recorded. The texts in this volume are far from consistent in their method of dealing with interjections within quotation or directly quoted speech. Sometimes an inserted 'he says' will be treated in the modern manner, with closing quotes before it and opening quotes after it for the continuation; sometimes the 'he says' or its equivalent will be inserted between parentheses to mark its separate nature from the surrounding quotation. Sometimes, however, simple commas substitute for the parentheses, so that technically there is no indication that the 'he says' is not a part of the quotation, and indeed ambiguities may occur. If any single system had been employed, the editor might have been content to follow it, as a feature of the period; but since the system varies even within individual texts, it has been thought convenient to normalize this textual situation by consistently adopting the compromise but acceptable method at the time, of enclosing all such interjected material in parentheses. However, each alteration of the text in this manner is recorded so that the exact reading of the copy-text can always be ascertained by those who wish this information. One special problem developed in *A Proper Answer*. Here the form within a line is always 'Falshood'; but when this word was broken at the end of the line it was the interesting custom of the printer to spell the first half 'False' so that the hyphenated form between lines would be 'False-|hood'. Since this spelling is clearly a convention dependent upon the hyphenation, each of its occurrences has been emended to 'Falshood' but listed for the sake of the record.

2. THE APPARATUS

All the textual apparatus is placed in appendices where it may be consulted at leisure by those who wish to analyse the total evidence on which the present text has been established. In the first appendix appears the List of Substantive Emendations. All verbal variation has been recorded here, and to the substantives have been added a very few examples of variant readings in the accidentals when these have influenced meaning in a strongly semi-substantive manner. Since the purpose of this list is to present at a view the major editorial departures from the copy-text, only the earliest source of the approved variant is recorded, together with the history of the copy-text reading up to its accepted emendation in the earliest source.[1] Certain emendations not found in the collated early texts have been assigned to W, that is, to the present edition, whether or not they actually originated here or with some preceding editor. By their nature they cannot be authoritative, even though they have proved to be necessary corrections, and hence a more precise record would serve little purpose, especially since minimal independent emendation has proved necessary in the substantives themselves. The basic note provides, first, the page-line reference and the precise form of the emended reading in the present text. Following the square bracket appears the identification of the earliest source of the emendation in the texts collated. A semicolon succeeds this notation, and following this appears the rejected copy-text reading with the sigla of the texts that provide its history up to the point of emendation. In these notations certain arbitrary symbols appear. When the variant to be noted is one of punctuation, a *tilde* ($\sim$) takes the place of the repeated word associated with the pointing. An inferior caret $\wedge$ calls attention to the absence of punctuation either in the copy-text or in the early text from which the alteration was drawn. Three dots indicate one or more

[1] An exception is the treatment of the readings in the variant states of *A Dialogue* where the total information is given in order to provide a complete record of the revisions.

omitted words in a series; *om.* means the matter in question was omitted.

The List of Accidentals Emendations follows on the record of substantive and semi-substantive emendation, and conforms to the same rules. The list includes all changes made in the copy-text except for those described as silently normalized. A list of word-divisions holds information about hyphenated compounds that will lead to an accurate reconstruction of the copy-text from the modern print. The reader may take it that any word hyphenated at the end of a line in the present text has been broken by the modern printer and that the hyphenation was not present in the copy-text unless it is separately listed and confirmed here. Correspondingly, when a word is hyphenated at the end of a line in the copy-text, the editor has been charged with ascertaining whether it is a true hyphenated compound or else an unhyphenated word that has been broken; the facts are then recorded in this list. Although certain of the editorial decisions in the matter of these copy-text readings approach the level of emendation, no record has been made of their treatment in editions other than the copy-text.

In all entries in the accidentals list, the forms of the accidentals to the right as well as to the left of the bracket accord with the system of silent normalization adopted for the edited text. Moreover, no record is made of variation in the accidentals that is not the matter being recorded. That is, if a punctuation variant alone is the question, the lemma of the word to which the pointing refers will take the form of the accidentals of the Wesleyan text regardless of the spelling or capitalization of the word in the text from which the punctuation variant was drawn. In this respect, then, the *tilde* to the right of the bracket signifies only the substantive and not its accidentals form in any edition other than the copy-text.

There are, strictly speaking, no true *editions*, other than the first, of any of the materials in the present volume. State *b* of *A Proper Answer* is merely a reimpression of state *a* with a minor addition in the title page; *The Jacobite's Journal* seems the product of a single impression; only *A Dialogue* exhibits impressions with any variants and these seem to have occurred during a single press run. For this reason there is no Historical Collation in the textual apparatus of the present volume.

3. COLLATION

In preparing the present text of *A Dialogue* Professor Coley collated the following copies of state *a*: British Museum (8026.C.51[3]), William Andrews Clark Memorial Library (*PR 3454/D51), Henry E. Huntington Library (305667), Harvard University Library (*EC7.F460.747d), Yale University Library (College Pamphlets 1039), Bodleian (2 copies—G. Pamphlets 1170 and 1918); of state *b*: Harvard University Library (*EC7.F460.747da); of state *c*¹: Newberry Library (J 54555.7021); of state *c*²: British Museum (102.c.43), New York Public Library (C p.v. 145 [no. 8]); of state *d*: Yale University Library (Fielding Collection 747d); of state *e*: John Rylands Library (R67092), Bodleian (Vet. A4 e. 1010). In preparing the present text of *A Proper Answer* Professor Coley collated the following copies of state *a*: British Museum (3 copies—1093.e.20, T.1791[3], and T.1632[5], which misnumbers p. 12 as p. 21), Bodleian (G. Pamphlets 1918), Harvard University Library (*EC7.F460.747p), William Andrews Clark Memorial Library (*PR 3454/P81), Yale University Library (College Pamphlets 1040), Henry E. Huntington Library (328825); of state *b*: Bodleian (22863 e. 31), Yale University Library (2 copies—British Tracts/1748/F461, and NZ/748Fi, lacking pages 37–44); Boston Athenaeum (Tracts B698), National Library of Scotland (Grindlay 222[5]). No press-variants appeared. For his own information, the editor collated copies of the Dublin reprint at Yale (Fielding Collection 747pc) and in the Huntington (356638) in order to establish the lack of authority in this edition.

In preparing the text of *The Jacobite's Journal* Professor Coley collated the following copies: Yale University Library (Z17/00455), numbers 8 and 12 of which are defective; British Museum (Burney 425), which lacks number 41; National Library of Scotland (Blk. 685), which lacks numbers 1–2, 12, 21–2, 37, 39–40, 44–6. Two press-variants were observed.

FREDSON BOWERS

A DIALOGUE

BETWEEN A

GENTLEMAN of *LONDON*,

Agent for two Court Candidates,

AND AN

HONEST ALDERMAN

Of the Country Party.

WHEREIN

The GRIEVANCES under which the Nation at prefent *groans* are fairly and impartially laid open and confidered.

Earneftly addrefs'd to the

ELECTORS of GREAT-BRITAIN.

LONDON:

Printed for M. COOPER, at the *Globe* in *Pater-nofter-Row.* 1747.

A
DIALOGUE

BETWEEN A

GENTLEMAN of *LONDON*,

Agent for two Court Candidates,

AND AN

HONEST ALDERMAN

Of the Country Party.

WHEREIN

The GRIEVANCES under which the
Nation at prefent *groans* are fairly and
impartially laid open and confidered.

Earneftly addrefs'd to the

ELECTORS of GREAT-BRITAIN.

By the Author of the *True Patriot*, and
A ferious Addrefs to the People of Great-Britain.

The SECOND EDITION.

LONDON:

Printed for M. COOPER, at the *Globe* in *Pater-nofter-*
Row. 1747.

A DIALOGUE

BETWEEN

A Gentleman from *London*[1]

AND

An ELECTOR in the COUNTRY.[2]

Gentleman.

Mr. Alderman, your most humble Servant. This Prevention of
my Visit is kind indeed.

Alderman.

My dear Friend, I no sooner heard you was in Town, than I
ran to embrace you. Our long Acquaintance and Friendship
ought not to be satisfied with cold Compliments; and, to say
Truth, I should have been better pleased if you had laid aside all
Ceremony, and had made my House your own.

Gentleman.

It was not, I assure you, that I doubted a hearty Welcome; but
the Occasion of my coming I feared might make such a Visit less
agreeable.

Alderman.

I am sorry my old Friend should come hither on any Occasion,
which he imagines would be disagreeable to me.

Gentleman.

Nay, now you misunderstand me. I mean my Business here is
of such a Nature, and will be attended with so many Followers,
that I must have been too troublesome a Guest at a private House.

---

[1] For evidence that the *Dialogue* was intended to have particular relevance for a particular
election see General Introduction above, pp. xxxiii–xxxiv.

[2] As the title page confirms, the reference here is primarily political. The elector is in the
'Country' or Opposition interest; as an alderman, he is a magistrate, perhaps also a Justice
of the Peace, of his town or borough. 'London' here represents the 'Court' or ministerial
interest. The dialogue between 'Court' and 'Country' is roughly that between Whig and
Tory.

Alderman.

Nay, nay, lay aside the Courtier, tho' you have a Place,[1] and speak out fairly.

Gentleman.

Sit thee down then, my Friend, and fill thy Pipe, and I will speak fairly and openly. I am come hither to espouse the Interest of two worthy Gentlemen, at the next Election, Sir *John Protestant*, and Mr. *English*;[2] they are strictly united, and I hope will succeed.

Alderman.

I must tell you then as plainly, I hope they will not; and I am sorry to find that one who hath always professed those honest Principles which I have heard so often from your Mouth, can espouse such a Cause.

Gentleman.

Why, do you know either of the Gentlemen, against whom you are so violent?

Alderman.

I know they are both Placemen, and that is with me a sufficient Objection to them.[3]

Gentleman.

Sure, my Friend, this is a very dangerous Doctrine. If the Service of the Public be so inconsistent with a Man's maintaining a good Character in his Country, I am afraid it will follow either that there must be an End of all Civil and Military Offices, and consequently of all Government; or that these must be entrusted to the most vile and infamous Hands.

Alderman.

You cannot so mistake my Meaning. I would only exclude *such* from the House of Commons.

[1] An administrative appointment or sinecure in the Government, a reward for political services. In alluding to his friend's 'Place' the Alderman manifests a typically Tory distaste for dependency upon ministerial favour.

[2] The names here assigned to the Court candidates in the Parliamentary elections of June–July 1747 reflect the Administration assertion that its opponents had Stuart inclinations and that the Stuarts would be hostile to the essential Protestantism of the country.

[3] Opposition Tories were particularly united in the belief that administrative and legislative functions should be separated, and that salaried posts should be reserved for persons not directly involved in electoral politics.

Gentleman.

Would you exclude them universally?[1]

Alderman.

Ay, universally.

Gentleman.

We must have then either a very sorry Parliament, or a very sorry Administration: For all Men of great Abilities, which enable them to execute either of these Trusts, and of great Fortunes, which are the best Security to the Public, for the faithful Execution of them, must be excluded either from the one or the other. A most dreadful Dilemma sure to this Nation. But do you not really see the utter Impossibility of carrying on the Business of Government, unless those who are concerned in the Administration of it, have Seats in that great Council, where all public Measures are to be canvassed and authorized? Can you imagine to yourself any thing more absurd than a Parliament whence every Man in public Business was excluded, debating and resolving Matters of which they must be *totally ignorant*? If the bare Mention of such a Parliament doth not shock you, ask any Member who hath sat there a single Session, and he must be candid enough to satisfy you, that the Business of the Nation cannot be (as it is) conducted in Parliament, unless those who are principally engaged in the conducting it, are Members of that Body.

Alderman.

Suppose I admit this, what a small Number of Placemen will on this Account become necessary?

Gentleman.

As to the Numbers, they are Matter of a different Consideration, and may become the Subject of our Discourse anon. If you admit it is necessary to have some Placemen in the House of Commons, it follows you can have no Objection to my Friends, merely on that Head, and therefore if you have no other, I shall

---

[1] The most recent Place Act (1743) specifically excluded 'the treasurer or comptroller of the navy, the secretaries of the treasury, the secretary to the chancellor of the exchequer, or secretaries of the admiralty, the under secretary to any of his Majesty's principal secretaries of state, or the deputy paymaster of the army, or . . . any person having or holding any office or employment for life'; 15 Geo. II, cap. 22, sec. 3; *Statutes at Large*, xviii. 36–7.

depend on your old Friendship to give me your Interest for
them.

Alderman.

To be plain with you, if they were never so unexceptionable, it
is not in my Power to serve them, for I am already engaged.

Gentleman.

And to whom, pray?

Alderman.

To Sir *Thomas Leadenhead* and Mr. *Toastum*;[1] Men of such
Worth and Honour, that I believe I may defy you to advance a
single Objection against them.

Gentleman.

Not any, I confess, stronger than what you might suggest to
yourself, especially against one of them; unless you have strangely
altered your Way of Thinking since I formerly knew you; for
sure I have often heard you maintain the most rigid Principles of
a Republican.[2]

Alderman.

I own it, and I promise you I am not altered in the least.

Gentleman.

Can you then require a stronger Objection to any Man, than
that he is a *known Jacobite*, which I take to be the case with Sir
Thomas? The other, indeed, calls himself a Whig;[3] but by uniting
his Interest with his Fellow-Candidate, I think he gives us the
strongest Reason to suspect his own Principles.

[1] The names point to the alleged inferiority of Jacobite programmes and candidates and
to the Jacobite reputation for hard drinking; see, for example, *JJ* nos. 1, 2, 6, below, pp.
91–5, 98–9, 124–7; and, for a specific allusion to the toasts drunk by the Independent
Electors of Great Britain, General Introduction above, p. xxx.

[2] On the use of 'Republican' as a term of opprobrium applied to extremist Whig elements,
see General Introduction above, p. lxv, and *JJ* no. 7 of 16 January 1748, below, p. 131.
The Gentleman is making a commonplace identification of Tories and 'real' Whigs in their
concern for safeguards against ministerial predominance by means of political patronage
and place-holding; see Caroline Robbins, *The Eighteenth-Century Commonwealthman*
(Cambridge, Mass., 1961), pp. 8–9, and *Dialogue*, below, pp. 17–23.

[3] A preliminary candidate for Westminster, Sir John Philips had accepted, briefly, a
place as Lord of Trade and Plantations in the 'broad-bottom' Administration which was
set up after Granville's ouster in 1744, but according to Philip Yorke 'seemed resolved to
give us an early specimen that he would be as troublesome a placeman as a patriot'; quoted

Alderman.

The Court, my Friend, hath long cheated us with Names; the Term *Jacobite* is a mere Bugbear, and hath served very well to deceive and to amuse the Multitude; but empty Sounds will not impose on me.

Gentleman.

You surprize me; I did not expect to hear this Language at present from any one. It seemed, I own, a strange Doctrine to me, which possessed many some Years ago, that the Spirit of *Jacobitism* was totally extinct among us: But now, when the Nation yet feels the Consequences of a cursed Rebellion,[1] for sure the most incredulous of your Friends, though they persisted so long in denying the Reality of that Rebellion, have now given up the Point; an Army of *Highlanders* advancing the *Pretender's* Banners into the very Heart of the Kingdom,[2] is a Proof, I think, that *Jacobitism* is no empty Sound.

Alderman.

And what Assistance, pray, did these *Highlanders* meet with in *England*?

Gentleman.

The usual Assistance which your Friends the *Jacobites* here lend to any Cause. It is true, indeed, they prudently refrained from drawing their Swords;[3] but it is as well known how gloriously and openly they *drew their Corks* in the *Pretender's* Favour.

Alderman.

I think, my Friend, I know you thoroughly; and I believe you so honest a Man, that though a Court may misguide, it cannot corrupt you. I will therefore venture to speak out; but first let me secure the Door, that no *Williams* may intrude himself.[4] I will now shew you my Confidence by the most

by Owen, *Rise of the Pelhams*, p. 252. See also Owen, pp. 72, 259, 335, and General Introduction above, p. xxxiv. By 1747, however, there can have been no doubt of his commitment to the Opposition. The reference here is undoubtedly designed to cover that other category of the Opposition, potentially disaffected Whigs.

[1] The Jacobite rebellion of 1745–6.
[2] On 4 December 1745 the rebels advanced as far as Derby, their deepest penetration into England.
[3] Contrary to Jacobite expectations, only one regiment (from Lancashire) was raised for service on behalf of the Pretender.
[4] John Williams, a Piccadilly innkeeper, was observed eavesdropping at the anniversary

explicit Language. I was bred, as you well know, in republican Principles, and I still retain them in my Heart; though I confess, I have long despaired of seeing any such virtuous Establishment in this Nation. Since then we must have a King, I am pretty indifferent as to the Person, and would in my Choice consult *the Good of Old England* only. Whenever therefore we want a *Redress of Grievances* under any King,[1] what can be so desirable as an Exchange? For by such Exchange we shall more probably be Gainers than Losers.

Gentleman.

You have now spoken out indeed, and I promise you shall not repent your Confidence. By what I can find then, you would turn away a King with less Ceremony, and perhaps for less Cause, than some prudent Men would dismiss a Servant. But how comes it, my Friend, since you have turned *Jacobite*, you have not learnt a little more Respect for this supreme Magistrate? I should rather have expected to hear something of divine, indefeasible, hereditary Right.

Alderman.

You know I have always despised such absurd Notions: I am a *Jacobite upon republican Principles*, I assure you.

Gentleman.

You astonish me no less, than if you was to call yourself an *Atheist upon Christian Principles*.

Alderman.

There is nothing so absurd in my Tenets as you would en-

feast of the Independent Electors of Westminster and was beaten for his pains; see General Introduction above, p. xxx.

[1] Cf. the Bill of Rights (1689), 1 Will. & Mar. session 2, cap. 2, sec. 13: 'And that for redress of all grievances, and for the amending, strengthening, and preserving of the laws . . .'; *Statutes at Large*, ix. 69. As a political cant phrase it is present in the sub-title of the *Dialogue*. In *TP* no. 19 of 4–11 March 1746 Fielding anatomizes the Opposition, 'in a Place not far from *Westminster*', and in particular 'a Gentleman they called the Elderman or Alderman', to whom are attributed sentiments like those of his counterpart in the *Dialogue*. Miriam Austin Locke (ed.), *The True Patriot* (University of Alabama Press, 1964), p. 172, conjectures that the earlier reference might have been to Alderman George Heathcote (1700–68), M.P. for London 1741–7, a leader of the Opposition in the City, who in September 1745 had unsuccessfully moved a redress of grievances against the ministry. See also *Yale Walpole*, xix. 107. In 1747 Heathcote was one of the stewards of the Independent Electors of Westminster; *GM*, xvii (1747), 150.

deavour to insinuate. I believe no King to have any Right at all, and therefore, whenever we have Grievances to redress, I would exchange him. This is an honest Doctrine, and a wise one.

Gentleman.

You will pardon me if I think it neither honest nor wise; nay, I hope to convince you it is not. You despise, you say, that indefeasible *Jacobite*-Principle of *indefeasible hereditary Right*.

Alderman.

I do from my Soul.

Gentleman.

Then you think King *James* the Second had no such Right, nor of Consequence can his Posterity derive it from him.

Alderman.

Certainly none.

Gentleman.

You will admit, perhaps, that if King *James* the Second had any Right which was defeasible, it was defeated by Forfeiture and Abdication. Perhaps you will be better pleased if I say the People did wisely and justly in *exchanging* him.

Alderman.

I admit all this.

Gentleman.

Then the *Pretender*[1] hath no hereditary Right.

Alderman.

None.

Gentleman.

Do you think it will follow from this Admission, that no other hath any Right to the Crown?

Alderman.

Do you really believe any one hath?

Gentleman.

Yes, faith, do I; and so clear and incontestable a Right, that

[1] James Francis Edward Stuart (1688–1766), only son of James II by Mary of Modena.

no honest Man, even though he was a Republican in Principle, would endeavour to divest him of the Possession. The divine Right to Crowns I shall treat with the same Contempt as yourself; but surely the human Rights of a King stand on the same Foundations of natural Reason and Justice with any other Rights whatever. What Right have you to your House, Mr. Alderman, for I think it is your own?

Alderman.

I am in possession of the Deeds, which is, perhaps, more than every Courtier can say.

Gentleman.

Doth not your Right consist in its being conveyed to you from those who had the absolute Property?

Alderman.

Why do you ask so plain a Question?

Gentleman.

And is not the King's Right to his Crown as plain?—In whom is all Civil Power originally and absolutely placed?

Alderman.

Certainly in the People.

Gentleman.

And will not the Voice, not only of our Law, but of Reason and Justice tell you, that whatever a Man possesses absolutely, he may dispose of, either in Part, or in the Whole, either absolutely or conditionally? That neither he, nor any who claim under him, can resume again what is thus absolutely granted without the Will of him to whom it was granted; or, if granted conditionally, till the Condition be broken?

Alderman.

This, I believe, is *Law*.

Gentleman.

And is it not *Reason* and *Justice*?

Alderman.

I cannot gainsay it.

Gentleman.

Surely you would think it highly unjust in the Person who sold you your House, or in his Heir, wantonly and of his own Will to turn you out.

Alderman.

I think I should.

Gentleman.

Have not then a Body of Men, or a whole People, the same Power of disposing of what they possess; and are not they, their Heirs and Successors, equally bound by their Grant?

Alderman.

There is great Difference between the Delegation of Power by a whole People, and the Disposition of Property by Individuals;[1] the latter being for the sole Advantage of the Persons to whom the Use is limited, whereas the former is delegated by the People solely for their own Benefit.

Gentleman.

For their own Benefit, I agree; but not *solely* so. Power, and Honour, and generally Riches, attend all Magistrates as the Emoluments of their Office, and this in Republics as well as Monarchies. But from your Distinction, I own, arises a tacite Condition; and this is well understood at present to attend the Crown of *England*, *viz.* That our Kings shall not go about to subvert the Laws, nor the Constitution of this Kingdom. Nay, this is even express'd in the Coronation Oath.[2] Now, till this Condition is broken, *the King of* England *hath as solid and as just a Right to his Crown, as any Subject can have to his private Property.* Let us see this in a lower and nearer Light. Would it not be against Law to deprive a subordinate Magistrate of any Office of

---

[1] The 'Difference' figured greatly in the parliamentary debates over the taking away of the heritable jurisdictions in Scotland; see General Introduction above, pp. xxvi–xxvii, and *Dialogue*, below, pp. 50–3.

[2] By the terms of the Coronation Oath Act of 1689 (1 Will. & Mar., C. 6) the oath read: 'Will you solemnly promise and swear to govern the people of this kingdom of *England*, and the dominions thereto belonging, according to the statutes in parliament agreed on, and the laws and customs of the same ?'; *Statutes at Large*, ix. 4. For a chart of the changes made by the Act of 1689 see Leopold G. Wickham Legg, *English Coronation Records* (London, 1901), p. xxxi.

Honour and Profit, unless he had forfeited it, or unless his Commission was expired?

Alderman.

Surely.

Gentleman.

Would it not be equally against Reason and Justice?

Alderman.

I see your Inference—and must frankly own to you, I have not much considered the Matter in this Light.

Gentleman.

I believe it: For you must now observe how necessary the absurd and exploded Doctrines of indefeasible hereditary Right, which we both alike despise, are to reconcile Treason against the present King, even to the Rules of natural Justice: For if the Sovereign Power devolved to the People by the Forfeiture and Abdication of King *James* the Second, the People have most certainly entailed the Crown on the House of *Hanover*, and his Majesty enjoys it in the Right of that Entail. Here then is a Title which every Republican must acknowledge. Those indeed, who at a time when the Throne was vacant, proposed other Forms of Government, argued perhaps honestly from their own Principles; but the Case is now altered, we are bound by the Act of our Ancestors in this as in every other Instance; and the Traitor, if he doth not hold indefeasible hereditary Right, must appear to himself in the detestable Light of a Rebel.

But this, tho' certainly of itself sufficient, is not all his Majesty's Title. The Parliament, in the Act of Settlement, made no arbitrary nor wanton Disposal of the Crown.[1] They adhered strictly to the Law and to the Constitution in which the Crown is held to be hereditary, though not indefeasibly so. His Majesty is the next Heir who is capable of enjoying it, being the next Protestant Heir; and he would not only have had an incontestable Right to

---

[1] 12 & 13 Will. III, cap. 2, enacted (1701) after Mary's death and that of the Duke of Gloucester, Princess Anne's son, upheld the hereditary right by going back in the Stuart pedigree to the daughter of the exiled Queen of Bohemia (herself the child of James I), the Electress Sophia of Hanover. By the terms of the Act, succession, after Princess Anne and her descendants and William's, was limited to the Electress and her descendants, 'being protestants'; *Statutes at Large*, x. 357–9.

the Crown; but by the Law of this Kingdom, would have been actually and *ipso facto* King, without any Act of Settlement whatever. So that this Act is to be deemed only as corroborative of his Majesty's Title, as an Affirmance of the Common Law, and of all the great constitutional Points enacted at the Revolution, particularly of that wholesome, necessary and excellent Law, by which Papists are excluded for ever from the Throne.[1]

Hitherto then I think this Doctrine doth not appear extremely honest. Is not a Traitor against this lawful and rightful Sovereign guilty, at least, of the same Injustice with a Robber? And if we add to this the Guilt of Perjury, which must attend all those who have sworn Allegiance to the present King, the Idea will, I apprehend, afford little Consolation on the Scaffold; nor can it produce much Honour to any Party, or to its Martyrs.

Alderman.

I own I cannot answer all this, and yet if you argue for the Right of Kings, it seems hard to deprive innocent Persons of their Right for the Fault of their Ancestors.

Gentleman.

I admit, to deprive any Person of his Right, is hard, and what is worse, unjust; and against this Injustice I have hitherto been arguing. But you are guilty here of a Misrepresentation: For instead of his Right, you should say what would have been his Right, had it not been prevented by the Fault of his Ancestors. This then is the Case of all Forfeitures; and have not the innocent Posterity of every Person attainted of Treason or of Felony, the same Reason to complain? But by the Forfeiture, a new Right accrues to another; a Right which stands on, and is guarded by, the self-same Rules of Justice which protect every other Right. Would it not be unjust to deprive the Son or Grandson[2] of one who was rightfully possessed of a forfeited Estate, and who hath now as good a Right as the Person had who originally forfeited

---

[1] Section ix of the Bill of Rights (1689) states that 'all and every person and persons that is, are or shall be reconciled to, or shall hold communion with, the see or church of *Rome*, or shall profess the popish religion, or shall marry a papist, shall be excluded, and be for ever incapable to inherit, possess, or enjoy the crown and government of this realm'; *Statutes at Large*, ix. 72.

[2] Charles Edward Louis Philip Casimir (1720–88), the Young Pretender, eldest son of James Francis Edward Stuart and grandson of James II.

it, and to restore it to the Son or Grandson of that Person, who hath now no Right to it at all? Compassion here pleads equally for both, and Justice only for one. On which Side then would be the Hardship? would it not be on that where it is coupled with the highest Injustice? This weak Argument, if it means any thing, goes to destroy all Forfeiture; and in your Case therefore it would maintain indefeasible Right, and in reality absolute Power.

Alderman.

I shall contend for no such Doctrine, I assure you; but you will admit, I believe, that if the Crown hath been forfeited, it may be forfeited again.

Gentleman.

I see no ill Consequence in the Admission.

Alderman.

I fancy you will admit too we have some Grievances to complain of.

Gentleman.

They must be Grievances of a very high Nature, Friend, which can amount to this Forfeiture. Such Grievances as must amount to a Breach of the Condition abovementioned, and to an Infringement of the Coronation Oath, by which the People are of consequence absolved from their Allegiance: For to think of this great and awful Magistrate with so little Veneration as to imagine him removeable, on every trifling and perhaps imaginary Complaint, at the Will, or indeed at the Caprice of a Party, is inconsistent as well with the Principles of a good Politician as with those of a good Christian. Indeed it is hard to say whether the Condition of such a King or of his People would be more lamentable; the one being constantly liable to the Loss of his Crown, and the other to a Confusion and Anarchy which always hath ended, and always must end in the Loss of their Liberty.

I think therefore it appears necessary for you to produce some Grievances of a very high Nature, if you would maintain the Honesty of the Principles you have avowed, or, indeed, if you would maintain their Wisdom.

Alderman.

Very well. Will you deny then that our Liberty is in Danger?

Gentleman.

First let me know what you mean by the Word *Liberty*; for
though this Word is in every Man's Mouth, I have often doubted
whether we have annexed to it any settled and certain Idea.
Many indeed seem to understand by it the Liberty of doing what
they please.

Alderman.

By the Liberty of an *Englishman* I mean the Enjoyment of all
those Privileges which the Law allows him.

Gentleman.

And can you shew me a single Instance where any Man hath
been abridged of this Liberty, under the present Administration,
or since the Establishment of the present Royal Family on the
Throne? Hath any one Man been executed, arraigned, or imprisoned contrary to the known Laws of this Realm? Have the
Estates or Properties of any (even of the lowest) Subject been
taken away? hath his Right been impeached or his Possession
been disturbed without the strictest legal Authority? Can we be
said then not to enjoy all the Privileges which the Law allows
us? On the contrary, do we not enjoy much more? Is not Treason
writ in our News-Papers; and talked and sung and toasted in
our Taverns every Day with Impunity? And yet if you consult
our Law Books, you will find there are very severe Laws for the
Punishment of all these Offences; and if you will turn over the
History of former Ages (particularly the Reigns of the *Stuarts*)
you will see very bitter Examples of these Punishments. Nay,
even of those Persons who have carried their Malice into Act,
and have appeared in open Rebellion, have any been convicted
without every Formality which the Law requires?[1] I dare appeal

---

[1] Although a number of commoners were tried and executed for complicity in the
Jacobite rebellion, the most controversial trials were those of four Scottish peers in Westminster Hall during the summer of 1746 and (Lovat's case) March 1747. For a detailed and
slightly hostile contemporary witness see Walpole to Mann, 1 August 1746 (*Yale Walpole*,
xix. 280–9). The Government was particularly anxious to observe all the legalities, but
objection was raised to the manner of indictment and to the fact that the Act of 1746 (19
Geo. II, cap. 9), which permitted the trial to take place 'in such county . . . as his Majesty
shall appoint', was not passed until after the date of the crime for which the peers were

to *Westminster-Hall* for the Integrity, for the Justice, for the Candour of all the Proceedings against them; so far were the Judges from shewing the least Partiality on the side of the Crown, that not one strained Construction of any Law, nor even one harsh or indecent Word fell from the Mouth of the King's Council against any one of the Prisoners. Compare this with the Proceedings of former Times, in Trials for Treason (and particularly with those in the Reigns of the *Stuarts*) you will find how much the Spirit of Liberty is strengthened among us by the present Establishment, by his Majesty's own Disposition, and by that of his Ministers. Lastly, to shew how mildly legal Powers in Favour of the Crown have been executed; when the *Habeas Corpus* Act was suspended by Parliament a whole Year,[1] not six Persons were Sufferers by its Suspension, though a dangerous Rebellion then raged in the Nation, and though many Persons were not only suspected, but publicly known to favour it, and only to wait a safe Opportunity of appearing in support of the Cause. Some of these may perhaps be called Instances of too great Mercy in the Royal Mind, and of too great Lenity in his Administration. But surely such amiable Blemishes will not be construed into Grievances, much less represented as Attacks on our Liberty: And I solemnly declare I know no other.

Alderman.

You mistake me. I have not said our Liberties were actually and openly attacked. I only said they were in Danger.

Gentleman.

This of *our Liberty being in Danger*, is a Cant Phrase invented for the same seditious Purposes with that ever-memorable Cant

being tried. The alleged clemency (or brutality) of the Government in its dealing with captured rebels lingered on as something of a political issue. Walpole wrote to Mann (12 August 1746): 'Popularity has changed sides since the year '15, for now the city and the generality are very angry that so many rebels have been pardoned'; *Yale Walpole*, xix. 296. As a result of the outcry over Lovat's being denied counsel for the purpose of examining witnesses, in June 1747 Parliament passed a Bill (20 Geo. II, cap. 30) allowing 'full defence by council learned in the law'; *Statutes at Large*, xviii. 409, and xix. 66–7; *Journals of . . . Commons*, xxv. 376, and *Yale Walpole*, xix. 396–7.

[1] During the Jacobite disturbances the Act had been suspended by 19 Geo. II, cap. 1 (21 October 1745) and further suspended by 19 Geo. II, cap. 17 (19 April 1746) and 20 Geo. II, cap. 1 (21 November 1746); *Statutes at Large*, xviii. 397, 443, and xix. [1]–2. The suspension expired on 21 February 1747. On the vehemence of Opposition objections see Coxe, *Pelham*, ii. 348–9.

Phrase of the Church being in Danger. Like that, it produces no direct Allegation, much less attempts any Proof; and consequently it admits of no Answer; but, like that, will by Time only be brought into universal Derision and Contempt. In private Life, the causeless Apprehensions of Danger from Persons who have given no Cause of such Suspicion, is thought a certain Symptom of Madness; in Public, they may be called the Phrenzy of the People; and this Words alone without Truth, nay, without Meaning, are always capable of raising. Thus it was remarked by a great Wit of the last Age; That instead of the *Church being in Danger*, it would serve altogether as well for the Purpose of raising a Mob to say the *Monument was in Danger*.[1]

Alderman.

This is Raillery; but you cannot in Reality imagine the Liberties of any People to be safe where Corruption hath spread itself so universally as among us.

Gentleman.

This is a second Grievance which you charge on the Government. Now admitting the Nation to be as corrupt as you please, do you really think the Government accountable for it?

Alderman.

Do I! ay surely: For who else distributes Places, Titles, Ribbands, Pensions, and all other Wages of Corruption!

Gentleman.

Hey! what a String of Words is here? Are then all Trusts and Rewards, which the Constitution of *England* hath lodged in the Gift of the Crown to be considered as the Wages of Corruption? This is very strange and new Doctrine.

Alderman.

Yes, when they are given to unworthy Men for bad Purposes.

---

[1] Swift, 'An Argument against abolishing Christianity', *Prose Works*, ed. Herbert Davis, ii (Oxford, 1939), 32: 'What, for Instance, is easier than to vary the Form of Speech; and instead of the Word *Church*, make it a Question in Politicks, Whether the *Monument* be in Danger?' The Monument, built by Wren to commemorate the Fire of London, bore an inscription which blamed the fire on the papists; Pope, 'Epistle III: To Allen Lord Bathurst', 339–40 and Pope's own note.

Gentleman.

True; but that is begging the Question. The Things themselves are no Corruption, and you give me no Proof of the bad
Purposes, or of the Unworthiness of those to whom they are
given.

Alderman.

Pensions, at least, you will grant must be Corruption.

Gentleman.

If these are clandestinely given to Members of Parliament,[1] I
will admit it; but do you know of any such? As to other Pensions,
they are a necessary Part of the Royal Bounty, and often most
laudably and wisely bestowed. But, my Friend, I find by Corruption, you mean Bribery; this is only one Species of Corruption; whereas this Word, when used generally in a political Sense,
must comprehend, I conceive, every thing which corrupts the
Minds of the People. Now Philosophy will tell you, that all our
Passions are equally capable of corrupting the Mind; and Experience must convince you that Envy, Malice, Anger, Hatred,
and Revenge, have as powerful a Dominion in the human Breast,
as Avarice or Vanity, to which two alone the Bribes you mention
can be applied. Are then the Arts of Corruption confined to a
Court? Are not the Heads of Parties, who are influenced by any
of the Passions I have mentioned to unite in an Opposition against
the Court, corrupt? What are the People who are misled and
inflamed by the grossest Misrepresentations, and blackest Falshoods against the King and his Administration? Are they not
corrupted in their Understanding, the most dangerous perhaps of
all Corruption? Lastly, what is public Favour and Popularity
obtained by inventing and circulating these Falshoods, under the
Colour and Pretence of Patriotism? Is not this Favour purchased
by Corruption?

---

[1] On 17 February 1747 a motion was made in the Commons 'to inquire whether any and
what Offices belonging to the Revenue are held in Trust, in the Whole, or any Part, for
others, and for whom; and whether any, and what, Deductions, Allowances, or Gratuities,
are made out of them to any Person or Persons, and to whom, in order to lessen the public
Expence, and to prevent any undue Influence in future Elections of Members to serve in
Parliament'; *Journals of . . . Commons*, xxv. 294. The motion was defeated, but Walpole
wrote to Mann (23 February 1747) that 'we had a warm day' on the debate; *Yale Walpole*,
xix. 370.

Alderman.

Most certainly; but I shall not so hastily grant that the Opposition have misrepresented the Court; it appears to me rather that you have misrepresented the Opposition. If you can prove to me indeed that all our Grievances are imaginary.

Gentleman.

If I should be so lucky, you will, I believe, grant that those who have endeavoured to inflame the Nation with imaginary Grievances cannot have acted from the Principles of Patriotism. We must then search after some other Motives to their Actions, and perhaps we need not search long to discover the Views of Men *who have formerly been in an Opposition, have grown popular from being so, have succeeded from that Popularity; have obtained the Power which they had opposed, have used that Power much worse than those whom they had opposed; have been removed from it again by their Country; have again set on Foot an Opposition, and have impudently applied a second time to their Country, hoping to corrupt even their Common Sense, and aspiring to a second Establishment in Power, by the Assistance of that Public, whom they have already so grossly betrayed, and who have already by unanimous Consent tumbled them from their Seat.*[1]

Alderman.

God forbid there should be many such.

Gentleman.

God forbid it too; but if there are any such, the Patriotism which they and their Partizans affect, may well, I think, be said to be pretended; and the Popularity gained by this Pretence, may well be imputed to the Corruption I have mentioned. Here then

---

[1] Alluding to the machinations of Granville (Carteret), Bath (Pulteney), and their adherents, who upon succeeding at last to Sir Robert Walpole's Administration deliberately excluded from office a number of their former associates in Opposition, among them George Lyttelton. By November 1744 the Pelhams, with the aid of the excluded members of the Opposition, forced Granville's resignation and undertook a 'broad-bottom' ministry. Granville retained the favour of the King, however, and when in February 1746 the Pelhams resigned in frustration, he attempted unsuccessfully to form a government, the so-called 'forty-eight-hour ministry'; see Owen, *Rise of the Pelhams*, Ch. VII. In 1747 there were Administration fears that the King might try to restore Granville in the new Parliament, and the Prince of Wales tried several times to recruit him for the new Opposition; see Archibald S. Foord, *His Majesty's Opposition, 1714–1830* (Oxford, 1964), pp. 256–63.

is one Corruption for which the Court is not accountable. Again, what shall we say to other Methods which, perhaps, carry with them least the Appearance of Corruption, and yet bring after them the same Consequences? Doth not the Country Gentleman, who uses the Power of his Fortune *arbitrarily* and *oppressively* to influence his Tenants and his Tradesmen, either in Boroughs or in Counties, equally destroy the Freedom of Election with him who pays so much ready Money for a Vote? Indeed every Attempt to deceive the People by misleading their Judgments, to inflame them by misinforming their Opinions, or to compel them by the Power of a private Fortune, are equal Corruptions to Bribery in their Nature, are more certain and efficacious in their Operation, and generally more dangerous in the End proposed.

Now in all these Methods of corrupting, the Opposition have greatly the Advantage of the Court; and are they freer even from that Species which you mentioned, from Bribery itself? Are Bribes distributed at an Election on one Side only? Are not the Cellars and the Coffers of the Country Party, as it is absurdly called, open on this Occasion? Are not the Wages of Iniquity distributed in as gross a Manner on that Side as on the other? Are there not as many and as bare-fac'd Instances on Record of Bonds and Notes by those who have espoused the Opposition and been espoused by them, as can be shewn on the Part of the Administration? Lastly, do not the Incumbrances on the Estates of Country Gentlemen, often to the Ruin of them and their Families, stand as perpetual Monuments of the Methods which they have pursued at their Elections? So that Corruption seems as unfairly to be charged on the Government, as a Plague would be, if such raged universally in the Nation.

Alderman.

I thank you kindly, Sir, for the Hint, since I believe you will acknowledge, that in the Case you mention of a Plague, our Governors wou'd deserve the highest Censure, if they did not immediately endeavour to prevent its spreading, and to put a Stop to it as soon as possible; especially if it should appear that the Way to effect this was easy, and chalked out to them.

Gentleman.

Is it so easy then to put a Stop to this universal Corruption?

Alderman.

I will venture to say it is; and that two Bills, for which the Public have long called, (I may say groaned) would effectually do it. You must know I mean the Place-Bill, and the Bill for annual, or at most triennial Parliaments.[1]

Gentleman.

Another Grievance then complained of is, that the present Administration have not given you that Idol (as you think it) of the Public, the Place-Bill. Now I am afraid there is great Superstition in the Worship of this Idol, and it would be equally unable with any popish Saint to bestow on its Votaries what they expected from it. However, I think, you have given up an universal Place-Bill.

Alderman.

I own the great Officers of State seem necessary to be allowed.

Gentleman.

And do you think there are no Place-Bills already?

Alderman.

Why, are there?

Gentleman.

Many, I promise you. There are several Offices which are at this Day inconsistent with Seats in Parliament. Nay, there is one Place-Bill enacted this very Parliament, by which great Numbers of inferior Place-Men are excluded from being hereafter Members of the House of Commons.[2]

Alderman.

I never heard, I assure you, of any such Law.

Gentleman.

Very likely not, nor would you hear of another if it was farther

---

[1] The Place Bill was a common eighteenth-century strategy of the 'Country' party in its fight to curb ministerial influence on the members of the Lords and the Commons; see above, p. 18, n. 1. Opposition hostility to septennial parliaments was based on the assumption that such a tenure entrenched government influence. For parliamentary debates on a 1744 motion for double-taxing places and pensions, and on a 1745 motion to reinstitute annual parliaments, see Hansard, xiii. 993–1050, 1056–1107.

[2] 15 Geo. II, cap. 22 ('For further limiting or reducing the number of officers capable of sitting in the house of commons'); see above, p. 5, n. 1.

extended; because it will never be thought by your republican or *Jacobite* Friends to have gone far enough, till it becomes an universal Place-Bill: But so many Restrictions of this kind have been already made, that unless we suppose some other undue Influence, the Court can never succeed in any unpopular Measures by this alone. The Number of Place-Men will hereafter be so inconsiderable, that we must suppose some undue Influence of another kind, or it could not be effectual: Nay, I will venture to say, there hath never yet been a Vote carried in the House of Commons in which great Numbers who have had no Places have not concurred. In proportion, therefore, as the Numbers of Place-Men abate, this other Influence must encrease. If, therefore, we can suppose a Minister capable of carrying Points by Corruption, we must see that this Corruption would be at the Expence of the Public, and consequently, the more general a Place-Bill is, the more it would enhance the public Expence by the Encrease of Pensioners:[1] For the Place-Men must be still paid; since you would not, I suppose, deprive the Government of Officers, though you would exclude these from Parliament.

Alderman.

But I fancy, my good Friend, you have heard of a Pension-Bill, as well as of a Place-Bill.[2] If we exclude Pensioners also, the Court will find it difficult, I believe, to procure a Majority.

Gentleman.

But this, I am afraid, is a harder Task than you imagine. I think I may call it impossible. Pensions and Gratuities may be given without Witness, and without being liable to any possibility of legal Proof: How will you guard against this? By Oaths? I am sorry to say sad Experience convinces us, that the Multiplication of Oaths serves to little other purpose than to the dreadful Propagation of Perjury. I might mention an Oath of much the same Nature enacted by Parliament to prevent Bribery at Elections,[3] and the bare mention of it is enough to fill any

[1] Those to whom government patronage took the form of money payments, as distinct from, or in addition to, appointments to 'Places' or offices. Cf. Johnson, *Dictionary* (1755), *s.v.* Pension: 'an allowance made to anyone without an equivalent. In England it is generally understood to mean pay given to a state hireling for treason to his country.'

[2] The two were frequent corollaries in Opposition strategy; see Foord, *His Majesty's Opposition*, p. 183 and note.

[3] 2 Geo. II, cap. 24 ('An act for the more effectual preventing bribery and corruption in

honest Man with Horror. This is indeed the most inadequate of all Methods to restrain Men from doing Evil; for when Interest hath once gotten the better of Honour and Honesty, the Sanction of an Oath will generally be little regarded. But admit that some Men should set to themselves a *ne plus ultra* in Iniquity, and tho' they may not be with-held by the Rules of Honour or Honesty, would yet be frightened by manifest Perjury; may not these Gratuities be called by so many Names, and conveyed in so many different Ways, that Consciences not over-scrupulous might find sufficient Evasions to satisfy themselves, and to explain away their Oath? Nay, admitting that some Consciences should be too nice for any Evasion whatever, and could by no Means be brought to accept any such Gratuity themselves, may not these, however, be as much influenc'd by Favours conferred on their Children, or on other Relations? In reality, these Bills have been represented to be of much more Consequence than they are; for Corruption is too stubborn an Evil to be cured, or even palliated by any such Remedies.

Alderman.

Corruption is certainly a very stubborn Evil, especially when it is so rooted, as it is at present in this Kingdom. But what can you say against annual Parliaments? The Reasons for our desiring these are, I believe, too strong for you to encounter; for indeed I have never heard any one attempt to give an Answer to them.

Gentleman.

Your present Acquaintances, the *Jacobites*, are much abler at Allegations than at Answers; for I think they have never yet been so good to give a single Answer to all which hath been advanced against their absurd Principles. Their Arguments and their Weapons are indeed one and the same; *Songs and Toasts, Curses and Huzzas.* Indeed in this they act consistently enough; for as it is a Cause in behalf of which no Man, though his Wit was ever so great, could say any thing, so is it a Cause for which no Man would fight who had even a single Grain of common Sense. I shall not therefore be deterred by their Example; but

the elections of members to serve in parliament'); *Statutes at Large*, xvi. 66–9. This Act required an oath of every voter, upon demand of a candidate or any two of the electors, and of every returning officer, to the effect that he received no gratuities, direct or indirect.

am as sanguine in my Hopes of answering this Grievance as much to your Satisfaction, as I seem to have answered the other. Let me ask you, then, what Advantage you propose from an annual Parliament?

Alderman.

That it would not be in the Power of a Minister to corrupt either the Electors or Elected.

Gentleman.

You think the Expence would be so great?

Alderman.

Certainly.

Gentleman.

So much the worse for us, for we must find the Money to corrupt them; but to confess the Truth, it would have no such Consequence. On the contrary, would you not be surpriz'd, could I convince you that this fine plausible Scheme would of all others bid the fairest for putting Parliaments absolutely into the Hands of a Minister, and that without giving him any Trouble at all with the Electors, and not much more with the Elected.

Alderman.

This would surprize me indeed.

Gentleman.

By what Right doth any Man sit in Parliament?

Alderman.

Why, by being elected by his Country.

Gentleman.

You should rather say by being *returned* elected; for if the Person so returned had not a single good Vote, he would have a Right to sit there, and the other Party would be driven to his Petition.[1] What then would be the Case, if a Minister could

---

[1] Election results could be petitioned in the Commons, 2 Geo. II, C. 24 stating 'That such votes shall be deemed to be legal, which have been so declared by the last determination in the house of commons'; *Statutes at Large*, xvi. 67. After the 1747 elections at least eight results were petitioned; *Debates and Proceedings of . . . Commons* (London, 1770), iii. 76, and *Journals of . . . Commons*, xxv. 423–6, 428, 481, 492.

corrupt such a Number of returning Officers as might, when joined to such of his Friends and Dependents as could be fairly elected, secure him a safe Majority in the House at their first sitting? This is no strange, forced, or improbable Supposition; on the contrary, this Majority, if we admit such universal Corruption as you complain of, must be with the greatest Ease obtained. The Persons necessary to be corrupted for that Purpose are neither considerable in Number or in Fortune. Reason will tell us, these Men are as liable to Corruption as any others; nay, Experience must convince us, that they have been corrupted in the most flagrant Manner. Now is it not certain, that before the Rights of ten Members could be adjusted, the Minister might have done his Business, and might send *his* Parliament about theirs?

And farther, though an annual Parliament might by such Methods become very dangerous to their Country, they would be very little formidable to the Minister himself. Long Parliaments have Opportunities to form Cabals, which have been often fatal to bad Ministers (and sometimes I am afraid to good ones.) It was principally owing to the short Date of Parliaments that they had formerly so little Weight in our Constitution. King *Charles* the First or his wicked Ministers seemed sensible of this, and were therefore willing to have pursued the old Road. And it was a Parliament, which from its Duration was called the *Long Parliament*,[1] which to their immortal Honour preserved the Liberties of this Kingdom, when they were *really in Danger*.

Alderman.

I honour that *Long Parliament* as much as any Man; and I frankly own you have said more against annual Parliaments, than I thought could have been suggested; but the Triennial Bill, I apprehend, is unexceptionable;[2] and this, perhaps, would equally

---

[1] The second of two Parliaments called by Charles I in 1640, it sat, with intermissions, for nearly twenty years and passed a Triennial Bill, impeached Strafford and Laud, passed an Act against abolishing Parliament without its consent, and adopted a number of other constitutional measures which mitigated the personal prerogative of the sovereign.

[2] In the Commons debate on an address of thanks for the King's speech opening the session (18 November 1746) Major Charles Selwyn (c. 1689–1749), M.P. for Ludgershall 1741–7, proposed a repeal of the Septennial Act and a 'triennial holiday' for the 'good people of South Britain', before going on to consider the ultimate desirability of annual parliaments; Hansard, xiii. 1430–1, and *GM*, xvi (1746), 622–3. For a 1745 motion for annual parliaments see *Journals of . . . Commons*, xxiv. 726.

secure us from the Danger of Corruption, with an annual Parliament.

Gentleman.

Perhaps it might; but why should we imagine either would be less corruptible than that which is Septennial? Do Men require so long time to be corrupted? Look into the History of those Parliaments, which have been suspected of undue Influence; are the first Sessions of those Parliaments less suspicious than the last?

Alderman.

It would not be worth a Minister's while to corrupt a Triennial Parliament.

Gentleman.

It must be evidently worth his while: For the Business of the Nation must be carried on in a Triennial Parliament, and the Minister may be destroyed by it.

Alderman.

It would not be worth the while of the Members to receive the Wages of Corruption.

Gentleman.

That is altogether as strange a Doctrine. All Wages are in Proportion to the Duration of the Service; and it is as good for the Labourer to receive his Hire for six Years under two Contracts, as under one. If we allow that a Majority is necessary to skreen a bad Minister, or to carry on his wicked Purposes; the only Question with him will be, can it be purchased or no? If the Members are above Corruption, so would they be if they were chosen for seven Years, as well as if chosen only for three. It should seem indeed, according to all Rules of Traffick, that a Majority in the Triennial would be bought cheaper; but admit the contrary, they must be had by a wicked Minister, if possible, whatever be the Price; and they themselves will enable him to defray it.

Alderman.

If Elections returned so frequent, it would be impossible to corrupt the Electors.

Gentleman.

As the Shortness of Time for which they are elected cannot

make the Members less corruptible, so neither would it, I conceive, effect this Alteration in the Electors. A Man who sells his Vote once in seven Years, will be equally ready to sell it once in three. If then we allow Corruption to have spread so deplorably as you imagine, would not this be a most effectual Means to spread it wider, nay, even to make it universal, since it would be a Trade constantly carried on. The Horror of all Crimes is lessened by frequent Examples of those Crimes before our Eyes; hence Offenders grow more hardened, and the Innocent are encouraged to become Offenders. Elections would thus in many Places be the Principal, if not the only *Trade* regarded, and the Price of Corruption, instead of being advanced, would probably be decreased; but let the Price be what it will, and the Market never so frequent, the Minister must go to Market and the Nation must pay.

But farther, if notwithstanding all the Arts of Corruption used on the other Side, the Court can out-bid the Country in a septennial Election, would not the Alteration proposed, be greatly in favour of the former? Do not Country Gentlemen already complain that they are undone by the Expence of an Election, once in seven Years; how much more unable would they be to support this Contention once in three Years? And as for all those other Arts which I have before mentioned, and shewn to be on their Side only, would they not be greatly weakened by the Triennial Scheme? So short a Period would hardly allow them time to enflame the People, to invent Grievances, and sufficiently to circulate Falshoods against the King and his Administration.

Alderman.

Do not attempt to be jocose, when you represent us to be in so melancholy a Situation.

Gentleman.

I only pursue that Opinion of general Corruption, which you asserted.

Alderman.

Can you lay your Hand on your Heart, and deny the Truth of the Assertion?

Gentleman.

As to the Corruption practised at Elections, it is so known and certain, that I should think no Man deserved the least Credit who denied it; but as to the Corruption of the Elected, I can lay my Hand on my Heart and declare, I believe it to be infinitely less than it hath been represented: However, admitting it was otherwise, and that Corruption was in both Cases universal, I think, I have plainly shewn that the Bills you have desired would be so far from curing it, that they would tend only to aggravate its ill Consequences.

Alderman.

Though I am not able to answer all your Arguments; it is difficult to persuade me that the Public should so eagerly desire what is hurtful to themselves, or that the Ministry should so obstinately adhere to the Good of the People against their own Consent.

Gentleman.

Neither of these are so improbable as you think. To deceive the People into mistaken Notions concerning their true Interest is no impossible (I am afraid, no difficult) Task. Whoever can put together a few pompous popular Words and pronounce them well, may, to use the Language of a very sensible Writer, *whistle the Public together, then get on their Backs and ride them at his Pleasure.*[1] And why should not the Ministry obstinately adhere to the Public Good? Is not the present Administration composed of a Number of Men of the greatest Property in this Kingdom? Who would be so great Losers by any Injury done to the Public; by enslaving or impoverishing the Nation, as those who have the largest Possessions in it? Can we believe that such Men would entail Slavery or Beggary on their Posterity? Can any rational Motive be assigned for such a Behaviour in Men to whom we may apply the Scripture Sentiment, with respect to our Souls; *What will they gain by the Loss of their* Liberty? *or, What shall they have in exchange for* it?[2] It seems, I think, not so very improbable that

[1] Robert South, 'The fatal Imposture and Force of Words: set forth in A Sermon preached on Isaiah v. 20', *Sermons Preached on Several Occasions* (Oxford, 1823), ii. 123: 'And he who will set up for a skilful manager of the rabble . . . may whistle them backwards and forwards, upwards and downwards, till he is weary; and get up upon their backs when he is so.'

[2] Cf. Mark viii. 36, 37; Matthew xvi. 26.

such a Ministry should obstinately adhere to the Good of the Public, even against their Consent. Their Situation in Business makes them the best Judges of this Public Good; and their larger Share of Property makes them the most interested in its Promotion.

But farther, how are you sure that the Ministry, if they desired to indulge the Public with their favourite Idol, contrary to Reason and good Policy, could however succeed in this Desire? The Interest which every Member hath in opposing such a Bill, seems too obvious to be mentioned; and what should induce them to pass such a Law? Not public Utility: For beside what hath been already advanced on that Head, a septennial Parliament hath great Advantage over the other two: For if the Liberty of this Country wholly consists in that Share of Power which is lodged in the Representatives of the People, it follows, that by how much the higher this Power is, and by how much the more Weight it carries in the Scale of our Constitution, so much the higher and stronger is our Liberty. Now to give this Body of our Representatives any Weight at all; or to make them more than nominally a Branch of our Constitution, some Degree of Duration is necessary; and the longer and more permanent this is, the greater will most certainly be their Power. I appeal to both Reason and Experience for the Truth of this: For Reason makes it plainly evident in Theory, that no Body which is eternally in a State of Fluctuation can acquire any political Strength; and Experience will shew this to be true in Fact, not only from the History of all other Countries, but from our own Annals, where we shall find the Power of the Commons, encreasing in our Constitution, as it hath encreased in Duration; and that long Parliaments only have been able to effect any thing notable in Defence of our Liberties: For what Weight indeed can a Body eternally fluctuating have in that Scale of Power where it is opposed to what is permanent and perpetual, as the other two Branches of our Constitution are known to be?

Alderman.

This Argument, I am afraid, proves too much, and will go to substitute a perpetual instead of a septennial Parliament. So that we should give up all future Right of Election, and make Seats in the House of Commons descendible to the Heir, as those of the Peers are.

Gentleman.

Est modus in rebus,[1] my Friend; such a House of Commons would be no longer Representatives of the People; and it is easy to see in that Case where the Balance of Power would lie, and what would be the Consequence of it. The Circumstance I have mentioned, however, serves to corroborate what I have here advanced: For as a perpetual Parliament would have more Power than a Septennial; so hath, for the same Reason, the Septennial over those for which you have above contended. The Perpetual would have too much, and the Annual and Triennial infinitely too little.

Alderman.

As I have not considered this Matter before, I cannot pretend to give it an immediate Answer.

Gentleman.

But the House of Commons would expect an Answer to it, as well as to all the other Matters I have mentioned on this Subject; and such Answers, in which the Arguments against septennial Parliaments should greatly preponderate, before they can be expected to pass a Law so visibly contrary to their own Interest. Would you have the Minister use any of that undue Influence which you have exclaimed against on this Occasion? But what Degree of Corruption must we suppose necessary to prevail on Men to sacrifice, not only their Honour, but their Interest, and the Good of the Public, to the Desire of a Ministry. Such a Degree of Corruption as this never hath yet, and I firmly believe never will infect our Legislature. There is a wide Difference, my good Friend, between such a Majority on the Side of the Government, as will suffer public Business to go on, by placing some Confidence in the Administration, and by assisting the Crown in pursuing vigorous Measures, when such are necessary, against its Enemies, on the one Hand; and such a Majority on the other, as will hearken implicitely to the Voice of a Minister without any Attention to the Good of the People. Without the former of these no Administration can stand a Moment, nor even the Government itself subsist. A Truth of which some hot-brain'd Men were lately so sensible, that they relinquished the

---

[1] 'There is a measure in all things'; Horace, *Satires*, I. i. 106 (Loeb).

Reins almost as soon as they had taken Possession of them.[1] But of a Majority of the latter Kind, I thank God our Annals can produce no Instance: For I may challenge the most malicious Malecontent during all the Time in which the Clamours against Corruption have run so very high, *that they have been ecchoed by the most corrupt Men amongst us*, to produce one single Instance of any Law which hath struck at the Root of our Constitution, or which hath attempted to undermine our Liberties: And what must be the Inference; but either that we have had no Minister wicked enough to aim at carrying any such Point, which few, I believe, will chuse to confess, or that his Influence in the Legislature was never sufficient to embolden him to attempt it.

Upon the whole, to deny that there is any Corruption in this Nation, would be to fly in the Face not only of Truth, but of public Notoriety. Indeed, to speak a bold political Truth, some Degree of Corruption always hath attended, and always will attend a rich and flourishing Nation. The virtuous Principles on which the *Roman* Commonwealth was founded, excluded this no longer than 'till Wealth flowed in upon them. Their Satyrist, you remember, introduces his Complaints of their Corruption by these Words:

> *Paupertas Romana perit——*[2]

and presently adds,

> *Prima peregrinos obscæna Pecunia mores*
> *Intulit; et turpi fregerunt secula Luxu*
> *Divitiæ Molles.——*[3]

Among us it had an early Introduction. My Lord *Clarendon* speaks of it as known long before his time, and very openly blames King *Charles* and his Ministers for not using it;[4] but in

---

[1] The Granville-Bath miscalculation of 11–13 February 1746; see above, p. 19, n. 1.

[2] Juvenal, *Satires*, vi. 295: *nullum crimen abest facinusque libidinis, ex quo paupertas Romana perit*; 'Since the day when Roman poverty perished, no deed of crime or lust has been wanting to us' (Loeb).

[3] Ibid., 298–300: 'Filthy lucre first brought in amongst us foreign ways; wealth enervated and corrupted the ages with foul indulgences' (Loeb).

[4] Book iv, section 76, *History of the Rebellion and Civil Wars*, ed. W. Dunn Macray (Oxford, 1888), i. 431: 'To which purpose [controlling a factious Commons in 1641], if that stratagem (though none of the best) of winning men by places had been practised as soon as the resolution was taken at York to call a Parliament . . . it is very possible they might either have been made instruments to have done good service, or at least been restrained from endeavouring to subvert the royal building.'

reality they despised the Power of the People too much, and hoped entirely to destroy that Power.

Nothing, I apprehend therefore, can appear more unjust than this Charge of Corruption on the present Government; which neither introduced nor can possibly cure it. And can we expect, that when the Enemies of the present Establishment, are so manifestly busy in employing every Art, fair and foul, open and secret, to corrupt the Nation; to mislead, inflame and bribe them against their own true Interest, and against the King and his Administration; that the Government should sit still and use no Attempts for its own Security. To defend yourself with the same sort of Weapons by which you are attacked, hath always been held lawful; and even Corruption, as the great Man I have above cited acknowledges, becomes justifiable when defensive.

Cato himself, the great Patron and Martyr of *Roman* Liberty, in this sense, not only admitted its Utility, but practised it. He was himself at the Head of a Subscription to bribe the *Romans* for their own Good, and to keep Men out of public Trusts, who attacked the Liberty of their Country,[1] and at last destroyed it, *by the same factious Methods,* and by the *same popular Outcries* which are now practised and raised within this Kingdom.

In this defensive Way only the present Government can be fairly said to apply to any Arts of Corruption; and in this sense, I sincerely think, every honest impartial Man will own, that some Degree of it may be necessary to preserve not only the King on his Throne, but the Religion and Liberties of this Nation; all which are by the blackest Corruption attempted to be undermined.

And in this defensive Sense only can any kind of Corruption be necessary to the present Government: For if the People were not deceived and misinformed; if they were not inflamed, and compelled and bribed by the several Parties who unite in Opposition; I think, I may with great certainty affirm, that their own Interest alone would biaſs them sufficiently in Favour of the present Government; and that Loyalty to his Majesty King GEORGE,

---

[1] Not located. Possibly an extrapolation (unwarranted) from Suetonius, *De Vita Caesarum*, 'The Deified Julius', i. 19, where it is recorded that the aristocracy endowed its candidate with election funds equal to those of Caesar's candidate, 'and even Cato did not deny that bribery under such circumstances was for the good of the commonwealth' (Loeb).

would be universally, as I hope it now is in most Places, the best Recommendation of a Candidate to their Election.

Alderman.

And do you really think this would be the Case, when the Nation is plunged over Head and Ears in an unnecessary, burthensome, grievous—I will call it *Hanoverian* War,[1] and when we are almost devoured by Taxes?[2]

Gentleman.

These two Charges, my Friend, amount but to one. Or rather I may say the latter is the necessary Consequence of the former. Every War must have Taxes to support it; and such a War as the present, must be supported by very high Taxes: For however it may deserve the other Epithets, which you have been pleased to affix to it, all must allow the War in which we are now unhappily engaged to be both grievous and burthensome. This is a Circumstance sure worthy to be lamented; but no Cause of Complaint against the Administration, unless the War shall appear to be really unnecessary, and unless it shall appear that the present Administration have involved us in it.

Now this being a complicated Question, as we are at present engaged in a War both with *France* and *Spain*, it may be proper to consider them distinctly.

First then, as to the War with *Spain*; this was most certainly undertaken at the earnest Desire of the *British* Merchants, who had long complained of the Insults and Encroachments made by the *Spaniards* on the Trade of this Nation.[3] It will not be said by

[1] A cant phrase of Opposition, to the effect that George II's partiality for his Hanover Electorate was responsible for both the undertaking and the prolongation of the war. The issue emerged in its most violent form during the debates over the expense of continuing Hanoverian mercenaries in English pay; see, for example, Hansard, xiii. 232–383. For the 1747 campaign the Commons had voted supplies to continue 18,000 Hanoverian mercenaries in British pay; *Journals of . . . Commons*, xxv. 256. When he was writing for the Opposition, Fielding satirized such subsidies; see *Some Papers Proper to be Read before the R—l Society, Concerning the Terrestrial Chrysipus, Golden-Foot or Guinea* (1743). Another satire on the same subject, *An Attempt towards a Natural History of the Hanover Rat* (1744), has been attributed to Fielding.

[2] *GM*, xvii (1747), 73, reprints from *The Craftsman* of 31 January 1747 an estimate that 'upwards of eight millions sterling will be raised by taxes on the people this year.'

[3] Cf. *Proper Answer*, below, p. 73. The South Sea Company in particular resented Spanish obstructions to trade with Spanish colonies. In 1739, after the Convention of Pardo had compensated England for 'right of search' violations, the mercantile interest, whose

any Man living, that this was either a War of Ambition, or enter'd into upon any Motives of ministerial Interest, or from any other Cause than a Regard to the Voice of the People, after long and repeated Endeavours to avoid it by amicable Means. But as you and your Friends have never complained of its being rashly *undertaken*, or unnecessarily prolong'd, but merely of its being *delay'd*, I need say no more upon this Article.

As to the War with *France*; the present Administration, at their first coming into Power, that is, when a certain great Earl had been obliged to lay down the Seals,[1] found the Nation already engaged in it, as well as in that with *Spain*. You will also observe, that War was declared not by us upon *France*, but by *France* upon us,[2] at the Instigation of *Spain*, after a Battle at Sea, in which she openly assisted that Crown, to whose Fleets she had before given Protection several times against ours;[3] not to mention a Design she had formed in the Year 1743, of invading this Kingdom in Favour of the Pretender;[4] and a Commission given to one of her Admirals in the *West Indies*, to have attack'd our Settlements there.[5] It cannot therefore be said that the *French* War ought to be charged upon this Administration, unless defending the Nation against the most open and outragious Attacks can be call'd

parliamentary spokesman was Pitt, urged war on the issue of expansion of trade in the colonial empire. Walpole reluctantly declared war on 19 October 1739. Even after the declaration his pacific tendencies continued to be the object of Opposition attacks.

[1] Under pressure from the Pelham–Hardwicke clique for not having brought the Dutch formally into the war, Granville resigned as Secretary of State on 24 November 1744.

[2] Louis XV's declaration was dated 15 March 1744 N.S.; George II's declaration was dated 29 March O.S.; see *GM*, xiv (1744), 154–5, 167–8.

[3] When the combined French and Spanish fleets emerged from Toulon, they were engaged on 11 February 1747 by a numerically superior English fleet under Mathews and Lestock and dispersed without significant damage, to the great indignation of the British public; see H. W. Richmond, *The Navy in the War of 1739–48* (Cambridge, 1920), ii. 1–57.

[4] Late in 1743 Marshal Saxe began making secret preparations at Dunkirk for an invasion of England, to be covered by the Brest squadron under Roquefeuil. During embarkation the great storm of 25–6 February 1744 destroyed a large number of transports and effectively frustrated the 'Design'. Pitt and other members of the Opposition attempted to discredit evidence of the invasion as hearsay, but Horace Walpole wrote to Mann (16 February 1744), 'Don't be surprised if you hear that this Crown is fought for on land.' See H. W. Richmond, *The Navy in the War of 1739–48*, ii. 74–8, 83–4; *Yale Walpole*, xviii. 376–9, 398–400; *Journals of . . . Commons*, xxiv. 568; Coxe, *Pelham*, i. 142–4.

[5] Presumably the Marquis de Caylus, who sailed from Cadiz in January 1745 for Martinique with a large fleet which, it was rumoured in England, was to attack the British colonies in the West Indies. In fact, de Caylus, who had been appointed Governor-General of the French Leeward Islands in October 1744, had no offensive mission. See H. W. Richmond, *The Navy in the War of 1739–48*, ii. 216.

involving it in a War. It must be farther observed, that, besides their Declaration of War against *England*, which left us no Option what Part to take, the *French* Arms were at that Time employ'd against *Flanders*.[1] By what Mistakes in our Conduct they were drawn thither, I will not say;[2] it is enough for the Defence of *this* Ministry, that these Mistakes cannot be charged upon *them*, as all who know any thing of the past Conduct of Business at home and abroad very well know. But into *Flanders* the War *now* was brought, and being there, what would you have had our Government do? Would you have had them allow the *French* to carry their Conquests on there without Opposition, till the whole seventeen Provinces,[3] for the Preservation of which we have formerly spent so much Money and Blood, had been quietly added to the Dominions of *France*? What, I say, in that case, would you have had our Government do?

Alderman.

I would have had them withdraw all our Forces from abroad, have carried on the War only at Sea, and have let the Continent go to the Devil.

Gentleman.

Friend, Friend; when the Devil is Master of the Continent, he will, let me tell you, be much too near a Neighbour to *England*. We shall have only the narrow Seas between Him and Us, and he must be a foolish Devil indeed if he can't find a way to get over to us in that Situation. I should think it much better Policy to keep him more at a Distance; for it is with States as with private Persons; they who do not resist him at his first Approaches,

---

[1] After the defeat at Dettingen (1743) and the expulsion of French armies from the Austrian Netherlands in that year, Louis XV adopted the conquest of Flanders as his main strategy for the 1744 campaign. In April 1744 the French began massing troops on the Scheldt–Sambre frontier, but by that time war had already been declared against England. See Lodge, *Studies*, pp. 85–6; J. W. Fortescue, *History of the British Army* (London, 1910), ii. 89, 103–7.

[2] Perhaps referring to Granville's aggressive foreign policy, which included the expedition of troops to the 'pragmatic army' in Flanders for the purpose of supporting Maria Theresa by creating a diversion against the French; see Fortescue, *History of the British Army*, ii. 82–3.

[3] The 7 'United Provinces' of the Netherlands (Holland, Zeeland, Utrecht, Friesland, Gelderland, Groningen, Overijssel) and the other 10 of Charles V's original 17, situated south of the major rivers. The latter had been captured by Philip II of Spain and after the partition of the Spanish Succession became known as the Austrian Netherlands. Saxe had conquered these for France in 1745–6.

are very ill able to do so when he hath broke into their Fences, and master'd their Outworks. But let me a little examine the Nature of your Proposition. In order to resist *France* and *Spain* (the two confederate Devils with whose joint Power we are now to contend) you are of Opinion that we should have thrown down our Arms upon the Continent, have left our Allies to take care of themselves, and have confined our Operations to a Sea War alone. Now the unavoidable Consequence of this would have been an immediate separate Peace, upon such Terms as *France* and *Spain* would have thought fit to give, between those two Crowns, the Empress Queen,[1] and the King of *Sardinia*. For if these Powers, with all the Assistance now given by *England*,[2] are but just able to stand out against *France* and *Spain*, how could they hope to do it effectually when that Assistance should be withdrawn? Another certain and terrible Consequence of our taking this Party,[3] would have been the Submission of the *United Provinces* to an entire Dependence on *France*, or, to speak plain, their being subjected to her; such a Dependence as must have ensued upon our acting that part, being indeed a Subjection, in softer Terms. I say, as must have ensued upon our acting that Part; for if the *Dutch* Government was ready to throw itself into the Arms of *France*, even with all the Spirit our Army could give to the honest Party there,[4] how impossible would it have been to have prevented their following the Bent of those Inclinations, if they had seen their Frontier entirely abandoned, and the very Heart of their Provinces at the Mercy of an Army ten Times superior in Strength to their own. What could the Fleet of

---

[1] Maria Theresa (1717–80), Empress (1745–80) and Queen of Hungary and Bohemia (1740–80), by the provisions of the Pragmatic Sanction succeeded to the Habsburg dominions on the death of her father, Charles VI. In the Convention of Turin (1742) and in the Treaty of Worms (1743) she entered into alliance with Charles Emmanuel III (1730–73), King of Sardinia and Duke of Savoy, against the Bourbon powers in Italy.

[2] In addition to whatever military assistance England provided simply by opposing their common enemies in Flanders and elsewhere, Maria Theresa and Charles Emmanuel III each received subsidies from England in accordance with the Treaty of Worms. In 1747 the Queen received more than £400,000, and the King received £300,000. Of a projected army of 140,000 men in Flanders in 1747, Britain was to supply 40,000, including Hanoverian and Hessian mercenaries. See *Journals of . . . Commons*, xxv. 262, 252.

[3] A decision on one side or the other, a determination, resolution (*OED*).

[4] The monarchists and anti-republicans who, after the revolution in Zeeland (April 1747), ousted the republican party which had governed for nearly fifty years and proclaimed the Prince of Orange Stadtholder, Admiral, and Captain-General of the United Provinces; see Lodge, *Studies*, pp. 247–50, and General Introduction above, p. xxiv.

England have done to hinder this, and how long, after such an Accession of maritime Power to *France*, would this Fleet have continued superior to those of that Crown and *Spain* united? No longer ago than in the Reign of *Louis* XIV. at the Time of the first Grand Alliance,[1] the combined Navies of *England*, *Spain* and *Holland* were barely a Match for the single Navy of *France*, tho' *Holland* was then a great maritime Power. What would the Inequality be of our Fleet alone, against the combined Force of *France* and *Spain*, when neither of these Powers would have any Thing else to do with their Money, but to apply it to strengthen their Fleets, assisted by all that would remain of the Shipping and Seamen of *Holland* and *Zealand*, which *France* must, in that Case, have entirely at her Disposition? And if our Fleets could not be sufficient to guard us against an Invasion, how could any Army we could keep up, be able to resist the whole Armies of *France* and *Spain*; for which they would then have no other Employment but to pour them at once into *England* and *Ireland*;[2] where they would be sure to be joined and assisted by all their *Popish* and *Jacobite* Friends, without a single Ally remaining to *England*, either to make any Diversion in favour of us upon the Continent, or to send us over any Succours against such a terrible and fatal Attack?

Alderman.

I protest you frighten me. I begin to think our withdrawing Measure not quite so safe as our Friends represent it.

Gentleman.

If your Friends mean to serve the Pretender, they cannot advise a better. But let us now, on the other hand, see what hath happened from our having acted a contrary Part. The King of *Sardinia* is still an useful Ally of *Great-Britain*, and a formidable Enemy to *France* and *Spain*. The ambitious Designs of the House of *Bourbon* in *Italy* have been hitherto disappointed.[3] The

---

[1] Signed at Vienna in May 1689 by the Dutch and Leopold I, and afterwards joined by William III as King of England, the alliance sought to promote English and Dutch influence in the election of Leopold's son, the Archduke Joseph, as Emperor and to support, against the French, the claims of the imperial house to the Spanish dominions.

[2] With Scotland, one of the presumed points of a French–Jacobite invasion, even after the failure of the Jacobite uprising of 1745. There were rumours of such an invasion in the English press as late as May 1747; *Yale Walpole*, xix. 261, 368, 376, 399.

[3] After the battle of Piacenza in June 1746 the French and Spanish forces in Italy were

Empire is fixed in the House of *Austria*; and her Arms, in Conjunction with ours, are now protecting the *United Provinces*. The Election of a Stadtholder there is an Event of the highest Importance, not only to the Issue of the present War, but to the future Safety and Welfare of that Commonwealth, and of *Great Britain*, by confirming and knitting more closely the Union of the two Countries, and by enabling the former to act with more Spirit and Vigour, whenever the Defence of the Common Cause shall hereafter require it; especially in the Support of the Protestant Succession established here in his Majesty's Family.[1]

Alderman.

I don't know whether, as a Lover of Liberty, I ought to rejoice at this Event. A Stadtholder may endanger the Freedom of the *Dutch* Commonwealth.

Gentleman.

True; but without a Stadtholder the King of *France* would be sure to oppress it. Lovers of Liberty are sometimes the Dupes of their own Zeal. Some such in *Holland* have been seduced by the *French*, as some here by the *Jacobites*, to do their Work for them, and carry on the Designs of absolute Power, out of an extravagant Passion for Freedom. *Servitutis odio in servitutem ruunt*.[2] But the *Dutch*, I thank God, have now opened their Eyes, and I hope the *English* will do so too.

Alderman.

If this Event be a happy one, it is not to be ascribed to the Government here, but to the Spirit of the People in *Holland* and *Zealand*.

Gentleman.

That Spirit could never have risen, or must have been instantly, and for ever subdued, if there had not been an Army of 110,000

driven out without having achieved the 'Bourbon' design of establishing Don Carlos and Don Philip in Naples and Tuscany respectively.

[1] The election of William IV of Orange as Stadtholder was warmly received in England for two reasons: the Prince was committed to a programme of increased Dutch participation in the war, and he was George II's son-in-law, which implied a concern for the support of the Protestant succession in England.

[2] 'In [their] hatred of slavery they rush into slavery.' Cf. Livy, *Ab Urbe Condita*, III. liii. 7: 'crudelitatis odio in crudelitatem ruitis.'

Men with a Duke of *Cumberland* at the Head of them, to raise and protect it.[1] Without that Assistance as well as the Help of our Ships, not the Prince of *Orange*, but the *French* King would have been, in effect, the Stadtholder of the *Seven Provinces*, and quiet Sovereign of the other *Ten*.

Alderman.

You think then that *France* hath been baffled in *Flanders*.

Gentleman.

No; she hath done a great deal in that Part of the World, but she hath been hindered from doing a great deal more. The *Dutch* are still independent, and *more so than they were when this War begun*; and though almost all *Flanders* hath been conquered by *France*, she hath not the same Hold of it as she would have had by the Submission of *Holland*, and by such a Peace must then have been made with her. She may now be compelled to make a Peace that will restore these Conquests again, and will provide for the future Security of the *Low Countries*, even better than before.[2] For it is not the Number or Fortifications of Towns, but an Army able and willing to defend them, that makes a real Barrier;[3] and if the Revolution which hath happened in the *United Provinces*, shall give them That, I shall think them in a much better State of Defence than they have been for some time; though some of the Towns that may be restored to them by the Treaty of Peace shall have been dismantled.

Alderman.

Will you pretend to persuade me that we are not in a bad State abroad?

[1] In accordance with the terms of The Hague Convention of January 1747 Cumberland had resumed command of the allied armies. At the time of the 'revolution' Zeeland was under considerable political and military pressure from the French and appealed to Cumberland for help. The latter, preparing to campaign against Saxe, could spare only a few Dutch battalions from the allied command; Lodge, *Studies*, pp. 246–8. Cf. Sandwich to Newcastle, 9 May 1747 N.S. (BM Add. MS. 32808, f. 130): 'They [the Dutch] have no resource but in England, all connection with France being at an end. It will depend on us to make them continue the war in whatever manner and as long as we please'; cited in *Yale Walpole*, xix. 395 n.

[2] By the Treaty of Aix-la-Chapelle (October 1748) France did in fact evacuate the Low Countries and restore to Holland her lost territories, but the prophecy, in June 1747, of this happy result must be put down to Fielding's firm design to support the Pelhams in their foreign policies.

[3] According to the terms of the Barrier Treaty of 1715 the maritime powers (England

Gentleman.

No, I will not. Our State is certainly dangerous. We have
Enemies to contend with almost too strong for us, the two
greatest Powers in *Europe*; whose Resources almost are in-
exhaustible, who neither value the Miseries or Complaints of
their Subjects, who force Money from them wherever it is, and
can make War much cheaper than we. Add to this, that one of
them hath not only an Army of 300,000 Men,[1] but is better
skilled in the Art and Science of War, particularly in Engineer-
ing,[2] than any other Power in *Europe*, of which we have felt the
Effects very severely. Besides the Strength of our Enemies, we
are also to struggle with the Weakness and Wants of some of
our Friends, with the partial Views, and wanton Ambition of
others, with their discordant Interests, with their mutual Jealousies, and with all those complicated Difficulties that weaken
Confederacies, and often defeat the best Measures, and wisest
Schemes for the common Good. If in the Issue of such a Contention we can come off without being undone, it is the utmost
we are to expect.

Alderman.

Methinks you give but a very indifferent Character of our
Allies.

Gentleman.

We must take them such as they are, not such as we wish
them to be. It is not in the Power of the *English* Government to
alter the State and Nature of Things. They can neither remove
these inherent Defects from the Alliance, nor prevent the ill
Consequences that necessarily flow from them.

and the Dutch) had handed over the Southern Netherlands to Charles VI on condition that
the Dutch should be allowed to occupy a number of border fortresses to protect themselves
against French attack; Roderick Geikie and Isabel A. Montgomery, *The Dutch Barrier*,
1705–1719 (Cambridge, 1930), Ch. VIII. During the negotiations leading up to Aix-la-
Chapelle the continued validity of the Barrier concept became a matter of dispute between
the maritime powers and Austria, thereby threatening the general treaty. The deprecating
reference in the *Dialogue* may represent a concessive anticipation on the part of the pacific
wing of the ministry to which Fielding seems to have been attached.

[1] Including forces in all theatres. Saxe's army in the Netherlands was estimated as high as
160,000 and as low as 110,000; *Yale Walpole*, xix. 395 n.

[2] Cf. *JJ* no. 4 of 26 December 1747, below, p. 111, and Fortescue, *History of the British
Army*, ii. 598: 'In truth the French engineers, in respect both of the skill of the officers and
the organization of the men, seem to have stood far above the rest of Europe, while the
British probably stood lowest of all.'

Alderman.

If we cannot mend such Allies, at least we may quit them.

Gentleman.

It would be very bad Policy to punish them by destroying ourselves. And to forsake the Alliance in our present Circumstances would certainly bring on our own Destruction.

Alderman.

I cannot but think, we ought by our Influence to check and correct their Follies or Faults.

Gentleman.

I think so too, as far as possible, and in some Instances this hath been done. The putting an End to the unhappy and ruinous War, between the Houses of *Austria* and *Brandebourg*,[1] which while it continued to rage, was the Triumph of *France*, and the utter Defeat of the Common Cause; the composing, I say, this fatal Quarrel, was entirely owing to his Majesty's Influence over the Councils of the Court of *Vienna*.[2] In advising which salutary Measure, it is as certain a Truth, that the present Administration have the greatest Merit to their Country, *as that the late Administration had none;*[3] *but are, on the contrary, justly responsible for all the ill Consequences of having thrown the King of* Prussia *into the Arms of* France, *by fomenting the Passions of the Court of* Vienna *against him; which was the original Cause of the War in* Germany: For it is sure that *France* would have never undertaken

---

[1] Citing as his major reason the British posture during the negotiations at Hanau (1743), Frederick II of Prussia (i.e. *Brandebourg*) resumed hostilities against Maria Theresa (*Austria*) in August 1744, thereby intensifying the animosity between Granville and the Pelhams; Owen, *Rise of the Pelhams*, pp. 227–33; Richard Lodge, *Great Britain and Prussia in the Eighteenth Century* (Oxford, 1923), pp. 32–61.

[2] A highly flattering estimate of George II's role in the secret Convention of Hanover (August 1745), which led to the Treaty of Dresden (December 1745) and peace between Frederick II and Maria Theresa. In fact George II's attitude was conspicuously anti-Prussian, as was that of his most trusted minister, Granville.

[3] Referring not to the abortive ministry of February 1746, but to the reorganized ministry (Dec. 1743–Nov. 1744) in which Carteret (Granville), who with the King's strong support had charge of the foreign policy, and the Pelhams were at loggerheads. Owen, *Rise of the Pelhams*, p. 237: 'By his persistence in assuming full responsibility for the conduct of the war, Granville had incurred the entire blame for the ill-successes of the past year.' By 1747 English policy was dedicated to getting Frederick II to join the alliance of the maritime powers and Austria.

that War, or have broken her own Guarantee of the *Pragmatick Sanction*,[1] if the Court of *Berlin*[2] had not been driven to act in Concert with her, by the Effect of these Councils. Who they were that advised these destructive Measures, and that have since talked of *Exterminating the King of* Prussia,[3] instead of healing the Differences between him and the *Imperial Court*, is very well known to all the World. But if those Differences had not been healed by *the Prevalence of more sober Councils*, instead of the King of *Prussia* being *exterminated*, the whole System of *Germany* had been destroyed, and *France* would, without Opposition, have made herself Mistress of *Italy* and of the *Seven Provinces*; the Preservation of both these is, indeed, owing to the Force, which, in Consequence of the Peace happily made between the Empress Queen and the Court of *Berlin*,[4] the former hath been able to send into those Countries.

Now let me ask you, whether in making that Peace the Interest of *Hanover* prevailed, or the Interest of *England*? Electoral Jealousies might have pursued the Weakening of a Rival Power in the Empire, even at the Risk of the Common Cause; but the Interest of *England* demanded a Union between the two Houses of *Austria* and *Brandeburg*, and that Interest, we see, was preserved by the Wisdom of his Majesty, and by the honest Zeal of his present Administration.

This Peace then is not *Hanoverian*. Let us see whether *the War* we now carry on be, as you call it, *Hanoverian*. Is *Hanover* or

---

[1] By which Charles VI attempted to secure the undivided Austrian (Habsburg) succession for his own daughters in preference to those of his elder brother. France had guaranteed it in 1735. See Lodge, *Great Britain and Prussia in the Eighteenth Century*, pp. 19, 26–7.

[2] The court of Frederick II of Prussia.

[3] Cf. *TP* no. 26 of 22–9 April 1746: '. . . this truly great and political Negotiation [the Treaty of Dresden, detaching Prussia from France] was steadily and laboriously pursued *in Opposition* to the Cabals of some Persons, who did not scruple to avow Schemes of a very contrary kind, and to denounce Vengeance against the King of *Prussia*, tho' it was as impracticable as impolitic to execute it.' The reference is to the anti-Prussian thrust of Granville's later policies and to his adherents' hostility to the increasingly conciliatory policies of the Pelhams.

[4] By the Treaty of Dresden (25 Dec. 1745 N.S.). In fact Maria Theresa was granted a larger subsidy by George II to permit her to increase her forces in Flanders to 30,000; *Journals of . . . Commons*, xxv. 119–20. In view of the enlarged subsidy (£400,000) the Queen offered to take into her own pay an additional 25,000 troops, for a total of 55,000 in Flanders by the end of April 1746; *Yale Walpole*, xix. 240 n. During the preliminaries of Aix-la-Chapelle, however, she was charged by the maritime powers with having failed to live up to her troop commitments; Lodge, *Studies*, p. 141.

England concerned in the Defence of *Flanders* and *Holland*? Is
Hanover or *England* concerned in opposing the Greatness of the
House of *Bourbon* in *Italy*, and in keeping the King of *Sardinia*
independent on[1] *France*? *The King of England* hath, no doubt, a
great Interest in the maintaining a powerful Emperor at the
Head of the *Germanick* Body, in order to form on that Side, a
considerable Barrier against the Power of *France*, and for the
Preservation of *Flanders*, in the Hands of the House of *Austria*;
but *the Elector of Hanover*, as well as some other Princes of *Germany*, might better find his Account in having a weak Head of
the Empire, to whom the Electors might give the Law. In
what Sense then can it be said, that the War carried on by the
Councils of those who are *now* his Majesty's Ministers, purely
upon Motives relating to *England*, with which his Electorate hath
nothing to do, is an *Hanoverian* War? As well may you call the
two last Wars made by King *William* and Queen *Anne*, *Hanoverian*.[2] This is entirely founded upon the same Principles. The
Cause, the Enemy, the Nature, and Objects of the War are the
same; with this only Difference, that none can complain of this
being prolonged, as that of Queen *Anne* was said to be, from
Views of Ambition, or a Desire of making great Conquests in
France. The present Councils of *England* are by no means infatuated with any such Dreams: As far as the Public can judge
of them, they tend to no more than to a good Peace; good, I
mean, in Proportion to the State and Condition of our Affairs,
to the Defensive Purposes, upon which alone we have carried it
on, and to our Engagements with our Allies, founded upon our
true Interests.

Alderman.

Do you hope to procure such a Peace as you here describe?

Gentleman.

The Practicability of it will greatly depend upon the Choice
of the new Parliament. If the Opposition prevails, we have two
Things to fear; either a shameful and fatal Desertion of our

---

[1] Independent of.

[2] Both 'King William's War' (1689–97) and the War of the Spanish Succession (1702–13) took the English into Grand Alliances which included the Electorate of Hanover. In the latter war George Lewis, the Elector and future George I of England, was an active general and a leader of the belligerent wing of the alliance. He encouraged Marlborough to persuade Anne against the preliminaries of Utrecht.

Allies and Interests on the Continent, which is the Scheme of some who are engaged in that Opposition, or a no less ruinous Forwardness to continue the War upon Objects or Passions in which the true Interest or Honour of *England* hath no real or weighty Concern, which the past Conduct of others who bear a principal Part in the same Opposition gives too much Cause to apprehend. Either of these would prevent our attaining such a Peace as I have described, and would plunge the Nation into infinite Difficulties and endless Calamities. But if the good Genius of *England* shall, as I doubt not it will, get the better of both, and such a Parliament shall be returned as will support the present Administration, while they continue to support the Cause of their Country, there is Reason to hope that they will bring us at last into a safe and happy Port. For we could never have weather'd such Storms as we have done, if the Ship had not been strong, and ably conducted. What a Hurricane did we go through, when, besides two great foreign Wars,[1] we had a Rebellion to contend with at Home! What an Advantage did that give to our Enemies! Yet, by the Blessing of God, by the Wisdom of his Majesty, by the Valour and Conduct of his Son, and by the Care of his Administration, that Danger hath been conquered, and his Throne and Kingdom, nay, I may say, the whole Constitution have gained an additional Strength from the Attempt so wickedly made to overturn them. This is an Earnest of what we may hope from the same Hands, if they are not obstructed in the great Work they have to do. On the other Side, with whatever Success our Enemies may have been crowned in some Parts of the World, during the Course of this War, they have failed and suffered as much in others; their Finances and Trade are almost ruin'd, their Wealth is become our Prize; nor can they long hope, without these Nerves of War, to pursue the Designs of their Ambition, or to resist the Efforts of a Confederacy, which they find they are not able to break or divide. We have a noble Army in *Flanders*,[2] led by a General who hath the Confidence and Love of his Troops, whose very Name is dreaded by theirs; and who, if the Enemy

---

[1] The so-called 'War of Jenkins' Ear' with Spain (1739–48), and the war of the Austrian Succession (1744–48) against France, primarily.

[2] In June 1747 Cumberland's army in Flanders was publicly estimated to be above 110,000 men. 'I believe I may safely assure you that so fine an army has not been anywhere assembled during this war'; Sandwich to Mann, The Hague, 1 May 1747 N.S. (SP 105/308, f. 121), quoted in *Yale Walpole*, xix. 409 n.

venture out of their Lines, will, probably, add to the Palm of *Culloden*,[1] a still nobler Wreath; but this he is too prudent to seek at too great Disadvantage, or to follow the Ardour of his Courage at the Expence of the Safety of his Country, and of that Common Cause which he defends. At Sea we have a most powerful and victorious Fleet, under two Admirals, who have retrieved the Glory of the Navy of *England*, and to whom we owe the greatest Advantages gain'd in this War.[2] All this must naturally incline the *French* and *Spaniards* to think of Peace, especially if *Genoa* should soon be taken, and another Irruption made into *France*:[3] Or if they should still obstinately reject all reasonable Terms, though no Man can answer for the Events of War, yet we have no Cause to believe, that the Campaign will be unfavourable or disadvantagious to the Allies. This we may depend on, that no Opportunity, either of making Peace or War advantagiously, will be lost, by those who now have the Conduct either of our Arms or Negociations.

Alderman.

You say a great deal for your Friends; but all do not see them in the same Light.

Gentleman.

No—for many see them in very false Lights; in the odious Colours that are thrown upon them by the Prejudice of Party, by the Malice of Enemies, or by the Envy of Rivals. But look at their Actions, and you will discern their true Characters. Consider the Difficulties they have had to contend with; the Firmness, the Temper, the Mildness, the Prudence with which

[1] Site of Cumberland's final and decisive victory over the Jacobite rebels on 16 April 1746. In fact Cumberland met Saxe's army at Laffeldt on 21 June 1747 and there lost the last battle of the war in the Netherlands. News of the battle seems to have reached London on June 27; *GM*, xvii (1747), 258. The *Dialogue* was published on June 23.

[2] Vice-Admiral George Anson (1697–1762), circumnavigator of the globe in 1744, had commanded the western squadron since 1746. On 3 May 1747 he defeated the combined squadrons of La Jonquière and St.-Georges off Cape Finisterre in the 'first decisive naval success of the war'; Richmond, *The Navy in the War of 1739–48*, iii. 93. Commodore Peter Warren (1703–52), who in 1745 had provided naval support in the taking of Cape Breton Island, was second-in-command at Finisterre. On June 13 Anson was created Baron, and on May 29 Warren was invested with a Knighthood of the Bath; *Yale Walpole*, xix. 414 n. On 1 July 1747 Westminster elected Warren as one of its two M.P.s.

[3] During the spring of 1747 Genoa, which had been the only direct land communication between Italy and the allied armies poised to enter Provence, was under ineffective siege by Austrian and Sardinian forces. It was not taken. For its role in a scheme to invade France, see General Introduction above, pp. xxiv–xxv.

they have acted; always pursuing a great National Plan, without stepping aside from it, either out of Resentment to those who opposed them, or from Flattery, or Fear, or any one private and partial Consideration. Have you considered the Persons of whom this Administration is composed? I will be bold to say, that if you look for the Men of the largest Property, of the longest Experience in Business, of the brightest, and of the most solid Parts, of the highest Reputation for Knowledge and Learning, of the most acknowledged Integrity in private Life, you will find them in this Administration.[1]

Alderman.

Indeed you surprize me; for their Adversaries talk of them as if they were a Collection of Blockheads, Knaves, and Beggars, without one Man of Sense, Virtue, or Estate, among them.

Gentleman.

I will not talk so of their Adversaries; but I will engage to make good what I have here asserted of *Them*; and can truly assure you, that I know very few who are not in the Administration, or Friends to it, whom it would be any great Gain to the Nation, to have employ'd in any Offices of Power or Trust.

Alderman.

But all this while you forget our Taxes; and unless we could forget them too, we shall not very easily be brought to think well of those who have laid them upon us.

Gentleman.

I would not have you think well of those who have laid them upon you; for they are the *Spaniards*, the *French*, and the *Jacobites*. The Part of the Administration hath been only to consider how they might be raised with least Inconvenience and Hurt to the Public. And on that Account, I am sure, they stand in a very meritorious Light to the Nation. For the Taxes are neither unequally, or partially, laid; nor prejudicial to Trade and Manufactures, nor expensive in the Collection, nor productive of any new Influence, nor particularly hard on the Poor; which are the

---

[1] A slightly altered version of this sentence is quoted in *JJ* no. 10 of 6 February 1748, below, p. 148.

only Objections that can fairly be made against necessary Taxes.
And that these were most necessary I have before sufficiently
proved. In the borrowing of Money, I am sure, that the Minister
at the Head of the Treasury hath more to boast of than perhaps
any of his Predecessors.¹ That after the Shock of so great a Blow
as Public Credit received the Year before,² and while the Nation
was still so deeply engaged in the Midst of such Perils and
Dangers, he should be able to raise so vast a Sum upon such
easy and moderate Terms,³ is what none would have believed to
be possible till convinced by the Fact; and what would not have
been possible to *any Minister, who was not possest, in the highest
Degree, of the good Opinion and Confidence of Mankind.*⁴ This is a
Triumph to one in his Station, as great and glorious as the most
decisive Victory can be to a General. And what a noble and disinterested Spirit, what an amiable Candour did he shew, in
coming so readily into the Scheme of a *Gentleman who had the

* Sir *John Barnard.*⁵

---

¹ Henry Pelham (1696–1754), M.P. for Sussex (1722–54), First Lord of the Treasury
and Chancellor of the Exchequer (1743–54).

² As a result, mainly, of the threat of a successful Jacobite invasion, culminating in the
near panic of 'Black Friday', 6 December 1745, the day the news of the rebel penetration to
Derby reached the public in London. Later in December there was a run on the Bank and
the directors decided to call in 20% from those who had subscribed to the last subscription:
see Sir John Clapham, *The Bank of England* (Cambridge, 1945), i. 233–4; *Yale Walpole*,
xix. 186. Pelham wrote to Trevor on 11 December 1745: 'our credit is in a manner totally
stopt; and though the public funds still keep up to a pretty good height, yet all the zeal
and endeavours . . . by many of the most substantial people in the city, cannot get the better
of the fears of mankind'; Coxe, *Pelham*, i. 283.

³ Philip Yorke to Joseph Yorke, 23 December 1746: 'Mr. Pelham opened ye Supply on
Friday last in a very able manner; We must raise this year for the public Service between
8 & 9 Million, an immense sum indeed, as the Speaker tells the King every Session'; B.M.
Add. MS. 35363, ff. 143–4, cited by John W. Wilkes, *A Whig in Power* (Northwestern
University Press, 1964), p. 109. In 1746 Pelham had also revived the national lottery; Coxe,
Pelham, i. 349–50, where a slightly larger figure is cited. For details of the 1747 subscrip-
tion see *GM*, xvii (1747), 528–9.

⁴ To make up the Supply for 1746 Pelham had arranged with the City for an advance of
£3,000,000. When the City learned of his resignation just prior to the 'forty-eight-hour
ministry' its response was, in effect, 'If no Pelham, no money'; *Egmont Diary*, iii. 315; Earl
of Ilchester, *Henry Fox, 1st Lord Holland* (London, 1920), i. 125; Wilkes, *A Whig in Power*,
p. 109. Coxe, *Pelham*, i. 350, notes that by the time of the raising of the Supply for 1747,
'such was the general confidence in . . . the skill and integrity of Mr. Pelham, that his plans
of finance were generally approved, and the subscription lists for the loans were filled.'

⁵ Barnard (*c.* 1685–1764), M.P. for London (1722–61), Sheriff of London (1735–6),
Lord Mayor (1737–8), knighted in 1732, a prominent City financier in the Opposition to
Walpole, was offered the Exchequer in the Bath–Granville 'forty-eight-hour Ministry', but

Year before opposed his;[1] and in lending him all the Weight of
his Power and Interest to render it feasible, as soon as he judged
that the State of public Affairs made it safe to venture upon such
an Experiment. It is hard to say which deserves best of the Publick, he, or the worthy Gentleman whose Scheme he adopted.[2]
Both of them equally shewed, that their Minds were superior
to all Party-jealousy, and actuated entirely by an honest Zeal for
the Good of their Country; but such a Conduct is still more rare
in a Minister, there being too many Instances of Men in that
Station rejecting and defeating Proposals, which they knew to
be right, only because they were not proposed by themselves.

Alderman.

If what you tell me be true, all the Abuse thrown out upon that
Gentleman, by some of my Friends, hath no Foundation at all.

Gentleman.

Pardon me; you are now too hard on your Friends. The
Foundation is great and apparent. It is the eminent Merit he had
in defeating the late Rebellion, by the early Advice that he gave
to bring over our Troops,[3] without which that Rebellion would

declined; *Yale Walpole*, xix. 212. After 1746 he seems to have been conciliated by Pelham;
Coxe, *Pelham*, ii. 78.

[1] *Egmont Diary*, iii. 315: 'This day [10 March 1746], the House of Commons debated
the scheme of Mr. Henry Pelham for raising the greater part of the supplies of this year,
which was carried by above 100 majority, though not so cheap for the nation as another
scheme offered by Sir John Barnard'; cf. Keene to de Castries (B.M. Add. MS. 43441, un-
folioed), cited by Wilkes, *A Whig in Power*, p. 249, n. 27. Of Pelham's scheme for the 1746
Supply, Richard Glover, *Memoirs by a Celebrated Literary and Political Character* (London,
1813), p. 50, remarked: 'Sir J. Barnard not only opposed it, but offered in Parliament,
that if the money must be raised by a job, he would undertake to furnish it half a million
cheaper. His opposition met with no success; however, Mr. Pelham had the discretion to
consult with Sir John Barnard on those matters ever after.' With Glover's additional
charge, p. 50, that Pelham gave 'Sampson Gideon, and other low-monied men, the most
abominable job for the loan of that year', cf. Coxe, *Pelham*, i. 289.

[2] Philip Yorke to Joseph Yorke, 23 December 1746: 'Sr. J. Barnard & Mr. P had
settled the Matter in concert, so that the money is borrowed at a cheap rate, & the Loan was
filled in 3 days, & a great deal more subscribed than was wanted'.

[3] In the absence of George II, who was once again out of the country visiting his Elec-
torate, Pelham persuaded the Lords Justices to issue orders for four regiments to return to
England, although Cumberland had previously ordered them into Flanders; Pelham to
Argyll, 20 August 1745, and Newcastle to Argyll, 21 August 1745, quoted by Coxe,
Pelham, i. 258, 260. Ten battalions of English troops were sent back on 4 September 1745;
Fox to Hanbury Williams, 5 September 1745, cited by Coxe, *Pelham*, i. 263–4. By the
terms of the Treaty of Utrecht the Dutch were obliged to send 6,000 men to England's

certainly have proved successful; when some who oppose him, and would be thought good Friends to the Government, affected to treat our Danger with Scorn, and the Measure of recalling our Troops to the Defence of their Country, as the Effect of a cowardly and pusillanimous Spirit.[1] Indeed, I make no doubt but Time will prove, that other Objections which have been made to his Conduct, by the same Gentlemen, have the same Foundation; and that his King and Country are greatly obliged to him for what hath been called Dullness, or Fear, by those who think wild and chimerical Enterprizes to be Proofs of superior Genius and Parts, or desperate Rashness and Folly, to be a Mark of Courage and Resolution.

Alderman.

Well, I must frankly own, either you have hitherto had a good Cause, or your Cause hath had a good Advocate.

Gentleman.

The very best Advocate a good Cause can have; which is plain-spoken Truth. But have you any more Grievances to complain of?

Alderman.

Grievances—Ay—let me see—Oh—Zounds! Why they say you have broken the Union.[2]

Gentleman.

That is a thundering Grievance indeed. But hark you, Friend, I hope your Allies, the *Jacobites*, do not complain of that as a Grievance, which was the first Act of their young Master's Regency, and his principal Merit to *Scotland*?[3]

---

assistance; they began to arrive on 17 September 1745. See *TP* no. 26 (22–9 April 1746), p. 1, col. 2, for a similar compliment to the foresight of the Pelhams.

[1] Granville, Bath, and the Marquis of Tweeddale, who was Secretary of State for Scotland, had long concerted in the view that fears of a rebellion were unfounded, and took steps to frustrate all attempts to send for troops. See Fox to Hanbury Williams, 5 September 1745; Coxe, *Pelham*, i. 264.

[2] That is, violated the terms of the 'Act for an Union of the Two Kingdoms of England and Scotland' (5 Anne, cap. 8); *Statutes at Large*, xi. 196–211. The Opposition charged in particular that Articles XVIII and XX of the Union would be violated by the 1747 Bill. See *Dialogue*, below, p. 50, and, for the debates on the Bill, Hansard, xiv. 9–57.

[3] The Young Pretender was appointed 'sole Regent of our Kingdoms' by a proclamation of his father's, dated from Rome, 23 December 1743, and first read at Glenfinnan on 19 August 1745. Charles's first 'manifesto', dated from Paris, 16 May 1745, but printed at

Alderman.

Look you, Sir, we have Wit enough to make it a Charge in some Parts of the Kingdom, against the present Government, that there is a Union between *England* and *Scotland*, and in others, that the Union is broken. But to be serious: Doth not the late Bill for abolishing Heretable Jurisdictions in *Scotland* infringe the Union?[1]

Gentleman.

How, pray?

Alderman.

Why, are not those Jurisdictions declared by the Union to be Rights of Property, and not to be alter'd, unless for the evident Utility of the Subject in *Scotland*?*

Gentleman.

Yes; and therefore, as Rights of Property, they are not taken away without a Compensation made to the Owners,[2] which is the Method used to reconcile private Justice with public Good in many Cases of a similar Nature, such as the Building of Bridges, making of Fortifications, and all other Acts where the Rights of Particulars are taken away for the Benefit of the Public.

* See the 18th and 20th Articles of the Treaty of Union.[3]

Edinburgh in July for distribution, does not in fact mention the Union. A second 'manifesto', dated 10 October and read in Edinburgh, states: 'With respect to the pretended Union of the two Nations, the King cannot possibly ratify it. . . .' Charles had already proposed to recognize the temporary independence of Scotland by summoning a Scottish parliament to meet on October 17. See James Browne, *A History of the Highlands* (Glasgow, 1843), iii. 20–3, 65–7, 104–7; Archibald Henderson, *The Edinburgh History of the Late Rebellion*, 4th ed. (London, 1752), pp. 15–22, 37–41; *Memorials of John Murray of Broughton*, ed. Robert Fitzroy Bell (Edinburgh, 1898), p. 159; William Law Mathieson, *Scotland and the Union* (Glasgow, 1905), p. 366; Walpole to Mann, 6 September 1745, in *Yale Walpole*, xix. 103.

[1] See General Introduction above, pp. xxvi–xxvii. On 17 June 1747 it became 20 Geo. II, cap. 43.

[2] Section vi of the 'Act for . . . abolishing the heretable jurisdictions' provided that 'reasonable and just compensation and satisfaction shall be made out of the next aids to be granted in parliament, for and in respect of every such justiciary . . . hereby taken away and dissolved'; *Statutes at Large*, xix. 129.

[3] Article XVIII stated that 'no alteration be made in laws which concern private right except for evident utility of the subjects within *Scotland*'; Article XX stated that 'all heretable offices, superiorities, heretable jurisdictions, offices for life, and jurisdictions for life, be reserved to the owners thereof, as rights of property'; *Statutes at Large*, xi. 206, 207.

Alderman.

But it will be necessary to shew the Utility of taking away these Jurisdictions before you will be clear of a Breach of the Union, upon this Principle, which I allow to be good.

Gentleman.

If the diffusing the Justice of the Crown over all Parts of the Kingdom, be for the Good of the Kingdom in general; if the freeing the Subject from any Oppression and servile Dependence upon his Fellow-Subject; if the removing all Interruption between him and the Fountain of Justice, the Crown; if the putting him, as the *English* Freeholder is, under the sole Protection of the King, and the Law; if all this, I say, be for the Benefit of the Subject in *Scotland*, then the Utility of taking away these Jurisdictions, is undeniably evident, and of a much higher Nature than in the Cases I mentioned before. Indeed such is the Utility of this Alteration; so much doth it concern the Publick Policy, and Common Weal of this Kingdom; that had not these Jurisdictions been expressly declared by the Treaty of Union to be private Rights, they might have been taken away without Compensation, as detrimental and dangerous to the State, or barely to bring the Course and Order of Government there to a nearer Conformity with that of *England*; which by the 18th Article is declared to be Reason sufficient for altering the Laws that concern Public Right, Policy, and Civil Government.[1] But surely to say that these Jurisdictions cannot be resumed, even upon due Satisfaction made to the Owners, is to suppose that they alone, of all Mankind, at least in civilized Countries, are exempted from the first Law of all Society, and from the great Maxim upon which all Government rests, that Private Conveniency shall give way to public Good.

Alderman.

Are not the Nobility of any Kingdom the great Guardians of Liberty; and the Powers enjoyed by them the best Restraints on that of the Crown?

---

[1] Article XVIII distinguishes between laws concerning 'public right' and laws concerning 'private right', and says of the former that they 'may be made the same throughout the whole united kingdom'. The Gentleman is here taking the line that the heritable jurisdictions are in fact matters of public, not private, right.

Gentleman.

No; by no means. The Liberty of the People is much better guarded by their own Representatives and by the Power of Parliament, than by that of the Nobles, who are as apt and more apt to oppress them, and to abuse their Power, than the King to abuse His in a well-ballanced and well-ordered Constitution. *That is the freest Government* (to use the Words of a noble *Scotch* Duke in the Debate on this Bill) *in which most People are free.*[1] Such is the Government here, and such by this Bill, and others past in this memorable Session of Parliament, will that of *Scotland* hereafter be.

Alderman.

But if these Jurisdictions be in their Nature so hurtful, as you suppose, how comes it about that they were not sooner taken away?

Gentleman.

Because all right Things in Government cannot be done at once; especially where particular Interests, and those of great and powerful Men, are concerned in preventing the Reformation; and because to effect such a Reformation, many things must concur which do not often fall out together: A great Occasion to awaken the Attention of the Legislature, great Authority in the Government, great Spirit, great Prudence, great Temper in the Administration, and above all, a stronger Regard to the preventing of future Evils than to the enjoying present Quiet and Ease, and to the patching up Matters for their own Times, a Virtue most rare in a Ministry.

Alderman.

But after all, was it wise in the Government to offend the *Scotch* at this time?

Gentleman.

Who told you they will be offended? On the contrary, I am persuaded that when they are rightly informed of the true Nature and Intent of these Bills; when they see how strongly they erred who had represented them as any Reflection or Punishment upon

---

[1] Apparently alluding to a speech by the Duke of Argyll, for a report of which see Hansard, xiv. 54–5. Archibald Campbell (1682–1761), 3rd Duke of Argyll (1743), had been political manager of Scotland for Walpole and the Pelhams. In 1747 he was using his considerable influence on behalf of the heritable jurisdictions Bill.

their Nation;[1] that on the contrary, they are given to them as national Benefits, and happy Fruits of the Union; I am persuaded, I say, that they will receive them with Satisfaction and Gratitude, and that the King and his Administration will be more popular there on this Account. Well, do your Friends complain of any thing more?

Alderman.

Complain! ay, believe me, do they, and loudly too, of this Dissolution of the Parliament.[2]

Gentleman.

What, the same Men who are so angry at Parliaments continuing so long? But is it the Power of the Crown they dispute, or the Expediency of the Measure?

Alderman.

As to the Power, there can be no Question, for there are many Precedents of such Dissolutions.

Gentleman.

Pardon me there; not of *such* Dissolutions. Many of our Kings have in Anger dissolved their Parliaments, often without any Intent of calling another for a considerable Period of Time, because these would not come into Court Measures, or would not give up some Points of their own, which the Court disapproved; and such Dissolutions, I grant you, were dangerous Things, and just Grounds of Complaint. But for a King to dissolve a Parliament, which hath distinguished itself by eminent Zeal for his Service, and with which he hath never once disagreed;[3] to abridge their Duration, and yet dismiss them with Praises and Thanks; of this no Precedent is to be found in our Annals.

Alderman.

What then is the Reason of so new a Proceeding?

[1] Chancellor Hardwicke, in introducing the Bill, and many of its proponents, in debating it, were careful to disclaim any punitive connection with the late rebellion; Hansard, xiv. 19, 47.

[2] The Parliament, which had first convened in December 1741, was dissolved by royal proclamation on 18 June 1747, a year before its normal expiry according to the Septennial Act; *Journals of ... Commons*, xxv. 412; see also General Introduction above, pp. xxx–xxxi.

[3] In fact George II was often at odds with Parliament, particularly with regard to his prerogative of choosing his ministers; Owen, *Rise of the Pelhams*, pp. 272–3.

Gentleman.

The Reason is this: It is necessary at this time, that as well our
Allies as our foreign Enemies should know the real Stability of
the present Government, and that our King reigns in the Hearts
of his People, contrary to the malicious Suggestions of *Jacobites*,
both at home and abroad. These have wickedly given out, that
not only the present Administration, but even the present Royal
Establishment subsists only by a corrupt accidental Majority, in
a Parliament almost expired; and that the People, when they
should have it again in their Power, would chuse such Representatives as will subvert them both. Hence our foreign Friends
are more timorous and jealous, and our Enemies more stubborn.[1]
To defeat these Misapprehensions in so dangerous a Season,
his Majesty hath thought proper to appeal a Year earlier to the
Voice of his People; depending on that Love and Fidelity of
theirs, which he so eminently deserves; and well assured they
will shew the World, that this Nation is not so mad or infatuated
as some at home have wickedly represented it, or some abroad
have foolishly believed it. But I will add no more on this Topic.
Read the King's Speech.[2]

Alderman.

I have, and must own it speaks a Language worthy of a King
of *Great Britain*.

Gentleman.

How noble a Confidence doth his Majesty express in the
Hearts of his People. Pray contrast this Dissolution with the
Prolongation of Parliament beyond the Time for which it was
chosen, which was so much complained of in the late Reign.[3]

---

[1] Cf. Horace Walpole's note in his manuscript Political Papers, f. 22: 'I have heard a
reason for this dissolution . . . that our allies would not have gone on, till they saw the
complexion of the next Parliament'; *Yale Walpole*, xix. 412 n.

[2] '. . . as nothing will give so much Weight and Credit to our Affairs abroad in the
present Conjuncture as to shew the Dependence I have upon the Affections of my People,
I have judged it expedient speedily to call a new Parliament'; reprinted in Hansard, xiv.
63–6, and *Journals of . . . Commons*, xxv. 408–9.

[3] In 1716 a predominantly Whig Administration argued that the Jacobite disturbances
of 1715 presaged further outbreaks, thereby affecting elections, and thus warranted a prolongation of the current Parliament beyond the tenure stipulated by the Triennial Act
(1694). Accordingly, on 7 May 1716 the Septennial Act (1 Geo. I, stat. 2, cap. 38) became
law, thus effecting a postponement until 1722 of an election due in 1718; *Statutes at Large*,
xiii. 282. There was further difficulty in 1719, when in the midst of renewed Jacobite

The only Reason assigned for that Prolongation, and indeed the only one that could excuse it in any Manner, was the danger of going to the Election of a new Parliament, the Year after a Rebellion, though we were then in Peace with all the World. A second Rebellion, and a more dangerous one still than the former, is but just overcome; we are in War with *France* and *Spain*; yet instead of prolonging this Parliament beyond its due Term upon that Account, his Majesty hath thought fit to shorten the Term of it by a whole Year. So much more confidently doth he trust in the Loyalty and Affections of his People, than his Father's Administration imagined it safe for that Prince to do.[1] The Reason is plain; the Royal Family then were new to the Nation, but now they are known to us; we have experienced their just and beneficent Government; and that Experience hath rooted in us a Love for the present Establishment, which no Arts of Sedition or Faction can be able to shake. At the same time I will venture to say, this Act of Confidence will yet more strongly establish his Majesty in the Hearts of his People; for it is natural to them to love the more, the more they are trusted.

Alderman.

They say, it is done because there are some very bad Measures now on the Tapis, which this Dissolution foretels.[2]

Gentleman.

The Presumption is strong the other way. Since, if there were any such Measures in View, they never would venture to trust them to the Judgment of a new Parliament, instead of one in which they have had so clear a Majority.

Alderman.

But is not this stealing a Parliament by Surprize?[3]

activity Stanhope and Sunderland tried unsuccessfully to bribe the Commons by proposing repeal of the Septennial Act itself, and prolonging the already extended tenure of the 1715 Parliament; see Basil Williams, *Stanhope* (Oxford, 1932), pp. 410–14.

[1] This much of the Gentleman's speech is reproduced in paraphrase by *GM*, xvii (1747), 294, which attributes the *Dialogue* to 'a ministerial writer'.

[2] Cf. *OE* of 20 June 1747: 'Some scheme not very white must have been in agitation'; as reprinted in *GM*, xvii (1747), 277. The author of the *OE* essay was Horace Walpole; see *Yale Walpole*, xix. 412 n.

[3] Cf. *OE* of 20 June: 'Surely, they are not insensible that the next election will be stolen away by surprize'; *GM*, xvii (1747), 278.

Gentleman.

I know but one way of *stealing* a Parliament, which is by a great Number of false Returns. Now, to obtain them, the Sheriffs and returning Officers must be so made as to be fit for the Purpose. Is that the Case this present Year? Look all over the Kingdom, and you will find it quite otherwise, which is the strongest Presumption, that nothing unfair is meant by the Court. And as to Surprize, did not all those who had a natural Interest in any County, City, or Corporation, begin making their Interest, before it was known that the Parliament would be dissolved, as is always done the Year before a general Election. Faction indeed will have less Time to work in, the People will sooner return to their Morals and Senses, and the Reign of Drunkenness, Idleness, and other Enormities attending Elections, will be abridg'd. Country Gentlemen will save the Expence of treating their Boroughs or Counties a Twelve-month more.[1] What of all this, I desire to know, can afford a reasonable Cause of Complaint?

Alderman.

Well, well, you may talk as you please, but it is the Right of the People of *England* to be discontented, and the Discontented have a Right to complain.

Gentleman.

The People of *England* in general are by no means discontented. Some Discontents there will always be, and I will tell you the Causes to which I ascribe those that subsist at present among us. First, to that universal Luxury, which hath flowed in like a Deluge upon the whole Nation, and is really the Cause as well of that Corruption of which you complain, as of that of which I have complained: For while every Man lives above his Degree, and runs into Expences beyond his Income, Wants and Distresses are every where generated in private Life; and when Men are uneasy there, they will not be easily pleased with the Public. The Tradesman finds his usual Profit unequal to the encrease of his Expence, and complains of the Decay of Trade. The Farmer is racked by his necessitous Landlord, who instead of

---

[1] Cf. *OE* of 20 June: 'but what shall I say to country gentlemen, who seem so glad to have the contest over, and the term of canvassing shorten'd, that they are silent spectators of the most fatal blow that can be given to their rights and privileges?' *GM*, xvii (1747), 278.

circulating his Cash back among his Tenants, drains all off either to the Capital, or to some other Place of public Resort and Pleasure, where the greatest Part is spent in foreign Luxury; hence the impoverish'd Country complains of the Weight of Taxes; which, tho' at best they would be burthensome, become thus intolerable. And, lastly, the Gentleman himself, having by such Means run out his Fortune, thinks of retrieving his Necessities by a Place; hence Murmurs against the Administration, which cannot supply the real Wants, or fancied Merits, of all Mankind. To these, if we add the Calamities and Load of Expence brought on us by the Ambition and Malice of our foreign and domestic Foes, we shall find the true Source of all our real Misfortunes, as well as of those chimerical Grievances, to redress which we are to extirpate at once both our Liberties and our Religion, by exchanging the best of Kings; a King respected all over *Europe, whom, if his whole People personally knew, they would all personally love*; for a tyrannical Papist to be introduced here by the Cabals of *Rome*, and by the Arms of *France*, and who hath dared to affect absolute Power even in his Declaration.[1] In his political Principles an Enemy to our Liberties; in his Faith, to our Religion; and in his Heart incensed against all our People, except a few desperate Rebels; dissolving the Union, and then mounting the Throne, under the highest Obligations to *France*, and to the worst Part of *Scotland*.

Alderman.

This is a frightful Picture indeed. I promise you his Friends represent him in a different Manner to our Party.

Gentleman.

And can you, or any Men in the Nation who call themselves Whigs, be the Tools and Bubbles of such despicable Wretches? For do not deceive yourselves; you are doing their Business, and and not they yours. The Republican doth indeed serve the Purpose of the *Jacobite*, as the Atheist doth that of the Papist: For to reduce this Nation to the Form of a Republic, is as wild a

---

1 The Old Pretender's declaration or 'manifesto', dated from Rome, 23 December 1743, read at Glenfinnan and later at Edinburgh, proclaimed his legitimacy against the Hanoverian usurpation, disavowed the Union, called for 'a free Parliament', granted immunity to all who declared for him, and commanded his subjects to assist him in the recovery of his rights. See, for a text, Henderson, *The Edinburgh History of the Late Rebellion*, pp. 15–18.

Scheme as to reduce it to Atheism; and thus, while the one assists in undermining our Government, and the other in undermining our Religion, the Schemes of Slavery and of Popery are in Fact carried on.

Alderman.

Yet surely you state the Case too strongly; the introducing Popery is not the necessary Consequence of introducing a popish Prince.

Gentleman.

Surely it is. No one Event can be more necessarily the Consequence of another. If you think this wants any Proof, let me recommend the Pamphlets to you writ at the Time of the late Rebellion,[1] and you will there find this Point fully demonstrated.* But admit the Danger to be never so small, why should we incur it? If we have no Grievances, we want no Exchange. If we have some, yet unless they were of the highest Nature, they can never justify either the Honesty of an Exchange, by which we must become perjured Traitors, or the Wisdom of it, since we must most certainly run the greatest Risque of both our Religion and our Liberties.

Alderman.

It would be a great Risque indeed; and I am not ashamed to own you have convinced me, it would be both dishonest and foolish in us to venture it.

Gentleman.

Give me your Vote then for those honest Gentlemen,[2] who will support an Administration which hath already preserved this Nation from Ruin, and under which the present Establishment, and of Consequence our Religion and Liberties, will be always secure.

* See the serious Address to the People of *Great Britain*, written by the Author of this Pamphlet.

---

[1] Cf. Fielding's own note in a similar context, *A Proper Answer*, below, p. 79. To the pamphlets Fielding lists there should be added his *A Dialogue between the Devil, the Pope, and the Pretender* (1745), esp. pp. 37–9.

[2] For the 'Earnestly address'd' electors of Westminster the choice of Administration candidates would have been Sir Peter Warren, hero of Finisterre, and Granville Leveson-Gower (1721–1803), self-styled Viscount Trentham, M.P. for Bishop's Castle (1744–7). Both were elected.

Alderman.

As to my Vote, I told you, it was engaged.

Gentleman.

Engagements into which you have been deceitfully drawn under false Colours and Pretences, cannot be binding. Will you vote for Men who have endeavoured to inflame you with a Cry of Grievances, which you now see to be wholly Chimerical? And what are these Men? One of them a notorious *Jacobite*,[1] and as notorious a Blockhead. The other a Person of known profligate Principles; a *Whig* in Name, but in Heart a Slave as all wicked Men are; one who hath joined with this *Jacobite*, and would join with the Devil himself, to work himself into Employment, which he despairs of being let into under the present Administration.[2]

Alderman.

My dear Friend, can I be safely free with you?

Gentleman.

You have already shewn that you think so.

Alderman.

Why then—I am almost ashamed to own it; but, O my Friend, mutual Promises have past between us. I have promised my Vote, and Mr. *Toastum* hath promised whenever his Party comes into Power to provide for my Son.

Gentleman.

As to the Conscientious Part, I think I have convinced you on which Side it lies; and as to the interested, I believe, I need very few Arguments to satisfy you, that my Friends are more likely to have it in their Power to serve your Son.

Alderman.

Let them do as they will, you have convinced me, that I cannot keep my Promise, and preserve my Duty to my Country. Here's a Health to our noble Sovereign King GEORGE; and I assure you

[1] Sir Thomas Leadenhead; see *Dialogue*, above, p. 6, and General Introduction above, pp. xxxiv–xxxv.
[2] See *Dialogue*, above, p. 6, n. 3.

no Enemy of his, or of my Country, shall ever have a Vote of mine.

Gentleman.

Fill a Bumper, my Friend, and I would pledge you, was the Glass ever so big. Believe me, it is under him and his Family only that our Religion, Liberties and Properties can be secure; and under him it must be our own Faults, if we are not a happy and flourishing People.

Alderman.

I really believe it.

Gentleman.

You see plainly now, the Views of your two Candidates; the one would destroy the Administration at the Hazard of the Government, to introduce himself into Power; and the other would destroy the Government, to introduce the *Pretender*. One or other of these Schemes is the real Motive of all the present Opposition, except among those who are merely the Dupes and Fools of the others. The two first Sorts of People know what they mean, and mean very ill; the latter would perhaps mean well enough, if they had but Sense to know *what they mean*. The first I detest; I pity the last; but both the Knaves and the Fools must be withstood and defeated at this critical Time, or between them the Nation will be undone. For my own Part, I have no Doubt but they will be defeated. And if we have a good Parliament, and can but see quiet Times, I make no Question but whatever is really amiss in the Government will be reformed, and that the Ministry will heartily join in the Work. But let us think of Safety before Reformation. And when we do reform, let it be soberly and temperately done; not according to the impracticable Schemes of School-boy Politicians, or to the furious Passions of Party Zealots; but with Knowledge, Judgment, and Impartiality; always remembring, *that we want good Examples more than good Laws.*

A PROPER
ANSWER
To A Late
Scurrilous Libel,
ENTITLED,

*An Apology for the Conduct of a late
celebrated Second-rate Minister.*

By the AUTHOR of the *Jacobite's Journal.*

Hic niger est, hunc tu, Romane, caveto.

LONDON,
Printed for M. COOPER in *Pater-noster-Row.*
MDCCXLVII.
[Price One Shilling.]

A PROPER
ANSWER
To A Late
Scurrilous Libel,

ENTITLED,

An Apology for the Conduct of a late celebrated Second-rate Minister.

By the AUTHOR of the *Jacobite's Journal.*

Hic niger est, hunc tu, Romane, caveto.

THE SECOND EDITION.

LONDON,

Printed for M. COOPER in *Pater-noster-Row.*
MDCCXLVIII.
[Price One Shilling.]

Advertisement.

The Author of the following ANSWER[1] would not be thought to conceive it possible, that some of the Insinuations in the APOLOGY could impose on any Man living;[2] the Intent of this Answer is to wipe off those odious Lights attempted to be cast on the late glorious Revolution, and to obviate a very false and dangerous Conclusion, which the wicked Author of the Pamphlet hath presumed to draw from the whole.

Indeed it was highly improper to suffer such an Attempt to pass unregarded, and yet it must be acknowledged highly difficult to give a serious Answer to a Writer who builds the deepest and blackest Designs, on Arguments in which he must be supposed to be only in Jest.

All that Part therefore is waved, as well as what relates to foreign Politicks, during the Administration of the late Earl of ORFORD:[3] For tho' many of the Objections here made are false, I know no Person who can be now called upon to refute them.[4]

---

[1] For the date of publication, a discrepancy in the title as first advertised in the press, and some of the early attributions of authorship, see General Introduction above, pp. xliv–xlv.

[2] See General Introduction above, pp. xxxix–xliii.

[3] Sir Robert Walpole (1676–1745), M.P. for Castle Rising (1701–2) and King's Lynn (1702–12, 1713–42), First Lord of the Treasury and Chancellor of the Exchequer (1715–17, 1721–42), resigned in February 1742 and was created Earl of Orford. The *Apology* devotes considerable space, pp. 30–46, to an 'explanation' of Walpole's foreign policy. Fielding's decision to omit discussion of this 'Part' may be due to two factors: the strong political ties between Walpole and Henry Pelham, on the one hand, and the discrepancy between the former's essentially pacific policy and the Pelhams' decision in 1747 to assume a militant posture, on the other. T. Manning, *A Review of the Late Mr. W———N's Conduct and Principles* (London, 1748), p. 67, observes that the *Apology* appeared just 'when a general Naturalization Bill was on the Tapis' and suggests that the pamphlet was designed to create in George II 'a Diffidence of the *English* in general', and thus to encourage him in the belief that his tenure depended on his being supported by foreign mercenaries.

[4] Walpole had died on 17 March 1745.

A PROPER ANSWER

To A Late

Scurrilous Libel,

ENTITLED

An Apology for the Conduct of a late celebrated Second-rate Minister, &c.

When Popery without a Mask stalks publickly abroad, and Jesuits preach their Doctrines in Print, with the same Confidence as when the last Popish Prince was seated on the Throne,[1] it becomes high Time for every Man, who wishes well to his Country, to offer some Antidote to the intended Poison.

There hath lately appeared a Pamphlet entitled, *An Apology for the Conduct of a late celebrated Second-rate Minister*, &c. This Pamphlet, for Impudence and Falshood, and, at the same Time, for the most secret and destructive Views, never had its Equal.

The two former of these make it the Object of Contempt and Ridicule; but the latter place it in a more serious Light, and call for some Antidote to the Poison this is intended to spread amongst the Multitude.

This Pamphlet asserts,

I. That the late Mr. *Winnington* was its Author.[2]

II. That not only he, but Sir *Robert Walpole*, and all the present Ministry; nay, that the Great Duke of *Marlborough*, and the Lord *Godolphin*, were *Jacobites*; and acted from a settled Design of introducing the Pretender into this Kingdom.[3]

---

[1] James II of England (1685–8).

[2] See *Apology*, Preface, pp. 3–6; and General Introduction above, pp. xxxviii–xxxix. For a similar list of charges see *GM*, xvii (1747), 574.

[3] Cf. *Apology*, pp. 25–6: 'most if not all the chief Ministers, since the Revolution, have had their Eye on the *old Constitution* . . . I am well satisfied, that Lord *Godolphin* and the Great Duke of *M———h*, wished as warmly to the *old Constitution*, as my Uncle *Harley*, and had wrought as arduously on their Plan, for its Restoration, as he did on his, or as I have on mine.' Sidney Godolphin (1645–1712), 1st Earl of Godolphin, held posts, including that of Secretary of State, under Charles II, corresponded with the Prince of Orange, advocated a regency after the flight of James II, corresponded with the latter at St. Germains, held posts as Commissioner and later First Commissioner of the Treasury under

III. That the late King was likewise a *Jacobite*, and intended to resign his Crown in Favour of that abjured, pretended Prince.[1]

IV. That the King of *France* is in the Interest of the House of *Hanover*; and not even a Well-wisher to the Cause of *Jacobitism*, or to the Family of the *Stuarts*.[2]

Such Assertions as these, no Man in his Wits will attempt to answer; nor no such Man will, I believe, desire to see them answered: But I must observe they greatly assist in answering all the rest; since they either prove the Author to be a Madman, or in Jest; or else that he is capable of asserting Falshoods blacker than Hell itself.

But black, and false, and wicked as this Pamphlet is, it contains some certain and undoubted Truths: Such are the Designs of Queen *Anne* and her Ministry, now first asserted and avowed in Print.[3] True, indeed, it is, that this unhappy, deluded Princess was, by wicked Ministers who acted under the Cabals of *Rome*, led into the most pernicious and destructive Schemes. To execute these, was that detestable Treaty of *Utrecht* made;[4] by which *France* was again re-instated in almost every Thing she had lost, and relieved from all she had to fear from her victorious Enemies. To these destructive Schemes were sacrificed the Fruits of so much Blood and Treasure, and all those glorious Consequences which might have been drawn from the unparalell'd Successes of our Arms, under the Conduct of the Great, the Protestant, the Whig Duke of *Marlborough*.[5] To carry on these

William III, was a confidant of Marlborough and like him was implicated by Fenwick in Jacobite conspiracies, was active in promoting union with Scotland, supported the Barrier Treaty with the Dutch, urged the impeachment of Sacheverell, and was dismissed by Anne with a pension in 1710.

[1] *Apology*, p. 22, speaks of George I as not having much 'liking to the Nation, and less perhaps to the H—r ap——t', that is, to the then Prince of Wales, and it implies abdication in favour of the Stuarts. See *GM*, xvii (1747), 574.

[2] *Apology*, pp. 44–5, attributes to Walpole the notion that France preferred the Hanoverian ministry because the latter was ruining England with debts and taxes; conversely, the French would never truly support 'patriot' schemes or the 'country' party because these would in fact strengthen England.

[3] *Apology*, pp. 19–20, describes Harley's secret plan to abet Anne, 'a weak, an irresolute and diffident Female Genius', in restoring the 'old Constitution' and the general spirit of Toryism, and speaks also of her appointing 'Fellow-Labourers in the hazardous Work'.

[4] The first in a series of interpolations; the Treaty of Utrecht (1713) is not alluded to by name in the *Apology*. It is a 'detestable Treaty' because it was part of a 'Tory peace'.

[5] Notwithstanding his political difficulties, Marlborough seems to have been something of a personal hero of Fielding's. *TP* no. 8 of 24 December 1745 praises his military

Popish Projects, that Great General was discarded;[1] our Allies, and with them the Protestant Cause of *Europe*, was abandoned;[2] and the Power of *France* restored, that she might be as able, as she was ready to assist, with that Power, in establishing the Throne in the House of *Stuart*,[3] and Popery in this Nation; to both which, as necessarily connected together, she, and all the other Popish Powers in *Europe*, had lent a helping Hand, during above half a Century.

Yet *weak* as this Princess was, the Minister, it is said,* *could not, with Safety, trust her with all the Secrets of his Plan*. What Secrets are here meant? To introduce the Pretender was her Desire and Design. Rather, therefore, say, She was not to be trusted with *the Consequences of this Plan*. WEAK indeed this Princess was, but she was HONEST. She would not have entered into this Scheme, could she have discerned it in its true Light. She would not have attempted to introduce a Popish Bigot, who hath no more Right to be King of *England* than he hath to be Emperor of *China*. She would not have made this Country a Scene of Bloodshed and Desolation; have brought Popery, with all its dreadful Horrors, upon us, and have subjected this Crown to be again dependent on the *French* King. I say *again*; for dependent it was during the Reigns of the three last Kings of the *Stuart* Line, and whom may that God, who alone can protect his

* In the Apology.[4]

'Sagacity'; see also the panegyric in *Of True Greatness* (1741) and 'Liberty. To George Lyttelton, Esq;' (1743).

   [1] Prior to the elections of 1710, and Harley's advent to power, Marlborough had been supported by the Whig junto in his bellicose position on the war. He resisted the preliminaries of Utrecht, which Harley and the Tories had agreed to. In 1711 the Tory Administration arraigned him on charges of peculation and dismissed him, with the Queen's support.

   [2] Without consulting her allies and despite a clause of the Grand Alliance (1689) prohibiting a separate peace, England agreed to preliminaries with France. After the two major powers had settled their differences, the allies were forced to accommodate as best they could, or continue the war without English support; Sir George Clark, *The Later Stuarts*, 2nd ed. (Oxford, 1955), pp. 230–7.

   [3] In fact, at Utrecht the French acknowledged not only Anne's title to the throne—at the beginning of the war it had been denied—but also the succession as regulated by the Act of Settlement (1701) to provide for the Protestant line. By 1715, however, Louis XIV was manifesting distinct, if informal, interest in Jacobite plans to invade England so as to restore James III.

   [4] p. 19: '. . . that he could not with Safety, trust even his royal Mistress with all the Secrets of his Plan, for answering her own principal Purpose'.

own Protestant Cause, grant to be the last of that Line, who ever shall reign in this Nation, or rather, who shall be ever the *French* Vicegerents here. Let me add, that to this Dependence is principally owing the present Grandeur of that ambitious Crown, which is the only great Sore of this Nation, and the chief Plague of *Europe*. Under this Dependence did those wicked Princes endeavour to subject this Nation to Slavery; chusing rather to be Viceroys over Slaves, than the limited Kings of Freemen: Nay, under this Dependence did *Charles* the Second, and *James* the Second, (and most openly and plainly the last) attempt not only to destroy our civil, but our religious Liberty, and once more to cast the intolerable Bonds of Popery upon us. But from Popery, and from *France*, and from the House of *Stuart*, the wretched Tool of both, we have been twice delivered, by the Sense and by the Bravery of our Ancestors: And shou'd we ever submit to (much more shou'd we court) these Chains again, what Animal upon Earth is there so low and despicable, that it would not suffer in Comparison with our Baseness or with our Folly?

And this, I think, our Jesuit is so kind to own:[1] For speaking of Sir *Robert Walpole's* Scheme (most absurd and ridiculous Supposition!) to introduce the Pretender, he says, "Another Branch of his Scheme, was to corrupt the Morals of the People generally, *in order to create an Indifference in them, towards Religion and Posterity. A Disregard for the latter* would plunge them naturally into Profusion and Luxury, which would necessarily hurry on Poverty *and Despair*; and a DISRELISH FOR RELIGIOUS WORSHIP IN GENERAL WOULD RENDER THEM LESS ANXIOUS AND AVERSE TO THOSE RELIGIOUS TENETS, that had given the best Colour for the late Change in the Constitution."[2] These are *verbatim* his Words;

---

[1] Cf. *JJ* no. 3 of 19 December 1747, below, p. 447: 'We are desired to return the Thanks of all the Jacobites . . . to Father Paul Maskwell of the Society of Jesus, for his excellent Treatise, called an Apology for a late celebrated Second-rate Minister &c.' Peter Murray Hill, Catalogue No. 88 (Spring 1964), pp. 22–3, § 154, records a copy of the *Apology* with a 12-line manuscript note (attributed to the original owner) stating that 'Mr. Murray the Author of Alethia told me that one Lynch an Irish Papist' from St. Omer wrote it. The note further states that, according to Murray, Lynch admitted to making over £100 by the pamphlet, and was congratulated by one of the Fathers at St. Omer for his service to the Pretender's cause. On St. Omer as a source see *Proper Answer*, below, p. 73. Cf. *The Patriot Analized* (London, 1748), p. 28: 'And yet see how one of our scribbling Champions dubs the Author a Jesuit. But little Notice is to be taken of one who, according to the *Comment*, wrote round the whole Compass of Parties'; see also pp. 36–8.

[2] *Apology*, p. 28, italics and capitalization supplied by Fielding.

and how they came to drop unguardedly from the Pen of a Jesuit may seem justly surprizing. But it is well observed by a sensible as well as worthy Writer, *That all Villains, if closely attended to, do, at one Time or another, betray themselves.*[1] Could the best and honestest Whig in the Nation have said more than this? Nay, have they not said this a hundred Times over? For is it not here confess'd, *totidem verbis,* that nothing but the utmost Indifference towards Religion and Posterity; nothing but a total Disregard for the latter, join'd with Despair, and an Indifference, nay, a general Disrelish for the former, could effectuate this horrid Scheme? Farther, is it not here confess'd and avowed, that the Success of this Scheme would be attended with the Restoration of those religious Tenets, (i.e. Popery) which are here acknowledged to have given the best Colour for the Revolution?

This is a Degree of Honesty which I did not expect in a Jesuit; but it is one of those political Flaws,

> ———*quas aut incuria fudit,*
> *Aut humana parum cavit Natura.*[2]

For none but the Devil himself is a Jesuit in consummate Perfection.

But what pray is meant by the Change in the Constitution? Or rather, what is meant by the Old Constitution, which was changed at the Revolution, and which any honest Man, or good *Briton,* would desire to see restored? What is this Old Constitution?

Is it the Constitution under the ancient Tenures, which was changed at the Restoration, given up as a Kind of postlimited Condition by *Charles* the Second, at his Return;[3] and in the

---

[1] Not identified. There is a similar dictum in Seneca, *Epistulae Morales,* xcvii. 13, which derives from Epicurus, 'Sententiae Vaticanae', no. vii, in Cyril Bailey, *Epicurus: The Extant Remains* (Oxford, 1926), p. [107]; cf. Morris Palmer Tilley, *Dictionary of Proverbs in England in the Sixteenth and Seventeenth Centuries* (Ann Arbor, Mich., 1950), T 117, p. 655.

[2] Horace, *Ars Poetica,* 352–3: 'which a careless hand has let drop, or human frailty has failed to avert' (Loeb).

[3] By the terms of 12 Car. II, cap. 24 ('An Act for taking away the court of wards and liveries, and tenures *in capite,* and by knights-service and Purveyance . . .') Charles II gave up his feudal dues from wardships, tenures *in capite* and other vestiges of the medieval system in which the monarchy was financed by its position at the head of the land-holding system. Since the effectual intermission of the Court of Wards and Liveries in 1645 many persons holding land of the Crown had disposed of said land; see David Ogg, *England in the Reign of Charles II,* 2nd ed. (Oxford, 1963), i. 158–61; *Statutes at Large,* vii. 472–86.

Hurry of Joy in which he then was, when perhaps it was little weighed or considered? Tho', to say the Truth, the Interest of the Crown was not concern'd in maintaining it:[1] For tho' the greatest Part of the People were in old Time Slaves under these Tenures, yet it was not a Slavery to the King, but to the great Men of the Nation, who, partly by these Means, were often too powerful for the King himself.

Is it then the Constitution under which the Barons lorded it, as well over the King as over the People, and which was destroyed by *Henry* the Seventh?

Is it the Tyranny of the Pope which we desire to restore, and which was abolished by *Henry* the Eighth?

Or lastly; Is it that Regal Tyranny, which four successive Princes of the House of *Stuart* had been endeavouring, by all the Means of Fraud as well as of Force, to erect and establish in this Kingdom?

To lay the Foundation of this Tyrannical *Babel*, did *Charles* the Second sell himself to *France*.[2] (I had almost said to the Devil.) With this View did he assist the *French* King, in the projected Extirpation of the Protestant Interest in *Europe*:[3] And with this View did he undermine both our Liberty and our Religion at Home. For this Purpose were the Laws perverted, to shed some of the best* and noblest Blood in the Nation; and the Pulpits corrupted to trumpet forth the Doctrines of absolute Power; in which Divines were found shameless enough to assert, that the King had an absolute Right to all that Subjects were possessed

---

* Lord *Russel*, *Sydney*, &c. murdered by Form of Law, for having been the Champions of Liberty, and of the Protestant Religion.[4]

---

[1] Cf. the preamble to the Act: 'Whereas it hath been found by former experience, That the courts of wards and liveries . . . have been much more burthensome . . . to the kingdom, than they have been beneficial to the King'; *Statutes at Large*, vii. 472.

[2] Most notably in the secret Treaty of Dover (1670), which provided that in return for a subsidy and armed assistance Charles II would declare himself publicly a Catholic.

[3] The Treaty of Dover also called for a new war against the Dutch, despite the terms of the Triple Alliance (1668), according to which England and the States General agreed to provide military assistance for each other in the event of attack. One of the secret clauses of the Triple Alliance called for England and the Dutch to declare war on France if the latter did not resolve her difficulties with Spain in the matter of the succession. In return for his participation in the joint attack on the Dutch Charles II was to receive an annual subsidy from Louis XIV for the duration of the conflict.

[4] The so-called 'Council of Six' (Essex, Hampden, Howard, Monmouth, Russell, Sidney), implicated in the 'Rye House Plot' (1683) to murder Charles II. William, Lord

of*; that he had Power to raise Taxes or Subsidies without Consent of Parliament; and that all his Subjects who resisted him would be damned†.

With the same Views did *James* the Second (the Foundation being thus laid) carry on the mighty Work openly, and above ground. Not to enumerate all the tyrannical Acts of his Reign, of which History is so full, and which are so recent, that they are universally well known, his assuming to himself the Power of dispensing with Laws,[1] a Power so unknown to our Constitution, was at once leaping (if I may be allowed the Expression) into the Saddle of Tyranny, and declaring himself absolute.

Now, this Fortress of arbitrary Power was, I acknowledge, totally overturned by the Revolution; and to overturn it was the whole End and Design of that Revolution.

* Dr. *Harsnet* made, for such Services, Bishop of *Chichester*.[2]

† Dr. *Maynwaring*, in a Sermon before the King, after which he was soon made Bishop of *St. David's*.[3]

Russell (1638–83), son of the 1st Duke of Bedford, Whig exclusionist and anti-Catholic, was tried for premeditating rebellion, pleaded not guilty, was sentenced, and executed at Lincoln's Inn Fields; Algernon Sidney (1622–83), a theoretical republican or 'real Whig', author of *Discourses concerning Government* (1698), was tried before Jeffreys on charges of treason, found guilty, and executed on Tower Hill.

[1] That is, of remitting or relaxing the laws in specific cases only. Of medieval origin, the dispensing power had not yet been invalidated by Act of Parliament, though in 1673 the Commons had persuaded Charles II to withdraw his Declaration of Indulgence. The exemplary instance of James II's use of the dispensing power involved Sir Edward Hales, titular Earl of Tenterden and self-declared papist, who was commissioned a colonel and later appointed Governor of Dover, although he had not taken the sacrament and oaths according to the Test Act (25 Car. II, cap. 2). His plea of king's dispensation was upheld by the King's Bench (1686) and he was later made Governor of the Tower of London and Master of the Ordnance. The Hales case was held to establish the right of papists to hold commissions as officers in the army; cf. *Tom Jones*, VIII. xiv. By his two Declarations of Indulgence (1687, 1688) James II generalized the dispensing power into a suspending power, whereby the laws themselves were remitted.

[2] Samuel Harsnett (1561–1631), Archbishop of York (1629), Fellow and later Master of Pembroke Hall, Cambridge, denounced as papist (1584), Vice-Chancellor of Cambridge (1606), Bishop of Chichester (1609), accused of popery by the Fellows of Pembroke and forced to resign, Bishop of Norwich (1619), sworn of the Privy Council (1629), and author of 'Considerations for the better settling of Church Government', which Charles I ordered to be circulated among the bishops (1629).

[3] Roger Maynwaring or Manwaring (1590–1653), chaplain in ordinary to Charles I, in which capacity he preached two sermons before the King in 1627, asserting (1) the peril of damnation for those resisting royal taxation, and (2) the indifference of parliamentary approval of the raising of financial aids and subsidies for the Crown; upon sentence of fining, imprisonment, and suspension, he recanted; Laud consecrated him Bishop of St. David's in 1635.

But what Change it hath introduced into our true Constitution, I am at a Loss to imagine. Indeed if we will acknowledge, with the base Flatterers who writ and preached in the Time of these *Stuarts*, that the King of *England* is, by the Laws of our Constitution, absolute, and can be controuled only by his own Will: In short, if the absolute Power exercised by some of the *Stuart* Family, and aimed at by them all, be really a Part of our Constitution, then I own the Revolution hath introduced a Change; a Change for which we ought forever to honour our glorious Ancestors, for having so hazardously purchased for us; since, without this Change, we should, in all Probability, have been at this Day the most wretched People that ever groaned under the heavy Burden of Popery and arbitrary Power.

Again, what means the Jesuit, when he says, "that those who had the earliest and principal Share in the Conduct of that mighty Affair, (the Revolution) had no View to such a Change as happened, nor intended to go such Lengths, as they were led into afterwards?"[1] Certainly they intended to have expelled this Popish Tyrant; for that was the first Step to be taken. Or was he only to be corrected; to have his absolute Power taken from him for a Time, and restored to him again? But what Degree of Weakness must we allow to Men whom we can suppose capable of such Designs, trusting one a second Time, who had already shewn he was not to be trusted, having broken the most solemn Promises, Vows and Oaths before?[2] Did they undertake this extremely hazardous Enterprize, at the certain Price of their Blood if they failed, in order, if they should succeed, to give up not only all for which they had contended, but themselves too, into the Hands of a Tyrant, who would most certainly punish them for what they had done? Did they rouse and incense the Lion, with a Purpose only of casting themselves into his Den?

How then can they be said to have gone greater Lengths than they intended? Were too beneficial Conditions stipulated for the Subject at this Time? Did the Declaration of Rights infringe the

---

[1] *Apology*, pp. 16–17. The parenthetical matter has been added by Fielding.

[2] Cf. Thomas Burnet, *History of the Reign of King James the Second* (Oxford, 1852), p. 7, where James II is reported to have promised his Privy Council 'that he would never depart from any branch of his prerogative' and that 'he would defend and maintain the church, and would preserve the government in church and state, as it was established by law'; *Tom Jones*, VIII. xiv: 'Besides this, he had dissolved his Subjects from their Allegiance by breaking his Coronation Oath.'

ancient Powers and Prerogatives of the Crown?[1] Was King *William* too circumscribed a Monarch? Sure no Jesuit would wish him to have had more Power; or have the Princes which have reigned since lost any of the Majesty of their Throne; or can they derive their Deprivation of any Right, with which our Constitution hath invested an *English* Monarch, from this Revolution.

And who are those People, who, in the very Moment of our Deliverance, and of that Deliverance to which they so gloriously, so dangerously contributed, repented them of the Good they had done, and of the Lengths into which they had been led effectually to free themselves from Popery and Tyranny? Here my good Jesuit *will pause,*[2] I apprehend, some Time, before he will be able to name any such Person. Struggles, I own, there were, very early ones, not in favour of *the old Constitution,* but in favour of that new one so lately attempted to be introduced, and so freshly abolished.[3] And these Struggles, I do agree with our Jesuit, were *highly to the Dishonour of those who had shamefully yielded to the Allurements of Court Favour and Power,*[4] and who were determined to involve their Country in Confusion, and, if possible, to sacrifice it to the Ruin it had so narrowly, so providentially escaped, in order to obtain such Favour and Power, or to revenge the Disappointment.

This, I am afraid, was too great a Source of that Opposition which arose in the early Days of the Revolution; and this hath been visibly in many Instances, and actually I conceive in most, the true genuine Cause of Opposition since.

[1] The document approved by both Houses of Parliament (12 February 1689), in which were stipulated the conditions under which the throne was to be offered to William and Mary. In particular the Declaration declared illegal the suspending power and the dispensing power ('as it hath been assumed and exercised of late'), upheld the right of subjects to petition the King without penalty of the law, declared illegal the right of the Crown to levy money for its own use without approval of Parliament and to raise or keep a standing army without similar approval, and upheld free and frequent elections of Parliament. In its final form as read to and accepted by William and Mary the Declaration was embodied in the Bill of Rights (1 Will. & Mar. session 2, cap. 2).

[2] Cf. *Apology,* p. 17: 'Here I paused a while, to see if I might not rest where so many great Men had taken their stand.'

[3] Alluding to the Jacobite intrigues of the 1690s, which included plans for an invasion and a plot on the life of William, implicating, at various times, Clarendon, Shrewsbury, Godolphin, Marlborough, Preston, and Fenwick. During this period the household of Princess Anne was also a locus of discontent.

[4] Cf. *Apology,* p. 17: 'and a Dishonour to those, who had shamefully yielded to the Allurements of present Favour and Power'.

But enough of this Skiomachy;[1] for so in Reality it is. I haste to the grand Point, to that poisonous Doctrine, which is endeavoured to be concealed in the Vehicle of all this Buffoonery, in all these monstrous and absurd Suppositions. "Shall we not," says this most impudent and malicious Writer, "arrive much sooner and more certainly at the Port of our Happiness, by sailing rather with, than against the Current of Power? Let all who are fond of War, and Parades on the *Continent*, be indulged. Let all who would maintain a large standing Corps of cherished foreign Mercenaries, have their way. Let those who would increase our Debts, be pleased. And let those who would prolong the War, to increase these Pledges, and for a Pretext to continue the aforesaid Mercenaries in our Pay, be praised and supported. In short, let all who would impoverish the People, in order to humble them, and corrupt them, in order to efface all generous Notions of Posterity, and their Country out of their Breasts; let those, I say, have Rope enough, and they will better answer our Purposes than *France*, even if she were sincere, and inclined to serve us."[2]

Every Article in the above Paragraph is a manifest Charge on the present Administration, and indeed on the present Establishment; and every one of these Articles is as false as any Charge which ever came from the College of *St. Omer's*.[3] I will examine them separately.

Let all, says the Writer, *who are fond of War, be indulged*. But how can the present Administration be charged with being fond of War? Why, because we are engaged in a War; a War undertaken at the repeated Sollicitations of the Merchants,[4] by the Advice of Parliament, and indeed desired, I might say demanded by the whole Nation. The then Ministry was forced into this War, against their Will,[5] they declined it to the very last, were

---

[1] A neologism, from the Greek σκιομαχία, fighting with shadows.

[2] *Apology*, pp. 48–9.

[3] Founded in 1593 by Robert Parsons (Persons), S.J., with the encouragement of Philip II of Spain, the Jesuit college for English Catholics had acquired during the Stuart machinations of the seventeenth century a reputation for political activism. It is here used by Fielding as a recognizable 'type' of sedition and disloyalty.

[4] The so-called 'War of Jenkins' Ear', declared against Spain in 1739. Cf. *Dialogue*, above, pp. 33–4; for some contemporary expressions of belligerence, see *GM*, ix (1739), 104–5, 535, 642–6.

[5] For the popular and parliamentary pressures on the pacific Walpole see Coxe, *Memoirs of the Life and Administration of Sir Robert Walpole* (London, 1800), iii, Chs. 51–3. 'It is recorded, that Sir Robert Walpole, hearing the bells ringing, inquired the cause of such

contemned and abused for having declined it so long, and were at last compelled to undertake it, by the united loud Voice of the People,[1] raised by the Trumpets of the Opposition, which had long blown nothing but War in the Ears of the Nation.[2] This is a Fact known, recent, and in the Memory of all Men. Nor were the late Administration more averse to the Commencement of this War, than the present have been desirous to put an end to it. Are they not known to be desirous of re-establishing Peace?[3] What Endeavours have they omitted for this End? Have they not gone every Length in advancing to this Purpose, which is consistent with the Honour of the Nation? nay, are not their Desires of obtaining a safe and honourable Peace so publickly known and acknowledged, that their Enemies have not scrupled to represent them as forward and willing to accept it on disadvantageous Terms?[4] How unjust then, nay how impudent is this Charge! Nor less so is that of *Parades on the Continent*. It is allowed by this Writer to be as clear as the Day, that the Rupture with *Spain* unavoidably involved us in a War with *France*;[5] where then is this War to be carried on? Are we desirous rather to make this Island than the Continent its Theatre?[6]

And that this Island would be the Seat of the War, if once our Out-works on the Continent were entirely in the Possession of the

---

rejoicings, and was informed that the bells were ringing for the declaration of war. They now *ring* the bells, he replied, but they will soon *wring* their hands'; Coxe, iii. 109 n.

[1] Cf. *TP* no. 30 of 20–7 May 1746, p. 1, col. 2.

[2] Prominent in the Opposition attack on Walpole's alleged pacifism were Lyttelton and Fielding himself, who as editor of *The Champion* (15 November 1739–? 1741) printed, if he did not himself compose, very severe remarks on Walpole's supposed failure to prosecute the war with vigour. See Coxe, *Walpole*, iii. 65, 81–3.

[3] In fact the ministry was badly divided on the issue of peace. By the time of *A Proper Answer* (December 1747) Newcastle had resumed his former militancy and with the support of George II was carrying this policy against a majority of the ministry, including Pelham and Chesterfield; Lodge, *Studies*, Ch. VII, and General Introduction above, pp. xxxviii, xlix. Cf. Walpole to Mann, 24 November 1747: 'Except Mr Pelham, the ministry in general are for the war; and what is comical, the Prince and the Opposition are so too'; *Yale Walpole*, xix. 448–9. The preliminaries of Aix-la-Chapelle did not commence in earnest until February 1748.

[4] Cf. *JJ* no. 10 of 6 February 1748, below, pp. 149–51.

[5] Cf. *Apology*, pp. 42–3: 'It appeared to me as clear as Day, that a Rupture with *Spain*, would involve us in a long and onerous War with France.'

[6] The rhetorical question is in response to a charge implicit in the phrase 'Parades on the *Continent*' (*Apology*, p. 49), namely, that for England a sea war is greatly preferable to a land war with its enormous expenditures of men and money and its handicap of entangling alliances. Cf. *Dialogue*, above, pp. 35–6.

Enemy, is demonstrable, and hath been demonstrated.[1] It could not indeed remain so long, and the Reason is no less obvious than shocking. Will not the very Nature of the Thing deter us from placing an entire Confidence in a Defence, which is subject to the Disposition of the Winds?[2] Will not History convince us how fatally this Protection of Situation and of maritime Strength have both been relied on; nay, will not even the Annals of King *William's* Reign shew us with how absurd a Vanity we boast our Superiority at Sea, over our present grand Enemy, and how capable he hath been, by a little Attention to his Marine, to dispute the Victory with us in that Element.[3]

If the Continent be of so little Concern to us, as some unmeaning, or rather ill-meaning, Persons have represented it, why hath so much Blood been spilt, and Treasure spent, on it, in the Days of our *oldest Constitution*, and in the Reigns of our best and ablest Princes? Why have Possessions on it been sought after, been so dearly won and maintained, and lost with so much Reluctance by us? If the utmost Extent of *French* Conquests there be so insignificant to this Nation, why hath it been thought, in all Ages, so plainly our Interest to confine that ambitious Crown within such narrow Bounds? Why did *Charles* the Second encourage and promote the Extent of those Conquests, in order to subdue his own Subjects, and to extirpate the Liberties of *England*?

Lastly, If it be so little our Interest to oppose these Successes, it as little becomes us to lament them. *France* hath certainly obtained no other Triumphs over us in this War. At Sea, where we are told we ought to do every thing, we have done every thing; for so entirely have we debilitated and ruined the Navy of *France*, that the very Ships we have taken from her are more than sufficient

---

[1] After the French successes of 1747, in particular the fall of Bergen-op-Zoom in September, the ministry concluded that public fears of an invasion would require the recall of a dozen battalions to defend the Kentish coast during the winter. See Newcastle to Sandwich, 20 October 1747 (B.M. Add. MS. 32810, f. 162), cited by Lodge, *Studies*, p. 292. Cf. Walpole to Mann, 20 October 1747: 'Holland seems gone!—how long England will remain after it, Providence and the French must determine!' *Yale Walpole*, xix. 442.

[2] Cf. *Dialogue*, above, p. 34, n. 4.

[3] After an inconclusive action at Bantry Bay while supplying James II's Irish campaign, the French fleet defeated Torrington's Anglo-Dutch squadrons off Beachy Head in June 1690, thereby commanding the Channel and greatly heightening English fears of an invasion. In 1691 James II did in fact project a landing of 30,000 men near Dover, to be under the protection of the French fleet in the Downs, but the Anglo–Dutch victory off La Hogue in May 1692 broke French sea power and nullified the invasion project.

to conquer those she hath left.[1] In this Light our Arms on the Continent must be allowed to be useful, nay, I must say success-ful; since they have at least engaged the whole Finances of *France* in the Land Service, and have diverted their Attention from their Marine.[2] Here then we ought to sing *Te Deum*, and to crown our Ministers with Laurels; but surely those who would represent us to have no Concern in the Affairs of the Continent, ought very little to lament our ill Success there; nor can Men who truly lament our Miscarriages there, very justly abuse the Ad-ministration, for having exerted their utmost Efforts to prevent them.

As to the base Suppositions concerning foreign Mercenaries,[3] they are inclusively answered already. If neither the entering into the War, nor the maintaining it on the Continent, can be im-puted as Faults to the Ministry, it will not surely be objected to them, that they do this in the easiest, cheapest and most effectual Manner; and that they are desirous to preserve both the Blood and Treasure of the Nation.

I come now to *the Increase of our Debts*.[4] That these are in-creased, is a melancholy Truth; but that there are any in the

---

[1] In particular, by the victories of Anson and Warren off Finisterre (May 1747) and of Hawke off Belleisle (October 1747); see H. W. Richmond, *The Navy in the War of 1739–1748*, iii. 78–115, and *GM*, xvii (1747), 486–7. Robert Beatson, *Naval and Military Memoirs of Great Britain*, iii (London, 1804), 82, 85, numbers the French fleet at 38 ships by the end of the war and the number of ships destroyed by the British at 32 by the end of 1747.

[2] *LEP* of 31 December 1747–2 January 1748 comments on this sentence: 'But by this Reasoning of our Author, it was worth our while to go over with inferior Numbers to be soundly b—t at Land, for the Sake of taking more easily some of their Men of War at Sea. This is deep indeed!'

[3] In particular, the Hanoverian and Russian mercenaries. Speaking of Granville, the *Apology*, p. 41, says, 'if he had been at the Helm in the late unhappy Troubles [the Jacobite rebellion of 1745], I should expect such an army of H———ns [Hanoverians] in the Bowels of our Country, as might be much easier brought hither than sent away.' By the terms of the St. Petersburg Convention (November 1747) between the maritime powers and Russia, the former undertook to subsidize the participation of 30,000 Russian troops in the war against France; *Journals of . . . Commons*, xxv. 486–91; Lodge, *Studies*, pp. 269–70, 283, 285; and, for Fielding's notice of the issue elsewhere, *JJ* no 14, below, p. 183.

[4] Cf. *Apology*, p. 49: 'Let those who would increase our Debts, be pleased.' *The State of the Nation, with a General Balance of the Publick Accounts*, 2nd ed. (London, 1748), pp. 4–5, breaks down the national debt of some £64 millions as of 31 December 1747, a figure which concurs with that given for the same date in *GM*, xviii (1748), 247; cf. Coxe, *Pelham*, i. 381–2, and *English Historical Documents, 1714–1783*, ed. D. B. Horn and Mary Ransome (New York, 1957), p. 337, which combines funded and unfunded debt into a figure of £69 millions. In 1739, the year the war began, the debt stood at £46 millions. For 1748 the Pelham ministry had to raise £13½ millions and did so, according to Coxe,

present Administration, who desire this Increase, is as impudent a Falshood. This is the Consequence of the War; of that War which the People desired, nay which they would not be denied; nor can the necessary Incidents of this War be charged on the Administration, with greater Justice than the unavoidable Accidents of it have been. A vast Part of this Debt was contracted long ago, even in the Reign of the beloved Queen *Anne*;[1] and the new Addition, though sufficiently deplorable, is however inconsiderable in the Comparison. Much the largest Share of it hath indeed been contracted in the Cause of the Revolution,[2] and if so, it hath been well and rightly contracted. Let it be imputed then to those on whom the Censure properly falls. The accursed *Jacobites*, who have supported the Machinations of *Rome* and *France* against their Country; Papists, who have attempted the Restoration of their Religion; and Protestants, who have long'd for they know not what; these are the Men who have obliged us to buy our Redemption from Popery and Slavery, at so high a Price; these are the Men who invited their dearly beloved King *James* to return to his loving Subjects; who afterwards spirited up the King of *France* to enter into a War in favour of his Son; and who have since encouraged that Crown, while at open Rupture with us, to send over his Grandson to this Kingdom, and to supply him with Arms, which we are to make use of against ourselves. *Rome* and *France*, the Pretender and his Adherents, have impoverished the Nation, and have loaded it with Debts and Taxes.

Possibly indeed some of his staunch Partizans here may have acted with the Views, which this Writer hath ridiculously imputed to the best Friends of the present Establishment. It is

Pelham, i. 382, 'without any other additional tax, than the increase of one shilling in the pound, on the duties of tonnage and poundage'. For Pitt's estimate that the War of the Austrian Succession increased the debt by £30 millions see John W. Wilkes, *A Whig in Power*, p. 107.

[1] The total funded and unfunded debt as of 1714 has been estimated at £36 millions; *English Historical Documents, 1660-1714*, ed. Andrew Browning (London, 1953), p. 356; see also Coxe, *Pelham*, i. 382. *The State of the Nation Consider'd, in a Letter to a Member of Parliament* (London [n.d.]), pp. iv-v, compares the expenses of the first seven years of 'Queen Anne's War' (£31·7 millions) with the first seven of the War of the Austrian Succession (£41 millions), 'whereby our Frugality is sufficiently explain'd'. This pamphlet, which is listed in *GM*, xvii (1747), 52 as among the January publications, was attributed by his contemporaries to Granville.

[2] The Jacobite 'revolution' of 1745-6. *The State of the Nation Consider'd*, p. 6, estimates them at £500,000.

now at least, credible that while they have attacked us by all the
Means of Force, they have still had this artful Design in Reserve;
intending if they should fail in the former to play this After-game,
and to gain our Affections by the very Methods which they themselves made necessary for our Defence. This is indeed so base and
jesuitical, that I should not easily have conceived it, had it not
been asserted in Print; but it now plainly appears, there is at
least one Man in the World wicked enough to suggest it.

But indeed I am apprehensive that if he hopes any Success
from this Scheme, he relies more upon our Folly, than I hope we
shall ever warrant; for it is much easier to shew the Falshood of
his Conclusion than it hath been to refute his Premises. In order
to do this, let us collect the scattered Argument, and reduce it to
some Appearance of Form. Thus then it stands. The Nation
under the present Establishment are burthened with Taxes, and
many other Grievances; by this Means they will become weary
of the present R—l Family; and will fly to the House of *St—rt*
for Redress. Here, must not our Jesuit allow that it is not enough
to prove the real Existence of the Grievances, in order to warrant
this Conclusion; nay, even if they could be brought home and
fixed on the present R—l F———y, (the contrary of which is
most certain) it doth not follow that we ought in Wisdom and
Prudence, to throw ourselves into the Arms of the other; for it
may be, that we may find no Redress of our Grievances by this
Means; nay, we may thus incur still greater and more intolerable
Mischiefs than we would avoid by this R—l Exchange:[1] For surely
no Jacobite is Fool enough to think, nor no Jesuit impudent
enough to assert that there are no Grievances greater than our
present. We must be allow'd at present to enjoy the greatest of all
Human Blessings, Liberty, in the fullest Extent, in which any
Nation ever did, or could enjoy it. Our Persons, and our Properties must be acknowledged to be secure from all kind of Violence;
nay, we think, we talk and we write whatever we please. Of the
last of these Liberties the present Apology is an Instance; for
had any Person attacked the established Government with equal
Virulence and Impudence, in any other Country, he would, in all,
have met with the most exemplary Punishment, and in many,

---

[1] The 'Royal Exchange' is cited in *JJ* no. 1, below, p. 92, as a favourite health of the
Jacobites. It involves a play on the mercantile building of that name and the Jacobite
desire to exchange George II for James III.

he would have been hanged. *Rara temporum Felicitas cum sentire qua velis, et qua sentias dicere liceat.*[1] A Happiness which we certainly enjoy.

And this Liberty, so perfect in Civil Matters, is no less uncontrolled in Religious. A Truth so manifest, so impossible to be contested, that it would be grossly mispending Time to offer a Syllable in support of it.

Now both these great Blessings (for such they are; tho' both are often applied to a very improper Use,) we may lose by a Change of that Government, under which we enjoy them; and that we should lose both by the Exchange here proposed, is as clear and evident as the future Consequences of any human Measures can be averred to be.

Let us look backwards to the Reigns of the *Stuarts*. A Family which were twice expell'd from the Throne within the Term of about 40 Years, for their open and violent Attacks on the Liberty of this Nation. If we have not Leisure to read over all the black Annals of these four Princes, who all lay in wait for our Liberties, as the Devil is in Scripture said to lay in wait for our Souls;[2] let us examine at least the Reign of *James* the IId. where every Engine that *Rome* could invent or furnish, was employed to extirpate all our Liberty and all our Religion.

Let us look forwards to what we may reasonably expect from a 5th Prince of the same Family, of the same Political Principles, and of the same Religion: *By Birth a* Stuart, *by Education a Papist; a Bigot under the Influence of the Councils of* Rome, *and under the Protection of* France: FOR BY THE ARMS OF THAT MONARCH ALONE HE CAN EVER BE ESTABLISHED HERE. And here is it possible to add one Argument to those*, which have been already advanced, and which none of their Party hath ever yet attempted to answer? And how trite and tedious must the Repetition of the same Arguments appear, to evince a self-evident Truth? Who

---

* See the serious Address published in the Time of the late Rebellion, and the Dialogue between an Alderman and a Courtier, published last Summer; both by the Author of this Pamphlet.[3]

---

1 Cf. Tacitus, *Histories*, I. i: *rara temporum felicitate ubi sentire quae velis et quae sentias dicere licet*; 'the rare good fortune of an age in which we may feel what we wish and may say what we feel' (Loeb).

2 e.g., Matthew x. 28. See also Robert South, 'A Sermon on Matthew 7: 26-7', in *Sermons Preached upon Several Occasions* (Oxford, 1823), ii. 338-42.

3 See esp. *Serious Address to the People of Great Britain* (1745), pp. 8-12.

can have the Patience to prove that it is the Nature of Fire to burn? But with what Indignation must we argue with Men, whom neither Reason nor Experience can convince of this, and whom not the Flames which have almost totally consumed their Ancestors, nor those which they see blazing in neighbouring Nations, can deter from desiring to apply a Firebrand to their own Houses. Can any *Man in his Senses* doubt whether *English* Liberty, and the Protestant Religion could probably, nay, possibly exist under a Prince bred up in the Principles of Popery and arbitrary Power; who must be introduced here, and must as certainly govern us, under the Influence and Protection of those Princes, who profess and practice that Policy and that Religion? If there be a Person capable of this Faith, how dreadful a Task must it be on any *Man in his Senses* to argue with him!

Without undertaking this Task then, I shall averr, that if the Premises asserted in this Apology were true, the Conclusion would be false; we must be infinite Losers in the Exchange, and consequently most wretched Fools to desire it.

Can any Price be bid up to the Value of our Religion and Liberties? Can any Advantages be offer'd to us in Exchange for these? Admitting they could, doth the Apologist offer us any such? What can he mean (if he means any thing more than to deceive the Multitude by Words) by the Restoration of the *old Constitution*,[1] unless it be to restore Popery and Slavery; the only Branches of *our Constitution*, which the Revolution and the present Establishment can be said to have lopped off! I defy him and all his Brother-Priests to mention another.

But it is tacitly insinuated, that by such Means the Nation would be relieved from its Debt. How! not by the Payment of it. Foreign Debts as well as foreign Obligations to our bitterest Enemies will be imported; but not a Farthing of foreign Coin. The national Debt is to be discharged by a Spunge,[2] *i.e.* by the Ruin of one half of our People.

---

[1] Cf. *Apology*, p. 24: 'The public Good being the common Object in View, neither of us [Harley and Winnington] could be justly blamed, for having made every other Consideration subservient to that one of restoring the Constitution. . . .'

[2] By cancelling or wiping out [the Debt] without payment (*OED*). The metaphor had traditional Stuart associations. See, for example, *Examiner* no. 15 (16 November 1710), where Swift describes Whig techniques for frightening the public with stories about the 'Pretender': 'Half a Score Stock-Jobbers are playing the Knave in *Exchange-Alley*, and there goes the *Pretender* with a *Sponge*'; *Prose Works*, ed. Herbert Davis, iii. 17. See also

How desirable this Event is, I leave to others, seriously to consider. Common Sense, I think must shew it in a very shocking Light to those who are to be ruined by the Expedient; and common Honesty, indeed common Humanity, will represent it in no very favourable Colours to the rest. But if this be a desirable Event, there is no Reason why we should purchase it at the Price of our Religion and Liberty, since it may be attained at a cheaper Rate; and surely this eligible and honest Purpose is as much in the Power of one Government to execute, as it can be in the Power of any other. If we will then ruin one half of our Fellow Subjects, let us not ruin all; nay, let us leave those who are to be thus deprived of their Properties, all the other Blessings of Society, and not cruelly take away their Religion and Liberties, in order to rob them of their Money.

As Power will always have Enemies, so in a free Nation we are always to expect Clamours against it. We are not therefore to wonder that our Apologist complains, of *tiring out the Nation with Debts, Taxes, coercive Laws, and Clogs upon Trade and Industry*;[1] we may rather be surprized that so fertile an Invention, employed with such wicked Views, should be able to find out no other popular, abusive, seditious Words than these, which may be reduced to two; namely, to coercive Laws, and to our national Debt, of which all the others are the necessary Consequence.

By the former of these, I solemnly declare I know not what is meant. I could point out many Laws made since the Revolution, in Affirmance and Protection of the Liberty of the Subject, besides the Declaration of Rights allowed and enacted at the Time of that Revolution, and which did indeed renovate and restore the true *old Constitution*, from the many Pollutions introduced into it under the *Stuarts*. But I defy this wicked Writer to name a single coercive Law enacted within this Period, which hath tended to enlarge the Power of the Crown, or in the least to abridge the lawful Liberty of the People.

Spectator no. 3 (3 March 1711). The metaphor was resurrected to describe what many took to be the implication of the Young Pretender's second 'manifesto' (10 October 1745), viz., that the National Debt had been contracted under an unlawful government and James II, although promising to 'take the Advice of his Parliament concerning it', would wipe it out. See Archibald Henderson, *The Edinburgh History of the Late Rebellion*, 4th ed. (London, 1752), p. 38.

[1] The italicized material is quoted from *Apology*, p. 27, where it describes Harley's '*Consumptive* Plan' for restoring 'the old Constitution'. The italics are Fielding's.

The Charge of *coercive Laws* therefore I reject as false in Fact.
As to our *great national Debt*, which, together with the War,
is the sole Cause of all our *Taxes*, and of all *Clogs upon Trade and
Industry*, it is a Truth which must be acknowledged by all; and
tho' Malignity only can represent this as a *Grievance to be complained of*,[1] it is surely a Calamity bitterly to be lamented; nor is it
more lamented by any than by the greatest of those now in
Power. Reason itself will tell us this; for it is the severest and
heaviest Clog on their Administration; nay, the Apologist tells it
us in every Page: For what is the whole Design of his Performance, but to prove that no Man can desire to increase or
aggravate this national Misfortune, but with a View to promote
the Jacobitical Scheme? The Charge then might be fairly retorted, and this Grievance might be fixed on the *Jacobites*
themselves, from the Words of their own Writer; and so far in
Fact, as hath been already said, they are chargeable; that
they and their Prince, and the great *French* Patron of that
Prince, have been the Occasion of laying us under this heavy
Incumbrance.

I am sensible that I have, in this Pamphlet, repeated the same
Thing more than once, but I am arguing with Men into whose
Heads common Sense must be, as it were, beaten, by frequent
Repetition.

All the Miseries which this Nation feels, or which she hath
to fear, are indeed, as the Apologist contends, strictly chargeable on that cursed Faction, which hath taken every Opportunity
to weaken the Hands of the Government at home, and the
Reputation of it abroad; which, from the Time of the Expulsion
of their Popish Idol,[2] even to this Day, a Period of near sixty
Years, have never rested from attempting the Restoration of him
and of his Family. During this whole Period, the Government
hath been constantly attacked, by the grossest, falsest, and most
malicious Calumnies, by the most groundless Murmurs, by
secret and assassinating Plots, by bold and open Rebellions, and
by Sollicitations of all the Assistance which the Cabals of *Rome*,
our ancient Tyrant, and of *France*, our natural Enemy, could
afford them. A just Opposition to these wicked Measures hath,

---

1 A political cant phrase; cf. *Dialogue*, above, p. 8 and note.
2 James II left England in December 1688, arriving at Ambleteuse on Christmas Day;
the *Proper Answer* was published on or about 23 December 1747.

of Necessity, increased our Taxes, and I will boldly add, hath increased Corruption; if to bribe the People to preserve themselves may, with Candour, be so called.

These are the only Evils under which the Nation groans, and these are most clearly to be imputed to the *Jacobites*. To charge them on the Government, is as monstrous an Injustice, as it would be to charge the Mischiefs brought on our Body by certain Remedies, (which however dangerous, are, in some inveterate Cases, allowed to be the only effectual ones,) to the Physician, and not to the Disease.

And now to speak aloud, should there ever come a Time when a wicked Administration should, in reality, pursue very pernicious Measures, the *Jacobites* would give those Measures the fairest Chance of Success: For while our Constitution is in such apparent Danger from this Party, wise and good Men would rather give up a great deal, than hazard the whole, by joining in an Opposition with Men, whose avowed Intention it is *to give up the whole*. It is indeed most certain, that no Grievances can be brought upon us by any Administration under the present Establishment, which may reasonably reconcile us to the Exchange proposed in this Apology; since it must be an Axiom with all Protestants, that a Protestant Tyrant is preferable to a Popish one, as it would be better to retain a religious Liberty than none at all.

But, in God's Name, can any such pernicious Measures be imputed to the present Administration? Is there a Man dishonest enough, or indeed impudent enough to assert, or even to insinuate, that one single Act of Power, unsupported by Law, can be charged upon them, or on their royal Master?

Lastly, Can the Nation complain of any one Evil, except these before-mentioned, and fairly and unanswerably accounted for? In all free Countries there will be Struggles for Power among the Great; nor will these Struggles be always conducted with the strictest Regard to moral Rectitude. One Instance of this Deviation is the Deceit constantly imposed on the People, by those who oppose, (that is who aim at obtaining) Power; for such constantly endeavour to annex the Colour of publick Interest to their own; but in Reality the People are less interested in this Contest, than the Tenants of a Manor commonly are in Competitions for the Stewardship; and are certain to be made only Tools and Bubbles of, when they enter with any Zeal into the Contention. In *England* we have never been without these Struggles, and from them must have been duly derived all those Clamours which Posterity only have seen to be groundless; and hence only, together with the destructive Schemes of Popish Priests, the most artful of Men, and of Protestant *Jacobites*, the silliest of Animals, have arisen all the base, and false, and wicked Aspersions, so industriously propagated against the honestest Ministry with which any Nation hath been blessed.

As to the Gentleman whose Name stands foremost, and who is maliciously hinted at by this Apologist to have succeeded to Sir *Robert Walpole's Influence*,[1] hath even the Apologist the Confidence to lay the least black Imputation upon him? His Virtues are too well known, too glaring, to encourage such an Attempt; and this the Silence of his worst Enemies on that Head have declared. He hath indeed a Mind which no Difficulties can conquer, nor any Power corrupt.

And why that not more invidious than false Reflection on his Parts?[2] Was it from his Want of Parts that the Apologist tells us, Sir *Robert Walpole* foresaw he was likely to succeed him? Was it owing to such Want that he did so far succeed him, as to take the Lead in the subsequent Administration, and to be regarded, submitted to, nay insisted on, as the most equal to this Lead, by the Heads of so many clashing and contending Parties? Do his Speeches in the H—— of C—— betray this Want of Parts? Or lastly, hath he shewn this by his great Support of the national Credit, at a Time when it was so severely attacked, so desperately despaired of, and so wonderfully preserved, by the Abilities of this Gentleman, and by the Reliance which the more sensible Part of Mankind had on these Abilities,[3] joined with the highest Integrity?——But I will restrain my own Inclinations from pursuing so amiable a Subject farther, and shall quit this truly great Man, with an Assertion which I have heard from one of the

[1] A distortion of the only reference to Pelham in the *Apology*; see the next note.

[2] Cf. *Apology*, pp. 32–3, where Walpole is said to have told Winnington: 'And as for P——m, the likeliest Man next yourself [to succeed Walpole], if the Opposition prevails not, whatever his private Sentiments concerning the *old Constitution* be, for I never had Confidence enough in him, to trust him with mine, he has not Parts equal to so arduous an Undertaking; and therefore I should suspect the glorious Work would miscarry in his Hands. . . .'

[3] See *Dialogue*, above, pp. 47–9.

wisest and greatest of his Intimates, *That he envied him on every Account except for his Power*.[1]

And here I would likewise have quitted this Apologist, had he confined himself to the Abuse of Civil Power; but the following Paragraph, which falls on the whole Body of the *English* Clergy, certainly deserves some Observation. "A Man (says the Apologist) may be a staunch Patriot, without thinking better of our spiritual Guides, than they deserve. How have they merited the Attention, or Approbation of Men of Sense and Candour? Churchmen, *before my Time*, may have had some Title to the Esteem of the People; but since I had any Knowledge of Men, *the Clergy have brought the C——h itself into C—t*."[2]

Here the Jesuit speaks out, and I hope all the Clergy of the Church of *England* will hear him. *Before my Time*, says he, *Churchmen may have had some Title to the Esteem of the People*. What is meant by this, or to what Time must he be understood to refer? Individuals may, perhaps, have deserved more Censure in some Ages than they have deserved in others; but I know no Reflection which can be justly cast on *the whole Body* within these last forty Years. The Clergy therefore, who may have had some Title to the Esteem of the People, were the Popish Clergy; by re-establishing those therefore, the Church is to be rescued from that Contempt which the Reformation hath laid it under. This, I think, is a fresh Intimation of what the Church of *England* may expect from the Success of these Jacobitical Schemes, to which, I am afraid, some of the Reformed Clergy have formerly given too great Assistance. Of such Folly, I gladly acknowledge, very few have lately been guilty; and this may indeed account for that intemperate Resentment against them, which hath above escaped a little untimely from the Pen of their Enemies, and which nothing but the highest Rancour could have led our Apologist out of his Way to introduce. But perhaps I injure him by saying he is led out of his Way, since we may so well connect his Arguments against the Church, with those which he hath urged against the State, and indeed with his general Purpose; for could he reconcile us to Popery, the great Work of

---

[1] Not identified. Possibly Lyttelton; less possibly Chesterfield. See General Introduction above, pp. xxii–xxiii, xlix–l, lxiii.

[2] See *Apology*, pp. 39–40. Fielding has added the italics. The 'disemvowelled' words are 'Church' and 'Contempt'.

Jacobitism might, for the future, be carried on without Fallacy or Imposition, and Men might be made *Jacobites*, without being first bereft of their Understandings. Beside, what can be more analogous than the Arguments here advanced against our Religion, to those which have been before urged against our Government: For do not the Faults of the Clergy afford as good and cogent Reason for abandoning the Protestant Religion in favour of Popery, as the Faults of an Administration under the present Establishment can possibly suggest for overturning that Establishment in favour of the Pretender?

The Imprudence and Malice of this Attack on their whole Body, who are here represented in a worse Light than any of their libertine Enemies have ever dared to represent them in, will, I hope, open the Eyes of all; and if any Members of the Church should yet remain weak enough to favour, even in their most fervent Wishes, the cursed Designs of this Party, they will now, I hope, be awakened to see, to detest, and to resent this injurious Treatment of their now open and unmasked Enemies. However they may be held by those, who in all their Writings* and Discourses treat them as *the sacrilegious Usurpers of their Right and Patrimony*, they will, I hope, never justify the Character given of them above, nor bring *themselves into Contempt, and their Church to Destruction*, by espousing the Cause of their most inveterate Enemies. On the contrary, I hope the Pulpit will henceforth resound with the Praises of that Government under which their Religious as well as Civil Liberty is secured, and the Church of *England* flourishes in all its just and legal Privileges.

Indeed, it is no less the Interest of the Clergy of the Church of *England*, than of the Religion they profess, to maintain and defend the present Royal Establishment in these Kingdoms. If they are wise, they must be themselves convinced, and if they are honest, they will endeavour to convince others, that A PROTESTANT CHURCH CAN BE ONLY SAFE UNDER THE PROTECTION OF A PROTESTANT KING, AND THAT THE INTRODUCTION OF A POPISH PRINCE MUST CERTAINLY BE ATTENDED WITH AN INTRODUCTION OF THE POPISH RELIGION.

I have now done with this Author, and I hope, have sufficiently exposed both him and his wicked Performance to the Contempt, or rather to the Detestation and Abhorrence of every Man, who

* This is the Term given to the Church of *England* by almost every *Popish* Writer.

hath any Regard for the Liberty and Religion now established in this Country; and which are as securely established under the Protection of the present Royal Family as the Wit of Man, or the Force of Policy can establish them. The Principles of Liberty and the Protestant Religion placed the Crown upon the present Royal Head that wears it; these Principles alone have hitherto maintained, and still must maintain it there. If that old Political Maxim, that the Interest of the King and People are the same, was ever true, it must hold so in this Instance. If our King or his Posterity will preserve their Crown, they must preserve our Religion and Freedom; if we will secure to ourselves the Possession of these Blessings, we must secure to our King and his Posterity the Possession of the Crown. I think, without presuming to violate the Sacred Person of his present Majesty with Panegyric, I may say, these Blessings are now entire in our Enjoyment; I may say farther, that we can as yet foresee no Time when any Prince of this august House would wish to deprive us of them;[1] but if such, in remote Times should arise, I will say, he must act contrary to his own Interest as well as ours. He cannot weaken our Religious and Civil Rights, without in the same Degree weakening himself. If he denies our Right to Liberty, he must deny his Right to the Crown; and who among us will be ready to defend the latter, when he is deprived of the former? *The Throne is established in the present Royal Family in Righteousness, and Righteousness alone can preserve it there.*

On the contrary, as the Principles of Popery and Slavery only can impose a Popish Pretender on us, so none but those Principles can preserve him here. If Popery and Slavery were not so firmly united in their Natures as they are, I believe it will readily be granted, that the former cannot be introduced here, till it is preceeded by the latter. As it is certain therefore that a Popish Prince will endeavour to make us Papists, it is as certain he would first endeavour to make us Slaves. Nay, this would be politically his Interest, even if Religion was out of the Case. For *Henry* the Seventh, who was introduced here by the Nobility, did all he could to weaken their Power, well knowing their Fickleness, and fearing lest they should expel him again: How much more justly

---

[1] Possibly a monitory glance at the Prince of Wales's Opposition party, one of whose principal journalists 'may be almost literally called the Drummer of Sedition, and said to beat up for Recruits in the Pretender's Cause'; *JJ* no. 17 of 26 March 1748, below, pp. 212–3.

may this Person suspect, that a Nation whom no Government can content, no Security can satisfy, would act by him as they had before done by others? How wise, and even how necessary must it be to govern those with a Rod of Iron, with whom every other Method had been found ineffectual? And what should restrain him from the Exercise of this Rod? The Friends of Freedom are not his Friends, neither can they justly tell him, that he owes his Crown to their Principles. The Liberty so stoutly contended for, and so strongly fortified by the Revolution, is by his Restoration abolished and superseded; and our *old Constitution*, that is, the Constitution as it existed under, and was left by *James* the Second, restored. He would not even have any Restraint on his Conscience, but would be in the same Seat of his Ancestors, with the same Rights, the same Reins, and the same Rod of Iron in his Hands, which they themselves so heartily exercised upon us.

But God forbid we should ever put this in the Hands of any one; and if our own Folly renders us unworthy of the Protection of Providence, may we be prevented from entailing such Curses on OUR INNOCENT POSTERITY.

THE
JACOBITE's JOURNAL.

By JOHN TROTT-PLAID, *Esq;*

SATURDAY, JANUARY 2, 1747.   NUMB. 5.

THE
JACOBITE's JOURNAL.

By JOHN TROTT-PLAID, *Esq;*

SATURDAY, DECEMBER 6, 1747.   NUMB. 1.

Woodcut frontispiece of the first twelve numbers. *Note the error in the dateline*
(December 6 for December 5) of the Yale copy of Number 1

——Ridiculum acri
Fortius et melius.——   Horace.[1]

If ever there was a Time when a Daily or Weekly Writer might venture to appear without any Apology to the Public, I think it is the present; for few Readers will, I believe, imagine it Presumption in any Author to enter the Lists against those Works of his Cotemporaries, which are now known by the Name of Newspapers; since his Talents must be very indifferent, indeed, if he is not capable of shining among a Set of such dark Planets.[2]

I do not therefore scruple to declare, that I conceive myself to be much better qualified for the Task of instructing and entertaining my Countrymen than any of these Writers; who, by their Productions, have vilified and degraded the Office of Censor as well as that of Historian; both which have formerly exercised the Pens of Men of true Learning and Genius;[3] nay, they have even furnished one Argument to the Enemies of the Liberty of the Press (if there be any such);[4] for the Badness and Baseness of the Manufacture hath been always held a good Reason for restraining it.

And as it seems to require no Apology to appear as a Writer, so neither can I persuade myself it requires any, at this Season, to appear as a Jacobite. A Title which Men assume in the most

[1] Horace, *Satires*, 1. x. 14–15: 'Jesting cuts hard knots more forcefully and effectively than gravity' (Loeb).

[2] In the first two numbers of the *JJ*, at the head of the columns of news items reprinted from other papers, Fielding supplies 'Marks' or cue titles for the following 'News-Writers': *Old England, Westminster Journal, Craftsman, London Evening Post, Whitehall Evening [Post], St. James's Evening [Post], General Evening [Post], Daily Advertiser, General Advertiser, London Courant, Daily Gazetteer.* The first four and the *Daily Gazetteer* seem to have been in the Opposition interest. *OE, LEP,* and the *Westminster Journal* were overtly hostile to the *JJ.*

[3] In particular, Addison and Steele, both of whom Fielding frequently acknowledges as models for his journalism. 'Isaac Bickerstaffe, Esq; Censor of Great Britain' was the *persona* used by them in the *Tatler*, no. 162 (22 April 1710) of which defines the office and its derivation from the Roman censor. Fielding first adopted the device in the *Champion* of 17 May 1740.

[4] See General Introduction above, pp. lvii–lviii, lxix–lxxi. Opposition writers had begun raising the issue of freedom of the press shortly after the elections of June 1747. Horace Walpole's *A Letter to the Whigs* (23 July 1747) claimed to see one of the first signs of repressive legislation in a statement in the *DA* of 28 May 1747.

public manner in Taverns, in Coffee-Houses, and in the Streets, may surely, without any Impropriety, be assumed in Print.

To say the Truth, our Party hath been very unfairly accused of having formerly concealed themselves from deep political Principles; whereas those who know us thoroughly, must know we have not any such Principles among us: For we scorn to regulate our Conduct by the low Documents of Art and Science, like the Whigs; we are governed by those higher and nobler Truths which Nature dictates alike to all Men, and to all Ages; for which Reason very low Clowns, and young Children, are as good and hearty Jacobites as the wisest among us: For it may be said of our Party as it is of Poets;

JACOBITA NASCITUR, NON FIT.[1]

In Reality, the Party hath so long chose to lay dormant, and have hitherto disavowed their Principles, from one or more of the following Reasons:

First, many have been afraid to reveal their Opinions, not from the Apprehension of Danger to their Persons, or of any Persecution on that Account; for I scorn to lay more to the Charge of the Whigs than is honestly their Due; but they have suspected that it might be some Objection to them in their Pursuit of Court-Favours, or Preferment, that they were desirous of removing the present King and his Family, and of placing another on the Throne in their stead. Moreover, they conceived, and that without the Help of any deep Politics, that Outcries against Ministers, on Pretence of their attempting to undermine the Liberty of the Subject, would not come with so proper a Weight from Men who profest the Tenets of indefeasible, hereditary Right, arbitrary Power, and prostrate Non-Resistance.[2] Again, they apprehended that Republicans,[3] who are an artful kind of People, might decline

---

[1] 'A Jacobite is born, not made.'

[2] The tenets adopted by a large body of the Church of England in the time of Charles I and elaborated into a 'Stuart' *de jure* or divine right theory after his death; David Ogg, *England in the Reigns of James II and William III* (Oxford, 1955), pp. 166–7, 506–7, and John Neville Figgis, *The Divine Right of Kings*, 2nd ed. (Cambridge, 1914), Ch. VII.

[3] On the Tory effort to impress 'republicanism' on the issue of monarchical succession, so as to depreciate the royal family, which, the Tories felt, had no just title to the throne, see David Hume, 'Of the Parties of Great Britain', in *Essays Moral and Political* (London, 1741), p. 135; also *Dialogue*, pp. 57–8; *TP* no. 26 (29 April 1746); and General Introduction above, pp. xl, lxiv–lxvi.

any Union with Men who wanted to exchange a limited for an absolute Monarch. And lastly, that the Dissenters would be extremely timorous on account of their Religion, and would rather chuse to tolerate a Church which tolerates them, than to run the Venture of being extirpated by the Popish-Christian Methods of Fire and Faggot.

2dly, There are others, and those perhaps not a few, who, tho' they have been very staunch Jacobites in their Hearts, have yet been ashamed of owning themselves so in all Companies; for though, when amongst one another, and while the Glass goes merrily round, they freely drink the Healths and talk the Language of the Party, according to the old Observation, *Defendit numerus,*[1] &c. yet in the Presence of wicked Whigs, who look grave at the King over the Water,[2] the Royal Exchange,[3] the three W's, (a great Health)[4] and other such witty Jests, a modest Man may be put out of Countenance, should he discover himself; for Men of Wit generally blush when their Jest is not laughed at. Besides, he may thus be drawn into Argument, and may be put on the Defence of those Doctrines by Reason, which are far above the Reach of it: For it may be truly said of Jacobitism (what a modern Writer,[5] with as much Malice as Falshood, says of Christianity) *that it is* NOT FOUNDED ON ARGUMENT.

3dly, Much the largest Part of our Body have declined the public Profession of our Principles, because they have really not known what they were.[6] We are not such severe Task-masters as to require of the whole Party, that they should search to the Bottom of the Matter. In all Mysteries, such as Jacobitism is,

---

[1] 'Safety in numbers'; often attributed to Juvenal, *Satires*, ii. 46.

[2] A favourite Jacobite toast to the King, in which 'each man having a glass of water on the left hand, and waving the glass of wine over the water' drinks in effect to James III in exile across the Channel; *GM*, xvii (1747), 150. Fielding may have wished to recall the controversy arising out of the annual feast of the Independent Electors of Westminster, held at Vintner's Hall on 19 March 1747; see General Introduction above, pp. xxix–xxx.

[3] See *Proper Answer*, above, p. 78.

[4] Not identified. John Doran, *London in the Jacobite Times* (Boston, [n.d.]), ii. 232, describes it merely as 'the very enigmatical toast'.

[5] Henry Dodwell the younger (d. 1784), author of the deistical tract, *Christianity Not Founded on Argument* (London, 1741).

[6] Cf. the note on p. 4, col. 3, of the original issue of *JJ* no. 1: 'We would not be supposed to imagine, that every Person who joins in the Designs of our Party is a true Jacobite; but as they contribute all in their Power to distress the Government, so we shall own them at present; and it will be time enough to pay them *their proper Wages* when they have done all our Work.'

Faith is sufficient, without the least Knowledge: And whoever wears a Plaid Waistcoat, roars at Horse-Races and Hunting-Matches, and drinks proper Healths in Bumpers, is a good and worthy Jacobite, tho' he should not be able to assign any Reason for his Actions, nor even to tell what he would be at.

Now from these Motives it hath proceeded, that so large a Body of Jacobites should have been (like Mr. *Bayes's* Army) so long *at the Door, and in Disguise*,[1] and not from any of those deep Designs with which our Enemies have charged us.

And here I cannot omit some of the various Conjectures, however ridiculous, which have been made concerning our sudden Appearance, at the latter End of last Summer.[2]

Some have imputed it to the extraordinary Heat of the Season, which, they say, filled the Air with great Numbers of *other* buzzing harmless Animals at the same Time;[3] the *English* Jacobites being in all things the Reverse of their Brethren in the Highlands, who are known never to creep out of their Holes but in cold Weather.

Some, again, will have this great Appearance of Jacobites to have been foretold by the great Plenty of good Liquor, neither Malt or Cyder having been ever cheaper than lately; and Nature hath been observed to produce no Creature, without providing it with proper Sustenance. For the same Reason the great Plenty of Game hath been urged as another Cause, or Sign at least, of their Appearance.

---

[1] *The Rehearsal*, v. 109: 'The army's at the door, and in disguise;/ Desires a word with both your majesties.'

[2] 'In the neighbourhood of Lichfield the sportsmen of the [Opposition] party appeared in the Highland taste of variegated drapery; and . . . they hunted, with hounds clothed in plaid, a fox dressed in a red uniform. Even the females at their assembly, and the gentlemen at the races, affected to wear the checquered stuff by which the Prince Pretender and his followers had been distinguished'; Smollett, *History of England, from the Revolution to the Death of George II*, III. i. 18. At the Tory race meetings in September 1747 the Duke of Bedford, Lord Trentham, and several other Whig politicians were horsewhipped. The episode received considerable and continuing attention in the press; *LEP* of 24–26 September, *OE* of 26 September, and *JJ* nos. 5 and 8, below, pp. 118, 139. See also Stephens, *Catalogue*, p. 652.

[3] A satirical commonplace, perhaps prompted here by the fact that during the summer of 1747 the newspapers had carried reports of an infestation of locusts in Transylvania and other places on the Continent; see *GM*, xvii (1747), 435, and *OE* of 19 September 1747. Cf. *Miscellanies* (1743), i. 204: 'I have been informed, that these Animals swarm in *England* all over the Country, like the Locusts, one in SEVEN Years [i.e. at election times]; and like them too, they generally cause much Mischief, and greatly ruin the Country in which they have swarmed.'

Others have derived this Swarm of Jacobites not from the Mildness of the Weather, but from the Mildness of the Government. In Support of which Opinion they observe, that this Spirit of Jacobitism began to rage, in a most extraordinary Manner, just upon the passing so general and extensive an Act of Grace,[1] that we can scarce find a Parallel to it in History. These add, that true *English* Jacobites fear Blood, as well as they love almost every thing else which is liquid. This Fear, say they, is so extensive, that the least shedding or sprinkling of Blood will disperse the greatest Numbers of Jacobites in a Moment; whereas they always appear more or less, in this Nation, in Times of a mild and bloodless Administration.

This, indeed, is representing us in a very odious Light; for nothing, I think, much worse than Ingratitude, can be laid to the Charge of the Devil himself; but, in Reality, none of these are the true Cause of our present Appearance. Perhaps it will, then, be asked of me, What is? To which I answer, That as Jacobitism itself is a Mystery highly above the Reach of human Reason, so are the Causes which, at particular Seasons, produce it. *Machiavel* himself believed the Stars to have a very great political Influence;[2] and tho' *Bacchus* be not among the Planets, yet *Ariadne's* Crown is among the Constellations.[3] Perhaps this might shine more bright than usual, and call us forth to drink at this Season, when our Civil War is just at an End; as was the Case in *Rome*, when *Horace* begins his Ode with

> *Nunc est bibendum*————.[4]

Perhaps the Moon itself, of whose Influence in terrestrial Affairs no one ever doubted, might occasion our Appearance. *It is the very Error of the Moon*, says *Shakespear*, speaking of

---

[1] 'An Act for the King's most gracious, general, and free pardon' (20 Geo. II, c. 52) was proclaimed at the closing of Parliament on 17 June 1747; *Statutes at Large*, xix. 170–84; *Journals of . . . Commons*, xxv. 408.

[2] 'Discourses', I. lvi and II. xxix, in *Works of the Famous Nicholas Machiavel*, 3rd ed. (London, 1720), pp. 320, 370–1. Baker, item no. 447, lists this edition among Fielding's books.

[3] The constellation 'Corona Borealis' or Northern Crown is identified with the garland or wreath, made by Hephaestus, which Dionysius gave Ariadne as a bridal gift. In Italy Ariadne became associated with Libera, the goddess of wine, and her festivals were marked by drinking and feasting.

[4] I. xxxvii. 1: 'Now is the time to drain the flowing bowl' (Loeb). The ode ('Ad Sodales') is about the death of Cleopatra and the consequent end of the civil war between Antony and Octavius.

epidemic Frenzy;[1] which indeed, in the Opinion of some People, is another Word for a Mystery, at least for most Mysteries.

But whether either of these, or whatever else, was the Cause of our Appearance at this Time, is, I believe, beyond the Reach of any human Understanding: I do solemnly declare it is greatly beyond mine. I do not pretend, therefore, to assert any thing with Confidence or Certainty on this Point; but will leave my Reader to his own Conjectures.

And this Course I shall frequently be obliged to follow in the Progress of the Work I have undertaken; I mean with regard to the Esoteric Doctrines of our Sect, which are perhaps as mysterious as those of Free Masonry itself. As to the Exoteric,[2] they will, I apprehend, be easy enough to explain, as indeed they principally consist in one Article, viz. *in Drinking*.

This the Comic Poet seems to have understood of us, when he says, "I would have every Man serve the King in the best manner he can. Parsons pray for him, Lawyers plead for him, Soldiers fight for him—and *Jacobites drink for him*."[3]

And it is well known, that our dearly beloved *Charles-Edward* P. R. saw us in the same inoffensive Light.[4] Indeed our Love never extends farther than to drink a Man's Health; nor our Hatred than to drink his D–m——n. As he would be a silly Fellow, therefore, who should be greatly ravished with us on Account of the former; so none, I think, but an ill-natured Churl, would desire to punish us very severely for the latter.

But, God be praised, there is no such Spirit at present in Power; and if a Man will only venture being laughed at, he may own himself a Jacobite without any other Danger: Now as I

---

[1] *Othello*, v. ii. 109.

[2] 'Exoteric' and 'Esoteric', neo-Pythagorean terms referring respectively to the public lectures and the private tutorials in the philosopher's own house, were taken over by Freemasonry to differentiate between the doctrine taught to recent initiates and that available to members of longer standing; Albert G. Mackey, *A Lexicon of Free Masonry*, 14th ed. (Philadelphia, 1872), s.v. 'Esoteric'; also *JJ* no. 3, below, p. 103. Fielding's analogy between Jacobitism and Freemasonry may have been suggested by the undoubted, if clandestine, communications between certain Jacobites in Great Britain and the York Rite lodges recently founded in France by, among other exiles, Andrew Michael ('Chevalier') Ramsay (1686–1743), Catholic convert and tutor to the children of James III; Calvin I. Kephart, *Concise Dictionary of Freemasonry*, 2nd ed. (Fort Worth, [n.d.]), pp. 144–7.

[3] Not identified.

[4] Referring to the relatively insubstantial support given by English Jacobites to Charles Edward Louis Philip Casimir (1720–88), the Young Pretender and nominal leader of the rebellion of 1745.

really love to make Men laugh, more than any other Person of my Acquaintance, so I have owned myself a Jacobite thus publicly, and have contrived a Method of appearing in my *Scotch* Plaid all over the Kingdom at one and the same time.[1]

In this Dress I intend to abuse the ***, and the ***, and the ***. I intend to lash not only the M——stry, but EVERY MAN who *hath* any P—ce or P–ns—n[2] from the G–v–rnm–nt, or who is *intrusted* with *any Degree of Power* or *Trust* under it, let his R–nk be never so *high*, his F–rt–n– never so *great*, or his Ch–r–ct–r never so *good*. For this Purpose I have provided myself with a vast Quantity of *Italian*[3] Letter, and Astericks of all Sorts: And as for all the Words which I *embowel*, or rather *emvowel*, I will never so mangle them, but they shall be all as well known as if they retained every Vowel in them.[4] This I promise my Readers, that when I have any Meaning, they shall understand it.

If therefore the poor Productions of *Grub-street* and *Billings-gate*; the low, quibbling, unintelligible Articles of a *London Evening-Post*; or the more than Cimmerian-Darkness of the Bellman of *Westminster*;[5] or of the *Argus*, with all his Eyes out,

---

[1] In reprinting this leader *GM*, xvii (1747), 579, annotates here as follows: 'It was sent free to every post town.' This is perhaps the earliest version of what was to become an Opposition commonplace, namely, that 'no less than 2000 of this *Court-Informer*'s weekly Labours are dispersed, by the special Order of his Patron'; *OE* of 5 March 1748. See also *OE* of 12 November, *LEP* of 6 February 1748, and above, General Introduction, p. lxxvi; and for details of government distribution of newspapers by means of the postal system, Laurence Hanson, *Government and the Press, 1695–1763* (Oxford, 1936), pp. 109–18, and Kenneth Ellis, *The Post Office in the Eighteenth Century*, pp. 47–51. In extending the provisions of 11 Geo. I, cap. 16 ('An Act for the more effectual disarming the Highlands'), the so-called 'Disarming Act' of August 1746 (19 Geo. II, cap. 39) stated that after 1 August 1747 'no man or boy, within that part of *Great Britain* called *Scotland* . . . shall, on any pretence whatsoever, wear or put on the clothes commonly called *Highland* Cloathes'; *Statutes at Large*, xviii. 526–7.

[2] 'Place or Pension'.

[3] Italic.

[4] Cf. *Tom Jones*, VI. ii: 'but I can read a Journal, or the *London Evening-Post*. Perhaps indeed, there may be now and tan a Verse which I can't make much of, because half the Letters are left out; yet I know very well what is meant by that'; and *JJ* no. 1, p. 4, col. 3: 'But it is sufficient for our Party to be told, that all Words gutted of their Vowels, and printed in Italick, are to be taken for Wit.'

[5] The Cimmerii were supposed to live in the westward lands of mists and darkness. For the Augustans they were a convenient 'type' of dulness; cf. *The Dunciad, in Four Books* (1742), iv. 532. The 'Bellman' was the editorial *persona* of the *Westminster Journal*. In London the bellman was a parish functionary, often the beadle, who served as a public crier and traditionally sought for tips and largesse by reciting doggerel verse.

of *Old England*;[1] if such Stuff as this can raise, inflame, and amuse our Party, how much better will all these Purposes be served by one, who hath more Wit and Humour in his Little Finger (according to a common Expression) than these Writers have in their whole Bodies. Nor will I yet disdain the poor Assistance of these weak Fellow-Labourers, whose Productions (such at least as tend to the Service of the Party) I will retail to you, and make as intelligible and pleasant as I can.[2]

In short, I am desirous to be laughed at for the Good of my Country; and there is no Man, who seriously wishes well to it, but will assist and promote so laudable a Purpose, by propagating and circulating this Paper to the utmost of his Power;[3] which, if the Opinion of *Horace* in my Motto, have any Justice in it, may be of so much Consequence to the Cause of that Truth which it espouses, and which I hope will, in the End, reduce all Men to be *as great and as sincere* Jacobites as myself.

SATURDAY, DECEMBER 12, 1747.   NUMB. 2.

> *Fœmina sylvestres Lapithas; populumque bimembrem*
> *Turpiter apposito vertit in arma mero.*
> *Fœmina Trojanos iterum fera bella movere*
> *Impulit in Regno, juste Latine, tuo.*   Ovid.[4]

As my Wife appears in her Plaid on *Ass-back* behind me at the Head of this Paper,[5] it will not, I hope, be imagin'd that I have brought her abroad only to take the Air, without assigning to her any Share in this Undertaking.

The *Mystery* of *Jacobitism* doth not, like that of *Free-Masonry*, exclude the Female World; for tho' all *Jacobites* are not, as some wicked Whigs have represented us, *old Women*,[6] yet Women we

---

[1] The editorial *persona* of *OE* at this time was 'Argus Centoculi'.

[2] A reference to the fact that one of the special departments of the *JJ* was devoted to the reprinting, with satiric commentary, of some of the more egregious items from the Opposition and other newspapers. See Appendix VI, below.

[3] See *JJ* no. 49, below, p. 425.

[4] *Amores*, II. xii (xiii). 19–22: ' 'Twas woman turned the sylvan Lapiths and the double-membered folk to unseemly arms o'er wine; 'twas woman moved the Trojans a second time to set new wars afoot in thy realms, O just Latinus' (Loeb).

[5] In the woodcut engraving on p. 1 of the first twelve numbers of the *JJ*; see General Introduction above, pp. lii–liii, and p. [89].

[6] Not identified, but see below, p. 98, n. 2.

have in great Numbers among us, who are as learned in the Knowledge of our Mysteries, and as active in the Celebration of our Rites, as any of the Male Species; and many of these are so far from deserving the Name of *old*, that their Age scarce yet intitles them to the Name of *Women*.

In our *Esoteric* Doctrines there is indeed no kind of Difference; for these (as I have observed in my first Paper) are so admirably calculated, that they are equally adapted to every Understanding: But in our *Exoteric* it is otherwise; for *Drinking* belongs principally to the Men, and Fighting to the Women. Not that I would insinuate that none of our Women *drink*; for, indeed, some do very plentifully: But this with them is maintained rather to be *Esoteric* than *Exoteric*; for whenever they exceed three or four of our principal *Joco-Treaso–* Healths, it is always performed in the *Sanctum Sanctorum*, where, when the Women are assembled alone, Rites are performed no wise inferior to those celebrated by our Men at their Mystical *Revels*; or, indeed, to those which were formerly instituted to the *Bona Dea*;[1] nay, perhaps, equal to the famous *Orgia* performed by the *Bacchanalian Women* of old Time.

I remember a certain Whig-Writer, whose Confusion we often drink, once boasted that the Beauties were all on his Side.[2] I believe I may, with more Truth, aver that all the Women of Spirit are on ours. What Female Whig hath ever exerted this high and excellent Quality equally with the famous *Jenny Cameron*,[3] and many others who marched forth with the Men,

---

[1] Roman goddess of fecundity, worshipped exclusively by women. Her proper name allegedly was Fauna, owing to her association with Faunus (Pan), and her ceremonies were marked by the use of wine and, in certain places, ritual abuse among the Vestals; Plutarch, 'Life of Caesar', ix. 3.

[2] Cf. Addison, *Freeholder* no. 8 (16 January 1716): 'It happens very luckily for the Interest of the *Whigs*, that their very Enemies acknowledge the finest Women of *Great Britain* to be of that Party'; also no. 11 (27 January) and no. 15 (10 February). *Freeholder* no. 24 (12 March 1716) characterizes the Tories as 'reduced to the poor Comfort of Prodigies and old Women's Fables'. Baker, item no. 22, lists the 1744 edition of the *Freeholder* among Fielding's books. Cf. also *TP* no. 2 (12 November 1745), p. 2, col. 1.

[3] Jenny (Jeanie) Cameron (d. 1772) was a middle-aged 'widow', daughter of Hugh Cameron of Glendessary, and among those present at the raising of the Stuart standard at Glenfinnan on 19 August 1745. According to the sensationalist literature of the time, she recruited a large body of men for the Young Pretender's service, fought beside him in battle, and became his mistress. Cf. James Ray, *A Compleat History of the Rebellion* (Bristol, 1750), pp. 22–9; *Tom Jones*, XII. ii; and Robert Forbes, *Jacobite Memoirs of the Rebellion of 1745*, ed. Robert Chambers (Edinburgh, 1834), pp. 22–3. *A Brief Account of the Life and Family of Miss Jenny Cameron* (London, 1746), p. 53, lists among the other ladies supposed to have marched the Duchess of Perth and Lady Ogilvie, who appeared 'to have disclaimed

in the same amiable Attire and Accoutrements which adorn my dear Wife above! Nay, to omit these warlike Atchievements, do the poor-spirited Wretches, in private Conversation, ever shew that Attachment to their Party which so nobly distinguishes the Petticoats on our Side? May you not often pass a whole Day in the Company of a Whig-Lady without knowing her political Principles, unless indeed that her Silence on that Head declares her not to be of our Party? Whereas, with our Women, it is hardly possible to sit an Hour, without incurring a Premunire[1] in Times of Whig-Government. The very Scandal at their Tea-Tables is political, and both the Esoteric and Exoteric Doctrines are constantly in their Mouths. Nor is this practised only by the more grave Matrons: Girls of Fifteen are as zealous and violent, and, what may appear surprizing, as deeply learned in the Mysteries as their Mothers or Grandmothers.

I remember a very strong Instance of this Kind, which I shall here give the Reader.

On *that melancholy Day* when the News of the Battle of *Culloden* arrived,[2] I happened to dine with some Whigs; where, however, was present a young Lady of our Party, who could not, I believe, exceed the Age of Sixteen. While several of the Company were exulting in the Account of the Victory, and some even expressed their Wishes that the Pretender, as they called him, would be taken, the young Lady could not refrain from declaring she heartily hoped he would escape, since he only pursued his Right. His Right! Miss, said a Gentleman present. *Yes, Sir,* answered she, *I say his Right; for if God made his Grandfather a King, how could any human Being justly dethrone him? Never tell me of his breaking his Coronation-Oath,[3] or of his endeavouring to*

all the Softness peculiar to their Sex'; see also 'The Fool: No. 49' (Monday, 10 Nov. 1746), as reprinted in *The Fool: Being a Collection of Essays and Epistles . . . Published in the Daily Gazetteer* (London, 1748), pp. 346–53.

[1] A writ by which the sheriff is charged to summon a person accused, originally, of prosecuting in a foreign court a suit cognizable by the law of England, and later, of asserting or maintaining papal jurisdiction in England, thus denying the ecclesiastical supremacy of the sovereign (*OED*). In the context of Fielding's irony here a Jacobite lady would issue a *premunire* against any person who invoked Whig (i.e. 'foreign') laws or assented to Hanoverian supremacy.

[2] The battle, whose loss signalled the final failure of the rebellion, was fought on 16 April 1746, but news of it seems not to have reached London before noon on 23 April; see *DA* of 24 April 1746.

[3] By the terms of the coronation oath then in effect James II was sworn to observe the laws and customs emanating from his royal predecessors, in particular those granted to the

overthrow the Constitution; what he did was only with his own, and who hath the Power to call any Man to account for doing what he pleases with his own? So much excellent Sense, such true Jacobitical Mystery, out of the Mouth of one so young, highly charmed me; tho' her Person and Face were not, I confess, any of the most beautiful.

As the Ladies therefore form so considerable (perhaps the most formidable) Branch of our Party, so will a very considerable Part of this Paper be allotted to their Use. Over this Branch my Wife will preside; and indeed she is excellently qualified for the Office, being as ready to draw her Pen as her Sword in the Service. For both these Nature hath endowed her with adequate Talents; for she hath a most masculine Spirit, and is a great Mistress of all that Wit and Humour which hath so notably distinguished and supported our Party. She hath coin'd the most facetious Healths, and hath invented many of those Stories which have been so industriously propagated and spread abroad by our faithful Friends and Allies the Popish Emissaries within this Kingdom. One Half, indeed, of those pretty F—bs which were so current at the Time of the Rebellion, were the Offspring of her Invention; as were several of the most acute unintelligible Articles which have been, from time to time, published in the *London Evening-Post*, to the great Entertainment and Edification of our Party.

It must give great Satisfaction to all the Jacobite-Ladies in the Kingdom, that their Interest will be espoused by one of such great Endowments; and more especially when they are informed that she is not more zealous in the Cause of Jacobitism than in that of her Sex, of whose Privileges she is most strenuously tenacious, constantly asserting that Women are, in every Consideration, equal to Men. Some of these Tenets did, I own, cause much domestic Disquiet in the early Days of our Matrimony; and I have often quoted Texts of Scripture, which I thought had commanded some little Obedience to Husbands; but she gave very little Attention to them, tho' she preached up the Obedience and Non-Resistance of Subjects on the same Authority. In Fact, I found the only possible Means of maintaining any Superiority

clergy by St. Edward, and to preserve for the churches committed to his care 'all Canonical Privileges, and due Law and Justice'; Leopold G. Wickham Legg, *English Coronation Records*, pp. xxvii–xxxiii, 287–316.

was by a manful Conquest of myself, and a generous Submission to my Wife: But no more of this, least I should give Offence where I would most avoid it.

In this Paper, then, it is the Purpose of my *Peggy* to supervise and direct all manner of Female Affairs, and to consult at once the Interest of her Sex and of her Party. The better to unite both which, she intends to convey a good deal of the Exoteric Jacobitical Mystery into Dress, which she proposes as much as possible to adapt both to Complexion and Principle; for it would be very hard on a Woman, if her Party should oblige her to injure her Beauty, especially if there be any Truth in what the Whigs (confound them) pretend, that our Women have so little to spare, and that all Female Loveliness is on their Side.

On this Account she admits the Excuse which several Women, otherwise well inclined, have alledged against wearing the *Scotch* Plaid-Petticoat, which is indeed a most unbecoming Dress for a fine Lady; tho' the little laced Waistcoat of that Kind sits very prettily on those Gentlemen, whose chief Ambition it is to distinguish their Abilities in Hunting and Horse-Racing, since it serves a double Purpose, and denotes at once the *Jacobite and the Jockey*.

The same Objection, she allows, lies against *White Roses*;[1] for the Colour of White doth greatly misbecome certain Complexions, and particularly those of such Female Votaries as have very devoutly applied themselves to the *Orgia*, or the *liquid Rites* celebrated in the *Sanctum Sanctorum*.

She hath taken these Matters into her serious Consideration, and is now busied in calculating something for this Purpose, which may serve, like the Frontispiece of this Paper, to convey proper Emblems of the Party, without making any Female Jacobite uglier than she is at present.

Jacobite Wit likewise will be circulated by her in this Paper; so that by diligently reading *us on a Saturday*, a Lady will be supplied with sufficient Entertainment for her Tea-Table during the whole Week; but, above all Things, proper and significant Healths or Toasts will be invented for the Use of the Ladies, who celebrate the Mysteries in higher and more generous Liquors than Tea.

And at the same time that my *Peggy* is thus employing her own

[1] The cockade or rosette of white roses was a principal emblem of Jacobite dress.

great Talents in the Cause, she will be as careful and industrious to commemorate the Services done by other Females: If, therefore, any Piece of Wit, Story, Health, or Jacobitical Emblem, either in Cloaths, Fans,[1] Nosegays, or otherwise, shall be exhibited by any Lady of the Party, who is desirous of distinguishing her Zeal, Care will be taken to record such Merit; and possibly (if the Service be very eminent) my Wife will dismount herself for a Day, in order to give her Place to the Lady, who shall ride behind me, ornamented with her own Devices: And this Justice I faithfully promise to perform with great Exactness to the Male Part of the Species, who shall intitle themselves to fill my Saddle, and mount the generous Beast in the Frontispiece.

Nothing, therefore, remains but that we both publish our earnest Desires to all Persons and Communities, that they will transmit to us a faithful Account of the meritorious Transactions as well of themselves as of others, in order to their being immediately inserted; for, indeed, to do *true* Honour to all Merit of this Kind is one of the principal Uses to which a public Paper may be applied.

And moreover, as the Task we have undertaken must be acknowledged to be very arduous, we think proper to solicit the kind Assistance of all our Friends of both Sexes, who are addicted to scribbling either in the Prosaic or Poetic Way; for they may be assured we shall, at all Times, be extremely ready to usher any Productions into the World which tend to the Service of our Party, provided we can do it with sufficient Safety to our Neck and Ears.

Nay, that we may not be taxed with too partial a Spirit, and with the least Apprehension of any Arguments which can be used against our Doctrines, (which Arguments our Party have indeed always despised too much to answer) we faithfully promise, that if any of the Whigs should be yet simple enough to aim at convincing an Individual among us by his Reasoning, we will give his Labours a Place in our Paper; tho', to say the Truth, I have always regarded such an Attempt as little less than an Affront: For surely, whoever endeavours to convince a Man, must presuppose him in an Error; and he who argues with another, at least presumes that it is possible the Person with whom he argues may change his Sentiments; but how fickle, how incertain, and un-

---

[1] Cf. *Freeholder* no. 15 (10 February 1716).

steady must his Principles be, which the Breath of Man can alter! True Jacobitism, on the contrary, is from Nature. It is born with us; it is bred with us; and thus nourished, becomes a Habit, which, like Instinct, defies all the Reasoning in the World to subdue.

SATURDAY, DECEMBER 19, 1747. NUMB. 3.

> *Favete Linguis, Carmina non prius*
> *Audita, Musarum sacerdos,*
> *Virginibus, puerisque canto.*
> *Regum timendorum* in proprios Greges;
> *Reges in ipsos imperium est Jovis.* Horace.[1]

Tho' I have divided the mysterious Doctrines of Jacobitism into Esoteric and Exoteric, in Imitation of the Doctrines of antient Philosophy, yet we do not imitate these Philosophers in revealing only the Exoteric to the Vulgar: In this Instance we rather resemble the Free-Masons, who communicate their whole inestimable Secrets to their whole Body; for, indeed, as they are equally adapted to the Understandings of all, there can be no Reason why they should be imparted only to the Few.

I know some impudent Whigs pretend, that we are ashamed of our Esoteric, or inward and spiritual Doctrines, as they have been so often confuted; but I would remind those Gentlemen, that there is something previously necessary to the Confutation of any Principle, which I believe they have never been able to arrive at, with regard to ours.

But to refute their Assertion of our being asham'd of our Tenets, I shall here publish some of the principal ones to the World; such as every Jacobite must, and doth, and will maintain,

---

[1] A conflation of *Carmen Saeculare*, 2–4, and *Odes*, III. i. 1–2: 'Observe a reverent silence! I, the Muse's priest, sing for maids and boys songs not heard before. The rule of dreaded kings is over their own peoples; but over the kings themselves is the rule of Jove' (Loeb). Philip Francis, *Poetical Translation of the Works of Horace*, 2nd ed. (London, 1747), II. 288–9, argues against the conventional assignment of the entire passage to *Odes*, III. i: 'Indeed it is ridiculous, that Horace should address an Ode to Children [*Virginibus pueris-que*], which was to teach them such Maxims of Morality, as were far above their Comprehension; while He excludes, from his Instructions, Persons of a more advanced Age, who alone were capable of understanding, and profiting by them.' Baker, item no. 558, lists Francis's translation among Fielding's books, and Fielding may well have been inspired by the satiric possibilities of the translator's argument.

in Defiance of all the Argument or Reason which hath been, or may be, urged against them.[1]

MYSTERY *the* FIRST.

That all Kings are by Divine Appointment; and that this Appointment is made in an invisible, incomprehensible Manner; sometimes by Conquest, sometimes by Knavery, and sometimes by Bribery. Sometimes by the Mob, against the Will of all wise and good Men; and sometimes by a few great Rogues against the Will of the People; and often against the Right, and through the Blood of the nearest Relations, and at the Price of the Lives of Millions. Some of these, so divinely appointed, are the vilest and wickedest, and others the weakest and sillyest Individuals that could be found in the whole Nation which they are to govern: Not that this Appointment hath been ever manifested in one single Instance, nor is it any where declared in Scripture,[2] unless in Words which can be understood of nothing but of all civil Power and Authority, and which are as applicable to a Constable as to any other Magistrate. Nay, the Divine Voice hath positively declared against it; as in the Case of the first King of the *Jews*.[3]

MYSTERY *the* SECOND.

That the Regal Right being divine, is consequently indefeasible. But the King of *England* is not absolute, but ought to govern by Law; but if he breaks the Law never so often, nay, if he attempts to subvert both the Law and the Constitution, as King *James* II. *of blessed Memory*, did in a thousand Instances, he is neither to be resisted, nor call'd to any Account for it. Breach of Word, or of Oath, even of his Coronation-Oath, must not be alleged in Excuse of Resistance: For as Dr. *Cartwright*, a good and true Jacobite, said in the Pulpit, of the Promises of the blessed King abovementioned, *The Promises of Princes are* DONATIVES,

[1] Cf. the Tory creed in *Freeholder* no. 14 (6 February 1716), from which also derives the name for the department of the *JJ* entitled 'CREDENDA', consisting of egregious and supposedly disloyal statements from the Opposition press.

[2] For examples of the Biblical texts commonly used to support the *de jure divino* theory of kingship see Robert Filmer, *Patriarcha* (1680), ed. Peter Laslett (Oxford, 1949), sects. iii–v, xxiii, pp. 57–61, 96–102; and John Neville Figgis, *The Divine Right of Kings*, pp. 7–8.

[3] Referring to the request of Israel to have a king to judge them despite the displeasure of the Lord; 1 Samuel viii. 4–22, and x. 18–19.

*and are not to be strictly examined or charged upon them; but we must
leave it to themselves to explain their own Meaning.*[1] But let a King
act as he pleases; let him set his Capital City on Fire, as *Nero* did;
or desire to extirpate all his People, as *Caligula*; or attack and
endeavour to deprive them of both their Religion and Liberty,
as did our dear King *James*, his Right is still intire and indefeasible, being divine; and he can neither be deprived by his Subjects, nor can himself abdicate his Crown.[2]

MYSTERY *the* THIRD.

*That Passive Obedience and Non-Resistance must be preserved by
Subjects to the Prince, tho' he should endeavour to erect a Tyranny in a
limited Monarchy, or to extirpate the established Religion of the Country.*
This is, indeed, included in the former; for to say we must leave a
King in Possession of his Power, let him make what Use he
pleases of it, is to affirm Passive Obedience and Non-Resistance
in the most direct Terms. This likewise implicitly contains an
Article of Jacobitical Faith, founded on long Tradition, and infinitely above all Reason, *viz.* That God hath been graciously
pleased to create many Millions of People for the sole Use and
Advantage, nay, for the Diversion of One; and this One, to
ordinary Eyes, which judge by the wandring Light of Reason
only, inferior in all human Excellencies to much the greater
Part of his Subjects, whose Lives and Properties are all to be at
his Disposal; for damnable indeed is that Acknowledgment of
*Grotius, That a Prince may be resisted should he attempt to destroy
any Part of his Subjects;*[3] and more damnable still that Position of

---

[1] Thomas Cartwright (1634–89), *A Sermon Preached upon the Anniversary Solemnity of
the Happy Inauguration of Our Dread Soveraign Lord, King James II, In the Collegiate
Church of Ripon, February the 6th, 1685/6* (London, 1686), p. 17: 'Princes must not be up-
braided with their Promises, much less threatned and menac'd with audacious Expostu-
lations, if they do not perform them; for their Promises are *Donatives*, and 'tis reason the
Doner should have the *explaining* of his *own mind*.' Cartwright, Dean of Ripon (1675) and
Bishop of Chester (1686), was one of James II's Ecclesiastical Commissioners and chief
Visitor of Magdalen College, Oxford, in the attempt of 1687 to enforce its submission to the
King.

[2] The so-called 'Convention Parliament', the elected body which was formed after
James II had fled the country, resolved (a) that the throne was indeed vacant, and (b) that
James II had in fact abdicated.

[3] *De Jure Belli ac Pacis*, ed. Joannes Barbeyrac (Amsterdam, 1720), i. 154 (I. iv. 11),
where Grotius cites Barclay to this effect and grants the point. Baker, item no. 68, lists
Barbeyrac's edition of Grotius among Fielding's books.

Melancthon, "That the Pretence of a Divine Right can neither excuse, nor justify his Crimes, nor the Dignity of his Office tolerate him to exercise a wicked and wilful Tyranny; but when his Impieties, and Injuries to his People, are evident, and insufferable, the Powers to whom God hath in such an Extremity committed the Sword to protect and deliver an oppress'd Nation, may remove him from the Government; as the *Romans* did *Caligula*, *Nero*, and other Monsters of Cruelty, who were not only Enemies to the Commonwealth, but to all Mankind."[1] But what is more wonderful, and consequently higher Mystery still, is, that God hath been pleased to subjugate his own Worship, and even Religion itself, to the Good Will and Pleasure of the Monarch; who may introduce Popery, (and why not Mahometanism as well) into a Protestant Nation, and that we ought not to resist it.

MYSTERY *the* FOURTH.

That a Popish Prince may be the Defender of a Protestant Church.
Tho' the third Tenet of unlimited Passive Obedience and Non-Resistance must extend as far as I have carried it, yet a Jacobite hopes and believes better Things; for tho' all Popish Writers* agree that every Prince ought to exterminate his Protestant Subjects; that the Omission of that Duty is damnable; and that putting them to Death is a just, meritorious Action. Tho' they all agree, that Heretics are to be sacrificed, and rooted out of the World by all Means whatever; tho' they have attempted this by a settled bloody Court of Inquisition, by constant Persecutions, and by the most cruel and general Massacres; nay, tho' the mildest of their Princes have been instigated to support this Cruelty of their Priests, and the bravest and most powerful have not dared to restrain it, we yet believe (and a noble Degree of Jacobitical Faith it is) that King *James* II. while he was introducing Popery at full Gallop, was keeping it out; that while he

---

* Beccan Theol. Scot. p. 1. c. 13. quæst. 5. c. 15. quæst. 6. Tho. Aquin, sumæ quæst. 10. Art. 3. Durand. Sancta Portian. quæst. utrum Hæret. sint tolerand. quæst. 5. Bellarmin de Lucis, l. 3. c. 21. Concil. Tolos. p. 46. Concil. Later. 4.

---

[1] Not identified. Possibly derived from 'De Magistratus civilibus', *Loci praecipui theologici* (1559), ii. 987, 998, reprinted in *Melanchthons Werke*, Band 11/2, ed. Hans Engelland (Gütersloh, 1953), 694, 708.

brought a Jesuit into the Privy Council,[1] made a profest Papist Secretary of State,[2] constituted two Popish Judges,[3] filled many of the most important Offices with Papists, put the Tower of *London* into the Hands of one of the rankest of all Papists,[4] brought Numbers of Papists into the Army,[5] made Popish Bishops,[6] placed a Society of Jesuits in the Savoy,[7] and erected

[1] Edward Petre (1631–99), Jesuit, clerk of the Royal Closet, superintendent of the Royal Chapel, and confessor of James II, was named to the Privy Council in 1687.

[2] Robert Spencer (1641–1702), 2nd Earl of Sunderland, Secretary of State under Charles II, was in fact merely retained in that position by James II. Sunderland's conversion to Catholicism, under the guidance of Edward Petre, did not take place until the summer of 1688; Sir James Mackintosh, *History of the Revolution in England in 1688* (London, 1834), p. 279; and David Ogg, *England in the Reigns of James II and William III*, pp. 192–4.

[3] Richard Allibone (1636–88), son of a Catholic convert, educated at Douai and Gray's Inn, King's Counsel and knighted by James II in 1686, was appointed to the King's Bench in 1687, from which he opposed the acquittal of the seven bishops; Robert Wright (d. 1689), associate of Jeffreys on the Bloody Assizes, who was appointed to the King's Bench in 1685, later became Chief Justice and the presiding judge at the trial of the seven bishops in 1688. Both Allibone and Wright had contemporary reputations as crypto-Catholics; Edward Foss, *The Judges of England* (London, 1864), vii. 209–10, 283. Samuel Boyse, *An Impartial History of the Late Rebellion in 1745* (Reading, 1748), p. 23, identifies the papist judges as Allibone and Christopher Milton (1615–93), the poet's brother, who was anti-Parliament during the Civil War; he was made deputy Recorder of Ipswich (1674) by Charles II, invested with the coif, knighted, and raised to the court of the Exchequer (1686) by James II, and transferred to the court of Common Pleas in 1687. See also W. S. Holdsworth, *A History of English Law*, 3rd ed. (London, 1922–4), vi. 509–11.

[4] In June 1687 Sir Edward Hales (1645–95), baronet, titular Earl of Tenterden, was made Lord Lieutenant of the Tower and Master of the Ordnance. A recent convert, Hales had acted as a Colonel of Foot without taking the required oaths, having been granted a dispensation by letters patent. See *Proper Answer*, above, p. 70, n. 1.

[5] There was in fact no law against enlisting Catholics as common soldiers, and the Hales case set the precedent for introducing Catholic officers into the English army. The Irish army, a separate establishment under the command of Richard Talbot, Earl of Tyrconnel, had already dismissed many of its Protestant men and officers, replacing them with drafts of Catholic recruits sent over from England; Sir George Clark, *The Later Stuarts*, 2nd ed. (Oxford, 1955), p. 122.

[6] In 1687 Pope Innocent XI divided England into four ecclesiastical districts and allowed James to nominate persons to govern them. The four bishops, who were publicly consecrated and sent out under the title of vicars apostolical, were John Leyburn (1620–1702), consecrated at Rome in 1685 as Bishop of Adrumetum, Vicar Apostolic of all England from 1685 to 1688, and of the London district in 1688; Bonaventure Giffard (1642–1734), Bishop of Madura and Parker's successor as President of Magdalen College, Oxford, consecrated Vicar Apostolic of the Midland district on 22 April 1688 by the papal nuncio in England; Philip (Michael) Ellis (1652–1726), Catholic convert, educated at Douai, brother to one of James II's Secretaries of State, consecrated Vicar Apostolic of the Western district in January 1688, also by the papal nuncio; and James Smith (1645–1711), educated at Douai, President in 1682, appointed Vicar Apostolic in 1688, consecrated as Bishop of Calliopolis *in partibus*.

[7] 'In the year 1687, Schools were set up and ordained here at the Savoy; the masters

Popish-Schools and Mass-Houses all over the Kingdom; while he did all this, and much more, contrary to Law, and to his own solemn Promises, we yet believe he intended to support the Protestant Church; and that his Son or Grandson, if restored, would do the same; tho' they are known to have hesitated even to make any such Promise.

Now there is scarce any thing in the whole Mystery of Jacobitism which may not be ranged under one or other of these Four Grand Principles, which every Jacobite must and doth believe; and these are all high Mysteries, infinitely above the Reach of human Reason, being indeed derived from the pure Fountain of Nature only. To say the Truth, they all flow from that one great natural Principle of the Divine Right of Kings.

And when we consider whence this great Principle arises, namely, from Nature herself, we shall not wonder to find it existing in the earliest Ages of the World; nay, before any Whig first broach'd those Notions of Liberty, which they pretend to support by Reason; absurdly supposing that God intended those to be universal Human Principles which must be supported by a Talent given to so few.

Nature taught this Mystery to the most antient Heathens. They saw there must be something divine in their Kings; which not being well able to account for, they at length imagined, not that the Appointment, but that the Person himself came from Heaven; and having exercised kingly Authority, and received kingly Honours here for a Time, returned back again to his State of Divinity. Hence the Apotheosis of *Uranus, Saturn*, &c. who being the most antient Kings, were, by the wise and Jacobitical Antients, considered as the most antient Gods.

It was not on Account of their Merit as Men, that these Divine Honours were assigned them, or Divine Worship paid to them; for had they been considered as Men only, many of them would have deserved rather Contempt or Detestation, as Robbers, Ravishers, and Murderers; but they were Kings, and therefore divine, and whether good or bad made no Difference. In Reality, they were all of the latter Sort; and it is remarkable,

whereof were Jesuits'; John Stow, *A Survey of the Cities of London and Westminster*, ed. John Strype (London, 1720), ii. 107–8 (Bk. IV, ch. vii). The Savoy palace was built between the Strand and the River by Peter, Earl of Savoy, in the thirteenth century. In the reign of Charles II it was converted into a military hospital and barracks; Henry B. Wheatley, *London Past and Present*, iii (London, 1891), 217–19.

that the *antient Greeks* had no other Word for a King but what signified a Tyrant;[1] one who had a Divine Commission to rule a certain Number of People, created only for his Use and Amusement.

In After-Ages, indeed, some wicked Whigs having started up in *Greece*, pretended to assert, from Reason, the Liberty of the People; and certain Cities having expelled their Kings, *only* because they were Tyrants, erected several Forms of Government, which they called Republics. Every Form of which, however detestable, is yet less absurd, and less inconsistent, than that strange new-fangled Monster of a Constitution, composed of an heterogeneous Mixture of Mystery and Reason, called a limited Monarchy, in which Kings are supposed to be circumscrib'd, and to govern by Law. This modern Whig-Notion is as incomprehensible and ridiculous as some of that Party have endeavour'd to represent that deep mysterious Jacobitical Emblem, namely, the Republican *Harrington*,[2] with the Arms of the King of *France* stamp'd on it, which we have tied to the Tale of our Ass in the Frontispiece of this Paper.

The antient Jacobitism was, however, greatly erroneous in one Instance; for tho' they believed their Kings divine, they never worshipp'd them till after they were dead: Now this Error we Moderns have corrected; for as we conceive the whole Divinity to consist in the Appointment, so by Death that Divinity ceases, or rather is transferr'd, together with the indefeasible hereditary Right, to the Heir.

Much of this Doctrine above set forth, will, I doubt not, appear shocking even to the Babes of our own Party, who perhaps have called themselves Jacobites, without ever examining into the Bottom of our Principles; but such they are, and by such he must both walk and drink who is desirous to be thought at once a good Jacobite and a good Protestant; or, to join the two Words, which, when joined together, make the profoundest Mystery, if he would deserve the Name of a P R O T E S T A N T-J A C O B I T E.

---

[1] ὁ τύραννος, an absolute sovereign, esp. one made by force; later, a tyrant or despot. See *JJ* no. 5, below, p. 121, and Aristotle, *Politics*, III. xiv–xv (1284*b*–1286*b*) and IV. x (1295*a*).

[2] James Harrington (1611–77), author of *The Commonwealth of Oceana* (1656), is used here and elsewhere in Fielding's writings of this period to represent the anti-monarchical emphasis of Republicanism, an emphasis which, according to contemporary Whig political writers, the Tory extremists were willing to encourage as part of the attack on the Hanoverian monarchs; cf. *JJ* no. 1, above, p. 91, and *Dialogue*, pp. 57–8.

SATURDAY, DECEMBER 26, 1747.   NUMB. 4.

Impius hæc tam culta novalia Gallus *habebit?*
Barbarus has segetes? EN QUO DISCORDIA CIVES
PERDUXIT MISEROS!   Virgil.[1]

To give an immediate Instance of that Firmness with which we shall maintain all our Promises,[2] we shall publish the following Letter; and this must at the same time convince the World of the Confidence we repose in our Party, and how little Danger we apprehend from the Force of Argument.

Sir,

Whether you are really a Jacobite or no, I will not presume to determine; for, however absurd and ridiculous the Principles of Jacobitism may appear in your Writings, you have done them no Injustice; and I think a little Knowledge of Mankind will convince us, that it is possible for a Man to hold certain Doctrines in Reverence, while he knows them to be Nonsense.

But it is not my Purpose to attack your Doctrines (either Esoteric or Exoteric) at present. I shall confine myself to one Point only, which is, to your Appearance at this Season.

Is this a Time, then, to raise internal Commotions? To disunite and divide the People, to embarrass and distress the Government, and, in a Word, to weaken the Nation? Shall we quarrel among ourselves, when the common Enemy of us all is at our Doors?[3] An Enemy whom we have every Reason to fear, and to oppose: Who, besides his boundless Ambition, hath an inveterate and implacable Hatred to this Kingdom, as it hath so often been the Scourge of his People, always the Rival of their Trade, and hitherto the principal Obstacle to their Pursuit of universal Empire in *Europe*.

Nor is this Enemy, whose manifest Views should give us such just Apprehensions, less formidable in his Power of executing

---

1 Altered from *Eclogues*, I. 70–2: 'Is a godless Gaul [i.e. a Frenchman] to hold these well-tilled fallows? a barbarian these crops? See to what strife has brought our unhappy citizens!' (Loeb). The accepted text reads *miles habebit.*

2 See *JJ* no. 2, above, pp. 102–3.

3 By December 1747 France, in addition to her mastery of the Austrian Netherlands, had taken most of the strong points in Dutch Brabant, thereby posing a threat to the rest of the United Provinces and to communication between the allied forces of England and of Austria; *Dialogue*, pp. 35, 39, and Fortescue, *History of the British Army*, ii. 150, 163.

them. He is Master of a vast, well-peopled Country,[1] whose Inhabitants are ready to pour forth all their Blood and Treasures at his Command; whose Glory it is to be Slaves themselves, and to make others Slaves to their Monarch. He is possess'd of an immense Army,[2] devoted to his Person, well disciplined, enured to War, and I must add, to Victory. This Army is commanded by great, vigilant, experienced, and enterprizing Generals;[3] and is follow'd by an Artillery, which, being in the Hands of the greatest Engineers which perhaps the World hath produced, may without *French* Ostentation be call'd invincible.[4]

To dwell no longer on Circumstances as well known as they are disagreeable—this Enemy is at our Doors: He is almost Master of our Outworks;[5] and shall we, at this time, lessen our Numbers, and weaken our Defence by intestine Divisions and Animosities?

The *Romans* in all Seasons, when their Neighbours suffered them to enjoy Peace abroad, fell presently into Civil Dissentions and Tumults; but no sooner was the Sword drawn by any foreign

[1] Contemporary estimates put the population of France at this time at roughly 23 million; Henri See, *Economic and Social Conditions in France during the 18th Century*, trans. Edwin H. Zeydel (New York, 1927), p. 8. The population of England and Wales together was between 6 and 6½ million, Scotland's about 1¼ million; *Abstract of British Historical Statistics*, p. 5.

[2] *Dialogue*, above, p. 40, estimates the French army at 300,000 men, presumably including auxiliaries in both the Dutch and Italian theatres. When the 1748 campaign in Holland began in earnest, the French had assembled about 115,000 men, and the allies, who by the terms of The Hague Convention of January 1748 had contracted for an army of 190,000 men, supplied only 35,000 to Cumberland for the siege of Maestricht; see Fortescue, ii. 163; *Yale Walpole*, xix. 466 n.; and *Journals of . . . Commons*, xxv. 489–90. During the recently concluded campaign of 1747, estimates placed the total number of effective troops in each of the contesting armies at slightly in excess of 100,000 men, but Walpole records a British concession of numerical inferiority; *Yale Walpole*, xix. 395, 409.

[3] In particular, Maurice, comte de Saxe (1696–1750), marshal of France (1743), commander-in-chief of the French forces in the Dutch theatre, victor at Laffeldt (Val) and, after Bergen-op-Zoom in September 1747, Governor of the conquered Netherlands; Count Ulrik Frederik Woldemar Løvendal (1700–1755), called Lowendahl, Russian (1738) and imperial (1741) count, soldier of fortune in the Saxon, Russian, and Austrian armies, under his friend Saxe's sponsorship admitted to the French army (1743) as lieutenant-general, one of the heroes of Fontenoy (1745), charged with reducing Bergen-op-Zoom, after which he was made a marshal. See Marquis de Sinety, *Vie du Maréchal de Lowendal* (Paris, 1867), i. 3–5, 115, 129, cited in *Yale Walpole*, xix. 395 n.; see also *GM*, xvii (1747), 450.

[4] Cf. *Dialogue*, p. 40 and note 2 there. Among the allies there was particular consternation at the way French engineers reduced the supposedly impregnable strong points of the Dutch barrier.

[5] Cf. *Dialogue*, p. 36 ('and master'd their Outworks'), and *Proper Answer*, p. 74 ('if once our Out-works on the Continent').

Enemy against them, than all domestic Discord ceased, and all united in the common Cause of *Rome*.

With what Contempt and Horror would that brave People have regarded any Faction among them, who should have chosen Times of Danger, when the very Liberty and Being of their Country was at Stake, to raise Commotions in the Commonwealth; nay, who should have endeavoured to avail themselves of the Arms and Force of an Enemy then at War with *Rome*, against their own Countrymen.

Doth, then, any Man deserve the Name of a *Briton*, who, at such a Season as this, endeavours to divide this Kingdom, and to inflame one Part of it against the rest? May not such Persons be more justly stiled the Enemies and Betrayers of their Country?

Nothing surely but the most inconsiderate Rashness, the most mad or drunken Zeal, can hurry any of us into such fatal Mischief; for I am unwilling to think there is one so despicable in his Principles, as knowingly and deliberately to sacrifice his Country to his Party; since, however slavish the Doctrines of Jacobitism may be, they incline *Englishmen* to be Slaves only to a King of their own: Tho' they believe God to have given them a King, the Grand Monarch[1] is not the Person. No Jacobite believes him to have any Divine Right to rule over and to enslave this Nation. Their very Attachment to the Family of *Stuart* must exclude the House of *Bourbon*; nay, I apprehend a thorough Conviction, that these Attachments are one and the same, would presently eradicate them both: For I can scarce entertain so mean an Opinion of any of my Countrymen, as to imagine they would wish to see the King of *Great Britain* the Vicegerent of the King of *France*.

I shall therefore, in the Remainder of this Letter, offer some Considerations, which, if your Party will lay aside their Cups a moment, and seriously attend to, must at least give them a very reasonable Suspicion, that this would be the Consequence of that Revolution which some may be, at present, weak enough to desire. And this, I think, will appear very plain, if it should be demonstrable that no such Revolution can ever be brought about, but by the Assistance of the Arms of *France*.

That it cannot be effected by his Friends here, must be allowed; since they are, in every Light, inferior to his Enemies. In Numbers;

[1] Louis XV of France.

for whatever may be the Boasts of your Party, it appears by all the Proof of which it is capable, that the Jacobites amount to a very inconsiderable Number, when compared to their Adversaries.[1] Nay, I much doubt whether, if the whole Nation could be poll'd, a Fiftieth Part would coolly and seriously give their Vote for either *Charles-Edward*, or his Father. Many Men act in Opposition to the Government from Hatred to Power, and many more from the Love of it. These are ready enough to join with you in pulling-down, but would widely sever from you in building-up. Nor would every one who wantonly drinks treasonable Healths, or foolishly puts on a Plaid-Waistcoat, go all your Lengths. It is true, that by so doing they well intitle themselves to ride in your Saddle; but very few of them have the Views you profess. In Fact, your Numbers are sufficient to embarrass the Government, and to lessen the Protection which that is desirous of affording us against the common Enemy. You may, perhaps fatally, encourage that Enemy to invade us, or may assist him if he should; but of yourselves alone, you are an inconsiderable Body. In Property again, the great Foundation of Power, you are no less our Inferiors. All the greatest and most powerful of the Nobility are known to be most zealously affected to the present Establishment: So are (except a very few suspicious Persons) all the richest of the Commons; and the most opulent City, not only of *Great Britain*, but of the whole World, hath most explicitly shewn itself on our Side.[2] A third Advantage, to which we lay Claim, is the Property of the Mind. This is, indeed, so much our Due, that I am ashamed to mention you in the Light of Competition. To speak Truth, Jacobitism is a Principle below the Dignity of Human Nature, and the very Beast you ride on hath an unworthy Burthen upon his Back. Again, it hath pleased God to intrust the Sword in our Hands; as well the Civil Sword as the Military. We have an Administration not consisting of one absolute Prime Minister, supported only by his Tools and

[1] See General Introduction above, pp. lxiii–lxv.

[2] In the 1747 elections, to the delight of the Administration leadership, the City of London, long regarded as an Opposition stronghold, gave two seats to the Administration; Owen, *Rise of the Pelhams*, p. 317 n. Fielding may also allude to the expedition with which the City merchants and bankers filled the subscription for the loan of £6,300,000 towards the Supply for the ensuing year, 'a subscription begun, and compleated, before even the report of it had reached the remote quarters of this metropolis'; *Westminster Journal* [21 November 1747], cited in *GM*, xvii (1747), 529; and Coxe, *Pelham*, i. 382.

Dependents, and obnoxious to the Great Men in the Nation;[1]
but an Administration composed really of all the Great Men,
whose Abilities of any Kind make them worthy of any Place in it;
supported by both Houses of Parliament, and, as appears by the
last Election, by a vast Majority of the whole People.[2] We have
an Army well disciplined and experienced, and whose Bravery is
renown'd all over *Europe*. This Army is not only known to be
inviolably attached to our Cause, but devoted to the Person of
their Royal General.[3] His Courage hath so engaged their Admiration, and his Justice, Generosity, and Affability have so won
the Hearts of the Soldiers, that their Officers aver they believe
there is not a Man in it, who would not go to the D—l at the
Command of his Royal Highness.

For the Truth of these several Matters, I need appeal no
farther than to the late Rebellion,[4] in which all that I have here
asserted appeared to the clearest Demonstration.

It is plain, therefore, that your Prince can have no Dependence
on the Power of his Friends in *Great Britain*; and it is as plain,
that he can borrow no foreign Force from any Power in *Europe*,
which he can convey hither, (the Force and Assistance of *France*
only excepted.)[5]

And this seems to be acknowledged by his own Conduct; for
would he have flown to the Protection of a Power whose Arms
are so obnoxious to, and at all times so justly suspected by *Great
Britain*; a Power then at War with us,[6] and visibly aiming at our

---

[1] Alluding to the comparatively exclusionist ministry set up by Carteret (Granville) and
Pulteney after the fall of Walpole (1742), and controlled by the former, with the support of
George II, against a generally reluctant Parliament.

[2] According to the analysis of the election results in the Newcastle Papers, the Administration won 341 seats, the Opposition, 216; B.M. Add. MS. 33002, ff. 440-6,
cited by Owen, *Rise of the Pelhams*, p. 317 n.

[3] By the terms of The Hague Convention of 12 January 1747 N.S. command of the
allied armies in the Low Countries was conferred upon the Duke of Cumberland; *Journals
of . . . Commons*, xxv. 251-6.

[4] The Jacobite rebellion of 1745-6.

[5] After the fall of Bergen-op-Zoom in September 1747 there was an alleged increase in
Jacobite activity, and rumours of an impending invasion from France brought pressure
to bear on Cumberland to withdraw 12 battalions of English troops from the Dutch theatre
for the better defence of the homeland; Newcastle to Sandwich, 20 October 1747 (B.M.
Add. MS. 32810, f. 166), cited by Evan Edward Charteris, *William Augustus, Duke of
Cumberland*, p. 335 n.; Pelham to Cumberland, 8 September 1747, cited by Coxe, *Pelham*,
i. 375. See also *Proper Answer*, above, p. 75, n. 1.

[6] In reply to an earlier French declaration (15 March 1744 N.S.) England had declared
war on France on 29 March 1744; see *GM*, xiv (1744), 154-5, 167-8. The Young Pretender

Destruction: Would he, I say, have endeavoured to introduce himself here, under the Banners of this Prince, if the Banners of any other Prince on Earth could have been spread in his Favour? Such an Assistance, he must well know, would render him odious to every reasonable Man in this Nation, and must animate every true *Briton* against his Cause, however he might otherwise be inclined.

Again, with what Views can we conceive that this Crown, the natural, the old, the certain Enemy of this Nation, would embrace his Party, or lend him any Assistance? Is it to aggrandize *Great Britain*, to enlarge our Liberties, our Trade, our Riches, our Strength? In a Word, is it the Design of *France* to make us more formidable to herself? Or may we not more justly suspect that she hath sufficient Assurances from this Pretender, that he will tread in the Footsteps of his Ancestors; and that by placing him on the Throne, she should again reduce this Nation to a Dependence on herself, and make it once more the Instrument of all her pernicious Schemes.

This, I say, is the least Mischief to us which *France* can intend, and what in all those Wars, which she hath undertaken in Support of this Family, she plainly hath intended; but she may *now* intend more. Her Successes have probably enlarg'd her Views, and no less than the intire Conquest of this great, this yet glorious Kingdom, may terminate her Prospect. Not to give us a dependent Prince, a Viceroy in Effect, but in Name too, may now be her audacious Hope.

This Hope, the bare Mention of which must be so shocking to a *British* Ear, if she hath dared to entertain it, she must build only on our Civil Dissentions. God forbid that I should raise a Blush in my Countrymen, by supposing that the united Strength of this Nation can be in Danger from any Enemy; but whatever Indignation the Idea may raise, (and without Indignation I would not have it read) I will assert, that if we suffer senseless Opinions and causeless Jealousies to divide, distract, and weaken us at this Time, the most ambitious Hopes of *France* are but too *reasonable*; *and a few Years will probably put an End to the very Being of this Country.*

landed in Scotland on 23 July 1745; Walter Biggar Blaikie, *Itinerary of Prince Charles Edward Stuart* (Edinburgh, 1897), pp. 2–4, and, for the extent of French aid, pp. 18, 84.

SATURDAY, JANUARY 2, 1748.   NUMB. 5.

Turba ruunt in me Luxuriosa——.

Ovid.[1]

Tho' my Paper, being appropriated to the Use of the Jacobite Party, may be rather considered as a private than as a public Vehicle; and no one consequently hath a Right to take a Place in it, as in the several Stage Papers which daily or weekly set out from the Press;[2] I shall, however, imitate the known Custom among Coachmen, who never scruple, when they have a proper Opportunity, to convert their Master's Coach into a Hack, and to take up a Fare. In like manner, when I have Leisure, and when the Business of my Masters doth not urgently call upon me, I shall usher into the World whatever Person or Goods I please. Without more Apology, therefore, I convey the following Letters to my Reader, the first of which only hath any Relation to Politics, and that too is written in Opposition to our Party.

Squire TROTT-PLAID,

I am deputed by my Sister *Jacobitesses* to represent the heavy Injury done us in the Frontispiece of your Journal, where you have ludicrously mounted a Female on an Ass, behind a Creature not one Bit better than the Beast he rides on. Had you, Squire *Trott*, considered our Case thoroughly, you had not placed us in so droll a Light: Such, I am convinced, you intend it; for I can never believe that one, who discovers so much good Sense, can be a Jacobite in Earnest, any more than are many of us whom I have called *Jacobitesses*; that is, Women who are obliged to talk the Nonsense of the Party, because their Husbands are of it. But now, as to those few who really believe they know not what, are they not rather the Objects of Compassion than of Ridicule? How should they know better? Neither their Fathers, nor Brothers, nor Husbands can instruct them in any Knowledge of the World, for they are intirely ignorant of it themselves; and as to any Instruction which they might get from Men of

---

[1] *Heroides*, i. 88: 'a wanton throng comes pressing about me' (Loeb).

[2] Public newspapers, particularly those friendly to the Administration, were distributed through the country, often *gratis* in the latter case, by the Post Office stages. See *JJ* no. 1, above, p. 96, n. 1; *Champion* of 5 February 1740; and Ellis, *The Post Office in the Eighteenth Century*, pp. 47–8.

Understanding and Experience, they are debarr'd from any such Conversation; for they are suffered to converse with no Whig. You cannot imagine how far this Prohibition is carried, especially in these Parts. We are not suffered to go to any Horse-Race, Ball, or Assembly, where a Whig Lord-Lieutenant or Member of Parliament presides, lest some Officer of the Army, or some other pretty Fellow (for positively all the pretty Fellows are Whigs) should dance us out of our Political Principles; since much good Argument, with us Women, may be made use of in Dancing. Nor are we only kept in Ignorance, and uninformed in most Things, but we are actually misinformed in many. The most malicious Lies which Popish Priests can invent, are propagated among us for Truth. One Family is set out in false Colours to raise our Compassion, and another is painted as disadvantageously and unjustly to create our Aversion.[1] Now that we may not discover the Falshood of this latter Misrepresentation, those among us, who are so happy to get to *London*, are for ever excluded not only from the Drawing-Room, but even from the Theatres on those Nights when any of the R—l Family appear there, least[2] our own Eyes should contradict the monstrous Lies told us by our Great Grandmothers, who are instructed by the Priests of our Popish Neighbours. You will not, I believe, be surprized at any gross Errors, or mistaken Notions, which Persons under these Circumstances may be capable of believing; I shall therefore send you the following Creed, which is absolutely held by every sincere Female Jacobite in this Nation.

The Creed of a Female Jacobite.

That King *James* II. was turned out by a Party of Presbyterians, to the great Prejudice of the Church of *England*, which he zealously maintain'd; and that all the reigning Princes since, except Queen *Anne*, who desired to restore the Pretender,[3] have been all Presbyterians, and Enemies to the Church of *England*; and that all Courtiers and Whigs are the same.

---

[1] The Stuarts and the House of Hanover. The latter was often attacked for its supposedly divided allegiance between England and the Electorate.

[2] In the eighteenth century an accepted form of 'lest'.

[3] Cf. *Proper Answer*, pp. 65–6.

That the greatest Part of the Money raised in this Kingdom is every Year sent to *H——r*.[1]

That the Church, which is now oppress'd, will flourish; that Taxes will be no more; that Liberty (of which, by the by, they have not the least Idea) will be restored; and that the merry Days of old *English* Hospitality will revive by the Restoration of the P——.

That this P—— is deprived of his Right in the same manner as a private Person would be, who was violently turned out of his Estate.[2] That he is protected and assisted by all the Popish Powers in *Europe*, only out of Compassion; and that he, and all his Family, tho' born and bred at *Rome*,[3] are true, good *Englishmen* in their Hearts, &c. &c. &c.

This, Sir, and much more of this Kind, is believed by some of the Sisterhood: But there are others, who, tho' they have the Misfortune to be yoked to a *Trott-Plaid*, have a sufficient Portion of Understanding, without much Improvement, to see through and despise the Principles, or rather the Nonsense of a Party, in which one would think it impossible any human Creature should be enrolled, who was not either mad, or (what most He-Jacobites are every Day) drunk.

> *I am, Sir, (with the utmost Contempt of the
> Party of which you profess yourself,)*

Litchfield,[4]   *Your humble Servant,*

Dec. 24.   STEWARTA STAFFORDSHIRE.[5]

Sir,

I am glad to find a Man of Learning and Genius once more in the Character of a public Writer. As to Politics, whatever may be your Principles, I shall not dispute them; for I have applied

[1] An allusion to the annual subsidy voted George II for support and maintenance of his Hanover troops. For estimates of the amounts involved see *Journals of . . . Commons*, xxv. 467, and Coxe, *Pelham*, i. 380.

[2] Cf. *Dialogue*, pp. 9–14.

[3] James Francis Edward Stuart, the Old Pretender, was in fact born in London (1688), the only son of James II and Mary of Modena.

[4] An allusion to the Lichfield race meeting disturbances in September 1747; see *JJ* no. 1, above, p. 93, n. 2.

[5] Staffordshire as a whole had a reputation as a Jacobite ('Stewarta') stronghold, a reputation it maintained in the 1747 elections, which at Lichfield itself were rumoured to have cost £30,000, and at Stafford produced riots and disorders which destroyed the house of Lord Chetwynd's brother. See above, General Introduction, pp. lxiii–lxiv.

none of my Time to that Study. Thirty Years ago, indeed, a general Cry that the Nation was undone,[1] created some Terrors in me, and had almost made me a Politician; but as I have heard that Outcry ever since, it hath long ceased to have any Effect, and I now enjoy my Fortune without any Apprehensions.

My chief Delight hath always been in reading; and as Works of Imagination afford me the greatest Pleasure, you may easily imagine that I have many Years ago run through all the Books (for they are not numberless) which ancient or modern Authors have produced of that kind. Indeed I have read them all so often, that their Beauties, from too much Familiarity, begin to pall upon my Mind.

How charmed am I therefore when I meet with a new Production in the Region of Fancy, capable of giving me the same Delight which I have received from my most favourite Authors at my first Acquaintance with them. The most learned Botanist, who discovers a new Plant; or the surfeited Epicure, who invents a new Dish, may perhaps have some faint Idea of my Pleasure, at perusing such Works from any of my Cotemporaries.

When I tell you I have lately received this Pleasure, you will not want me to inform you that I owe it to the Author of *CLARISSA*.[2] Such Simplicity, such Manners, such deep Penetration into Nature; such Power to raise and alarm the Passions, few Writers, either ancient or modern, have been possessed of. My Affections are so strongly engaged, and my Fears are so raised, by what I have already read, that I cannot express my Eagerness to see the rest. Sure this Mr. *Richardson* is Master of all that Art which *Horace* compares to Witchcraft,

[1] Referring to various Tory and Jacobite turmoils following the unsuccessful rebellion of 1715, notably the formation of a 'Leicester House' Opposition around the Prince of Wales (1717–18), rifts within the Whig coalition favouring George I, Gyllenborg's projected invasion of England by Swedish forces (1717), and finally another projected invasion, by Jacobite forces, under the Duke of Ormonde and by plan of Cardinal Alberoni (1719).

[2] The first two volumes of Richardson's novel were published anonymously on 1 December 1747, with a title-page statement '*Published by the Editor of* Pamela'; William Merritt Sale, Jr., *Samuel Richardson: A Bibliographical Record* (New Haven, Conn., 1936), p. 49. The volumes were advertised in *JJ* nos. 2 and 3; Andrew Millar, Fielding's publisher, was among the booksellers distributing it. In the 'Court of Criticism' of *JJ* no. 14, below, pp. 187–8, there is a letter commending the novel and this notice of it. Cf. Fielding to Richardson (*c.* 15 October 1748), printed by E. L. McAdam, Jr., 'A New Letter from Fielding', *Yale Review*, xxxviii (1948), 304–6. Compared with *Pamela*, *Clarissa* received relatively little published criticism from contemporaries.

——*Pectus inaniter angit,*
Irritat, mulcet, falsis terroribus implet,
Ut Magus——.[1]

With what Indignation do I therefore hear the Criticisms made on this Performance. *Clarissa* is undutiful; she is too dutiful. She is too cold; she is too fond. She uses her Father, Mother, Uncles, Brother, Sister, Lover, Friend, too ill, too well. In short, there is scarce a Contradiction in Character, which I have not heard assigned from different Reasons to this poor Girl; who is as much the Object of Compassion as she can be, and as good as she should be described.

Do, pray, Sir, now and then lay aside your Politics, and take upon you to correct our Critics. Advise these Snarlers, of both Sexes, to improve their Heads a little, before they venture to sit in Judgment on the Merit of an Author. I wish likewise before they read any more of this Author, they would amend their Hearts; for this, I take it, is an Axiom: *That a* bad *Heart cannot taste the Productions of a* good *one.*

I am, Sir,

Yours, &c.

Welcome, old *Trot*, welcome into the World, under whatever Title thou dost please to appear; Champion, Patriot,[2] Jacobite, any thing; I rejoice when I hear thou art stirring; I am then sure to laugh. Thou art the comicallest, pleasantest, merriest, best-humoured Fellow in the Universe. Thy Father laughed when he begat thee. Thy Mother laughed when she bore thee. Thou didst certainly come laughing into the World, and wilt go laughing out of it. I laugh with thee. I laugh at thee. And when thou art hanged, as thou wilt most certainly be, should the Jacobites ever succeed, I shall laugh ready to split my Sides.

Yours in a Horse-laugh,

HA! HA! HA!

Mr. *Trott,*

I do not wonder at the Ignorance of such a Jacobitical Rascal as yourself; but pray, Sir, be pleased to correct the Blunder in

[1] *Epistles,* II. i. 211–13: 'With airy nothing wrings my heart, inflames, soothes, fills it with vain alarms like a magician' (Loeb).

[2] Fielding had previously edited *The Champion* (1739–41) and *The True Patriot* (1745–6).

your third Journal, where you tell us the Greeks had no Name for a King but what signified a Tyrant.

Indeed, Sir, the *Greeks* had no other Name for such Kings as the *Stewarts*, and particularly the last Minion of that Party, were; but Kings of a different Stamp were by the *Greeks* distinguished by an Appellation which imported them to have been the Basis or Fundamental of the Community. I would send you the Name in *Greek*,[1] but that I suppose neither you nor any of your Party could read it.

Your Humble Servant,

Hanover for ever.

Trott-Plaid,

D—n you, place the following Motto from *Martial* before your confounded Jokes on the News-papers for the future.

> *Sunt bona, sunt quædam mediocria, sunt mala plura*
> *Quæ legis hic.——*[2]

Yours,

TOM TICKLE.

Mr. *Tickle,*

Be pleased to add the remainder of the Line.

> ——*Aliter, non fit, Avite, Liber.*[3]

Yours,

JOHN TROTPLAID.

SATURDAY, JANUARY 9, 1748.   NUMB. 6.

> *Ecce Mimallonides sparsis post terga capillis,*
> *Ecce* leves Satyri, prævia Turba Dei.*
>
> Ovid.[4]

**Anglicé,* Highlanders, or wild Men in their Dresses.

Having in a former Paper endeavoured to explain (as far forth as Mysteries may be explained) some of the Esoteric, i.e. the

---

[1] ὁ βασιλεύς.

[2] *Epigrams,* I. xvi: 'There are good things, there are some indifferent, there are more things bad that you read here' (Loeb).

[3] 'Not otherwise, Avitus, is a book produced' (Loeb).

[4] *Art of Love,* i. 541–2: 'Lo! Bacchanals with tresses streaming behind them, lo! wanton Satyrs, the god's forerunning band' (Loeb).

inward and spiritual Part of Jacobitism,[1] we shall now proceed to give the Reader a Taste of the Exoteric, or that which is outward and visible.

Many ignorant People resort no higher for the Original of Jacobitism, than to the Abdication of the late King *James*, deriving, I suppose, the Name of our Sect from the Word *Jacobus*: But as we have already shewn our internal Doctrines to have their Foundation in the remotest Antiquity, I shall here evidently demonstrate, that our external have still a clearer Right to the most ancient Origination, and are indeed no other than the famous *Orgia* of old, celebrated in honour of the God *Bacchus*, of which we gave an obscure Hint in our first Paper.[2]

Now that this God was called *Iacchus* is well known; hence plainly the Word *Iacchites*, or, according to the *English* Pronunciation, *Jackites*, which, being abridged, is *Jacks*, our ancient Appellation, and by which at this Day we are commonly distinguished; for though all the Doctrines of Jacobitism are very ancient, yet the Word itself is certainly modern, and a very easy Corruption from the genuine Name: Perhaps this Corruption was introduced at the cursed Revolution,[3] as a Compliment to our beloved Monarch, who was then apotheozed,[4] and began like *Alexander* to receive divine Honours in his Life-time;[5] and like *Alexander* received no more after his Death; but his Son hath from that Time been worshipped in his stead. For in this Instance, as hath been said, we Moderns differ from the Ancients of our Order.

Some learned Men have attempted to draw a Parallel between *Bacchus*, or *Iacchus*, and *Moses*, whom they have conceived to be one and the same Person.[6] Others again have imagined that our *Bacchus* is no other than *Nimrod*; and others that he is the same

---

[1] *JJ* no. 3, above, pp. 104–8.   [2] See also *JJ* no. 2, above, p. 98.

[3] The earliest instance noted by the *OED* (*s.v.* 'Jack' sb⁵) dates from 1695.

[4] Emended from copy-text's *apotheized*, which is just possibly Fielding's neologism. The emendation seems preferable to the only alternative (*apotheosized*) for two reasons: it presumes a misprint of one letter as opposed to the omission of two letters; the *OED* lists no usage of *apotheosize* or its cognate forms prior to 1760.

[5] In 331 B.C. Alexander was saluted by the priests at the temple of Jupiter Ammon in Libya as the son of that god, an event to which Fielding makes Diogenes allude scoffingly in the 'Dialogue between Alexander the Great and Diogenes the Cynic', *Miscellanies* (1743), i. 228.

[6] Abbé Banier, *Mythology and Fables of the Ancients Explain'd from History*, ii (London, 1740), 441–4, develops the parallel, which he credits to Vossius. Baker, item no. 219, lists the translation of Banier's *Mythology* among Fielding's books; and see below, p. 127, n. 2.

with *Noah*.[1] And all these learned Men have been led to their several Conjectures by the strict Resemblance between the Heathen God and the several Persons recorded in Scripture. Now was not *Moses* the first Politician, *Nimrod* the first great Hunter, and *Noah* the Inventor of the Vine?[2] Is not here then the clearest Account of our Mystery; which consists at this Day, as it did then, in a Mixture of Politics, Hunting and Drinking*?

Diodorus Siculus tells us,[3] that the Army which *Iacchus*, or, if the *English* Reader pleases, *Jackus*, led to the *Indies*, consisted as well of Women as of Men, both alike armed with the *Thyrsus*,[4] a Weapon we may suppose like that of *Pallas* in the *Rehearsal*,[5] which was filled with Wine; whence the Poets feigned that an *Iacchite* or *Jackite* striking with his Weapon, could make a bubbling Fountain of Wine spring from the Earth†.

Nor was *Jackus* only the Founder of the Vine; the same *Diodorus* tells us likewise,[6] that he was the first Inventor of Beer; which is indeed the Liquor chiefly used in the Celebration of the *English* Mysteries.

And if in some Particulars, our present *Orgia*, or, as they are called, *Jacobite Meetings*, should differ from the ancient, how little is such Innovation to be wondered at in so long a Succession of Ages. It will be, I think, much more astonishing to consider, how much of the old Mystery we have preserved pure; indeed so as to have lost nothing which can be thought essential; and what little Differences are, must perhaps be considered rather as Improvements than Corruptions; as will appear, when we proceed, as we

---

* *See* Bannier's Mythology, *Book* I. *Chap.* 17.[7]

† Euripides, *cited in* Bannier, ut supra.[8]

---

[1] Banier, *Mythology*, ii. 443, gives the evidence and the sources of both the Nimrod and the Noah identifications.

[2] Genesis ix. 20: 'And Noah began to be an husbandman, and he planted a vineyard'; cited by Banier, ii. 443.

[3] *Biblioteca Historica*, III. lxv. 3–4, and IV. iv. 2–3. Fielding owes the reference to Banier, ii. 440, 445.

[4] Banier, ii. 449, describes the army of Bacchus as armed with *thyrsi* which, when struck to the ground, caused springs of wine to bubble up.

[5] IV. 1: 'Lo, from this conquering lance, / Does flow the purest wine of France.'

[6] *Biblioteca Historica*, iii. lxxiii. 6 and iv. ii. 5, refers to a drink prepared from barley which takes the place of wine in places where the vine does not grow successfully.

[7] An error for Book II, Chapter 17.

[8] *Bacchae*, 706–9.

now shall, to take a View of the particular Ceremonies used, as well by us, as by our ancient Predecessors.

First then we are told, that in the old Celebration of the Mysteries, it was usual for the Performers to counterfeit Persons drunk:[1] This Ceremony we must be allowed to have improved as much as the Reality exceeds the Appearance of any thing. In our Songs which we sing, like the Ancients, in Chorus, at our Meetings, we have certainly the Superiority; for as theirs were only composed in honour of Drinking, ours contain the threefold Mystery above hinted; being partly political, partly in honour of Hunting, and partly of Drinking.

"The Women who celebrated the Festivals of old (says the famous Abbé *Bannier*) were called *Bacchantes*, from the Howlings and Noise which they made: *Mimallonides*, because they prattled with an unbounded Freedom, and *Thyades*, because heated with Wine they roamed about like mad*." Our Women, who do all this, are distinguished by one Name only, viz. *Jacks*, or *Jack-Women*, which includes an Idea of the whole.

Ovid, in his *Metamorphoses*, tells us, that one of the Ceremonies used at these Mysteries consisted in calling Names.

> ——*Bacchumque vocant, Bromiumque Liæumque*
> *Ignigenamque Satumque iterum, solumque Bimatrem.*
> *Additur his Nyseus, indetonsusque Thyoneus*
> *Et cum Lenæo genialis consitor uvæ,*
> *Nycteliusque Eleleusque parens, et Iacchus et Evan,*
> *Et quæ præterea per Graias plurima gentes*
> *Nomina Liber habet.*[3]

We likewise call Names very liberally at our Meetings: For first, in imitation of these our Predecessors, we invoke our Deity

---

* Bannier, ut supra.[2]

---

[1] Banier, ii. 460, describes the orgiastic procession in part as follows: 'The *Phallophori* followed them with a Chorus of *Ithyphallophori* habited like Fauns, counterfeiting Persons drunk, and singing in Honour of *Bacchus* Songs suitable to their Functions.'

[2] *Mythology*, ii. 449.

[3] 'Calling on Bacchus, naming him also Bromius, Lyaeus, son of the thunderbolt, twice born, child of two mothers; they hail him as Nyseus also, Thyoneus of the unshorn locks, Lenaeus, planter of the joy-giving vine, Nyctelius, father Eleleus, Iacchus, and Euhan, and all the many names besides by which thou art known, O Liber, throughout the towns of Greece' (Loeb). The passage is from iv. 11–17, and is quoted by Banier, ii. 448 n.

by the Name of *Ascanius, The Wanderer, The Adventurer, The Chevalier*;[1] and as we grow warmer with Worship, we attribute to him still more sacred Names, and ascribe to him those Honours, which our Mysteries hold to be divine. To this likewise we have added, by way of Improvement, certain Names of an abusive Signification, which we cast on the Enemies of our Order, such as *Whig, Roundhead, Sh–tsack, Republican Hanoverian Dog, Bitch,* &c. &c. &c.

The ancient *Bacchanalians* are recorded to have drest themselves like Satyrs, *i.e.* wild Men;[2] we dress ourselves like the wildest Men we are acquainted with, namely the *Highlanders*.

Now as to the more mysterious Part of these Rites we shall find the modern in most Particulars to agree exactly with the ancient. The *Iacchites* are said to have made the Air resound with the Words EVOHE IACCHE:[3] Now do not the modern *Jackites*, or *Jacobites*, at all their Meetings, make the Air ring with the same Word *Evohe*, or *Evoy*, and that as well at the Performance of the Drinking, as of the Hunting Rites; and who hath not heard the Words EVOHE JACK, frequently used on these Occasions, especially when the Person hath been, what may properly be called *drunk* with Devotion.

Many of the Appellations of the ancient Deity, as well as of the modern, contain inexplicable Mystery. Most of those which are capable of Explanation may be equally applied to either. Such are the *Satus iterum, Solusque Bimater*; *i.e.* that had two Mothers;[4] which as clearly allude to the famous Story of the Warming-Pan,[5] as to the no more unaccountable Birth of *Bacchus*.

[1] Contemporary names for the Young Pretender, commemorated in the pamphlet literature of the time by such titles as *Ascanius; or, the Young Adventurer* (1746), *The Wanderer* (1747), *The Young Chevalier* (1750). Ascanius, son of Aeneas and Creusa, accompanied his father to Italy after the fall of Troy.

[2] Banier, ii. 459, describes 'People drunk, dress'd like Satyrs, Fauns, and Silenus's'.

[3] Banier, ii. 459, records this shout of the Bacchantes to their god; cf. Ovid, *Art of Love*, i. 563, where Bacchus is given the epithet 'Euhian'.

[4] 'twice born', 'child of two mothers'; see Ovid, *Metamorphoses*, iv. 12 (*satumque iterum solumque bimatrem*) and p. 124, n. 3, above.

[5] When after 15 years of childlessness James II's wife, Mary of Modena, gave birth in June 1688, it was widely rumoured that a supposititious child had been smuggled into the labour room in a warming pan; Bishop Burnet's *History of the Reign of King James the Second* (Oxford, 1852), pp. 287–96, 362–7. In January 1746, during the height of the Jacobite rebellion, Burnet's and Lloyd's account of the birth of the Old Pretender was republished; *GM*, xvi (1746), 48.

One of the Epithets of *Bacchus* is *Biformis*.[1] How well this must be adapted to a Popish Prince at the Head of a Protestant Church cannot want a Comment, any more than it needs one to apply *Bicorniger* or Double-horned;[2] which so evidently denotes the two Mysteries of Hunting and Drinking; both which are performed with Horns.

The Hunting-Match said to have been celebrated at the latter End of last Summer, in which drunken Men rode about the Country in the Dress of Satyrs, *i.e.* of *Highlanders*,[3] was a most perfect Imitation of the *Orgia*. It is true, indeed, these were not, in the manner of the ancient *Bacchanalians*, mounted on Asses,[4] the true Reason of which was, that so many Asses were not to be found; but this Omission was abundantly supplied by their whole Behaviour; for though they did not ride upon that Beast, yet they so well imitated him in all their Actions, that it is universally acknowledged, they all behaved like perfect Asses.

As for our Drinking-bouts, they do indeed in every Particular, bear so exact a Resemblance to the ancient *Bacchanalian* Revels, that could one of those *Bacchanals* return to Life, and should he be immediately introduced into some of our Clubs, he would most certainly imagine himself present at the Celebration of one of his old Feasts. Perhaps, indeed, he would not be so well able to understand some of our mysterious Toasts; but these he might very well conclude were a slight Diversification of the Ceremonies (for they were not formerly in all Places the same). This, at least, he could not fail to conclude from our whole Conversation, as well as from our Actions, that if we did not attempt, like the ancient *Bacchanalians*, to personate Men out of their Wits, we were in reality in that Condition.

I cannot quit this Subject without transcribing a Passage from the excellent Author who hath been of such Use to me in unravelling the most secret Mysteries of *Jacobitism*, and which will hereafter be of still greater Use.[5] "All the Nations of *India*

---

[1] Banier, ii. 447, derives the 'biform' Bacchus from the fact that 'he was sometimes represented like an Infant, sometimes like a bearded Man.'

[2] Banier, ii. 448: 'from the Horns which he sometimes wears, the Symbols of the Beams of the Sun, which this God represented'.

[3] At the Lichfield race meetings of September 1747. See *JJ* no. 1, above, p. 93, n. 2.

[4] Banier, ii. 449, describes the procession of the Orgies: 'Followed next a Company mounted upon Asses, which was attended with Fauns, Bacchanals, *Thyades*, *Mimallonides*, *Naiads* . . . .'

[5] In *JJ* no. 9, below, p. 146, and *JJ* no. 12, below, pp. 164–6; also *Tom Jones*, XII. i.

(says he) among whom *Bacchus* travelled, decreed divine Honours to him; and none but the barbarous *Scythians* refused to worship a God who had propagated a Drink which so frequently levelled Men with the Beasts*."

In like manner I may say, all the Counties of *England*, over which King *James* tyrannised, decreed divine Honours to him; and none but the barbarous *Whigs* refused to worship a King who had endeavoured to propagate a Religion which levels Men with the very worst of Beasts.

The Reader therefore will cease to wonder, that Mysteries which so nearly resemble each other in their Original, should differ so very little in the Manner of their Representation; or that the drunken *Jacks* of our Days should so exactly conform to the Manners of their ancient Brethren.

Whereas it hath been represented unto us, as well by the Letters of several of our Correspondents, as by the humble Petition of many of the most reputable Booksellers, and doth otherwise sufficiently appear, that a great Number of loose, idle, and disorderly Persons, calling themselves Authors, have lately assembled at a certain Ale-house of ill Fame in *Grub-street*, commonly known by the Name of the *Pen and Pitcher*,[1] and have there conspired together to mix up great Quantities of Ribaldry and Nonsense; and have afterwards endeavour'd to their utmost to spread the said Mixtures abroad among the People, often under false Names and Colours; and by means of a certain wicked, base, deceitful and diabolical Art, vulgarly call'd Puffing, to the great

---

* Bannier, *Vol.* II. *Page* 446. *Note, all the Quotations from this Author are from the* English *Translation, which is a most excellent one.*[2]

---

[1] Not identified. The name may be fictitious, alluding, as it does, to the vocation and supposed avocation of wretched writers.

[2] The translation (1739–41), which was apparently reissued by Andrew Millar in 1748, is advertised in this and succeeding numbers of the *JJ*; see *JJ* no. 9, below, p. 146, n. 3. Cross, ii. 106 n., without giving his evidence, states that 'Fielding appears to have written the advertisement', and offers the further 'surmise that William Young made the translation under Fielding's supervision'; iii. 336. It should be noted that Fielding was by no means above 'puffing' both Millar and Cooper books generally, including many in which he could not possibly have participated. If Cross, ii. 92, is also correct in his guess that Parson Young was Fielding's assistant on the *JJ*, there would have been additional reason for 'puffing' the translation. However, the euhemerist thrust of Banier's anti-mythology, like that of Pierre Bayle's *Dictionary*, may have been sufficient recommendation in itself to a satirist of Fielding's capability.

Annoyance of his Majesty's good Subjects, often to the great Prejudice of the Reputation of Men of the best and most solemn Characters, and always to the Loss of both the Money and Time of the Reader; to the Prejudice of all honest Booksellers, to the utmost Abuse, Disgrace, and Discouragement of Literature, and, lastly, to the great Scandal of this Nation.

And whereas the said wicked Persons, tho' often within the Intent, are not literally within the Description either of the Black Act,[1] or of the Act against sending threatning Letters;[2] nor can the said Mixtures be sufficiently suppress'd, nor the Mischiefs intended by them be obviated by any Laws now in Being, We have been therefore humbly requested, as well by our Correspondents as by the Booksellers aforesaid, to erect a Court of Criticism for the well-ordering and inspecting all Matters any wise concerning the Republic of Literature, and for the due Correction and Punishment of all Abuses committed therein. All which doth belong, and from Time, whereof the Memory of Man is not to the contrary, hath belonged to that high Censorial Office, with which, for very wise Causes and Considerations, we have thought proper to invest ourselves.

Having therefore duly weigh'd the Premises, and being well convinced of the great Necessity of immediately reviving the said Court, to the long Suspension of which (even from the Time of our most dear Predecessor *Isaac Bickerstaff*, Esq; of facetious Memory)[3] may justly be imputed all the Abuses above complain'd of, we have graciously determined forthwith to revive the said Court; and do hereby give Notice, that the said Court will be held on *Thursday* next at our Bookseller's Shop, between the Hours of Twelve and Two; and with the Proceedings thereat the Public will be acquainted in this our Paper, between the Foreign and Domestic Articles of News.

In this Court we intend, moreover, to recommend all Books

---

[1] 9 Geo. I, cap. 22, also called the Waltham Black Act because of its occasion by depredations near Waltham by persons with blackened or disguised faces; Giles Jacob, *Law-Dictionary*, rev. by T. E. Tomlins, 2nd ed. (London, 1809), *s.v.* 'Black Act'; and *Statutes at Large* xv. 88–94. Lawyer Dowling cites the Black Act to Allworthy in *Tom Jones*, xviii. iii.

[2] 9 Geo. I, cap. 22 also contained provisions which made sending a letter without a name, or with a fictitious name, demanding money or other valuables, a felony without benefit of clergy; *Statutes at Large*, xv. 88.

[3] See *JJ* no. 1, above, p. [90], n. 3.

and Writings, which have the least Merit in them, to the Public:
And do hereby strictly charge the said Public not to purchase any
modern literary Productions whatever, till they have first read
our Approbation.

> *Given at our Bookseller's Shop,*
> *this* 10*th of Jan.* 1748.[1]

JOHN TROTT-PLAID.

ARTICULI JACOBICI:

Or, *Articles of Jacobite Faith invented and spread for the Use of
our Party; and which every good Jacobite is either to believe, or say
he does.*

I. That the Ministry are desirous of making a bad Peace when
we are able to carry on an advantageous War.

II. That they are desirous of carrying on a disadvantageous
War in order to purchase a bad Peace.

III. That all the bad Consequences which have attended the
War; the Burden of Taxes at home; the Infidelity and Weakness of our Allies abroad, &c. are all justly to be charged on the
same Ministry.

IV. That a Desire of obtaining the best Peace in their Power,
from these and other Considerations, is to be imputed as a Crime
by those who clamour against Evil which we suffer by the War.

V. That a Great Peer is about to resign his Place, and a Great
Commoner is gone discontented to Bath.[2]

Such things as these can never be inculcated too often by those
Jacobites who are not afraid nor ashamed to serve their Party
at the trifling Expence of Modesty, and of Truth.

---

[1] The date of this issue of the *JJ* is 9 January 1748.

[2] Contemporaries would have recognized here an allusion to the efforts made by the
Opposition press to exploit the growing friction between Chesterfield and Newcastle, and
the growing restiveness of William Pitt (the 'Great Commoner'), chafing under the
relatively minor assignment of Paymaster-General of the Forces. Chesterfield did in fact
resign as Secretary of State on 6 February 1748; see, for example, *GM*, xviii (1748), 90.

SATURDAY, JANUARY 16, 1748.   NUMB. 7.

>   ———*Pauci dignoscere passunt*
> *Vera bona, atque illis multum diversa, remota*
> *Erroris nebula: quid enim Ratione timemus,*
> *Aut cupimus? quid tam dextro pede concipis, ut te*
> *Conatus non pæniteat, votique peracti?*
> *Evertere domos totas optantibus ipsis*
> *Dii faciles. Nocitura Toga nocitura petuntur*
> *Militia.*———   Juvenal, *Satire* 10.[1]

As Jacobitism is a very high unintelligible Mystery, and as it is the Glory of our Party to maintain their Doctrines in Opposition to Reason and Argument, all Attempts to shew the Inconsistency of these Doctrines with Reason contribute only to raise and spread our Triumph.

We shall therefore make no Apology to our good Friends for publishing the following Abstract from the Dedication to the Electors of *Great Britain*, which is prefixed to a late Pamphlet called an *Historical Essay upon the Ballance of Civil Power in England*;[2] since no Author hath better illustrated our Doctrines, nor more conspicuously placed them in the glorious Light abovementioned.

The Author having complimented the Electors on their late Choice of Representatives, proceeds thus: "You may now rest secure, that under the present Administration supported by a Whig Parliament, every Thing will be done for the Common Good, which the hazardous Circumstances of the Times will permit. 'Tis not in the best-laid Schemes, or the wisest Mortals to command Success; all that can reasonably be expected from our Governors, is, that every thing be done which may deserve

---

1 Juvenal, *Satires*, x. 2–9: '. . . there are but few who can distinguish true blessings from their opposites, putting aside the mists of error. For when does Reason direct our desires or our fears? What project do we form so auspiciously that we do not repent us of our effort and of the granted wish? Whole households have been destroyed by the compliant Gods in answer to the masters' prayers; in camp and city alike we ask for things that will be our ruin' (Loeb).

2 This anonymous pamphlet was published *c.* 9 January 1748, and has been attributed to Samuel Squire (1713–66), Archdeacon of Bath, chaplain to the Duke of Newcastle, and later Dean of Bristol and Bishop of St. David's. See *GM*, xviii (1748), 48; the 'Court of Criticism', below, p. 134; and *JJ* no. 9, below, p. 145, n. 2. The quotation which follows is from pp. xxv–xxx of the Dedication 'To the Freeholders, Burgesses, and other Parliamentary Electors of *Great Britain*'.

it.——No! Gentlemen! you may at all times assure yourselves, that you have no internal Dangers to fear for your darling Constitution, but from Tories and Republicans. When either of these Parties, thro' some fatal Co-incidence of Circumstances, shall gain the upper Hand, shall get the Superiority, 'tis then indeed time for you to look about you, to ring the Alarm-bell, to put yourselves upon your best Guard, and to watch every Motion of the desperate Enemy.

"The *Republicans*, indeed, act entirely upon Principle; 'tis their great and especial Business to raise and encourage Differences between the King and his Subjects, to introduce Confusion into the State, and thereby to pave the way for their *Oceanas* and *Utopias*. Only the Gentlemen in this Way of Thinking would do well to reflect a little more attentively, than they usually do, upon the present State of *Great Britain*, 'That it is too far advanced in Luxury, Magnificence, great Estates, and high Titles, to return to a Commonwealth in any Shape whatsoever; that the Envy, Emulation, and Ambition of the proud and popular Landholders would be a perpetual Occasion of their tearing one another, and their Country to pieces, were they not all subordinate to one supreme Head.'——'Without a previous Agrarian, says Mr. *Harrington*, there can be no equal Commonwealth:' And 'a vicious and corrupt People, as *Machiavel* well observes, is not so much as capable of one.'[1]

"As to the *Tories*, considered as such, their political Conduct is all over weak and self-contradictory. Their Principles and Practice are at a perpetual Strife and Variance with each other. They soberly maintain the Divine Right of Kings to their Thrones, and yet are ever railing at the Succession in their own State, and labouring all they can, with Safety to their Persons, to weaken and subvert it.——They pretend to be the most zealous Advocates for the Prerogative of Princes, yet are always attempting to lessen that of their own.——They profess a passive as well as active Obedience to the supreme Power; yet strenuously oppose every Measure, which is thought to come from it, whether right or wrong.——They only are the true Friends of *Old*

[1] *The Oceana and Other Works of James Harrington, Esq;*, ed. John Toland (London, 1737), p. 55: 'An equal Commonwealth . . . is a Government establish'd upon an equal Agrarian'; 'Discourses', Bk. I, ch. xviii, in *Works of the Famous Nicholas Machiavel* (London, 1720), p. 292: 'therefore arises the difficulty (or rather impossibility) in a corrupt City, to maintain a free State, much less to erect one'.

England, tho' at the same time they are perpetually murmuring at, and complaining of every vigorous Step which is taken by the Administration, for preventing the ambitious, faithless, and encroaching *French* from becoming Masters of the whole neighbouring Shore, &c.——Their Words, 'tis true, are the Words of Patriots and honest Men, but their Actions are the Actions of concealed Jacobites. I would by no means be thought to fix this odious Appellation upon the Generality of them; for we have their own Words, as well as their most solemn Oaths for it, that they from their Souls detest, and abhor, both the Thing as well as the Name.——If it be absurd therefore, as the Author of the *Dissertation upon Parties* tells us it is, to impute to the Tories that now are, the Principles which were laid to their Charge formerly, is it not, at least, incumbent upon the Gentlemen of this Denomination, either freely to own that they are now become downright Republicans, or else to give us a more certain Clue whereby we may be able to trace out and explain the Grounds of their present political Conduct? For that they are not Whigs, nor desire to be looked upon as such, the Healths they drink, the Songs they sing, the Insinuations they are continually dropping, and a thousand other Circumstances, will sufficiently inform us.

"Nor let the *Whigs* be charged with Inconsistency, and accused of having receded from the Principles which they formerly professed, when they become Advocates for the Crown, and Assertors of the Royal Prerogative. They always were, and every true Whig still is, for maintaining an equal Ballance of Power between the several Orders of the Legislature. This is the sure Characteristic by which you may always know them; they are against an over-bearing, a domineering, an unconstitutional Power, in whatever Hands it may chance to be lodged. Does the Ballance seem to incline to the Crown? they are for lightning that Scale: Does the Side of the Nobility, or Commons, preponderate? they are for throwing more Weight into the other Scales.——'Tis Tyranny, 'tis Oligarchy, 'tis Confusion they oppose; 'tis the Constitution which they are always labouring to preserve free and inviolate. 'These are they who walk, as it were, the Perambulations of the Government, and who think it their Duty to keep the true and old Boundaries and Landmarks of the State, and not to set up new. These are they who guard Prerogative, Privilege and Liberty, so as none of them intrench upon the other:' These are they who preserved you from the threatning Dangers of the last Rebellion, and from whom alone you must expect Relief, should the same threatning Alarms once more attack you: These are they who are continually watching for the Preservation of *Europe*, and from whose steady Counsels and Advice to their Sovereign, you can alone hope to put an honourable End to this burthensome, though necessary, War.

"In short, a true and consistent Whig is a Ballancer, a Mediator; always against Violence, and against Encroachment from whatever Quarter it is derived——Under a *Henry* VIIIth, a *Charles*, or a *James*, he is a Countryman; under a *William*, or a *George*, he is a Courtier——Still a Friend to Law, Truth, Justice, and the Establishment. Such were the great *Clarendon* and *Southampton*; such the Lords *Somers* and *Godolphin*; such was the late Earl of *Orford*; and such are those illustrious Persons, who are, at present, generally supposed to enjoy the greatest Share of his Majesty's Favour and Counsels."

Proceedings at the Court of Criticism, *held on* Thursday, Jan. 14, 1747. *before* JOHN TROT-PLAID, *Esq; Censor of* Great Britain.

Several Persons applied to his Honour in order to obtain Offices in the said Court; most of whom being rejected, departed grumbling, and threatened to go into the Opposition.

A Petition from Orator *Handlie*[1] was read, praying to be Crier of the Court, offering to write, preach, or swear any thing, and to profess any Party or Religion, at a cheap rate; rejected.

A Petition of a small Body of Critics, signed THE TOWN, humbly praying that his Honour would take the Playhouse under his Inspection, was presented and read. Upon which the Court

---

[1] John ('Orator') Henley (1692–1756), eccentric Nonconformist preacher, harangued the London populace in sermons, orations, and lectures on 'science' from his gilt-and-velvet pulpit or 'Tub' in Lincoln's Inn Fields, near Clare Market. Employed by Walpole to edit the Whig newspaper *The Hyp-Doctor* (1730–41), ridiculed in *The Dunciad*, caricatured by Hogarth, Henley was also the butt of Fielding's satire as early as *The Author's Farce* (1730). On 4 December 1746 Henley was apprehended, by order of Chesterfield (then one of the Secretaries of State) 'on a charge of endeavouring to alienate the minds of his majesty's subjects from their allegiance by his *Sunday*'s harangues, at his *Oratory Chapel*'; *GM*, xvi (1746), 666. On 19 June 1747 Henley and his bail appeared before the court of the King's Bench and were discharged; *DA* of 20 June 1747, cited by *Yale Walpole*, xix. 341 n. See also Stephens, *Catalogue*, pp. 620 ff., esp. no. 2823 ('The Brazen Faced O——r or Popish Incendiary').

said, They would consider thereof; and the Managers of the said Playhouses were ordered to attend on *Thursday* next.

M. Cooper presented to the Court a Pamphlet entitled *An Historical Essay upon the Ballance of Civil Power in* England, *&c.* which was read.[1] And it was ordered that an Extract from the Dedication be immediately printed in this Paper,[2] and that the said Pamphlet be recommended to the Perusal of the Public.

The Court was moved on the Behalf of the Paper Manufacture; which it was said would be considerably injured by that general Prohibition published in our Journal of the 9th Instant.[3] It was suggested by a learned Council that, If so be, that how, a Book was perfectly inoffensive, it might be permitted to be suffered to be read. And besides that how a Book might have some Degree of Merit, without having sufficient to entitle it to the high Honour of the Recommendation of the Court. Why therefore then, it would be better to qualifie the generality of the Words of the Clause of the Prohibition; and to confine it then to this, that how, if so be, a Book be condemned by the Court, why therefore then, in that Case, nobody should be permitted to read it.

This Motion was opposed by a Council who said he was employ'd by the Pastry-Cooks and the Makers of Trunks and Bandboxes,[4] who were more concerned in Interest to support the beforementioned Order in its full Extent, than the Paper Manufacturers could be to abridge it. He said it was true, that the Morals of the People, or the Reputations of Individuals, could not be injured by Books merely inoffensive; but that such might nevertheless rob the Public of both their Time and Money. He likewise urged, that it was not the printing, but the reading only of such Books, which was prohibited; and that he conceived there would not be one the less printed on account of the Prohibition; for as all Authors, good or bad, have the same good

---

[1] Mrs. Cooper advertised the pamphlet in *JJ* nos. 6 and 7; Strahan printed it, but charged Andrew Millar, not Mrs. Cooper; see B.M. Add. MS. 48800, f. 58ᵛ; also General Introduction above, pp. xxxv, n. 2, and liv.

[2] An extract from pp. xxv–xxx of the *Essay* makes up the leader of this issue of *JJ*.

[3] In *JJ* no. 6, above, pp. 127–9.

[4] Pastry cooks used waste paper to wrap pies in; trunk-makers used it to line trunks and boxes. Both were convenient Augustan emblems of the fate in store for dull or unsold writings. See, for example, Dryden's *Mac Flecknoe*, vv. 100–1, and Pope's *Dunciad, In Three Books*, i. 136. Fielding defines both usages in *CGJ* no. 6 (21 January 1752), referring, in the latter case, to Hogarth's *Beer Street.*

Opinion of their own Works, not one would despair of the Court's Recommendation to the Public. The principal Consequence, he said, would be, that his Clients the Pastry-Cooks, &c. would be served at a cheaper rate.

The Court, conceiving this to be a Matter of great Moment, were unwilling to determine hastily, and therefore gave Day to the several Parties concerned in Interest, to wit, Thursday fortnight, when they will hear the Merits of the Cause on both sides.

After which the Court adjourned to Thursday next at 12 of the Clock.

SATURDAY, JANUARY 23, 1748. NUMB. 8.

Est iniqua in omni re accusanda, prætermissis bonis, malorum enumeratio, vitiorumque selectio.

Cicero, *De Legibus*, Book 3.[1]

Sir,

I agree with one of your Correspondents in your 5th Journal, in hoping that you will take upon you the Office of Criticism; or, in properer Words, will place yourself at the Head of *English* Critics. Indeed, to supervise and correct these Gentlemen is more closely connected with the Political Scheme than perhaps it appears to be at first Sight. The Spirit of Criticizing, and the Spirit of Opposition, are extremely alike; and the sour ill-natured Snarler, whose Pride and Pleasure it is to revile, very seldom, I believe, excepts the Government out of his Censures.

To say the Truth, I question whether the two Characters may not often concenter in one Person. When a Man becomes infamous in the higher Circle, and is, as it were, dethroned by the Public from his Patriot Tyranny, why may he not be supposed, like the famous *Sicilian* Tyrant of Old,[2] to condescend to exert the same Talents, and to vent the same Venom, in a lower Sphere? Thus probably the Political Snarler, who hath hiss'd at the

---

[1] *De Legibus*, III. ix. 24–6: 'in an attack on any institution it is unfair to omit all mention of its advantages, and enumerate only its disadvantages, picking out its special shortcomings' (Loeb).

[2] Perhaps most apposite to the career of Dionysius II, Sicilian tyrant of the fourth century B.C., who after surrendering Syracuse to Timoleon is said by some writers to have been reduced to supporting himself as a schoolteacher.

Government for many Years, when he can be no longer heard with Attention, turns the Edge of his Spleen another Way, and commences the Damner of Plays, and a Writer of Weekly Libels.

Nothing indeed seems easier than to run an exact Parallel between them.

First, then, if we examine the Matter well, we shall find these Snarlers in the Republic of Letters to be composed of the same Ingredients with their Fellow Labourers in the State. These are principally Ill-nature and Envy, and, above all, Disappointment; for as bad Authors, who have been disappointed in the Pursuit of Fame, or perhaps of something more substantial, are always the severest Critics on such of their cotemporary Writers as are in Possession of what they aimed at; so discarded, rejected, disappointed Statesmen are ever the bitterest Patriots.

The Reader will pardon my using the Word Patriot as well as Critic, in a very inadequate and improper Sense. The Persons who have, without any just Pretension, assumed these Characters, must answer for the disadvantageous Light in which they have placed these Words; and while I pursue such Impostors, none but themselves will represent me as endeavouring to derogate from the great Merit of those who, with equal Talents, fill up either Character; and these, I will venture to say, are commonly, in both Instances, the very Persons who are vilified and traduced by the Pretenders to each.

And as these pretended Patriots and Critics arise from the same Source, so they act in the same manner. The Business of both is apparently, and almost professedly, to find Fault. Is this the only Office of Criticism? Did *Aristotle*, *Horace*, *Quintilian*, or even *Scaliger*, the sourest of all good Critics,[1] write with such an Intention? Again, is it the Office of a Patriot only to censure and revile? Have the greatest and truest Patriots, either antient or modern, taken this Method of expressing their Love to their Country? There is perhaps scarce a Writer extant without some Degree of Merit; nor have we had, I am sure, within our Memory, any Minister who deserved no Commendation; yet what Praise ever flows from the Pen of a modern Critic, or of a modern Patriot? How contrary is such a Spirit to the amiable Temper of *Horace*.

---

[1] Cf. Swift, 'Battle of the Books', *Prose Works*, ed. Herbert Davis (Oxford, 1939), i. 161: '*Bentley* having spoken thus, *Scaliger* bestowing him a sower Look . . .'.

Nempe incomposito dixi pede, currere versus
Lucili. Quis tam Lucili Fautor inepte est
Ut non hoc fatiatur? at idem quod sale multo
Urbem defricuit Charta laudatur eadem.[1]

What can be fairer than this? On the contrary what more barbarous than to point out the Faults of an Author, or of a Man, to the World, and at the same time, by concealing their Excellencies, to insinuate that they have none. The World wants our Assistance more to enable them to discern what is lovely than what is odious; why then should we with-hold it from them? In God's Name let us speak out honestly, and set the good against the bad, that the Public may judge which preponderates. This would be a fair Method; and this Men would pursue, if Truth, and not Spleen, Rancour, Malice and Revenge guided their Pens.

Indeed, not only Truth and Justice require this, but even Policy seems to suggest it. This would carry at least an Appearance of Impartiality, and would gain the Ear and Attention of the Public; which never pays any Regard to the Censures of a Writer, when once it is known that his Purpose is only to blame and vilify; and what can be more manifest than this Purpose in Men who have attacked the present Administration during a Course of Years, and have never touched upon a single Excellence in the bright Characters of a *Pelham* or a *Hardwick*?[2]

Another most cruel Method practised by both the abovementioned Persons, is to condemn a Work or a Man as vicious, because they are not free from Faults or Imperfections. Whoever looks for any human Person, or any human Performance, absolutely perfect and without any Blemish, searches after

A faultless Monster which the World ne'er saw.[3]

[1] *Satires*, I. x. 1–4: 'To be sure I did say that the verses of Lucilius run on with halting foot. Who is a partisan of Lucilius so in-and-out of season as not to confess this? And yet on the self-same page the self-same poet is praised because he rubbed the city down with much salt' (Loeb). The accepted text reads *fateatur*.

[2] Philip Yorke (1690–1764), cr. Baron Hardwicke (1733), Lord Chancellor (1737–56), was attacked by the Opposition for his alleged harshness as the Lord High Steward at the trial of the rebel lords, and for his introduction of remedial legislation dealing with the 'heretable jurisdictions' in Scotland and with the disarming of the Highlands. Fielding had 'anticipated' Hardwicke's judicial mercy and probity, in *TP* no. 33 (17 June 1746), as reprinted in *The London Magazine*, xv (1746), 298.

[3] John Sheffield, Earl of Mulgrave, *An Essay upon Poetry* (1682), l. 235.

Paradise lost, the noblest Effort perhaps of human Genius, hath its Blemishes, which Mr. *Addison* finely compares to the Spots in a Map of the Sun.[1] Neither *Socrates* nor *Brutus* were without Faults, and some of the most admired Characters, both antient and modern, have had very glaring ones.

Horace will teach us to judge of Writings,

> ——*Ubi plura nitent in Carmine, non ego paucis*
> *Offendar Maculis——*.[2]

By the same Rule we must form our Judgment of Men. Candour, nay Humanity requires us to controll our Censures in this Manner. The snarling Critic who condemns the Works of his Cotemporaries if he can find any Faults in them, declares only that they are of human Original; and the virulent, raging, pretended Patriot, who exclaims against the Ministry because they reach not consummate Perfection, exclaims against them only because they are Men; or rather, I believe, to speak a plain honest Truth, *because they are Ministers.*

> I am, Sir,
> Yours, &c.
> CANDIDUS.

Mr. *Trott*,

I send you a Motto from *Horace*, which you may prefix to your inimitable Bill of Mortality.

> *Hic miseræ Plebi stabat commune sepulchrum,*
> *Pantolabo Scurræ, Nomentanoque nepoti.*[3]
> Yours

Mr. *Trott-plaid*,

Your gay Appearance at this Time is as surprizing and un-accountable, as it was unexpected; and the random Conjectures of the wondering World demonstrate that your *Jacobite Phyz* hath as much Political Mystery in it as your *Jacobite Principles.*

Some, that you have honoured with your weekly Visits, pretend that your Squireship makes this drunken Frolic in Memory of

---

[1] Cf. Addison, *Spectator* no. 303 (16 February 1712): 'I have seen in the Works of a Modern Philosopher, a Map of the Spots in the Sun.' The 'Philosopher' has not been identified.

[2] *Ars Poetica*, 351–2: 'when the beauties in a poem are more in number, I shall not take offence at a few blots' (Loeb).

[3] *Satires*, I. viii. 10–11: 'Here was the common burial-place fixed for pauper folk, for Pantolabus the parasite, and spendthrift Nomentanus' (Loeb).

the Affair of *Preston-Pans* and *Falkirk*;[1] but I think this a very idle Conjecture; these happy Scenes indeed might enlarge and open wide the Circumference of your Mouth for a Season, but the decisive Battle of *Culloden*[2] one would think must closely contract, if not for ever shut, it.

Others imagine, that the pleasing Effects of Riots and Horse-races are the Reasons of your Mirth and Jollity; but this is a Conjecture full as idle as the former; for in a Society where if one Member suffers, all the Members condole and suffer with him, how is it possible that such a *True Blue*[3] as Mr. *Trott* should madly rejoice at those unhappy Exploits that have brought the *Staffordshire Heroes* upon their Knees,[4] a Posture which no Jacobite ever made use of before, but in the mysterious Worship of toasting his Idol P—ce.

Your Friends, Sir, who must be allowed to understand the Reasons of your Mirth better than any of us, pretend that upon the falling off of some rotten Members,[5] you merrily christened them *Turn-coats*, and still continue to laugh at their Disgrace; but if the turning of a Coat, or the falling off of your Members be the true Source of your Mirth, I am persuaded that I shall see you merrier and merrier still; for even a *Jacobite* must allow, that if a Man has his Coat on with the wrong Side outward, all the World may justly pronounce him a Fool if he does not turn it. I therefore sincerely wish that you and your Party may never be a Day without the entertaining Mirth of a Turn-coat; and if in the general Defection your unerring Guide in the hempen-Girdle should forsake you, I hope you'll still be conducted the

---

[1] On 21 September 1745 the Young Pretender defeated Sir John Cope at Prestonpans (Gladsmuir) in the first major confrontation of the Jacobite uprising; on 17 January 1746 the Young Pretender defeated General Hawley at Falkirk, near Stirling, in the last significant rebel victory before the final withdrawal.

[2] See *JJ* no. 2, above, p. 99.

[3] Specifically applied to the Scottish Presbyterian party in the seventeenth century (in contradistinction to royalist 'red'), 'blue' was later affected by Tories and political conservatives in general as emblematic of their staunchness of principle.

[4] See *JJ* no. 1, above, p. 93, and note 2 there.

[5] Representatives of boroughs whose makeup had so decayed as to deprive them of any real constituency to represent, and hence, as the allusion implies here, of any responsibility to the voters, thereby making them more susceptible to defection. The 'falling off' referred to may have been the Prince of Wales' failure to secure the loyalty of a number of boroughs traditionally Tory in complexion; see Owen, *Rise of the Pelhams*, pp. 314–18. There was a further loss to the Opposition of a number of disputed elections which were adjudicated by Parliament after it reconvened in November 1747.

right Way by some other dexterous Gentleman of the Order of the Rope.

Llahnelle,[1] *Staffordshire,*
Jan. 11, 1747. PHILAROTHES.[2]

SATURDAY, JANUARY 30, 1748. NUMB. 9.

————*congestaque eodem*
Non bene junctarum Discordia semina Rerum.

Ovid.[3]

It may seem astonishing that there should be an Art in general Practice among us Moderns, to which no Language hath ever yet assign'd a Name. As I am necessitated therefore to give it an Appellation of my own, I shall call it the Art of Contrariety; or, if the Reader pleases, the Art of Forestroke and Backstroke; which latter Term may possibly convey the easiest Idea to the *English* Vulgar, as their favourite Exercise of Cudgel-playing must immediately place a very familiar Instance of it before their Eyes. By this Forestroke and Backstroke the ingenious Champion puts his Adversary beside his Guard, and commonly triumphs over a broken Head in a few Minutes.

Similar to this is the Practice of the sagacious Lawyer, who, as the Phrase is, *lays his Count different Ways*, either in a Declaration or an Indictment; that is, in plain *English*, charges the miserable Defendant with different Crimes before the Judge: Nor is he contented with this, but adds at last what he very properly calls a *Drag-Net*, a kind of summary Charge, which no Innocence can possibly escape.

The Physician is no less apprised of this wonderful Secret. He mixes up different Ingredients in the same Potion, that if the Doctor should unhappily miss the Disease, some at least of his contrariant Medicines may hit it.

My Reader will, I believe, easily suggest to himself Instances of the like Nature in most of the known Sciences and Professions:

---

[1] Anagrammatic of Ellenhall, a town in west central Staffordshire and here intended to represent unregenerate Jacobitism.

[2] From the Greek compound φιλο-ρόθος, a 'lover of tumult'.

[3] *Metamorphoses*, i. 8–9: 'and warring seeds of ill-matched elements heaped in one' (Loeb).

I shall therefore confine the Pursuit of this Subject to one Order (or indeed rather several Orders) of Men, who have lately instituted a new Science or Profession among us, which is at present well known by the Name of THE OPPOSITION. In this the above-mentioned Art is brought to the highest Degree of Perfection, to the no small Praise of those whose Labours have brought it to this Height, as it promises the most notable Advantages to our Party; nay, without it, indeed, the present Opposition could not subsist a Moment.

But by this Art Men of all Tempers are gained over to our Side. There are some among us of so *Quixottish* a Disposition to War, that they would never willingly sheath the Sword, till we were become Masters of the whole Trade of *France*; that is in other Words, till we had extirpated the *French* Nation. *Delenda est Gallia* is their Maxim,[1] and they would carry on the War *ad internecionem Gentis*, (to the Destruction of the one or the other People) without once considering which would be the likeliest to succeed. Again, there are others (and these I must say much the more reasonable Men of the two) who, with *Cicero*, prefer the most unjust Peace to the justest War.[2] Now what but the great Art of Contrariety, can engage these different Parties in our Favour? For if we, the Anti-ministerial Writers, apply ourselves to one Side of the Question only, let us belie the Administration never so heartily, it is manifest, that, in Proportion as we inflame some Men against them, we shall reconcile them to the Favour of others.

In the next Place, by this noble Art we take away all Power of Defence; for tho' neither of the contradictory Accusations may be true, yet an Answer to the one is a kind of tacit Admission of the other; at least we find it easy to insinuate this to the Public, whose Judgment of itself is sufficiently distracted with these different Censures. Thus if the Ministry, when abused for having involved us in the Miseries of War, answer, that they did not begin it; that they lament the Calamities it hath brought upon us, and the Ruin with which it threatens us, and are therefore desirous of putting an End to it;[3] we immediately turn our Accusation to

---

[1] Cf. *Delenda est Carthago*, the obsessive advice of Marcus Porcius Cato (234–149 B.C.), the Censor, to the Roman senate; Plutarch, 'Life of Marcus Cato', xxvii. 1.

[2] *Epistulae ad Familiares*, VI. vi. 5; see also *Letters to Atticus*, VII. xiv. 3.

[3] Cf. *Proper Answer*, pp. 73–4.

the direct Contrary, and libel them with endeavouring to procure a disadvantageous and dishonourable Peace.

But the greatest Use derived from this Art is, that by such Means, Men of all Characters, Principles, and Parties are able to join in an Opposition; or, to speak more truly, the Opposition is by this Art enabled to assume all the different and repugnant Principles of Men of all Denominations. Thus Jacobites and Republicans, Tories and Whigs, Churchmen and Dissenters, exclaim all at once against the Administration, throw out contradictory Abuses against Power, and all, from Motives directly opposite to each other, join in one common Opposition.

In short, this noble Art of abusing on both Sides of the Question is one of the highest Refinements in Policy; and may be truly called the greatest Improvement which this learned and sagacious Age hath produced. I do not, indeed, challenge to[1] the Times in which I live the total Honour of the Invention; but this I may fairly say, that we have (in Politics at least) abundantly added to the Discretion of our Forefathers, and have at present carried the Art to a Pitch, which it will be very difficult for those who come after us to exceed. I have already, in the Course of this Paper, done Honour to the many Labours of my Cotemporaries in this Way, particularly with regard to War and Peace. I shall now subjoin two Letters, which have led me into these uncommon Thoughts, and which will sufficiently both illustrate and prove all I have above advanced.

Thames-street,[2] *Jan.* 20, 1748.

Mr. *John Trott-Plaid,*

Sir,

Having observed that yours is the only political Paper regarded, have thought proper to advise you, on a Matter of great Consequence to the Public, *viz.* touching the Exportation of Wheats to *France* at this present.

If there be any Truth in the common Report upon 'Change, that such an Exportation will be permitted or connived at,[3]

---

1 'claim for', 'arrogate to'; an archaism (*OED*).

2 On the north bank of the Thames, extending from Puddle Dock, Blackfriars, to the Tower, it was a suitable address for an exporter of grains.

3 During January 1748 the London papers were full of speculation that at last the anomalous exportation of cereals ('corn') to France would be prohibited by law. On 26

what can we think of our M———y, which will thus supply the
Enemies of their Country with the Means of carrying on a
War with us; and will cast away an Advantage which Providence
seems to have given us over these Enemies; indeed, will relinquish
the only Means that may probably offer of bringing them to
Reason!

What can the most candid Man alive think of such a M———y,
but that they are blind, or supinely inattentive to the true Interest of the People?[1] But shall not we be justified in still severer
Censures, and in suspecting, that how dear soever the *French*
may pay for their Corn, the whole M——ey which it costs them
is not paid aboveb——rd?[2]

Do, Sir, be so good as to tell them, that whoever is concerned
in such an Exportation, or whoever hath the Power of preventing
it, and doth not, is a Tr——tor to his Country, and justly answer-
able for all the future Miseries which we may suffer in this
ruinous War.

I am,

Your humble Servant,

Thomas Urban.

N.B. You need not take any Notice of the Exportation of Wheat
to *Leghorn*,[3] in which self and Co. are concerned.

January the Commons passed a resolution, *nemine contradicente*, to the effect that 'the
Exportation of Corn to Foreign Parts is very beneficial to this Kingdom; and ought not to
be prohibited at this Time'; *Journals of . . . Commons*, xxv. 492.

[1] Cf. Coxe, *Pelham*, i. 386, quoting Newcastle to Sandwich, 29 January 1748: 'An un-
lucky accident has happened in the House of Commons, relative to the exportation of corn.
Some officious designing fools had given out, that in order to prevent carrying corn to
France, there must be a total prohibition of all exportation. The country gentlemen, and
some others, were so alarmed at this, that, without considering the consequences, or knowing what had passed in Holland, they came to a resolution against prohibiting the exportation of corn; but this is only general and cannot authorize the carrying it to France, which,
as all commerce is, is prohibited by the declaration of war. This has given me a good deal of
concern. . . .'

[2] For an example of the Opposition commonplace that the Administration was in some
way making a profit out of the proposed exportation of corn to France, see 'The Conjurors',
in *GM*, xviii (1748), 22, which alludes to the fortunes to be made by 'two *jobbers*', presumably the 'two Brothers', Newcastle and Pelham.

[3] The Tuscan seaport, from which, it is implied, the wheat might be clandestinely
transshipped to France or her allies.

To *Mr*. John Trot-Plaid, *Esq*;

Hampshire, *Jan*. 20, 1747–8.

Squire,

Tho'f[1] I am your Name-sake, I do not pretend to claim Kindred with so great a Gentleman as your Worship; but I hope you will be so kind as to publish this Letter, that it may be read by those whom it concerns.

Here is a Report in this Naybourhood, that a Proclamaytion is going to be against expurting Corn to *France*.[2] If this Repuort be true, what can we Varmers think of the Government, that will lay Taxes upon us, and prevent us at the same time of all the Meanes to pay um. When the Blessing hath sent this Scarcity of Corn among our Naybours, as it were, to help us off with what hath lain so long upon our Hands, would it not be the hardest Thing in the World, that we should be deprived of the only Meanes of paying both our Rent and our Taxes.

Varmer *Hogsworth*, who is a Government Man, and always votes on that Side, cannot help shaking his Head at this Matter. He zays, that the great Volks at Court pay no Consideration to the Good of the Land; and that, provided they can get Money in *London*, they care not a Brass Varden what becomes of all the Varmers in the Country. This he spoke last *Zunday* at Vestry; but a Squire in the Naibourhood, who is a Man of great Learning and Parts, told me privately that the true Reason why we must not be zuffered to zell our Corn into *France*, is, that it may be all saved in order to buy it afterwards cheap, and zend it to *Handhover*.

As you tell us that you are a Friend to the good old Cause, do, worthy Squire, abuse the Government about this Matter. Mahap you may frighten them from this Proclamation. Do tell um, that to prevent the Nation, and especially the poor Varmers, who want it more than any Bodi, vrom getting above a Million of Money in these bad Times,[3] is the direct Way to cause another Rebellion; for a Man had e'en as good be hanged as starved, and that must be the Consequence of shutting up the Corn in

---

[1] Here and in other 'dialect' letters (e.g., *JJ* no. 11, below, p. 156) Fielding uses this genuine dialect spelling of *though*. Cf. *Tom Jones*, VII. xiii.

[2] On 19 February 1748 George II issued a proclamation expressly forbidding trade with France 'without a licence in that behalf'; reprinted in *GM*, xviii (1748), 71.

[3] It was reported in the press that France had applied for permission to import 400,000 quarters of English wheat at £2. 10s. per quarter; *GM*, xviii (1748), 30.

our Barns, to be all defoured by a Parcel of *Handhover* Rats.[1]
So this is all at present from, Noble Squire,

Your Worship's humble Servant, to command,

George Trott.

Thus we see what notable Use the Art of Contrariety will draw
from every Event. The more difficult and problematical the
Question is, the easier will it be to make it a Handle of this two-
fold Abuse, which will operate both Ways with equal Success,
while the Matter is under Deliberation; and thus two opposite
Parties may, with a most admirable and commendable Cunning,
be wrought up to wish the Destruction of their Governors, while
these are breaking their Rest, and employing their utmost Care
and Endeavours to pursue all the Good, and to prevent all the
Evil apprehended by either Party.

Proceedings at the Court of Criticism, Thursday Jan. 28.

The great Cause between the Paper Manufacture and the Makers
of Trunks and Band-boxes came on, and after a full Hearing the
Court came to the following Resolution; That the Public may,
if they are willing to be imposed on, purchase other new Books
and Pamphlets, besides those recommended by this Court.

A Letter to *John Trott-Plaid*, Esq; from *Duncan Mac-Carte, a
Highlander*, concerning the History of *Thomas Carte*, an *Englishman*, was read;[2] and being found to contain Wit and Humour,

---

[1] One of the bits of evidence that Fielding might have been the author of *An Attempt
towards a Natural History of the Hanover Rat* (1744), an anonymous pamphlet attacking
the maintenance of the Hanoverian mercenaries; see Gerard E. Jensen, 'A Fielding Discovery', *Yale University Library Gazette*, x (1935), 23–32. It may seem curious that Fielding should call attention to his *volte face* on such a controversial issue, but cf. *Tom Jones*,
VI. xiv.

[2] *A Letter to John Trot-Plaid, Esq; Author of the* 'Jacobite Journal', *concerning Mr.
Carte's* 'General History of England', by 'Duncan MacCarte, a Highlander', was published *c.* 23 January 1748 by Mrs. Cooper; see *GA* of 23 January 1748. The *Dictionary of
National Biography* and Cross, ii. 88, attribute this ironic pamphlet to Samuel Squire.
However, it is not listed among Squire's works in the manuscript account of his life written
by his son, nor is it in the four-volume compilation of Squire's works (in the B.M.) to
which the manuscript account is prefixed. The *Letter* seems to have been confused with
another Cooper pamphlet of the same month, *Remarks on Mr. Carte's Specimen of his*
'General History of England', which is altogether more sober in tone and style. The latter
is advertised in *JJ* nos. 7 and 8. It is listed among Squire's works by his son's manuscript
account.

was ordered to be recommended.[1] And the said Book of *Thomas
Carte* the *Englishman* was ordered to be taken into Custody.[2]

Mr. *Addison*, to whom the Mythology and Fables of the
Antients, explained from History by the Abbé *Bannier*, lately
advertised in this Paper, was referr'd, reported to the Court that
he had read the same, and found the Character given the said
Work in the Advertisement to be strictly true.[3]

Ordered, That the said Mythology be strongly recommended
to the Public, as the most useful, instructive, and entertaining
Book extant.

The Court being informed that THE TOWN and the Playhouse
Managers attended without in the Entry, they were ordered to
attend on *Thursday* next, when the Managers of *Drury-Lane*[4]
were ordered to prepare themselves to shew Cause why Mrs.
Clive[5] (who in Comedy is certainly the best Actress the World

[1] The *Letter* itself alludes to issues of the *JJ* and, pp. 9–10, congratulates 'Trot-Plaid'
for his project.

[2] Thomas Carte (1686–1754), non-juring clergyman with a record of Jacobite involvement going back to 1715, published the first volume of his *General History of England*
(1747–55) on or about 1 January 1748; see *Remarks on Mr. Carte's Specimen* (1748), p. 49.
The *Letter to John Trot-Plaid*, p. 12, inquires if 'Trot-Plaid' has seen Carte's volume and,
p. 13, mockingly invites him to 'puff it'.

[3] The relevant paragraph of the advertisement, which first appeared in *JJ* no. 6, reads
as follows: 'This comprehensive Work, which may be justly called a Key to all the Classic
Authors, so greatly facilitates the rightly understanding those Authors, that nothing can be
a more proper Introduction to the Studies of Youth, nor indeed can be better calculated to
retrieve a true Classical Knowledge in such as have for a long Time disused and neglected it.
Lastly, no Book can be more pleasant or profitable to an unlearned Reader, as it may be
said to contain the very Marrow of all ancient History, with the most entertaining and
instructive Parts of which, it is of itself alone sufficient to make us acquainted.' See *JJ* no.
6, above, p. 127, n. 2.

[4] Since 9 April 1747, when they signed an agreement to be co-partners in the patent,
David Garrick (1717–79) and James Lacy (d. 1774); James Boaden, *Private Correspondence of David Garrick* (2 vols., London, 1831–2), i. 50–3. Lacy, who had been with
Fielding's company at the New Haymarket in the 1730s, was in charge of the Drury Lane
properties and wardrobe, and Garrick superintended the acting; Genest, *Some Account of
the English Stage* (Bath, 1832), iv. 228. Fielding and Garrick may have been friends as
early as 1740; see Charles B. Woods, 'The "Miss Lucy" Plays of Fielding and Garrick',
PQ, xli (1962), 299 and n. 10.

[5] Kitty Clive, née Catherine Raftor (1711–85), noted comedienne at Drury Lane during
Cibber's management, was one of Fielding's favourite actresses and the star of a number of
his plays, one of which (*The Intriguing Chambermaid*) he dedicated to her. Her predilection
for high-comedy roles may have been the occasion of a supposed quarrel between her and
Fielding; see 'Verses Occasion'd by a quarrel between Mr. Fielding and Mrs. Clive, on his
intending for her the part of the Bawd in his own Play called "The Wedding Day" ',
Works of . . . Sir Chas. Hanbury Williams, ed. Edward Jeffery (London, 1822), ii. 190. This
poem, which was first printed in *The Foundling Hospital for Wit*, No. I (1743), p. 1, repre-

ever produced) is excluded from any of her Parts, and particularly from that of the Lady *Lurewell*;[1] and why such a Part as that of *Tag* in *Miss in her Teens* is imposed upon her.[2]

(*Adjourned.*)

SATURDAY, FEBRUARY 6, 1748. NUMB. 10.

An cum Tibicines iique qui fidibus utuntur, suo, non multitudinis Arbitrio, Cantus modulantur, vir sapiens, multo arte majore præditus, non quid rectum sit, sed quid velit vulgus, exquiret?

Cicero.[3]

Sir,

One principal Reason of that universal Contempt with which the Labourers against the Government are at present received by the Public, may possibly arise from that visible Partiality in their Writings observed by one of your late Correspondents: For, as he well remarks, "the World seldom gives much Attention to a Critic when they have once discovered that he desires and designs only to find fault."[4]

To avoid this Error therefore, and in order to make some very rank Abuse which I intend to cast on the Ministry the more palatable to my Reader, I shall introduce it with a short Declaration in their Favour.

sents Mrs. Clive as priding herself on 'the lady's part'; cf. *JJ* no. 10, below, p. 152-3, and *Tom Jones*, IX. i.

¹ A role in *The Constant Couple; or, A Trip to the Jubilee* (1700) by Farquhar. For its first performance in the season of 1747-8 Mrs. Clive played Lady Lurewell (24 October 1747), but was replaced in succeeding performances by Mrs. Pritchard; see *London Stage*, Part 4, i. 12, 17, 27, 44.

² At the Drury Lane première of this controversial farce by Garrick the role of 'Tag', which during the preceding season at Covent Garden had been the property of Mrs. Pritchard, was taken by Mrs. Clive (24 October 1747); *London Stage*, Part 4, i. 12. According to a hostile review in *The Anatomist and New Regulator* of 31 January 1747, the actress who plays 'Tag' is 'the most to be pitied; if it is a disagreeable task to be brought upon the stage for no other purpose than—*to talk bawdry*'; reprinted in *GM*, xvii (1747), 72.

³ *Tusculan Disputations*, V. xxxvi. 104: 'Are flute-players and harpists to follow their own tastes, not the tastes of the multitude in regulating the rhythm of music, and shall the wise man, gifted as he is with a far higher art, seek out not what is truest, but what is the pleasure of the populace?' (Loeb). The conventional reading has *numerosque moderantur* for *modulantur*, and *verissimum* for *rectum*. Fielding uses the passage as the motto of *TP* no. 19 (4-11 March 1746).

⁴ A curiously inexact quotation from *JJ* no. 8, above, p. 137: 'the Public; which never pays any Regard to the Censures of a Writer, when once it is known that his Purpose is only to blame and vilify'.

First then I do agree with the Author of a modern Pamphlet* "that in the large Circle of the present Administration are to be found the Men of the largest Property, of the longest Experience in Business, of the brightest, and of the most solid Parts, of the highest Reputation for Knowledge and Learning, and of the most acknowledged Integrity in private Life."[1]

I do agree that for such a Body of Men as this to conspire together to ruin or injure their Country, *i.e.* to ruin or injure themselves, is so morally IMPOSSIBLE, that as there is scarce a Degree of Folly capable of believing, so one would think there should be no Degree of Impudence equal to the asserting so monstrous and absurd a Falshood; for the worst or weakest of Men do not wade through the deepest Mire of Villainy or Folly without a Motive.

On the contrary, I agree, and so must every honest Man in his Senses, that the present Administration hath struggled hitherto through Difficulties which cannot be paralleled in History. They found this Nation at their Access to Power immerged in an immense Debt,[2] and torn and divided with Faction, a mad Man pushing by every Method to reinstate himself in Power,[3] many Parties endeavouring to set their Country in a Blaze, hoping from its Ashes to produce each his own favourite pernicious Scheme of Government; all the Heads of these Parties satisfied with the highest Probability of public Ruin, provided they could but discern the lowest Probability of converting it to their own private Interest; and the whole Body of the People debauched with Luxury and Licentiousness; their Resentments fired with imaginary Grievances, their Hopes raised with vain Expectations, surfeited with Ease, and desirous of Change.

---

* *A Dialogue between a Gentleman and an Alderman.*

[1] Cf. *Dialogue*, p. 46: 'I will be bold to say, that if you look for the Men of the largest Property, of the longest Experience in Business, of the brightest, and of the most solid Parts, of the highest Reputation for Knowledge and Learning, of the most acknowledged Integrity in private Life, you will find them in this Administration.'

[2] After the resignation of Granville (Carteret) in November 1744 the new 'Broad Bottom' coalition confronted a National Debt estimated variously from £53,679,247 (*Journals of . . . Commons*, xxv. 53) to £56,967,689 (*State of the Nation for the Year 1747, and respecting 1748* [London, 1747], p. xi). See also *Proper Answer*, above, p. 76, n. 4.

[3] Alluding to the supposed machinations of Granville, whose influence with George II remained powerful enough to vex the Pelhamites until after the failure of the 'forty-eighthour ministry' in February 1746. See *Dialogue*, above, p. 19, n. 1.

Under these and other dreadful Circumstances at home, they found this wretched Nation engaged in a War with a most powerful Enemy; they found this War undertaken and carried on against a Force greatly superior to our own Strength, and that of our Allies, all of whom were weak, some of them indifferent, and those who were most in earnest, were pursuing Interests separate from that of the common Cause.[1]

In this War they found the Debt of the Nation encreasing, our Reputation sinking, our Credit in Danger, our Outworks mouldering away into the Hands of our Enemy,[2] Rebellion within holding the Sword to our Throats, and Invasion hourly threatning us from without.

In such a Situation, what but the highest Love for their Country, and the justest Sense of the great Stakes they themselves had in it, could have emboldened any Men to attempt our Preservation! What but the highest Abilities, the greatest Prudence and Firmness, could have enabled them, or can still enable them, to preserve us!

Though this Picture, I solemnly declare, hath not to my Knowledge a flattering Feature, yet it must be allowed by all the Friends to the Administration, to have done them Justice; I hope therefore I shall be thought impartial when I proceed, as I now will, to lay open their Faults with the same Freedom.

Here then let me ask this honest Administration, why they do not put an immediate End to this ruinous War?

That the War is ruinous, and may probably end in our Destruction is apparent; nay this is admitted by their best Friends; for the Proof of which I need only refer myself to a Pamphlet lately published, entituled *The Case restated,* &c. which in plain Language delivers this certain Truth.[3]

The only Answer which the Ministry, if they would completely defend themselves, can make to this accusatory Question is, That they could obtain no Peace; but the contrary of this is known, nay the Pamphlet last above cited asserts, that *France* hath offered not only an honourable Peace, but what every

---

[1] Cf. *Dialogue,* pp. 34–7.
[2] Cf. *Dialogue,* pp. 35–6, and *Proper Answer,* pp. 74–5, for similarities of phrase.
[3] *The Case Re-stated; or, An Examine of a late Pamphlet, intitled* 'The State of the Nation for the Year 1747' (London, [n.d.]), pp. 49–50. This Cooper imprint is listed among the January 1748 books by *GM,* xviii (1748), 48.

reasonable Man must allow to be, in our present Situation, as desirable and as advantageous on our Side, as we ought to expect she should either offer or accept.[1] Why hath not this Peace been embraced?

That we have been hitherto victorious in this War must not be pretended; for then we must retract all the Abuse that we have cast on the Ministry for the Conduct of it. Now if we have been unsuccessful, what can we hope or desire more than to conclude the War by restoring all things to that Situation in which they were when it begun?

Can we imagine that *France*, the more she enlarges her Conquests will be the more generous in her Concessions? Should she (as most probably she will if the War continues) add *Holland* to her own Dominions, will she be as ready to resign that Province, as she hath been to resign *Flanders*?[2] Or will she give up both upon better Terms than she hath already offered to give up one?

This will appear surely too absurd a Confidence, and will be denied. Are we then to expect, till we have humbled our Enemies to our Wish, and beaten them into such Concessions as Policy will better than Humanity countenance us in exacting? Shall we never sheathe the Sword till we have first plunged it into the Heart's-Blood of *France*, and have possess'd ourselves of all her Trade, (as the Author of the *State of the Nation* hath it)[3] and of all her Towns, which we shall be Masters of at the same Time.

This is going a Step farther in Madness than Don *Quixote* himself; for tho' perhaps, a few Years ago, the Knight might, with his Brother *Gr——le*[4], have thought himself equal to the Conquest of *France*, he would certainly have learnt Wisdom from

[1] *Case Re-stated*, p. 53, refers to 'such Overtures of Peace made to us by *France*, as might be embraced even in a successful War'. For the so-called Saxe-Ligonier overtures after the battle of Laffeldt see General Introduction above, p. xxxvii, and Lodge, *Studies*, pp. 267–304.

[2] As early as the summer of 1747 France had indicated a willingness to restore all conquests in the Netherlands; B.M. Add. MS. 32711, f. 589, as cited by Lodge, *Studies*, p. 268 and note.

[3] *State of the Nation for the Year 1747, and respecting 1748* (London, 1747), pp. 24, 30–2. This anonymous pamphlet, which was published during December 1747, appears to derive from the *State of the Nation Consider'd*, announced in *GM*, xvii (1747), 52, as a January 1747 publication. The latter pamphlet was frequently attributed to Granville, as Fielding, in his next paragraph, seems also to do with the former.

[4] The comparison of Granville with Quixote was apparently a commonplace; see the *Westminster Journal* of 13 February 1748, reprinted in *GM*, xviii (1748), 77; also *JJ* no. 45, below, p. 405.

Experience; and would have concluded, e'er this, that he had been enchanted, and that the Adventure had been reserved for some other Knight.

Sure our Ministry cannot reason in this Manner. What then; will they say that, sensible as they are of the Necessity of making Peace, and of the Happiness of doing this, upon tolerable Terms, they still refuse it for fear, lest a Set of Incendiaries should endeavour by misrepresenting their Measures, to enflame the People against their Preservers, and to make them as angry with those who put a final End to this War, as they were formerly taught to be with the Administration which declined the Beginning it?

But how weak an Apprehension is this! Can we believe that a People, who have so sufficiently suffered for that Delusion into which they were then led, will be so soon liable to be again deceived?

With how much greater Ease will these Incendiaries be able, should we be unsuccessful in the ensuing Campaign, to inflame the Nation against those who concurr'd in the Continuance of the War? To them will be imputed any Infidelity or Weakness in our Allies, the Chances of War, nay, the very Accidents of Wind and Weather.

Have our present Ministry so little Experience in these public Incendiaries, as to hope from any Conduct to silence their Invectives; or do they want still more Experience of the Contempt, with which such Invectives are received by the People?

But I will admit that it was in their Power to do all the Mischief their rancorous Hearts desire; that two or three of the lowest Inhabitants of *Grub-street*, abetted and encouraged by some who ought to be shut up in *Bedlam*, and by others who deserve a more ignominious Confinement, should be able to raise a Storm, which should become dangerous to a Minister, nay, which should overwhelm him, while he is pursuing the Good, nay the Preservation of his Country;[1] I hope still there will be found in the present

----

[1] In thus adumbrating the issue of the liberty of the press Fielding may have been responding to Opposition charges that the ministry contemplated some restraints. *OE* of 28 November 1747 initiated a series of six leaders on the subject; see General Introduction above, p. lxix, and the 'Court of Criticism' in *JJ* no. 15, below, p. 198. Coincidentally, on the day of the present issue of the *JJ* (6 February 1748) Chesterfield suddenly resigned the seals as Secretary of State for the Northern department. His resignation, which was the result of an irreparable breach with Newcastle and in no sense chargeable to political journalism,

Administration a Spirit equal to the glorious Attempt. Ease and Safety are the Rewards of private Virtues, and the Blessings of a private Station; of public Virtues, the Rewards are Tomb-stones, Monuments, and every Honour which Posterity, in Verse and Prose, can fix on the Memory of Heroes and Patriots. Rewards so great and glorious, that they can only be purchased by Care and Fatigue, by Difficulty and Danger, with the Slander of all the Vile, the Foolish, the Wicked, and the Mad. Thus says *Horace*, speaking of the Peace-making Worthies of old:

> *Romulus et Liber Pater et cum Castore Pollux,*
> *Post ingentia facta Deorum in Templa recepti*
> *Dum Terras Hominumque colunt Genus,* ASPERA BELLA
> COMPONUNT, *&c.*
> *Ploravere suis non respondere Favorem*
> *Speratum Meritis.*[1]

And such Rewards, however dearly they may be purchased, I will venture to assure that Person who shall give a tolerable Peace to this bleeding Country.

Proceedings at the Court of Criticism, Thursday Feb. 4.

After hearing Council for and against the Managers of *Drury-Lane*, the Court came to the following Resolutions.

1. That the Part of *Tag* in *Miss in her Teens*, is a much better Part than that of Lady *Lurewell*; and that the whole Play of the *Trip to the Jubilee* is a wretched Performance, and ought to be banish'd from the Stage.

2. That the true Reason why Mrs. *Clive* hath been less liked in the Characters of fine Ladies than in others,[2] hath been, that these Characters being monstrous Pictures of Affectation, without

had been rumoured even before the 1747 elections; see Walpole to Mann, 5 June 1747 (*Yale Walpole*, xix. 412), and Newcastle to Bedford, 14 January 1748 (*Bedford Correspondence*, i. 308), cited by Lodge, *Studies*, p. 307 n.

[1] *Epistles*, II. i. 5–10: 'Romulus, father Liber, Pollux and Castor, who, after mighty deeds, were welcomed into the temples of the gods, so long as they had care for earth and human kind, settling fierce wars . . . lamented that the goodwill hoped for matched not their deserts' (Loeb).

[2] Cf. *A Letter of Compliment to the ingenious Author of a Treatise on the Passions* (London, 1747), p. 33: 'Mrs. C—E, who has had her share of Popularity, and once was esteem'd the PHAENIX of the Age, seems now to be of little Consequence; her Laurels are all wither'd; her Friends grown cold; and the repeated Acclamations that us'd to welcome her Appearance, are now no more.' *GM*, xvii (1747), 156, lists the *Letter* among the March 1747 books.

Wit, Humour, or Nature, have given her no Opportunity of exerting her great Talents for true Comedy, or of answering the great Expectation which the Audience always entertain from her Performance: And that if ever she fails of pleasing, it is owing to the Author, and not to herself.

3. That the Business of an Actor, as well as of a Writer, is to copy Nature, and not to imitate the Excellencies of their Predecessors: That Mr. *Garrick*, Mr. *Quin*,[1] Mrs. *Cibber*,[2] Mrs. *Clive*, and Mrs. *Woffington*,[3] are all, in their several Capacities, Examples of this Merit.

4. That the Audience be at Liberty to carry Books to the Theatre; and that whenever an Actor presumes to add Conceits of his own to his Part, any one of the said Audience may hiss him off the Stage.

5. That by over-acting a Part, true Comedy is turned to Farce, and Tragedy into Burlesque. And that this Fault, if ever so little given way to, soon becomes incurable; and the Actor is afterwards fit only for *Bartholomew* Fair,[4] or to give Tea.[5]

---

[1] James Quin (1693–1766), actor at both Covent Garden and Drury Lane, was a great rival of Garrick's at the former theatre during the 1745–6 and 1746–7 seasons. According to Genest, *Some Account of the English Stage*, iv. 247, Quin 'had retired to Bath in disgust at Garrick's success'; he seems to have given only two performances at Covent Garden during the 1747–8 season; see *London Stage*, Part 4, i. 5. Quin had acted in Fielding's *Universal Gallant* (1735), and the latter's numerous references to him are laudatory; see Dudden, i. 375–6, and *Joseph Andrews*, p. 262 n.

[2] Susannah Maria Cibber (1714–66), married to (1734) and separated from (1738) Fielding's old antagonist Theophilus Cibber; opera singer and tragic actress, in 1747–8 she was a member of the Drury Lane company. In *Tom Jones*, ix. i, Fielding groups Garrick with Mrs. Cibber and Mrs. Clive ('these two most justly celebrated Actresses') as having 'all formed themselves on the Study of Nature only; and not on the Imitation of their Predecessors'.

[3] Margaret Woffington (*c.* 1714–60), Irish-born actress, engaged by Rich for Covent Garden (1740), later (and in 1748) with the Drury Lane company, acted in Fielding's *The Wedding Day* (1743); referred to favourably in his modernization of 'Part of the sixth Satire of *Juvenal*' in the *Miscellanies* (1743), 93, to which she, Garrick, and Clive were all subscribers.

[4] One of the oldest fairs in London, Bartholomew Fair ran from the last Wednesday to the last Saturday of August, in Smithfield. Although leading players from the London stage set up booths at the fair and put on 'old favorites', the fair was chiefly noted for its pantomimes, juggling acts, rope-dancing, and the like. Here Fielding uses it as a symbol of vulgar, overstated acting mannerisms, and the last resort of the failing actor.

[5] Samuel Foote (1720–77), actor, dramatist, and in 1747 Fielding's distant successor as manager of the 'New' Haymarket, evaded the provisions of the Licensing Act by advertising his frequently libellous mimicries of living persons as concerts, auctions, 'diversions': 'At the request of several Persons who are desirous of spending an Hour with Mr. Foote, but find the Time inconvenient, instead of Chocolate in the Morning, Mr. Foote's Friends are

6. That an Actor of *Drury-Lane* Theatre be privately admonished of both these Imperfections;[1] and acquainted, that if he doth not reform, he will shortly be apprehended, and publicly tried for the same at this Court.

7. That Mr. *Garrick* be discharged from the Accusation brought against him;[2] and that he do receive the Thanks of this Court for his great Improvement of our Theatrical Entertainments, not only by his own inimitable Performance; but by his proper Regulations of the Theatre under his Direction.[3]

It was then moved, that Mr. *Rich* might be admonished for suffering private Characters to be ridiculed by Mimickry and Buffoonry upon his Stage.[4]

Resolved, that all such Mimickry is indecent, immoral, and even illegal; and Mr. *Rich* was admonish'd accordingly.

One *Horse-piss*, alias *Horse-dung*, alias *Horse-lie*, alias THE FOOL,[5] was convicted of Scurrility, and received Sentence of CONTEMPT.

The Trial of Mr. *Carte's* History was appointed for this Day Fortnight.

(Adjourned.)

desir'd to drink a Dish of Tea with him, at half an Hour after Six in the Evening'; *GA* of 1 June 1747, as reprinted in *London Stage*, Part 3, ii. 1314. See also Mary Megie Belden, *The Dramatic Work of Samuel Foote* (Yale Studies in English, lxxx, New Haven, Conn., 1929), pp. 50–8, and, for Fielding's relations with him during 1748, *JJ* no. 22, below, pp. 261–6.

[1] Not identified. For a list of the actors employed by the Drury Lane during the 1747–8 season see *London Stage*, Part 4, i. 3.

[2] In *JJ* no. 9, above, p. 146.

[3] Fielding may be attempting here to support Garrick against various charges of mismanagement at Drury Lane. See, for example, *A Letter to Mr. Garrick, on his having purchased a Patent for Drury Lane Play-House* (June 1747); *Mr. Garrick's Conduct as Manager . . . Consider'd in a Letter Address'd to Him* (October 1747); and especially *D—ry L—ne P—yh—se Broke Open. In a Letter to Mr. G.* (February 1748). Cf. *JJ* no. 11, below, p. 162.

[4] John Rich (1692–1761), actor, pantomimist, manager of Lincoln's Inn Fields (1714–32) and Covent Garden (1732–61), an old competitor of Fielding's and a present one of Garrick's, is here berated for permitting Foote, a member of the Covent Garden company, to put on satirical performances like 'Tea' as afterpieces in that theatre. Foote's earliest performance of 'Tea' at Covent Garden was on 11 November 1747; his most recent on 3 February 1748. See *London Stage*, Part 4, i. 13–17, 20–2, 26–8, where a total of 18 performances before February 6 is listed.

[5] 'The Fool', an essay series originating in the *Daily Gazetteer* as an expression of that paper's editorial views, appeared in a collected edition in January 1748; see *GM*, xviii (1748), 48. By *Horselie* Fielding evidently meant William Horsley, a writer on economic subjects and translator (1753) of *The Universal Merchant*; see Robert L. Haig, *The Gazetteer, 1735–1797* (Carbondale, Ill., 1960), p. 21, where the attribution to Horsley is credited to a reported manuscript memorandum in Alexander Chalmers's copy of *The Fool*.

SATURDAY, FEBRUARY 13, 1748.　　　　NUMB. 11.

Fælix qui propriis ævum transigit in Arvis;
Ipsa Domus puerum quem videt, ipsa senem.
Non freta Mercator timuit, non classica miles,
Non rauci lites pertulit ille fori.
Indocilis rerum, vicinæ nescius urbis.

Claudian.[1]

Tho' the following Letter comes a little too late for the Occasion, I cannot forbear giving it a Place in my Paper, as it breathes that honest hearty *English* Spirit, which distinguishes the Country Gentlemen of this Island from all other People in the World. I have often thought what a glorious Nation we should be, if we could once see a Majority in our Senate of this kind of Men; for if Honesty be the best Policy, we should then be the ablest of all Politicians.

I am sorry, however, to premise, that as the Naturalization Bill was not supported by the Ministry,[2] I could not possibly abuse them on that Account. I know, indeed, it is usual with some of our Party not only to misrepresent those Measures in which the Administration are really concerned, but to libel them for Schemes which never once entered into their Head. This is doubtless a commendable Zeal, and hath often produced very wholesome Effects; but it is never wisely extended to Matters of public Notoriety; for tho' L—ng is a Quality absolutely necessary for the Support of the present poor Opposition, yet we should take care never to advance such Lies as every Reader is capable of contradicting.

Thus then runs the Letter, in the very Words of the Writer.

---

[1] *Shorter Poems*, xx (lii), 1–2, 7–9: 'Happy he who has passed his whole life mid his own fields, / he of whose birth and old age the same house is witness./ . . . He was never a trader to fear the seas nor a soldier to dread the trumpet's call; / never did he face the noisy wrangles of the courts' (Loeb). The accepted text reads *transegit* and *tremuit* (for *timuit*).

[2] On 4 December 1747 a Bill for naturalizing foreign Protestants was brought into the Commons for a first reading. The Bill was designed to supply certain manpower defects occasioned by the war and to encourage certain branches of manufacture. On 16 December the City of London petitioned against it, and Pelham, unwilling to alienate the monied interests, 'professed to take no interest in the fate of the bill, though he approved the general principle'; Coxe, *Pelham*, i. 386–7. On 4 February 1748 the Bill was read for a second time and defeated; see *Journals of . . . Commons*, xxv. 459, 499; Hansard, xiv. 133–48; *GM*, xvii (1747), 590.

Trott-Plaid,

Are you asleep? What, not a Word of the NATURALATION Bill? Is the Devil in you to let *slep* so fair an Opportunity of abusing the *Ministry*? Have not all the News-writers bin at them with your *Hightalicks* about bringing in a Set of *rascally Forenners* to underwork the poor *English*? A *Pack* of *Dogs* that can live on an *Inion* or a *Turnup*, and will be glad to work for *Dripence* a Day, when a poor *Englishman* in this Time of *Taxses* can hardly support himself for a Shillin. D—n all *Forenners*. Is this a Time, says Sir *John Bumper*, to *bring overzee* a Set of *ragged Muffins*, when they be at War with us, od rot em and confound em, to ete up all the *Remanes* of *English* Beef now the Distemper too is among us.[1] Who knows, cries Tom *Toastaway*, but that the King of *France* may naturize his hole Army, and so cut all our Throtes; but an if he dus unt, there be others that may; put that in *Hightalicks, there be others that may.* What do Forenners come over here for but after the Riches of *Old England*? and thof[2] they be never so ragged when they come over here, then they soon grow rich; for they tell me there's a hardly a poor Man in all *Spittle Fields*,[3] thof I am sure we haf poor enuff in the Country.—So poor they are, that I can't get a Man who can afford to go to Day-Labour under a Shillin a Day.[4] If you don't abuse the *Ministry* for this I shall think you are a *Com over*.[5] Its a thing impossible you shud ever haf a better *Handel*. Stick to the Point; do but put in some-

---

[1] Distemper among the horned cattle had been a serious problem for some years. On 13 February 1746 George II gave the royal assent to a Bill making regulations to prevent the spreading of the distemper; *GM*, xvi (1746), 105. On 5 February 1747 it was felt necessary to strengthen the Act of 1746, and Orders in Council, stipulating particular measures for dealing with the disease locally, were issued from time to time throughout 1748; *Journals of . . . Commons*, xxv. 274, and *GM*, xviii (1748), 41, 91, 137.

[2] See *JJ* no. 9, above, p. 144 and note 1 there.

[3] Spitalfields, a London district taking its name from St. Mary's Hospital, outside Bishopsgate, was settled, after the Revocation of the Edict of Nantes, by French Protestant silk-weavers, who founded there the English silk industry, as was pointed out by the supporters of the naturalization Bill during the debates in Commons; Hansard, xiv. 136.

[4] Arthur Young, *A Six Months' Tour through the North of England* (London, 1770), i. 445–6, estimated the general average prices of day labour from 7*s*. 2*d*. to 5*s*. 8*d*., depending on the distance from London. Fielding's figure is shockingly, deliberately low, a reflection on the character of the letter writer and on one of the principal arguments in favour of the naturalization Bill, viz. that the health of the national economy depended greatly upon a 'frugal' and 'parsimonious' work force; Hansard, xiv. 137–40.

[5] One who practises a dodge or trick, or tries to impose by craft. *OED* cites no use as substantive.

thing about Forenners that's enuf. Confound em, *Old England* never gets any Good by em. Why do we meddle or make with their Matters? why don't we zend out a great *Vleet* and vetch home all their Tread among ourselves, as a Book called *The State of the Nation* advises us to do?[1] When we have got all their *Tread* and their Ships let um vite it out in *forren Parts* as long as they please, what's that to us? If we haf got once hold of all their Ships, they can never come over hither. Never tell me of a Parcel of *Duch* Sons of *B——s*. Let the King of *France* haf um, they deserve no better. What signifies it to us when we have got Possession of all their *Tread*, as the Book says; and I know a Naybour of mine who thinks it would be better for us if *Holland* was once concurred than not. For then he says we should have all the Herrin Fishery to ourselves. But I suppose this *Naturalation* Bill was to have brout a Parcel of *Duchmen* upon us if they be *concurrd* in their own Land, to ete up ours, and to take the *Tread* out of the Mouths of our own Peple after we have bin at the Truble to vetch it from abroad. But I hope *Old England* will be too hard vor um all; and as every *Englishman* can beat *dre* o um, I hope they shant always get the better o us by their *Treats* as they say they do. A true *Englishman* would scorn to be *treated* by any o um. Let us once get all their Tread, I desire no more. Never till then shall we have a good Piece, says the Book *about the State of the Nation*,[2] and therefore I never would make a Peice before that Time. What signifies if we owe thirty or forty Millions more, as the Book says; when a Man's once in vor the Plate, what signifies its going a little varder. If we can raise Muny without a Lan-tax, I don't care a hapenny. I don't care vor parting with a Zum at once; but as vor twopence or *dripence* the more in a Commodity, I falue it as little as another. As vor a new Window-Tax, I falue it not of a Rush.[3] I put out one haf

---

[1] See *JJ* no. 10, above, p. 150 and note 3.

[2] *State of the Nation for the Year 1747*, p. 31.

[3] The 1747 Act imposing a window tax (20 Geo. II, cap. 3) charged houses having 10–14 windows at 6*d*. per window, those having 15–19 windows at 9*d*. per window, and those with 20 or more at 1*s*. per window; *Statutes at Large*, xix. 2–18. According to the report of the tax commissioners, 'The general Practice of Stopping up Windows and Lights hath likewise been one of the greatest Prejudice to this Revenue, as the same hath been done only with loose Bricks or Boards, which may be removed at Pleasure, or with Mud, Cow-dung, Mortar, and Reeds, on the Outside, which are soon washed off with a Shower of Rain, or with Paper or Pasteboard on the Inside, to evade the Payment of these Duties'; *Journals of . . . Commons*, xxv. 561. A further broadening of the tax base and a tightening of the

of my Windows last Year, and if there comes another Ile put out t'other haf.——D—n me a Man may drink in the Dark, and mayhap he may then be the buolder in toasting honest Healths. If it be vor the Good of *Old England*, let um raise what Muny they will, zo that the Taxes bent burdensum, as they call it, to *Tread*, nor the *landed Interest*. I am too true a Hart ever to grumble about it. I have a good 1500 l. a Year; and the *landed Interest* and *Tread* are all that I am concerned for; let us keep out all Forenners, and take away all their Tread, I desire no more.

Write therefore, honest *Trott-Plaid*, about this Matter of *Naturalation*, and give um zum *Stingers* about *Forenners*; and don't forget HANNOVER RATS;[1] for I promise you I've a zeed um, and larger Rats they be than ever were a zeed in *England*, till of late Years; and they tell me several Ship-loads have been brought over directly from *Hannover*. I am,

> *Dear* Trott,
> *Thine very heartily,*
> Humphry Gubbins.[2]

Dear Trott,

Tho' I have always called myself only a Tory, I am a hearty Well-wisher to the Jacobite Scheme; but I have terrible Scruples about reconciling Rebellion against the present Government to the Doctrine of Passive Obedience and Non-Resistance.

I wish therefore, for my Sake, as well as for the Sake of many others, who can scarce have avoided seeing this Objection, you would inform us by what Method you yourself got over this Difficulty; and how many Ages the Crown must have remained under any Settlement, or in any Family, before the Royal Family obtains hereditary Right.

I hope you will give us full Satisfaction on this Point; for it would be very hard to be hang'd and d—n'd too for any Principle.

> *Your humble Servant,*
> Tory Rory.[3]

---

regulations were introduced in the Commons in March 1748 and passed into law at the close of session on 13 May; *Journals of . . . Commons*, xxv. 564, 581, 658.

[1] See *JJ* no. 9, above, p. 145 and note 1.

[2] *OED, s.v.* 'Gubbins', gives (a) fish parings or fragments; (b) a contemptuous name formerly given to inhabitants of a district near Dartmoor, who had a reputation for primitivism. *CGJ* no. 32 (21 April 1752) has a letter signed 'Humphry Gubbin'.

[3] Roaring, uproarious, boisterous, with an allusion to the political party. *OED* cites only adjectival and adverbial usages.

Sir,

Jacobitism is not founded on Argument.

Yours,

John Trott-Plaid.

To the Author of the Jacobite Journal.

Sir,

You have very facetiously ridiculed the News-Writers for troubling the Public with the Marriages and Deaths of People of no manner of Consequence; but there is a worse Custom than this, and that is the publishing of Treaties of Marriage between Persons of the first Rank, often with little or no Foundation.

Besides the Offence which this sometimes gives to the nice Delicacy of a young Lady of Fashion, it may possibly do her a real Injury.

Be pleased therefore to desire these Writers, for the future, never to insert that any young Lady is married 'till they are sure of the Fact, unless it be one of those whose Names no more than their great Beauty, Merit, and Fortune,[1] were ever heard of before.

I am, Sir,

Yours, &c.

Proceedings at the Court of Criticism, Thursday Feb. 11.

The Court heard a Cause between the Corporation of *Grub-street*, Plaintiff, and the Corporation of *Billingsgate*, Defendant, concerning the Property of a late Pamphlet intitled, *A Critical Address,* &c.[2] in which it was set forth, on the Behalf of the Plaintiff, that the Corporation of *Grub-street* had, from time immemorial, a Right to claim all low, scandalous Invectives, without the least Wit, Humour, Argument, or Fact; and then they proceeded to give undeniable Proof, that the aforesaid Pamphlet contained such Invectives, and that there were only two Facts charged on the Ministry, *viz.* Attempting to take away the Liberty of the Press, and to naturalize Foreign Protestants,

---

[1] Cf. p. 4 of the original issue of *JJ* no. 11: 'MARRIED. Mess. —— —— all eminent, to the Misses —— —— very agreeable young Ladies of great Beauty, Merit, and Fortune.'

[2] *A Critical, Expatiatory, and Interesting Address to a Certain Right Honorable Apostate* (London, [n.d.]) is listed by *GM*, xviii (1748), 96, among the books for February 1748.

both which were notoriously false.[1] It was farther urged, that the said Pamphlet was a mere Catch-penny; and in order to cheat the Public by raising it to the Price of a Shilling, the Pages were number'd to 51; whereas, in Fact, it contain'd but 42;[2] all which were said to be certain Proofs of its belonging to *Grub-street*.

The Defendant on the contrary urged, that when these Invectives proceeded to the Use of opprobrious Terms, and to downright calling Names, such Works had always been adjudged to be the Property of *Billingsgate*. And the Court being of that Opinion, they proceeded to read in Evidence Page the 2d (in Print the 11th)[3] unparalleled Perfidy, *pretended* Friends, Corruption, lamentable Degeneracy, Public Calamity. Page 3d. Domestic Grievances, iniquitous Schemes, dark Designs, Ambition, Corruption, Destruction of Trade, impoverishing our People, pernicious Views, destructive Practices, iniquitous Power, calamitous, dreadful Threats. Page 4, Ambition, Avarice, Rapaciousness, Venality, Credit decaying, Commerce destroyed, Liberties endangered, wicked Practices, shameful Misconduct, flagrant Treachery, arbitrary Wretches, motley Crew, notorious Supporters of Corruption, detestable Relics of the old Fathers of Iniquity, shameless mercenary Band of Prostitutes. Infamous Deserters of Honour, base Betrayers of their Country, Men without Genius or Capacity, insolent Intruders, arrogant Supporters, presumptious Power, mean Degeneracy, iniquitous Apostacy, abandoned shameless Creatures, profligate corrupt Services. Page 4.[4] Imps of Power.——At which Words the Corporation of *Grub-street* being ashamed of their Cause withdrew their Pretensions, and the Court decreed the said Pamphlet to belong justly to *Billingsgate*, and indeed to be the most *Billingsgate* Performance ever exhibited in any Language.

Porcupinus Pelagius, who was convicted of having writ a Panegyri— Satyri— Serio— Comi— nonsensi— unintelligi— Poem, called *The 'Piscopade*,[5] was brought to the Bar, and his

---

[1] pp. 11–12, 22–3 allude to a threat against the liberty of the press; pp. 27–36 argue that the naturalization Bill was designed by the Administration to introduce cheap foreign labour, so as to permit English commercial interests to compete more successfully with France in foreign markets.

[2] The actual text of the *Address* is on pp. 9–51, a total of 43 pages, not 42.

[3] It is in fact p. 10 of the printed text. [4] An error for p. 5.

[5] *The 'Piscopade: A Panegyri—Satiri—Serio—Comical Poem* by 'Porcupinus Pelagius' (London, 1748) is listed by *GM*, xviii (1748), 96, among the February books. 'Porcupinus

Council in Arrest of Judgment took Exception to the Indictment. 1. That the Word *Poem* was a Misnomer; for that whatever was not written in any Numbers could not be called a Poem, which being allowed to be good Critical Law, he produced several Passages, and particularly the two first Lines.

> *The Cabinet summoned in Council conven'd*
> *Prodigious Constituents*, answering the End.

2dly, That the Word *Satiri* or *Satirical* is improperly used on this Occasion; for that an unmannerly Abuse of a whole Body of Men, (as here on the whole Bench of Bishops)[1] is Scandal and not Satire.

3dly, That *de minimis non curat Lex*, and That such Stuff as this is too low for the Consideration of so high a Court of Critical Justice. To support this he referred to the Lines above cited. He likewise cited Line 8. *This here and that there*. Line 17. *Strangely bedumpt took his Place at his Heels*. 20. *As tho' he seem'd griev'd he went down to the Race*. 22. *He follows his Sire like a Tantony Pig*.[2] 28. *Cheek by Jowl with his Brother*. 35, 36. *His old Brother Authors look'd on him oblique. Pair'd his Coat with Don* Juan's *and thought them alike*. 45, 46. *Ready to take what Impression he'd give. So the S—f—d Petition he might but survive*.[3] 62. *To pay the just Debt which to pay he was born*. 64. *Let us gain him, quo' he, for a Friend if we can*, &c. &c. &c. 4thly, That this unknown Scribbler, having in a former infamous Work, dared as impudently as unjustly to abuse the noble Person who at present so illustriously presides in *Westminster-Hall*,[4] and who in his

Pelagius' was one of the editorial *personae* of *OE* during this period; see *JJ* no. 15, below, pp. 197–200.

¹ *The 'Piscopade* satirizes the political jockeying which it alleged was contaminating the selection of Archbishop Potter's successor in the primacy; cf. Stephens, *Catalogue*, pp. 656–62.

² A pig which very closely and obsequiously follows another, St. Anthony being the patron of swineherds and represented generally as accompanied by a pig.

³ The 1747 elections at Seaford were 'managed' for the Treasury by Newcastle, and duly returned court candidates despite the active opposition of the Prince of Wales; Owen, *Rise of the Pelhams*, p. 317. On 20 November 1747, over the petitions of Lord Middlesex and William Hall Gage, it was set forth to the Commons, 'That, on the Day before the said Election, a noble Person of this Realm did invite to, and entertain at, his House, most of the Voters for the said Town and Port; and, in the Room where they were assembled, spake to them one by one, and did solicit and influence them with respect to giving their Votes at the said Election'; *Journals of . . . Commons*, xxv. 429.

⁴ *The Causidicade: A Panegyri—Satiri—Serio—Comic Dramatical Poem* by 'Porcupinus Pelagius' (London, 1743) attacked the ministry and many eminent men of law for alleged

high Office doth so much Honour to his Country, all the Scandal of such a Writer for the future is to be deemed Panegyric.

Tho' these Objections were all allowed to be true, the Court said they would not be bound by any other Rules but by those of Equity, and pronounced Sentence of Contempt upon the Author and all his Works.

Ordered, That the Applause of this Court be signified to Mr. *Garrick* and Mrs. *Cibber* for their inimitable Performance in the Play of *Venice preserved*.[1]

M. Cooper moved the Court against one *Thomas Snouch*[2] of *Grub-street*, Printer; for having grubbed[3] a Pamphlet entitled *Drury-lane Playhouse broke open*, to the great Damage of the Author, who had writ it to get a Penny which he very much wanted.

Resolved, That the said Pamphlet is the lawful Property of *Grub-street*, and that they have a Right to grub the same.

Ordered, That the Pamphlets entitled *The State of the Nation*, and the *Critical Address*, together with the Poem called *The 'Piscopade*, be forthwith grubbed, at one Halfpenny each, or if possible at a less Price.

(*Adjourned.*)

SATURDAY, FEBRUARY 20, 1748. NUMB. 12.

Sacra recognosces Annalibus eruta priscis. Ovid, *Fasti*.[4]

When a Man deviates pretty much in his Tenets from the general Road of Thinking, it is common for such of his Adversaries as are

political expediency in the appointment of William Murray (1705–93), later 1st Earl of Mansfield, but a Scot and therefore a 'presumed' Jacobite, as Solicitor-General in place of Sir John Strange (1696–1754), who had resigned. The poem was particularly hard on Chief Justice Willes and on Hardwicke, Lord Chancellor and the 'noble Person who at present so illustriously presides in *Westminster-Hall*'; see *JJ* no. 8, above, p. 137 and note 2, and no. 20, below, p. 238. In his Preface to the second edition (1744) of Sarah Fielding's *Adventures of David Simple*, I. v–vi, Fielding notes with indignation that he had been rumoured as the author of *The Causidicade* and charged with 'down-right Idiotism, in flying in the Face of the greatest Men of my Profession'. He categorically denied the charge.

¹ Otway's *Venice Preserv'd* (1682), with Garrick as the male lead (Jaffier) for the first time, and with Mrs. Cibber as the heroine (Belvidera), played at Drury Lane on 8 February to great applause; *London Stage*, Part 4, i. 29.

² 'Snouch', a jibe, jeer, or scoff (*OED*).

³ Not recorded in quite this sense. The context here suggests that 'Snouch' is being accused of having pirated or perhaps illegally remaindered the pamphlet, which in fact bore the Cooper imprint. See also *JJ* no. 10, above, p. 154, n. 4 and no. 13, below, p. 177.

⁴ *Fasti*, i. 7: 'Here shalt thou read afresh of holy rites unearthed from annals old' (Loeb).

too polite, to call him either a Fool or a mad Man, to suppose him in Jest. A provoking Method, by which the most serious Arguments are, in a Moment, turned into Ridicule; and *Socrates* himself becomes, from a grave Reasoner, a very comical merry Fellow.

It is sufficiently apparent to me, as well from the Letters of my Correspondents as from other Instances, that my Jacobitical Writings have been hitherto seen in this Light. It hath been conceived impossible, that I should in Earnest hold the Principles I have asserted; and this for no other Reason, but because they are directly repugnant to common Sense.

How poor and trivial is this Objection? Have no Doctrines been propagated and received in the World, but those which were reconcileable to Common Sense? Are not all the Opinions of the Ancients concerning the Soul, which are preserved in the first Book of *Aristotle* on that Subject,[1] (if I may be allowed the Expression) stark staring Nonsense?

And yet these were held by the Philosophers, and by them delivered as solemn Truths, to be believed and cultivated by their several Pupils. Doth *Cicero* think it impossible for a Human Being, and a wise Human Being too, to believe in Nonsense, when he declares, that there is no kind of Nonsense which hath not been avowed and maintained by some Philosopher or other?[2] What was the ancient Theology (in which, as we have before shewn,[3] much of the Mystery of Jacobitism was contained) but so many Systems of errant Nonsense? And lastly, what is the Alcoran, now held in Esteem and Adoration over so large a Part of the World, but a Heap of Nonsense from the Beginning to the End?

Why then, shall not a very inconsiderable Portion of Mankind, and those, for the most part, of the lowest Understandings, be supposed to believe in Jacobitism, only because it is Nonsense? And why may not there be one in this Number who is able to read and write?

But instead of attempting to argue with such self-sufficient Contradiction of all Experience, I shall proceed to account for the

---

[1] *De Anima*, i. ii.

[2] *De Divinatione*, ii. lviii. 119. Also cited in *The Champion* of 21 October 1740 and, probably, in *CGJ* no. 19 (7 March 1752).

[3] See *JJ* no. 3, above, pp. 104–9.

Rise of this nonsensical Sect, as it is call'd, and as it must be allow'd to be, if whatever is contradictory to Human Reason must
be so named. And herein I shall pursue the Method of the celebrated Abbé *Bannier**, where he accounts for the Origin of
Fables; since, to say the Truth, the Mystery of Jacobitism may
be derived from much the same Sources.

One Source of Fables (says that excellent Author) is human
Vanity:[1] Now Obstinacy, which is a considerable Branch of
Vanity, is the great Source of Jacobitism; for if Men had not
obstinately adher'd to their own Opinion, against all Reason and
Argument, we must have long since yielded to the Malice of our
Enemies.

Another Source of Fables is said to have been the Want of the
Use of Letters.[2] The same may be said of Jacobitism; for surely
our Party may as properly be said to want the Use of Letters
as those who lived before their Invention, since, by the Use of
Letters, cannot be meant barely being able to read, which perhaps
some Jacobites are. Those only may be properly said to have
made a due Use of Letters, who have laid up from them a Fund
of Knowledge and Learning, by which they are enabled to direct
their Thoughts in the Pursuit of Truth. Superficial Learning is
indeed worse than none at all, and serves only to darken and confound the Understanding; for, as Mr. *Pope* rightly observes,

A little Learning is a dangerous Thing.[3]

And very little indeed is, I believe, the Portion of all Protestant
Jacobites.

What the learned Abbé adds on this Head, may likewise be
applied to us. "The Fathers," says he, (to which we may add
Mothers and Grandmothers) "related Actions to their Children;
and as it is the Custom never to say things to young People in a
simple Way, they intermix'd in their Narratives Circumstances
that served to imprint them strongly on their Minds; and thus
the Memory and Imagination of Children were fill'd with high

---

* *Mythology, Book* I.[4]

[1] *Mythology*, I. iv. 33–4.

[2] Chapter IV ('Conjectures about the Origin of Fables'), i. 32–48, postulates some 16
sources of fable.

[3] *Essay on Criticism*, ii. 215.

[4] *Mythology*, I. iv. 32–3. Millar repeats his advertisement of the Banier translation in this
and the following number of the *JJ*.

Notions; and they coming in Course to relate the same Stories, added still some other Circumstance to them."¹ This he calls a confused distorted Tradition; but adds, they were obliged to make Use of it.

A third Source of both is the false Eloquence of Orators. "It was an ancient Custom (says *Bannier*)² to praise the Heroes (Kings) after their Deaths, and upon Festival Days (as the 29th of *May*, 10th of *June*, &c.)³ in studied Panegyricks, where the Orators gave themselves full Liberty to feign and invent, making it their Business to represent the Heroes (or Kings) not what they had been, but such as they ought to be; and never failing to exalt them to (or to bring them down from) Heaven, and to confer Divinity upon them, without the least Reserve." Here I cannot omit an Observation of my Author: "If one was so absurd (says he) even now a-days, to compile a History of our own Heroes from most of their Panegyricks, it would be no less fabulous than those of Antiquity."⁴ How applicable this is to us, will, I doubt not, more fully appear when the learned Mr. *Carte* shall come down to the Reigns of the *Stuarts*.⁵

A fourth Source of Fables, according to our Author, are the Lies of Travellers.⁶ Nor do I doubt but Jacobitism hath received much Advantage from this Fountain.

Another Original of Fables is drawn from the ancient Ignorance in Philosophy.⁷ To the modern Ignorance in the same may likewise be ascribed much of Jacobitism. It is a Maxim in Philosophy, that the same Cause operating through the same Medium, must produce the same Effect. Of this all Jacobites are ignorant, or how could they deny that a Popish Prince operating through, or rather operated upon by, his Priests, will always attempt to introduce Popery. The Antients being ignorant of the various Phœnomena of Nature, attributed them all to the

---

¹ *Mythology*, I. iv. 34.

² *Mythology*, I. iv. 34; the quotation is by no means exact, the parenthetical matter having been added by Fielding.

³ Charles II was born on 29 May 1630; James Francis Edward Stuart, the Old Pretender, was born on 10 June 1688.

⁴ *Mythology*, I. iv. 35, with some alterations of phrase.

⁵ See *JJ* no. 9, above, p. 145. At this time only the first volume ('Containing an Account of the first Inhabitants of the Country, and the Transactions in it, from the earliest Times to the Death of King John, A.D.') of Carte's *History* had appeared.

⁶ *Mythology*, I. iv. 36–7.

⁷ *Mythology*, I. iv. 45–8.

Influence of certain Deities. From the same Ignorance the Jacobites have always imputed scorching Summers, hard Winters,
bad Harvests, Famine, Pestilence, &c. to the Revolution. *What
wretched Philosophy*, says our Author, *was this? but it was the best
they had.*[1]

I shall mention but two more, which, of all others, have chiefly
contributed to introduce and to support our Sect, as our Author
tells us they did antient Fables.

The former of these is the misunderstanding Sacred Scripture.[2]
By the Perversion of which, God hath been represented as sending a Tyrant from Heaven to plunder, pillage, and destroy his
People, and to subvert his own Holy Religion; and this in Opposition to Reason, to Fact, and to his own Holy Word. Texts,
which can be understood only of all Civil Authority, have been
applied to the Persons of Kings; and temporary Precepts given
to the primitive Christians, in order to regulate their Conduct
under Heathen Princes, and in the Times of Persecution, have
been urged as the Rules of our Conduct under a Christian Prince,
in a Country where God hath graciously pleased to establish his
own Religion.——But I will pursue this Point no farther, as
so many Divines have handled it already.

The latter, and the last which I shall produce, is Ignorance of
History. Ignorance of antient History, faith the learned Abbé,
was the most plentiful Source of Fables.[3] In like manner Ignorance of modern History, *viz.* of the Reigns of All the *Stuarts*,
but more especially of that of *James* II. is the most plentiful
Source of Jacobitism. Perhaps indeed some few Jacobites, who
can read, may have perused the Annals of those Times; but to
read History without any Portion of Historial[4] Faith, is as
ineffectual as to read the Scriptures without Religion. If a Man
sits down to read over the Times of *James* the Second, with a
thorough Resolution to believe, against all Evidence, that he was
a good King; that he govern'd according to Law; was merciful
to his Enemies, that is, to Protestants; and intended no Harm to
the Church of *England*; he will rise with no more Alteration in
his Opinion from what he reads, than one who is determined to

---

[1] *Mythology*, I. iv. 47.   [2] *Mythology*, I. v. 51–8.
[3] *Mythology*, I. v. 58–64.
[4] 'Historical'. Perhaps the text should be emended, as the obsolete form here printed is a
century later than the latest instanced in the *OED*.

think *Paul* an Enthusiast or an Impostor, will receive from the late excellent Treatise on his Conversion.[1]

Can any Protestant, without such a pre-conceived Resolution, attend a Moment to the numberless Facts by which that Prince endeavoured to introduce Popery, without the utmost Alarm on account of his Religion? Can any Man, who hath any Zeal for our Constitution, unless from such a Resolution, see that Monarch assume a dispensing Power, by which one Act all our Laws were trampled under Foot, and not be fired with Apprehensions for his Liberty? Lastly, can any Man of common Humanity, without this Resolution, smell (for they stink in History) the rotting Limbs of hundreds of his Countrymen exposed in all our Highways, and not melt with Compassion; while he burns at the same time with Indignation and Abhorrence against the Tyrant, who hath thus feasted his wanton and luxurious Revenge in the Blood of his Subjects.

Very well, Sir, perhaps it will be said by some Whig Reader, I admit all this to be true; and can you believe and know these Things, and yet remain a Jacobite? Yes, Sir, I do believe and know all this, and yet am a Jacobite. I am resolved to be a Jacobite, and will be so in spite of all the Reason and Evidence in the World. I was born a Jacobite, and I was bred one. My Father was a Jacobite before me, and so have been all our Family, and so am I, and so I will always be, because I will, and because I dare.[2]

> *To the Author of the Jacobite Journal.*

Sir,

As the Dispute about the Inspiration of the primitive Fathers runs high, between the truly learned Dr. *Middleton* and the very zealous Dr. *Chapman*,[3] give me Leave to decide the Controversy in favour of the latter.

[1] *Observations on the Conversion and Apostleship of St. Paul. In a Letter to Gilbert West, Esq.* (London, 1747), by Lyttelton, had appeared on 13 May 1747; see Rose Mary Davis, *The Good Lord Lyttelton*, pp. 148–56.

[2] *The Rehearsal*, IV. i: 'I drink, I huff, I strut, look big and stare;/ And all this I can do, because I dare.'

[3] Conyers Middleton (1683–1750), contentious cleric and scholar, had engaged in controversy with John Chapman (1704–84), Archdeacon of Sudbury and writer on classical antiquities, over the relative merits of primitive and miraculous Christianity, on the one hand, and the sufficiency of Scripture, on the other. Middleton's *Introductory Discourse to a Larger Work . . . concerning the Miraculous Powers* (London, 1747) attacked Chapman's

There is a Prophecy of St. *Jerom*, which the present Inclemency
of the Season proves to be true, and that he certainly was, as Dr.
Chapman contends,[1] an inspired Person. It is not therefore mar-
vellous, that such a Saint should demolish a Dragon big enough
to swallow a Bull.[2]

The Prophecy:

Cum Sol splendescat, Maria purificante;
Tunc Glacies fuerit magis aspera, quam fuit ante.[3]

Thus English'd in the Stile of The 'Piscopade.

On *Candlemas-Day*, if the Sun shines out,
The Frost will be harder than it was, no doubt.

Note,

Sol splendebat, currente anno, Maria purificante.[4]

Yours,

SCRIBLERUS.

Proceedings at the Court of Criticism, Thursday Feb. 18.

Thomas Carte, Englishman, was indicted, for that he, not having
the Love of Truth before his Eyes, nor weighing the Duty of
an Historian, but being moved and seduced by the instigation
of the wicked Spirit of *Jacobitism*, in the Month of——at *Bristol*
one false, foolish, ridiculous, and absurd Story, concerning one
Christopher Lovell being cured of the King's Evil, by the Touch

Popery the Bane of True Letters (London, 1746) for its 'discovery' of a Jesuitical plot to
subvert the Reformation by introducing hypercriticism of Scripture and ecclesiastical
history, a thesis to which Chapman returned in his *Jesuit-Cabal Farther Opened* (London,
1747). The controversy was apparently still warm in 1748; see *GEP* of 13–16 February
1748 for an advertisement of *Remarks on Two Pamphlets Lately Publish'd against Dr.
Middleton's* 'Introductory Discourse'.

1 In, for example, *Popery the Bane of True Letters*, pp. 6, 22.
2 Not identified. Presumably alluding to the fabulizing that grew up about the person of
Jerome after his death, particularly with regard to the miracles reported of him. Fielding is
here satirizing the proponents of a primitive and miraculous Christianity.
3 More commonly, *Si sol splendescat . . . Major erit glacies post festum quam fuit ante.* See
Sir Thomas Browne, *Pseudodoxia Epidemica*, Bk. IV, ch. iv, where it is referred to as the
'proverbial distich'. Fielding's attribution of it to Jerome is intended to reflect satirically on
Dr. Chapman's use of Jerome as an exemplar of the supposedly miraculous character of
primitive Christianity. The feast of the Purification of the Virgin Mary (Candlemas Day)
is on February 2.
4 'The sun was shining, in the current year, on the [Feast of the] Purification of Mary.'

of a certain *then* un-anointed, eldest, lineal Descendant of a Race of Kings, *&c.* the Property of certain old Women unknown, did steal, take, and, in a vast folio Book, called *A General History of England*, did insert and publish,[1] with a manifest Intention of imposing on weak and credulous People, in Defiance of Common Sense, to the evil Example of all bad Writers of Romances, and against the Truth of History, its Stile and Dignity.

To this Indictment the Prisoner pleaded Not Guilty.

The History was then produced, and Page 291 was read, where, in a Note, this silly Story was found, attested by the Prisoner.

Then the *General Evening Post* was likewise produced and read, by which it appeared, that this ridiculous Story was false in Fact: For that the said *Christopher Lovell* was so far from being cured, that he afterwards died of that Distemper.[2]

The Prisoner made the usual *Old-Bailey* Defence. First, said, *that he found it*; and then offered to impeach one Doctor *Lane*, and Mr. *Samuel Pye*.[3] But the Court gave but little Attention to such idle Stuff, and pronounced him Guilty of the Indictment.

Then the Court proceeded to Sentence in the following Manner:

Thomas Carte, an *Englishman*, you are convicted of a very high Offence; no less than that of perverting the Intent of History, and applying it to the sordid and paltry Use of a Party.

This is so much the more inexcusable in you, as the Intent with which you inserted this foolish Story manifestly appears, from many Observations you have very properly made on the

---

[1] In his *History*, I. iv. 291 and note, Carte, in order to illustrate the unction of kings and the gift of healing the 'scrophulous humour call'd the king's evil', presented a modern case of a cure by touch, 'which could not possibly be ascribed to the royal unction', the case of a Christopher Lovell, whom Carte had met personally 'in the week preceding St. Paul's fair' at Bristol. Lovell had been 'touched' by the Old Pretender at Paris in 1716. Carte was careful to say that 'this descendant and next heir of their blood had not, at least at that time, been either crowned or annointed'; but his meaning was wrenched into Jacobitism.

[2] *GEP* of 14–16 January 1748 printed a letter, signed 'Amicus Veritatis' and dated from Bristol on 13 January, to the effect that the supposed cure of Lovell was brief and his disease soon mortal. The letter sneers at what it calls 'an idle Ja——te tale, calculated to support the old thread-bare notion of the divine hereditary right of a certain house'; reprinted in *GM*, xviii (1748), 14.

[3] Carte, *History*, I. iv. 292, states that 'Dr. Lane, an eminent physician in that place' [Bristol], told him of the cure and led him to 'Mr. Samuel Pye, a very skilled surgeon . . . who had tried in vain, for three years together, to cure the man by physical remedies'. Samuel Pye was the author of *Some Observations on the Several Methods of Lithotomy. In a Letter to Dr. J. Lane* (London, 1724).

Credulity of the Vulgar, particularly in Page 390; where speaking of an idle Report which was current among them, you justly add: *So apt are they to swallow the absurdest Stories that can be invented, if they flatter, in any Respect, their Wishes, Passions, or Prejudices.*[1]

Now surely no more absurd Story was ever invented than this of which you are convicted. When, pray, was this healing Power given to Kings? Or is there any Authority to suppose it was ever given? Doth the Scripture make any mention of such a Gift? If it doth not, are we not forbidden in Scripture to believe any such Power of working a Miracle?

Is this Gift bestowed on all Kings indifferently, or is it confined only to those who are Christians? If to the latter, *Charles* the Second, I am afraid, could have no Title to it, if what Bishop *Burnet* says of him,[2] and what his Life so well confirmed, be true, that he was a Deist.

For what Purpose was it given? Not as a Manifestation of Hereditary Right, as you would seem to think. For neither *Edward* the Confessor, nor Queen *Anne*,[3] nor, indeed, one half of our Kings, who have pretended to this Power of healing the Evil, had any such Right. Nay, indeed, when we consider the numerous Offspring which must have proceeded from the many Persons who have been excluded from this Hereditary Right, it is more than possible that no such Right ever rested in the Family of *Stuart*.

At what Time do Princes come to the Possession of this Gift, if it be an Incident inseparable from that Divinity with which

---

[1] I. iv. 390, noting an 'idle report' that after the Battle of Hastings Harold, whose body had been returned to his mother for public interment, in fact lived on for many years in a religious retreat.

[2] Cf. *History of My Own Time*, I. i. 93: 'He [Charles II] seemed to have no sense of religion: both at prayers and at sacrament he, as it were, took care to satisfy the people that he was in no sort concerned in that about which he was employed . . . He said once to my self, he was no atheist, but he could not think God would make a man miserable only for taking a little pleasure out of the way'; cf. III. xvii. 614. Burnet does not seem to have implied that Charles II was a deist, but the King did have such a reputation among contemporaries; see C. E. Whiting, *Studies in English Puritanism, 1660–1688* (New York, 1931), p. 3, and *Poems on Affairs of State*, vol. ii, ed. Elias F. Mengel, Jr. (New Haven, Conn., 1965), p. 429.

[3] Edward, after the Danish royal line came to an end with the death of Harthacnut, was elected King by popular acclamation, thus restoring the ancient native dynasty. Anne succeeded William III in accordance with the exclusionist provisions dictated by Parliament in the Bill of Rights (1689) and the Act of Settlement (1701).

some think a Crown invested, and which seems the ancient Opinion, then cannot they exercise it 'till they are in Possession of the Crown; and, consequently, your Story must be, as it hath been proved to be, as false, as foolish and absurd.

Let me ask you one Question; Would you be thought to believe this Story, or to disbelieve it? If the former, what an Historian will you be thought? If the latter, what a Man must you be?

Nothing now remains but that you receive the Judgment of this Court, which is, That your History be forthwith grubbed, for the Use of those for whom it is calculated; and that you, *Thomas Carte*, an *Englishman*,[1] be, and do remain, under the Contempt of this Court.

Other Indictments were preferred against him, for having endeavoured to prove, that a King is not bound by his Coronation Oath, *&c.*[2] but the Court refused to hear them.

Note. He endeavoured to recommend himself to his Honour as a *Jacobite*;[3] but his Honour said, He would always do strict Justice in this Court, without Regard to any Party or Person whatever.

The Court being informed that THE TOWN behaved in a very indecent Manner on *Saturday* last, at the Representation of the New Comedy,[4] to the great Terror of the Actresses, and of several

---

[1] Fielding harps on Carte's nationality because it was prominent on the title-page of his *History* and in the advertisements for it.

[2] *History*, I. v. 392, states: 'This variation in the form of the *English* coronation oaths, and the late introduction of them into practice, afford sufficient reasons to presume, they had nothing in them of the nature of an original contract'; see also I. v. 396, and vi. 785.

[3] Cf. *Diary of the First Earl of Egmont*, iii (London, 1923), 312, *sub* 18 January 1746: 'He [Carte] is a determined Jacobite and fled twice from justice for being concerned in rebellious practices, but by the lenity of the Government was allowed to return without prosecution: wherefore there is reason to believe that his history will be wrote to support the doctrine of indefeasible hereditary right, in order [to] serve the Pretender.' See also John Nichols, *Biographical and Literary Anecdotes of William Bowyer* (London, 1782), pp. 191 n.–204.

[4] *The Foundling*, by Edward Moore (1712–57), had its première at Drury Lane on 13 February 1748, with Garrick, Macklin, Barry, Mrs. Cibber, and Mrs. Woffington in the cast. In his Dedication of the first edition Moore wrote: 'The Disapprobation, which the character of Faddle met with the first Night, made it necessary for me to shorten it in almost every scene'; as quoted in *London Stage*, Part 4, i. 30. *JJ* no. 15 of 12 March 1748 reprints a news item from the *London Courant* to the effect that a reference in one of Faddle's speeches to an indecent contemporary poem entitled 'Adollizing' 'was the true Reason why such Endeavours were used to interrupt the Run of the Play'. There is a reference to disturbances at an unnamed 'new' play in *Tom Jones*, XIII. xi. The manuscript diary of Richard Cross, the Drury Lane prompter, records a disturbance also at the performance of 22 February 1748; see *London Stage*, Part 4, i. 31. Walpole wrote Mann about another on February 25; *Yale Walpole*, xix. 469. See also *Some Unpublished Correspondence of David Garrick*, ed. George Pierce Baker (Boston, 1907), p. 55.

Ladies of the first Quality among the Audience, it was ordered, that *the said Town* be forthwith apprehended, and the Court resolved to proceed against *the said Town*, on *Thursday* next, for the said Offence.

It being humbly represented to the Court, on the Behalf of several Booksellers of Credit, who are Proprietors of a certain *Grub-street* Paper called the *London Evening-Post*,[1] that they are intirely ignorant of the scandalous Matters inserted in that Paper; with which the Writer, Printer, and Publisher are only chargeable. The Court ordered, That the said Booksellers be discharged from all Censure, on Account of every past Offence committed in that Paper; but that they do immediately relinquish their Shares in the same, or do change their said Writer, &c. for the future, on Pain of seeing their Names gibbeted in this Journal, together with those of the said Writer, Printer, and Publisher.

(*Adjourned.*)

SATURDAY, FEBRUARY 27, 1748.   NUMB. 13.

——*Velari Pictura jubetur.*

Juvenal.[2]

There is scarce any Thing more provoking than to be totally misunderstood, and by that means to have our Compliments received as Affronts, and our Panegyrick converted into Satire.

It cannot therefore be wondered at, if I am not well pleased with that gross misunderstanding of the Emblematical Frontispiece so long prefixed to my Paper, which hath generally prevailed, and which, among other good Reasons, hath at length induced me to displace it for the future.[3] By this Error of the Public, a Contrivance of mine, (the Expence of much laborious

---

[1] The proprietors have not been identified. According to its colophon the printer of *LEP* at this time was 'J. Meres, in the *Old Baily* near *Ludgate*'. John Meres (d. 1761), printer of the *Daily Post* as well as *LEP*, had been arrested in 1740 for improper remarks, and released with a warning about his conduct of the latter paper; see Plomer, *Dictionary*, p. 167, and *JJ* no. 17, below, p. 214.

[2] *Satires*, vi. 340: 'the picture must be veiled' (Loeb). The allusion is to the displacement, beginning with this issue, of the frontispiece.

[3] See General Introduction above, pp. lii–liii. The original issue of *JJ* no. 12, p. 4, col. 1, carried the following note: 'Our Readers are desired to take their Fill of our Frontispiece this Week, as we intend to displace it for the future.'

Thinking) to do Honour to the Jacobite Party, hath been represented as the Means of vilifying and degrading it.

But seriously, could the Art of Man have carried the Glory of Jacobitism higher than it was carried in this Print, where a Jacobite of either Sex was seen cloathed in Mystery, and riding on one of the most honourable Beasts in the Universe, whilst Popery servilely attends, leading it by the Halter, and *France* and the Republican Party are dragged after its Heels. Is not here depictured that notable and mysterious Union of *French* Interest, Popery, Jacobitism, and Republicanism; by a Coalition of all which Parties this Nation is to be redeemed from the deplorable State of Slavery, under which it at present labours?

It would be endless to enumerate all the Mistakes and ridiculous Conceits entertained on this Occasion. Some have imagined we intended to insinuate that the Protestant Jacobites were led by the Nose by Popery, and spurr'd on by *France* and the Republicans; whereas nothing can be more certain in Fact, than that Popery and *France*, and the Republicans, have ever been the mere Dupes and Tools of the said Jacobites.

Many have endeavoured to discover Resemblances to real Persons in the Figures there exhibited. By the Popish Priest, it hath been said we design to represent the old Chevalier;[1] and by the Figures on the Ass, the young Chevalier his Son and the famous *Jenny Cameron*.[2]

Others have found out Likenesses of less Importance, and several Squires and Country Gentlewomen of *Staffordshire*, and other Counties, who never travel beyond the Limits of a Fox-chace, have been supposed to ride, once a Week, Post all over the Kingdom in this Paper.

But the most egregious Errors have been committed in Misconstructions concerning the Ass. Several ingenious and witty Printers of News-Papers have very facetiously taken Occasion to call the Author himself an Ass;[3] supposing, probably, that as

---

[1] The Old Pretender was alternatively designated the 'Chevalier [de] St. George'. The designation apparently dates from 1708, the year of a projected invasion of England that was to have been led by the Old Pretender with the backing of Louis XIV, who endorsed the 'transparent incognito then used for the first time'; Alistair and Henrietta Tayler, *1715: The Story of the Rising* (London, 1936), p. 7, and *The Old Chevalier* (London, 1934), pp. 21, 38.   [2] See *JJ* no. 2, above, p. 98 and note 1 there.

[3] For example, by *LEP* of 16–18 February 1748, which offered a motto to replace the frontispiece Fielding had dropped: 'Ass as thou art, Thou woulds't not have to eat,/ Did not the LONDON EV'NING give thee Meat.'

Scripture informs us an Ass once spoke;[1] so certain Descendants of the same Family might write, which Faith, perhaps something within their own Experience, might sufficiently encourage them to receive.

To mention no more of these absurd Conjectures, I must here inform my Reader, that by the Body of the Ass we intend to figure the whole Body of Jacobitical Doctrine.

Now as there was no Symbol among the Antients, of which the Emblematical Meaning was so plain and easy to be discovered, our Party could never have so universally mistaken it, had it not been from that Want of Learning among us, which I lamented in my last Paper. Hence, being misled by those erroneous Opinions, which the Moderns have propagated to the great Disadvantage of Asses, the Jacobites have been unwilling to discover any Resemblance between themselves and an Animal which the wise Antients saw in so respectable a Light, and which the Ignorance of latter Ages hath highly dishonour'd by odious Comparisons with certain Individuals of the Human Species.

Thus *Homer* is well known to have liken'd one of his principal Heroes to this noble Animal;[2] which was in such Esteem among the antient *Jews*, that he was not only an Object of their Devotion, but they are said to have preserved his Figure in massy Gold in the Temple of *Jerusalem**.

If the Transfiguration of *Midas* in the *Metamorphoses*,[3] doth but little Honour to the Ears of our Symbol, the Story of *Lotis*, which the same Poet tells in his *Fastorum*,[4] is greatly in Praise of his Braying, by which the Chastity of that Nymph was rescued from the wicked Designs of her insidious Lover.

In such Esteem hath this noble Beast been held among the Learned, that I have seen a Book composed in his Favour, and

---

* Bannier's *Mythology*, Book 6, Chap. 4.[5]

---

[1] Numbers 22: 30: 'Am I not thine ass, upon which thou hast ridden ever since I was thine unto this day?' With this reference Fielding may have inspired a particularly pointed attack on himself by 'The Fool, No. 261', which draws analogies between Balaam and his ass and Pelham and *his* ass (Fielding); reprinted in *LEP* of 27 February–1 March 1748.

[2] *Iliad*, xi. 558 ff. Homer likens Aias (Ajax), son of Telamon and 'bulwark' of the Achaeans, to a lazy ass being driven out of a corn field by small boys.

[3] xi. 157–93.

[4] i. 415–40, where the nymph Lotis is wakened by the braying of an ass just in time to escape ravishment at the hands of Priapus.

[5] p. 548.

entitled *Laus Asini*;[1] not to mention the celebrated Performance of *Apuleius*, to which he hath given the Name of the *Golden Ass*.

Instead therefore of being displeased with the Emblem, our Party have great Reason to be vain on this Occasion; nor do I think there can be a juster Comparison than of a Protestant Jacobite to an Ass, or one more to the Honour of the former.

First, what can so well answer to that noble and invincible Obstinacy, which I have more than once celebrated in our Party, as the intractable and unalterable Nature of this Animal, which gave Rise to an antient Proverb alluded to by *Horace* in his Satires,

> ———*Ut si quis Asellum*
> *In Campo doceat parentem currere frænis.*[2]

> ———Your Art
> As well may teach an Ass to scour the Plain,
> And bend obedient to the forming Rein.

And again in his Epistles:

> *Scriptores autem narrare putaret Asello*
> *Fabellam surdo.*[3]

> *Democritus* would think the Writers told
> To a deaf Ass their Story.———

which may most strictly be applied to all those Writers, who have endeavoured to convince the Jacobites by Argument.

Again, what can give us a more adequate Idea of that Firmness, with which we have supported all the ill Usage of the worst of Sovereigns without Resentment, than the laudable Indifference which an Ass hath for the same; whom you may beat, whip, kick, and spur as long as you are pleased, he still trudges on without altering his Pace.

To omit many other obvious Resemblances, such as *Braying*, &c. the famous Story of the Countryman and the Ass, briefly

---

[1] Probably the *Laus Asini . . . ad Senatum Populumque eorum, qui, ignari omnium, scientias ac literas hoc tempore contemnunt* (Lugduni Batavorum, 1623), attributed to Daniel Heinsius.

[2] I. i. 90–1. The translation which follows is that of Francis, *Poetical Translation of the Works* (1747), iii. 15.

[3] II. i. 199–200. The source of the somewhat literal translation of this passage has not been found. It may be Fielding's.

touched upon by *Horace* in the Epistle address'd to his own Book,[1] is so perfect a Picture of Jacobitism, that I have been inclined to think, as the Antients are known to have inveloped all their Mysteries in Fable and Allegory, that no less than Jacobitism itself was intended to be couched under this Story.

"A certain Countryman observing an Ass making towards a Precipice, ran to him, and catching hold of his Tail, endeavoured with all his Might to withhold him from Destruction; but the more the Countryman attempted to preserve him, the more obstinately the Ass contended against his kind Preserver, and the more eagerly was bent upon accomplishing his fatal Purpose. The Countryman at last, wearied out with his Endeavours to save an obstinate Beast against his own Will, and having probably received some Thanks from his Heels for his intended Kindness, instead of pulling any longer, gave the Ass a Push, and tumbled him headlong down the Precipice which he had been so industriously pursuing."[2]

I make no doubt but many of our good Enemies the Whigs, who have well imitated this Countryman in the former Part of his Behaviour, would imitate him likewise in the latter, was it not that they cannot precipitate us without tumbling down themselves at the same time.

These are the Mysteries, then, which have been couched under my Frontispiece, and which, tho' their Meaning must now appear to have been so plain, have nevertheless stood exposed so long at the Head of this Journal, without having been, as I can find, understood by any.

Perhaps I shall be asked, why I have now displaced them, since, after so large and full an Explanation, they cannot fail of being highly agreeable to that Party, for whose Use chiefly this Paper is calculated; and who would, for the future, worship my Ass with the same Veneration with which the *Jews* of old did theirs.

Now, tho' the Indignation which I have exprest in the Beginning of this Essay at the many gross and absurd Misconceptions which have been vented by the Public, would alone very well

---

[1] *Epistles*, I. xx. 14–16. The 'famous Story' derives ultimately from an Aesopian fable (Helm no. 335, Chambry no. 278); see Benedict Einarson, 'Horace, *Epistles* I, 20, 14–16' *Classical Journal*, xxviii (1932–3), 611, who lists some proverbial analogues.

[2] The immediate source of this version of the 'famous Story' has not been identified.

justify the Discontinuance of my Emblem so much abused, there are, to say the Truth, two other Reasons which have had a stronger Weight with me in producing this Determination.

The former of these is, that the Ass and his Retinue do indeed take up too much Room, and must oblige us either to suppress Part of our own Lucubrations, or some of those material Articles of News which we weekly transcribe from others; or lastly, those Pieces of Intelligence called Advertisements, which, tho' not always the most entertaining to our Reader, do afford very agreeable Entertainment to ourselves.

A second and a very strong Motive with us, is to lend all the Assistance in our Power to a very worthy and willing, tho' weak Brother, the learned and facetious Novelist Mr. *Carte*; whose great Romance, tho' in our Court of Criticism, where we shall always act impartially, we have been obliged, like other Judges, to condemn, contrary to our own Inclinations, to be grubb'd,[1] we shall always privately esteem as a Work calculated solely for the Use of our Party. As we have therefore, to our great Concern, received very credible Information that the said Work begins already to be considered only as a Heap of waste Paper,[2] we have thought proper to lend our Frontispiece to our good Brother, in order that it may be prefixed to the future Volumes of that great Work, advising him to omit the Words *London Evening-Post*, and to insert *English History* in their stead. This will not fail of greatly recommending his Performance to our Party, who never willingly read any thing but what an Ass may at least be supposed to have bray'd.

I could wish moreover, that the learned Novelist would take our Advice in another Instance, and for the future deal forth his excellent Work in weekly Portions or Numbers; I do not mean in such a Form as the real History of *England* is now publishing by Mr. *Waller*;[3] but in the same manner with those true and

---

[1] See *JJ* no. 12, above, p. 171.

[2] On 7 April 1748 the City of London withdrew its annual subsidy to Carte for his *History*. See *JJ* no. 27, below, p. 298, n. 3.

[3] T. Waller, of the Mitre and Crown, opposite Fetter Lane, Fleet Street, was publishing 'Mr. Guthrie's *History of England*' in weekly numbers at 6*d*. *LEP* of 25–27 February 1748 advertised as 'This Day publish'd' at 6*d*., 'No. X of the Third and Last Part of Mr. Guthrie's History of England'. William Guthrie (1708–70), author and journalist, brought out his *General History of England* in 3 folio volumes (1744–51), with the imprint 'D. Browne for T. Waller'; see also George L. Lam, 'Note on Guthrie's "History of England" ', *N & Q*, clxxxiii (1942), 71–2.

delectable Histories of *Argalus* and *Parthenia*, *Guy* Earl of *Warwick*, the *Seven Champions*,[1] &c. in which Form, at the Price of 1*d*. each, when embellished by our Frontispiece, I make no doubt of assuring him as universal a Sale, as the inimitable Adventures of *Robinson Crusoe* formerly had throughout this Kingdom.

To the Honourable JOHN TROTT-PLAID, *Esq; Censor-General of* Great-Britain,

The Humble Petition of John Pudding,[2] *Gentleman, on Behalf of himself and his Brethren, the antient and incorporated Society of Merry-Andrews.*

Humbly Sheweth,

That your Petitioners are an ancient and respectful Corporation,
Who daily labour, as well for the Health, as for the Pastime of the Nation,
At the Expence of a very learned and costly Education.
And yet there is great Danger that our Society should fall,
Thro' a Set of Interlopers, that never had any Education at all.
Every Squire in every Parish, to your Petitioners great Dolour,
Thinks to rank as Merry-Andrew, only from wearing a Coat of our Colour.
If the Coat can make you the Thing, altho' you have nothing in ye,
Then the Skin may make the Lion, and the Glitter make the Guinea.
Do those Squires, like us, shew any Learning in their Discourses?
Do any of them ever tumble, except it be from their Horses?
Do they abound, like true Andrews, in the genuine *Attic* Salt?

---

[1] Cf. *Joseph Andrews*, I. i. 18: 'our own Language affords many ['biographies'] of excellent Use and Instruction, finely calculated to sow the Seeds of Virtue in Youth, and very easy to be comprehended by Persons of moderate Capacity. Such are . . . that of an Earl of *Warwick*, whose Christian Name was *Guy*; the Lives of *Argalus* and *Parthenia*; and above all, the History of those seven worthy Personages, the Champions of Christendom.' These popular romances were hawked about in the form of chapbooks 'at the Price of 1*d*. each'.

[2] Cf. *Jack-Pudding*, a buffoon, clown, or merry-andrew; esp. one attending on a mountebank (*OED*). *JJ* no. 12, p. 4, col. 1, had anticipated the petition: 'The Petition of *John Pudding* shall be inserted in our next.' Cf. *Spectator* no. 47 of 24 April 1711, and *CGJ* no. 10 of 4 February 1752.

Or, tho' they can drink up the Hogshead, thro' its Hoops can any
of them vault?
They boast indeed with us the same tutelar Saint,
But believe me, honour'd Sir, this is all but a Feint.
The Pig-nut in Merit,[1] is not more below the Cherry,
Than is St. *Andrew* of the *Highland* below St. *Andrew* the *Merry*.[2]

Now, in as much as this Grievance is of late so common grown,
That almost every Parish has a Squire Andrew of its own,
To compleat our Misfortune, 'tis but one Thing we lack,
That every Curate, on his Part, should set up for a Quack.

Wherefore, in these impending Dangers, your Honour's
Aid we humbly crave,
The true original Professors of Mirth and Medicine to save,
And your Petitioners shall ever pray, and in particular
your faithful Slave,

JOHN PUDDING.

Proceedings at the Court of Criticism, Thursday Feb. 25.

The Officers to whom the Warrants for apprehending THE
TOWN were directed, return'd, that *the said Town* could not be
found; but one of the Officers said, he had narrowly miss'd them,
at an obscure Coffee-house near *Hounsditch*;[3] upon which the Court
awarded another Process, as is usual in Cases of that Nature.

The Court were moved on Behalf of the History of *Thomas
Carte*, an *Englishman*, which received Sentence of *grubbing* on
Thursday last. It was said, that the Historian had, in the *General
Evening Post* of *Tuesday* the 23d. alledged in his Defence:[4]

---

[1] The tuber of *Bunium flexuosum* or earthnut, which when the rinds are peeled off are
eaten raw by country people; sometimes applied also to the acorn. Cf. *Spectator* no. 69 of
19 May 1711.

[2] Almost certainly a fiction, although the etymology of *merry-andrew* is in fact uncertain. The association of St. Andrew the Apostle is with Scotland as a whole; Fielding has
narrowed the reference to emphasize the Jacobite aspect.

[3] Not identified. The obscurity of the coffee house and its disreputable location suggest a
fiction. Percy Fitzgerald, *The Life of Mrs. Catherine Clive* (London, 1888), p. 4, refers to a
Bell Tavern in Hounsditch, kept by a Mr. Watson, a boxkeeper at Drury Lane, said to have
been a meeting place of the Beefsteak Club.

[4] GEP of 20–23 February 1748 printed a letter signed 'Tho. Carte' and dated 'Dean's
Yard, Feb. 13, 1748'. John Nichols, *Literary Anecdotes of the Eighteenth Century*, ii. 508 n.,
cites 'a tract, intituled, "A Second Letter to Trotplaid, Esq. Author of the Jacobite
Journal, concerning Mr. Carte's General History of England"; plainly shewing, that the
Letter in the General Evening Post, Feb. 23, 1748, signed "Thomas Carte", could not have
been wrote by Thomas Carte the Englishman'.

1. That this was inserted in a Note, *only to refute* the erroneous Notion concerning that Sanative Virtue of Touching.

2. That in Order to refute this Notion it was there inserted, *without any Design of publishing it.*

3. That this Note (tho' it hath many apparent Marks of a recent Performance, and manifestly refers to a Transaction long ago) being long since inserted, and unhappily, *without a Mark directing it should be copied*, was transcribed for the Press, and never seen by the Author 'till sent in the Proof Sheet.

4. That the Person touching not being named, what is said of him here *must be agreeable to more than one*, namely, to all the eldest Sons of the late King *James*, tho' he had never so many.[1]

5. That tho' he hath not some Books, nor *a thousand others*, now by him, out of which he hath made Transcripts, he thinks *he may make Use of his Transcripts*; and tho' he should mistake the Name of the Author, or the Book quoted, *that is not material.*

6. That "he passed some Days, about 26 Years ago, with Mr. *Anstis*[2] at *Mortlake*, when a Pamphlet, wrote by a Surgeon, about the King's Evil, was advertised in the News-papers, and had a good deal of Discourse with him on that Subject; and by what was then said, he (*Carte*) was perswaded, that Mr. *Beckett's* Enquiry into the Antiquity and Efficacy of touching for the King's Evil,[3] printed in 8vo, *A.D.* 1722, (according to the Book-sellers Stile, who begin their Year even before *Christmas*) was the Pamphlet in question; tho' he never saw it, and had entirely forgot the Surgeon's Name, when having Mr. *Anstis's* Discourse[4] abovementioned before him, and consulting a learned Gentleman, who had studied and practised Physic above 40 Years, and transcribed his (*Cart's*) Note for the Press, about the Name of the Surgeon referred to by Mr. *Anstis*, it was either by the Doctor's

[1] The *GEP* letter reads simply: 'for the Person touching is not named, and what is said of him agrees to more than one Person.'

[2] John Anstis (1669–1745), Garter King-at-Arms, author of works on heraldry, imprisoned for supposed intrigue with the Pretender in 1715, later cleared.

[3] William Becket (1684–1738), F.R.S. (1718), surgeon to St. Thomas's Hospital, Southwark, original member of the Society of Antiquaries, and author of historical and practical works on surgery, including the *Enquiry* here mentioned. See Nichols, *Literary Anecdotes of the Eighteenth Century*, v. 278.

[4] The *GEP* letter describes 'a MS. Discourse on Coronations, which he [Anstis] left at his Death unfinished'.

Opinion, or by his own Inadvertence, that he put down *Tucker* for the Name of the Surgeon."[1]

Here the Council being told by the Court, that he did not make himself understood, answered, That he could not help it; for he read Mr. *Carte's* own Words, which he could not pretend to say, he understood very well himself.

He then concluded with saying, He hoped the Court would take Pity on an old Man, who appeared to labour under the Incapacities betrayed in the said Letter, and change the Word *Contempt* in the Sentence into *Compassion*; especially as he was willing to submit to be grubbed: For that *since he had published his first Volume*, and found it did not sell, *he was willing to deliver it to such as would subscribe for it in any Manner they pleased.*

The Court having perused his Letter in the *General Evening Post*, took his Infirmities into Consideration, and ordered their Clerk to erase the Word *Contempt*, and to insert, that the said *Carte* be, and is considered by this Court *as an Object of their Compassion*.[2]

Resolved, That it appears to this Court, that the Author of *The 'Piscopade* and the Author of *Old England* are one and the same Person.[3]

Ordered, That Mrs. *Cibber* do prepare a good warm Box at her Benefit,[4] for the Reception of Ourself and our fair *Peggy*, where we both intend to appear in our Plaids.

(*Adjourned.*)

---

[1] William Tooker (1558 ?–1621), Fellow of New College, Oxford, chaplain to Queen Elizabeth, Dean of Lichfield, and author of *Charisma sive Donum Sanationis* (1597), which vindicates the royal power of 'touching' for the king's evil. See Nichols, *Literary Anecdotes of the Eighteenth Century*, viii. 413. In his *History* Carte refers to a book by 'Tucker' as providing instances of cures by 'touching'. The *GEP* letter states that the reference should have been to Becket's *Enquiry* instead.

[2] That part of the 'Proceedings at the Court of Criticism' which pertains to Carte was reprinted in *GEP* of 5–8 March 1748.

[3] This attribution has not been substantiated; *OE* of 5 March 1748 ridicules it. The *'Piscopade* has been associated tenuously with William Kenrick (1725 ?–79), miscellaneous writer, dramatist, and later (1751) an enemy of Fielding's; Cross, ii. 4–5, 387–8, 409–10. The statement in *JJ* no. 11, above, p. 161, that the same author wrote *The Causidicade* (1743), if taken seriously, would appear to rule out Kenrick as too young. *The Causidicade*, on the other hand, has been attributed to Macnamara Morgan (d. 1762), Irish dramatist and lawyer; *N & Q*, 2nd Ser. iv. 94 (1 August 1857). Morgan may well be the 'Morgan Scrub' referred to in *JJ* no. 41, below, p. 388, n. 2, as the editor of *OE*, and the lawyer charged with writing the '*Causidicade, Processionade, Triumvirade, 'Piscopade*, and *Old England*', in *JJ* no. 15, below, p. 197. For other candidates, see *JJ* no. 17, below, p. 214.

Note 4 on p. 182

SATURDAY, MARCH 5, 1748.   NUMB. 14.

Quoquo modo audita pro compertis habet.

Tacitus. *Annales.*[1]

The following Letter evidently demonstrates the great Services
done to our Party by those inflammatory Writers, who have
lately dispersed their Lucubrations over the Kingdom. My
Cousin *Gubbins*, (as well as most other Country Gentlemen)
being the Pupil of these Writers in Politics, speaks the Language
of his Master; and whoever will take the Pains of searching into
the Anti-ministerial Papers and Pamphlets during the last half
Year, will, I am convinced, find every Sentiment in his Letter,
printed in one or other of those Performances.

Cousin Jan Trott-Plaid,

I am again azat down to write to ye about National Concerns;
for zure, zince *England* was *England*, such Times as these were
never azeed before.

Is this a time to be a carrying on a War, when the Nation is
soused over Head and Ears in Debt in such a manner? I know
there be zum ministerial Rascals that call it the Marchants
War.[2] Tis a d—nd Lie; the Marchants never intended to have
any War, but at Zee. Tis the Ministry that went to War upon
the Kontinent, and what is the Consequence? Have not the
King of *France* agot all *Flanders* by it, and t'other Pleace there,
what d'yee call it, *Bravebant*?[3] Do you think he would ever
athoute of carrying his Army thither, if we had unt a zent over
our Men to show un the Way? Besides, an if he had, wueld not
the *Duch* have bin very able to defend themsels if our Men
had unt been there? And if our Ministry would have a Land
War on the Kontinent, why did unt they take care to have good
A Lies?[4] Why did unt they vollow the Method of my L—d
G——,[5] why did unt they bully the King of *Prussia* a little

---

[4] In *Venice Preserv'd* at Drury Lane on 7 March; *London Stage*, Part 4, i. 34. The
benefit was advertised in *GA* of 16 February 1748.

[1] *Annals*, III. xix. 7: '[one school] admits all hearsay evidence, whatever its character, as
indisputable' (Loeb).

[2] Cf. *Dialogue*, above, p. 33: 'this [war] was most certainly undertaken at the earnest Desire
of the *British* Merchants . . .'.   [3] Brabant.   [4] Allies.

[5] Carteret (Granville), who had detached Frederick II of Prussia from the combination
hostile to Maria Theresa in 1742, with the Treaty of Westminster, was considered by
Frederick to be pursuing an essentially anti-Prussian policy, particularly in the negotiation

muore,[1] and then he wud ha comed in; but to gu to carry on a War without Men enow, they might as well think of running down an old Fox with a Harl of Dogs*. As for the *Duch* and the Queen of *Hungry*, we might have known they would deceive us; for is it not plain now that they have deceived us?[2] And now we have agot a Parcel of *Hessians* and *Switch*,[3] and *Hannoverians* and *Rushions*,[4] and who the Divil is to pay um? Old *England* pays for all.

But zay the Ministerial Rascals, we would ha a Piece.—Ay and zo woud we ha a Piece too; but than it must be a good Piece, and a lasting Piece, and a Piece that it shall never be in the Power of *France* to brake again. If *France* be a minded to make a Piece, we'l gi it her. Let her restuore all she has unjustly a taken upon the Kontinent, and let us keep *Cape Britoon*, which we got fairly at Zee by the Vallur of *Englishmen*,[5] and then every *Englishman* will be vor a Piece; but after zuch an expensive War, which has almost a ruind us, and in which we have bin a beaten from the Beginning, to think we will accept of a bad Piece after all, why what the Devil must they think of us, but that we be either mad or Fools. No, no, we will never part with *Cap Britton*— Tell um that.—We will never part with *Cap Britton*. As for all the rest we have a got by the War, they may have it again with

---

* *A Sportsman's Phrase for three Dogs.*[6]

of the Treaty of Worms (1743); see Richard Lodge, *Great Britain and Prussia in the Eighteenth Century*, pp. 40–56.

[1] On the charge of bullying Prussia, cf. *Dialogue*, above, p. 42.

[2] Alluding to the failure of the Dutch and Maria Theresa to deliver the number of troops agreed to by the allies in convention. See *Dialogue*, above, p. 42, n. 4.

[3] There is no record of parliamentary disbursements for Swiss mercenaries in 1748. To an eighteenth-century audience, however, Swiss soldiers were a veritable 'type' of the mercenary; see *Pasquin*, v. i: 'These are Swiss soldiers, I perceive, Mr. Fustian; they care not which side they fight on'; Henley, xi. 221. A Swiss regiment was formed in 1744 from among the Swiss servants in and around London, for service in case of the expected invasion from France; *GM*, xiv (1744), 166, and Walpole to Mann, 1 March 1744 (*Yale Walpole*, xviii. 409). Swiss mercenaries served under Marshal Wade in the Forty-Five; *Journals of . . . Commons*, xxv. 136.

[4] For the expenses of maintaining the Hessian, Hanoverian, and Russian auxiliaries, see *Journals of . . . Commons*, xxv. 771, and *Proper Answer*, above, p. 76, n. 3.

[5] Louisburg and with it Cape Breton Island, fell in June 1745 at the hands of a New England colonial force escorted by Commander Warren's ships; H. W. Richmond, *The Navy in the War of 1739–1748*, ii. 200–16.

[6] A leash of hounds (*OED*), that is, a set of three, an insufficient number in this case. Cf. *Hounslow-Heath; A Poem* (London, 1747), p. 21 n.: 'A Couple and half, or a pair of Couples; two of them buckled together is an Harle of Hounds.'

all my Heart; but rather than part with *Cap Britown*, I woud gi my Vote to carry on the War to the End of the World, provided it could be done, (as to be sartain it may by those who know how to do it) without the Ruin of the Nation.

If the present Ministry don't know how to do this, why wont they go away, and let those cum in that do know. To be zure there be zuch men, thof we, who live altogether in the Country, don't know um; but Ould *England's* Journal, t'other Day, signified as how he did.[1] I wish methinks he would have named um, that we might a drank their Healths, that would ha been zome Satisfaction in these bad Times.

Prithee, Cousin *Jan*, how comes it about that zuch a Zet of Bl–ckheads, as the present Mins—y be, (for that you do all agree they be) should ha outwitted many wiser Peple than themsels, and ha got all their Power? What the Devil, be they Conjurers: for they zay the K— don't like um,[2] nor the P— don't like um,[3] nor the Peple don't like um. How the Devil comes all this about? I can never believe that dree, or vour, or half a Score Men can keep out the Pretender, (as he is a call'd) if the——and——and every Body else was for bringing un in.

What a Pox, shall zuch a Parcel of Fellows as these go on to carry on a bad War, and to make a bad Peace, and to level Tacses, and to take away the Liberty of the Press, and all the rest of the Liberties of the Nation, and to zend away all our Corn, and to bring over Forenners.[4] I say they must be Conjurers, and I can never believe the contrary.

But now I mention the Liberty of the Press, prithee, do tell us, how long it was a taken away, or if 'tis not yet adun, when 'tis to be, and what the Ministry have begun about it. And about other Liberties too I should be glad to know, why don't you

---

[1] Not identified. *OE* of 13 February 1748 compared the Pelham ministry unfavourably with Granville's, but without 'naming' the latter.

[2] After the failure, in February 1746, of the joint attempt by George II, Bath, and Granville to form a ministry exclusive of the Pelhams, it became an Opposition tactic to hint at the King's enduring resentment of the Pelhams. For evidence of a reconciliation by 1747 see Owen, *Rise of the Pelhams*, p. 318.

[3] Perhaps alluding to the 'fracas, the cabals at court', and the scuffle for power subsequent to Chesterfield's sudden resignation as Secretary of State on 6 February 1748. However, contemporary testimony agrees that from an Administration point of view the session of Parliament ('the P——') was generally 'tranquil and satisfactory'; Fox to Hanbury Williams, 17 February 1748, cited in Coxe, *Pelham*, i. 390; see also i. 388.

[4] Cf. *JJ* no. 9, above, pp. 144–5, and *JJ* no. 11, above, pp. 156–8.

always mention Particulars, and name every Liberty as often as tis a taken away. I fancy you despise us Peple in the Country too much to let us into any Secrets: for these 20 Years last past that they have bin a taking away our Liberties,[1] none of you Writers have ever mentioned one single Particular; zu that when the Ministerial Rascals ask what the Devil we mean by our Liberties being endvaded, we look like Fools, and know not what to anser, but that it is zu put down upon the Peaper.

Prithee, do let us a little into the Secret of Matters; for it is very hard for a Man to be told every Day that his House is a-vire, and to believe it is a-vire, and yet neither to be able to see any Flame, nor to smell any. What must his Naybours think of such a Man, who complains for twenty Years together, and when he is asked in what Part of his House the Flame is, can only anser, I heard a Fellow in the Street cry Fire.

I would not have you to think, that either I or the rest of our Friends want this Information upon any other Account, than to be abel to anser the Rascals: for I promise you we believe every thing oursels as much as if we knowd it. So no more at present, from,

Dear Cousin Jan Trott-Plaid,

Your affectionate Cousin and Servant,

Humphry Gubbins.

To the Author of the Jacobite Journal.

Bissextile, or Leap-Year.   Vincent Wing.[2]

Sir,

The learned Author from whom I take my Motto, assures us, that this Year there will be a Day added between the 28th of *February* and the 1st of *March*. An Event so extraordinary, (which I find, by searching the Records of Times past, has not been known to happen above once in four Years) certainly deserves the Attention of the Public; and therefore I shall offer

---

[1] Fielding is here quietly making the point that the Prince of Wales's current Opposition party is in direct line of descent from the Bolingbroke–Pulteney–Carteret clique which quickly gathered around the Prince on his first arrival in England in December 1728.

[2] Wing (1619–88), astronomer and compiler of almanacs and calendars, was the source of a long series of later compilations bearing his name. The motto comes from *An Almanack for the Year of our Lord God 1748. Being Bissextile or Leap-Year. By Vincent Wing* (London, [n.d.]).

some few Observations that occur to me upon this important Subject.

This is a Matter of Consequence to the money'd Men of this Kingdom: For those who have Money out at Interest by the Year, will lose 1 336th Part of that Interest.¹ For which Reason, I am inform'd, that many eminent Usurers of the City of *London*, as well *Jews* as *Gentiles*, intend to keep a solemn Fast on *Monday* next,² to bewail the Disaster brought upon them by that Day, and to balance it as well as they can, by a Parsimony somewhat greater than usual. On the contrary *Jack Courtly* tells me, that he and his Friends have already bespoke a grand Entertainment at the *King's Arms* in *Pall-mall*,³ in Commemoration of their having Money one Day, without paying Interest for it.

But let us leave these curmudgeonly Usurers and the rakehelly Spendthrifts their Counterparts, and turn our Eyes to the Ladies, whom we shall find no less affected in a Point as dear to them as Money is to the Usurer. Prince *George* of *Denmark* was born on the 29th of *February*,⁴ and, by a just calculation of Chances, one Woman in 1741 may be supposed to be born on that Day. Therefore, whenever I see a Miss who has lived as many Years in the World as an old Man, I take it for granted that she had the same Birth-day with that illustrious Person, and that 'till she has seen 20 Birth-days, she reckons herself a Miss in her Teens,⁵ and consequently intituled to as many Lovers as she can get.

I am afraid this Calculation will hardly be sufficient to account for the Number of young Ladies born a good while ago: If not, we may add an equal Number of those born in Leap-Years, late on the 28th of *February*, or early on the 1st of *March*; who,

---

¹ Apparently an error for 1/366th, itself only an approximate figure, unless some sort of compounding is implied, or else some 'excluded' days.

² Fielding's invention. For the business community as a whole March 7 was a working day. The most recent public fasting day seems to have been February 17.

³ Located on the north side of Pall Mall, near the Haymarket, this tavern is perhaps that referred to in *Amelia*, IV. v, and X. v and vii, as well as in *Journal of a Voyage to Lisbon*, *sub* Wednesday, 26 June 1754. See J. Paul de Castro, 'Principal London Coffee-Houses, Taverns, and Inns in the Eighteenth Century', *N & Q*, 12th Series, vi. 105 (10 April 1920).

⁴ According to his coffin plate, George, Prince of Denmark (1653–1708), youngest son of Frederick III of Denmark and consort of Queen Anne (1683), was born on 2 April 1653. However, the date is elsewhere given variously as 29 February and 11 and 21 April; see G. E. Cokayne, *Complete Peerage*, rev. ed., iii (London, 1913), 571. The February 29 date is given by Sir Charles Cotterel, *The Whole Life and Glorious Actions of Prince George of Denmark* (London, 1708), p. 2.

⁵ Alluding to Garrick's play, *Miss in Her Teens*; see *JJ* no. 9, above, p. 147.

by a favourable Report of their Midwives may claim the same Privilege.

But you will say, how does this conduce to our Great End? Truly what I have said hitherto, was only to draw in the Reader by a little Amusement, and fix him at last upon the main Point. I, who am a Practitioner of the Law, know, as well as you Political Writers, that any Thing may be made out of any Thing, and indeed out of nothing, notwithstanding an obsolete mistaken Maxim to the contrary.[1] And now you shall see how easily this great Work is brought about. Let us only suppose the Government to be a huge Debtor for the Interest of all the public Funds, and that the Interest of all those Funds for a Day amounts to *   Is it not apparent that this Sum is sunk upon us? And is it not apparent, that, unless they divide that Sum between you and me, there will be, and there must be, and there ought to be a most outragious Clamour against them?

Now I am got into my Interrogatories, give me leave to ask a question or two more. Is not the 28th of *February* usually the Day before the 1st of *March*? Is not the 1st of *March* postponed by this additional Day? Is not the 1st of *March* the Grand Anniversary Feast of the Ancient *Britons*?[2] Are not the Ancient *Britons* choleric? Are they not brave? The Tendency of these Questions is very plain. Believe me, it would be no difficult Matter, if we could find any great Man of that Country who would join us heartily, so to incense those inflammeable Gentlemen, by a warm Representation of the Indignity offered to their Country and tutelar Saint, as to * * * * Our Friends will understand the rest.

Yours,

Ephemeridius.

* I have purposely omitted the Sum, not doubting that our Friends will suppose it greater than it is.

Proceedings at the Court of Criticism, Thursday March 3.

The following Letter was read, and approved, and the Thanks of the Court were ordered to be return'd to the Writer.

1 *Ex nihilo nihil fit*. Cf. Fielding's 'Essay on Nothing', *Miscellanies* (1743), i. 180: 'There is nothing falser than that old Proverb . . . *Ex Nihilo nihil Fit*.' See also Henry K. Miller, *Essays on Fielding's 'Miscellanies'* (Princeton, N.J., 1961), pp. 298–312.

2 The commemorative day of St. David, patron saint of Wales. In what follows Fielding alludes to the incendiary potential of the Opposition centred on the Prince of Wales.

To John Trott-Plaid, *Esq; Censor of* Great Britain.

The Observations on *Clarissa* in your 5th Journal[1] gave me very great Pleasure, not only as being (in my Opinion) extremely just, but as giving me Hopes that something, besides Abuse of an Author, might possibly be received and relish'd by the Publick. But how was I mortified in almost every Set of Company I went into afterwards, by hearing it said with a Sneer, that *Clarissa* was finely *puff'd* in the last *Jacobite Journal*. Pray, Sir, is it fair to call all Commendation *Puffing?* As you have undertaken the Office of Censor, I wish you would endeavour to convince the World how unjust and cruel a Thing it is to give a Name of Reproach to the most deserved Praises that can be bestowed; and at the same time not only to suffer, but to encourage all Sorts of Abuse that can be thrown on the most ingenious Productions of the Age.

This, I am afraid, is a Proof of too much Ill-nature in the Human Composition; but as you have evidently shewn the very Reverse in the Proceedings at your Court, (though I declare you have not, I think, bestowed any undeserved Praise on either Book or Person) I hope by your means to see Commendation and Censure placed upon such an Equality, that neither shall be deem'd other than the Effect of an impartial Perusal; unless upon due Examination it shall be found, that one is the Effect of Malice, Envy, or Ill-nature, or that the other is (that only true Puff) the Breath of Flattery purchased by a Bribe. I promise you I am only an Advocate, and no Party concerned in this Cause; for, unless you think well enough of this short Letter to publish it, I never shall, by appearing in Print, experience the Bitterness of the present prevailing Humour of Criticism, nor the Benefit of a Reformation, should you effect one, being no Writer, but only your constant Reader, and

Humble Servant, &c.

The Pamphlet advertised as written by the Author of the *Dissertation on Parties*,[2] in order to insinuate that it was the

---

[1] See *J.J.* no. 5, above, pp. 118–20.

[2] *GA* of 27 February 1748 advertised the pamphlet *Good Queen Anne Vindicated* as 'By the Author of *The Dissertation on Parties*', i.e. Bolingbroke.

Performance of that celebrated Hand, was read, and condemned
as a meer Catch-penny, and an Imposition on the Public.
(*Adjourned.*)

SATURDAY, MARCH 12, 1748.   NUMB. 15.

Qui mihi Discipulus, puer, es, cupis atque doceri
Huc ades; hæc animo, concipe, dicta tuo.[1]

The following is a Parody on the first Book of *Ovid's Art of Love*;
for which Reason we recommend a new Translation of that
Book[2] to the unlearned Reader, where he will find all the Precepts of the Original modernized, and rendered agreeable to
the present Times, and where he will be better enabled to relish
the Beauties of this Performance; for which we thank the Writer,
and desire a Continuance of his Correspondence.

To the Writer of the Jacobite Journal.

Sir,
You have here a Translation of a *Latin* Poem, intitled, *De Arte
Jacobitica*, in three Books. I have sent you the *English* Version of
the first Book, because I have been told that Jacobites are no
Scholars, and understand no *Latin*. If you like this, you may
hereafter receive the Translation of the second Book. Mean time,
I remain yours, &c.

M. O. A. J.[3]

Horace wrote the Art of Poetry, *Ovid* the Art of Love, and I

---

[1] 'You who are a pupil of mine, boy, and are desirous of instruction, come hither; take
these words to heart.' The source, if any, of this epigraph has not been identified. Fielding
may be parodying the didactic forms of address that are characteristic of Ovid's *Ars
Amatoria*, e.g. ii. 498–9.

[2] *Ovid's Art of Love Paraphrased, and Adapted to the Present Time*, although advertised
in *JJ* no. 15 as 'This Day is published', was first published in February 1747; *GM*, xvii
(1747), 108. Millar lists it among Fielding's works, in the publisher's advertisement prefixed (p. vii) to the 1754 edition of *Jonathan Wild*, and again in the 1758 edition of Sarah
Fielding's *Cleopatra and Octavia*. The 1756 Dublin issue of *Ovid's Art of Love Paraphrased* makes the first explicit title-page attribution to Fielding; see review of *The Lover's
Assistant, or, New Art of Love* (1760), ed. Claude E. Jones, in *PQ*, xli (1962), 587–8.
Millar, whose name appears in the 1748 advertisement in *JJ* no. 15 but not on the original
1747 title-page, may have been trying to 'remainder' the original issue; no title-page dated
1748 has been discovered.

[3] Perhaps 'Master of the Order of Ancient Jacobites'.

write the Art of Jacobitism.——Come, *Tisiphone*,[1] from Hell, bring with thee ill-judging *Zeal*, and obstinate *Bigottry*, and inspire me with all thy Furies, while I teach the black Art of Jacobitism. 'Twas thou that didst instruct the holy Inquisitors, and those Miscreants that belyed the sacred Name of *Jesus*, to embrue their Hands in Christian Blood: Nor hast thou been unmindful of the *English* Nation: We too can boast our *Lauds*,[2] our *Sacheverils*,[3] our **ok*[4] *ippen*[5] [*Here several proper Names were doubtless in the Original, but the Rats or Moths have devoured them.*]

First of all learn the Art of Lying, and Misrepresenting. Fling Dirt enough, and some will certainly stick. You may venture to abuse the King himself; but do this with Caution, for the Sake of your Ears and Head. But spare not his Ministers; give a wrong Turn to their most plausible Actions. If they prosecute the War with Vigour, swear they are neglectful; if they desire a Peace, call them Cowards; if War, call them bloodthirsty, and Seekers after the Ruin of their Country. 'Twas by such Arts as these that the brave *Marlborough*, and the just *Godolphin*,[6] fell a Victim to the Intrigues of *Harley*[7] and ***. You may add Perjury to your Lies. *Jupiter*, 'tis said, laughs at the Perjury of Lovers;[8] he has many a time forsworn himself to

---

[1] The invocation to Tisiphone is apposite, because the Furies were avengers of crime, especially crime against the ties of kinship; here, by extension, crime against country.

[2] William Laud (1573–1645), Archbishop of Canterbury, is listed here among the Jacobite 'martyrs' by reason of his impeachment by the Long Parliament and subsequent execution on grounds of high treason.

[3] Henry Sacheverell (1674 ?–1724), Fellow of Magdalen College and incendiary preacher in the High-Church cause, was impeached for two sermons (1709) affirming non-resistance and opposing toleration and occasional conformity. His trial (1710), which ended in a close verdict against him, took place in an atmosphere of public rioting and ideological dispute, and eventually led to the fall of the Whig ministry. He became a virtual exemplar of High-Church sentiment and Tory principle. See, for example, *Spectator* no. 37 (12 April 1711) and no. 57 (5 May 1711), and *JJ* no. 21, below, pp. 248–9.

[4] Henry St. John (1678–1751), Viscount Bolingbroke, Secretary of State (1710) under Queen Anne, was dismissed from office on the accession of George I and attainted.

[5] William Shippen (1673–1743), the 'downright *Shippen*' of Pope's imitation of Horace (*Sat.* ii. i. 52), for many years leader of the Jacobite wing of the Commons, was imprisoned in the Tower in 1718 for expressions reflecting on George I.

[6] See *Proper Answer*, above, p. 64, n. 3.

[7] Robert Harley (1661–1724), 1st Earl of Oxford, in 1710 architect of the dissolution of the Whig ministry and of the Tory victory in the general elections, head of the ministry which charged Marlborough with peculation and succeeded in dismissing the latter from all his offices in 1711. Harley is one of the 'heroes' of the pseudo-Winningtonian *Apology*; see General Introduction above, p. xl, and *Proper Answer*, above, p. 65.

[8] Ovid, *Art of Love*, i. 633–6.

Juno. You have *Jupiter* for your Example: What can a Pagan, like yourself, desire more? The next thing you are to remember, is to feign a Love to your Country and Religion: The less you have of both, the better you can feign both. O Liberty, O Virtue, O my Country![1] Remember to have such Expressions as these constantly in your Mouth. Words do Wonders with silly People: But don't too openly discover your Design of ruining your Country by changing the Religion of it, and introducing arbitrary Power and a Popish King. Don't be caught in your own Trap. Remember the End of *Perillus*, who was burnt in his own Bull;[2] and you may be ruined yourself before you bring about the Ruin of your Country. Keep therefore to general Terms, and never descend to Particulars: You may wish things went better.———*You can't tell, but surely 'twas better in good Queen Anna's Days—or in the Bacchanalian Times of Charles—or, in the Holy Martyr's Reign.* At the mentioning the Martyr, you may drop a Tear; and, if you are sure of your silly Company, you may swear the present Ministry cut off his Head. An Anachronism in Politicks is no more faulty than an Anachronism in Poetry. If you are among good and orthodox Churchmen, you may swear the Church of *England* is in Danger under a Church of *England* King, and cannot be secure unless the Popish Pretender is restored. Paradoxes in Conversation are to be supported with Confidence and Sophistry. Remember likewise, that you frequently inculcate the Divine Right of Kings to do Wrong; and that they are accountable to God only for being Devils upon Earth.

Various People are to be taken by various Methods; and a wise *Proteus* will turn himself into all Shapes. This *Proteus*, the Fables say, was an *Egyptian* Conjurer,[3] and transformed himself into what monstrous Appearance he pleased: He roar'd a Lion, he grinn'd a Wolf, he flash'd a Fire, he flow'd a River. This *Proteus* be thou; roar, grin, flash, and flow. Spread thy Nets,

---

[1] Cf. Cato's 'Rome is no more' speech in Addison's Cato, IV. iv. 106.

[2] Inventor of the brazen bull in which Phalaris, the celebrated Sicilian tyrant, was said to have burned his victims alive, Perillus was the first to perish by his own invention; see Ovid, *Art of Love*, i. 653–4, and *CGJ* no. 19 of 7 March 1752.

[3] Homer, *Odyssey*, iv. 385 ff., identifies Proteus as an Egyptian *daimon*, servant of Poseidon and resident of the island of Pharos. Virgil, *Georgics*, iv. 387 ff., follows Homer in the account of Proteus' powers of transformation, but locates him on Carpathos, between Crete and Rhodes.

and catch the various Fry with various Baits. Consider a little the Dispositions of Mankind; the Young are open and honest, the Old are cautious and wary. Old Birds are not to be caught with Chaff; and an old Hare will be sure to double.¹

But you will ask perhaps where the proper Persons are to be found, to make Proselytes of to Jacobitism. This is an Enquiry worthy a Sportsman: For he is a bad Huntsman who would beat about the *Royal-Exchange* for a Hare or a Fox; and not a much better Gunner or Fisherman, who goes a shooting in *Somerset-Gardens*, or attempts to angle in the magnificent Bason there.² As those all know the Places where their Game resort, so must you. You have no Occasion to go with Parson *Whitefield* to *Georgia* after a young Jacobite;³ but you may go with Parson *Whitefield* to *Kennington-Common*,⁴ or *Bagshot-Heath*,⁵ or *Hounslow*,⁶ in quest of one; for Want has made many a Man a Jacobite, Revenge more, and Ignorance thousands. Want and Penury bid you hope for Change. Revenge works stronger in the human Heart than even Penury. Who can bear to see a Rival prevail? Hence the affected Patriotism of *** and ** and *. [*Here likewise are many proper Names lost, never to be retrieved but by Conjecture.*] Ignorance

¹ Cf. *Ovid's Art of Love Paraphrased* (1747), p. 87: 'Old Birds are not taken with Chaff; and an old Hare will be sure to double.' There are a number of striking verbal parallels between the 'Paraphrase' of 1747 and the 'Parody' printed in *JJ* no. 15.

² Cf. *Ovid's Art of Love Paraphrased*, p. 9: 'For he is a bad Huntsman who would beat about the *Royal-Exchange* for a Hare or a Fox; and not a much better Gunner or Fisherman, who goes a shooting in *Somerset-Gardens*, or attempts to angle in the magnificent Bason there.' The gardens, which were laid out by William Goodrowse early in the seventeenth century, on the Thames-side of Somerset House, contained a water-garden with fountains and statuary; Henry B. Wheatley, *London Past and Present*, iii (London, 1891), 270, and John Timbs, *Curiosities of London* (London, [1867]), p. 736.

³ George Whitfield (1714–70), leader of the Calvinistic Methodists and famous open-air preacher, had been evangelizing in America since 1744. Appointed minister of Savannah by the Georgia trustees, he had founded an orphanage in that city. *GM*, xviii (1748), 329, records his return to London on 4 July 1748. For some of Fielding's allusions to Whitfield and to Methodism see Dudden, i. 270 n.

⁴ In the manor of Lambeth, this common was the customary place of execution for Surrey, and it was here that the so-called 'Manchester officers' were executed for their part in the Forty-Five. After the churches began to close their pulpits to Whitfield, c. 1739, he took to open-air preaching at places like Kennington Common, Moorfields, and Black-heath. See John Gillies, *Memoirs of Rev. George Whitfield* (New Haven, Conn., 1834), p. 43; *GM*, xvi (1746), 383; John Doran, *London in Jacobite Times*, ii. 158–78.

⁵ In west Surrey, not far from Windsor Great Park, with an unsavoury reputation as a hangout of highwaymen.

⁶ A large heath in southwest Middlesex, between Brentford and Staines, also with an unsavoury reputation as a hangout of highwaymen.

is the Mother of Jacobitism. Hence the rural Sportsmen and Foxhunters will fall an easy Prey; and the Country will afford sufficient Plenty of younger Brothers, whose Eyes their good Mothers have kept betimes from poring on *Greek* and *Latin* Authors; those *Greek* and *Latin* Authors, which have been the Bane of the Jacobite Cause, and inspired Men with the Love of *Athenian* Liberty and old *Rome*, and taught them to hate Tyrants and arbitrary Governments. *London* too has all Sorts of Game for the Net. Whores and Rogues abound there; many are ruined, and most in a fair Way of being so. How many disappointed out-of-Place poor Rogues do we every Day meet? And what universal Ignorance, attended with complicated Impudence? In short, the Variety is so great, that it will even distract your Choice.

But above all, in Times of publick Calamities, then remember your Lesson; say God himself is turn'd our Enemy. And if, by Chance, our Monarch should meditate new Triumphs, and resolve on the Punishment of *France*; then, when *William* the Avenger[1] is abroad, do thou raise Commotions and Tumults at home. Whilst he, *all Gold*, shines in the *Gallick* Plains, carrying in his Hand his Father's Thunder; do thou, *all Lies*, walk the dirty Streets of *London*: And remember, I repeat it again, fling Dirt enough; blacken, lie, and defame. Perhaps some *Jack Cade*[2] may arise in the glorious Cause of Jacobitism, and shake the Throne itself; while Swarms of Locusts and Caterpillars come from the North, and devour the Fruits of *England*.

Part of our Undertaking still remains, and Part is finish'd: Here, then, let us cast Anchor, and moor the Ship.[3]

To the Author of the Jacobite Journal.

Dear Brother Trott-Plaid,

I have herewith sent thee thy Genealogy and mine, to let the Whiggish Rascals know that our Rise and Pedigree are not so

---

[1] One of the contemporary names for the Duke of Cumberland, conqueror of the Jacobites in the Forty-Five, who in March 1748 was back in Flanders ('*Gallick* Plains') preparing to meet Marshal Saxe; Charteris, *William Augustus, Duke of Cumberland*, p. 340. Cumberland had left England on 24 February 1748; *Yale Walpole*, xix. 464.

[2] John Cade (d. 1450), leader of the rebellion now bearing his name, defeated Henry VI's army at Sevenoaks and briefly entered London, where he beheaded the Lord Treasurer before being driven out.

[3] Cf. the concluding sentence of *Ovid's Art of Love Paraphrased*, p. 87; also, Ovid, *Art of Love*, i. 772.

mean as they are apt to imagine, and insinuate to the thoughtless World.——Please to publish it in thy next Journal, and thou wilt oblige many of thy honest Readers, and particularly thy sincere Friend, and hearty Well-wisher, (which is all the same)

Jan. 15th,   *Cambr. Britannicus.*[1]

1747–8.

The Genealogy of a Jacobite.

The Devil begot Sin, Sin begot Error, Error begot Pride, Pride begot Ignorance, Ignorance begot blind Zeal, blind Zeal begot Superstition, Superstition begot Priest-craft, Priest-craft begot Lineal Succession, Lineal Succession begot Indelible Character, Indelible Character begot Blind Obedience, Blind Obedience begot False Worship, False Worship begot Infallibility, Infallibility begot the Pope and his Brethren in the Time of *Egyptian* Darkness,[2] the Pope begot Purgatory, Purgatory begot Auricular Confession, Auricular Confession begot Renouncing of Reason, Renouncing of Reason begot Contempt of the Scriptures, Contempt of the Scriptures begot Implicit Faith, Implicit Faith begot Carnal Policy, Carnal Policy begot unlimited Passive Obedience, unlimited Passive Obedience begot Non-resistance, Non-resistance begot Oppression, Oppression begot Faction, Faction begot Patriotism, Patriotism begot Opposition to all the Measures of the Ministry, Opposition begot Disaffection, Disaffection begot Discontent, Discontent begot a Tory, and a Tory begot a Jacobite on the Body of the Whore of *Babylon*, when she was deem'd past Child-bearing.

To the Author of the Jacobite Journal.

Mr. Trott-plaid,   *Manchester,*[3] *March* 5.

Several Jacobites in these Parts cannot help thinking, that you are

---

[1] A Welsh-Briton. Cambria (Wales) was anciently and erroneously supposed to have got its name from Camber, legendary son of Brute, legendary founder of the British race. Here again Fielding is glancing at the Prince of Wales, leader of the Opposition.

[2] Exodus 10: 21–3. The analogy is between the supposed growth of the notion of infallibility during the Mosaic jurisdiction and a similar growth of the same notion in the Christian Church after it had been carried away from the Scriptures and subjected to the 'tyranny' of the papacy. See Martin Luther's *Babylonian Captivity of the Church* (1520), *passim.*

[3] The city had a contemporary reputation for disaffection, in great measure the result of its having raised a regiment in support of the Young Pretender during the Forty-Five.

a little too severe upon our good Friend Mr. *Carte.* Pray why should you endeavour to discredit the Story of *Christopher Lovell,*[1] so much to the Advantage of our Cause? The Whigs would have done this with Pleasure; but from you, it does not come so well. Besides, let me tell you that you go upon very poor Evidence. *Christopher* died of the King's Evil: What then? *Christopher,* as he was a very careless drunken Fellow, might have lost the little Piece of Money, which is always hung about the Neck of the Patient when touch'd;[2] in which Case it is notorious and frequent, and an Event always expected, that the Sores will break out again; so that, unless it could have been proved that *Christopher* died possess'd of the Piece of Money aforesaid, his dying of the King's Evil is of very little or no Importance; and notwithstanding what has been said against it on this Account, this Instance will still remain a Proof of pure Blood, since neither Coronation nor Anointing could have any Share in the Cure.

As to the Power itself, the numberless Instances on Record put that beyond all Doubt; and to pretend to argue or reason against Matters of Fact fully proved, and evidenced in the highest Manner by Records, is very ridiculous, and will never pass. In short, Sir, we Jacobites are very clear in these Points, and are resolved, notwithstanding your critical Censure, to approve and applaud Mr. *Carte's* Work, and to have his Name in the highest Esteem and Veneration. Immortal *Carte!*

O may some Poet rise, in future Times,
Worthy to sing thy Praise, that soaring high
Above th' *Aonian* Mount, or Sky-dipt Top,
Or *Snowden's* Brow, that, if compar'd, would make
Pindus a Wart; thence, on *Miltonian* Wing
Mounting a-loft, may reach the Stars of Heaven,
And there inscribe thy never-dying Name;
That as the *Greater Bear,*[3] so call'd of old,
Was chang'd by Moderns to the *Charles's Wain,*[4]

[1] See *JJ* no. 12, above, pp. 168–9.
[2] A coin or medal (originally a gold angel, in later times specially struck for the purpose) given by the sovereign to each person 'touched' for the king's evil (*OED*).
[3] Here apparently restricted to the seven brightest stars of *Ursa Major,* which form the 'Plough' or 'Big Dipper'.
[4] Applied to the seven brightest stars of *Ursa Major,* the name appears to arise out of the verbal association of the star-name *Arcturus* with *Arturus* or Arthur, and the legendary

The Lesser may be call'd from thee the *Cart*:[1]
There may'st thou roll within thy narrower Orb,
Attendant and regardant; nor e'er set,
Nor setting, fall beneath the Ocean's Brine.
As the blind *Grecian* Bard divinely sings
Self-taught. There may'st thou ever shine, to guide
The *British* Sailor o'er th' *Atlantic* Deep,
Homewards returning from each distant Clime,
And point his Course out to his Native Strand;
Where safe arriv'd, he jocund leaps on shore,
Roaming in search of Wine and buxom Lass,
His Solace from long wat'ry Way return'd.
    Whilst *Thames* does flow, whilst *Albion's* chalky Cliffs
Do brave the Ocean's Surge; whilst she reigns Queen
Among the Sea-girt Isles, so long secure
Thy Name, thy Honour, and thy Praise shall last;
But never from thy Patron's Praise disjoin'd.
Prince of Historians, to thy greater Worth
The antient *Greek*, of History stiled the Sire,[2]
Resigns submiss his Title; and he too,
*Olorus' Son, his everlasting Claim.
Great *Livy*, bowing low, shall own thee far
His greater: E'en *Guthry*[3] himself, tho' loth,
Reluctant tho', must yield.—*Cupidum pater optime vires
deficiunt——.*[4]

  * Thucydides, *who calls his History an everlasting Possession.*[5]

Go on, great Author, and in thy next Book give us a Dissertation on *Jacob's* Stone brought from *Scotland* by *Edward* I.

---

association of Arthur and Charlemagne; what was originally the wain of *Arcturus* became at length the wain of Carl or Charlemagne (*OED*).

  [1] The Lesser Bear, *Ursa Minor*, is also called 'The Waggon', and hence, by extension, '*Cart*'. The constellation is connected mythologically with the Arcadian nymph Callisto, whom Zeus placed among the stars under the name of *Arctos*. The first four letters of the latter name can be made, anagrammatically, into '*Cart*'.

  [2] Herodotus, Greek historian of the fifth century B.C., was called the father of history by, among others, Cicero (*De Legibus*, i. 5).

  [3] See *JJ* no. 13, above, p. 177, n. 3.

  [4] Horace, *Satires*, II. i. 12–13: 'Would that I could, good father, but my strength fails me' (Loeb).

  [5] *History*, i. 22.

and now placed under the Coronation-Chair at *Westminster*.¹
Demolish our Adversaries with this Stone; be very particular
about the Prophecy *Ni fallat Fatum Scoti*, &c.—which has always
been looked on to have had a primary Completion, when the
Stuarts first ascended the Throne.² The second may be clear'd
up full as much to the Satisfaction of every intelligent Reader,
as you have done the aforesaid miraculous Power; and let us see
who can hold up their Faces against the united Force of both of
them, or what the minute Criticks in their fictitious Court can
pretend to say to the contrary.

Your very humble Servant,

True Blue.

P.S. Mr. *Trott-plaid*, play the fair and impartial Part now, and
print this. I should be sorry to be forced to send to the *London
Evening-Post* to have it inserted there, and let the World know
that you refused it a Place in your Paper, because it was against
you, which I think would not be for your Reputation.

Proceedings at the Court of Criticism, Thursday March 10.

A third *non est inventus* being returned upon the Warrant to
apprehend THE TOWN, Process of Outlawry was issued against
the *said Town*.

One *Porcupine Pillage* came into the Court, and crying out,
I am the Author of the *Causidicade, Processionade, Triumvirade,
'Piscopade*, and *Old England*, threw a great Shovel-full of Dirt
at his Honour,³ but luckily none of it hit him. He was immediately

¹ The Stone of Destiny, more familiarly the Stone of Scone, was supposed to have been
brought originally from Tara in Ireland to Scone in Scotland, where it was used as the
coronation stone of Scottish kings until Edward I removed it to England at the beginning
of the fourteenth century. In Irish legend the stone of Tara was said to be that on which
Jacob rested his head at Bethel. Cf. *Spectator* no. 329 of 18 March 1712.
² For the full text of this ancient prophecy, which foretold that when the Stone was
removed from Scone the sovereignty of Scotland would soon follow, see *The Whole Pro-
phecie of Scotland* (Edinburgh, 1615), as reprinted in *Collection of Ancient Scottish Prophecies*
(Edinburgh, 1833), p. 64. The Latin prophecy is said to have been inscribed on the Stone
itself; *Sconiana* (Edinburgh, 1807), p. 9; but cf. Arthur Penryn Stanley, *Historical Memoirs
of Westminster Abbey*, 5th ed. (New York [n.d.]), i. 78. The 'primary Completion' here
referred to took place when James VI of Scotland became James I of England. The
'second' would be the hoped-for restoration of the Stuart line.
³ *OE* of 5 March 1748 devotes its entire leader, signed 'Porcupinus Pelagius', to a vicious
personal attack on Fielding. See *JJ* no. 11, above, pp. 160–2.

seized, and being brought to the Bar, the Court delivered themselves as follows:

I am very sorry to see, in an Age when the Liberty of the Press is pretended to be in Danger, such an Abuse made of this Liberty, as must give the greatest Encouragement to its Enemies (if there were any such) to attempt a Restraint of it: For wise and good Men will, by these Means, be brought to esteem this Liberty rather as a Nusance, than as a valuable Privilege to the Society.

Nothing ought to be, nor indeed generally is more dear to a Man than his Reputation; and if it be in the Power of every anonymous Scribbler to defame private Characters, and to publish Scandal over the Nation, without Regard either to Truth or Decency, I am apt to think every honest Man will soon wish to see this Power taken from them; and will lose all Aversion to a Law, which shall protect so valuable a Property as Reputation. For when this barbarous and wicked Practice becomes general, the Apprehension of it will reach those who have not yet been attacked, since, according to the vulgar Phrase, Men in a public Calamity know not whose Turn it will next be to suffer.——Thus *Horace*, speaking of the same abominable Custom, says:

> ——*Jam sævus apertam*
> *In rabiem verti cœpit jocus et per honestas*
> *Ire minax impune domos: doluere cruento*
> *Dente lacessiti; fuit intactis quoque cura*
> *Conditione super communi: Quin etiam lex,*
> *Pœnaque lata, malo quæ nollet carmine quenquam*
> *Describi, &c.*[1]

Thus translated by the Rev. Mr. *Francis*:[2]

> ——Cruel Wit soon turn'd to open Rage,
> And dar'd the noblest Families engage.
> When some who by its Tooth envenom'd, bled,
> Complain'd aloud: Others were struck with dread
> Tho' yet untouch'd, and in the public Cause,
> Implor'd the just Protection of the Laws,

---

[1] *Epistles*, II. i. 148–54.
[2] *Poetical Translation of the Works of Horace*, iv. 171. Of the note at the conclusion of the passage below, only the sentence immediately following the colon is from Francis.

Which from injurious Libels wisely guard
Our Neighbour's Fame.*

Do not affect to misunderstand nor misrepresent me. No Man
is more averse to the Destruction of the Liberty of the Press than
myself; but I am likewise an Enemy to the Abuse of this Liberty:
and it is from this Abuse alone it can ever be destroyed.

Now I must tell you very plainly, that, of all others, you have
been the most guilty of this Abuse. In your *Causidicade*, *Processionade*, &c. you have attack'd the most eminent Men in the
Profession of the Law, and particularly, I once more repeat it,¹
that great and admirable Person who is at the Head of it, and
whose Character soars as much above my Panegyric, as above
your Slander. Slander, indeed, on such a Character, is, by *Plutarch*, well compared to a Dart thrown against a solid Object,
which flies back into the Face of the Darter:² For, as *Seneca* well
observes, *Qui talibus maledicunt sibi ipsi convicium faciunt.*³

In your *'Piscopade*, you have at once fallen upon the whole
Privy-Council, and upon the whole Bench of Bishops, whom you
have traduc'd in a manner not only never permitted with Impunity, but, I believe, never attempted in any Nation.

Consider a Moment with yourself, whether you can imagine
any thing more absurd than for one in your Station of Life to
pass Censure on all the greatest and most sacred Characters in
the Kingdom, of whom you must be entirely ignorant, as you
cannot be supposed to have had Access, even to their upper Servants.

As to your Talents as a Writer, I tell you very sincerely and

---

* The Law was this: If any one sing, or compose Verses injurious to the Reputation of
another, let him be punished with Death.⁴ And it is remarkable, that this Law was introduced at a Time when the *Roman* Liberties were at the highest.

---

¹ For earlier notice of the attacks on Hardwicke see *JJ* no. 11, p. 161, n. 4 above. *The
Processionade* (1745) was a satirical poem attacking the Lords Justices and Hardwicke, the
Lord Chancellor.
² Cf. 'De Herodoti Malignitate' 8, *Moralia*, 855C. For a similar sentiment, without the
simile, see *Moralia*, 88D, and *Tom Jones*, XIV. vii.
³ Apparently adapted from the pseudo-Senecan work known as 'De Moribus', where the
accepted text reads: *multi cum aliis maledicunt sibi ipsis convicia faciunt.* See Seneca, *Opera*...
Supplementum, ed. Fr. Haase (Lipsiae, 1902), p. 64. Fielding's version may be translated:
'Those who slander worthy men bring censure upon themselves.'
⁴ For the law see Cicero, *De Republica*, IV. x. 12, and Pliny, *Natural History*, XXVIII. iv.
18.

very candidly too, they range you in the lowest Class. As your Ribaldry is unworthy of the Name of Wit, so your Numbers are no less undeserving of the Honour of Poetry. And if such truly contemptible Stuff should have been more propagated than it ought, do not plume yourself on that Account: For, believe me, no one of any Taste will ever read you with Approbation; nor will you ever be ranked even among the indifferent Poets which this Age produces. The Vulgar are eager after Scandal, from the same Curiosity that makes them flock to Executions; and in either Case their Curiosity is highest when their Superiors are the Sufferers; but the Author, like the Hangman, is so far from gaining their Admiration, that he is hardly ever considered by them. I advise you therefore for the future to lay down your Pen, or to exercise it in your own Profession,[1] where, in the low Branch to which you was bred, you will require no Genius to enable you to succeed. For you need not apprehend having drawn on yourself the Anger of that Great Man, whose high Station must exclude you from his Notice, and whose high Mind will secure you from his Resentment.

However, your abusive Behaviour here, and your Contempt of this Court, must not go without some Punishment. It is considered therefore by this Court, that you, *Porcupine Pillage*, be committed to the Bridewell of *Billingsgate* for the Space of a Month, and that you do stand in the Pillory of our Journal on *Saturday* next, all Day long, with these Verses of *Ausonius* pasted over your Head:

> *Nec posthæc metues ubique dictum.*
> *Hic est Theon* Poeta falsus.*[2]

The Court then proceeded to hear Council for and against the

---

* The Character which *Erasmus* gives of this *Theon* is, that he was a certain Poet of outragious Loquacity, and most petulant Scurrility, whence Persons whose Names had been scurrilously treated, were said to be bit with *Theon's* Tooth.[3]

---

[1] Presumably the law, in view of the allusion to Hardwicke, the Lord Chancellor, in the next sentence. Macnamara Morgan, one of those sometimes associated with 'Porcupinus Pelagius' and *OE*, was an attorney by training. See *JJ* no. 13, above, p. 181, n. 3.

[2] 'Epistles', xiv. 102–3, *Opuscula* xviii: 'no more hereafter shalt thou dread the universal cry: "This is that feigned poet, Theon"' (Loeb). The generally accepted text reads: *nec iam post metues ubique dictum: / Hic est ille Theon poeta falsus.*

[3] 'Adagiorum, Chil. II, Centur. II, Proverb. LV' (*Dente Theonino rodi*), in *Opera Omnia* (Lugduni Batavorum, 1703), ii. 466, where he cites Horace, *Epistles*, I. xviii. 82.

Foundling, and said, they would deliver Judgment on *Thursday* next.

Ordered, That Mrs. *Woffington* do prepare a good warm Box at her Benefit on *Monday* next,[1] for the Reception of Ourself and our fair Consort *Peggy*, her Namesake.

(*Adjourned*.)

SATURDAY, MARCH 19, 1748.   NUMB. 16.

——*Nos hæc novimus esse nihil.*

Martial.[2]

To shew our Contempt of all Arguments drawn from Common Sense, we shall freely print the following Letter, which we received last Week.

> *Lost is his God, his Country, ev'ry thing,*
> *And nothing left, but Homage to a King.*

Pope.[3]

Sir,

If the Notoriety of the Fact did not exclude all Argument to the Contrary, it would be hardly possible to conceive that any Body of Men, (professing themselves Protestants) could be so blind to their own Interest, so thoroughly in Love with Slavery and Tyranny, or such Enemies to the Church of *England*, as to wish to exchange the wise, just, and moderate Government which we have at present the Happiness to live under, for Popery and Tyranny under a cruel and bigotted Pretender, whose Principles, as well as his Interest, must oblige him to introduce and protect the Religion of the Church of *Rome*: Much less could any one believe it possible, if sad Experience had not taught it him, that any Body of Men could be so entirely divested of every Principle of Humanity, and so abandoned to every Kind and Degree of Wickedness, as to involve themselves and their native Country in the Guilt and Horror of a Civil War; to imbrue their

---

[1] At Drury Lane on 14 March 1748, with Peg Woffington in the title-role of *Jane Shore* for the first time; Fielding's *Intriguing Chambermaid* was the after-piece; *London Stage*, Part 4, i. 36.

[2] *Epigrams*, xiii. ii. 8: 'I know these efforts of mine are nothing worth' (Loeb).

[3] *Dunciad* (1742), iv. 523-4. The letter which follows may not have been written by Fielding.

Hands in the Blood of their Neighbours and Countrymen, to violate the most sacred Oaths, and incur the horrible Guilt of wilful Perjury;[1] in a Word, to introduce universal Horror and Desolation into the Land; and all this, meerly for the Sake of a few, abandoned, long exploded Principles, which the Jacobites themselves seldom chuse to own, and can never defend; nay, when hard press'd, do not scruple to disavow.——A Reflection upon this, has led some People to imagine, that great Numbers who pass under the Denomination of your Party, have no settled Principles at all; and that others of them hold such as they dare not profess, and, under the Guise of Jacobites, are, in Reality, *Roman* Catholicks. Of those, who have no Principles at all, there are many Sorts; some, for Instance, whose Disaffection does not proceed from a particular Hatred to the present, or a particular Attachment to any other Family or Government; but meerly from an Abhorrence of all Government, and a Desire to break through all the Restraints of Religion, Morality and Laws, and to give an unbounded Loose to every brutal Passion, and every inordinate Lust, without Fear of human Punishment, or Dread of Divine Vengeance. In a Word, to reduce us to that blessed State of Nature which the *Hotentots*,[2] and some other Nations, live in at this Day; where every Man doeth what seemeth right in his own Eyes, and is at full Liberty to practise every Vice, and gratify all his Passions, without Disgrace or Controul. Others there are, and of these not a few, whose Disaffection proceeds meerly from a Desire of Change, no Matter in whose Favour, or by what Means it is effected.——Men of broken Fortunes, and ruined Reputations, who have nothing to hope for under the present, and nothing to fear under any Alteration of Government: Whose Affairs, in short, are so desperate that no Change can be to them for the worse; and their Morals so loose

---

[1] By the provisions of the 'Act imposing the Abjuration Oath' (13 Will. III, cap. 6) and later Acts (e.g., 2 Geo. II, cap. 31) extending and particularizing its provisions, an oath abjuring the Pretender was imposed on office holders, ecclesiastical persons, foundation members of colleges, teachers in the universities and schools, lawyers and persons of sundry other categories; *Statutes at Large*, x. 399–406. The 'sacrament of the Lord's Supper according to the usage of the Church of England' had been required of even minor office holders and functionaries since the first Test Act (1673). An Act had been passed on 3 May 1744 making it treason to correspond with the sons of the Pretender; *Journals of . . . Commons*, xxiv. 680–1.

[2] An Augustan 'type' of primitivism, usually of the pejorative sort. Cf. *CGJ* no. 9 of 1 February 1752, and *Spectator* no. 389 of 27 May 1712.

and depraved, as to make it indifferent to them what Form of Religion or Government is established—whether Popery or Protestantism, absolute or limited Monarchy.——In a Word, (so as they can but serve themselves by it) whether we shall be Freemen or Slaves.——Lastly, the remaining Part of those who compose this goodly Fellowship, (and indeed the only honest Men among them) are the ignorant and illiterate Vulgar, who, by the grossest Lyes, the vilest Insinuations, and the most scandalous Misrepresentations that the Malice of Jacobites, or the Cunning of Jesuits could invent, have been deluded into a Party, whose Principles (if they knew them) the most Ignorant could not chuse but despise, and whose execrable Designs in Favour of Popery and Slavery they would certainly abhor. The former of these would be a Disgrace to any Doctrines but those of Popery, any Cause but that of Tyranny, and any Party but that of Jacobitism. The other is (I flatter myself) far from being so numerous as the Jacobites would insinuate; and indeed the few of that Rank who joined the Pretender in his late Attempt, and the Horror that prevailed so universally among them, at the Rumour of his Approach, seems to me an undeniable Proof, that their Number is indeed very inconsiderable. The Truth is, the good People of *England* begin to see they have been abused: Their Eyes are opened; the Delusion is wearing off a-pace, and will daily more and more, the more universally the Jacobite Principles are known, and their Consequences considered. What Thanks therefore do you deserve from all Well-wishers to their Country, for so publick and open a Declaration of the Principles of your Party, which seems so fair a Prelude to their utter Extinction in this Land. These Principles which have hitherto shunn'd the Light, and sculk'd about in Corners, or at best have been but insinuated, often deny'd, and seldom openly profess'd, are now publickly avow'd in a News-Paper,[1] and communicated through the whole Island. And whatever Advantages to the Cause you or the Jacobite Party may expect will result from it, I believe you will find yourselves mistaken; and tho' I shall ever be ready to acknowledge your Candour and Ingenuity in this Procedure, (which I the more admire as they are Qualities very rarely to be met with in one of your Party) yet you must excuse me if I still insist, that a more likely Expedient to overthrow all

[1] *The Jacobite's Journal.*

future Hopes of the Party, you could not possibly have invented. ——For what! Can the most rank Jacobite be stupid enough to flatter himself, that the Freeborn People of *England*, remarkable above any other Nation for Good Sense and Love of Liberty, will ever be brought to swallow that monstrous Absurdity, so repugnant to the Common Sense of Mankind, so derogatory to the native Freedom of Human Creatures, so opposite to all the Principles of our Constitution, and so contrary to the express Declaration of Holy Writ—*That Kings are by Divine Appointment, and consequently their Title indefeasible.*[1] If they are so, let them produce their Charter, and at least condescend to tell us the Marks, by which we may discover the Real from the Counterfeit. If they cannot do this, let them be assured that, in the mean time, as we were born free, we will maintain our Liberty; as we were created rational, we will follow the Dictates of our own Reason; as we are bless'd with an excellent Constitution, we will preserve it inviolate; and as we yet enjoy the Use of the Bible, to that we will adhere. We will entertain more honourable Conceptions of that Eternal Being, the supremely merciful God, than ever to let that become an Article of our Belief; the very Mention of which fills us with Horror,—That the greatest Tyrants that ever plagued Mankind, in all their horrible Impieties, in all their excessive Cruelties, in all their foul Murders, in all their abominable Lusts, in all their monstrous Villanies, in all their general Devastations, in every Act of publick Oppression, or private Injustice,—acted by Divine Appointment.——A most daring and impious Assertion.——Let the Jacobites duly consider of it, and they will be filled with Confusion at its Blasphemy. For to what doth this blasphemous Assertion amount to less, than that the supreme all-merciful God hath given a Divine and Indefeasible Right to Kings to murder out of Wantonness their own Subjects, as a late Emperor of *Morocco*, who is said to have slain Forty thousand of his with his own Hands;[2] or to proscribe, without any Process of Law, as many of the Nobility and Gentry as are obnoxious to them, in their arbitrary and wicked Designs;

---

[1] Cf. *Dialogue*, above, pp. 9–14.

[2] In *Freeholder* no. 10 of 23 January 1716 Addison credits Muley Ishmael, recently deceased Emperor of Morocco, with having slain 'above Forty Thousand of his People'. Addison cites as his major source Pidou de St. Olon's *The Present State of the Empire of Morocco* (1695), but the author of the letter in the *JJ* probably took the example directly from the *Freeholder*.

as *Augustus Cæsar*, who, for this Reason, proscribed great Numbers of the principal Senators of *Rome*;[1] or to sacrifice to their Lust, or their Vanity, to their Pleasure, or their Revenge, as many of their Fellow-Creatures as they think fit; as *Nero* did Hundreds of the *Romans* of all Ranks,[2] of every Age, of each Sex, not sparing even his own Mother or Brother, his Wives, or their Children, Citizens or Foreigners, Friends or Enemies, Senators or Plebeians, Kindred or Strangers, Old or Young, Men or Women, all perish'd alike; Death was the Lot of all, tho' the Means were various: Not to insist on a thousand Instances of the like Nature, of Butcheries that heretofore have been, and are at this Day acted, and acting in divers Parts of the World by the sole Command, and meerly to gratify the Lust, or satiate the Revenge of these annointed Tyrants. But if the abominable Lives of these Tyrants are not sufficient, methinks at least their terrible Deaths should destroy all their Pretence for Divine Commissions. Such were the Deaths of *Antiochus, Seleucus, Demetrius*, and others among the antient *Syrians*; of *Cambyses, Ochus, Sefi, Solyman*, and others among the antient and modern *Persians*; of *Tiberius, Caligula, Galba, Vitellius, Otho, Domitian*, &c. among the *Romans*; of the *Amuraths, Bajazets, Mahomets, Selymus's*, among the *Turks*; with numberless others, needless to mention, in all Parts of the World, and some not very far from hence.[3] Methinks, I say, the Remembrance of the Tragic End of these Prodigies in Impiety, should make even Jacobites blush at least, if not tremble, in asserting that they acted by Divine Appointment.

As one Absurdity naturally begets another—hence hath arisen that monstrous Principle of unlimited passive Obedience and Non-Resistance.——Twice within the Space of a Century, have our Constitution, our Liberty, and our Religion, been in Danger of being destroyed, by these very Principles, in the Reigns of King *Charles* the First, and of his Son *James* the Second. In the former, a strict Adherence to them, on the Part of the King,

---

[1] See Suetonius, 'Divus Augustus', *De Vita Caesarum*, II. xxvii.
[2] See Suetonius, 'Nero', *De Vita Caesarum*, VI. xxxvi–xxxvii.
[3] Perhaps a reference to, among others, Charles XII of Sweden (1682–1718), whose 'Fall', in Samuel Johnson's words, 'was destin'd to a barren Strand,/ A petty Fortress, and a dubious Hand'; *The Vanity of Human Wishes* (1749), 219–20. In his later years Charles, who was for the eighteenth century a 'type' of the modern tyrant or despot, intrigued with the French and the Jacobites against the Electorate of Hanover so as to menace George I.

against the Sense of the Nation, and in open Violation of the undoubted Rights of the People, joined to a rigorous Exercise,
and ill-timed Enlargement of ecclesiastical Discipline, occasioned
at length a Civil War, which ended in the Death of the King,
and in the temporary Ruin of the Constitution. In the latter, they
led the weak and unhappy King, by Nature a Bigot, and by
Education a Papist, in Defiance of his Coronation Oath,[1] to
attempt the introducing Popery into the Church, and Tyranny
into the State. God be praised, he failed! and the Popish Emissaries who spurred him on, were probably a Means designed by
the good and all-directing Providence of God, to bring about the
glorious and ever-memorable Revolution; a most auspicious
Event, by which our Liberties, our Constitution, and our Religion, were established on so firm and solid a Foundation, that
we trust the Malice of all our most inveterate Enemies, will
never be able to prevail against either:—That neither the Pope
and the Pretender, nor their Emissaries and Tools, the Jesuits
and Jacobites, with all their wicked, impious, and ignorant
Adherents, combined together in the same hellish Scheme,
against our Religion, Laws, and Liberty, will ever succeed in
their flagitious Attempts, as long as there are any Remains of
Good Sense, any Zeal for the Constitution, any Love of Liberty,
or any Regard for the Protestant Religion in Being among us.
In short, 'till the whole Body of the People shall become so depraved in their Understandings, so debauch'd in their Morals,
so corrupted by Wickedness, and enervated by Luxury, as to prefer Darkness to Light, Slavery to Liberty, Popery to Protestantism, and a despotic Government to our present happy Constitution. But God be praised, this Scene of Desolation is, in all
likelihood, as distant, as I am sure it would be terrible. The
Principles that lead to it lose Ground daily, and will, I flatter
myself, be soon extirpated out of the Land; and neither the
Principles themselves, nor the Party that espoused them, be
hereafter mentioned, but with Detestation, or heard of but in
Derision.——Yes, I have that good, and, I hope, just Opinion
of my Countrymen, that wherever any Party shall presume to
maintain such absurd Doctrines as these; Doctrines that lead
directly to Slavery, and would subject us to Popery, and include
in them Blasphemy; and especially if the Party that espoused

[1] See *JJ* no. 2, above, p. 99, n. 3; also *Proper Answer*, above, p. 71, n. 2.

such Doctrines, stood out in direct Contradiction to their own Principles; and while, with the most shameless Impudence, they were inculcating the slavish Doctrine of Passive Obedience to a bigotted Tyrant, should yet be so superlatively wicked, as to engage in open Rebellion against a most excellent King, in direct Contradiction to their own Principles, and in willful Defiance of the solemn Oaths that Numbers among them had taken: Whenever, I say, such Principles shall be espoused, and by such Men, (Principles so absurd, and Men so abandoned) I doubt not but my Fellow-Subjects, as true *Englishmen*, good Christians, Friends to the Church, and Lovers of their Country, will not fail to treat both the Doctrines themselves and their Defenders, with that thorough Contempt, and utter Abhorrence, they so justly deserve.

I am, Sir,

Your most humble Servant,

A Friend of the Church of England.

Proceedings at the Court of Criticism, Thursday March 17.

The Court upon Motion delivered the following Opinion concerning the *Foundling*.[1]

The Incident upon which this Play is founded, is Mr. *Belmont* bringing into his Father's House, at Midnight, a young Woman who, tho' unknown to the Family, is there received as a Ward of his, left to his Care by a Friend. The Father makes no Objection, nor much Enquiry into the Matter, and the Sister immediately contracts an Intimacy and Friendship with her.

This is too improbable.[2] Some better Story should have been forged by the young Gentleman, or Credulity should at least have been made the Characteristic of the Father; tho' even then the Imposition would have been almost too gross, especially in an Age which doth not greatly relish very *outrés*[3] Characters. The

---

[1] See *JJ* no. 12, above, p. 171, and note 4 there.

[2] The charge of improbability was a common one. See, for example, 'Remarks upon the *Foundling*' in *GM*, xviii (1748), 114–15, and *A Criticism on the Foundling. In a Letter to the Author* (London, 1748), p. 4.

[3] The *OED* records only two earlier usages in English, one of them Fielding's in his Preface to *Joseph Andrews*, p. 6.

Conduct of the Sister is still more unnatural. A young Lady of Fashion would never have been brought even to converse with a Woman under these suspicious Circumstances; nor have been contented with so absurd a Tale, which plainly appears to be, as it really is, a trumped-up Story: The Beauty of *Fidelia* would have been no Recommendation of her to any of her own Sex, particularly to such as *Rosetta* is described to be; nor have taken off those bad Impressions which the most candid must have received upon her first Appearance.

The Character of *Faddle* is likewise exceptionable:[1] For tho' I do admit, that some very sorry Fellows have been admitted among their Betters, in the Light of Buffoons, who perhaps have been as great Rascals as *Faddle* himself, yet they do not thus openly and plainly appear so. Nor do I believe such a Woman as *Rosetta*, or indeed any other young Lady, ever did or wou'd make Choice of a Fellow of this kind to create Jealousy in a Lover; since she must greatly demean herself by such Conduct. Again, the Behaviour of the Colonel to *Faddle*, in the Presence of his Mistress, is altogether as improper, and foreign to the Manners of upper Life.

These I think are the principal Objections; indeed all which appear to me of any Moment.

Now, on the other Side, the Story of *Fidelia* is extremely pretty and interesting: Her Character is highly amiable, her Distress very tender and affecting, and the Incidents which occasion it are very naturally and artfully contrived. The Character of young *Belmont* is very finely drawn. The Struggles between a virtuous Disposition and vitious Habits are most nobly and usefully painted: The Redemption from evil, by the conscious Shame which results from having a base Action set before him in its true and genuine Deformity, shews great Knowledge of Human Nature in the Author; and perhaps something which is yet more to his Honour.

The Change from bad to good is, I think, more artfully brought about here, than in any other Play, and the Scene which leads to it is one of the finest upon our Stage.

The whole Play abounds with generous and worthy Sentiments, and the Diction is every where lively and full of much Wit and Spirit.

[1] See *JJ* no. 12, above, p. 171, n. 4.

As to the malicious Insinuations of Plagiarism,[1] they do not deserve an Answer: They are indeed made in the true Spirit of modern Criticism.

Of the same Kind is all that hath been said concerning the Confusion in the unravelling the Plot. Indeed the Art with which the Plot is conducted, the Degrees by which it opens, the Incidents which occur in the Progress, and which at last produce the final Discovery, deserve great Commendation. To say Truth, the Want of Clearness is, I apprehend, not in the Author but in the Critic.

It hath been said that this is improperly called a Comedy; for that there is much to make you cry, and little to make you laugh. I would remind these Gentlemen of that famous Line in *Horace*, a Book of the highest Authority in this Court.

Interdum tamen et vocem Comœdia tollit.[2]

It is indeed true, that some good Writers, who have chosen a grave Fable for their Comedy, have intermixed inferior Characters of Mirth, as *Steele* in the *Conscious Lovers*:[3] But it must be admitted, at the same Time, that there are Precedents to the contrary, particularly in *Terence*,[4] an Author whom we shall always mention here with the utmost Respect.

Upon the whole, we do adjudge the Comedy of the *Foundling* to be a good Play, and that it do continue to be represented and received as such—and that *the Town*, for their false Clamour, be in our Contempt, &c.[5]

The following Paragraph out of the *London Evening-Post* of *Tuesday*, was then ordered to be read.[6]

[1] Cf. Walpole to Mann, 16 February 1748: 'I like the old *Conscious Lovers* better, and that not much; the story is the same, only that the Bevil of the new piece [i.e., Belmont] is in more hurry, and consequently more natural'; *Yale Walpole*, xix. 465. Presumably the 'Insinuations' referred to in the *JJ* were by word-of-mouth; John Homer Caskey, *The Life and Works of Edward Moore* (New Haven, Conn., 1927), pp. 39–47, implies that plagiarism was not a common charge in the printed criticisms of the play.

[2] *Ars Poetica*, 93: 'Yet at times even Comedy raises her voice' (Loeb).

[3] e.g., Tom, servant to Bevil Junior, and Phillis, maid to Lucinda, who were added after the main body of the play was complete; George A. Aitken, *The Life of Richard Steele* (London, 1889), ii. 277–8.

[4] Especially in the *Andria*, which Steele took as the model for *The Conscious Lovers*.

[5] 'The character which is given of this play by the author of the *Jacobite Journal*, is extremely to his honour and advantage'; 'Remarks upon the *Foundling*', GM, xviii (1748), 259.

[6] It is from a letter, signed 'Guglielmus', in the issue of 12–15 March 1748.

To the AUTHOR, *&c.*

"*Sir,*   *Saturday, March* 12.

As the known pension'd Scribler for the M——try, the Author of *The Jacobite Journal*, has this Day openly thrown off the Mask, and declar'd himself an Advocate for taking away the *Liberty of the Press*, Mankind can no longer doubt of the Designs of his Patrons; and he is not only for taking it away, but for inflicting *Death* on those who make use of this truly *English* Privilege, as appears from a Note at the Bottom of the second Page."[1]

After which the Court recommended to the Public to revise the Passages in the last Court of Criticism here misrepresented, and then to determine what the Author of the said *London Evening-Post* is, and what he deserves.

My Wife *Peggy* hath prevailed with me to go to one Benefit more, *viz.* on *Monday* next, to the *Provok'd Wife*, for the Benefit of Mrs. *Clive*,[2] where my Wife tells me, I shall be sure to see all the Ladies who have any true Taste for Wit and Humour.

(*Adjourned.*)

SATURDAY, MARCH 26, 1748.   NUMB. 17.

——*Amoto quæramus seria Ludo.*

Horace.[3]

When the Ass disappeared from this Paper, it might be reasonably concluded that the Jacobite would not stay long behind.

In plain Fact, I am weary of personating a Character for which I have so solemn a Contempt; nor do I believe that the elder *Brutus* was more uneasy under that Idiot Appearance which he assumed for the Sake of his Country,[4] than I have been in the

---

[1] The allusion is to the 'Court of Censorial Inquiry' in *JJ* no. 15, above, pp. 198–9, where Fielding attacked the standards of Opposition journalists.

[2] At Drury Lane on 21 March 1748, with Garrick as Sir John Brute and Mrs. Clive as Lady Fanciful, the latter, 'by Particular Desire', to do the Irish song 'Ellen a Roon'; *London Stage*, Part 4, i. 38.

[3] *Satires*, I. i. 27: 'jesting aside, let us turn to serious thoughts' (Loeb).

[4] Lucius Junius, nephew of Tarquinius Superbus (King of Rome), was surnamed 'Brutus' because he feigned idiocy to escape the fate of his brother, who had been put to death by their uncle; later (*c.* 510 B.C.) Brutus led the rising against the Tarquins and liberated Rome, of which he then became consul. See *TP* no. 25 of 15–22 April 1746, p. 2, col. 1, where Fielding quotes Virgil's compliment to Brutus (*Vincit amor patriae*) from *Aeneid*, vi. 823.

Masque of Jacobitism, which I have so long worn for the same amiable and honest Purpose; in order, if possible, to laugh Men out of their Follies, and to make them ashamed of owning or acting by Principles no less inconsistent with Common Sense, than detrimental to the Society.

And even the Jacobites themselves (if there be really any Persons weak enough to maintain such Tenets in Earnest) cannot tax me with any Unfairness. If they will reflect seriously, and confess ingenuously, they must be forced to allow, that it is impossible for any Man to unite the contradictory Doctrines of a Protestant and a Jacobite, without being guilty of all the glaring and monstrous Absurdities which I have endeavoured to assign to that motley Character.

Here then I shall pull off the Masque, and openly avow that I *John Trott-Plaid*, Esq; notwithstanding my Name, do, from my Heart, abhor and despise all the Principles of a Jacobite, as being founded on certain absurd, exploded Tenets, beneath the lowest Degree of a human Understanding.

Many Reasons, besides my great Abhorrence to this Character, have urged me to lay it down for the future.

First, I have observed that tho' Irony is capable of furnishing the most exquisite Ridicule; yet as there is no kind of Humour so liable to be mistaken, it is, of all others, the most dangerous to the Writer. An infinite Number of Readers have not the least Taste or Relish for it, I believe I may say do not understand it; and all are apt to be tired, when it is carried to any Degree of Length.

A second Reason is, that there is no Species of Wit or Humour so little adapted to the Palat of the present Age. I am firmly persuaded, that if many of those who have formerly gained such Reputation this Way, were to revive and publish their Works *de novo*, they would have few Readers, and acquire but little Credit. This is indeed too plain and simple a Food, and wants all that high Seasoning which recommends the Works of modern Authors. Ridicule is not sufficiently poignant; nothing but downright Abuse will whet up and stimulate the pall'd Appetite of the Public; nor will the World at present swallow any Characters that are not well ragoo'd and carbonaded. The general Taste in Reading, at this Time, very much resembles that of some particular Men in Eating, who would never willingly devour what doth not stink.[1] When a new Book, Pamphlet, or Poem is published, the Enquiry is not, as formerly, What is the Subject? Who writ it? Is there Wit or Humour in it? But, who is abused? Whom is the Author at now? Doth he lay about him well? and such-like; and according to the Answer received to these Questions, the Performance is cherish'd or rejected.

A third Reason which hath induced me to the above Resolution, is a Conviction that the Principles which I attack are really improper Subjects of Ridicule; for as some Persons and some Topics may be too high and solemn, so, in Reality, others may be too low and contemptible to be treated this Way. Indeed, if to ridicule any thing it be necessary to lower it by a Comparison to something else,[2] I believe it will be very difficult to find such a Comparison for Jacobitism.

But the last and strongest Motive to me hath been, that the Matter is past a Joke; for, however absurd and despicable the Principles of Jacobites may be, the Designs of the Party, and their Consequences, are of a very serious Nature. When every Attempt, with which Malice can supply Invention, is employ'd to undermine and blow up the Constitution; when conceal'd Popish Traytors are crept into the Seminaries of Learning, and endeavour to taint the Minds of our Youth;[3] and when the most bare-faced Libels are every Week spread all over the Nation, in order to spirit up the Vulgar to rise and cut the Throats of their Betters; it is high time to speak in a plainer Language than that of Irony, and to endeavour to raise something more than Mirth in the Mind of the Reader.

One of these Incendiaries in particular may be almost literally called the Drummer of Sedition, and said to beat up for Recruits

---

[1] Cf. *Tom Jones*, i. i, and the letter signed 'Heliogabalus' in *TP* no. 5 of 3 December 1745, p. 4, col. 2.

[2] Cf. *Tom Jones*, v. i.

[3] 'Whereas there have been lately some very tumultuous disturbances and outrages committed in the publick streets of *Oxford*, by young scholars of the university, particularly on the 23d of *February* last past, amounting to a notorious insult on his majesty's crown and government...', from a public declaration of 'the Heads *of* Houses, *and* Proctors *of the* University *at* Oxford, *on* Monday April 11, 1748'; printed in *GM*, xviii (1748), 214, and *JJ* no. 24 of 14 May 1748, p. 3, col. 1, over the signature of John Purnell (*c.* 1708–64), Warden of New College and Vice-Chancellor of Oxford (1747–50). See also *GM*, xviii (1748), 234, and *Yale Walpole*, xx. 6 and note. Oxford had a reputation for Jacobite sympathies dating from the seventeenth century; cf. the letter from 'a Nonjuror to his Son at *Oxford*', *TP* no. 24 of 8–15 April 1746, p. 1, cols. 2–3.

in the Pretender's Cause.[1] He hath in very direct Terms addressed himself to the People, and very plainly (tho' with all the Affectation of Eloquence) advised them to rise and do themselves Justice.[2] In this, indeed, he differs from the famous *Vaux*, that as the Assassin, already upon Record, attempted clandestinely to blow up King, Lords and Commons, this Gentleman would effect the same Purpose, in a fairer and more open Manner, and would encourage the People to take up Arms against the Government, with this Motto on their Banner,

NIL DESPERANDUM.[3]

This Conduct may perhaps be thought fair and open; but we shall not find him in all Respects equally honest: In two Instances, indeed, (and these pretty considerable ones) he deviates a little from this Plain-dealing; for he beats up for Recruits to serve the Pretender in the Name of his present Majesty; and fights in the Cause of Popery and Slavery, under the Standard (as he pretends) of the Constitution.

To consider such Attempts as these in a ludicrous Light, would be as absurd as the Conceit of a Fellow in *Bartholomew-Fair*, who exhibited the comical Humours of *Nero* ripping up his Mother's Belly;[4] and surely a Man who endeavours to rip up the Bowels of his Country, is altogether as improper an Object of Ridicule.

[1] James Ralph (1705?–62), Fielding's former colleague in the theatre and on *The Champion*, who under the pseudonym of 'George Cadwallader' was editing *The Remembrancer* for the Prince of Wales's Opposition party. The first number appeared on 12 December 1747, one week after the *JJ* began publishing. See *GM*, xviii (1748), 130: 'But in order more effectually to defeat the views of the *Remembrancer*, whom he [Mr. Trott-Plaid] proclaims (*March* 26) a dangerous enemy, because a writer of some abilities, he lays aside his ass, and his character of a Jacobite, renounces irony . . . and formally engages this potent antagonist, charging him with having for hire, and against his conscience, deserted a party which he formerly defended . . .'.

[2] Perhaps *Remembrancer* no. 13 of 5 March 1748, but the general sentiment is common to a number of other issues, e.g., no. 11 of 20 February, and, with particular reference to the Latin motto below, no. 12 of 27 February.

[3] 'Never despair.' *Nil Desperandum* was the motto of *The Remembrancer*. Cf. Horace, *Odes*, I. vii. 27–9: *nil desperandum Teucro duce . . . / certus enim promisit Apollo / ambiguam tellure nova Salamina futuram.*

[4] Cf. Fielding's Preface to *Joseph Andrews*, p. 7: 'What could exceed the Absurdity of an Author, who should write *the Comedy* of Nero, *with the merry Incident of ripping up his Mother's Belly* . . . ?' No such droll has been identified, and the language of the *Joseph Andrews* reference suggests that the example is imaginary. For Nero's assassination of his mother, Agrippina, see Tacitus, *Annals*, xiii. 8.

And what makes the Matter still more serious, with regard to this Author, is, that he is far from being like the rest of his Fellow-Labourers, void of all Abilities. Such Persons as the Writer of *Old England*,[1] the Printer of the *London Evening-Post*,[2] and the poor *Fool*,[3] can do neither Good nor Harm to any Cause or Party; for tho' a Sword is said to be a dangerous Weapon in the Possession of a Madman, a Pen is never dangerous but in the Hands of a Man of Sense.

Here perhaps the candid Reader will say, Why did not the Ministry secure such a Writer to themselves, or at least purchase his Silence, when he offered himself to them? Especially since they have experienced his Abilities in writing already on more Sides than one?[4] Why is an Author obliged to be a more disinterested Patriot than any other? And why is he, whose Livelihood is in his Pen, a greater Monster in using it to serve himself, than he who uses his Tongue to the same Purpose?

To confess the Truth, the World is in general too severe on Writers. In a Country where there is no public Provision for Men of Genius, and in an Age when no Literary Productions are

---

[1] See *JJ* no. 13, above, p. 181 and note 3 there. For additional identifications, see Theophilus Cibber, *Lives of the Poets* (London, 1753), v. 313–14, where it is suggested that John Banks (1709–51) was the editor of *OE* about this time; Thomas Birch to Phil. Yorke, 23 June 1750 (B.M. Add. MS. 35397, ff. 251ʳ–252ᵛ), where a Hugh Morgan, attorney of Clifford's Inn, is called 'the original Author'; and a manuscript note in a contemporary hand on p. 30 of the B.M. copy of the 'Second Edition' of *The 'Piscopade*, glossing line 490 with the statement that William Guthrie was the author of *OE* and had a pension for not writing. Laurence Hanson, *Government and the Press*, p. 119, demonstrates that Guthrie's pension began in 1746. John Burke Shipley, who supplied the Birch MS. reference above, points out that Birch may well have been confused between the attorney Hugh Morgan, the sometime printer of *OE* (H. Morgan), and Macnamara Morgan.

[2] See *JJ* no. 12, above, p. 172, n. 1.

[3] Fielding attributes this pseudonym to William Horsley in *JJ* no. 10, above, p. 154.

[4] Ralph seems to have written for at least one Walpole paper, *The Daily Gazetteer* (1735 ?–97); see Robert L. Haig, *The Gazetteer: 1735–1797* (Carbondale, Ill., 1960), p. 5 and note. Ralph also wrote for the anti-Walpole *Common-Sense* (1738–9) and *The Champion* (1739–43 ?), and may have joined the anti-Pelham *OE* in 1743; see John Burke Shipley, *James Ralph: Pretender to Genius* (unpublished Ph.D. dissertation, Columbia University, 1962), Ch. x. No support has been discovered for Fielding's assertion here that by 1748 the Pelham ministry had had an opportunity to buy off Ralph. Coxe, *Pelham*, ii. 485, prints a letter from Pelham to Newcastle, 20 July 1753, in which the former says of Ralph, 'I could have had the fellow if I would; but his conduct, when in pay, was such, that I should have been ashamed to have corresponded with him.' Pelham may have been referring to the overture made on Ralph's behalf by Bubb Dodington sometime after the death of the Prince of Wales (1751); see *Diary of the late George Bubb Dodington*, ed. Henry Penruddocke Wyndham (Salisbury, 1784), p. 237; also Shipley, pp. 504–5.

encouraged, or indeed read, but such as are season'd with Scandal against the Great; and when a Custom hath prevailed of publishing this, not only with Impunity but with great Emolument, the Temptation to Men in desperate Circumstances is too violent to be resisted; and if the Public will feed a hungry Man for a little Calumny, he must be a very honest Person indeed, who will rather starve than write it.

In a Time therefore of profound Tranquillity, and when the Consequence, at the worst, can probably be no greater than the Change of a Ministry, I do not think a Writer, whose only Livelihood is his Pen, to deserve a very flagitious Character, if, when one Set of Men deny him Encouragement, he seeks it from another, at their Expence; nor will I rashly condemn such a Writer as the vilest of Men, (provided he keeps within the Rules of Decency) if he endeavours to make the best of his own Cause, and uses a little Art in blackening his Adversary. Why should a Liberty which is allowed to every other Advocate, be deny'd to this?[1]

But at a Season when the Kingdom is engaged in a most dangerous War; when we are in the most critical and perillous State; when it is become a Question, and that soon, as it seems, to be decided, whether we shall be any longer a Nation; and when indeed this in a great measure depends on our Unanimity among ourselves. At such a Season to blow the Trumpet of Sedition, to labour at re-kindling the scarce extinguish'd Coals of Rebellion, to blacken and misrepresent the best of Governments, and to harangue the People with false, plausible, and popular Alarms, into a Distrust of those great and good Men, who are, of all, most desirous and most able to preserve them; is an Action which deserves a worse Name than I am willing to stain this Paper with.[2]

To treat such Men and such Measures in a ludicrous Manner, or to consider a serious Design of setting the Nation on Fire, in order to scramble something out of the Flames, as a Jest, must surely be thought very absurd and foolish: Here therefore I lay

---

[1] For Fielding on the right of the man of letters to change his politics, see 'The Present History of Great Britain' in *TP* no. 25 (15–22 April 1746), p. 3, cols. 1–3.

[2] According to Dodington, *Diary*, pp. 20–1, the Pelham ministry ordered the printer and publisher of *The Remembrancer* to be taken up for the issue of 18 November 1749, but the paper was permitted to continue publishing. There is no evidence that the ministry contemplated action against it in 1748.

down my Character of Jacobite; tho' I shall still retain the Name of the Paper, as it is for the Use of that Party for which it is designed; and tho' they are not to be ridiculed out of their Folly, I hope still to be able to reason them into Sense.

Proceedings at the Court of Criticism, Thursday March 17.

One B—— and one B——, two Jacobites, came into the Court, and complain'd of the Revd. Mr. *Warner*, that he had preach'd a very improper Sermon on the 30th of *January* last, before the Right Hon. the Lord Mayor and the Aldermen of *London* at St. *Paul's* Cathedral;[1] and the said B——s alledged, that this Day hath always been understood as a Jacobitical Day;[2] and that the Sermons preach'd on that Occasion should savour of Jacobitical Doctrine; but, on the contrary, that Mr. *Warner*, among many other Paragraphs, had ventured to preach the following:

"There is great Reason to conjecture, that the Guilt we have been now lamenting, had been never perpetrated, could The People have foreseen the Progress of their Crimes, or in the Beginning have suspected, that the Enemies of The King, had been capable of an Action, which they at last committed; could they have thought that the Great Defenders of English Liberty— contending only for Redress of Grievances—would have proceeded by a Stretch of Power against the Common Rights of Englishmen, to deliver them up to Sedition, Confusion, Tumult, and—*when they look'd for Righteousness—Oppression**;[3] in short, could they have ever thought, that a Day would come by Their means, when, amidst the Commiseration of All his Subjects— the Few *Sons of Violence* excepted—their Sovereign could be arraign'd in his own Courts of Justice, imprison'd in his Palace, and executed in the Capital of his Country?

"Let these Things, therefore, fill our Minds with a Cautious Dread, (for That is the End of this Day of Remembrance) of encouraging any Reports, or harbouring any Complaints, and of

---

¹ Ferdinando Warner (1703–68), rector of the united parishes of St. Michael Queenhithe and Holy Trinity, published his *Sermon Preach'd before the Right Honourable Lord Mayor . . . on Saturday, January 30, 1747-48* (London, 1748) during March; *GM*, xviii (1748), 144.

² The date of their anniversary fast commemorating the 'martyrdom' of Charles I.

³ In Warner's *Sermon* the note designated by the asterisk (not reprinted in the *JJ*) refers to Isaiah 5: 7.

propagating any Jealousies, which may have a Tendency,—
tho' but a Distant one—to weaken our own Affections for His
Majesty, or to alienate those we converse with from their true and
sworn Allegiance."[1]

All which he said was in Favour of the Diabolical Cause of
Whiggism, and contrary to our Allegiance to our Sovereign
Lord——, his Crown and Dignity.

The Court then, having first perused the Sermon, adjudged,
That the said Sermon be, for its Loyalty, recommended to the
Public; and that the said *B*——*s*, for their false Clamour, be in
the Mercy of the Court, &c.

Note, It was said that the printed Sermon differ'd from that
which was preached; but this, on Examination, was found to be
false.

(*Adjourned.*)

SATURDAY, APRIL 2, 1748.   NUMB. 18.

Quid non audebis, perfida Lingua, loqui ?

Martial.[2]

As the following concerns the Vindication of a Gentleman,[3]
whose Character is very dear to all who have the Honour of his
Acquaintance, and ought to be no less so to the Public, we shall
postpone every other Matter to give it an immediate Place.[4]

To the Author of the Jacobite Journal.

Sir,

I have lately read a Pamphlet intitled, *A second and third Letter
to the Whigs*.[5] The Scurrilities in it are below any Body's Notice,
and so are the Reasonings; but I think it worth while, in Answer

---

[1] The quoted matter is from Warner's *Sermon*, pp. 18–19.

[2] *Epigrams*, VII. xxiv. 2: 'what wilt not thou, perfidious tongue, dare to say ?' (Loeb).

[3] George Lyttelton (1709–73), at this time one of the junior commissioners of the
Treasury. In the Dedication of *Tom Jones* to Lyttelton Fielding calls him 'my Patron'.

[4] This seems to represent a significant change of editorial policy. Among the news items
in *JJ* no. 17 (26 March 1748) appears the following notice: 'The Author of two Letters
concerning a certain Writer, must excuse us from meddling with any thing so much below
our Notice.' If these 'two Letters' are *A Second and Third Letter to the Whigs* cited below, it
may be inferred that the decision to examine them came from Lyttelton himself.

[5] Published anonymously on 26 March 1748, the pamphlet is by Horace Walpole; see
Yale Walpole, xiii–xiv. 18–19 and note.

to the Assertions of that impudent Libeller, to mention to you some Facts which I certainly know to be true: First, that the Gentleman abused in that Pamphlet under the Name of *Selim*, did not write the *Letter to the Tories*; nor ever saw, or heard of it, till he read it in Print.[1] This I affirm upon certain Knowledge, and this, one would think, no Man could doubt of, who reads that Letter, meerly from the Matter contained in it, without needing any other Proof. Yet upon the absurd Supposition of his having writ it, that Gentleman is aspersed by the Author of the *Letters to the Whigs*,[2] as designing to attack the Liberty of the Press, agreeably to a Paragraph in the *Letter to the Tories*, which does indeed call for such a Restraint.[3] And upon the same groundless Supposition, much more Abuse in the first *Letter to the Whigs*,[4] and in those two lately published, is thrown upon him by the same dirty Hand. 2dly, I must take Notice, that the last Edition of the *Persian Letters*, corrected by the Author, was not published since he came into his Majesty's Service, but in the very Beginning of the Year 1744, having been revised by him in the Year 1743;[5] so that the Alterations then made were agreeable to his Sentiments while he was in Opposition, and not made with any Regard to his being in Office, as this Writer suggests;[6] by which three Parts in four of the Wit and Raillery in the second

---

[1] *A Letter to the Tories* (London, 1747) appeared anonymously during June 1747; *GM*, xvii (1747), 300. It was generally attributed to Lyttelton; see *GM*, xviii (1748), 520, for a poem to Lyttelton in which he is named as the author of the *Letter*. However, Horace Walpole was less certain of it later, and George Ayscough did not include the *Letter* in the 1774 edition of Lyttelton's collected works; see *Yale Walpole*, xiii–xiv. 18 n., and Rose Mary Davis, *The Good Lord Lyttelton*, pp. 197–8. 'Selim' was Lyttelton's *persona* in his *Letters from a Persian in England to his Friend in Ispaham* (1735).

[2] p. 10.

[3] p. 17: 'They might, without any danger, exert with spirit and vigour the full power of legal government, check and even suppress the infamous licence of the press (unknown to all other ages and nations, and destructive of all civil society) . . .'.

[4] Published anonymously on 23 July 1747; *Yale Walpole*, xiii–xiv. 19. Walpole's first answer to the *Letter to the Tories*, it attacked the Pelham ministry and defended the freedom of the press.

[5] The fifth edition of the *Letters from a Persian*, published early in 1744, was revised in the spring and summer of 1743; Davis, *The Good Lord Lyttelton*, p. 198. Lyttelton joined the Pelham ministry in December 1744 as one of the junior commissioners of the Treasury; Davis, pp. 124–5.

[6] *Second and Third Letter*, p. 17. Walpole collated the third and fifth editions of the *Letters from a Persian* and attributed the changes to a difference between the Lyttelton of 1735, defender of the Constitution, and the Lyttelton of 'his Majesty's Service', after his conversion to the Administration.

Letter to the Whigs falls to the Ground. 3dly, I affirm, that this Gentleman, while in Opposition, never *had a Hand in a private Printing Press*, as this Writer asserts *p.* 34; nor ever *writ* or *countenanced* any *immoral* or *irreligious* Paper or Book, or *seditious Libel*, or *personal Scurrilities*, or *private Anecdotes* of Defamation;[1] but always exprest the utmost Abhorrence of all such Writings, as all who knew him then can attest, and as even those who were most prejudiced against him then have since been convinced. He had indeed the Misfortune to have such Writings sometimes imputed to him, upon no better Grounds than the *Letter to the Tories* is now; and against that kind of Defamation there is no Security to the best Man in the World.

Next, I assert, that neither he nor his particular Friends did ever *speak* or *vote*, while in *Opposition*, against *Septennial Parliaments*, as the Writer of this Libel asserts, *p.* 30;[2] and for the Truth of this I appeal to all the Members of the two last Parliaments; not to take notice, that his Opinion upon this Point stands just the same in the *first* Edition of the *Persian Letters* as in the *last*, though in the *last* he has added some Arguments to enforce his Opinion, which the Importance of the Subject seem'd to require.[3]

Lastly, I must observe, that the Words quoted *p.* 10, from one of the *Persian Letters*, to prove a Conformity of Opinions between the Author of them and of the *Letter to the Tories*, viz. "That the Licentiousness of the Press was grown of late to such a dangerous Height, as to require extraordinary Remedies; and that, if it were put under the Inspection of some discreet and judicious Person, it would be far more beneficial to the Public." I must observe, I say, that these Words are not there delivered as the Opinion of the Author himself; but, on the contrary, are

---

[1] p. 34: 'He [Lyttelton] has formerly had a Hand in a private Printing-press, whence has issued many a Tract little short of Treason.' In his *OE* essay of 23 April 1748 Walpole located the printing press in question 'at a great House in Bloomsbury Square', apparently referring to some involvement with the Duke of Bedford; see Davis, p. 199, and, for Walpole's authorship of the *OE* essay, *Yale Walpole*, xiii–xiv. 18. Similar charges are made in the *Second and Third Letter to the Whigs*, p. 8.

[2] However, the *Memoirs and Correspondence of George, Lord Lyttelton*, ed. Robert Phillimore (London, 1845), ii. 799–803, does print an undated speech of Lyttelton's on Triennial Parliaments.

[3] Cf. 'Letter LXVIII' in the first edition (1735), p. 205, with 'Letter LXVI' of the fifth edition (1744), pp. 267–8. Davis, p. 37, sees Lyttelton's shift as from a 'wavering' to a 'settled' position.

immediately answer'd in a very strong manner, agreeably to the Tenour of the whole Letter, (*see Persian Letters, last Edition, Epist.* 48, *p.* 248.)[1] which Answer this honest and candid Writer has quite supprest, and only taken this Part of the Dialogue, in order to make good his Charge upon the Gentleman by whom those Letters were writ.

I could mention many more Facts affirm'd in this Pamphlet, in relation both to this Gentleman and to his Friends, with no more Regard to Truth than those I have already taken Notice of, particularly that execrable Falshood of *their publishing Loads of Scandal against his R. H.*;[2] but it is unnecessary and irksome to follow such an Author through all his Lies. The World will judge by these of the rest, and he has past Sentence upon himself.——— Speaking of the Gentleman whom he calls *Selim*, he says (*p.* 34) *If I have once misquoted him, or ascribed to him one detestable Doctrine which is not his own, I am willing my Writings should incur the Stigma that I call for on his.* So far is just; but when he adds, that on this Condition he would consent *to abolish the Liberty of the Press,* and erect an *Index Expurgatorius,* he goes beyond what either that Gentleman or any of his Friends will ever consent to, on any Account. The Abuse of the Press, so far as it is personal to themselves, they see with Contempt: If it offends in a higher Manner, there are Laws in Being to punish those Offences, and *let those Laws take their Course*; but let nothing be done, even for the Security of Government, by which Liberty can be hurt.

POSTSCRIPT.

Upon Enquiry I find that the Bookseller, for whom the *Persian Letters* were printed, has, without the Knowledge of the Author, for some End of his own, lately publish'd a very few of them with a new Title-Page, put to them last Year, and dated 1747;[3] but the 5th Edition, *with all the Alterations that are in them now,* was publish'd very early in the Year 1744, as will appear by the Books sold at that Time; was revised and corrected in the Spring and Summer of the Year 1743.

---

1 In the fifth edition (1744) the passage quoted from 'Letter XLVIII' is in fact on p. 208.

2 *Second and Third Letter to the Whigs,* p. 8.

3 The bookseller of the fifth edition was John Millan (*c.* 1704–84), near Whitehall, publisher of Thomson and certain heraldic works, sometime associate of Mrs. Cooper; Plomer, *Dictionary,* pp. 170–1. The assertion of a 1747 title-page has not been verified.

As Truth, Justice, and Public Good are the Principles on which this Paper is founded, the ensuing Letter wanted no Recommendation to us; nor do we apprehend it will want any to our Readers.[1]

Sir,

Having read in your Paper of the 19th Instant a Plan or Proposal for the Improvement of the Highlands of *Scotland*, by erecting 50 Townships or Villages there, with sundry Encouragements and Conditions tending to promote Industry in that uncultivated Part of this Island; and being convinced that such a Measure would produce the most salutary Effects, I cannot help communicating to the Public, by your means, a Hint for the more ready Execution of the Plan abovementioned, which occurr'd to me on hearing that a Bill was on Foot for the Relief of insolvent Debtors.

It is notorious, that there are several thousand Persons now confined for Debt in the Gaols of this Kingdom, who are not only unserviceable to the Public, but are also a dead Burthen upon it, as they must be supported by the Labour of others; and as these Persons might be render'd useful Members of Society, it is certainly very just and reasonable that the Legislature should occasionally interpose, and give them that Relief by a Special Law, which they cannot have by the Law in general.

But as this Relief has never been administer'd, except on Condition of yielding up all their Effects to their Creditors, the Consequence is, that Numbers of unfortunate and indigent Persons are turn'd adrift at once, without having the immediate Means of Subsistance: A Circumstance attended with obvious Inconveniences, which often frustrate the good Intentions of those insolvent Acts of Parliament.

This Observation is so trite, that I have often wonder'd it should never have produced something, either to cure or palliate so palpable an Inconvenience, which may very probably be owing to the Difficulty of the Case, especially on former Occasions; as no Fund may have existed which could be appropriated to their Support, consistent with the Justice due to their Creditors.

By the abovementioned Plan for improving the Highlands, two Acres of Land in Property and Flax-seed are to be assign'd to each of the first Inhabitants, or Planters of the Villages to be

---

[1] The letter which follows does not appear to be by Fielding.

erected, which, attended with the Advantages of Situation and the Cheapness of the Country, might of itself afford to an industrious Family the necessary Means of beginning the World with Advantage.

But as some small Stock for the Purchase of Houshold Furniture and the Implements of Husbandry, or of any useful Manufacture, would greatly contribute to the Success of the Adventurer, nay must be necessary to his Subsistence at first; I cannot think that the Creditors of any insolvent Debtor, willing to settle as abovementioned, and to become industrious, would begrudge a small Share of his Effects to enable him to do so; or perhaps some other small Fund may, by the Wisdom of the Legislature, be appropriated to that Purpose.

Upon this Supposition, I propose that each insolvent Debtor, who shall give Security to go and settle in one of the Villages to be erected in the Highlands, with his or her Family, and to abide there for the Space of   [1] Years, shall have the Benefit and Advantages pointed out by the Plan abovementioned; and upon the Surrender of his or her Effects to the Creditors, shall be absolutely discharged.

If these Encouragements should induce a considerable Number of industrious *English* to settle in the manner above specify'd, I am confident they would soon reap the Fruits of their Labours, and that they would not be tempted to abandon those Benefits, which Nature would teach them to transmit to their Children.

And such a Settlement would have further Advantages: It would afford a Nursery for the *English* Language in those Parts; would strengthen the Union of the two Nations by the Coalition of their natural Interests, and would prove an additional Bulwark to our most happy Constitution, *&c.*

London, March

26, 1747.   *I am,* &c.

Proceedings at the Court of Criticism, Thursday March 31.

The Author of the 2d and 3d *Letter to the Whigs*, being brought upon his Tryal, pleaded to the Jurisdiction of the Court, and as the famous *Coke*, who being indicted on the *Coventry* Act,

---

[1] Both the B.M. and the Yale copies print blank at this point.

urged, that his Design was Murder and not Mayhem;[1] so did the Prisoner insist, that his Crime was of too atrocious a Nature for the Cognizance of this Court.

This Objection was over-ruled by his Honour, who said, That every Abuse of the Press was subject to his Censures; that he had indeed a kind of concurrent Jurisdiction, as the Judgments of Contempt or Infamy, which are given in this Court, do very well stand with those Punishments which are inflicted in any other.

Then the Council for the Prosecution, having first opened the Indictment, which was for outragious and malicious Calumny, proceeded to his Proofs, in the following Manner:

And first he alledged, that the Culprit not only every where asserts, that the Author of the *Persian Letters* and the Writer of the *Letter to the Tories* is one and the same Person; but that, in Page 6 he says he will prove it. By which it is maliciously insinuated that this Fact is here proved upon the Person calumniated; (nay, in Page 21 he says, no Man living can doubt of it:) Whereas there is not, in the whole Letter, one single Proof attempted of it.

Again, in Page 8 this excellent Person is charged with having been the Author of much personal Scurrility,[2] (nay, indeed, he and his Friends of all the Personal Scurrility) published from the Year 1734 to 1747, without producing any Evidence to support so black a Charge; and the Falshood of which is only to be equalled by that of another Calumny in the same Page, where the same Person and his Friends are accused *of publishing a Load*

---

[1] On 13 March 1722 Arundel Coke (Cooke), son of Richard Cooke of Little Livermore, Suffolk, and member of the Middle Temple, was indicted for having hired and then abetted one John Woodburne, a labourer, in the attempted murder of Coke's wealthy brother-in-law, Edward Crispe, who escaped with severe facial disfigurement. The prosecution argued that the offence was created by an Act 'usually call'd Sir *John Coventry's* Act' (22, 23 Car. II, cap. 1), to prevent malicious maiming and wounding. Coke tried unsuccessfully to make the legal point that his intention had been murder, not disfigurement, and that therefore he was not punishable under the Coventry Act. See *The Tryal and Condemnation of Arundel Coke, alias Cooke, Esq.* (London, 1722) and *An Exact and Peculiar Narrative of a Cruel and Inhumane Murder attempted on the Body of Edward Crisp, Esq.* (London, 1722); also *Statutes at Large*, viii. 331–4, and *A Complete Collection of State Trials*, comp. T. B. Howell, xvi (London, 1816), 53–94.

[2] *Second and Third Letter to the Whigs*, p. 8, refers particularly to 'a private Anecdote in the old Minister's [i.e., Robert Walpole's] Family, or a scandalous Tale of a certain noble Earl and his Wife'. For the latter, see *The Court Secret* (London, 1741), which deals with the private life of the Earl of Scarborough; see also Davis, p. 198.

of Odium and Scandal against his R. H. This is again repeated
Page 14, and again, in the most impudent Manner, Page 16.
*Who can spirit up a Son against a Father, then a Father against a
Son, and perhaps when desperate with each, foster up a Brother to
dictate to both.*[1] What Odium, or what Scandal is here meant?
If any such hath been published, (for I have read none) the
excellent Person here accused is most innocent of it; and he and
his Friends may defy the malicious Calumniator to name any one
Instance of their having published, or having encouraged the
publishing of any Thing of this kind. And as for the last malignant Reflection of having fomented any Divisions of this tender
Kind, here basely, and without the least Colour of Evidence,
insinuated, cursed may they be who have attempted it, if there
are any such; and as cursed those who charge that Guilt on the
Innocent.

I omit the Scurrility of this Writer. His calling Men, Page 11,
the most profligate Characters that ever existed. P. 17. One *dis-
gracing Patriotism with Irreligion.* P. 18. *An Animal so swoln with
Poison, that he shou'd, like the Scorpion, carry about him the Antidote
to his own Venom.* P. 23. *A profligate Incendiary, who hopes to build
his own Fortune on public Confusion.* Ib. *Ingrafting Canting upon
Prophaness.* Ib. *Cataline and Cromwell.* P. 24. *Ambitious Boy,
with a bad Heart, successfully wicked.* Ib. *Scribbler.* P. 27. *Revolted
Patriot, Adopter of Persecution, who would massacre his Opponents,*
&c.

The Way he makes out the latter Part of the Charge is incomparable. The Author of the *Persian Letters* had said, You
should pull down at once these Ensigns of Party, which are
indeed false Colours hung out by Faction, and set up instead of
them one National Standard, which all who leave, by whatever
Name they may call themselves, should be considered and used
as Deserters.[2] Now, says this acute Reasoner, *Death is the Punishment of Deserters,* and *consequently* that Gentleman *would inflict
that Punishment on all Men in Opposition.* P. 46.[3] But further,
the Author of the *Persian Letters* calls for *Justice upon Public*

---

[1] *Second and Third Letter,* p. 16, accuses Lyttelton of widening the severe breach between
George II and Frederick, Prince of Wales, and of setting the Duke of Cumberland against
both. The reference is presumably to Lyttelton's activities as secretary to the Prince of
Wales prior to December 1744; Davis, pp. 48–52, 75–6.

[2] 'Letter LVI', 5th ed. (1744), p. 230.

[3] An error for p. 26.

Offenders.[1] Upon which this Writer in a Fury cries out, *If a Man so void of every Sentiment of* English *Good-Nature, that amiable Word, for which no other Language has a synonymous Term, so adulterated to every Opinion that is essential to* English *Liberty: If such a Man does not deserve to be stigmatized, Satyr has lost its Province, and Praise and Reproach may be Words without Meaning.*[2] The bare repeating this Nonsense explodes it better than any Observations upon it can do. But thus it is, that throughout this Pamphlet, the Accusations brought against this Worthy Gentleman are proved and supported. In short, no Man who hath the least Acquaintance with this Gentleman, in public or private Character, can read this Letter without being equally astonished at the Malice and Folly of the Writer.

The Culprit appeared contumacious, and made no Defence, saying, if his Proofs were not sufficient, he could produce no better; upon which the Court adjudged him guilty of Calumny, and pronounced Sentence of Infamy against him.

Falshoods and Calumnies of as black a Nature, against other Hon. Gentlemen, were also proved upon this Writer in his *Third Letter.* But we want room to insert the Proceedings upon them in this present Paper.[3]

(*Adjourned.*)

SATURDAY, APRIL 9, 1748.   NUMB. 19.

Nihil est, Antipho,
Quin male narrando possit depravarier.

Terence. *Phormio.*[4]

It is impossible for a Minister, or for a Man, so to conduct his Ways, as effectually to silence all the Clamours of Envy and Malice; since these Vices, like the green-eyed Monster Jealousy, in *Shakespear, can mock the Meat they feed on.*[5]

As no Ministers since *Adam* have, I believe, given less Food to these malignant Passions in their Enemies than the present, so

---

[1] 'Letter LXXX', 5th ed. (1744), p. 324.

[2] *Second and Third Letter*, pp. 26–7.

[3] For a fuller discussion of this contretemps between Fielding and Horace Walpole see W. B. Coley, 'Fielding and the Two Walpoles', *PQ*, xlv (1966), 170–7.

[4] *Phormio*, IV. 696–7: 'There's nothing, Sir [Antipho], that can't be made worse by the telling' (Loeb).   [5] *Othello*, III. iii. 165–7.

never did this creative Art in their Enemies exert itself in more ample manner; insomuch that four or five Writers (who seem otherwise not to have very fertile Inventions) have, by this alone, been able to support themselves for several Months together.

To say the Truth, this, which I have called the Art of Creation, should rather perhaps be stiled the Art of Perversion, or Misrepresentation; for I would not allow to these Writers a Power which many of the Antients were unwilling to attribute to the Supreme Being, of making Something out of Nothing; but they can so magnify or diminish, so change, pervert, and misrepresent whatever they undertake, that when it comes from their Hands, it seems no very hard Expression to call it the Work of their own Creation.

A very singular Instance of this, and one indeed scarce to be parallell'd, we have had in the late Contest between the Towns of *Buckingham* and *Aylesbury*.[1] In this Instance, an Affair of very little Consequence hath been represented as of the utmost Importance to the Nation; a Matter, of which there have been a hundred Examples, hath been called unprecedented; an innocent and strictly legal Measure, hath been stigmatized with the opprobious Term of an arbitrary Job; nay, hath been insinuated to be an actual Infringement of the Royal Prerogative:[2] And

---

[1] On 19 February 1748 Richard Grenville (1711–79), M.P. for Buckingham borough, brought in a Bill to the Commons for transferring the summer assizes for the county of Buckingham from Aylesbury to the county town of Buckingham. The Commons then heard a petition from Aylesbury which told of threats by Grenville that if the town petitioned against the Bill, he would 'not only remove the Summer Assizes, but the Winter Assizes also, and carry the Quarter-Sessions where he thought proper'. Horace Walpole characterized the Bill as part of 'some attacks . . . made by the Grenvilles on Lord Ch[ief] Justice Willes' and 'a derogation from the rights of the Judges, who have a right to fix the Assizes'. In the parliamentary debates over the Bill its proponents made the charge that the summer assizes, which by custom had been held in Buckingham, were in 1747 transferred by Chief Justice Willes, in whose circuits the towns lay, as a family favour to his son, Edward Willes, who had been elected M.P. for Aylesbury in the 1747 elections. 'So vigorous an opposition was made to this Bill, and such warm Debates attended every step, 'till it passed (on the 15th Inst. 155 to 108) that the curiosity even of our distant readers, occasioned a request to see what could be said upon an affair of such vast importance to the nation; in comparison of which, Bills *seemingly* of a more public concern were carried unexamined'; *GM*, xviii (1748), 104. See *Journals of . . . Commons*, xxv. 512, 530, 538, 561–3, 570, 617, 620, 659; *Yale Walpole*, xix. 470–1; Hansard, xiv. 202–46; and Lewis M. Wiggin, *The Faction of Cousins* (New Haven, Conn., 1958), pp. 124–9. On 13 May 1748 the Bill passed into law (21 Geo. II, cap. 12); *Statutes at Large*, xix. 214–15.

[2] As reported in Hansard, xiv. 208, Sir William Stanhope (1702–72), Lord Chesterfield's younger brother and at this time M.P. for Bucks., made the charge of infringement of the royal prerogative; however, this and other printed versions of the speech appear to derive

lastly, the Behaviour of an Hon. Gentleman on this Occasion, while he acted by all the Rules of Justice and Honour, hath been attack'd, traduced, and even attempted to be ridiculed.[1]

And that this is the Case will appear in the most incontestable Manner to all those, who, after having read the Misrepresentations of this Matter, shall consider it in the following plain and simple Light.

The C A S E.[2]

Notwithstanding the many Misrepresentations that have been employ'd against this Bill, the following plain Facts will sufficiently shew to any impartial Person, that it is, in every respect, highly just and reasonable, and calculated to prevent the Administration of publick Justice from being made subservient to private Purposes.

The Town of *Buckingham*, from whence the County of that Name was denominated, is the Place where formerly all the Business of the County was transacted for many Ages together, without any Inconvenience, or Complaint, that appears; and continued so, until, by the Partiality of Lord Chief Justice *Baldwin*, who purchased the Manor of *Aylesbury* towards the

---

from *The Original Speech of Sir W———m St———pe, on the First Reading of the Bill for Appointing the Assizes at Buckingham, Feb. 19, 1748*, which was published on 3 March 1748 and claimed as his own by Horace Walpole: 'I formed part of the speech I had intended to make into one for Sir William, and published it in his name'; *Yale Walpole*, xiii. 21.

[1] Although the printed attacks were especially severe on Richard Grenville, who had introduced the Bill in the Commons and with his brother George had borne most of the personal opprobrium, the reference here is probably to Pelham, whose lack of title may be reflected in the 'Hon. Gentleman'. Walpole to Mann, 11 March 1748, relates that after being attacked in the Commons for leaguing with the Grenvilles on the Bill, Pelham 'rose with the greatest emotion, fell into the most ridiculous passion, was near crying, and . . . fell upon the Chief Justice (who was not present) and accused him of ingratitude'; *Yale Walpole*, xix. 471. In the debates, apparently, much was made of Pelham's alliance with politicians who had been among those responsible for the downfall of Sir Robert Walpole, Pelham's political mentor.

[2] Although *LEP* of 7–9 April 1748 professes to think Fielding was the author of the 'Case', the latter seems to be a reprint, with minor variations, of a three-page pamphlet entitled *The Case of the Town and County of Buckingham: Reasons for Passing the Bill now depending for fixing the Summer Assizes at the antient County-Town, where they have usually been holden* (London, 1748). The title of this pamphlet suggests a date of composition prior to 15 March, when the Bill passed the Commons, or, at the very latest, 6 April, when the emendations made by the Lords were accepted; *Journals of . . . Commons*, xxv. 618, 629. If Fielding had written the 'Case', it seems likely that he would have published it in the *JJ* earlier than 9 April, that is, in time to affect the pending Bill.

End of the Reign of *Henry* VIII. Part of it was, for his private Advantage, removed by him from *Buckingham* to *Aylesbury*.

The County-Gaol was at the Castle of *Buckingham*, as appears by many Books and Records, till that Castle went to Decay.

By the 11th *H*. VII. *c*. 4. intitled, The Names of the Cities and Towns limited for the keeping of Weights and Measures, amongst all the other County Towns assigned for that Purpose, *Buckingham* is assigned for the County of *Buckingham*: Which is a Proof, that the Parliament considered it as the County Town, at that Time.

By the 6th *R*. II. *c*. 5. the Assizes are directed to be holden in the principal Towns where the Shire-Courts were holden.

From what has been shewn before, there can be no Doubt, but that the principal Town of *Buckinghamshire* was, at that Time, the Town of *Buckingham*.

By the 11th *R*. II. *c*. 11. reciting the former Act, it is provided, That the Chancellor of *England* for the Time being, shall have Power thereof, to make and provide Remedy, by Advice of the Justices, *from Time to Time, when Need shall be,* notwithstanding the former Act. This Act does not repeal the former Act, but only provides a Remedy *from Time to Time, when Need shall be*; which must be understood of extraordinary Cases, which are likewise provided against in the Bill now proposed. It is plain this was the Opinion of Lord Chief Justice *Hale*, who, in his Pleas of the Crown, treating of this Subject, quotes the 6th *R*. II. *c*. 5. as being in full Force; but distinguishes it by saying, That it is *directive* to the Judges, and not *coercive*.

By the 14th *H*. VI. reciting the Act of the 6th *R*. II. *c*. 5. for holding the Assizes in the principal Towns of every County, as being in Force, and that the same Statute ought to be observed and kept, the Assizes for the County of *Cumberland* are therefore directed to be holden at *Carlisle*, the principal Town of that County: Nor was this *occasioned by the Situation and Strength of that Place*, from the Apprehensions of a neighbouring Enemy, as is suggested in the printed Case against this Bill; for it is expresly provided by the Act itself, That this Regulation is only to take place *in Time of Peace, and of Truce*.

By the 1st *Eliz*. the Assizes for *Staffordshire* are directed to be holden at the County-Town of *Stafford*: And there are *a Multitude of Instances*, on the Journals of the House of Commons, in almost every Reign, of Bills for fixing the Assizes at particular Towns.

June 3, 1614, a Bill was brought in, for fixing the Summer Assizes at this very Town of *Buckingham*; but the Bill was lost by the sudden Dissolution of that Parliament, Four Days afterwards.

By all these Examples, it appears how little Truth there is in the Assertion, That this Power of the Judges, of transferring the Assizes from one Town to another, at their Pleasure, *has been exercised for Four hundred Years, without any Complaint.*

In *Prynn's* Observations on the Fourth Institute, there are many Instances given of Patents for fixing the Assizes and Shire-Courts at the Extremity of their several Counties; particularly one to *Launceston*, at the very Extremity of the County of *Cornwall*, which continued in Force till the First of his late Majesty, when a Power was given to the Chancellor, with the Advice of the Judges, to appoint the Assizes at any convenient Place in *Cornwall*: But notwithstanding this, the Assizes were still holden at *Launceston* till a few Years ago, when a Bill pass'd the House of Commons for fixing the Summer Assizes at *Bodmyn*; and tho' that Bill was afterwards dropt, yet the Assizes have ever since been holden alternately at *Bodmyn* and *Launceston*; which is all that is contended for in the present Case, with regard to *Buckingham* and *Aylesbury*.

In the first printed Case against this Bill, it appears by the Gazettes, That from the Year 1666 to 1720, the Summer Assizes had been holden 25 times at *Aylesbury*, 21 times at *Buckingham*, and 9 times at *Wicomb*. From the Year 1720 to 1747, which is 26 Years, it is admitted, That they have been always holden at *Buckingham*. So that, in the 81 Years, from 1666 to 1747, the Summer Assizes were holden 47 times at *Buckingham*, 25 times at *Aylesbury*, and 9 times at *Wicomb*: And yet this Bill to fix them, according to an uninterrupted Usage of 26 Years, and the Usage of the far greater Number of Times for 81 Years backwards, is treated as an extraordinary Act of Violence and Oppression upon this County, tho' there never was, during that long Period, any one public Complaint, or Remonstrance, of the County, or even of the Town of *Aylesbury*, against it.

The Town of *Buckingham had not the Happiness of having any Judges in their Neighbourhood* till 1722 or 1723, and have now been deprived of that Advantage for several Years last past: So that it may be reasonably presumed, if the Judges who went that Circuit before, and those who have so frequently gone it since, had thought this a grievous and oppressive Act upon the whole County, that they would not, for the Sake of any particular Borough, have continued in the Practice of it for such a great Number of Years; nor would the County itself have acquiesced under it, without the least Complaint, if they had felt those heavy Inconveniencies which have been so fully and so industriously displayed.

The great Arguments made use of against this Bill, are drawn, First, from the Inconveniency and Situation of the Town of *Buckingham*; and, Secondly, from the County-Gaol being lately built at *Aylesbury*.

Buckingham is, in every respect, as good a Town, and very near as large, as *Aylesbury*. It has more in Number, and larger Inns, for the Reception of those who attend the Assizes, than *Aylesbury* has. The Town-Hall, where the Courts of Justice are holden, is a large Building; and both the Civil and Criminal Courts are better, and more convenient, than in any of the other Counties upon the same Circuit, except *Norfolk* and *Suffolk*. The Judges and the Counsel have never complained of their Reception or Usage there; on the contrary, 'tis well known, that they have frequently declared, that they are more commodiously lodged and accommodated, in all respects, at *Buckingham* than at *Aylesbury*.

The County of *Buckingham* is, in Length, from South to North, near 60 measured Miles; and, in Breadth, from East to West, in general, about 10 or 12 Miles. From *Uxbridge*, which lies pretty near the Southern Extremity of the County, to *Aylesbury*, is 18 computed, and 27 measured Miles; from *Aylesbury* to *Buckingham*, going Northward, is 12 computed, and 17 measured Miles; and from *Buckingham* to a little beyond *Olney*, which is the Northern Extremity of the County, is 14 computed, and 21 measured Miles. As to the Breadth of the County from East to West, it is as broad at *Buckingham* as at *Aylesbury*, or at any other Part; and tho' it is true, that *Buckingham* lies within Three or Four Miles of *Oxfordshire* and *Northamptonshire*, to the West and North-west, it is equally true, that *Aylesbury* lies within Four or Five Miles of *Hertfordshire*, to the East and South-east. By this State of the Situation of that County, and by looking into the Map, and appealing to those who live in it, for the Truth of it, it will appear how false and groundless the Insinuation is, upon which the great Opposition to this Bill is founded; to wit, that *Buckingham* lies in the extreme Corner of the County; tho', if that were true, the having one of the Assizes there, is no more than is practised in many other Counties, in the like Circumstances; particularly in *Norfolk* and *Berkshire*, where the Assizes are alternately holden at *Norwich* and *Thetford*; and at *Reading* and *Abingdon*; tho' both *Thetford* and *Abingdon* are at the utmost Extremity of their respective Counties, which is likewise the Case of *Launceston*, as has been mentioned before; and in those Counties where both the Assizes are fixed by constant Usage at one Place, the greater Part of them are far from being in the Middle of their several Counties, and a great many of them much less so than *Buckingham*: The Truth of which will appear to anybody who will examine what the Assize-Towns are, and look into the Maps for their Situation.

As it stands by the Bill now proposed, *Aylesbury* is left in Possession of the Winter Assizes, and of the Four Quarter Sessions; so that the Inhabitants of that Part of the County which lies South of *Aylesbury* have the Administration of publick Justice distributed to them Five times at *Aylesbury*, and the Inhabitants of that Part of the County which lies North of *Buckingham*, have it once at *Buckingham*. Surely this is a very reasonable Request; especially when every Person acquainted with that County must own, tho' the Distance is less, that it is a harder Day's Journey from the Northern Extremity of the County *in Winter* to *Aylesbury*, than from the Southern Extremity of the County *in Summer* to *Buckingham*.

It is true that the Goal was begun at *Aylesbury*, by a Rate made at the Quarter Sessions there, and levied contrary to Law upon the County; but this was completed no longer ago than the Year 1736; till which Time, it appears by the Petition for the Bill then passed, that there was no County-Goal at *Aylesbury*. The Town of *Buckingham* was then, and continued for 10 Years after, in the uninterrupted Possession of the Summer Assizes, without the least Application from the County then, or at any time afterwards, to alter them; nor was it ever imagined, at the time that their Consent to this Act was applied for, out of Compassion to the poor Workmen who had been employed in that Work without any legal Authority, and who could not otherwise have been paid, that this friendly Compliance would have been made use of as an Argument for taking away the Summer Assizes, which they had so long enjoyed.

It has been industriously reported upon this Occasion, that the County is to be charged with raising a considerable Sum for building a new Goal at *Buckingham*: But this is a direct Falshood, since 'tis well known, that the Town of *Buckingham* has always had a Goal of their own, which is now actually beginning to be rebuilt, without raising One Shilling upon the County for that Purpose. It has been said likewise, that the County is put to a Charge in carrying the Prisoners to *Buckingham*: But this is a Mistake; for it is allowed to the Sheriff at the Exchequer, and is not defrayed by the County; and this Expence, which has been so strongly insisted upon, amounts by the Accounts in the Exchequer to a Demand of 10 *l.* and to an Allowance of 5 *l.* a Year, and no more. The Circumstance of the Assizes not being holden at the same Place where the County-Goal is established is not peculiar to this County, but is in common with a great many others; particularly *Surry*, *Norfolk*, *Kent*, *Berkshire*, *Cornwall*, and *Somerset*; and consequently ought no more to be urged as a Reason in this Case, than it is in those.

It has been said, that the Prerogative of the Crown is concerned in this Question; and that the King has the Power of appointing the Places for holding the Assizes: But it is plain, from the Acts of the 6th and 11th of *R.* II. that the Crown has divested itself of this Power by Law; and that the Assizes are fixed in the principal Towns, except in cases of Need; when, by the latter Act, the Chancellor with the Advice of the Judges had a Power to provide a Remedy. It was not reckoned an Invasion upon the Prerogative of the Crown in the Time of Queen *Elizabeth*, when the Act for settling the Assizes at *Stafford* was passed; and it will not be said, that the Prerogative was not as high then as it is now.

By the 7th and 8th *W.* III. *c.* 25. it is provided, That the County-Courts for the Election of Knights of the Shire shall be holden where the same have *most usually been for* 40 *Years last past.* This Act was occasioned by the Removal of the County-Courts, for the Purposes of Elections; of which there was an Instance in *Buckinghamshire*, where the County-Court was removed at the

Time of the Election from *Aylesbury* to *Newport,* in Favour of Mr. *Hackett,* who, in the Parliament of *James* II. was a Candidate for this County against Mr. *Wharton*: And there was an Instance of the same Kind a few Years after, in the County of *Surry.* It will not be denied, that the County-Court is the King's Court, and holden by his Officer as much as the Assizes are by the Judges; and the Prerogative of the Crown is as much concerned in the one as the other: Notwithstanding which, it was thought proper to fix them where they had been most usually holden, without considering whether they were in the Middle of their Counties, or in all other Particulars the most convenient Places, and without apprehending a Monopoly; tho' all these Arguments must certainly hold much stronger in Cases of publick County-Elections, than in the Case of the Assizes. How does this materially differ from the present Purpose? In this instance, the Summer Assizes were removed, in the very Week of the Elections, from the antient County-Town, *where they had been most usually holden for more than* 40 *Years*; that is to say, for the greatest part of Eighty-one Years last-past, as appears by the Admission of the printed Reasons against this Bill. They were altered without the least Colour of Complaint, or application from the County for whose sake it is pretended this Bill is opposed. But whatever Reasons may be now assigned, the World will judge, under these Circumstances, whether they ought to have been changed; and consequently, whether the restoring them is not an Act of Justice, and not of *private Favour against publick Utility.*

This Bill has been represented as a Hardship upon the County *for the sake of a particular Borough.* What the Sentiments of the County are about it has been shewn by the Petitions to the House of Commons for and against it; by which it appears, that the greater Part of the Property in the County, with near 1500 Freeholders, have desired that this Bill may pass in order to fix the Administration of Justice in this County for the future in its usual Channel, and to prevent the Assizes from being removed from one Borough-Town to another at Pleasure.

Thus far the Case.

Now will any unprejudiced, or ingenuous Man say, that it did not become the Members of the Town of *Buckingham,*[1]

---

[1] The two M.P.s for Buckingham borough were Richard Grenville and George Grenville (1712–70), a junior Commissioner of the Treasury.

or any one Member of *Buckinghamshire*,[1] or Gentleman of that County,[2] to support the Town in a Cause of this kind; in which, beside any Pretension to Favour, they seem to have so clear a Claim of Right, that we may at least suppose any impartial Person would incline to their Side?

To speak out honestly and plainly, Can those Gentlemen who have an Interest in the Town of *Buckingham* be blamed for taking Part in such a Cause, or for making it their own? Who is there who will lay his Hand upon his Heart, and declare he would not, in the like Circumstances, have done the same? Nay, might not even a Casuist have censured him if he had acted otherwise?

Now what must that Man be, who sitting in an Assembly where the Cause of his Friend is try'd, refuses him his Vote, I will add his Interest, when Justice demands it? To support a Friend in a very doubtful Case, is, I believe, no uncommon Act of Friendship; nor doth it, in truth, deserve a very harsh Appellation; but to desert his Cause, when he is manifestly in the Right; to forsake not only your Friend, but Truth and Justice at the same Time, and this from the paultry Fear of the malicious Slander of his Enemies, would argue a very pitiful Mind indeed.

The good Man will love his Friend; the Man of Honour will adhere to Justice; and the Man of Spirit will exert himself in Support of both. Let therefore the Case under our Consideration be, for once, of the utmost Importance, by being made the Test of all these Qualities in a very Honourable Gentleman, and he will be found in this Instance, as in all others, to have maintained the Dignity of his high Station, and of his higher Character.[3]

---

[1] The two M.P.s for Bucks. were Sir William Stanhope and Richard Lowndes (*c.* 1707–75). Stanhope opposed the Bill; therefore Lowndes must be meant, although he was by background an Opposition Tory; see Owen, *Rise of the Pelhams*, p. 66 n. Wiggin, *Faction of Cousins*, p. 67 n., cites the *Verney Letters* (London, 1930), ii. 255, to the effect that in June 1746 Lowndes 'abused Pelham and the Grenvilles'.

[2] Not identified; but see Wiggin, *Faction of Cousins*, p. 125.

[3] This and the preceding paragraph are in defensive praise of Pelham, whose support of the Grenvilles and whose 'high Station' as Chancellor of the Exchequer and principal minister of the Government seem to be referred to.

SATURDAY, APRIL 16, 1748.   NUMB. 20.

Mordear opprobriis falsis, mutemque colorem?
Falsus Honor juvat, et mendax Infamia terret
Quem nisi mendosum et mendacem?

Horace.[1]

When I first undertook to defend the present Royal Establishment, I very little apprehended that I should, by that Means,
subject myself to public Abuse. Whatever other good Appellation my Design may be favoured with, I frankly own it had no
better Claim to Heroism, than the Prowess of the Champion at
a Coronation; since I concluded myself equally safe with him,
in asserting the Right of the King on the Throne.[2]

But in this, it seems, I have been greatly mistaken; for before
my Paper hath reached the 20th Number, a heavier Load of
Scandal hath been cast upon me, than I believe ever fell to the
Share of a single Man. The Author of the Journal was soon
guess'd at;[3] either from some Singularity in Style, or from the
little Care which, being free from any wicked Purpose, I have
ever taken to conceal my Name. Of this several Writers were no
sooner possessed, than they attempted to blacken it with every
kind of Reproach; pursued me into private Life, *even to my boyish
Years*; where they have given me almost every Vice in Human
Nature. Again, they have followed me, with uncommon Inveteracy, into a Profession, in which they have very roundly
asserted, that I have neither Business nor Knowledge: And
lastly, as an Author, they have affected to treat me with more
Contempt, than Mr. *Pope*, who had great Merit and no less

---

[1] *Epistles*, I. xvi. 38–40; a more generally accepted text reads *mutemque colores* and, by
emendation, *mendicandum*. 'Ought I to be stung by such lying charges, and change
colour? Whom does false honour delight, whom does lying calumny affright, save the man
who is full of flaws and needs the doctor?' (Loeb).

[2] At a coronation the office of the Champion of the King is to ride armed into Westminster Hall and challenge to combat any one who disputes the king's title to the crown; cf.
Tatler no. 17 (19 May 1709).

[3] Perhaps the earliest attribution to Fielding is in *A Free Comment on the Late Mr.
W——G——N's Apology for his Conduct* (London, 1748), p. 48 of which bears the dateline
'December 14, 1747'; this pamphlet is listed among the December 1747 books in *GM*,
xvii (1747), 596, and is advertised in *GA* of 21 December 1747. The earliest attribution to
be found in the newspapers themselves seems to be that in *LEP* of 9–12 January 1748, which
publishes a poem identifying the author of *JJ* as the author of 'Tom Thumb', *Joseph
Andrews*, and *Pasquin*.

Pride in the Character of a Writer, hath thought proper to bestow on the lowest Scribbler of his Time. All this, moreover, they have poured forth in a Vein of Scurrility, which hath disgraced the Press with every abusive Term in our Language.[1]

I do not here intend to tire the Reader with a Defence, which he must know it is impossible for the most innocent Man alive to make; and which, if he cou'd make, the best-natured Man would hardly have the Patience to read. I shall therefore rest contented with these Consolations: That the Works of all these Authors will have a very short Existence: That those who know me, will not take their Opinion of me from those who know me not: That even to a Stranger, their Calumny carries two strong Antidotes with it; from its own Weight, which is sufficient to sink it; since it is scarce possible to believe that such a Monster exists; and from its apparent Inveteracy, which must raise the Candour of every worthy Man on my Behalf.

Here, I think I may fairly ask these Authors, whence all this inveterate Rage and Malice proceed? I am not conscious of having injured any Human Being, much less can I be supposed to have injured those with whom I am not acquainted. The Productions of one of these Men, indeed, I have charged with Scurrility; a Charge which he acknowledges to have been of such Service to him in propagating his Labours, that it kept his Printer at Work for a whole Fortnight.[2] But there is another who hath libelled me twice or thrice a Week, ever since the Commencement of this Paper, without having received the least previous Provocation, or, indeed, scarce any Return to his Abuse, which, if transcribed, would fill this whole Paper.[3]

Am I to derive all this from a natural Malevolence of Disposition, and to imply the same universal Malice in these Libellers, as the Law doth in those who kill without Provocation; who

[1] For a survey of newspaper attacks on Fielding's private and professional life (in law and letters) see General Introduction above, pp. lxx–lxxi, lxxiv–lxxxii.

[2] In *JJ* no. 11, above, p. 161, 'Porcupinus Pelagius' was charged with having scurrilously abused Hardwicke and the bishops in *The 'Piscopade*. In *OE* of 5 March 1748 'Porcupinus Pelagius' replied: 'However, my Book-seller is not a little obliged to him [Trott-Plaid]; for in dismounting the original *Spanish* Figures, and replacing the Niches with *English* ones, he has helped on the Publication so far as to keep my Printer in full Employ ever since . . .'.

[3] Presumably *LEP*, if 'previous Provocation' means provocation previous to the first number of *JJ*, which ridiculed *LEP* in both text and frontispiece.

are to be presumed, says Lord *Hale*, to be *hostes humani generis*?[1]

Shall I be indulged the Vanity of applying to myself the Marks which some eminent Writer (I think Dr. *Swift*) tells us always attend a Man of Genius; who, at his first Appearance in the World, is sure to be attacked by all the Insect-Reptile-Scribblers of the Age?[2]

Or lastly, is it the Cause, and not the Man, which is obnoxious? Are these Writers such zealous Jacobites in their Hearts, and so firmly attached to the Pretender's Interest, that they cannot bear to see his Party, and their absurd Principles, ridiculed? It is (to use the flagitious and nonsensical Words of the Letter-writer to the Whigs) *come to the Crisis of a Question, whether these Scribblers will suffer a Prince of the House of* Hanover *to sit on the* British *Throne*.[3] It was in Defence of this illustrious House that I drew my Pen, and in their Defence I have drawn on myself all the Scandal and Scurrility, which the blackest Degree of Malice could rake out of the Kennels of *Grub-street* and *Billingsgate*. Honestly, I am sure, I may say in their Defence; for much of this Scurrility was cast on the Author of the *Jacobite Journal*, before he had touched on a single Ministerial Question. Nay, even to this Day, so very little of that kind hath been made the Subject of this Paper, that those who will call it Ministerial, must acknowledge, that to defend the King and the present Administration, are one and the same Thing.

To despise unjust Calumny, and to be totally insensible of it, are very different Matters. The latter I do not affect, nor do I believe any good Man ever did: For to have a great deal of this metaphorical Dirt and Ordure thrown on your Character, can be no more agreeable, than to have a Quantity of literal Filth thrown on your Person. Both of these Injuries arise from the same Kind of People, and both produce the same Effects, a little

---

[1] Matthew Hale, *Historia Placitorum Coronae* (2 vols., London, 1736), i. xxxvii. 455: 'When one voluntarily kills another without any provocation, it is murder, for the law presumes it to be malicious, and that he is *hostis humani generis* . . .'. Baker, item no. 131, lists this edition of Hale among Fielding's books.

[2] 'Thoughts on Various Subjects', *Prose Works*, ed. Herbert Davis, i (Oxford, 1939), 242: 'When a true Genius appears in the World, you may know him by this infallible Sign; that the Dunces are all in Confederacy against him.'

[3] *Second and Third Letter to the Whigs*, p. 50: 'It was almost come to the Crisis of a Question, whether the Nation would suffer a Prince of the House of *Hanover* to sit upon a *British* Throne.'

temporal Uneasiness and Disguise; for tho' the Mob should cover a Gentleman with Dirt, they could never persuade those who know him, that he was either a Chimney-sweeper or a Tom-T—dman, as I have been more than once called;[1] and those who did not know him before, as soon as they are informed who he is, will pity the Gentleman, and detest the Mob who have used him so.

But besides the Contempt which I really have for this Metaphorical Dirt, and besides the Consolations under it which I have mentioned above, I have further Reason to be contented with the Fate of every Great Man at present among us, for all have been insulted by the undistinguishing Virulence of these Writers. Not to mention one who, in certain Things which he calls Poems, hath indiscriminately libell'd the whole Privy Council, the whole Bench of Bishops, and all the Judges, with my Lord Chancellor at their Head;[2] nor the Author of the *Letter to the Whigs*, whom we handled a little in our last; in the *Old England* of last *Saturday* the Reader is plainly told, that neither of two noble Dukes hath any Head;[3] besides other Insinuations equally witty, equally civil, and equally true.

Who or what this most malignant Writer is, I will not determine.[4] Let the polite Reader judge of his Degree by the Good-Breeding, of which we have just given an Example. Let the Scholar judge of his Literature by his last Performance, in which there is scarce one Paragraph of good *English*; and let the Lawyer pronounce how capable he is of discoursing of the Laws of our Country, who hath joined a Writ of Formedon and Ejectment together, and hath told us, that an uninterrupted Possession of 20 Years is a Bar in both. That he may not tax me with doing him an Injury, I will quote his Words: *The Wisdom of the Law assures us, that twenty Years uninterrupted Possession* (very barbarous Language by the By) *is a Bar against a Writ of Formedon*

---

[1] *OE* of 19 March 1748 printed an acrostic on TROT-PLAID of which the first line reads: 'T signifies *Tyburn*, Tomt—dman, and Trot.' The poem was also printed in *LEP* of 17–19 March 1748.

[2] For the 'Poems' of 'Porcupinus Pelagius' see *JJ* nos. 11 and 15, above, pp. 161, 197.

[3] *OE* of 9 April 1748 called Pelham and Newcastle the 'two Hey-Dukes' and stated that when the writer came to look more closely at them, 'I found that neither of them had a Head.' A heyduke is a robber, marauder, brigand (*OED*), which explains its application to Pelham, who was not in fact titled.

[4] But see *JJ* no. 13, above, p. 181, where the author of *OE* is said to be 'one and the same Person' as the author of *The 'Piscopade* and other 'Poems'; also *JJ* no. 15, above, p. 197.

and Ejectment.[1] Now I must inform this Writer, that the Years in a Formedon are to be computed from the Time of the Title accrued, and that the Possession is totally immaterial in this Action; and so he will find it in 21 *Jac.* 1. *c.* 16.[2] I should not have troubled the Reader with this Remark, had not the World been assured in this Paper, that the Author of the *Jacobite Journal* was a Lawyer, but had never read a Syllable of the Law.[3]

Now surely, without being possessed of the Spirit of *Cadwallader*, who tells us, *that the Miserable find Consolation in seeing others as miserable as themselves*,[4] (a Sentiment neither very Christian, nor very humane) a Man may be permitted some Satisfaction in finding that the same Writers who have abused him, have likewise abused Persons of the highest Distinction, and of the greatest Characters; for it is not that he draws hence the pitiful Comfort which an ungenerous Thief feels at the Gallows from having Fellow-Sufferers, who are to undergo the same Fate; but because, in Reality, the Writers do, by such impolitic Means, utterly destroy their own Credit, and their most malicious Calumny becomes perfectly inoffensive: Indeed we may apply to them a common Phrase which, tho' Vulgar, they have most probably both heard and used in the Streets, *That their Tongues are no Slander*.[5]

Since I have bestowed so much of this Paper (for the first and last time) on Writers who have abused me, the good-natured Reader will perhaps pardon my Vanity in publishing the following Letter, which I received last Week, when I acknowledge that I fear my Writings are here treated as much too kindly, as the other Authors have treated me too scurrilously.

---

[1] *OE* of 9 April 1748. A writ of Formedon is that brought by persons who claim land under a gift in tail when the land is in possession of a person or persons not legally entitled to it; a writ of Ejectment is available only to persons entitled to the possession of land under a lease or other chattel interest. See William Allen Jowitt, *Dictionary of English Law*, ed. Clifford Walsh (London, 1959), s.v.

[2] *Statutes at Large*, vii. 273–5: 'all writs of *formedon* . . . shall be sued and taken within twenty years next after the title and cause of action first fallen.'

[3] For example, in *OE* of 5 March and 2 April 1748.

[4] In *Remembrancer* no. 18 of 9 April 1748. For 'Cadwallader' see *JJ* no. 17, above, p. 213, n. 1. Cadwaladr, so-called 'last King of the Britons', defended Wales against the Saxons and later the Angles. Merlin prophesied his return at some future date to expel the enemies of his country.

[5] Tilley, *Dictionary of the Proverbs in England*, T389, p. 674, cites no example with 'their'.

To John Trott-Plaid, *Esq;*

Sir,

* * * * *"Ridiculum acri fortius et melius"*[1]—may, at proper Seasons, be an useful Lesson; and yet surely there is a Time when *Banter* ought to cease, when it should give Way to *Truth* and *Reason;* to cut the Throat of Madness or obstinate Folly with a Feather, is a Task to which even your Pen is not always equal; and when the soft and gentle Methods of Allegory and Fiction fail in their Attempts to check a spreading Evil, Recourse should be had to the Force and Influence of serious Argument:

"Cuncta prius tentanda, sed immedicabile vulnus ense recidendum est."[2]

It is admitted, Sir, that no Writer of our Age has carried the Power of *Humour* to an higher Pitch than you have done; and if you have fallen any thing short of the great *Cervantes,* in your several Portraits of Human Nature, (which possibly no masterly Critick will readily allow) you have undoubtedly excelled all other Authors of the Utile-dulce Class;—but as a continued Sameness of Sentiments (even the most lively Sentiments) is apt to cloy the Understanding of a Reader; and as the Sting of Humour, (the most sprightly Humour) by a Frequency of Action, is worn, as it were, into a State of Bluntness, and loses its Effect, a constant Writer will, to keep up the Spirit, and to preserve the Dignity of his Paper, find a Time to drop his Humour, and to become *serious:* This Time, Sir, you have found, and have answered the Expectations of your Friends and Admirers, by discarding your *Ass,* laying aside your *Fool's Coat,* renouncing a *ridiculous Character,* which had exhausted our whole Stock of Laughter, and resuming that of a *Man of Sense,* a *genuine Patriot,* a *real Englishman;* with this generous Turn of Mind, in this amiable Character proceed and prosper! Exert your happy Talents in the *open* and *avowed* Service of your Country: Load yourself with Labour to increase the Number of her Friends, and rob yourself of Rest to defeat the wily Views, to obviate the determined Malice of her infatuated Foes. To this End paint the

---

[1] Horace, *Satires,* I. x. 14–15, where the completed sentiment is to the effect that ridicule is often more effective than gravity.

[2] Ovid, *Metamorphoses,* i. 190–1: 'I swear I have already tried all other means. But that which is incurable must be cut away with the knife' (Loeb). The accepted modern text has *temptata* for *tentanda, corpus* for *vulnus,* and omits *est.*

Protestant Jacobite (if such a Monster breathes) as *your* Pen can paint him;—place his Absurdity in a glaring Light, make him blush, make him tremble at his own Image, correct, convince, reclaim, and save him.

Your Predecessors, of living Memory, the *Spectator*, the *Tatler*, and the *Guardian*, in their Labours to please and to improve Mankind, did not disdain the Assistance of a lower Order of Pen-men, but rather encouraged a general Correspondence, accepting every Mite thrown in to swell their Magazine of *Letters*, *Virtue*, and *Religion*. If such are your Sentiments, Mr. *Trott-Plaid*, you have only to intimate your Disposition "to bestow a Minute or two on a *Post-paid* Letter;" and when you happen to meet with one to your Taste, it may perhaps save an Hour's Labour to your Head and your Eyes; both which, for the Sake of the Public, it is incumbent on you, now-and-then, to relieve.

I am, Sir,
Your most humble Servant,

March 3,[1]

1748.   Walter Wishwell.

P.S. It is to be hoped that a formal Cession of your Jacobitism will not give Birth to any Revolution in the *Court of Criticism*; but rather that such Incident will confirm your Title to the *Chair* in that august Assembly; continue to be a Terror to *Knaves*, a Lash to *Fools*, and a warm Opposer of the *Cart*esian[2] System of Politicks.

Proceedings at the Court of Criticism, Thursday April 14.

The following Letter to his Honour was read, and ordered to be printed.

To the Author of the Jacobite Journal.

Sir,

I heartily agree with you, that the Cause of *Jacobitism* is become too serious an Affair, at this Time, to be treated in a ludicrous

---

[1] Apparently a slip for *April* 3. 'Trott-Plaid' did not in fact 'pull off the Masque' until *JJ* no. 17 of 26 March.

[2] Playing on the name of Descartes and that of Carte, the historian. See *JJ* no. 15, above, pp. 194–7.

Manner; and therefore am very well pleased that you have put off the *Fool's Coat*, and re-assumed your *Orange* Colours.[1]

You very well observe—"That every Attempt, with which Malice can supply Invention, is employed to undermine and blow up the Constitution; that Popish Traytors are crept into the Seminaries of Learning, and Libels are dispersed all over the Nation."[2]——But among the latter, I think, there is one that more particularly deserves your Attention.

There is very diligently dispersed, by the Papists, all over this Country,* a Pamphlet called *The* State *preferable to the* Church; *or, Reasons for making Sale of the whole present* Property *of the* Church *in* England *and* Ireland, *for the Use of the* State, *&c.*[3]—— If *Ithuriel's* Spear be applied to this Piece, I fancy it will startle you,

So sudden to behold the grizly King.[4]

The Author has put on an *Orange* Dublet, and in that Guise labours, with Might and Main, to set Priests and People together by the Ears; insisting upon it as necessary, that the former part with their Glebe and Tythes to the latter: This he expects will throw the Nation into a Ferment, and raise a dreadful Outcry of the Church's Danger, which may perhaps pave the Way for his darling Point—a Restoration.

He then tries to remove those Obstacles that may at last possibly prevent his pernicious Intention.——The Church-Lands in Lay-Hands are indeed a main Hindrance, which, as it deserves his utmost Care to remove, so he has bestow'd most Pains upon it, from *p.* 22 to the End of his Book; and has endeavoured to prove, that these Lands are more secure to Laymen under a Popish Administration, than they are, or can be, under the present Government; as being not only confirmed to them by Act of Parliament, but settled on them by the Popish Bishops

---

* If needful, I can swear that I received this Book out of the Hands of a Papist.

---

[1] The Whig or 'loyal' colours, as opposed to the Tory or Jacobite 'true blue'. Orange was chosen because of the accidental coincidence of its name with that of the town of Orange, which formerly belonged to the house of Nassau, the ancestral house of William III of England. The wearing of orange ribbons, scarves, cockades and the like was a symbol of attachment to the principles of the Revolution settlement of 1689.

[2] A somewhat compressed quotation from *JJ* no. 17, above, p. 212.

[3] *GM*, xviii (1748), 48, lists this Cooper pamphlet among the January 1748 books.

[4] *Paradise Lost*, iv. 821, referring to Satan after he has been touched by Ithuriel's spear.

and Clergy, and established to them by the unalterable Decrees of the Popes of *Rome*, by their Legate, and in their own proper Persons.

But that you may not mistake this Author's Intention, take it in his own Words, *p. 59, &c.* "Before I take Leave of you, permit me to make an Observation which arises from the Subject I have been treating of: I have shewn, that if we had continued Papists, the Dispensations of *Rome* would have intirely quieted our Consciences, as to our Possession of Church-Lands; and our Minds, as to any Claim the Clergy might vainly set up, hereafter, to such Possessions: And I have endeavoured to shew likewise the moral Impossibility of an *English* Legislature's repealing that solemn Act, passed the second of *Philip* and *Mary*,[1] to confirm the Rights of those Possessors so dispensed with by the Court of *Rome*.

"We should have found all these Precautions necessary, if we had remained in Communion with the See of *Rome*; and should our present Infidelity ever throw us back into that mysterious Communion, we shall find these wise Precautions of our Fathers so many impenetrable Bulwarks, behind which our Possession of Church Lands rests as firm and secure as the THRONE itself; as in *Saxony*, where, *tho' the Prince and his Family be Papists*,[2] his *Protestant* Subjects are, and *think themselves for ever secure**, in the Possessions of their Church-Lands.

"The Protestant Possessors likewise of Church-Lands in the *Palatinate*, the Dutchies of *Wirtenberg*, *Baden*, and several other States of *Germany*, are no less secure in their Possession of such Lands, tho' their respective Sovereigns BE RETURN'D to the *Roman* Communion. All are tranquil, all are safe and secure in the Empire, with Regard to Church-Lands: Nor is there any, THE LEAST COLOURABLE PRETEXT FOR OUR BEING OTHERWISE HERE IN *ENGLAND*, EVEN THO' OUR SOVEREIGNS SHOU'D SWERVE FROM THE ORTHO-DOXY OF THE REFORMATION.

---

* Mind the Lyer; True Protestants in *Saxony* do not, nor cannot, think themselves for ever secure.

---

[1] 1, 2, Phil. & Mary, cap. 30; *Statutes at Large*, vi. 40. The Act confirmed the dispersion of Church lands to lay persons during the reign of Henry VIII.

[2] Frederick-Augustus III (1696–1763), Elector of Saxony and King of Poland (1733–63). His father had become a Catholic in 1697 in order to obtain the throne after the death of Sobieski.

"And, Sir, the Observation I would make before I conclude is this, That as we have the Pleasure to find, and think our Possession of *Church-Lands* to be secure at all Events, UNDER ANY KING, AND OF WHAT RELIGION SOEVER HE MAY BE, so have we likewise the Satisfaction to look upon our Properties in the FUNDS to be equally solid and secure. *I admit that Corruption has taken deep and dangerous Root among us of late Years*; but, Sir, as it was seldom known that a Man would be corrupted to his own Undoing, nay to the Undoing of his Friends and Relations, in short, of all that he holds dear; how can we suppose that an *English* Legislature will, or can, be corrupted to wipe off any of our Property in the *Funds* with a Parliamentary Sponge? And sure I am, that no Prince, ever so little versed in our Annals, and acquainted with our Tempers, will venture to lessen that Property *without Consent of Parliament**.

"As I take such a Violation to be morally impossible, I should be extremely easy as to the Disposition and RELIGION OF OUR *FUTURE* RULERS, even if the Prospect before us had been less flattering than it is. The Royal Progeny IN VIEW†, promise all the Good we can hope for; but my Comfort shall be always this, THAT LET WHO WILL BE KING, the People will have the Power; and I am sure, they never can want the *Will* to secure their Properties in the *Funds* and *Church-Lands*."

Now, Sir, who could have thought that an impudent Papist could have found a Way, in the very Face of the Court, to promote the Interest of the Pretender, and calm the Fears of his Friends? Yet this is done in the Piece before you.———Upon the Whole, it appears plain to me, that there is at this very Time A MOST DANGEROUS PLOT laid against his Majesty, his Crown, and Dignity; and that this Piece is published to prepare the Way for the Execution of it, by setting Clergy and People together by the Ears, and removing those Obstacles that have hitherto been an effectual Bar to a Popish Succession.

I therefore desire, that you'll please to bring this Libel before

* This is copied from the young Pretender's Declaration in *Scotland*.[1]
† It would have been too plain to have said, *The Prince in View*.

---

[1] His second 'manifesto', dated 10 October 1745, states in part that with regard to the Funds his father 'is resolved to take the Advice of his Parliament'; *The Edinburgh History of the Late Rebellion*, 4th ed. (London, 1752), p. 38. Cf. *Proper Answer*, above, p. 80 and note 2 there.

your next *Court of Criticism*, and there thoroughly sift and examine it, in order to your approving, or condemning it, as you in your great Wisdom shall think it deserves.

I am, Sir,

Your humble Servant,

LANCASTRENSIS.[1]

P.S. Would you plainly see a Jesuit in Disguise, look at these Expressions:

Page 59. "The Clergy of *England* are looked upon by very many, to have sought more the Things of this World, than those Things of *Jesus Christ*; for the obtaining of WHICH (*i.e.* Things of *Jesus Christ*) *their* Romish *Predecessors under* Philip *and* Mary, *had spontaneously released all Claim to those Things of this World that had been taken from them.*"——Here the Devil appears very plain.

Page 46. "The Pope, PERHAPS, more tenacious of the Things of this World than he ought."——A Jesuit durst say no more.

Page 31. "For my own Part, *whose whole Estate is Church-Land*, I look upon myself to be signally indebted to the cautious Care of my Ancestors, *&c. &c.*"——This is plain Truth in *Jesuitical* Language.

The Court, instead of passing Sentence, recommended the Author to the Notice of higher Courts of Judicature.

(*Adjourned.*)

SATURDAY, APRIL 23, 1748.   NUMB. 21.

——*Pueris dant Crustula blandi*
Doctores, elementa velint ut discere prima.

Horace.[2]

The Reader will perceive that the following Letters have lain by me some Time, and were received before I threw off the Mask of Jacobitism.

---

[1] A native of Lancashire; here, by loose analogy with the state of the English Crown during and after the Wars of the Roses, a supporter of the House of Hanover (Lancaster) against the aspiring Stuarts (York). It was an eighteenth-century commonplace to compare the Stuart Pretender with another scion of the White Rose, Perkin Warbeck (d. 1499).

[2] *Satires*, I. i. 25–6: 'Teachers . . . give cookies to children to coax them into learning their A B C' (Loeb). Francis and other 18th-century editors print *Pueris olim dant*.

The first of these, I am assured, is a genuine Letter. It will appear as well from that, as from the second, how truly the Letter-writer to the Whigs, and some other such Miscreants, have represented the Spirit of Jacobitism to be extinct in this Nation.[1] It will appear likewise from both, in what Hands the Education of our Youth (the true Source of this Spirit) is entrusted, and how necessary some public Enquiry into that Matter is become.

A Letter from a Jacobite in one Part of the Kingdom, to his Quondam Tutor dwelling in another Part.

Dear Sir,

I am sorry to acquaint you, that my old Friend and School-fellow, and your old Scholar, *John Turncoat*, has revolted from our Party, and apostatized from our Tenets. But, to curtail this stinging and doleful News, it fell out on this wise.

You remember that *John Turncoat* (for I shall now neither call him Master or Esquire, tho' we used to flatter him formerly with those Appellations) was frequently soliciting Sir *John True-James* to procure him a Post in the Customs.——Yesterday he came to me with a more thoughtful Air than Common.——*Jemmy*, says he, Sir *John* hast at last got me a Grant of—— Collection; and ever since I received his Letter, various have been the Commotions and Perturbations of my Mind.——About what, crys I?——Says he, I am informed that I must take a Sacrament-Oath (before I can be admitted into Business) that I believe *G——* has a true Title to the Crown of *England*,[2] as well *de jure* as *de facto*; which, continued he, you know I can't do without Perjury: What shall I do, says he?——You Fool you, reply'd I, how have I done? Have not I taken that Oath, and what of all that? It's an imposed Oath, which we are obliged to take *Nolens Volens*; there can be no Sin in not performing it as to serving him faithfully; or in taking it, in Regard to your Belief of his Title being just or not. By all Means, *Jack*, says I, accept of the Place; never mind

---

[1] See esp. *A Second and Third Letter to the Whigs*, pp. 76–7.

[2] Cf. the 'Act imposing the Abjuration Oath' (13 Will. III, cap. 6): 'I A. B. do truly and sincerely acknowledge profess testify and declare in my Conscience before God and the World That our Sovereign Lord King [i.e. George] is lawfull and rightful King of this Realm . . .'. See *JJ* no. 16, above, p. 202, n. 1; also no. 27, p. 298, n. 1, and no. 33, p. 344, n. 1.

the Oath.——Then says he, in a damn'd sneaking Tone, "God will be angry if I live in a forsworn State." Pshaw, pshaw, says I, the sacred *James* has more Interest with his Holiness the Pope, than to suffer the Hierarchy of Heaven to impute that to you for a Sin, which you did in Favour of his Holiness his beloved Minion. I hope, said he, you don't think me a *Roman*, to accept of the Pope's Absolution: I assure you Sir, I am a true Protestant.—— Pho, answered I, what signifies what Religion we are of, if we can live in Splendor, and have our Ends in this World? Did not I answer him right in that Point? I am sure those are the Principles you formerly inculcated into me, and all your Scholars. But to go on, after many fruitless Arguments and Exhortations, I was forced to bring him to the Rev. Mr. *Robert Artful*, our good and learned Divine, as also Schoolmaster in this Town,[1] who came here after you left this Place. He is a good and firm Jacobite, and as the late Master, Mr. *Honesty*, shewed an Inclination to Whiggism, we got him (Mr. *Artful*) into the School, and dismiss'd the other; for this you know is our chief Aim in all public Schools. I say, I brought him to this worthy Divine, who, as well as I, advised him to take the Commission however, and did all we could to baffle his Conscience about the Heinousness of Perjury; the Reverend Gentleman adding, that he himself had taken this very Oath, which was imposed upon him; and that, tho' in his Prayers in Public he named King *G—ge*, in his Heart he meant, and in his private Devotions always named *J—s*: Nay, continued the old Gentleman, I take Care to bring up all my Pupils in that Way of thinking, and have convinced many of the Smallness of the Crime, (if it be any) in perjuring oneself in that Case; for which I hope to be well rewarded in this World, and to come off well enough in the next. But some old Woman or other had so prepossessed him with the Thought of the Sin, that he was immoveable, and in fine said, that he had impaired his Estate with entertaining *J—s's* Friends, and was now forced to accept of the Place. But since he must take the Oath, he would be for the future as rigid against us, as hitherto he had been firm for us, for his Oath's Sake, as he call'd it forsooth. On which the good Father's Wrath was so kindled, that had I not prevented him, I believe he would have chastised his Folly and Insolence.

[1] As both an ecclesiastical person and a schoolmaster, Mr. Artful was a member of *two* of the classes for which the abjuration oath was specifically required.

I am sorry any who have had the Happiness of drinking the Milk of your Instructions in their Youth, should afterwards let it turn sour in their Minds. But be assured I shall always remain what you bred me up, a staunch Jacobite,

And am, &c.

Derbyshire, Jan. 30th, 1747.[1]

'*Squire Trott-Plaid,*

It is with no little Pleasure I find a Person of your Consequence appear so publickly in the Interest of our Party. Though I have not had an Opportunity to peruse all your valuable Productions, I am inform'd (by those that have) that you promise to dismount for a Stage or two, for any Person who can prove his Services for our Cause adequate to so great an Honour.

Therefore not only out of a Desire of making myself conspicuous to the Party, but also to show in what Manner I think myself intituled to mount before *Peggy,* I here give you some Account of myself, and then hope you'll think I merit what I sollicit for.

Know then that I am at the Head of one of the largest Schools in this C——y,[2] and have Noblemen's and Gentlemen's Sons from most Parts of the Kingdom under my Tuition. In these Circumstances you may easily imagine I have great Opportunities to season their tender Minds with all the Mysteries and Principles of our Party; and I can assure you, I don't let the Opportunity slip, for I bestow (its well known) more Pains on this Head, than I do to bring them up in the Principles of Christianity. 'Tis for that Purpose I have collected a few of our Mysteries, and form'd them into a Creed, which I teach my Pupils by Heart, and explain it to them as Occasion requires: Here follows a Copy.

---

[1] A satirical dateline. Derbyshire is named because of its associations with Henry Sacheverell, the High-Church extremist of Queen Anne's day, so much admired by the signatory of this letter ('Philo-Sacheverel'). Sacheverell, who claimed Derbyshire connections, preached an incendiary assize sermon at Derby on 15 August 1709. It was one of the two sermons directly responsible for the impeachment proceedings against him; see *JJ* no. 15, above, p. 190. The date, January 30, is that of the death of Charles I, the Stuart 'martyr'.

[2] Derbyshire had a lingering reputation for Jacobitism, but there is insufficient evidence that Fielding here meant to refer to a particular school, e.g., Repton, whose first usher betrayed Jacobite sympathies during the Forty-Five; *Victoria History of the County of Derby,* ed. William Page (London, 1907), ii. 241.

I BELIEVE King *James* II. had a Divine Right to govern this Nation as he pleas'd, without Controul; and that no one in these Realms ought to oppose him, or his Heirs, in such their Government, on Pain of D———n. I BELIEVE, that tho' this good old King was driven hence by his rebellious and disobedient Subjects, his Heirs will sometime be happily restor'd to their Rights. Then shall our Taxes cease, and the Debts of the Nation be paid with a Sponge.[1] I BELIEVE it is my Duty, and every Individual's within these Realms, to endeavour such a Restoration. And I most FIRMLY BELIEVE, I should stick at nothing to serve the Cause, nor to alienate the Hearts of the People from the present Government.

Thus, Sir, I have let you know what Station of Life I'm in, and how far serviceable to the Cause; and with Pleasure I can assure you, I have had no bad Success; therefore don't doubt but you'll think me of so much Use as to merit your Saddle for one Day: But if that be too great an Honour, pray let me take the Place for the same Space, of that sarcastick Gentleman (to whom I'm nearly ally'd) who leads your Beast,

And you'll much oblige, Dear Sir,
Your Admirer and Humble Servant,
Philo-Sacheverel, *alias* True-Blue.

Squire Trott-Plaid,

As you profess yourself an honest *Jacobite,* and we believe able to advise us in the Matter we are going to propose to you, we beg you wou'd give us your Opinion about it. We read (that is such of us that can read) in the News-Papers, an Extract taken out of Parson *Carte's* History, how that one *Christopher Lovell* was cured of a very bad Distemper,[2] by going we know not where, a great Way off, to you know who. Now as a very bad Distemper or Evil, has just now entered the Borders of our County, and afflicts our Cattle sorely,[3] we want your Advice, whether it wou'd not be right for us to send our Cattle to the same Person, wherever

---

[1] For the traditional association of this metaphor with an alleged Stuart intention of 'wiping out' the National Debt, see *Proper Answer,* above, p. 80, n. 2.

[2] According to *GM,* xviii (1748), 13, which reprints it, the extract was published first in *GEP* of 7 January 1748; see *JJ* no. 12, above, pp. 168–71.

[3] See *JJ* no. 11, above, p. 156 and note 1 there.

dispersed, and however distressed, and still unanointed, (God knows) to be touched by the same Hereditary Hand that cured *Christopher Lovell,* or that of the Heir-apparent, and we promise, if it succeeds, and the latter should come into this Country again, we will use him better than we did the last Time. If we had thought of this at our Meeting at *Litchfield* in *September* last,[1] we cou'd have got Persons of greater Rank to have joined with us in this our Application, but now we can only subscribe,

The Jacobite Farmers of Staffordshire.

Proceedings at the Court of Criticism, Thursday April 21.

That Court of Criticism in which we preside is so far from being a Court of Damnation only, that one main End of its Institution is to correct a malevolent Spirit, which at present too generally prevails, and which seems to go about *seeking what it may find Fault with.*

The Part, indeed, of the Critical Office in which we are most delighted, is that which consists in giving Praise and Recommendation to Merit; and this we shall extend to every new Scheme and Invention whatever, that anywise tends to public Utility.

After this Declaration we shall make no further Apology for printing the following Letter. We do indeed agree with the Writer, that had we suppress'd a Plan of so noble a Charity, we should have deserved his severest Censure; nor will those whom it chiefly concerns to carry it into Execution, deserve that Censure less, if they pass it over unregarded, or indeed if they omit immediately setting their Hands to so useful a Work.

The Letter which was read in Court, and ordered to be recommended, is as follows:

Most Noble 'Squire Trott-Plaid,

To penetrate into the Heart of so comical, so odd, and so unaccountable an Animal as you seem to be, is beyond all human Art, and a Task too hard for the D——l himself. Were I to judge of your Principles by what I can gather from a Paper, which has lately made its Appearance in the World under the Title of

---

[1] See *JJ* no. 1, above, p. 93 and note 2 there.

the *Jacobite Journal*, which, to your immortal Honour, they say you are the Author of, I should take you to be a downright honest Man, and a true *Briton*; one who has the Interest of your Country, and the Good of Mankind, sincerely at Heart. But I may be deceived, tho' I must confess that nothing has so much the Appearance of Honesty as that Warmth with which you recommend any Thing that has the least Shew of public Benefit. I do not know how I can try you better than by offering a Scheme to your Consideration, which, in my Opinion, must be of great Advantage to this Nation, *viz.* For raising a Fund for maintaining the Widows and Children of inferior and distress'd Clergymen.[1] Now if you are that generous, candid, and well-disposed Creature, that you profess yourself to be, I do not doubt but the Sequel will meet with your Approbation. But if, on the Contrary, you are a sad Dog in the Shape of Goodness, both myself and my Scheme will be the Object of your Ridicule and Contempt: So— without farther Apology here goes—*Parturiunt Montes, nascetur ridiculus Mus.*[2]

In the first Place I will tell you how this Project came into my Head. You must know, then, that some time ago I went with a Friend of mine to visit the Widow of an Officer, who, for the sake of living cheap, is settled in our Neighbourhood. She has two Children, a Boy about eight, and a Girl about ten Years old; and I think a fonder Mother, and more dutiful or lovely Children, I never saw. When we came in, the little Boy was reading to his Mamma, and Miss was working; and, as I found afterwards, they had no other Instructor. I was so charmed with the obliging Behaviour of this Lady, and the Pains that the little ones took to imitate their Mamma, that I could not help saying that I thought she was quite happy in having such Children. She answer'd with a Smile, mix'd with Concern, "Poor Things, if they had not lost their Papa, it would have been happier for them; but now they have no Friend but me. However, if it should please God to let me live till they are grown up, I hope, tho' I have nothing but my Pension to live on, that I shall be able to give them a virtuous

---

[1] Cf. Fielding's note in *Tom Jones*, IV. xiv: 'This [Mrs. Honour] is the second Person of low Condition whom we have recorded in this History, to have sprung from the Clergy. It is to be hoped such Instances will, in future Ages, when some Provision is made for the Families of the inferior Clergy, appear stranger than they can be thought at present.'

[2] Horace, *Ars Poetica*, 139: 'Mountains will labour, to birth will come a laughter-rousing mouse' (Loeb).

Education; and all I desire is to see them get a Livelihood in an honest Way, tho' a mean one."——Here I could not help reflecting how happy it was that Women, who were so often left destitute as Officers Widows were, should have such a Provision made for them, as prevented both them and their Children from falling into those Vices, to which Necessity is so irresistable a Temptation. She went on with saying, "That if she was to begin her Life again, she would not marry an Officer; for, besides the Inconveniency of their frequent Absence from their Families, they seldom left any thing behind, except Children: But still she thought their Widows were happier than the Widows of the Generality of the Clergy, especially the inferior ones, who very often leave a numerous Issue behind them, to be maintained by the Charity of well-disposed People. A meagre Subsistence indeed!" This put me upon thinking, that if the same Thing was done in the Church as is done in the Army, Distresses of this Nature would be easily remedied. I suppose you know, that the Pensions of Officers Widows are paid out of a Fund raised by their giving one Day's Pay in the Year for that Purpose.[1] Now if every Ecclesiastick, from the Archbishop down to the Curate, was to do the same, I'm sure it would raise a Fund large enough not only to maintain the Widows, but likewise to provide for many of their Children. I have mentioned this Scheme to every Parson that I have seen for these three Years last past, which they all to a Man approved; and as it would be a Trifle to each Individual of that Society, and of such infinite Advantage to the Whole, I cannot help thinking, if you would consider, improve, and recommend this Project, but that it would be soon carried into Execution. And what flatters me in this Opinion is, the peculiar Happiness of this Nation at present, in having an Archbishop of so public a Spirit, and so extensive a Benevolence, as Dr. *Herring* is universally acknowledg'd to be:[2] And I doubt not but his Majesty's known Goodness will incline him to give Sanction to a Thing so likely to prevent all that Misery, which at present

[1] For 'Pensions, for the Year 1748, to Widows of reduced Officers of Land Forces and Marines', Parliament estimated £3,886; see *Journals of . . . Commons*, xxv. 771.

[2] Thomas Herring (1693–1757), Archbishop of Canterbury (1747). As Archbishop of York during the Forty-Five he earned an enormous contemporary reputation for militancy, because of his vigour in organizing his diocese against the rebels and his having raised some £40,000 from Yorkshire to assist the Government. Upon his death Herring left benefactions to the sons of the clergy.

is felt by many of the Members of this Society for want of such a Provision. I could tell you of a thousand Instances of this sort of Distress, which I have been Witness of.——But this, to a Man who has seen so much of the World as you have, would be impertinent, and only serve to shock your Humanity. And here I might likewise offer some Arguments to recommend this Scheme, as it has the Appearance of public Good, to your Patronage, did not I take you to be one who has too sincere a Pleasure in doing Good, to need any other Incitement to it than the Knowledge of any Object: And as the best of Hearts and of Heads seem to be happily united in you, I hope, as well for your own Interest as the Service of your Country, that you may continue to employ them for the excellent Uses for which they were designed by the Author of them.

With regard to the collecting or paying this Money, I would have none employ'd but either Parsons or their Children; and, to prevent Expence, it may be paid in twice a Year at the Visitations,[1] together with their Procurations.[2] And as for the three first Years, I would have nothing paid out to any one, in order to raise a good Fund at first. Another Advantage that would accrue from this, would be an Opportunity of breeding up to the Church, now-and-then, a Boy of promising Parts, tho' he should always be the Son of a Clergyman. I took the Liberty to give you these Hints, which you may make what Use of you please; and I hope the Goodness of my Intention will excuse my Impertinence. Tho' I must tell you, that if you should bring this to bear, it would give me great Satisfaction, whose Circumstances will not admit of my doing any other Good to the Miserable than that of wishing them well. So——*Si quid novisti rectius istis—candidus imperti; si non, his utere Mecum.*[3] And now, Sir, out of pure Compassion to your Patience, I shall conclude with a Saying of an ingenious Orator, (whom it would be the highest Presumption in me to imitate in any Thing but his Modesty) who, after having made a pathetic Speech on a public Occasion, ended it with these

---

[1] Visits by an ecclesiastical person (or body), generally a bishop or archdeacon, to examine into the state of a diocese, parish, etc.

[2] The provision, in the eighteenth century already commuted to payments in money, of necessary entertainment for the bishop, archdeacon, or other visitor, by the incumbent diocese, parish, etc.

[3] Horace, *Epistles*, I. vi. 67–8: 'If you know something better than these precepts, pass it on, my good fellow. If not, join me in following these' (Loeb).

Words, *Si quid recte dixi, hoc est quod volui; si non, hoc est quod potui.*[1]

Yours sincerely,

Philanthropos.[2]

P. S. I assure you, on my Honour, I am not a Parson.[3]

My Wife hath prevailed with me to go once more to the Play this Season, *viz.* on *Monday* next, to the *Provoked Wife*, for the Benefit of Mr. and Mrs. *Mills*.[4]

As Mr. *Garrick* hath very kindly agreed to assist this Benefit with his own Performance[5], we have no Fear that the Town will do a Violence to their own Pleasure, in order to do the same Violence to their Good-nature.

Mr. *Mills*,[6] who, from his peculiar facetious and good-humour'd Disposition, retains still the Name of *Billy Mills* among his Familiars, is a strong Example of the Fickleness and Inconstancy of Fortune. He hath, by slow Degrees, risen to the Top of Theatrical Greatness, and by as slow Degrees tumbled

---

[1] 'If I have spoken to the point, that is what I intended [to do]; if not, that is the best I was able [to do].' The quotation has not been identified.

[2] Cf. p. 4, col. 1, of the original issue of *JJ* no. 20: 'We have received a Letter from *Philanthropos*, which we shall consider in our next.'

[3] There are, however, some curious resemblances between this letter and Ferdinando Warner's *Scheme of a Fund for the better Maintenance of the Widows and Children of the Clergy* (London, 1752), the Introduction of which states (p. 5) that 'about Eight years ago' Warner drew up the present scheme and 'communicated it to Those, who, from their Stations in Life, and the Nature of this particular Charity, I thought were the most likely to give it any Attention'. The date squares with the statement in the *JJ* letter, 'I have mentioned this Scheme to every Parson that I have seen for these three Years last past.' Furthermore, Warner's *Scheme*, which is dedicated to Archbishop Herring, speaks both of the provisions for widows of army and navy officers (p. 6) and of a subscription from within the ranks of the clergy themselves (p. 13). Fielding makes an undoubted and complimentary reference to Warner in *JJ* no. 17, above, pp. 216–17.

[4] At Drury Lane on 25 April 1748, with Mills as Heartfree and Mrs. Mills as Belinda. 'Mr. and Mrs. Mills take but one benefit this year that they may not be troublesome to their friends'; *GA* of 20 April 1748, as cited by *London Stage*, Part 4, i. 49.

[5] Garrick performed the role of Sir John Brute; *GA* of 25 April 1748.

[6] William ('Honest Billy') Mills (d. 1750), son of a more famous Drury Lane actor, John Mills (d. 1736), seems first to have performed in London at St. Martin's Lane in the spring of 1712; *London Stage*, Part 2, i. p. xxx. Later, as a member of Drury Lane, the younger Mills played in a number of Fielding's plays, including *The Miser*, in which he had played Clermont as recently as 3 February 1748. Apparently an old acquaintance of Fielding's, he is mentioned in *Joseph Andrews*, I. viii. 40, *Tom Jones*, VII. i, and *CGJ* no. 15 of 22 February 1752. See also 'Partridge's Vile Encomium: Fielding and Honest Billy Mills', *PQ*, xliii (1964), 75–8.

down again. He succeeded to the grave Parts in Comedy of
Booth,[1] and to the gayer Characters in which *Wilks*[2] had shined,
and maintain'd both with equal Ability.

In Tragedy he hath likewise been very considerable; where,
not to dwell on every particular Excellence, he is thought of all
others to have made the best Appearance through a Trap-Door:
For which Reason those Characters which are in some Part of the
Play to enter upon the Stage Head-foremost, generally fell to his
Lot.

He was at all times a very safe Actor; and as he never shock'd
you with any Absurdity, so he never raised Horror, Terror,
Admiration, or any of those turbulent Sensations, to that dangerous Height to which Mr. *Garrick* (however good a Man he may
otherwise be) hath been guilty of carrying them.

From the Pinnacle of Theatrical Greatness, where he was
once seated, he hath by degrees fallen; not through his own
Demerit, (for he is now as good as ever he was)[3] but by the greatest
Misfortune in the World, namely, successful Rivals.[4]

This Reverse of Fortune he hath born with Heroic Constancy,
and with Christian Resignation. He hath indeed continued
always *Honest Billy Mills*; nor have Envy, Malice, or any other
Species of Malignity, been able to taint his natural good Disposition.

Indeed his Character in private Life is so amiable, that if the
Ladies will patronize one of the best and kindest of Husbands;

---

[1] Barton Booth (1681–1733) acted at Lincoln's Inn Fields, the Haymarket, and Drury
Lane. He was noted for his performances in tragedy, particularly in Shakespeare. The
'Court of Censorial Enquiry' in *CGJ* no. 10 (4 February 1752) comments on his manage-
ment of Drury Lane as part of 'that famous Triumvirate, Booth, Wilks, and Cibber'.
See also *Joseph Andrews*, III. x. 260, and *Miscellanies* (1743), i. 27, 64.

[2] Robert Wilks (1665–1732), first popular at the Smock Alley theatre in Dublin, then at
the Haymarket and Drury Lane, in both of which he had a share of the management. He
was noted for comedy; see *CGJ* no. 15 of 22 February 1752. Fielding satirized Wilks and
Cibber in the 1730 *Author's Farce*, and Wilks is the subject of an anecdote in *Tom Jones*,
IV. i. See also *Miscellanies* (1743), i. 5.

[3] Cf. the obituary in *GA* of 18 April 1750: 'a person formerly well esteem'd in his profession, and if his infirmities in the latter part of his life render'd him less useful to the stage,
yet he amply made amends for it, in the deserv'd character of an Honest man, and an
indulgent Husband'; reprinted in *London Stage*, Part 4, i. 191. See also Genest, *Some
Account of the English Stage*, iv. 296.

[4] In his important role as Claudius in *Hamlet*, for example, Mills had been replaced by
William(?) Bridges about 1744. In 1748, Bridges being with Covent Garden, Luke Sparks
had taken over the role for Drury Lane; *London Stage*, Part 4, i. 8, 11, 17, 19, *et passim*.

and the World in general will encourage an honest, good-natured, inoffensive Man, he and his little Family[1] will owe many a future happy Hour to the Public on *Monday* next, and his Benefit, tho' one of the last, will not be one of the least.[2]

(Adjourned.)

SATURDAY, APRIL 30, 1748.   NUMB. 22.

Train up a Child in the Way he shall go; and when he is old he will not depart from it.

Proverbs.[3]

The Letters which I presented the Public last Week, naturally led me into some Reflections on Education, which I believe can never be published at a more seasonable Time than the present.

Diogenes being carried into *Crete*, there to be sold for a Slave, the Crier asked him in what Art he was skill'd, or how he should recommend him to a Purchaser. "Proclaim (said *Diogenes*)[4] that you are about to sell a Man who understands the Government of Children." This Crier, who was it seems a Wit, immediately bawled through the Streets, *Is any one willing to buy a Master?* *Laertius* informs us, that one *Xeniades*, a *Corinthian*, being taken with the Novelty of the Thing, went directly to *Diogenes*, and having examined into his Qualifications, purchased him, carried him home, and delivered his Children to his Care. The same Author adds, that the new-bought Master very fully answered the Character he had given himself; and instructed the Youth committed to his Charge, in the liberal Arts, and in all those bodily Exercises which conduce to Health, Strength,

[1] *London Stage*, Part 4, i, p. cclxii, and pp. 61, 318, 376, lists a Miss [Theodosia ?] Mills among those performing in the minor theatres during the 1748–9 season and at Drury Lane itself from 1752 to 1754.

[2] Each season the major theatres regularly scheduled benefit performances for individual actors or actresses, followed by those for the treasurer, minor actors in groups, and theatre staff. On the order of precedence in benefits, based on a combination of rank, seniority, and special talents, see *Private Correspondence of David Garrick*, ed. James Boaden (London, 1831–2), ii. 40. *London Stage*, Part 4, i. 49, prints the receipts and the house charges for the Mills benefit.

[3] 22: 6.

[4] The following anecdote of Diogenes the Cynic is taken from Diogenes Laertius, *Lives of Eminent Philosophers*, vi. 74–5.

and martial Atchievements: Lastly, he inculcated into their Minds the true Principles of Philosophy, and confirmed them in the strictest Habits of Virtue.[1]

Here the Novelty or Jest, I suppose, consisted only in the Phrase of *buying a Master*; for the Education of Children was, by the wise Antients, considered as a Matter of such great Importance, that we can conceive no Absurdity in the Recommendation; nor could *Xeniades*, at almost any Price, have been thought by them to have made a bad Bargain. The great Lawgiver of *Sparta*, when it was objected to him that he gave a Sallary to certain Rhetoricians, who instructed his Boys in the Study of Eloquence, answered, "If any Man will undertake to *improve the Morals* of my Children, I will not only give him a Thousand Drachms, but will willingly bestow upon him half of what I am worth."[2] Indeed, if I should transcribe the many excellent Passages from the best old Authors on this Head, it would more than fill my whole Paper. "No Man can doubt (says *Aristotle* in his *Politicks*) but that the Education of Youth ought to be the principal Business (μάλιστα πραγματευτέον) of the Legislature; and that great Mischief arises to the Polity of those Cities where this is neglected."[3] And *Cicero*, "Those who do not rightly instruct and educate their Children, do not only an Injury to their Children, but to the Public."[4]

And yet unnecessary and unpleasant as it may seem to stay any longer in so hackney'd a Road, as is this Part of the Subject; and tho' all sober Men have so unanimously agreed in the Advantage which accrues to every Community from a right Education of the Youth; yet what this right Education is, appears to be still an undecided Point. *Aristotle* tells us,[5] there were many different Opinions in his Days on this Head; and, to say the Truth, that Book of his *Politics*, in which this Matter is treated, is much the worst of that whole Work. He himself hath ranged

---

[1] The outline of Diogenes' curriculum is from vi. 30–1, 70.

[2] The source of this statement, presumably by Lycurgus, has not been identified.

[3] VIII. i (1337a11–13). This passage is given in the original Greek and translated in a slightly different way in *TP* no. 13 (21–8 January 1746), in a letter signed 'Abraham Adams'.

[4] Possibly altered from *Verrine Orations*, II. iii. 69, 161. The motto of *TP* no. 13 of 21–8 January 1746 provides this text: *Qui non recte instituunt atque erudiunt liberos, non solum liberis sed et Reipublicæ faciunt injuriam.*

[5] *Politics*, VIII. ii (1337a35–b3).

Education under four Heads only, *viz.* Letters, Exercises, Music*, and Painting.[1]

Other good Authors speak very generally and indefinitely on this Point. Every Man will, I believe, agree with these Apothegms which are recorded in *Plutarch*,[2] That the Instruction of Children ought not to be confined to those superficial Parts, which will be of no Use to them when they grow up: And again, That they ought principally to learn what will be of Service to them hereafter. With such Axioms as these, which require no Ghost to come from the other World to teach us, antient Writers every where abound; but none have left us any Thing regular or systematical of this Kind; for as to the *Offices* of *Cicero*, they are rather Instructions to a Son already educated, than a regular System of Education: And the Precepts of *Quintilian*, in his truly excellent *Institutions*, are rather calculated to breed learned Men, and expert Orators, than sound and good Members of the Commonwealth in private Stations.

A Task, therefore, which all these great Pens seem industriously to have avoided, may be justly thought extremely nice and difficult to execute; and so, perhaps, it is to lay down such a System of Education as may serve for all good Purposes, and which may so cultivate the Human Mind, that every Seed of Good in Human Nature may be reared up to full Perfection and Maturity; while all which is of evil Tendency is weeded, and, as it were, pluck'd by the Roots from the youthful Disposition, before it spreads, and is strengthened by Time.

But, however difficult it may be to draw an exact Plan of every Thing which is to be done on this Occasion, it is surely very easy to assign many Errors which ought to be avoided, particularly with Regard to those Parts of Education in which the Public is principally concerned. Some of these Errors are indeed so gross, that it is astonishing they should ever have escaped the Observance, or Correction, of the Magistrate in any Society where there was the least of Order or Discipline.

---

* The *Greeks*, by the Word μουσική, generally mean more than we understand by the Word Musick. The *Latins* translate it better by *Artes Canoræ*, and to this Sense[3] *Plato* always uses it; but *Aristotle* seems here to apply it in a more confined Sense, as in the 7th Chap. he expressly distinguishes it from Poetry. See *Quintilian, Lib.* I. *cap.* 17.

---

[1] VIII. ii. 3 (1337ᵇ23–5).   [2] 'Apothegmata Laconica', in *Moralia*, 213D, 224D.
[3] 'to this effect'. *OED* records only 'to that sense'.

As the main End of Learning is to investigate and discover Truth, it seems extremely rational to season and prepare the Minds of Youth with those generally known and received Doctrines, which may be considered as Axioms, and which may be inculcated into tender Minds as Principles, upon which to found their future Enquiries; but if the Omission or Neglect of this should be connived at, and the whole Care of the Master employed only in laying the Foundations of Learning, and thus enabling the Youth to make these Discoveries hereafter themselves, (as is the Case in some public Schools) surely it must be most preposterous to suffer the Masters in others, to sowe the Seeds of Falshood and Erudition at one and the same time; or indeed, to drop all Metaphor, to fix false Principles in young Minds, and afterwards to instruct them with Learning, that they may be enabled by plausible Arguments to support such Principles; and this in those weighty and important Branches of Religion and Politics.

With regard to the former, what can be more absurd than to suffer a Religion, which we acknowledge not only to be false, but dangerous to the Commonwealth, to be publicly taught in Schools in this Kingdom. I say publicly; for I would by no means rob a Roman Catholic of his Child, or oblige him to educate him in an Opinion contrary to his own; but this Indulgence should be used tenderly and privately, where it may be free from the Danger of Example, or of spreading the Contagion.

Again, as we are a free People, who have recovered our Liberties by the Revolution, and have confirmed and secured them by an Establishment of the Throne in the House of *Hanover*, shall we suffer our Youth to be bred up in the Belief of Doctrines not only repugnant to common Sense, but to our Constitution? Shall the indefeasible Hereditary Right of Kings, Passive Obedience, and Non-Resistance, the Illegality of the Revolution, and the Injustice of the Act of Settlement, be taught as Principles in our Seminaries of Education?

If there were no other Proof that this hath been done, it plainly appears from the very Existence of Jacobitism, which is a horrid Composition of all this Nonsense, (which Existence since the recent Adventures in *Staffordshire*,[1] and those more recent

---

[1] The disturbances at the Lichfield (Staffordshire) race meetings in September 1747 are referred to in *JJ* no. 1, above, p. 93 and note 2 there.

at *Oxford*,[1] no Man can have the Front to deny;) for Absurdities of this monstrous Kind can only be imbibed when the Mind is young and tender, and susceptible of any Impression; and when the ignorant uninformed Boy is yet to be fashioned either into a Christian or a Pagan, a Papist or a Mahometan.

But in Reality, the Fact itself that the Education of many of our Youth is in the Hands of such Teachers, is clear and certain; and it is no less certain, that an immediate Stop ought to be put to so pernicious and growing an Evil, which may so strictly be called a Matter *dignum Lege regi*.[2] If we have already no Law adequate to the Purpose, it is to be hoped our Legislature will think it worthy their Consideration, and give us such a Law.

The Administration is at present happily in the Hands of Men of more sensible and more liberal Principles; of Men who have been and are the Guardians of those Liberties, which these poisonous Doctrines endeavour to undermine. If they are desirous to deliver down these Liberties safe to our Posterity, it behoves them to take especial Care, that our Posterity should be taught to relish the Blessing which will be transmitted to them, that they likewise may maintain and preserve it.

This can be only done by a thorough Inspection and Scrutiny into the Characters of all those who are intrusted with the Tuition and Instruction of Youth, from their earliest Season of Erudition, till they become their own Masters; by utterly disqualifying all such as, by open Profession, maintain any of the above exploded Doctrines; by laying Offences of the beforementioned Kind under the severest Penalties; and lastly, by restraining every School, with greater Strictness than at present, to a Licence, and that Licence to be granted in a manner which may exclude any Possibility of Favour or Connivance.

But my Warmth carries me too far, and I am hurried to direct those whom it is my Intention only to alarm. If my Labours shall happily have the Success aimed at, in turning the Thoughts of the Legislature to this important Subject, they will with Ease be able fully to prevent the future bad Effects of what hath hitherto proved so dangerous a Disease, and hath more than once threatned the Destruction of our Constitution.

I cannot here omit a short Quotation from an Epistle of

---

[1] See *JJ* no. 17, above, p. 212, n. 3, and *JJ* no. 24, below, pp. 278–81.
[2] 'fitting for crown law'.

Erasmus to a Schoolmaster:[1] "I agree (says he) that your Function is laborious; but that it is wretched, or deplorable, I deny. The Instruction of Youth is an Office inferior only to the first in a Government. Can you conceive that to be a sordid Employment, which consists in embellishing the tender Minds of your young Citizens with Learning and Religion, and in forming so many good and great Men for the Service of your Country? Fools may perhaps see so eminent a Character in a mean Light; but if, in the Opinion of the antient Heathens, it was great and glorious to deserve well of the Republic, I declare boldly, no Man can deserve better of his Country, than he who is employed in fashioning the rude Minds of Children, if he be qualified for that Office, and discharges it with Integrity."

To conclude; as *Sparta* and old *Rome* will for ever stand as Examples of a right Political Education, I am sorry to say, in *England*, we have seen the equal Force of what is wrong in this Regard. To the virtuous Principles infused into their Youth it was owing, that their Citizens, however otherwise vicious in their Dispositions, were all true Patriots; and to the pernicious Doctrines sucked in by our young Gentlemen, can only be imputed, that so many of them are, *at this Day*, staunch Jacobites.

Proceedings at the Court of Criticism, Thursday April 28.

Samuel Fut,[2] of the Parish of St. *Giles's*,[3] Labourer, was indicted, for that he being a Person of an evil Mind and Conversation,

---

[1] From paragraph two of 'Erasmus Ioanni Sapido Liberalium Artium Doctori S.D.' See *Opus Epistolarum Des. Erasmi Roterodami*, ed. P. S. Allen, ii (Oxford, 1910), 154.

[2] Samuel Foote, actor and mimic, during the 1747–8 season was both a member of Rich's Covent Garden company and manager of his own small troupe at the New Haymarket theatre, where from time to time during the regular season and for sustained runs during the summer he put on dramatic burlesques and mimicries in defiance of the Licensing Act. From 28 March to 2 June 1748 Fielding ran his own puppet theatre in Panton Street. In the *GA* of 14 April 1748 he had an advertisement for a performance on 18 April of a puppet drama called 'Fair Rosamund', one of whose satirical targets was 'Mimicking', i.e. Foote. The latter seems to have retaliated instantly; his advertisement for the performance to which Fielding refers here is in the *DA* of 15 April: 'Monday next at his Auction Room, late new theatre in The Haymarket, Mr. Foote will exhibit for the satisfaction of the curious a choice Collection of *Pictures*, all warranted *Originals*, and entirely new'; reprinted in *London Stage*, Part 4, i, p. clxxxii. Martin C. Battestin, 'Fielding and Master Punch in Panton Street', *PQ*, xlv (1966), 191–208, gives details of Fielding's puppet theatre and of his interchange with Foote. On 21 April a notice in the *GA* stated that to 'Fair Rosamund' would be added 'the Comical Execution of *Mr.* PUPPET FUT, *Esq*;

Notes 2 and 3 continued overleaf

and not having the Fear of either Law or Gospel before his Eyes, but being moved and seduced by the Devil, or some of his Imps, on the 18th of *April*, and at divers other Times, at a Place called and known by the Name of the *Scandal-Shop*, in the *Haymarket*,[1] one Justice of the Peace,[2] one Orator,[3] one Poet,[4] one Lord,[5] one Auctioneer,[6] and divers other Persons, did steal and take off, and with a certain Instrument, called a Hatchet-Face, value Three-halfpence, which he the said *Samuel Fut*, before a certain wooden Head, then and there did wear, and hold, them the said Justice of the Peace, *&c.* in a certain Part called the Character, then and there wickedly, diabolically, and ridiculously, did maul and hack; and other Injuries to them did, against the Peace, *&c.*

The Prisoner pleaded Not Guilty.

Grocer and Mimick. With a New Scene *representing* TYBURN'; reprinted in Battestin, pp. 202–3. See also Mary Megie Belden, *The Dramatic Work of Samuel Foote*, Ch. II, and *JJ* no. 10, above, p. 153, n. 5.

[3] An attempt to 'place' Foote amid contemptible surroundings. St. Giles's parish, which included Drury Lane and much of the squalid district around the theatres, was the 'location' of Hogarth's *Harlot's Progress* and *Gin Lane*.

[1] 'The New, or Little, Theatre in the Haymarket operated sporadically after the Licensing Act either by the subterfuge, occasionally, of a "Concert", or "Entertainment" with a play given gratis during the intermission, or for one night stands "by permission" or "by authority" for benefits, or for a series of summer performances which would not compete with the business of the patent theatres'; *London Stage*, Part 4, i, p. lxx. Prior to the Licensing Act of 1737 Fielding himself had associations with this theatre: his *Don Quixote in England* (1734) opened there, and in 1736 he organized his 'Great Mogul's Company of Comedians' in the New Theatre and did *Pasquin*.

[2] Sir Thomas De Veil (*c.* 1684–1746), one of Fielding's predecessors as Justice of the Peace for Westminster; for details of his colourful career see *Memoirs of the Life and Times of Sir Thomas Deveil* (London, 1747).

[3] 'Orator' Henley, who in 1747 had engaged in exchanges of buffoonery with Foote on the stage of the Haymarket theatre; see Belden, *The Dramatic Work of Samuel Foote*, p. 55 n., and *London Stage*, Part 3, ii. 1305–6.

[4] Not certainly identified. At Covent Garden on 28 March 1748 *The Mouse Trap, or, Foot's Vagaries* seems to have ridiculed Garrick's *Miss in Her Teens*; see *London Stage*, Part 4, i. 40. But Foote's only identified mimicry of Garrick was of the latter's acting mannerisms; Belden, p. 51. The 'Poet' or author may well have been Fielding himself. Without giving their evidence, both Cross (ii. 89) and Battestin (p. 202) identify Foote's performance of 18 April 1748 as the one in which the latter first mimicked Fielding; see also Belden, p. 57, and *London Stage*, Part 4, i. 46.

[5] Not identified. Presumably the 'young Nobleman of great Honour' referred to below.

[6] Christopher Cock (d. 1748), famous London auctioneer, with rooms in Covent Garden; at his death in December 1748 Cock was apparently Justice of the Peace for Hertfordshire; *GM*, xviii (1748), 572. Fielding had ridiculed Cock in his *Historical Register* (1737), and there are passing allusions to him in *The Champion* of 19 February 1740, in *Joseph Andrews*, III. vi. 240, and *Miscellanies* (1743), i. 113.

Then several Lords and Ladies were produced,[1] and sworn, who proved the Fact beyond any Possibility of Doubt. After which the Prisoner being called upon to make his Defence, began to mimick the Court, pulling a Chew of Tobacco from his Mouth, in Imitation of his Honour, who is greatly fond of that Weed.[2]

For this indecent Behaviour he was gently rebuked by his Honour, and advised to consider seriously of his Defence, if he had any to make. But he remaining silent, or rather contumacious, and performing many ridiculous Gestures, he was at last pronounced to be guilty of the Charge.

His Council then moved in Arrest of Judgment. 1. That the Prisoner being on many Accounts obnoxious to the Law of the Land, and having committed this Offence in open Defiance of an Act of Parliament,[3] as well as of the Government, which had refused to license this immoral Performance,[4] was liable to the Censure of higher Courts of Justice, and consequently could not be try'd here. 2. That some of the Persons mimicked were dead, and could not be sensible of any Injury done to their Characters. That Part of the Indictment therefore was vicious, and if Part, the Whole.

To the first of these it was answered, That this Court had a concurrent Jurisdiction, to be exercised at their Discretion: And if the Government are at present too busily employed in Matters of greater Moment, to attend to such Offences, and to give them due Punishment, it becomes more necessary for this Court to

---

[1] In his advertisements, as in his private life, Foote made a point of cultivating the patronage of 'Quality'; see Belden, p. 6. Fielding returns to the attack in *JJ* no. 23 (7 May 1748), p. 2, col. 3, where he comments on the nomination of governors for Bridewell and Bethlehem hospitals: '*If proper Officers were to attend every Morning at Mr. Foot's Scandal shop, they might take up more than* 100 *Persons, some of which are of Quality and Distinction, all proper to be the* Governed *at those Hospitals.*'

[2] Fielding's habit of chewing tobacco was frequently satirized in the hostile press; for example, by *OE* of 23 April 1748, which apparently altered Horace Walpole's original copy to describe its victim's 'Bacco-protuberating under Lip', and *DA* of 23 April, in a piece perhaps by Foote himself, with its reference to Fielding as 'a dirty Fellow, in shabby black Cloaths, a flux'd Tye-Wig, and a Quid of Tobacco in his Jaws' (cited by Battestin, p. 203).

[3] The so-called Licensing Act of 21 June 1737 (10 Geo. II, cap. 28); *Statutes at Large*, xvii. 140–3.

[4] No evidence has been adduced to support this statement; nor is it known whether Foote even attempted to procure a licence for his 'Collection of Pictures'. In April 1747, however, he had been closed down by the constables for his 'Diversions of the Morning'; see Belden, pp. 7–8.

exercise that concurrent Jurisdiction; and a Case lately adjudged here was cited, which was exactly in Point.[1]

To the Second; That if any of the Persons mimicked were dead, the Offence was thereby heightened rather than extenuated; since to drag Persons out of their Grave, in order to ridicule them, could be only justifiable in the Case of notorious Criminals; whereas, on the contrary, one of these was a young Nobleman of great Honour, and the other a Magistrate, to whose Care the Public were highly indebted, for having brought many notorious Rogues to Justice; many, perhaps, of the Prisoner's intimate Acquaintance; and had he been now alive, the Prisoner, through his Means, would certainly have shared the same Fate.

The Objections being fully answered and over-ruled, his Honour proceeded to Sentence in the following Manner:

Samuel Fut, You stand convicted of a very high Crime; a Crime not only contrary to Law, but certainly *contra bonos mores*.[2]

I know not for what Reason, unless, as the Council hath said, because the Government is concerned in more weighty Matters, that you have been suffered to go on so long with Impunity; for surely the Act of Parliament, which was made to prevent Theatrical Abuse, was made on a much less Occasion than you have afforded.[3] Persons have been formerly ridiculed under fictitious Fables and Characters; but surely since the Days of the Old Comedy, none, 'till your Time, have had the Audacity to bring real Facts and Persons upon the Stage: Nay, you have gone even beyond that Old Comedy, which was by Law banished from *Athens*, as an intolerable Evil; since the Representation by Mimickry is much stronger than that by Painting on a Mask.

---

[1] See *JJ* no. 18, above, p. 223, where the author of *A Second and Third Letter to the Whigs* was judged to come under the 'concurrent Jurisdiction' of the 'Court'.

[2] 'contrary to good manners'.

[3] A widely-held contemporary opinion derived the passage of the Licensing Act of 1737 from the effects on the Walpole Administration of Fielding's 'Masques drawn from Life' (*Champion* of 11 December 1739), notably *Pasquin* (1736) and *The Historical Register* (1737). The classical statement of this opinion is that of Colley Cibber, *Apology for the Life of Mr. Colley Cibber, Comedian* (London, 1740), p. 164. In an undated manuscript note on p. 164 of his own copy of the 1740 *Apology* Horace Walpole wrote: 'He [Fielding] had written a piece called the Golden Rump, which was an outrageous satire on the King and Queen and it was going to be acted; but Sir Robert Walpole got a copy of it and stopped it —and then procured the Licensing Act, to prevent such gross abuse of the Stage.' Cf. Walpole's statement in his *Memoirs of the Reign of George the Second* (London, 1846), i. 13–14. The supposititious 'Piece' has never been found, and there was contemporary scepticism about the circumstances of its composition; see Cross, i. 227.

Against this Kind of Buffoonry no Innocence can be secure. The most inoffensive Particularity may subject Men to Ridicule; nay, by Means of mixing up much Falshood with some Truth, a very good and worthy Man may be actually exposed to Infamy.

Nor doth this Buffoonry require any Capacity, unless that of mimicking the Voice, Features, and Gestures of another Man, the meanest and vilest of all Arts. Had those Parts which form either an Author or an Actor been necessary, you know, by Experience, how unequal you must have found yourself to the Task.

And here I must take leave to mention a short Word to those who have encouraged you in this wicked Undertaking, since I find some Persons of Figure have not been ashamed, in giving their Evidence, to own they have more than once been your Spectators.

It no more becomes a Gentleman,* says an ancient *Greek* Author, *to admit Slander willingly at his Ears, than to give it vent at his Tongue.*[1] And I am inclined to believe, that many (the Ladies especially) would not have been seen at your Slander-Shop, had they suffered themselves seriously to reflect on the Barbarity to which they became in a Manner Accessaries; and in this barbarous Light they would have presently seen your Mimickry, had they but for a Moment made the Case their own; a Circumstance which may perhaps happen to some of them, if this outragious Licentiousness continues to meet with Reward instead of Punishment: For let me tell you there are many as good Mimicks as yourself, and there are some who can supply those Mimicks with better Food than is in your Power.[2]

As for you, happy would it have been for you, and so will the Event prove it, if you had continued to deserve the Addition of Labourer, by which you are indicted; and had endeavoured to get your Bread rather by the Labour of your Hands, than by that of your Face.

---

* In *Greek* a *modest Man*; by which they meant the same as the *French* do by an *honest Man*, or as we by the Compound *Gentleman*.

---

[1] Cf. Thucydides, *History*, VI. xli. 2. Fielding's note seems to require a text containing some form of σώφρων, meaning 'prudent', 'self-controlled', 'moderate'. Herodotus, *History*, VII. x. 7, records a similar sentiment but lacks the key form.

[2] Fielding did in fact continue to spar with Foote, as he here threatens to do. See Belden, p. 57 n.; *London Stage*, Part 4, i. 48, 53; and Battestin, pp. 205–6.

But I spend too much Time on one so despicable, and at the same time so incorrigible. I shall proceed therefore to pronounce the Judgment of the Court; which is, that you *Samuel Fut* be p–ssed upon, with Scorn and Contempt, as a low Buffoon; and I do, with the utmost Scorn and Contempt, p–ss upon you accordingly.

The Prisoner was then removed from the Bar, mimicking and pulling a Chew of Tobacco from his Mouth, while the P–ss ran plentifully down his Face.

(*Adjourned.*)

SATURDAY, MAY 7, 1748.   NUMB. 23.

————*Culpa docentis*
Scilicet arguitur————.

Juvenal.[1]

The following Letters, as the Reader will perceive, are all occasioned by my last Paper, which I am pleased to find hath excited some Attention in the Public.

Sir,

I have long since been well convinced, that the Passage in *Aristotle's Politics*,[2] referr'd to in your last, is corrupt. Can we suppose so wise a Man would have included Painting in the four most essential Parts of Education? I must confess I cannot well cure the Text by any Reading, similar to the Word γραφικήν,[3] perhaps some such Word as μεθικήν,[4] or πιθικήν,[5] (for possibly those occur in Authors, tho' I will warrant neither) should be restored.

But to wave a *Greek* Controversy, which I am afraid would, at present, be little understood by most of your Readers, I am well satisfied the *English* Translation of the Beginning of the third Chapter of the 8th Book should run thus:

[1] *Satires*, VII. 158–9: 'It is the teacher's fault, of course' (Loeb).

[2] VIII. ii. 3 (1337ᵇ23–5). See *JJ* no. 22, above, pp. 257–8.

[3] 'graphics' or drawing.

[4] In view of the subsequent emphasis on the Jacobite fondness for drink, a playful, false etymology from μέθυ, meaning 'wine'.

[5] A similarly playful etymology from πίθος or 'wine jar', an etymology which may have also pleased contemporary Hellenists because of its resemblance to πίθηκος, ape or monkey; hence, perhaps 'jackanapics'.

"But there are about four Things in which they usually instruct Children; Letters, and Exercises, and Music; to which some add Drinking," (not Painting, as some sober Coxcomb hath foster'd into the Text.)[1] Would *Aristotle* have reckoned Painting among the Necessaries or Conveniencies of Life, as he immediately after concludes all these to be? And doth he not, in the 5th Chapter, join Drunkenness and Music together, and expressly tell us, that both these are equally useful to drive away Care?[2] Who is there so ignorant as not to have heard of the antient Συμποσίαι,[3] or Drunken Bouts, and the Laws and Regulations made concerning them? It would be surely Matter of Wonder, if the Youth were left totally uninstructed in a Matter which was so justly thought to be of such Consequence; and what is more likely than that this fourth Part of their Institution was calculated with a View to this Study?

Now, Sir, in what doth the true *English* Jacobitical Education differ from that prescribed by this great Philosopher? Of Letters, which is the first Ingredient mentioned, you will not, I suppose, pretend to say that our Youth are ignorant; since there is scarce a Squire who doth not know the whole Four-and-twenty;[4] indeed, so as to be able to read pretty tolerably well. In Exercises, there can be no Doubt but we keep up strictly to the Precepts of *Aristotle*. Such are Horse-racing, Hunting, &c. which make the most considerable Part of the Education of our Youth: And as to the two last, which, in Imitation of the great Master, we join together, it must be allowed that all possible Care is taken to finish the Erudition of young Gentlemen in both these Branches. Are not particular Places set apart for this noble Purpose only, where the hard Students sit up all Night for Years together, in order to perfect themselves in these necessary Parts of Education? In which *Bouts* of Study no Pains are omitted to adhere to the Rules of the old *Greek*, who says,* that "in Rhimes and Songs

---

* Ἔστι δ' ὁμοιώματα, &c. cap. 5.

[1] Aristotle, ibid. 1337ᵇ25 has 'drawing'.

[2] 1339ᵃ19–21: 'And for this end [to drive away care] men also appoint music, and make use of all three alike—sleep, drinking, music—to which some add dancing'; *Works of Aristotle Translated into English*, ed. W. D. Ross, x (Oxford, 1921), loc. cit. [n.p.].

[3] The 'symposia' or convivial meetings for drinking, conversation, and general intellectual entertainment among ancient Greeks.

[4] 'I' and 'J' were conventionally considered as one letter; so too were 'U' and 'V'.

consist chiefly the Resemblances of the true Nature of Anger and Gentleness, of Courage and Modesty, and of those Affections which are the Reverse of these, and of all other Ethics. This is plain from their Operations," &c.[1] And for this Reason he says it is plainly *necessary all Youth should learn these Rhimes and Songs*, which, as he tells us in this very Chapter, serve us, together with Drink, for such excellent Remedies *to drive away Care*, according to the Words of *Euripides*,[2] and of an old *English* Ballad.[3]

Henceforth, my Friend, I hope it will be no more said that *Aristotle is fallen into Contempt or Disuse* at a certain Place,[4] since the Education there carried on so exactly pursues the Methods laid down by this great Antient, the Tutor of that mighty *Alexander*,[5] who, among other heroic Arts, hath left more than one upon Record, which proceeded from the Drinking Precepts he probably received in his Youth; and who is recorded by *Plutarch* to have instituted one of the greatest Prize-Drunken-Bouts ever known, in which no less than 42 of the Combatants fell, and the Victor himself, who drank 18 Quarts of Wine, was one of the Number.[6]

I am, Sir, *yours*, &c.

A Staggerite.

Sir,

I am surprized that so learned a Man as you seem to be, when you mention the good Consequences of *Spartan* Education, should have forgotten to derive it from its true Source, *Exempli Gratia*, from that admirable Correction of their Lads, for which the *Spartan* Masters were so renown'd.

You cannot be ignorant that several of these Boys were scourged to Death upon the Altar of *Minerva*:[7] Now this Altar

---

[1] *Politics*, VIII. v (1340ᵃ19–23).

[2] 1339ᵃ19 alludes to Euripides, *Bacchae*, 381: 'And the children of care have forgotten to weep' (Loeb).

[3] Apparently altered from *Begone, dull care*: 'Come, you shall dance, and I will sing, so merrily we will play, / For I hold it one of the wisest things to drive old care away'; see William Chappell, *Popular Music of the Olden Time*, ii (London, [n.d.]), 689.

[4] Oxford University; see *JJ* no. 17, above, p. 212, n. 3.

[5] In 342 B.C. Aristotle accepted the invitation of Philip of Macedon to be the tutor of the latter's young son, Alexander.

[6] 'Life of Alexander', LXX. i. Promachus, the victor, drank four pitchers of wine, which according to modern calculations amounts to about 12 quarts.

[7] At Sparta it was to stain with human blood the altar of Artemis Orthia, not Minerva, that the boys underwent the ritual flogging known as 'diamastigosis', supposed to have been

of *Minerva*, I take to be a figurative Expression, and to mean no other than the Block which was used in their Schools, (as it is at present in some of ours) for the Purpose of Flogging.[1]

This, tho' perhaps an Error on the right Side, was carrying the Matter rather too far, and may be almost called Severity; since surely a Castigation somewhat short of Death may be sufficient for all good Purposes.

But, alas! how deplorably are we fallen into the other Extreme in our Schools. In the very best, Correction is confined to nine or ten, or at most a dozen Lashes; and in others the Master is in a manner disarmed; so that the Tree of Learning will, in a short time, be converted to no other Use than to supplying Brooms for the ignoble Services of the House-maid. So true is that most pathetic Line of Mr. *Pope*:

And Birch shall blush with noble Blood no more.[2]

I believe it is needless, after what I have here said, to inform you, that I am myself a Schoolmaster; an Office, as *Erasmus* very rightly observes,[3] of the highest Dignity in the Commonwealth, next to that of the Sovereign. This Office I have so well discharged, that I have whipt more *Latin* and *Greek* into the Lads under my Care, than most of my Cotemporaries of the same Profession. When I first enter'd upon my School, I laid it down as a Rule that every Boy can learn, as every Horse can draw; but that the Slow requires more Scourging than the Sprightly: And again, that there is neither Horse nor Lad but which sometimes wants to be whipt. Indeed none, however circumspect, hath escaped from me untouch'd, and most of them bear my Mark about them to this Day.

In Correction, however, I have always confined myself to that Part which Nature seems to have intended, and to have well supplied for this Purpose. *Ovid* would persuade us, that old *Chiron* used to flog *Achilles* on the Hand.

initiated by Lycurgus; Plutarch, 'Life of Lycurgus', XVIII. I, and 'Ancient Customs of the Spartans', cap. 40, in *Moralia*, 239; also Pausanias, *Description of Greece*, III (Laconia), xvi. 7–11.

[1] Cf. *Tom Jones*, XIII. i.: 'To thee, at thy birchen Altar, with true *Spartan* Devotion, I have sacrificed my Blood.' See Cross, i. 48, for the institution of the 'birchen Altar' at eighteenth-century Eton.

[2] *Dunciad* (1728), iii. 330; and (1742), iii. 334. Pope's line begins 'Till . . .'.

[3] See *JJ* no. 22, above, pp. 260–1.

Quas Hector sensurus erat poscente Magistro
Verberibus jussas præbuit ille manus.[1]

And many Masters I have known to follow his Example; but surely with too little Reason: For Nature would never have furnished any Part with little Flesh when she had intended a great deal should be scourged away; and there is a Passage in *Quintilian* which plainly intimates the other Method to have prevailed among the *Romans*. "Besides, (says he) many other Circumstances, from Pain or Fear, happen to Boys at the Time of Correction, which are indecent to be mention'd, and which may afterwards put him to the Blush."[2] I know *Quintilian* is an Enemy to the Rod; but he confesses that the Contrary was the received Opinion in his Time, and that *Chrysippus* himself was a Friend to Birch.

Cicero, who was wiser than both, advises much Castigation. His Words are, *Hi sapienter faciunt qui adolescentes maxime castigant.*[3] And *Solomon*, who was the wisest of all, hath told us, *that he who spares the Rod, spoils the Child.*[4] The first Principle therefore of good Education is Scourging, which must be confest by all who have ever been well scourged; in other Words, who have ever been at School; and this, I think, must have been your Case.

I am, Sir,
Your humble Servant,
Roger Strap.[5]

Mr. *Trott-plaid*,

You very facetiously tell us in your last, that Jacobitism, the Existence of which no one can at present deny, is an Argument a Posteriore of the vicious Education of our Youth: Now, Sir, give me Leave to say that this vicious Education, the Truth of which I think altogether as impossible to be controverted, is an Argument a Priore of the plentiful Existence of Jacobitism.

---

[1] *Art of Love*, i. 15–16: 'Those hands that Hector was to feel, he held out to the lash obediently, when his master bade' (Loeb). Copy-text prints *prosecute* (for *poscente*) and *Verboribus*.

[2] *Institutes*, I. iii. 13–16. Chrysippus (*c.* 280–207 B.C.), the Stoic convert named below, was Cleanthes' successor as head of the Stoa at Athens.

[3] *Ad Herennium*, IV. xxv. 3–4: 'they act wisely who chastise the young with especial severity' (Loeb).   [4] Proverbs, xiii. 24.

[5] For Fielding the name 'Roger' may have had more than its slang connotations. It is the name of Thwackum, another cruel schoolmaster, whose 'Meditations were full of Birch'; see *Tom Jones*, XVIII. iv; also III. v.

You, Sir, who so well know what the nonsensical Principles of this Sect are, and have, in your fictitious Character, so notably exposed their monstrous and absurd Folly to the World, must readily agree, that nothing can be so well calculated for the Support and Propagation of these Doctrines, as that slender Stock of Knowledge which is acquired by great Numbers of our Youth, while they remain in what the Law calls their Infancy. Without pointing at Individuals, or any Species of Men, I think I may aver, that all of the Jacobitical Stamp are furnished with this half (or rather half-quarter) Learning, which makes the human Soil just rich enough to bear this Kind of Fruit.

It may be averred, nay, I believe, it may be demonstrated, that there never was, nor never can be, one single Man of Sense, or of true Erudition, capable of holding such Tenets. I am pleased to say, Experience convinces us, that the merely illiterate Vulgar are not of the Party. These Doctrines are, as I have said, the Fruit only of that shallow Learning, (I had almost said Ignorance) which is taught at Seminaries half-reformed from Popery, and which are ready, on the first Occasion, to return to the Bosom of that *Alma Mater*. Doctrines hoarded up in the Repositories of Luxury, Laziness, Bigottry, and Error, where Learning consists in Words, Wit in Quibble, Religion in Grimace and Superstition, and the most refined Policy centers in the dark Interests of Priestcraft.

While our Youth are thus educated, the Consequences are certain: For while they here suck in bad Principles, together with bad Wine, tho' the Strength of bodily Constitution may prevent any future ill Effects from the one, few of them will have sufficient Strength of Mind to overcome or eradicate the Poison contracted from the other.

You will excuse me, Mr. *Trott-plaid*, if I think you have been a little too tender on this Head. The Fact is too notorious to be any longer concealed, and the Evil is too great and dangerous to be any longer born. However inveterate the Disease hath been suffered to become, by being too long temporized with, it must now be cured, or it will destroy our whole Constitution; and in such a Case, if harsh Medicines are necessary, they must be applied.

I am, Sir,
Your sincere Wellwisher,
BRITANNICUS.

Proceedings at the Court of Criticism, Thursday May 5.

The following Letter was read and ordered to be printed.

Sir,

I could have wished your Correspondent, who, with so much just Indignation, has given us an Account of the *Pamphlet*, in which an impudent Assertion, concerning the Safety of *Church-lands* in *Lay-hands*, in the Church of *Rome*, is contained,[1] had likewise shewn the Falshood of it: Or that you yourself had thought proper to have supplied his Defect. But as you have turned him over to *higher Courts of Judicature*, give me leave, thro' your Means, to inform the World, that tho' the *Papists* have many Times asserted the *same* Thing, and have referr'd us, with this Author,[2] to *Germany* for a Proof of it; yet 'tis well known, that the Church of *Rome* condemns,[3] and has protested, in the most solemn Manner, against the Liberty allowed by the Treaty of *Munster* in this Matter. For Pope *Innocent* published a Bull just after, to null the said Treaty, as prejudicial to the Catholic Religion, to the Apostolical See, to Churches, and other holy Places and Persons, and ecclesiastical Rights. In the Body of the Bull he saith, that his Nuntio there (*Chigi*, who was afterwards Pope *Alexander* the Seventh) did protest against these Articles, as void, null, unjust, and agreed upon by Persons who had no Power, and that they were to be so looked on by all. But the Pope did not think this sufficient, but declares all those Articles that related to the Liberty of Religion, *Church-lands*, or any ecclesiastical Rights, or that brought any the least Prejudice to them, or which might be thought or pretended so to do, to be null, void, invalid, unjust, damned, reprobate, vain, and without any Force or Power, and that they shall remain so for ever: And that no Person, tho' *ever so much sworn* to observe those Articles, shall be bound by such Oath; nor any Right, Title, Plea, Prescription, shall accrue to any by Virtue of them. And therefore, out of the Plenitude of Apostolical Power, he doth absolutely

---

[1] *The State Preferable to the Church*; see the 'Court of Criticism' in *JJ* no. 20, above, pp. 242–5.

[2] *State Preferable*, pp. 59–61.

[3] The remainder of this sentence and the next four sentences are taken, with some modification, from the General Preface to Edward Stillingfleet's *Answer to Several Late Treatises, Occasioned by a Book entituled a 'Discourse concerning the Idolatry Practised in the Church of Rome'* (London, 1673), e1r–e2r.

damn, reprobate, null and cassate all those Articles and Protests before God, of the Nullity of them; and restores all Persons and Places to their ancient Possessions, notwithstanding them; with very much to the same Purpose. This was dated at *Rome, apud sanctam Mariam majorem sub annulo* 3 *Jan.* 1651, in the eighth Year of his Pontificat. Vid. *Stillingfleet's* Defence of his Idolatry of the Church of *Rome*, Part 1st. in the General Preface. Here you see the most ample Condemnation of this Writer's Assertion, which 'tis fit you should let Protestants see, in order that they may indeed know what they are to expect from a *Romish* Prince and Clergy. If you think proper to publish this, you may probably expect to hear farther from a

True Protestant.[1]

(*Adjourned.*)

SATURDAY, MAY 14, 1748.   NUMB. 24.

———*Pax optima Rerum*
Quas Homini novisse datum est: Pax una Triumphis
Innumeris potior.———

Silius Italicus.[2]

Whoever will be pleased to cast his Eye backward for one Month only, and recollect the gloomy Prospect which the Situation of public Affairs then presented; the dreadful Apprehension which prevailed in every Mind, and discovered itself in every Countenance; arising from the daily Decline of national Credit,[3] from the apparent Strength of our Enemies, and from the manifest Weakness or Perfidy of our Allies, must be obliged to own, when he compares it with the pleasing Scene now shifted on the Stage, that no Nation hath ever had a quicker Transition from Evil to Good. Now as this happy Alteration of our Affairs is intirely

[1] The identity of the 'True Protestant' is not known; the letter does not appear to be Fielding's.

[2] Silius Italicus, *Punica*, xi. 592–4: 'Peace is the best thing that man may know; peace alone is better than a thousand triumphs' (Loeb).

[3] 'Although the subscriptions for the new loan had been nominally filled, with such unexpected alacrity, yet an alarming decline suddenly took place in the money market, and the contractors were consequently precluded from making good their stipulated advances'; Coxe, *Pelham*, i. 393. For a contemporary estimate of the causes of this decline see *London Magazine*, xvii (1748), 175.

owing to the Preliminaries of Peace lately signed,[1] surely we ought, with one Accord, to cry BLESSED ARE THE PEACE-MAKERS.[2]

And, indeed, there is sufficient Reason to think that the Nation in general is well enough inclined to join in this Exclamation; for surely no People were ever more sick, more weary of a War, than we were of this. As I would here particularly avoid any thing of an invidious Kind, I shall not enter into the Question, By whom we were driven into this War? However we came into it, two Things must be allowed by all, that it hath been very expensive,[3] and very unsuccessful;[4] if, therefore, there be any Truth in these Words of *Cicero*, *Ut circumspiciamus omnia quæ Populo grata sunt atque jucunda, nihil* tam populare *quam pacem reperiemus**, we may surely conclude that this Peace will procure the utmost *Popularity* to those glorious Patriots who have obtained such a Blessing for us.

Some Individuals however there are, who cannot be expected to concur in this general Thanksgiving. No Evil can attend Society from which some particular Members do not derive a Benefit; and few of these are so generous and disinterested as gladly to sacrifice their own private Views to the public Good.

And first, those Sons of *Mars*, who are commonly called the Food of Gunpowder, tho' Gunpowder may more properly be said to be their Food, may be supposed to receive little Satisfaction from the Approach of Peace. War is their Calling, and consequently in Times of Peace they may well be apprehensive of a Stagnation of Trade; by which many will be *broke*, and others,

---

* Pro Lege Agraria cont. Rullum.[5]

---

[1] On 30 April N.S., by the English, Dutch, and French; Coxe, *Pelham*, i. 497. The signing was announced by a royal proclamation dated 5 May 1748; *GM*, xviii (1748), 204. George II also announced it in his speech closing the session of Parliament, on 13 May 1748; *Journals of . . . Commons*, xxv. 660. [2] Matthew v. 9.

[3] In 1739, the year of the outbreak of war with Spain, the total funded and unfunded debt stood at c. £46 million; in 1744, the year of the outbreak of war with France, the figure was c. £57 million; in 1748 it was c. £76 million. See *Abstract of British Historical Statistics*, ed. B. R. Mitchell (Cambridge, 1962), p. 401. By 1748 England was paying roughly £1,750,000 in subsidies to her allies and auxiliaries; *Journals of . . . Commons*, xxv. 771. See also *Proper Answer*, above, p. 76 and note 4 there; and *JJ* no. 48, below, p. 422, n. 3.

[4] For the disappointment of Allied expectations with regard to the number of troops they were actually able to put in the field, see Coxe, *Pelham*, i. 405–15.

[5] *De Lege Agraria*, 1. viii. 23: 'in examining everything which is pleasant and agreeable to the people, we shall find nothing so popular as peace' (Loeb).

(to carry on the mercantile Stile) will be able barely to get a Livelihood. These therefore, and especially the younger Sort, who fear less to be knocked o' the Head themselves than they hope to see their Seniors share that Fate, may be reasonably imagined to be Enemies to a Peace.

Again, those who have lived for some time past in constant Hopes of seeing the major Part of this Nation knocked o' the Head, in order to introduce the Pretender to the Throne, cannot but view with the highest Concern a Measure which seems to threaten the intire Destruction of all their present and future Schemes, and to make their Game absolutely desperate.

Besides these, there are a third Sort of Men, who are indifferent either to War or Peace; who in their Hearts have no more Attachment to one King than to another;[1] and would willingly vote the Devil upon the Throne, provided they might be promoted to the Dignity of being his Imps. All the Hopes of these Men lie only in Change, and their End is to accomplish it: The Means consequently are to cry out against the Things that be. If we are engaged in a War, then is the War said to be undertaken upon unjust or weak Grounds, to be carried on in an improper Manner, to be attended with intolerable Expence, and to be dangerous and ruinous to the Nation. If we make a Peace, then is it base, dishonourable, injurious: Our Successes in the War are magnified, in Defiance of manifest Truth and Experience, and in direct Contradiction to what they themselves had just before asserted; and to make the Terms we have accepted disadvantagious, we are in a Moment elevated to a Situation of giving Laws to all *Europe*.

Such as these we cannot expect to be pleased, or to say they are pleased with this Peace, whatever Terms our Ministers may have obtained for us; but surely the Conditions must be very bad indeed, upon which this War is to be ended, if they do not give a general Satisfaction to this Nation.

As I am yet ignorant what these Conditions are,[2] I shall not presume to guess at them; much less shall venture to praise, tho' others have been rash and foolish enough to condemn, in the Dark.

---

[1] Fielding elsewhere labels this sort of men 'Republican'; cf. *Dialogue*, pp. 8–9 above.

[2] Abstracts of the 24 preliminary articles appeared in *GM*, xviii (1748), 220–2, and *London Magazine*, xvii (1748), 226–7, as well as in the newspapers of 12–14 May.

But tho' I cannot affirm what the Preliminary Articles of this Peace are, I think I may, with sufficient Certainty, mention some Particulars which they cannot possibly be supposed to contain.

First, I believe, in general, this will not be such a Peace as was by *Henry* the Vth made in the Cathedral of *Troys*:[1] I am pretty confident there is no Stipulation that after the Death of *Lewis* the XVth, King *George* the IId shall be King of *France* peaceably, and hold the Crown to him, his Heirs and Successors; and because the said *Lewis* the XVth, by reason of his Infirmities, is unable to govern, King *George* the IId, during the Life of *Lewis*, shall rule and govern the Realm of *France*, to the Profit and Honour of the same King *Lewis**. I say, from some particular Reasons which I shall keep to myself, I am convinced there will be no such Clause in the ensuing Treaty.

Again; we cannot expect the present Negotiators on Behalf of *Great Britain* should obtain such Concessions as *might* have been obtained by our Plenipotentiaries at the Treaty of *Utrecht*;[2] and for this likewise I have my Reasons.

In the next Place, I am apt to suspect that *France* will not be brought to give up all her fresh-acquired Conquests, and at the same time to consent that we shall retain whatever we have taken from her.[3] If this was to be insisted upon, I cannot say but our Peace is premature; we should have waited at least 'till we had gained half a Dozen more compleat Victories, nor would perhaps even those have been sufficient.

Nor am I sanguine enough to hope that this politic Power will acquiesce in delivering up her whole Trade into our Hands. This, I am afraid, we shall never be able to effect by Negotiation, as Affairs at present stand; nor indeed till we have made an absolute Conquest of *France*, which, however probable it may

---

* Such Clause was inserted in the Peace of *Troys*.

---

[1] By the terms of the Treaty of Troyes (1420) Henry V was to inherit the French Crown upon the death of Charles VI; in the interim, as Charles VI was in poor health, the regency was to be exercised immediately by Henry V, with counsel from certain French statesmen. See E. F. Jacob, *The Fifteenth Century* (Oxford, 1961), pp. 184–6; and for a text of the treaty, Thomas Rymer, *Foedera*, ix (London, 1729), 916–20.

[2] A 'Tory' treaty; hence Fielding's emphasis on *might*. It had been preceded by relatively successful Allied campaigns under Marlborough and Prince Eugene. Cf. *Proper Answer*, above, pp. 65–6.

[3] For the intensified belligerence about surrendering Cape Breton see, for example, *OE* of 7 May 1748.

appear to some, I much question whether the King of *Prussia* would sit still and overlook.[1]

Now, without any of these Concessions, into which I fear we have neither beaten, nor shall be able to argue our Enemies, I cannot help looking on this Peace as a very desireable one, if Matters are restored by it to a kind of Statu quo. If our Ministers have saved us from the Ruin with which we were so visibly, so confessedly threaten'd; if they have helped us out of all those Difficulties in which our own Folly had involved us, a Folly and Rashness of which those who had been most guilty were become most sensible;[2] I will say such Ministers deserve every Honour, and every Commendation, which is in the Power of a grateful People to bestow.

Those who are guilty of an Error must expect to be Losers by it. This will be commonly the Consequence in private Affairs; in public it is certain; for here is no Generosity nor Pity towards the Conquered, and one Nation will never be ashamed to take all Advantages of the Weakness of another. If our present Ministry therefore, which found us plunged in a destructive War, that we were unable to carry on, have been able to put a safe and honourable End to it; if they have preserved us from that Ruin, which we were at the Brink of when they undertook our Cause, surely we ought to rejoice and be thankful. In such a Situation we must be mad to expect to purchase any Thing more than Experience, by all the Expence into which we have hurried ourselves.

In such a Situation, I once more repeat, Blessed must be the Peace-makers; as it is almost impossible they should have made any Concessions contrary to our Interest, or even to our Honour, since to obey the Dictates of Prudence and Necessity can never

---

[1] At this moment Henry Bilson Legge, the British envoy in Berlin, was trying unsuccessfully to detach Prussia from her alliance with France. Furthermore, the Allied plan to defeat France now depended upon the arrival of 30,000 troops marching overland from Russia, and Frederick II was extremely fearful of Russian intervention. See Lodge, *Great Britain and Prussia*, pp. 65–6.

[2] Perhaps alluding to the *volte face* of some of the belligerent wing of the ministry, led by Newcastle and often accused of seeking to perpetuate the aggressive foreign policies of Granville, who was, until near the end, a supporter of Newcastle in the decision to seek peace. 'That which gives me the greatest comfort is to say that my lord Granville, and all those who have been the greatest supporters of the war and favourers of our system, approve greatly what is done'; Newcastle to Sandwich, on the signing of the preliminaries, 24 April/ 7 May 1748 (B.M. Add. MS. 32812, f. 118), as cited in Lodge, *Studies*, p. 342. See also *Studies*, p. 304.

be dishonourable to any Nation. We have been overpower'd by Numbers, while we have acquired real Glory in the Field; and surely we may acknowledge this, without losing any Honour in the Cabinet.

From what is here said the Reader will suppose that I do not conceive this Peace, however desireable in our present Circumstances, to be conceived in the highest Terms in our Favour; nor such as, had we been Conquerors, we might have expected to impose on our Enemies. I cannot therefore imagine there is any Truth in the printed* Accounts of these Preliminaries; for if the Conditions of this Pacification be but almost as good as they are there represented, surely we say with him in *Virgil*,

> ———*quod optanti Divum promittere nemo*
> *Auderet, volvenda Dies en attulit.*———[1]

Whether we are to impute these Articles (if they are true) to the Intervention of Providence, to the reasonable Disposition of our Enemies, or to the Wisdom and Watchfulness of our own Ministers, I will not determine. If to the first of these, sure it must inspire us all with Thanksgiving; if to the second, it should for the future abate our Animosity to a Nation which hath at last repaid us the Generosity which we have exerted towards them in former Treaties; but if the last be the Case, we must be the most ungrateful of all Nations, if we do not give such glorious Benefactors the Praises which are so justly their Due, and henceforth treat all Cavil and Slander against them with more Contempt, if possible, than those great Men have themselves hitherto treated it with.

Proceedings at the Court of Criticism, Thursday May 12.

The Court being sat, there appeared at the Bar a venerable Figure of a Man, whose silver Beard, extending to his Girdle, demanded a Sort of Veneration, and whose Countenance discovered an intelligent Mind, though at that Time somewhat

---

* See this Account in the first Article of the Foreign News.[2]

[1] *Aeneid*, ix. 6–7: 'that which no god had dared to promise to thy prayers, lo the circling hour has brought' (Loeb).

[2] Under a dateline from The Hague of 12 May, *JJ* no. 24, p. 2, col. 1, reprints 'in Substance' the 24 Articles.

clouded by a large black Patch on his Forehead, such as distinguished some of our Countrymen after the Battles of *Preston-pans* and *Falkirk*.[1] His Honour for some Time gazed with Eagerness on this Figure, and at length, with a Mixture of Astonishment and Pleasure, reconnoitred an old intimate Acquaintance, whom he saluted by the Name of *Priscian**, and desired to know his Business at that Tribunal. To this the old Gentleman, with a becoming Decency reply'd, that "He came as a Suitor to the only Court in *Britain*, wherein Grievances, such as his were, could be properly redressed.——Your Honour must know, (continued he) that for time beyond the Memory of any Man living besides myself, I have had the good Fortune to be esteemed (I had almost said respected) in a certain Manour, situate, lying, and being on the Banks of the River *Isis*,[2] and occupied, in joint-tenancy, by nine Coheiresses, with whom your Honour is well acquainted, and some of which you have heretofore addressed. ——I hope, Sir, you will not charge me with Vanity, if I find it necessary to remind you, that in the Figure made by these Ladies in the World, they have not disdained my Assistance; and such is the external Respect paid to me, even at this Time, that, by the Custom of our Manour, a public Panegyric on me and on my Profession, is twice in every Week, pronounced from a Rostrum erected for that Purpose,[3] and the Panegyrist rewarded for his Labours by an annual Stipend.——Now, may it please your Honour, my humble Remonstrance and Complaint is, that the Premises notwithstanding, on the 11th Day of *April* last past, a certain Number of Literati assembled at a Place called *Golgotha*,[4] within the Manour aforesaid, and having or pretending

---

* *Priscian* was a great Grammarian, and those who spoke or writ false Grammar, were proverbially said to break *Priscian's* Head.

---

[1] Alluding to the Ash Wednesday ceremonial of putting ashes on the forehead as a symbol of sorrow for the believer's sins, in this case the two signal triumphs of the Young Pretender's army, at Prestonpans and Falkirk. See *JJ* no. 8, above, pp. 138–9.

[2] From its source to its junction with the Thame, below Oxford (the 'Manour' referred to here), the Thames is called the Isis.

[3] According to the 1740 edition of *Parecbolae sive Excerpta e Corpore Statutorum Universitatis Oxoniensis*, p. 3, a *praelector grammatices* (or *grammaticae*) lectured publicly two days in every seven, in Latin, from the works of Priscian, Linacre, and other grammarians.

[4] At a meeting on 11 April 1748 the Vice-Chancellor, the Heads of Houses, and the Proctors of Oxford University resolved on a public proclamation condemning the riotous disturbances at the University on 23 February and outlining certain prohibitions to prevent their recurrence; see *JJ* no. 17, above, p. 212. The proclamation, which was given wide

to have Authority for that Purpose, caused me to be apprehended, and brought before them: And albeit I was an absolute *Stranger* to all and each of the said Literati, and in no wise conscious of having ever given the least Offence or *Trouble* to any one of their Number; yet did they then and there lay violent and *rude* Hands upon me, committed many notorious Insults to me, obliquely accused me of having my CHAMBERS always attended with great Intemperance and Excess;[1] and LIKEWISE LAYING a very heavy Blow on my Forehead;[2] and then forced me, against my Will, to give something under my HANDS,[3] and bruised me, in a most *barbarous* Manner, with a certain *heavy, blunt, wooden* Weapon, which I think the Assailants called a Πρόγραμμα.[4] Unsated with these Acts of *Barbarity*, and insensible of my Groans, they then caused me to be exposed to the View of the Public, to be led in Triumph, and to bleed afresh in sundry Places within the Liberties of the said Manour—an open Insult on *Human Literature*, an Offence committed against the *Peace* and *Purity* of *Grammar*, and the Dignity of Common Sense.——Such, may it please your Honour, is my Complaint; my Evidence of these Facts is the *whole Letter'd World*. A suitable Redress for such manifest Injuries, is to be expected only from a Judgment to be given by you, at the Head of this august and awful Tribunal." Here *Priscian*

press coverage, was printed on pp. 2–3 of the original issue of *JJ* no. 24, with a note referring the reader to the 'Court of Criticism'. Also reprinted, immediately above the proclamation, was an item from *GA* of 7 May 1748: 'Yesterday the three Students, brought up some Time ago from Oxford, in Custody of a Messenger, for drinking the Pretender's Health, were admitted to Bail.' The Oxford disturbances were eventually used by the Pelham Administration in an attempt to control the chancellorship of the University, and hence its political complexion as well. Two of the three students taken into custody were found guilty and imprisoned, and the Vice-Chancellor, John Purnell, was tried, unsuccessfully, in February 1749; see *GM*, xviii (1748), 521–2; Richard Blacow, *Letter to William King* (London, 1755); Aaron Tozer, *A Blow at the Root* (London, 1749), pp. 58–60; and *Yale Walpole*, xx. 6, 18.

[1] As reported in the press, the relevant part of the Oxford proclamation reads: 'And whereas many of the disorders complained of have been chiefly and immediately owing to scholars having private entertainments, and company at their chambers, which are generally attended with great intemperance and excess . . .'. See *GM*, xviii (1748), 214.

[2] Cf. the public text: 'and likewise laying a mulct on the master or mistress of such house or houses'; *GM*, loc. cit., which annotates the phrase by reference to the 'likewise laying a very heavy Blow' of *JJ* no. 24.

[3] The close of the proclamation reads: 'Given under our Hands the Day and Year abovementioned'.

[4] A public proclamation or edict; the term was used in the public announcements of the proclamation.

made a profound Reverence to the Bench and ceased. His Honour then ordered the Evidence subpœna'd by the Complainant to be *called*; the *Letter'd World* instantly appeared, was sworn and examined, and verified every Article of the Complaint: Whereupon the Court without any Deliberation adjudged,

First,—"That the outragious Assailants of poor *Priscian* should one and all be taken into Custody by the *Usher* of the B—— *Rod* attending at *Westminster*[1]—and proceeded against as in Offences of the like Nature." Secondly, "That a Mandamus should issue out of this Court, directed to the *Prælector Grammaticæ*,[2] in the Manour of the Muses, peremptorily requiring him, the said *Prælector*, to prepare a proper Cataplasm, and to apply the same, in due Manner and Form, to the Wound received by the innocent Person thus injuriously assaulted."

(*Adjourned.*)

SATURDAY, MAY 21, 1748.   NUMB. 25.

Namque ego hominem homini similiorem nunquam vidi alterum
Neque aqua aquæ, nec lac est lacti, crede mihi usquam similius.
                                        Plautus, *Menæchmi*.[3]

I have often amused myself with comparing the People called *Jacobites* with the People called *Jews*; between whom I find a stricter Analogy than perhaps can be discovered between any other two Sects.

Both of these are well known to found their whole Faith on certain Traditions, the Truth of which they take for granted, tho' never so contradictory to Reason, or to the Nature of Things. The *Jewish* Rabbins have, indeed, shewn a more fertile Genius than the *Jacobite*, in the Number of their Inventions, and a happier Cast of Thought in the Pleasantry of them; but in one Instance, I think, they rather fall short; for the *Jacobite* Traditions

---

[1] The Gentleman Usher of the Black Rod was so called from the black wand surmounted by a golden lion which he carried as a symbol of office. As Chief Gentleman Usher of the Lord Chamberlain's department of the Royal Household and as Usher to the Lords, he would be responsible for presenting persons for trial before the latter body.

[2] The lecturer in grammar or, more precisely, classical philology.

[3] *Menaechmi*, v. ix. 29–30: 'For I never did see two men more alike. No drop of water, no drop of milk, is more like another, believe me' (Loeb).

seem to me rather more surprizing and miraculous than the *Jewish*.[1]

To mention one only; the *Jacobite* Rabbins tell us, that on *Friday, Feb.* 6. 1684,[2] one of the Angels, I forget which, came to *Whitehall* at Noon-day, without being perceived by any one, and brought with him a Commission from Heaven, which he delivered to the then Duke of *York*, by which the said Duke was indefeasibly created King of *England*, *Scotland*, and *Ireland*, to have and to hold the said Kingdoms, with all the People thereunto belonging, their Religion, Liberties, Privileges and Properties, to him and his Heirs, and to the sole Use and Behoof of him and his Heirs for ever; and with full Kingly Right and Authority to do with the same, at his Will and Pleasure, all natural Rights of the said People, and all Common Sense, Reason, and even the divine Word itself to the contrary notwithstanding.[3] By Virtue of which Commission the said *James* enter'd on his Kingly Authority, and did what seemed good in his own Eyes, and what seemed Evil in the Eyes of most others, for the Space of three Years and more; 'till in the Year 1688, the Devil enter'd into the Heart of one *William*, Prince of *Orange*, and caused him, the said Prince, with a mighty Army, and with the Assistance of the King's own Subjects, or rather Slaves, to march to the Royal Palace, where the aforesaid Angel, who now thought it high Time, made a second Appearance, and thence, in a second Attempt (the first proving fruitless)[4] convey'd away the King, together with his divine Commission, to another

---

[1] In its précis of this leader *GM*, xviii (1748), 223, alludes parenthetically to 'the 2 volumes lately published' on the religious traditions of the Jews, i.e. J. P. Stehelin, *Rabbinical Literature; or, the Traditions of the Jews* (London, 1748). This allusion is apparently in the nature of a 'puff' of some sort, for there is no substantive connection between these volumes and Fielding's leader. According to Martin C. Battestin, 'Tom Jones and "His *Egyptian* Majesty": Fielding's Parable of Government', *PMLA*, lxxxii (1967), 74–6, a more likely model might have been Bishop Hoadly's 'The Happiness of the Present Establishment and the Unhappiness of Absolute Monarchy' (1708). Hoadly draws parallels between the Jews and the Jacobites which are not unlike some of those drawn by Fielding, and Hoadly's sermon seems to have been the only one published since the Restoration with the text from 1 Samuel 8 which the *JJ* leader makes use of below.

[2] Charles II died about noon on 6 February 1684/5, and James II was proclaimed King.

[3] See *JJ* no. 3, above, p. 104, esp. notes 2 and 3 there.

[4] James II first attempted to leave England on 11 December 1688, but was captured at Feversham and sent back to London under military guard. He was then forced to leave Whitehall a second time, for Rochester and imminent exile to France, on 23 December. See David Ogg, *England in the Reigns of James II and William III*, pp. 218–20.

Country, where the said King afterwards dy'd, seized of the same Commission, which descended, in an invisible Manner, to his Heirs, who from time to time, one time or another, are to be restored to the full Exercise of the same indefeasible, divine, lawful, lawless Authority.

This, I say, is one Tradition of the *Jacobites*, and this I conceive to be rather more miraculous than all the Stories which the *Jews* have told us of *Adam* and *Eve*, the Tree of Knowledge, the Expulsion from Paradise, &c.

Again, it is the unhappy Fate of both these People, who have been alike deprived of their own divinely constituted Kings, to live under Governments which they hold to be damnable and diabolical, and no Allegiance nor Submission to be due to them: But, on the contrary, are daily hoping and looking for their Destruction. For another Instance in which they exactly resemble each other, is their constant Expectation of the Arrival of their Messiah; for whose Coming they have both many Prophecies, on which, with equal Faith, they rely. Both have frequently suffered Disappointments, which have not been able to mortify or lessen the Confidence of either, and, in all human Probability, one Hour will complete the Happiness of both the *Jew* and the *Jacobite*; tho' this Hour seems at present to be at some Distance.

Thunder and Lightning, Storms and Tempests, are the Seasons when the *Jews* expect the Arrival of this Blessing. In Times of War and public Danger, which may be called Political Tempests, the *Jacobites* look for the coming of their Lord. The Ceremonies performed at their Seasons are somewhat different: The *Jews* are said, on all such Occasions, to set open their Windows; the *Jacobites* open their Barrels, Bottles, and every other Vessel which contains Liquors. Of neither of these Ceremonies will I venture to assign the Reason.

Both must be allowed to be a very extraordinary kind of People, and like to no others that the World hath ever produced. The Divine Being, it is true, hath not yet set any particular Mark on the *Jacobites*, as he is thought to have set on the *Jews*;[1] but they

---

[1] In view of Fielding's reference to it below, as 'another Instance' of imitation, circumcision is apparently not meant here. The 'Mark' may therefore derive from some aspect of the covenantal relationship between Jehovah and the Israelites which stresses the favoured or 'chosen' status of the latter. But cf. Moses Lowman, *A Rational of the Ritual of Hebrew Worship* (London, 1748), pp. 16–17, 21–2: 'God appointed a visible Mark, as a Seal of a

have at last found the Means of supplying this Deficiency in the Resemblance, having lately put a Mark on themselves, which bears some Affinity to that Party-coloured Distinction that once used to denote a Set of People who formerly existed among us under the Denomination of F—ls; but as these are all included in the *Jacobite* Party, so the former Name is now entirely lost and absorbed in the latter.

Some, I know, imagine that the *Jacobites*, when they set this most surprizing Mark on themselves, had a View to imitate the *Jews*; and this the rather from their having so confessedly imitated them in another Instance; I mean in the Humour of Circumcision, which at present so universally prevails among the *Jacobites* equally with the *Jews*. The Original of this Practice was set on Foot, as I am told, soon after the Battle of *Culloden*,[1] and was performed in Memory of that Victory, or as they call it Massacre, which derives its Name from that Place. From that Day the Custom hath been universal; and I am credibly informed there is not a *Jacobite* now in *England* who is uncircumcised.

The *Jews* were by the Antients accounted the most superstitious of all People; but in this the *Jacobites* of our Days are at least their Equals. In the worst of Times, and when their Hopes have seemed to lose all Foundations, a River having too much or too little Water in it,[2] a Man born with an extraordinary Member,[3] an Eclipse,[4] a Comet,[5] an Aurora Borealis, or any such ordinary or extraordinary Phenomenon, is sufficient to support their drooping Spirits, and is interpreted to be a Fore-runner of him they look for.

There is one very remarkable Instance, in which both these strongly resemble each other, and at the same time differ from

Covenant between himself and *Abraham*, and God said unto *Abraham* . . . *every Man-child among you shall be circumcized* . . . a constant sensible Mark of Consecration to *Jehovah*.'

1 See *JJ* no. 2, above, p. 99.

2 *GM*, xviii (1748), 223, annotates this phrase by referring to the 'Historical Chronicle for March, 1748' (ibid., p. 136), in which a 'Letter from . . . Scotland' describes the sudden drying up of several rivers there.

3 Perhaps a reference to Thomas Hall, the celebrated 'gigantic boy' from Willingham, near Cambridge, who at 3 years of age was four feet tall and, *in partibus generationis*, was remarkable even at birth; *GM*, xv (1745), 50. He died in September 1747 and his case history was written up by T. Dawkes as *Prodigium Willinghamense* (London, 1748), a Cooper pamphlet listed among the February 1748 books by *GM*, xviii (1748), 96.

4 There was to be an eclipse of the sun on 14 July 1748.

5 The newspapers carried numerous accounts of a comet seen between Cassiopeia and Andromeda in mid April 1748; *GM*, xviii (1748), 151, 166–7, 177.

all the rest of Mankind, who are said by Nature to be addicted to Self-Interest, and to pursue their own Good: Now whoever hath read the History of either of these Sects with any Attention, must be persuaded that their principal View hath always been to work out their own Ruin, in direct Opposition to the most indulgent Dispensation of Providence; and (which is most observable) this perverse Attachment to their own Destruction, as well in the one Sect as in the other, hath arisen from a strange Desire of being enslaved, as well as their Neighbour Nations. "We will have a King over us, and be like all other Nations," said the *Jews* to *Samuel*.[1] "We will have a King over us, and be like the *French* Nation," would the *Jacobites* say, if they durst.

And as there is so great an Analogy between the *Jews* and the *Jacobites*, so hath there been the same Likeness between their Kings. Indeed the Words of the Prophet, in the Eighth Chapter of the First Book of *Samuel*, are equally applicable to their *Jacobitical* as well as *Jewish* Majesties.

"This (saith *Samuel*) shall be the Manner of the King that shall reign over you: He will take your Sons and appoint them to his Chariots, and to be his Horsemen, and some shall run before his Chariots. He will make them his Captains over thousands and over fifties; and to sow his Ground, and to reap his Harvest, and to make Instruments, and the Things that serve for his Chariots. He will also take your Daughters, and make them Apothecaries, and Cooks, and Bakers. And he will take your Fields, and your Vineyards, and your best Olive-Trees, and give them to his Servants. And he will take the Tenth of your Seed, and of your Vineyards, and give it to his Eunuchs, and to his Servants. And he will take your Men-Servants, and your Maid-Servants, and the chief of your young Men, and your Asses, and put them to his Work. He will take the Tenth of your Sheep, and ye shall be his Servants."[2]

Hitherto the Resemblance is exact, but in what follows the *Jacobites* have been happier than their Counterparts; for *Samuel* tells the *Jews*, "That they shall cry out in that Day, because of the King whom they have chosen, and the Lord will not hear them in that Day."[3] Now the contrary hath befallen the *Jacobites*;

---

[1] 1 Samuel viii. 19–20.   [2] 1 Samuel viii. 11–17.

[3] 1 Samuel viii. 18: 'And ye shall cry out in that day because of your king which ye shall have chosen you; and the Lord will not hear you in that day.'

for they did cry out, and that loudly too; (witness the Affair of *Magdalen-College* in particular)[1] their Cries were heard, and the Tyrant they had chosen was driven from the Throne.

But no sooner was the Rod taken from their Backs, than (like the *Jews* after every Deliverance) they began again to long for its Stripes; and, like them, rebelled against their Deliverer.

Both have been always a stubborn Generation, and both have always refused to hear the Voice of their Friends; but here the Obstinacy of the *Jacobites* seems, I think, rather the most outragious; for the *Jews*, at least in the Instance abovementioned, could not be said to have experienced the Evils which were threaten'd them; and tho' their Disbelief of the Prophet, whose Divine Commission they were so well assured of, was inexcusable, yet it seems somewhat short of the Folly of those who fly in the Face of Conviction, and would again cast themselves into the Pit of which they have already essay'd the Horrors,[2] and whence they so narrowly, so miraculously, and I may say so providentially, have escaped.

In After-Ages, indeed, the headstrong Temper and wilful Blindness of the *Jews* cannot be equal'd; and yet even here the *Jacobites* have approached as near to their Perverseness as possible. The clearest Light of Reason, and the strongest Force of Argument, they have with heroic Constancy resisted. Every Blessing of Government they have tasted to allure them, and some few of its Terrors have been employed to affright them, and both alike to little Purpose. Miracles are the only Proofs which they cannot, with the *Jews*, boast of having withstood.

Thus, I think, I have pretty well made out the strong Analogy

---

[1] Upon the death of its President in 1687 Magdalen College, Oxford, one of the richest foundations in Europe, was issued a *mandamus* from James II to appoint a particular successor, and a dispensation relieving the Fellows of their statutory obligation to choose one of their own number. Oxford, having recently (1683) made public its support of the doctrine of passive obedience, was expected to offer little resistance to James II's design, but in fact the Fellows of Magdalen disregarded his *mandamus*, elected one of their own, and carried their election, according to the statutes, to the Bishop of Winchester, who confirmed it. Ultimately, the King expelled the new President and 25 recalcitrant Fellows, and installed the pluralist Bishop, Samuel Parker. Parker died shortly afterwards and was succeeded by Bonaventure Giffard, one of the four new Vicars Apostolic, under whose tenure Magdalen became almost altogether Roman Catholic. According to Hume, *History of England*, Ch. LXX, *sub* 1687, 'This act of violence, of all those which were committed during the reign of James, is perhaps the most illegal and arbitrary.' See also *JJ* no. 27, below, p. 297 and note 1 there.

[2] In the Jacobite rebellion of 1745–6.

which I have above asserted to exist between these two extraordinary Sects; and surely it is a reasonable as well as charitable
Hope, in Favour of the *Jacobites*, that as they unhappily resemble
the *Jews* in so many unfortunate and blameable Instances, they
will at least bear the same Resemblance to them in the only
chearful Circumstance which attends their Story.

Now we are told, that the *Jews* shall one Day be converted to
the Truth;[1] this therefore I hope we may be allowed to prophesy
of the *Jacobites* also. So far, then, I will take upon me to be a
Prophet, that whenever the Conversion of the one shall happen,
that of the other will not be far off. How distant this Day is, is
beyond the Power of my Divination to ascertain: I will content
myself therefore with foreseeing clearly, that it seems at present
more likely to arrive than the Messiah of either the one or of the
other.

Note, *Last Thursday being Ascension-Day, on which there are no
Sittings in Westminster-hall, there were no Proceedings in the
Court of Criticism.*

SATURDAY, MAY 28, 1748.   NUMB. 26.

*Quid referam Ticidæ, quid Memmi Carmen; apud quos
Rebus abest omnis, nominibusque pudor?*

Ovid, *Tristia*.[2]

There are two Instances in which it will be always more judicious
to leave the venomous Bites of Slander, however malicious and
cruel they may be, to the slow but certain Cure of Time, than
to endeavour, by answering them, to apply any immediate
Remedy. Wounds from these Bites, tho' they may smart very
severely, are seldom deep; and will, if let alone, most surely heal
of themselves: But if a Writer attempts to handle them, even with
the most gentle Touch, it often happens, as when a Surgeon is
called in to a small Cut, by opening and letting in Air the
Orifice is spread wider, and a Scar is left behind, where there
would have been none, if the Patient had used no Application;
but had trusted to pure and innocent Blood for the Cure.

---

[1] A tradition based on Romans ix–xi.

[2] *Tristia*, ii. 433–4: 'Why allude to the verse of Ticidas or of Memmius, in whom
things are named—with names devoid of shame' (Loeb), reading *adest* for copy-text *abest*,
the latter surviving into the eighteenth century on the authority of Bentley.

The former of these is in Cases of an extreme nice and delicate Nature; such as is the Chastity of a young Woman of Fashion, against which, if any barbarous general Aspersions be cast, it will be wiser in the injured Person to endeavour to stifle them by Silence, than to aim at vindicating herself, or at punishing the Offender, if this be in her Power; tho' indeed there is scarce any Punishment adequate to the Crime; and to the Glory of our Law be it spoken, they have inflicted no direct Punishment upon it.

There is perhaps nothing amongst Men which can equal the tender Instance I have here given, as it relates to the Interest of an Individual; but as it concerns the Welfare of the Whole, there may be some Slanders of a still more delicate Nature; for there are some Characters which ought to be held so sacred, and preserved so inviolate, that we ought rather to stifle and bury every Reflection on them in Oblivion, than to attempt to canvas and refute it in Public.

This Distinction between the Character of the Magistrate and of the private Person is made by the Law of God, *Exod.* xxii. 28. "Thou shalt not raile upon thy Judges; neither speak Evil of the Ruler of thy People:" Which Verse St. *Paul* quotes, *Acts* xxiii. 5. and pleads Ignorance of the Dignity of the Person against whom he had spoken lightly, tho' after the highest Provocation, as the only Excuse for such Behaviour.[1]

Our own Laws are well known to make the same Distinction; witness the Action of *Scandalum Magnatum*:[2] For every Peer of this Realm hath, as a Lord of Parliament, a public as well as private Capacity. Nay, and my Lord *Coke*, in his Comment on the first Statute upon which the above Action is founded, confines the Purport of it to such Rumours whereby Discord may arise between the King and his People;[3] and this was the original Intent and Foundation of the Law, tho' perhaps it hath been

---

[1] Acts xxiii. 5: 'Then said Paul, I wist not, brethren, that he was the high priest: for it is written, Thou shalt not speak evil of the ruler of thy people.'

[2] 'The making of defamatory statements regarding persons of high rank, such as peers, judges, or great officers of state . . . and the person guilty of it was liable, not only in damages, but also to punishment under the statutes . . . The action for damages lay, without proof of special damages, in respect of words which ordinarily were not actionable without such proof'; Jowitt, *Dictionary of English Law*, ed. Clifford Walsh, ii. 1589.

[3] *Second Part of the Institutes of the Laws of England*, 'Stat. de Westminster I', cap. xxxiv; for a similar comment on 2 Ric. II, cap. 5, see *Reports*, part iv, f. 13*a*, and part xii, ff. 133–4.

since carried a little farther in Protection of the Reputations of Great Men.

But notwithstanding the severe Damages which have been sometimes given in this Action of *Scandalum Magnatum*, we find our Nobles have very seldom resorted to any such Remedy. In short, the Case is of too nice a Nature to bear the public Proceedings of a Court of Justice, much less is it a proper Subject for a Paper Controversy, and to be transmitted from the Press all over the Kingdom.

Nay, besides the gross Inconvenience which my Lord *Coke* tells us these Laws were made to prevent, namely, "That Discord which so oftentimes in the Reign of *Henry* III. break out into fearful and bloody Rebellions;[1] (and agreeable to this is the Rule by which the Court of *King's-Bench* grants Informations of Libels, because they directly tend to provoke Men to the Breach of the Peace;)[2] there is another good Reason why all Scandal against Great Men and Magistrates should be more effectually restrained than private Slander, *viz.* because it directly tends to lessen all that Respect from the common People, which is a necessary Attendant on Government, and which can only create Authority. The Honour which begets Respect is of too nice a Composition to bear an Attack from the rude Breath of Slander; nor can it afterwards be sufficiently purified by the clearest and strongest Defence. It is no Satisfaction to the Character of a Great Man to be acquitted of Dishonour; but he may apply to himself what *Cæsar* said of his Wife, *It is enough that he was ever suspected.*[3]

For this Reason much of the Scurrility which the mean unknown Scribblers of these Times have dared to cast on some of the greatest and noblest Characters, hath past unanswer'd, and often without any Notice taken of it in this Paper; more especially when contrary to the Precepts not only of Religion and Law, but even of common Decency, the scurrilous Dart hath been

---

[1] *Second Part of the Institutes,* cap. cit.: 'And this discord and scandal did oftentimes in the raign of that king [Henry III] break out into fearful and bloody Wars and Rebellions.'

[2] The King's Bench considered libels and actions *de scandalis magnatum* as public or general acts, involving the general welfare, and would take notice of them without the usual preliminary pleading. Informations in such cases were often granted *ex officio* by the Attorney General or suitable Crown Officer instead of at the relation of a private individual. See Coke, *Reports,* part iv, f. 13*a.*

[3] A commonplace. Cf. Plutarch, *Lives,* 'Caesar', x. 6, and 'Cicero', xxix. 7; Suetonius, 'Divus Julius', *De Vita Caesarum,* lxxiv. 2; and *The Champion* of 23 October 1740, a 'Lilbourne' essay and hence probably not by Fielding.

levell'd at the highest Mark, at that Sacred Head which the wise Preacher[1] forbids us to malign even in our Thoughts.

When therefore one of these Writers (as hath been lately the Case) shall dare to break into the Royal Closet, and thence to proclaim Falshoods to the World,[2] we dare not follow him thither to contradict him. The *Sanctum Sanctorum* of Government, as well as of Religion, is a Place too sacred to be polluted by vulgar Eyes; nor are the Secrets there transacted the proper Subjects of News-Papers and Pamphlets. In a Free Country the People have a Right to complain of any Grievance which affects them, and this is the Privilege of an *Englishman*; but surely to canvas those high and nice Points, which move the finest Wheels of State, Matters merely belonging to the Royal Prerogative, and in no wise affecting the Body of the People, in Print, is in the highest Degree indecent, and a gross Abuse of the Liberty of the Press.

If we have among us Men so extremely profligate as to attempt getting a little Money of the public Curiosity by this worst of Ways, or to endeavour by such Means to make their Court to the worst of Men, it is a Grievance which must, I am afraid, be submitted to. It is a Subject, as I have said, of too great Nicety to be reduced to a Controversy in Writing; nor can such mean, indecent, and most highly criminal Slanderers be brought to public Justice, from the same Reason which silences the Writer.

To enter therefore into no Particulars, but to retire from this delicate Subject with the same Caution with which we have advanced to it, I shall now endeavour to give my Reader some general Antidotes, which may serve as well against some late poisonous Libels of this Kind, as against any which may hereafter be dispersed.

First, it is manifest that the Writers of these Libels are not, nor cannot be Gentlemen; but must be sought after (if any one hath so mean a Curiosity) only among the lowest Dregs of the People,

---

[1] St. Paul. See above, p. 288, n. 1.

[2] Perhaps *The Court Spy; or, Memoirs of St. J—M—S's* (London, [n.d.]), an anonymous shilling pamphlet listed among the April 1748 books by *GM*, xviii (1748), 192. It purports to be an intimate account of the affairs of the Hanoverian mistresses, the rivalry of George II and Cumberland for a French opera singer, and Chesterfield's involvement with the Countess of Yarmouth, the King's mistress. Page 7 refers to the falsehoods and contradictions of partisan journalism, 'from the pension'd Ministerial Author of the *Jacobite Journal*, to the low Hack in the *Daily Advertiser*'.

who are destitute of all Advantages of a liberal Education, and who can alone be supposed capable of transgressing all the Rules of Decency in so notorious a Degree.

Again, it is as plain that such Writers cannot be good Men, since the evil Consequences of propagating such malicious Slanders among the People, must be apparent to Men of much less natural Understanding than the Composers of these Libels; nay, the very End proposed (if it be any other than that of getting their Bread) must be of the blackest and basest Kind.

And who, without a Mixture of Contempt and Abhorrence, can read the Productions of such Men as these? Nay, who would read them at all, especially when he must, on the least Reflection, be convinced, that it is impossible there should be any Truth contained in a Performance, the Author of which cannot possibly know any thing of the Subject on which he writes? What indeed (to omit every other Consideration) can be so absurd as to imagine a Fellow in his Garret in *Grub-street*, (or in *Pall-mall*, if you please)[1] treating of Transactions to which only four or five of the principal Persons in the Kingdom can be supposed to have been privy. If there be a Man weak enough to throw away a Moment in perusing the political Reveries of such a Writer, is not the Reader worthy of an Apartment in that College,[2] where the Affairs and Interests of all the Princes in *Europe* are discuss'd, by Gentlemen who have never been nearer to the Cabinets of those Princes, than the Writers I have mentioned above can be presumed to have been to the Royal Closet, which they have the Audacity to violate.

A sensible and honest Reader will indeed give the same sort of Answer to such Libels as was once given by a good Christian to an impudent Unbeliever, who, after a very blasphemous Description of Heaven, very impiously preferr'd Hell to it: Lookee, Sir, said he, as to the latter Place you may challenge some Credit while you speak of it; but as to the former, all you say must go for nothing, since every one must be convinced that you have no Acquaintance in any such Place.[3]

---

[1] Presumably an allusion to the second part of the title of *The Court Spy*, St. James's being at the west end of Pall Mall and an impossibly presumptuous address for a writer more properly belonging to Grubstreet.

[2] That is, Magdalen College, Oxford. See *JJ* no. 25, above, p. 286, and *JJ* no. 27, below, p. 297, n. 1.   [3] Not identified.

In Reality, there is so much Weight in this last Argument, that, if rightly attended to, it would not only overthrow all this superlatively atrocious Scandal; but indeed all the Abuse which the lowest Set of Scribblers, who ever handled a Pen, do at present so liberally bestow on their Superiors. If the Reader would once fairly and candidly ask himself this Question; How is it possible this Fellow should know any thing of the Matter? I will venture to affirm that neither the Author, nor any for him, could give the least satisfactory Answer.

This is, indeed, so obvious an Objection to all that anonymous Scandal with which the Press at present swarms, against every truly great Man in the Nation, that it can scarce escape any honest and candid Reader. None indeed but Minds tainted with Envy and Malice, that lend an easy and willing Faith to Abuse, can be imposed on by these Writers; and such may be said rather to impose on themselves; being desirous to think that true, which they desire should be so.

Such Persons as these have been always reputed to be Partakers of the Guilt, and a kind of Accessaries to the first Inventor of the Slander. *Thou shalt not receive a false Tale*, says the Divine Lawgiver.[1] Indeed all moral Writers have considered this lending a ready Ear to Detraction, as little less culpable than Detraction itself; to which Purpose there is a fine Passage in *Menander*;

$$\text{ὅστις δὲ διαβολαῖσι πείθεται ταχὺ}$$
$$\text{ἤτοι πονηρὸς αὐτός ἐστι τοὺς τρόπους}$$
$$\text{ἢ παντάπασι παιδαρίου γνῶμην ἔχει.}[2]$$

"He who easily gives Credit to Slanders, must either be a very faulty Man in his own Morals, or absolutely be possessed of no more Understanding than an Infant."

In either Case it would be lost Labour to endeavour to reason him out of his Belief. This indeed affords a good Reason why we should never trouble ourselves to answer any Slander; but surely it holds in the strongest manner against answering such as I have above described.

There is a second kind of Slander with which it is very unsafe

---

[1] Exodus xx. 16, and xxiii. 1.

[2] Fragment 577 ('De Calumnia'); see *Menander: The Principal Fragments*, trans. Francis G. Allinson (London, 1921), pp. 498–9. The source of the translation in the *JJ* has not been identified.

to meddle; but as this is, of all others, the most cunning and mischievous, I have not Room to consider it sufficiently at large in this Paper.

Proceedings at the Court of Criticism, Thursday May 26.

Complaint was made to the Court, on behalf of several Booksellers, against the Author of *Observations* ON THE PROBABLE ISSUE OF *the Congress at Aix-la-Chapelle*,[1] for having fraudulently taken a vast Quantity of Abuse against the Ministry, the Property of the said Booksellers, being contained in divers Pamphlets lately published by them; all which Abuse the said Author hath publickly vended as his own.

It was farther set forth, that the said Author, not content with this Theft, had broke open the Garrets of no less than three Gentlemen now employed by the said Booksellers at the high Rate of one Guinea per Sheet, to compose certain Essays, vulgarly called Libels, against the said Ministry; and had there taken and carried away every Thing which the aforesaid Gentlemen had to say on the Subject of the Peace, whatever it should be; the said Observations not containing a single Line, which is not the Property of the said Booksellers, save only two or three in the Title-page,[2] which neither they nor their Authors can read, and of which consequently they do not know the Purport.

Several Affidavits were then read, in Support of the Complaint, upon which it was ordered that the said Author do, on *Thursday* next, shew Cause why he should not be severely censured for these Proceedings.

It was then moved that all Persons might be forbid buying the said Book in the mean Time; but his Honour said there was no Precedent for such Prohibition, and that he believed it was as much in his Power to stop the Progress of Wild-fire.

One *Catchpenny* was indicted for publishing *Remarks on the Preliminary Articles of Peace, as they were lately transmitted to us from the Hague*, &c.[3] by which Title he had taken in divers of his

---

[1] Advertised in *LEP* of 10–12 May 1748, this anonymous pamphlet was 'printed for R. Montagu in Wild Street, near Drury-Lane, and sold by M. Cooper'. With a profession of impartiality it affects to survey the major arguments for and against the peace negotiations.

[2] An epigraph from the Greek of Demosthenes; see *JJ* no. 27, below, pp. 302–3.

[3] The *Remarks* was published by C. Corbett, one of the booksellers involved in the *JJ*, and was advertised in *LEP* of 17–19 May 1748. If it is to be taken seriously, the indictment

Majesty's unmeaning Subjects in the Sum of one Shilling each, the said Pamphlet in reality containing nothing at all.

He was convicted on the fullest Evidence; but Judgment was arrested, the Indictment being for publishing Remarks on the Preliminary Articles, whereas there are no such Remarks in the Pamphlet.

The said *Catchpenny* was again indicted for publishing a certain execrable Collection of Stuff called *The Foundling Hospital for Wit*;[1] in which he had endeavoured to impose on the World certain Bastards of *Grub-street*, as the true and legitimate Off-spring of Wit, to the great Scandal of all such legitimate Off-spring, and contrary to the Statute made against TAKING IN, &c.[2]

Of this Offence he was convicted; but as he pleaded his Poverty in Excuse, and alledged that he did it only to get Bread for his Family, the Court, instead of punishing him, gave him half a Crown; but ordered his Book to be grubbed by the common Grubber attending the Court, under the true Title of *An Hospital for Nonsense*.

The Court then ordered the following Proclamation to be read and publish'd:

"Whereas the Number of those People who call themselves Authors encreases daily, to the great Scandal of Learning, and to the no less Prejudice of Trade and Husbandry, both which are thereby deprived of many useful Hands; to the great Loss of the Time, as well as Money, of several well-disposed Persons; and to the great Terror of all who are much known in the World, and have any Regard for their Reputations. And whereas it is

against 'Catchpenny' would have to be against the author, not the publisher or printer, of this anonymous pamphlet; see the next note.

[1] *The Foundling Hospital for Wit, No. V*, by 'Timothy Silence', was advertised as pub-lished, in *GA* of 5 May 1748, and is listed among the April books by *GM*, xviii (1748), 192. Printed for W. Webb and sold by M. Cooper, this number of the periodical anthology of satirical verse and prose may have caught Fielding's attention because it reprinted 'The Fool No. 261', a letter signed 'Slabber Bib', which anatomized the supposed relationship between Palaam (Pelham) and his ass (Trott-Plaid). Among other charges, it claims that Fielding worked for Pelham 'at the Bar, on the Stage, and in the Press'.

[2] i.e., against cheating, tricking, or imposing upon, in this case, the reader, by means of a title-page which in no way reflects the true nature of the text. The 'statute' is, of course, a satirical fiction of the 'Court'; see the proclamation below, and cf. William Kenrick, *The Town: A Satire* (London, 1748), p. 14: 'Who takes th' Advantage of a senseless Age,/ And cheats the Reader with a Title Page'. The 'statute' is invoked again in the 'Court of Criti-cism' of *JJ* no. 33, below, p. 345.

impossible for any one Man to read all the Nonsense which is every Week published, and advertis'd in the News-papers; this Court doth earnestly recommend it to all his Majesty's Subjects, who shall happen to have been *taken in* by any of the said People calling themselves Authors, or who shall have other just Matter of Complaint against them, and shall not have Opportunity personally to appear at the said Court, to transmit an Account, by Writing, of the Name and Title of the said pretended Authors, or of their Works, in order that due Proceedings may be had against them, and that the said pretended Authors may be sent back to their respective Trades or Handicrafts, or to the Plough's-Tail, from whence they came."

(*Adjourned.*)

SATURDAY, JUNE 4, 1748. NUMB. 27.

———*Exemplo trahenti*
Perniciem veniens in ævum.

Horace.[1]

If Vanity was my prevailing Foible, I should not be a little pleased to see the two Universities, in a manner, under my Cognizance, as will appear by the following Letters, the first of which I have received from *Oxford*, and the latter from *Cambridge*. Out of Respect, therefore, to those learned Bodies, I shall, in Preference to them, postpone my own Lucubrations 'till the next Week.

To JOHN TROTT-PLAID, *Esq;*

Sir,

The Declaration filed in your Court of Criticism, on *Saturday* the 14th Instant, in the Cause of *Priscian* against certain Literati, seems to be well founded in Facts;[2] and the Evidence of those Facts is possibly sufficient to justify the Resolution of the Court, droll as that Judgment seems to be, which directs, "that a Bench

---

[1] *Odes*, III. v. 15–16: '[when he revolted] from an act destined to bring ruin for the time to come' (Loeb).

[2] Cf. *JJ* no. 24, above, pp. 278–81. There are two discrepancies in Fielding's recollection: first, no such judgment as that quoted below was given, except perhaps by implication; second, the 'Court' itself was under dateline of 12 May. The 'Board of Areopagites' refers to the meeting of the Heads of Houses and proctors which issued the ungrammatical πρόγραμμα signed by the Vice-Chancellor and ridiculed by the 'Court' of *JJ* no. 24.

of *Areopagites* should be sent to School, and chastized into a Recollection of the first Rudiments of *Grammar*."

But, Sir, without Attention to Matters of such little Moment as the Impropriety of a Particle, or the ungrammatical Turn of a Period, I must tell you, that every Friend to his Country is pleased to see even this feeble Stream of Loyalty[1] issuing from a Fountain of Learning; and to find a considerable Body of Men, at length throwing in their Mite, towards the Support of a Government, by which they are, and by which alone they can be protected in the Enjoyment of many and great Advantages peculiar to their Situation in Life.

Now, Sir, if the Edict or Programma, which your old Friend and Acquaintance has so minutely sifted, does not altogether come up to every Expectation of the *Letter'd World*, from a Community of Scholars, let it, however, have its whole Weight and Influence; let it be received as a Profession of political Faith and Obedience, and be esteemed as a public Declaration of a sincere Abhorrence and Detestation of all seditious Practices. In this Light I am willing to look upon it, and the View makes me as willing to conclude, that these Programmatists will not disdain the following Hints, calculated as well to advance their special Honour, and promote their Interest, as to vindicate the Cause of Justice and Truth, the Cause of *Britain*.

First, then, let this venerable Body of Men openly and publickly, and in their corporate Capacity disavow, revoke, and make void, a certain System of Slavery, a certain Series of political Nonsense and Absurdities, handed into the World by their Predecessors, in the Year 1683, and known by the Stile and Title of the *Oxford Decree*:[2] The astonishing Tenets whereof have now, for almost Time out of Mind, been exploded and laughed at, by every Man of Sense and Honour in the Kingdom.[3]

---

[1] The public statement or πρόγραμμα.

[2] On 21 July 1683 an official Convocation at Oxford University publicly decreed as false and blasphemous some 27 propositions found in books which sought to limit the power of kings. The books in question were interdicted to all members of the Oxford community and were ordered to be publicly burned 'in the Court of our Schools'. The decree was presented to Charles II on 24 July and published in the *London Gazette* of 23–6 July 1683; see also Charles Edward Mallet, *History of the University of Oxford*, ii (London, 1924), 448–56.

[3] The Oxford decree enjoined all readers, tutors, etc., to instruct their students in the necessary doctrine 'of submitting to every Ordinance of Man for the Lord's sake, whether it be to the King as Supreme, or unto Governors'.

As a reasonable Motive to such a Procedure, be it observed that this pernicious Decree was virtually repealed in so short a Space of Time as five Years after its Publication, by those very misguided Men who made it; when finding themselves insulted by the lordly Power of Popery, and feeling themselves wounded, crushed, and sinking under the Iron Rod of arbitrary Power, they made a glorious Stand for Liberty, in the very Presence of the reigning Prince;[1] and no sooner were they convinced that Reason and Truth, humble Remonstrances, and every conscientious Submission, were unavailing Advocates for their Safety, than to their confessed Honour, with one Heart and one Voice, they concurred in Addresses for Protection to another Prince,[2] who came to make them free, and in the earliest Measures devised by a steady, a resolute, a Protestant People, to secure the Blessing of Liberty to themselves, and to transmit it down to their Posterity. ——Again,

Be it remember'd, that this erroneous, this shameful Decree, was, in fact, refuted by a more cogent Decree of the House of Lords, who, on *Thursday* the 23d Day of *July*, 1710, first re-solved, "That the Judgment or Decree of the University of *Oxford*, passed in their Convocation on the 21st Day of *July*, 1683, contained in it several Positions contrary to the Constitution of this Kingdom, and destructive to the Protestant Succession, as by Law established."—and then ordered, "That the said Judgment and Decree shou'd (together with certain other Productions of the like Import) be burnt by the Common Hangman, in the Presence of the Sheriffs of *London* and *Westminster*."[3]

Secondly,—Let those of this Community, who have taken upon them the Office of Tutors, and to whom more especially is committed the immediate Care of forming the Minds, guiding the Understanding, and fixing the Principles of young and un-experienced Scholars, bestow a Reflection on the Importance of

---

[1] In September 1687, during the controversy over the presidency of Magdalen College, James II went down to Oxford to bully the Fellows, who with two exceptions protested their inability to obey. Ultimately, troops had to be sent in. See Mallet, *History of the University of Oxford*, ii. 452–6; J. R. Bloxham, *Magdalen College and King James II* (Oxford, 1886), pp. x–xxx, 242–71; and *JJ* no. 25, above, p. 286 and note 1 there.

[2] The University published its congratulations to Prince William, 'Illustrissime atque invictissime princeps', on 17 November 1688; Mallet, ii. 458.

[3] The interrupted quotation given here represents a conflation of separate passages in Fielding's source; see below, p. 299, n. 1. For the published text of the Lords' decree, which was delivered on 23 March 1710, not in July, see *Journals of the House of Lords*, xix. 122.

this Trust, and be watchful and diligent in preparing their Pupils for the Service of their Country: In this laudable View their Instructions will more effectually take Place, if attended by incidental Lessons of Loyalty, and of Obedience, to an established Government: And nothing surely can be more reasonable, nothing more necessary, than such a Procedure; since it is well known that the first and lowest Academick Honours are not conferred without a previous and public Administration of the Oaths of Allegiance and Supremacy;[1] and that no Emoluments can be legally enjoyed by any Member of a College, without his solemn Subscription to the Oath of Abjuration.[2]

Lastly,—The Rulers of this Community are vested with full Authority to follow the Example of the Governors of the Metropolis, by reclaiming the annual Stipend or Pension by them (for the Encouragement of Learning) rather too hastily granted, to a pretending, unequal Writer of History, to enable him to begin, continue, and perfect a Labour, the First-fruits of which, tho' relative to Facts of the earliest Times, discover a Turn of Mind hurtful to the present Age, and a Spirit of Faction and Calumny, to be abhorred by every Reader, who really is, what this trifling Writer calls himself, an *Englishman*.[3]

To resolve and execute such reasonable and expected Measures, will be making a just and becoming Use of the extensive Powers and valuable Privileges, by which, under the Favour and Protection of the Crown, and by the Indulgence of the Laws, these Schools of Knowledge, Virtue and Religion, have been so justly distinguished.

I am, Sir, Yours, &c.

Oxford, May 23,

1748. ANONYMUS.

---

[1] By the terms of 1 Will. & Mary, cap. 8, which imposed the oaths of allegiance and supremacy, all schoolmasters were required to take the prescribed oaths under penalty, ultimately, of being forbidden to hold any office; *Statutes at Large*, ix. 5–11. See also 1 Geo. I, stat. 2, cap. 13.

[2] 13 Will. III, cap. 6; *Statutes at Large*, x. 399–406, and *JJ* nos. 16 and 21, above, pp. 202, 246.

[3] 'A court of common council at *Guildhall*, on a motion made by Sir *W. Calvert*, seconded by Sir *J. Barnard*, unanimously resolved to withdraw the subscription of 50 *l.* per *Ann.* granted *July* 7, 1744, to Mr. *Carte*, in order to enable him to procure materials for a complete history of *England*'; *GM*, xviii (1748), 185. See also John Nichols, *Biographical and Literary Anecdotes of William Bowyer*, pp. 199 n., 200, 567 n., 572 n.; and *JJ* no. 13, above, p. 177.

N. B. The *Oxford Decree* of 1683, may be found at large in the Body of the folio Edition of *Sacheveral's* Tryal; and the Judgment of the House of Lords thereupon, at the End of that Tryal.[1]

Cambridge, May 4, 1748.

To John Trott-Plaid, *Esq;*

Sir,

In spite of all the *dirty Ink* that has been spent to *asperse* your Character as an *Author*, I can't help admiring, and at the same time espousing, the Principles you have all along maintained in your *Journal*. To expose the *Weakness* of Jacobitism (to give it no worse a Name) is a Task truly laudable at this Time of Day. But, above all the rest of your Performances, your Paper now before me of the 30th of *April*, gives me the greatest Satisfaction, as you are pleased to handle a Subject of the utmost Importance, *viz.* the *proper Principling* (if I may be allow'd the Expression) of Youth. Tho' some of our *Fraternity* may not be over well satisfy'd to hear you propose to the Consideration of the *Legislature* a *thorough Inspection and Scrutiny into the Characters of all those who are intrusted with the Tuition and Instruction of Youth*, yet I am intirely of your Opinion, that the Danger of so *pernicious* and *growing an Evil*, as that of inculcating or encouraging *Jacobitical Principles*, is a Matter that loudly demands the timely *Restraint of Laws*.

Every one must be sensible that the Strength, the Security, and the Reputation of the State depends, in a great measure, on the wise Erudition and sound Principles of the *growing Generation*. If the Minds of Youth get a wrong Biaſs in their first Institution, and, by the *Corruptness* of Instructors, be taught to receive *Doctrines* and *Tenets* diametrically opposite to the Wholsomness of our *present Establishment*, what can we expect from them, when they are come to be the *maturer* Members of the Community, but *Discontent, Sedition*, and well if not *Rebellion* too, against our happy Administration? For my Part, I have always laid it down as a Rule, and more particularly since our late *Northern Troubles* rouz'd our Attention, to instil Notions of Attachment to our *Government*, and Loyalty to his *Majesty* and the *Protestant*

---

[1] *The Tryal of Dr. Henry Sacheverell before the House of Peers for High Crimes and Misdemeanours* (London, 1710), pp. 162–5 (Oxford decree), 326–7 (Lords' resolution).

Succession, with the same steady Regard that I would *Principles of Religion,* or any *System of Morals.*

Tho' Classical Learning, 'tis own'd, be the principal Business of Schools, and a competent Stock of *Greek* and *Latin* the chief End and Pursuit of Youth, yet the *Love of our Country* (which, *Tully* says, *comprehends all other Endearments*)[1] and an Affection for our *King* and the *Act of Settlement,*[2] are by no means useless Lessons of Instruction. If I might *advise* (for I pretend to no Authority to *enforce* my Opinion) I would have the Youth at our public Schools constantly mix with their other Exercises some Subjects on Loyalty—Liberty—with all the various Duties and Obligations they lay under, for the Defence of our most *happy Constitution*: And thus, by being early taught, and knowing the Blessings they enjoy under the best of Governments upon Earth, they will learn betimes to set a due Value on them. For, notwithstanding the Veneration I bear to the *Ancients,* and the Gratitude I owe to all those *modern* helping Hands, that have, by their united Labours, contributed to facilitate the Business of Education, yet I declare from my Heart, I had rather have my Son a *loyal* and *well-affected Subject* than the deepest *Logician,* or the greatest *Scholar* in the Universe.

I could wish to find, that your late Paper may produce some further Sentiments on this Subject; and am Mr. *Trott-Plaid's*

Most constant Reader,

CUMBRIENSIS.[3]

Proceedings at the Court of Criticism, Thursday June 2.

The Court delivered the following Opinion concerning the *Castle of Indolence,* lately published by Mr. *Thomson*:[4] "This is a

---

[1] *De Officiis,* I. xvii. 57: *sed omnes omnium caritates patria una complexa est.*

[2] 12 & 13 Will. III, cap. 2, secured the succession of the Crown to the House of Hanover by certain further, specific determinations, to the exclusion of all Roman Catholic claimants, of both the Orleans and Palatine lines; *Statutes at Large,* x. 357–60.

[3] Literally 'of Cumbria', i.e. of Wales. However, the letter is announced as from Cambridge ('Cantabriensis'), which suggests that the false etymology may be intended as a hit at the deficient Latinity of the academic correspondent. On the relations between the Government and the two Universities, see General Introduction, above, pp. lxvi–lxvii.

[4] *The Castle of Indolence. An Allegorical Poem, Written in Imitation of Spenser* was entered at Stationer's Hall on 6 May 1748 and published the following day; Alan Dugald McKillop (ed.), *James Thomson: 'The Castle of Indolence' and other Poems* (Lawrence, Kans., 1961), Introduction, p. 56. Thomson's poem, which was a Millar publication, was advertised in half a dozen issues of the *JJ,* beginning with no. 25 (21 May 1748).

noble allegorical Poem, and truly breathes the Spirit of that Author which it professes to imitate.

"The Description of the Castle is truly poetical, and contains every Image which can be drawn from Nature, suitable to the Occasion. The Author hath, with wonderful Art, brought together all the Inducements to Slumber; and at the same time hath taken sufficient Care that they shall have no Effect on his Reader.

"No less Genius appears in the Wizard's Speech.[1] The *Epicurean* System is here enforced with Arguments of such seeming Solidity, that we cannot wonder if it captivated the Hearers. Their Entrance into the Castle is finely described in the 28th Stanza, and illustrated with a beautiful Simile.

"The Inside of the Castle is described with wonderful Power of Fancy. The Subjects of the Paintings are happily chose, and in the exact Spirit of the Antients. The Music likewise is adapted with much Knowledge and Judgment.

"Nothing can be imagined with more Propriety than the Amusements of this Place. The Crystal Globe, in which all the Inhabitants of the Earth are represented, is really a Master-piece, and would have shined in *Homer*, *Virgil*, or *Milton*; nor is the Execution here unequal to so noble a Hint.[2]

"I shall pass over those Parts where the Author hath chosen to pay a Compliment to some of his Friends; tho' I cannot help saying that these are extremely delicate; and what is contained in the 65th and 66th Stanzas, I know to be extremely just;[3] nor less so is, I believe, the Author's Description of himself, tho' the Character is certainly amiable.[4]

"The Prosopopeia, with which the first Stanza[5] concludes, is a fine Allegory, and contains an excellent Moral; and the Introduction of the Diseases into the Castle by secret Treachery, is one of those nice Touches which, tho' they principally constitute a great Writer, pass often unobserved by the Generality of Readers.

"The Poet's Lamentation at the Beginning of the 2d Stanza; the Generation of the Knight of Arts and Industry; his Edu-

---

[1] Canto I. ix–xix.   [2] I. xlix–lv.
[3] I. lxv–lxvi compliment Lyttelton, Thomson's friend and principal patron during the 1740s.
[4] I. lxviii.   [5] Here, and in the succeeding paragraph, an error for 'Canto'.

cation and Accomplishments; his Introduction into *Britain*, and Establishment here; the Mischiefs wrought by Indolence; the Description of the Page; the Sally; the Conversation between the Knight and his Bard; the Attempts of the Wizard; the Bard's Song; the Destruction of the Castle, with the different Fates of those who have suffered under different Degrees of the Enchantment of Indolence; the Erection of the Hospital by the Charities descending from Heaven; and lastly, the Descriptions of Beggary and Scorn, form the principal Incidents of the 2d Stanza; nor is there one of all these which doth not deserve great Commendation.

"Upon the whole, there is much Merit in this Performance; and I do order, that the Thanks of this Court be forthwith signified to Mr. *Thomson*, the Author, for his excellent Composition."[1]

The Court then proceeded to hear Council on Behalf of the *Observations on the probable Issue of the Congress at Aix-la-Chapelle*.[2] It was admitted that the Book did contain much of the Abuse which hath been already published, and which will hereafter be published against the Ministry; but it was said, that the Author did not look on this as the Property of any particular Bookseller, because it had all been already printed twenty times over by different Persons, and that he therefore imagined it to be *nullius in Boni*, like every Thing else of a base Nature. The Council farther said, that when there was not a single Fact to charge on the Ministry, the only way to write against them must be by general Slander; and unless there was a Liberty granted of transcribing from one another, this would soon be totally exhausted; that such a Restraint therefore would affect the Liberty of the Press, the most valuable Privilege of which is to abuse the Government: Nor could any Injury be thus done to the Proprietors of Libels, since it was manifest by Experience, that the Public will buy the same Scurrility a hundred times over. He said it had been always held lawful to quote the Words of an Author, in order to answer or to expose them; that this was the plain and honest Intention of the Book under Consideration, as would have appeared from the Motto, had the Booksellers or their Authors understood it; for

---

[1] According to McKillop, ed. cit., p. 61, Fielding's review was 'the first full appreciation' of *The Castle of Indolence*.

[2] See *JJ* no. 26, above, p. 293.

that the literal Translation of it was, "It is natural to all Men to listen with Pleasure to Calumnies and Accusations; but to be themselves grieved at the Praises of others."[1] A Disposition which, he said, greatly prevailed in this Nation at present.

The Court stopt him from proceeding farther, saying, they had perused the Book, and did recommend it to the Public as a true Piece of political Humour, well worth their Perusal; and the Complaint was dismiss'd with Contempt.

(Adjourned.)

SATURDAY, JUNE 11, 1748.   NUMB. 28.

Atque ita mentitur, sic veris falsa remiscet.

Horace.[2]

In a former Paper, I have treated of that Slander which is too nice and delicate in its Nature to admit of any Handling;[3] I shall now endeavour to expose a second kind, with which it is very dangerous to meddle, from the Difficulty, or, indeed, Impossibility of giving it an Answer. This is that Slander, of which the Foundation is cunningly laid in Truth; and this is much more artful and mischievous, than those bold, impudent, and injudicious Calumnies, which the blind Inveteracy of Malice and Envy sometimes encourages rash Men to discharge; and which seldom do any Injury, unless to the Credit of their Author, on whom they often recoil with their utmost Force. At worst, the solemn Denial of a Man of good Character is always sufficient to refute them.

Thus it happened with the flagitious, unknown Author of *Three Letters to the Whigs*.[4] He had falsely charged a Gentleman of the most unblemish'd Honour, with having written a Pamphlet called, *A Letter to the Tories*; and, upon this Supposition, built many unjust Accusations against that Gentleman: But here, the Foundation being absolutely false, the whole Superstructure fell

---

[1] Demosthenes, 'De Corona', 3; for the Greek text and comparable translation, see *Demosthenes: De Corona and De Falsa Legatione*, trans. C. A. Vince and J. H. Vince (London, 1926), p. 21.

[2] *Ars Poetica*, 151: 'and so skilfully does he invent, so closely does he blend facts and fiction' (Loeb).

[3] See *JJ* no. 26, above, pp. 288–92.

[4] This pamphlet by Horace Walpole had accused Lyttelton of proposing censorship of the Opposition press; see *JJ* no. 18, above, pp. 217–20, 222–5.

to the Ground, and, being solemnly denied,[1] was never afterwards believed by a single Person.

But in the Case abovementioned, the Slander'd is laid under
much greater Difficulties. The least Mixture of Truth excludes
him from this easy Manner of rescuing his Reputation. His
Honour will not suffer him to return a general peremptory
Denial to the Charge: He is here obliged (as the Lawyers call it)
to plead specially; to divide the Accusation, to separate Truth
from Falshood, to admit the one, and to award[2] only the other.

Now this is a Matter that requires great Pains and Skill in the
Advocate; and, what is worse, as such an Enquiry must be always
attended with great Trouble to the Judge, it is no easy Matter to
engage, as far as is necessary, the Attention of the Public, before
whom the Defence is to be made. Truth and Falshood are indeed
sometimes so blended together, that it requires great Care and
Time to separate the one from the other; much more commonly
of both than the World will be kind enough to bestow: For this
Judge cannot be compelled to attend; and Compassion, or the
Love of Justice, are seldom Motives sufficient to induce him. On
the contrary, I am afraid, his Affections are often engaged on the
Side of the Accuser; since all ethic Writers have concurred in
remarking the ready Assent which Human Nature is inclined to
give to Calumny, and our own Observations too well confirm
this Opinion. How much must this Inclination be strengthen'd,
when Part of the Accusation is known and acknowledged to be
true! When this Part hath once taken Possession of the Mind,
how easily doth it draw all the rest after it! Who hath not often
heard such Expressions as these: "Indeed, I believe it all; for I
myself know the Truth of this or that Circumstance.——Nay, he
cannot deny that himself, &c." Thus a Molehill of Truth (if I
may be allowed the Expression) sometimes creates a Mountain of
Falshood. And some trifling, inconsiderable Fact gives Credit to
the blackest and most malicious Stories.

It is really shocking to consider the wicked Purpose to which
this Art of mixing up Truth and Falshood together hath been
applied, and the many dreadful Effects which have been produced
by it, to very innocent and good Men. The Destruction of the
excellent *Socrates*, will be an eternal and shameful Example of the

---

[1] See *JJ* no. 18, above, pp. 217–20.

[2] 'to examine a matter and adjudicate upon its merits' (*OED*).

Efficacy of these Means. In the Slanders spread abroad against him among the *Athenians*, as well as in his Accusation before the *Areopagi*, there was some Mixture of Truth, tho' no Man was surely more innocent of all Impiety than he.

Nothing, indeed, can equal the Force of this strange Composition, in which as the least Particle of Truth is capable of transmitting its Colour to never so much Falshood, so the least Infusion of Falshood is able to communicate its rancorous and poisonous Quality to all the Truth with which it is blended.

By this Method, the greatest and most admir'd Characters which the World hath ever produced, may be easily blackened and overthrown; and the most renowned of all Actions may be vilified, and rendered the Objects of Contempt and Abhorrence.

Socrates shall serve for an Instance of this. The learned Reader knows, that he might, if he had pleased, have made his Escape from Prison.[1] *Plato* likewise tells us, in his *Phædon*, that the Morning of this great Man's Execution, when his Wife, the famous *Xantippe*, was lamenting over him, he turned to one of his Friends, and desired him to take away that troublesome Woman.[2] Why may we not suppose that the *Athenian Evening Post*, or the *Old Athens*, or the *Fool*, (for I presume there were Fools there as well as here) or some other *Athenian Grubstreeteer*, inserted the following Paragraph on the Occasion.

"WE HEAR the famous Atheist *Socrates*, who was lately condemned for Impiety to the Gods, refused to go out of Prison, tho' the Doors were set open, and defied the Government to execute him; a fresh Instance of his Obstinacy. He persisted likewise in uttering the most horrid and shocking Blasphemies to the last; and when his Wife, who, WE HEAR, is a Woman of remarkable Sweetness of Temper, and whom he hath very cruelly used on many Occasions, went to take her Leave of him, he abused her in the grossest Language, called her by several opprobrious Names, and at length prevailed on one of his Gang, who were there to visit him, to kick the poor Woman down Stairs; so that she now lies ill of the Bruises she received."

In this Example I have followed the modern Fashion, and have greatly embellished the real Fact with many Circumstances of Invention; but much less than this is necessary to subvert

[1] In his *Crito*, 44B–46A, Plato tells of a plan of escape devised by Socrates' friends.
[2] *Phaedo*, 60A. Xantippe was famous for her shrewishness.

Truth. We may often adhere strictly to the Letter of a Story; and yet, by forging the Motive only, so far misrepresent the Person who is the Subject of it, that from deserving our highest Commendation, he shall be exposed to the utmost Infamy. Thus we may say, that the elder *Brutus*, from Pride and Cruelty, put his own Sons to Death;[1] that the younger *Brutus*, from Ambition, and a Desire of supplanting him in his Power, stabb'd his Friend;[2] or, to mention but one more, and him perhaps the most glorious of all Mankind; that *Timoleon*, being jealous of his Brother's Power, and from the Motive of Rivalship, destroyed him; and, as an especial Mark of his Hatred and Cruelty, employed *Satyrus*, who had married his own Sister, for that detestable Purpose.[3]

But, indeed, the Dealers in Scandal seldom use this Moderation. They are not contented with false Glosses and malicious Comments; nothing less than an actual Misrepresentation of Facts will generally satisfy them; for the Truth of which I need only appeal to the numberless scurrilous Libels, which have, within this last Twelvemonth, disgraced both the Press and the Nation.

Few of my Readers want to have any particular Instances pointed out to them; nor can they well expect this of me, after what I have asserted above, that such Scandal is not to be meddled with. However, I shall venture to name two; since these have, I believe, been already spread as wide as it is possible to spread them, and the Malice and Falshood of both are now as universally known.

The first of these flagrant Instances (indeed the most flagrant that any Age or Country hath produced) was exemplified in the

---

[1] L. Junius Brutus, liberator of Rome from the Tarquins, was said to have put to death his two sons, who had attempted to restore the Tarquins; see also *JJ* no. 17, above, p. 210.

[2] Marcus Junius Brutus, the so-called tyrannicide, was a trusted friend of Caesar's as well as a political idealist; he was persuaded to join the conspiracy to assassinate Caesar on the grounds that only thereby might the republic be re-established.

[3] Timoleon, son of Timodemis and Demariste, was so ardent a lover of liberty that when his brother Timophanes attempted to tyrannize their native city of Corinth (c. 365 B.C.), Timoleon joined with some friends in killing the tyrant. According to Plutarch, 'Timoleon', iv. 4, Satyrus, one of the tyrannicides, was not related to Timoleon by marriage, but was simply 'his friend the seer whose name, according to Theopompus, was Satyrus, but according to Ephorus and Timaeus, Orthagoras' (Loeb). Fielding may have confused him with the third tyrannicide, Aeschylus, who in Nepos's 'Life of Timoleon', i. 4, is the husband of Timoleon's sister, and in Plutarch is called the brother of Timophanes' wife. See H. D. Westlake, 'The Sources of Plutarch's *Timoleon*', *Classical Quarterly*, xxxii (1938), 65–6.

monstrous Lies propagated concerning an Affair, which happened
at the End of last Summer; where a Nobleman of the highest
Rank and Dignity, and eminent for the most exalted public as
well as private Virtues, was in Danger of being insulted by a
riotous, factious, Jacobitical Mob.[1] The distinguished Bravery of
this Nobleman made it, indeed, probable that something very
tragical might have happened on this Occasion; but as to what
really did happen, besides the Insolence of the Mob, (which in
England is no strange Matter) it was not of any Consequence or
Importance: No sooner however did the News of this Affair
reach *London*, than the Ten thousand Tongues of Slander began
all to bellow at once. The Press, the Streets, and the Highways all
rung with Libels cramm'd with Lies, and array'd in all the Wit of
Grub-street and *Billingsgate*. Nor were the Writers contented with
venting these Falshoods for a Week or a Month, the latter of
which may be considered as an extreme old Age, to which few of
their Calumnies arise;[2] but have lately bound them up in a
Pamphlet,[3] and, as it were, revived them from the Grave of
Oblivion, where they had long lain buried.

The Bill concerning the Town of *Buckingham* is another
notorious Example of this Kind.[4] Here every Art, which Wit and
Malice united could invent, was employ'd to represent a Matter
in which the little County of *Buckingham* was alone concern'd, as
of universal Import to the Public. A Bill petitioned for by much
the greater Number of Freeholders, was said to be opposed by

[1] During the disturbances at the 1747 Lichfield race meeting the Duke of Bedford was
assaulted and struck at by members of the 'mob', including one Toll, a dancing-master;
see *GM*, xviii (1748), 378, for the conviction at the Stafford assizes in August 1748 of 13
rioters; also *JJ* no. 1, above, p. 93. John Russell (1710–71), 4th Duke of Bedford, First
Lord of the Admiralty (1744–8), and at this time Secretary of State for the Southern department, is praised in both capacities by the *JJ* (no. 9 of 30 January 1748, and no. 12 of 20
February 1748, both *sub* 'Domestic News'); see Appendix VI, below, pp. 456, 459. Bedford,
who had been a subscriber to the 1743 *Miscellanies*, was to bestow upon Fielding the 'princely
Benefactions' noted in the Dedication of *Tom Jones*, namely, the post of Justice of the Peace
for Westminster later in 1748, and the 'several Leasehold Messuages or Tenements' necessary
to the extension of his jurisdiction to include Middlesex county as well; see G. M. Godden,
Henry Fielding, pp. 195–7. Fielding's own note to the Introduction of his *Journal of a
Voyage to Lisbon* (1755), p. 26, credits his patron, Bedford, with having got him 'a yearly
pension out of the public service-money'. [2] 'attain'.
[3] Perhaps *The Foundling Hospital for Wit, No. V*, which appeared in late April or early
May 1748, and printed two poems on the Lichfield rioting (pp. 1–6). See *JJ* no. 26, above,
p. 290 and note 2 there.
[4] See *JJ* no. 19, above, pp. 226–33.

the County in General. A manifest Opposition to all Jobs, and a Defence of the Freedom of Elections, were, by a kind of Legerdemain, construed into the very Reverse. And lastly, the Conduct of a noble Gentleman,[1] who exerted many of those exalted Qualities of which he is possess'd on this Occasion, was traduced in a Language which we shall not repeat in this Paper.

I shall conclude this Essay in the Words of a learned and witty *English* Divine; who, in his Sermon on this Text in *Isaiah, Woe unto them who call Evil good, and Good evil, that put Darkness for Light, and Light for Darkness,* &c. hath the following excellent Passage. "Detraction (says he) is that poisonous Arrow, drawn out of the Devil's Quiver, which is always flying about and doing Execution in the Dark; against which no Virtue is a Defence, no Innocence a Security. It is a Weapon forged in Hell, and formed by that prime Artificer and Engineer, the Devil; and none but that Great God who knows all Things, and can do all Things, can protect THE BEST OF MEN against it."[2]

The Court of Criticism met as usual; but nothing past worth communicating to the Public; and having sat half an Hour, the said Court adjourned to Thursday *next.*

SATURDAY, JUNE 18, 1748.   NUMB. 29.

Ambubaiarum Collegia.——

Horace.[3]

If it be admitted that Slander, in the two Instances we have given of it,[4] which indeed comprehends almost every pernicious Species, is not safely either to be answered in Writing, or prosecuted in a Course[5] of Justice; an honest Man may perhaps answer, What then? Are a Set of unknown paultry Scribblers to vilify and asperse the Characters of every great and good Man in the

---

[1] Cf. *JJ* no. 19, above, p. 227, where the person presumably Pelham, is called 'an Hon. Gentleman'.

[2] Robert South, 'The Fatal Imposture and Force of Words: set forth in a Sermon preached on Isaiah V, 20, May 9, 1686', *Sermons Preached on Several Occasions* (Oxford, 1823), ii. 135, 137. The two sentences are somewhat separated in South's text, which is also quoted in *The Champion* of 6 March 1740, and in *Miscellanies* (1743), i. 170.

[3] *Satires*, I. ii. 1: 'The flute-girls' guilds' (Loeb). The phrase forms part of the motto for *TP* no. 4 (26 November 1745) and *CGJ* no. 8 (28 January 1752).

[4] See *JJ* no. 26, above, pp. 287–93, and *JJ* no. 28, above, pp. 303–8.

[5] i.e. a judicial or justiciary proceeding. That the emendation to 'Court' should be resisted seems clear from Fielding's *A Serious Address to the People of Great Britain* (1745), p. 12: 'Can any Man take from him an Acre, or a Shilling, but by a due Course of Law ... ?'

Kingdom at their Pleasure, and are such Scurrilities neither to be answered nor punished?

I am sorry I must reply in the Affirmative. This is an Effect of that Licentiousness which will always, in some Degree, spring up in the same Soil where Liberty flourishes; nor can the nicest Hand of the Legislator totally pluck up and eradicate the former, without doing, at the same Time, some Injury to the tender Root of the latter.

For this Reason, those illustrious Persons in whose Service this Paper hath been said to be retained,[1] because it doth not, like all the rest, most scurrilously abuse them, have rather chose to over-look and despise all those malicious Howlings, with which the Press hath resounded against them, than to endeavour to restrain it by Law; nay, they have, to their immortal Honour, avoided this Method, even while they have patiently submitted to bear all the Obloquy which the false Imputation of such an Attempt could cast upon them.

But while I am commending them for abstaining from harsh or coercive Methods, I must acknowledge they seem worthy of some Censure, for neglecting others of a very different Kind, which seem obvious enough, and which would, in all Probability, soon put a final End to this Evil, without any possible Injury to Liberty; nay, even with Emolument to the very Offenders themselves. And this Method of remedying publick Mischief by Lenitives will be always most agreeable to a wise and good Legislator or Magistrate, who must be considered as free from all Motives of Pique and Resentment, and never desirous of punish-ing those whom he can otherwise reclaim.

In Truth, then, I do not question the Efficacy of gentle Measures on this Occasion; not that I would be understood here to agree intirely with the Opinion of some, who, acknowledging the dangerous Consequences which may arise from the present growing Spirit of Slander, and detesting all harsh or coercive Means of abolishing it, have proposed to take off three or four of the Capital Slanderers, by bringing them at once into the Minis-try, and placing them in the most considerable Posts of the Government. This I object to, as directly contrary to my Master *Aristotle*, who says μεγάλων γὰρ κύριοι καθεστῶτες, ἂν εὐτελεῖς ὦσι

---

[1] The Pelham ministry, through the particular offices of Lyttelton; see, for example, *OE* of 2 April and 11 June, and *LEP* of 4–6 and 16–18 February 1748.

μεγάλα βλάπτουσι.* Anglicé, *Set a Beggar on Horseback, and he'll ride.*[1] Besides, it may be doubted whether these Gentlemen may be perfectly well qualified for those Offices of State which require the Knowledge of Languages; and I am afraid it is a Maxim in Politics, not to trust Authors in any Treasury. Nor can I readily concur with the more moderate Proposition of erecting the Authors of *Old England*, the *Fool*, and the Printer of the *London Evening-Post*, into a Board called *the Board of Supervisors*; and that the Ministry should constantly, from time to time, be obliged to lay all their Measures before this Board, previous to their being carried into Execution. But however plausible this may appear to some, I cannot help objecting, that as the present Forms of our Government subject our Councils to too much Delay, and often to some Danger of Discovery, this Scheme would greatly increase both those Inconveniences; which would perhaps more than counterballance the great Sanction which, it is urged, would be thus given to all our Political Transactions abroad.

Besides, I am apprehensive of some Mischief which might accrue to these honourable Gentlemen themselves, if any of their best-concerted Measures should be unsuccessful; since probably they might not be so well able to stem the Torrent of Faction, which in such Case would rage against them.

And of this, indeed, those Authors seem sensible. One of them hath several Times told his Readers, That he hath no Concern in the Management of Affairs, and is entirely indifferent who is at the Helm, provided they act for the Interest of his Country; which he hath often assured us is not the Case at present.[2] Another very flatly desired the Public last Winter to take Notice, that he had given the Ministry due Warning and Advice, with Regard to their Conduct in the *West-Indies*, and very cautiously

---

* Pol. Lib. 2. cap. 9.[3]

[1] For this proverb see Tilley, *Dictionary of the Proverbs in England*, B239, p. 40.

[2] Not identified. However, as reprinted in *LEP* of 25–8 June 1748, No. 255 of 'The Fool' begins: 'To convince them (the M——y) how much I am in Earnest, as to the not being attach'd to any Party, I will freely tell the Gentlemen in Power . . .'. This suggests an earlier, perhaps fuller, statement of political neutrality, but the file of the *DG* for this period is far from complete.

[3] A mistake for ii. 11 (1272^{b}41–1273^{a}1). A more literal translation: 'Such officers have great power, and therefore, if they are persons of little worth, do a great deal of harm'; *Politics*, trans. Benjamin Jowett, *Works of Aristotle*, ed. W. D. Ross, x (Oxford, 1921), 1272^b.

added, that if they now neglected to pursue his Directions, they only (and not he) were to be blamed.[1]

Again, should either of these Methods, or any other such be pursued, it could by no means answer the End; but would rather aggravate than lessen the Evil: For if you should take off three or threescore Writers of this Sort, you would probably encourage as many hundred new Scandal-mongers to take up the Pen; since every Man, who can barely write, is equally capable with the present Set of becoming Authors.

To omit therefore all other Proposals on this Head, most of which seem less to deserve an Answer, I shall proceed to lay my Plan at once before the Reader; and this is no other than to erect an Hospital for Sc—NDR—LS.[2]

As I was apprehensive that the Reader might be startled at a Word which is sometimes used in no very good Sense, I have chosen to follow the Method of some of the ingenious Gentlemen who are the Subjects of this Plan, in not printing it at length; but indeed I could not find any other Word which might be so safely used, and so little liable to any Doubts or Difficulties in Law, as to the Qualification of future Candidates, as this. Wit, Learned, Author, &c. might perhaps have implied more than I mean; but surely it can be no Question, whether every mean illiterate Fellow, who gets his daily Bread by spreading Lies all over the Kingdom, by defaming the greatest and best of Men, nay even by robbing any single Man of his Character, is or is not included within the Term abovementioned.

But why should I make any Apology for the Use of a Term which is not held scandalous in our Law, especially when I apply it to those who endeavour to persuade us, that the greatest Personages in the Nation deserve it?

But before I enter into a particular Detail of my Plan, I shall

---

[1] Not identified. The extant files of the Opposition Journals for this particular period are incomplete.

[2] This proposal elicited a violent rejoinder from Horace Walpole, in *OE* of 25 June 1748, also reprinted in *LEP* of 25–8 June. Walpole's piece, the second such attack by him on Fielding in 1748, compares the latter's proposal of a hospital for scoundrels to the mad Dean Swift's proposing a hospital for lunatics, and describes 'Trott-Plaid' as Foote mimicked him—shirt out, holes in his 'Galligaskins', with his familiar, Mr. Punch, on one side of him and a picture of 'Selim Slim' (Lyttelton) on the other. Walpole also recounts the embarrassing anecdote about Fielding's attendance at the theatre in the company of his second wife, his former maid. See General Introduction, pp. lxxix–lxxx and *JJ* no. 18, above, pp. 217–20, 225 n. 3.

consider every Objection which may be raised against it; to all which I hope to give a satisfactory Answer.

First, it may be said, that I am proposing a Reward for them, who, of all others, most deserve a whipping Post.

This I have partly obviated already, by observing, that neither the Legislator, nor the Magistrate, have ever recourse to Punishment from vindictive Motives, and would be always better pleased to do their Business an easier Way.

But, indeed, tho' the Consequence of this Evil be very pernicious to Society, the Motive to it is not generally among the worst Ingredients of the human Composition. Necessity is a severe Task-Master; and notwithstanding the Precepts which most of us receive in our Youth to learn and labour honestly to get our Living, the Temptation must be allow'd very strong, when much larger Wages are offered us for Idleness and Iniquity, than for honest but hard Labour. When therefore the Mason, the Bricklayer, the Carpenter, &c. offer no more than half a Crown *per diem*, and the Printer, at least, doubles the Price, while he requires but half the Work, it requires no ordinary Degree of Virtue to chuse the former.

Again, I am perswaded that these Writers are far from being sensible of the Pain they give, or the Mischief they are doing. The Rank of these People may almost be said to be below Reputation; and one may apply to such Fellows the same callous Want of Feeling which *Macduff* remarks of one who had no Children, and consequently knew not the Tenderness of a Father;[1] when therefore such Persons hack and hew the Characters of their Fellow-Creatures, we may say of them,

Alaſs! they have no Character to lose.[2]

This must be at least the Case of every Author while he remains unknown; and I believe, if I should never so grosly abuse any of the three Authors abovementioned, I might safely ask many Thousands of my Readers, Whom have I injured?

Another Objection may possibly be, that as no other Name would, with sufficient Certainty, include all the Authors I would

[1] *Macbeth*, IV. iii. 216: 'He has no children'; remarked of Malcolm by Macduff after the former attempted to comfort him concerning the murder of Lady Macduff and her children. Fielding parodies the remark in *Tom Jones*, XI. i.

[2] Cf. La Bruyère, 'Of Man', *Works*, 6th ed. (London, 1713), ii. 252; Pope, *Moral Essays*, 'Epistle II. To a Lady', 2; and *Tom Jones*, XIV. i.

provide for, so this would probably include many more; nay, possibly some Men of Fortune would become liable to be shut up in my Hospital.

This Objection, I own, hath much Force, and can only be answered by proposing a restraining Epithet to be added to the Substantive, such as scribbling, scandalous, &c. and for the absolute Security of all Men of Fortune, it may be enacted, that no Man of——a Year, shall be capable of being a Sc—ndr—l, let him write, or do whatever he pleases.

A third Objection will, I suppose, be the Expence to the Public, which must arise from this Hospital; but this will appear extremely frivolous, when I come to lay down the Particulars of my Plan. In the mean time, I shall only observe, that if the Buyers of all the scandalous Nonsense vented every Day, should agree to pay the same Money to the Hospital, which they now pay for nothing, a very large Fund might be raised for the Purpose; and they might have the Satisfaction of thinking they contributed to the Support of a few worthless, but indigent People; instead of assisting, in doing an Injury to many worthy Men, and that an Injury of the most cruel Nature.

Other Objections shall be considered hereafter, when we shall think proper to resume the Subject.

Proceedings at the Court of Criticism, Thursday June 16.

The Court of Censure was adjourned to this Day Fortnight.

The Court of Recommendation was moved, that his Honour would please to resume the Subject of a charitable Provision for the Widows and Children of the poor Clergy; and a Letter from a Dignitary of the Church of *England*, highly approving the Scheme formerly printed in this Paper,[1] was read.

It was then said, That this Scheme was by no Means a new or unprecedented Matter; for that something very nearly resembling it was already instituted in more than one Diocese; and that other grave and good Men, besides his Honour, had lamented the Distress and Misery in which many worthy Clergymen were unavoidably necessitated to leave their Families, and had consider'd the Neglect of making any Provision for them, as a Reproach to the whole Nation.

---

[1] See *JJ* no. 21, above, pp. 250–4.

A Book written by the learned Dean *Prideaux* was then produced, and the following Quotation from it was ordered to be read and printed;[1] where the learned Writer, having offered his Objections to a particular Method proposed for raising such Charity, proceeds thus:

"But here you will say, Must there then be no Regard had to the poor Widows, and Children of deceased Ministers? Must no Compassion be shewn towards them, or any Provision at all made for them? To this I answer, None shall be more ready, than I will always be for the providing of all suitable Relief for them in a justifiable Way. I reckon this is, what we in this Kingdom are defective and faulty in. Most other Protestant Churches in other Parts of Christendom have Provisions for the Wives and Children, which their Ministers may leave behind them at their Decease, stated and settled by Law. And no Christian State is more obliged to this, than we in this Kingdom, because by that great Number of Alienations of Tythes, which were made from the Church into the Hands of the Laity at the Reformation, a Multitude of our Livings are so impoverished, as not to be sufficient to provide a Minister with a tolerable Competency, while he lives, much less to enable him to leave wherewith to support a Family after his Decease. But is there no other Way of finding Relief for them, but by robbing God, his Church, and the next Successor? Are there no other Means of providing Charity for their Support, but at the Price of Simony, Sacrilege and Oppression? It is against this Evil and Impious Way only that I argue: Find out any other, that is justifiable, and honest, and I shall be most ready heartily and zealously to concur with you in it. For I truly think it a great Defect among us, and a Reproach to the whole Nation, that so little is done in it already, since so many Reigns are now past since the Reformation, in all which it hath been continually complained of, and never yet redressed. And I think we cannot be excused, 'till some legal Method be settled by the Government to make Provision herein. And because my destroying your Way may not be thought to be from any Design of

---

[1] Humphrey Prideaux (1648–1724), Dean of Norwich (1702–24), is here quoted from 'The Justice of the Present Establish'd Law', *Ecclesiastical Tracts Formerly Published,* 2nd ed. (London, 1716), pp. 271–3. The tract here quoted is signed and dated 25 March 1703. Baker, item no. 551, lists the 1716 [–18] edition of Prideaux's most famous work, *The Old and New Testament Connected in the History of the Jews and Neighboring Nations,* among Fielding's books.

obstructing so good a Work, I will supply you with another, which after my most serious Thoughts on this Matter, seems to me the most proper for the Purpose, as being not only free from all the Objections, which I have made against that, which you have proposed, but that which, in all likelyhood will prove the most effectual to answer the End intended, and all this without grieving or oppressing any Body. And an Act of Parliament can establish this Way, as well as that, which you propose. And therefore, if you will alter your Petition, and put this way into it, instead of the other, you shall have both my Hand and my Heart to concur with you in it. I will propose it to you in these following Articles,

I. "That the whole Body of the Clergy do equally take upon them this Charge of providing for their own Poor, that is, the Poor Widows and Children of Clergymen deceased, in the same Manner, as every Parish provideth for those that fall into Poverty in it.

II. "That in order hereto, the Clergy of every County be incorporated, and have stated Meetings and proper Officers appointed to manage this Matter.

III. "That the Officers appointed do annually lay an equal Rate upon all the Ecclesiastical Benefices in the County, for the maintaining of those Poor belonging to the Clergy, in the same Manner as the Overseers of the Poor do in every Parish, make a Rate for the maintaining of the Poor belonging to the said Parish.

IV. "That a License of Mortmain be granted every such Corporation to purchase and hold Lands to a Value in Proportion to the Number of Parishes, which are in the said County.

V. "That all Parishes be discharged from making Provision for any such Poor, as the Clergy are to be charged with according to this Proposal, and that in consideration hereof all Ministers of Parishes be discharged from all Poors-Rates in their said Parishes for their Ecclesiastical Benefices, and be charged for them only to the maintaining of their own Poor, and none other."

(*To be continued.*)

SATURDAY, JUNE 25, 1748.　　　　　　　NUMB. 30.

Vetuere Patres quod non potuere vetare.

Ovid, *Metamorphoses.*[1]

Aristotle, in his *Ethics*, tells us, that "the *Persians* exercised as severe a Tyranny over their Children, as over their Slaves;"[2] and by *Seneca*, *Lactantius*, and *Servius*, we are told, that "the Condition of the Children of *Roman* Parents, was worse than that of their Servants:"[3] It is doubtless then highly to the Honour of *British* Liberty, that the Power of a Parent is circumscribed, as well as that of a Magistrate. I am led into this Reflection by a Letter just receiv'd, (apparently in a Female Character) and which I shall put into the Reader's Hands exactly as it came to mine.

To JOHN TROTT-PLAID, *Esq;*

> *Houndly-Hall*, near *Litchfield*,
> *Staffordshire*, *June* 11.[4]

Sir,

I am a constant Reader, and determined Admirer of your *Saturday* Lecture to the Political and Moral World, and am well pleased with your own Productions, and with those of your Epistolary Friend; but, to my huge Mortification, I have not yet caught you stooping to a Female Correspondent: And, to speak the Truth, your public and solemn Divorce of Mrs. *Margaret Trott-Plaid*, (at the Time when you got rid of your Ass)[5] has created in me a Sort of Suspicion, that you have no extraordinary Esteem for her Sex,—a Flaw, indeed, in the most masterly Understanding!——— But it cannot be: And when, with Delight, I reflect on your avowed Friendship for that whimsical, worthy Creature Parson *Adams*; on your Labours in Defence of honest *Joseph Andrews*; and, above all, on your generous Protection afforded to poor

---

[1] iv. 61: '[their] parents forbade what no parents could forbid' (Loeb). The accepted text punctuates with a colon after *patres*.

[2] VIII. x (1160^{b}27-8).

[3] Not identified. The use of direct quotation may imply an intermediate source.

[4] The dateline raises once more the reproach of Tory Jacobitism in connection with Lichfield and Staffordshire; see *JJ* no. 1, above, p. 93. According to *GM*, xviii (1748), 281, June 11, 'being the anniversary of his majesty's accession to the crown in 1727, was observed with the usual rejoicings'.

[5] See *JJ* no. 13, above, p. 172. The headpiece depicting the ass appeared on the first twelve numbers only.

Mrs. *Hartly*,[1] I am eager to perswade myself, that your confessed Humanity must carry you into a Concern for any domestic Distress; and that, like your great Patterns, *Addison* and *Steel*, you could find a Time for Attention to the reasonable Complaints even of a Cookmaid. Under this Perswasion, of your Friendship for Human Nature, I offer you an artless Recital of *real* Grievances.

I am, Sir, the only Daughter of a Gentleman of some Distinction in his Country, and quite happy in the Friendship of an only Brother, somewhat older than myself, a Man of Virtue, Sense, and Honour:—Sometime ago, my Brother was visited by an intimate Friend of his, whom (without assuming the Air of a Romance-Writer) I must ask Leave to call *Philander*. How earnestly do I wish that my whole Tale was, like this borrow'd Appellation, *Romanesque*?[2] But, Mr. *Trott-Plaid*, the Truth is, that this same *Philander* had a Person to please the Eye, and a Manner to win upon the most wary of my Sex, not destitute of Taste; and as his Visit continued two Months, possibly scarce one of them was expir'd, before Nature whisper'd to my Mind, something like a *Wish* to be his Friend, but, at the same Time, I must tell you, that Powerful Art stept in to my Assistance, insomuch, that I am sure the Secret was with me alone. A pretty frequent Recourse to the *English* Shelves in my Brother's Study, supply'd me with Matter for General Conversation with *Philander*, in which he came up to my highest Expectations, from a Man of modest Knowledge, and unaffected Virtue, a satisfying Judgment, and sprightly Parts: At length the expected Moment arriv'd; and in the prettiest, the least embarrassing, the most engaging Manner, a Declaration was made of something more particular. I was prepared to reply, that "a Father had a Property in me." *Philander* bowed, and look'd as if he thank'd me, which made me fear I had said too much; and, possibly, this Fear was legible in my Cheeks, for, with a Delicacy of Manners, he instantly changed the Subject, and relieved me. My Father's Opinion, at that Time, of this agreeable Man, opened an easy Passage to

---

[1] A slip for Mrs. *Heartfree*, an important and sympathetic female character in *Jonathan Wild*. If the slip is not due to a misreading of copy, then it suggests that Fielding is not in fact the author of the 'Letter just receiv'd (apparently in a Female Character)'. Cross, ii. 92, attributes it, tentatively, to Sarah Fielding, whose *Adventures of David Simple* (1744), Bk. IV, ch. vi, makes a somewhat similar slip.

[2] Characteristic of a romance or fictitious narrative remote from 'real' life. The *OED* records no such usage.

his Approbation: In a word, *Philander's* Moral Character, his Estate, and his proffer'd Settlement, answer'd every Inquiry, and every Expectation, and I (to my huge Satisfaction) was commanded, by a Parent, to treat a Man whom I loved, as one whom I was soon to obey. This I did with a chearful Innocence, and then thought myself as happy as I now feel myself to be wretched. It would possibly be a Task, even to your Penetration, Mr. *Trott-Plaid*, to suggest any Evil, inferior to the Death or Treachery of *Philander*, which cou'd at once destroy my pleasing Hopes, and yet he lives, is faithful, and I, alas, am undone!——It was but last *Monday*, (dismal *Monday*!) that my Father sent for me to his Closet, and the Moment I enter'd, without the least Preface to soften my Sentence, "Child, (says he) you must think no more of your Sweet-heart."——Your own Humanity, Mr. *Trott-Plaid*, will represent to you my Astonishment, better than my Pen can paint it.——"Not think of *Philander* more, Sir?" reply'd I, (and I wonder how I cou'd be so bold,) "You must then give me leave to say, that as your Commands gave Birth to any Disposition in me to think of that Gentleman at all, I hope I have a Right to know, for what Crime in him, or in me, those Commands are recalled?"——"Why, Child, (says he) I have Reason to suspect his *Principles*."——"His Principles, Sir? What says my Brother, who has known him long and intimately? Nay, what say you, Sir, who lately thought so favourably of him, that I heard you call him a Pattern of Probity? Then for his Religious Sentiments"——"Prithee, Girl, don't cant to me about *Philander's* Religion and Probity, when I tell you I dislike his *Principles*; and since your Prejudice in his Favour, seems likely to carry you into an indecent Opposition to my Will, I must silence you at once, by telling you, that I have lately discovered, that his Great-grand-father, being a Member of the *Oxford* Parliament in 1681,[1] was one of those Republican Rascals, who promoted the *Bill of Exclusion*;[2] and determined I am, that the Blood of the *Hunters*

---

[1] Charles II's fifth and final Parliament met in Oxford in March 1681, so as to remove itself from the incendiary influences of London aldermen and the London mob during the debates over 'exclusion' *versus* 'limitation' (by means of a regency).

[2] The third of three such Bills (1679, 1680, 1681), it resolved 'to exclude *James* Duke of *Yorke*, and all Popish Successors, from inheriting the Imperial Crowns of *England* and *Ireland*'; *Journals of . . . Commons*, ix. 711–12. The Bill was read for the first and only time on 28 March 1681. Charles II dissolved the Oxford Parliament before the Bill could be passed into law.

shall not be corrupted by a Mixture with the Spawn of any Whig in Christendom." By this I must confess I was effectually silenc'd; for having no Idea of the Nature of the Crime committed by *Philander's* Great-grand-father, I cou'd not offer at any Reply, and so the Conference ended.——This Resolution, with the Reason for it, was, by the same Authority, imparted to my Brother, who took the Liberty to reply, that "As Matters had proceeded so far between his Friend and his Sister, and with his Father's Concurrence, he cou'd not discover the Weight of this Objection, which he feared wou'd, in Case of a Rupture, be insufficient to vindicate the Honour of the Family." For this modest, this rational Remonstrance, this Act of Humanity, he likewise was charged with the Crime of Whiggism, and loaded with the Infamy of communicating the dreadful Decree to *Philander*, who, after an apparent Shock, collected himself, and reply'd, that "He had never made a Secret of his Political Creed, and from this Treatment found no Sort of Cause to renounce it." With eager Steps he then made his Way to my Apartment. Oh! Mr. *Trott-Plaid*, the Situation of my Heart at his Approach!—— "Madam, (says the worthy Creature) your Father's Lunacy has distracted me; I struggle for a Moment's Calmness, in which to tell you, that his Treatment rather heightens than impairs my Love for you, and for my Country.—My Estate is ample, and unencumbred; I never had a Thought about your Fortune, and shall, with Rapture, receive your Commands to execute the proffer'd Settlement, without receiving a Shilling from your Father's Purse."——My only Reply was a Stream of Tears, and I think I discovered something very like a Moisture on the Cheeks of the generous *Philander*, who, with a just Indignation, instantly left the House.——This, Mr. *Trott-plaid*, is my real Case. Under a Weight of unmerited Woe, I call aloud for your Protection and Advice.——You must know the Nature of the Crime committed by *Philander's* Ancestor: Was it really of so deep a Dye, as to stain the Honour of a Family in the Fourth Generation? If not, what Answer shall I make to his last Proposal? Surely, when Happiness and Honour invite, a Daughter has some Sort of Power to pursue the Path pointed out by her own Reason.——But where am I rambling?——Disobedience to a Parent's Will is certainly a Crime:—And yet perhaps there is a Law requiring an Exercise of that Will, by the Rules of

Justice. I am lost in Doubt.——Good, dear Mr. *Trott-plaid*, what is to be done by the unhappy

HONORIA HUNTER?

I think the Conduct which my fair Correspondent ought to pursue is so obvious, that it would be mere trifling to give her my Opinion; and I am convinced, that before these Moon-light Nights are over, any Advice of mine would be needless, and come too late.

Proceedings at the Court of Criticism, Thursday June 21.

The Court being sat, the Clerk proceeded to read the Remainder of the Quotation from Dean *Prideaux*.[1]

"All the Difficulty in this Proposal will be to get the Clergy excused from being rated for their Benefices to the Parochial Poor. But since hereby the Clergy discharge the Parishes from so many Poor, as belong to them, it is but equitable, and reasonable, that the Parishes should discharge them, on the other hand, of so much of the Parish-Rates as is laid upon their Benefices, in order to maintain them. And the Widows and Children of Clergymen, when reduced to Poverty and Want, by their Decease, have a very just Claim to the publick Charity of the Nation, in that they, who left them in this Condition, died in the publick Service of it; and that especially since the Reason, why they were not better provided for by the Deceased, for the most part, is, because they themselves were not sufficiently provided for while living in the Station in which they served. Had not the State taken from the Church so much of its former Endowments, by impropriating them into Lay-Hands at the Time of the Reformation, Ministers would have been in a Condition to have provided for their Families themselves, and therefore the State being the Cause of that Poverty, in which Clergymen so often leave their Families behind them when they die, I reckon they are under a more than ordinary Obligation to take care of a suitable Provision for them. To turn them over to the Allowance of the Parochial Poor, will be too hard for Persons of their Condition. The Character of those they were so nearly related to, and the Rank which the Dignity of their Function did put them in, while they were living, do require,

---

[1] See *JJ* no. 29, above, pp. 314–15. *GM*, xviii (1748), 274, prints a condensed version of the extract from Prideaux, 'From the *Jacobite Journal*, June 18 and 25'.

that they should be maintained in a better manner than this, after their Decease. It was a Rule of Charity among the *Jews*,* that if a Person of the better Rank should fall into Poverty and Want, he was to be relieved in a manner suitable to his former Condition; and there is Reason for it, because when Men have been habituated to a plentiful and opulent Way of living all their Lives past, they will need more Things, even for the necessary Support of Life, than other People, who have been more hardily bred; and therefore, if allowed no more than what is given the meaner Sort, barely to keep them from starving, they cannot be maintained by it. And therefore since the Character of the Minister, while he lived, the Dignity of his Function, and his Station in the publick Service of the Church, in which he minister'd, did put him and his Family above the ordinary Sort of People, it is reasonable that his Wife and Children, which he leaves behind him at his Decease, if afterwards reduced to Want, should be considered and provided for in a Manner suitable to their former Condition; and not be brought down so low, as to be put on the same Level with the meanest of Beggars, and the vilest Scum of the People in a Parochial Allowance. As this will be a Disgrace to the Function, and a Dishonour to the Order, of which the Person was, to whom they were so nearly related, so also will it not only be insufficient to relieve their Need, but moreover carry with it such a Load of Indignity, and Contempt upon the Persons themselves, as none of them, considering their former Condition, will ever be able to bear or submit to. And therefore, as long as there is no Provision for them, but in such a Way as this, which they cannot accept of, and which also would be insufficient for them if they could, it is the same thing as if they were not provided for at all; and it still lies upon the Nation to take that Care of them, which Charity and Justice do require. And in what better Method can it be done, than in this, which I now offer unto you? For if they be put into the Hands of the Clergy themselves to take care of them, you may be sure they will be provided for in such a suitable and sufficient Manner, as every one of them will be glad to accept of, and so all will be fully relieved, and comfortably supported by it. And what less can the Nation do towards it, than appropriate what the Ministers usually pay for their Benefices to the Rates for the Parochial Poor, for

* Maimonides in Tract. Metanoth Anijim, cap. 10.

this Purpose? We do not ask a new Rate, or a new Tax for this Charity; but only a Part of that which is already established, and this for the Maintenance of a Part of the Nation's Poor, which they are bound to provide for, as well as the other. Neither do we ask any Ease for the Clergy in this Matter, because if they take upon them the whole Charge of providing for the Clergy's Poor, that is, for the Widows and Children of Clergymen deceased, that are left in Want, and do it in such a manner as is suitable to their Condition, as well as their Needs, as it ought to be done, the Expences which the Clergy must be at herein, will rather exceed than any way fall short of that which they are now charged with in the Poors-Rates of their Parishes. And therefore what can be more reasonable and just than that, when they take upon them, in the Manner as I have proposed, the Burden of wholly providing for the former Sort of Poor, they be wholly exempted from being charged any thing to the latter; and that at the same time they discharge the Laity of the Poor, which they take into their Care, the Laity discharge them of the other? For otherwise the Clergy will be charged double to what others are charged only single, which is by no means intended by this Proposal."

The Court will give their Opinion in our next.

(*Adjourned.*)

SATURDAY, JULY 2, 1748.   NUMB. 31.

——*Nil ortum tale.*

Horace.[1]

It is not only unfair, but highly injudicious to deny to an Adversary the Possession of such Excellencies as appear in him in the most eminent Degree. An Endeavour of this Kind is not, indeed, so injurious to him as it is affronting to our Reader, whose Senses and Understanding are thus very grosly contradicted; and the Lie is flatly given to that Opinion, which he must have necessarily preconceived.

For this Reason I have often thought Mr. *Pope's* Resentment hurried him too far, when he attempted to persuade the World

[1] *Epistles*, II. i. 17: 'nothing like you . . . has arisen' (Loeb).

that Mr. *Cibber* was a dull Fellow.¹ Had he scrutinized very narrowly into his Works, he might possibly have found some Objection, which might have given my Friend more Trouble to refute;² but when he was arraigned of Dulness, every Man of his Acquaintance was ready to bear Testimony of his Side, and the Accusation retorted all the Ridicule on the Accuser.³

Whether it proceeds from the Fairness of my Temper, or from Judgment, I will not determine; but I have, in the Course of my Writings, been extremely cautious to avoid this Error. So far, indeed, from doing any glaring Injustice to the Authors whom I have opposed, or from shocking any Preconception of my Reader in their Favour, I have never offered to animadvert on a single Imperfection, which hath not been as visible (to use a common Expression) as Light; or rather as Darkness, in the Divine Language of Milton.⁴ Indeed I have often thought that they themselves must, in their cooler Hours, acknowledge my great Candour towards them; since I do not remember to have said more of them, than that they are obscure unknown Scribblers, who appear, from their Works, to be neither Gentlemen nor Scholars; and that their Writings contain neither Wit nor Humour, Sentiment nor Language, Truth nor Politeness; every Word of which their greatest Admirers must certainly admit to be evident.

I shall now extend my Courtesy a little farther to these Writers, and will make use of that stubbed Broom which one of them last Winter put into my Hand;⁵ with which I will sweep out the

---

¹ Colley Cibber (1671–1757), actor, dramatist, theatre manager, and in 1748 still poet laureate, was installed by Pope as the 'more considerable Hero' of the *Dunciad in Four Books* (1743), replacing Lewis Theobald, hero of the earlier versions. Fielding reverts to the example of Cibber's conviction of dulness in the *Dunciad*; see *Journal of a Voyage to Lisbon*, *sub* Monday [July 22].

² No friend to Cibber in 1748, Fielding generally attacked him for supposed defects of character (vanity, sycophancy, sexual promiscuity), or of style and idiom. However, in *CGJ* no. 10 of 4 February 1752 Cibber's management of Drury Lane is said to have been characterized by a deliberate suppression of talented younger actors. For a survey of his relations with Fielding see *Joseph Andrews*, I. i. 18 n.

³ Contemporary opinion seems to support Fielding in this assertion. Much of the published criticism of the *Dunciad* in the eighteenth century argued that Pope had made a faulty conviction of Cibber in this respect; see *The Dunciad*, ed. James Sutherland (London, 1953), pp. xxxvi, xliii, and W. L. MacDonald, *Pope and His Critics* (London, 1951), pp. 206–10.					⁴ *Paradise Lost*, I. 63.

⁵ A letter signed 'Porcupinus Pelagius' in *OE* of 5 March 1748 describes 'Trott-Plaid' as 'busying himself in the Kennel, with his Stump-Broom in his Hand'.

Kennel as clean as possible, in order to see if nothing of any Value can be found at the Bottom, since it is to be hoped that Monster never lived, which *Juvenal* tells us is,

——*nulla virtute redemptum*
          A vitiis.[1]

And here, I think, I discern a very eminent Degree of Spirit. I do not mean that kind of Spirit which is supposed to constitute a Writer; but that which is, perhaps, the principal Ingredient in the Composition of a Hero. That Courage, which, according to Mr. *Pope,*

—— *knows no Fears*
Of Hisses, Blows, or Length or Loss of Ears.[2]

This great Virtue is indeed as manifest in most of our Writers at present, as any of the beforementioned little Imperfections can possibly be, and I might fairly appeal to their whole Works for the Proof of it. I shall however produce one Instance of a most notable Kind, and to which, I believe, no Age can boast a Parallel. It was transcribed from the Works of one *Fool* into those of another, and was published in the *London Evening-Post* of *Saturday, June* 13.[3]

          From the FOOL. N°. 295.
Dear Coz,

I send you underneath a few Lines, found upon the Door of the H—— of C——, which I suppose was intended for their Knowledge and Service, and therefore hope your inserting them will oblige them, as well as,

                    Dear Coz,

                              Yours,

                                        BRITANNICUS.

"In antient Times this Honour'd H—se did hold
Men who preferr'd their Country's Good to Gold;
But now, alas! this Sacred H—se contains

---

[1] *Satires*, iv. 2–3: 'of wickedness without one redeeming virtue' (Loeb).

[2] *Dunciad* (1728), i. 44–5; (1743), i. 47–8: 'knows no fears /Of hisses, blows, or want, or loss of ears'.

[3] An error for the issue of 16–18 June 1748. The 'Britannicus' letter and the 'few Lines' of poetry which follow are reprinted accurately from this issue of *LEP*. The 'castrated Words' are: House of Commons, Walpole, Pelham.

Those who would sell their very God for Gains;
If any Fool, inquisitive, should pray
To know the Reason of this great Decay;
W–lp—e began, and *P——m* plays his Part,
To fix Corruption's Standard in their Heart.
Evil is put for Good, and Bitter, Sweet;
And ev'ry Virtue does Oppression meet:
They've introduced a most luxurious Way,
That far exceeds the Income of the Day,
Which makes these Wretches poor, and hunger after Pay." }

What can be bolder, or more full of Spirit, than for two obscure News-Writers to fly in the Face of a third Part of the Legislature? (to omit the Libel not only against the Dead,[1] but against one of the greatest Men now alive;) and very plainly to assert that the Standard of Corruption is fixed in their Heart; that they put Evil for Good, and Bitter for Sweet; that they oppress every Virtue; that they are poor Wretches, hungering after Pay, and would sell their very God for Gains?

This, I say, is here very boldly and plainly asserted; for as to the castrated Words, they might as safely have been writ at Length; since there is scarce a single Fool who is not capable of supplying the omitted Letters; and (as it was once well said in the *King's-Bench*, in the Case of a Libel) it would be hard that the four Judges there should be the greatest Blockheads in the Kingdom, and the only Persons incapable of understanding what an Author meant.[2]

I think I may challenge the World to give an Example of Candour equal to what I have shewn on this Occasion; since the Spirit I have mentioned is certainly the only Semblance of Good which can be extracted from these Lines; and the Office I have undertaken, may not improperly be compared to that of extracting Spirit from Ordure: For surely the Idea which I have here kindly assigned, no more appears to the common Reader, than

---

[1] Sir Robert Walpole had died on 18 March 1745. Pelham is censured, in the *LEP* poem, for acting like Walpole's creature in his management of the House of Commons.

[2] Not identified. Although a printed source cannot be ruled out, Fielding may have been drawing on the MSS. of his maternal grandfather, Sir Henry Gould; see William B. Coley, 'Henry Fielding's "Lost" Law Book', *MLN*, lxxvi (1961), 408–13. The apparently determinative function of the judges implies a case of seditious libel or perhaps *scandalum magnatum*.

the Idea of Gin doth on viewing any of the Filth from which it is said to be often distilled.[1]

The first Thought which must occur to the most friendly Reader, on perusing the abovementioned Lines, is, that they are some of the worst which were ever writ, and do truly lie at the very Bottom of the *Bathos*; deeper indeed than either *Sternhold* or *Hopkins*, or any Bellman in the Kingdom, ever dived.[2]

The next Thing apparent is the Abuse; and here let me observe, that every one will not have sufficient Candour and Good-Nature to interpret this in the same favourable manner with myself: What I have termed Spirit, they will, I am afraid, be apt to call Impudence; for, tho' it may be thought a little too severe, it would surely be no Injustice to see it in that Light.

A third Idea which may arise is, that this flagrant Kind of Scurrility is really very impolitic, as it tends rather to serve the Party at whom it is levelled, and to injure only that which can be thought to vent or to espouse such Stuff; for unless we can suppose the Nation to be sunk into the lowest Abyss of Stupidity, as well as Rancour, we must imagine, however keen may be their Appetite for Scandal, they will reject such coarse Food, which must indeed turn the Stomach of the most Indelicate.

However as I have, for once, undertaken the Cause of these Gentlemen, I will endeavour to take off the Edge of all those Aspersions, which, I am convinced, great Numbers of Persons must have cast on them and their Works; particularly on the little Poem I have here inserted.

And here, tho' I must agree that this Poem is as bad as it is possible to represent it, yet why should we not suppose the

[1] *OED*, s.v. 'Geneva', cites Sir J. Hill, *Mat. Med.* (1751), II. v. xxi. 487: 'but at present only a better Kind [of] that is made with the Juniper Berry, what they commonly sell is made with no better an Ingredient than Oil of Turpentine . . . and with the coarsest Spirit they have.' Fielding had a considerable contemporary reputation of expertise in the matter. *LEP* of 9–11 June 1748 prints a poem entitled 'On the Parodies in the *Jacobite's Journal*', the last line of which refers to 'Trott-Plaid's "fav'rite Gin" '.

[2] Thomas Sternhold (d. 1549) and John Hopkins (d. 1570), joint versifiers of a metrical version of the Psalms which was still enormously popular in the eighteenth century, were ridiculed by Dryden, Rochester, Pope, and others as the very models of inferior poets. Cf. Pope to Swift, 15 October 1725: 'My name is as bad an one as yours, and hated by all bad Poets from Hopkins and Sternhold to Gilden and Cibber'; *Correspondence of Alexander Pope*, ed. George Sherburn (Oxford, 1956), ii. 334. For the identity of the 'Bellman', see *JJ* no. 1, above, p. 96 and note 5 there. As bad poets, all three are here associated with the Art of the *Bathos*, or Profund'; see Pope's *Peri Bathous* (1728), Ch. IV. Fielding attributed this Scriblerian work to Swift; *CGJ* no. 18 of 3 March 1752.

Author himself intended it to be so? I believe there have been few Writers capable of writing any thing so ill, tho' they endeavoured it never so earnestly and heartily; and shall we imagine that this Author could by chance, nay, even against his own Will, arrive at such an Excellence in the Profound! Sir *Richard Steele* profess'd that he was often dull by Design;[1] and what is more natural than to think, that the Author of the above Lines had the same dull Design, in order the more to degrade and vilify those who are the Subjects of his Satire? This is agreeable to a Rule of *Longinus*, which hath been practiced by many great Wits.[2]

The Abuse I likewise acknowledge to be as gross as the most malicious Critic can insinuate; but surely this can never be deemed Impudence, while the Author hath the Caution to conceal himself. Had he set his Name to such a Poem, I allow, he would have been the most impudent of all Men; but on the contrary, so modest are all these Authors, and such especial Care have they taken to conceal themselves, that they have never, I believe, exposed their Names to twenty Persons in the whole Kingdom.

And as to the last Surmise, that such rank Scurrility is prejudicial to the Party which it espouses; if I grant this likewise, how can it be called impolitic in Men, who can be supposed to be no more attached, either in Interest or Affection, to one Party than to another? The certain Fact is, that these Authors write with no other View than to get their daily Bread; an End which is undoubtedly good and justifiable; and so will the Means be, in Proportion, as they can injure and expose the wicked Party whose Cause they pretend to espouse. For though in the Properties of *Great-Britain* these Men have no Concern, and some of them, I am afraid, but very little in the Liberties, yet I am convinced they are not so vicious and depraved in their Hearts, as to desire to ruin or enslave the Nation. Their only Design is to eat; and Men

---

[1] For example, in *Tatler* no. 38 (7 July 1709) and no. 234 (7 October 1710). Steele's profession of deliberate dulness is alluded to in *The Champion* of 22 May 1740; *Tom Jones*, v. i; and *CGJ* no. 1 of 4 January 1752.

[2] Probably to *Peri Hupsous* ('On the Sublime'), xv. 11: 'By a sort of natural law in all such matters we always attend to whatever possesses superior force . . . And it is not unreasonable that we should be affected this way, for when two things are brought together, the more powerful always attracts to itself the virtue of the weaker'; *Longinus on the Sublime*, ed. & trans. W. Rhys Roberts (Cambridge, 1935), p. 91. Cf. *Peri Bathous*, Ch. v, p. 19: 'He ought therefore to render himself Master of this happy and antinatural way of thinking to such a degree, as to be able, on the appearance of any Object, to furnish his Imagination with Ideas infinitely below it'; and *Tom Jones*, v. i.

who are obliged to rake their Bread out of the Dirt of *Grub-street* and *Billingsgate*, are rather to be pitied than detested.

In this Light they have hitherto been seen by the noble Persons at whom they have so long endeavoured to throw their Dirt; but at so great a Distance, that they have not once been able to reach or annoy them: For this must be acknowledged by the most malicious Enemy of the present Administration, either that they have no Power to punish Offences of this Kind, which surely none will say, or that they have overlook'd them with a Lenity and Dignity, not to be parallel'd in History.

Proceedings at the Court of Criticism, Thursday June 30.

His Honour was pleased to deliver the following Opinion, in the Cause of the Widows and Children of Clergymen.[1]

There is no Nation, I believe, where public and private Charity have more nobly prevailed, than in this Kingdom;[2] and yet it is as lamentable as strange a Truth, that this generous and truly Christian Spirit, hath been so generally misguided, as seldom or never to be directed to its most proper Objects; which, to me, appear to be those Widows and Children of Gentlemen, who, from the adverse Fortunes, or sometimes, perhaps, through the Faults of a Husband and Father, are left in the most distressful and destitute Circumstances.

How much more these are the Objects of Compassion and Charity than those of the lowest and meanest Rank, who are understood to be included under the General Name of the Poor, can possibly be, will appear from many Considerations.

For, in the first Place, such Poor have no Wants beyond those Necessities which would arise in a pure and simple State of Nature; and these are so few, and so easily supplied, that, in a well-regulated Society, scarce an Individual, unless from Sickness, Lameness, Old Age, or Infancy, can be destitute of them. And for the Support of Persons under any of these Disabilities, so small a Fund is really necessary, that it can hardly be supposed, even if there was no legal Provision, but that a Nation, where

---

[1] First raised in *JJ* no. 21, above, pp. 251–4, and continued in the 'Court of Criticism' in *JJ* nos. 29 and 30, above, pp. 313–15, 320–2.

[2] Cf. Fielding's *Enquiry into the Causes of the late Increase of Robbers* (1751), section iv, esp. pp. 31–2; and his *Proposal for Making an Effectual Provision for the Poor* (1753), Introduction, pp. 8–11.

Christianity is established, and where Good-Nature so remarkably flourishes, would voluntarily contribute what would be abundantly sufficient for their Sustenance and Preservation.

On the contrary, Education and Habit may add greatly to those Wants, with which we are at first born, and may make many Things, without Affectation, or Delicacy, or Extravagance, absolutely requisite, not only to our Well-being, but even to the Preservation of our Being itself. Hence the mere Necessaries of Life, to Persons who have been educated and have lived in a superior Manner to the Vulgar, do greatly exceed those of the lowest Poor, and must, consequently, require a larger Fund to provide for them; a Fund, to which as the Superfluities of their wealthy Neighbours can never be adequate, we cannot expect to see often effectually supplied by any voluntary Contribution.

Again, if Persons so educated could reduce their Wants to the Standard of the lowest Vulgar, and would willingly condescend to supply themselves by the same Labour; they are, in general, absolutely disqualified for it, by the Tenderness and superior Delicacy in which they have lived; and while they really want much more, they would be enabled to gain much less than the meanest of the Poor; to whom, moreover, they are as inferior in Skill, as they are in Strength. Nor are Persons of Condition in Distress, from bodily Wants only more miserable, and more the Objects of Compassion, than the ordinary parochial Poor. How much more tender are the Sensations, which more refined and polish'd Minds are capable of feeling! What must be their Sense of that Contempt and Shame to which the most sordid Degree of Poverty, however unjustly, subjects them! With what Agonies, what Heart-akes must they behold those innocent, helpless Babes, on whom they have entailed a State of such exquisite Misery!

There is one Circumstance too, in which the Case of an impoverish'd Gentlewoman must seem most remarkably deplorable. Society affords many Professions and Trades, to which Men may apply themselves, to procure a bare and common Sustenance at least; nay some, by great Abilities and Industry, have, from the lowest Condition, risen to great Prosperity and Affluence: But the Fate of a Gentlewoman is much harder. Every Profession, and almost every Trade is shut against her, and she hath no Method of acquiring a Livelihood, but what is too shocking to mention; and yet, shocking as it is, many have, by absolute Necessity, been driven to it; and thus the younger and handsomer have been exposed to Vice and Shame,[1] while others, without any possible Resource, have been abandoned to Beggary, to Starving, to Goals, and to broken Hearts.

Is it not therefore astonishing, that in a Nation where, besides many voluntary Charities, at least two Millions in a Year are raised for the Support of the lowest Poor,[2] not one public Charity (except to the Widows of Officers)[3] should subsist, in Behalf of the Objects I have here pointed out; and, indeed, very few Benefactions of a private Kind.[4]

What I have hitherto said, may seem equally to affect the Case of all Gentlewomen and their Children in Distress; I now come to consider more particularly the Widows and Children of the Clergy.

The Remainder of this Speech will be in our next.

SATURDAY, JULY 9, 1748. NUMB. 32.

I know my Friend Mr. *Adams*[5] so well, that I am convinced he will pardon the few Alterations I have made in the following Letter, which I shall now communicate to the Public.

[1] On the tendency of daughters of clergymen to become vicious through want, see *JJ* no. 32, below, p. 338, and Fielding's note in *Tom Jones*, IV. xiv.

[2] If this statement be taken in its literal sense as excluding proceeds from donative or 'voluntary Charities', the figure seems high. In his *Proposal for . . . the Poor*, Introduction, p. 9, Fielding estimates the poor rate for the nation at roughly £1 million, a figure which has been accepted by a modern authority, Dorothy Marshall, in *The English Poor in the Eighteenth Century* (London, 1926), p. 77. Cf. B. R. Mitchell, *Abstract of British Historical Statistics*, p. 410, where an average annual figure for the years 1748–50 is estimated at £730,000.

[3] See *JJ* no. 21, above, p. 252.

[4] For example, the annual 'Feast of the Sons of the Clergy', which in 1748 was held on May 5 with proceeds of £907; as reported by *GM*, xviii (1748), 234.

[5] Abraham Adams, the 'Parson Adams' of *Joseph Andrews*. It is just possible that the reference to 'Alterations . . . in the following Letter' ought to be taken seriously, in which case the letter might have been written by Fielding's learned friend William Young (1702 ?– 57), the original of Parson Adams and, possibly, an assistant on the *JJ*.

To JOHN TROTT-PLAID, *Esq;*

*

Sir,

Going to dine with Mr. *Booby*[1] in *Whitson-Holidays*,[2] I happened to observe two *Dissertations* of yours lying in his Hall-Window. In one of these you labour to assign the Etymology of a late favourite Title in some Parts of *Great-Britain*, that of *Jacobite*.[3]———And in the other you run a Parallel between the People of this Sect and that of the *Jews*.[4]

With regard to your Parallel, I freely allow you that both these Sects look upon the Governments they live under to be damnable, that they are both alike stubborn, and both equally superstitious. But here I think it my Duty to observe, that your Derivation of the Word *Jacobite* is neither agreeable to your usual Penetration, nor to the Analogy of language. You draw it from *Jacchus* or *Bacchus*. Now although your Conjecture may be so far approved, as some Authors affirm that *Bacchus* had two Mothers—Or as others, that he dropt from his Sire's Thigh, without any Mother at all[5]—Or farther, as they all agree, that in the Celebration of his Festivals *Bacchus* makes his Sons and Servants frantic and foolish —Yet, Sir, let me tell you, had this Sect been derived from him, they had been stiled *Jacchites*. The middle Syllable in *Jacobites* could never have got into the place where it now stands.———And, pray Sir, show a little Respect to the Rules of Grammar, in this Case.———Well, therefore, according to all those Rules, the Word must come from *Jacob*—(in *Hebrew*)—which is, in plain *English*, a *Supplanter*. And here, Sir, you have both the Name and Thing —and all our Rules entire. Beside, apply we to them likewise

---

* Note, *The Motto being in* Hebrew, *neither Mr.* Trottplaid *nor his Printer could read it.*

[1] Nephew of Lady Booby and the late Sir Thomas Booby, and husband of the 'charming Pamela', he had 'presented Mr. *Adams* with a Living of one hundred and thirty Pounds a Year'; *Joseph Andrews*, IV. xvi. 344.

[2] The holidays associated with, and usually following, Whit Sunday, the seventh Sunday after Easter, which is observed as a festival of the Christian Church in commemoration of the descent of the Holy Spirit on the Day of Pentecost. In 1748 Whit Sunday fell on 29 May. [3] See *JJ* no. 6, above, pp. 122–7.

[4] See *JJ* no. 25, above, pp. 281–7.

[5] For the covert allusion here to the so-called 'Warming-Pan' episode, see *JJ* no. 6, above, p. 125 and note 5 there. This and the two adjacent affirmations concerning Bacchus are derived from Abbé Banier's *Mythology* and applied satirically to the Old Pretender, in *JJ* no. 6, above, pp. 125–7.

what *Abigail* said of *Nabal, As his Name is, so is He. Nabal is his Name, and Folly is with him.*[1]——So, Mr. *Trottplaid*, say I of these Gentlemen,—*Jacobites* is their Name, and Supplanters they are.

I have often lamented your Ignorance of the *Hebrew*; to which Ignorance alone it must be owing that you missed so plain an Etymology; an Etymology which would have opened to you their whole Character. You would not then, my Friend, have been content with observing (as you do) that these People are *ever looking and hoping for* the Destruction of the Government.[2] You would have found them in their Synagogues, not supinely looking, but zealously and fervently *praying for* our Destruction. ——You would have seen them in common Life, not barely *hoping*, but urging and exhorting, swearing and forswearing, writing and fighting for our Ruin.

As this Sect resembles the *Jews*, then, in deriving from *Jacob*— So you see, Sir, they differ from them too as they still retain the original patriarchal Name; while, on the other hand, the *Jews* reject it, and glory in the Stile of *Israel.*[3] A material Distinction this, between the one and the other: For as, by their Conduct, these *Supplanters* prove themselves the Sons of *Jacob*; why might not the Foresight of their Behaviour give one Occasion of the Patriarch's Name being changed into *Israel?*——Had he been called, during Life, by his first Name, his Posterity after him had all equally to this Day have been dignified by the Title of *Jacobites*. But had this been the Case, please to observe, Sir, what had been the Consequence?——Instead of an *Israelite* indeed—*Nathaniel* must have been pronounced a *Jacobite* indeed, (*i.e.* a *Supplanter*) in whom is no Guile![4]—With what Face, think you, could I have read with an audible Voice, either from the Desk or the Pulpit, such a glaring Contradiction to the Experience of my People? What *Polyglotts* and *Synopses* must I have consulted? How must I have expounded the Text quite away, before I could remove the Offence which every modest Ear would take at it? What Matter of Triumph would such a Text have afforded to the *Jacobites?* And, on the other hand, how would even the Infidels glory in

---

[1] 1 Samuel xxv. 25. In Hebrew *Nabal* means 'fool'.

[2] Cf. *JJ* no. 25, above, p. 283: 'But, on the contrary, are daily hoping and looking for their Destruction.'

[3] Genesis xxxii. 28: 'And he said, Thy name shall be called no more Jacob, but Israel.'

[4] John i. 47: 'Jesus saw Nathanael coming to him, and saith of him, Behold an Israelite indeed, in whom is no guile!'

comparing the Inconsistency of *Jacobitical* Conduct with such a Declaration?——But as by a timely Change of *Jacob's* Name there is this happy Difference made between this Sect and that of the *Jews*; so you perceive, Sir, by the same Means, are we of the Clergy, and all his Majesty's good Subjects, happily delivered from all these Embarrassments; and the Mouths of Gainsayers effectually stopp'd.[1]——And give me Leave to tell you, Sir, that I have had the Honour to receive both Mr. and Mrs. *Booby's* Compliments upon this Discovery, and their Congratulations too upon this Deliverance.

To proceed, therefore:—From what I have advanced it appears, that the Character of *Supplanting* is the true Mark of a *Jacobite*. And let me add, it is the *only true and essential one*—and that all the other Marks, you mention, are not definitive of, but only contingent to that Sect.

Thus, for Instance, they may (beside the Reason you assign for their wearing party-colour'd Coats)[2] affect therein to imitate the Coat of *Jacob's* favourite Son[3]—(and it would be little Cruelty, I presume, if they, like him, were sold for Slaves on that Account:) —But then, like Friars of different Orders, you may spy *Jacobites* too cloathed in every Kind of Habit. The most inveterate and poisonous Sort of them are found, I believe, on the Banks of the River *Isis*—and are commonly seen in black—*Hic niger est.*[4] Others, I am told, are sometimes seen in more costly Attire; so that by their Garments you cannot distinguish them; and these Garments serve to hide that Mark in the Flesh with which, as I learn from your Writings, they have chosen to distinguish themselves since they were smote at *Culloden*.[5] Indeed it is well they wear the Mark of any Religion; for a Rebel to such a Government as ours is at present, bears no Mark of a Christian about him.

---

[1] Cf. Titus i. 9–11; Luke xxi. 15.

[2] See *JJ* no. 25, above, p. 284.

[3] Genesis xxxvii. 3: 'Now Israel loved Joseph more than all his children, because he *was* the son of his old age: and he made him a coat of *many* colours.' Another satirical allusion to the late and unexpected birth of the Old Pretender, only child of James II and Mary of Modena, in 1688.

[4] Horace, *Satires*, I. iv. 85: 'that man is black of heart' (Loeb). The topical application is to the black gowns worn by the Oxford academicals; see *JJ* no. 17, above, p. 212. Fielding uses this Horatian tag as the epigraph of his *Proper Answer*.

[5] The general circumcision 'supposed' to have been performed by Jacobites after the 'Massacre'; see *JJ* no. 25, above, p. 284.

Howbeit nevertheless this Sign, for the Reason above-mentioned, can never sufficiently demonstrate them; and indeed, all the others by which you have endeavoured to point them out are like the popish Marks of the true Church, uncertain and indeterminate. The only full and adequate Notion of their Character is, that they are by Nature, or at least by Principle, SUPPLANTERS. This alone can account for their endeavouring to supplant one of the best Governments under Heaven.——This alone can account for their attempting foolishly to rob themselves, and wickedly to deprive their Country of her Liberties and her Religion: A Character so particular, that neither *Jew*, nor *Gentile*, nor any, but themselves, can be their Parallel.

Among the *Gentiles* I have read of an honest *Socrates*; in *Nathaniel* a *Jew* was found without Guile; and in the Pale of the *Papists*, *Erasmus* was a good plain-spoken Man.——But of *Jacobites* (by the very Term) none can be righteous, no not one. King *David* was tolerably well acquainted with them and their Cabals; when he could say, *Deceit and Guile go not out of their Streets*. That in the Evening they return, grin like a Dog, and run about through the City.——*They run*, says he, *here and there for Meat, and grudge* (or *stay all Night*, as the Margin has it) *if they be not satisfied.*[1]

Their History, therefore, from first to last, is comprehended, as I may say, in their Title-page. And what *Job* said of his three Comforters, may, with great Propriety, be affirmed of *Jacobites* in general, *Miserable Deceivers and Supplanters are ye all.*[2]

There are, 'tis said, at this Time, in the eastern Parts of the World, near 50000 Families of *Jacobites*; the most learned of whom did formerly profess Obedience to the Pope, and do still (like their brethren in *Europe*) differ from the *Roman Catholics* merely in Expression.[3] They circumcize their Children, moreover, and (because the Baptist foretold that the Messiah should baptize—*with fire*)[4] they also baptize their Children by applying a

---

[1] Psalms lv. 11 and lix. 6, 14, 15.   [2] Job xvi. 2. Cf. *Tom Jones*, XIV. iii.

[3] Members of a Monophysite Christian sect of Syria and Mesopotamia taking its name from Jacobus Baradaeus of Edessa, who revived the Eutychian heresy that the human nature of Christ was lost in the divine. The Jacobites acknowledged a patriarch of Antioch as their head and used a liturgical rite also used by Syrian Christians in submission to Rome, which, although it regarded the Jacobites as heretical, did in fact recognize Jacobite orders and sacraments.

[4] Matthew iii. 2, and Luke iii. 16.

red-hot Iron to their Foreheads.¹ Now I could here wish, methinks, that we had a Law, or that without a Law our *Jacobites*
would use the same Ceremony of Indiction²: That whereas their
Forehead appears only cloudy and gloomy, (*ceu marsya victus*)³ we
might, by such a Mark in their Front, recognize them, at first
Blush, for Fire-brands and Incendiaries.——But what I would
chiefly observe here, is, that however the several Branches of this
extensive Family may otherwise differ; at least they all agree, *in
eodem tertio*,⁴ in the fundamental Doctrine of supplanting and
undermining—By which all Commentators understand—not
barely tripping up their Neighbour's Heels, (*flinging him*, as the
modern Phrase is) and deceiving him to his Damage—but over-
throwing the Foundations on which all Society stands, and
destroying Order, Law, and Liberty itself.

But I have already filled up my Portion of Paper. I shall
reserve, therefore, what I have farther to say till some other
Opportunity.——I cannot, however, conclude, without expressing to you my sanguine Hopes of seeing the Day, when the
unfair Practice of *Supplanting* (like that of Smuggling)⁵ will be
abolished—When there shall be a Conversion of this Sect; and
Jacobitism be no more. You seem to apprehend this Day as very
distant: But be of good Courage, Sir.—A northern Correspondent of mine tells me, that out of 200 officiating Ministers of
that Profession in *Scotland*, there have lately a whole Half-dozen
submitted.⁶ A great Point gain'd, my Friend! A noble Prospect

¹ *OED*, s.v. 'Jacobite', cites Ephraim Pagitt, *Heresiographie*, ed. of 1661, p. 21: 'The
Iacobites . . . mark their children with a hot Iron with the signe of the Cross, alluding to
the words of Saint John.'

² 'indication'. This obsolete usage is almost a century later than that cited by *OED*.

³ Juvenal, *Satires*, ix. 2 (*ceu Marsya victus*): 'like a vanquished Marsyas' (Loeb).
Marsyas, satyr and musician, challenged Apollo to a contest of music, lost, and was
flayed alive. His statue in the Forum was apparently noted for its expression of pain; see
Horace, *Satires*, I. vi. 119–21.

⁴ 'in the same third [case or point]', the previous two, in which they do not agree, being,
presumably, circumcision and baptism.

⁵ Smuggling was much publicized in the press after the notorious Hawkhurst gang
broke open the customs house at Poole (Dorset) on 7 October 1747 and later tortured to
death two witnesses who intended to testify against them; Lord Teignmouth and Charles
G. Harper, *The Smugglers* (London, 1923), i. 50–112; and *GM*, xvii (1747), 494, 591, and
xviii (1748), *passim*.

⁶ Cf. Hansard, xiv. 277, where during debate on an amendment to an Act of 1746
relating to letters of ordination for episcopal ministers in Scotland, Lord Hardwicke is
reported to have said, 'from the list on our table it appears, that in all Scotland there were
but six episcopal ministers that took the oath in pursuance of that act.' The debate in the

this! Hail ye First-fruits[1] of a general Harvest! Six Converts, already, out of 200! And they Ministers too.——Why, Sir, six a Week will bring in the whole Number by next *Easter*; and never fear, but their Flocks will soon follow their Shepherds. From this Beginning, moreover, I hope for some Concessions of the like Kind in the southern Part of the Island; and in this Hope I do and will rejoice, and desire you, Sir, also to rejoice, with your hearty old Friend,

ABRAHAM ADAMS.

From my Study, the 11th of June,
  being the Day of his Majesty's Accession.[2]

Proceedings at the Court of Criticism, Thursday June 30.

Conclusion of the Speech begun in our last.

First, then, the Families of the Clergy seem more especially to deserve our Consideration, as it much more frequently happens to them, than to any others, to be left in this distress'd and destitute Condition: Of which the Reasons are as obvious as the Fact is certain. I shall mention only one; which is, that great Numbers being raised to the Rank of Gentlemen, by taking upon them the sacerdotal Office, can be supposed to bring with them no hereditary Fund, nor to have any other Means of living than what this Office supplies them with. And this, in many thousand instances, is so bare, that great Frugality only can enable them to discharge their own ordinary and requisite Expences. It is hardly possible for these poor Clergymen to support a Family out of this scanty Income, much less can it be expected (even by the most rigid Man alive) that they should be capable of laying up a future Provision for their Wives and Children.

Now when, by the Death of such a Clergyman, the whole Income of his Family ceases, and they are left in the most extreme Poverty; the Hardship of their Case is, in one Circumstance, highly aggravated, beyond that of the Widow and Children of most other poor Gentlemen; for they are commonly as

Lords, which commenced on 10 May 1748, provoked considerable opposition among the bishops, who saw the amendment as a threat to the principle of episcopal ordination.

[1] A clerical allusion to the tax or payment, usually representing the amount of the first year's income, paid by each new holder of an ecclesiastical benefice to some superior, at this time the Crown.

[2] Of George II's accession to the throne in 1727. See *JJ* no. 30, above, p. 316, n. 4.

destitute of Friends as Money. They have no rich Relations, no proud Head of a Family, who thinks his Honour, at least, concerned, in preserving any Branches of his House from utter Beggary or Starving. The Father of this little Family was the first of his Name who ranked among Gentlemen. The utmost Assistance which his Relations could lend him, hath already been bestowed on his Education; and there is none among them, to whom his Widow can now apply for Relief.

And yet, notwithstanding the ill-natur'd or haughty Reflections which may here arise in the low-minded Pride of some, this Priest, however low his Extraction, was, by his Office, a Gentleman. Regard to this holy Office obliged him, when alive, to support some Dignity of Character, and some genteel Appearance, not only in himself, but in his Family. His Wife was to be maintained, and his Children educated in a Manner superior to what is practised by the Vulgar; or he himself must have sunk in the Opinion of all his Parishioners; he would have brought a Contempt on his sacred Function, and have lost all that Respect which every Man must preserve, who, with due Efficacy, will discharge the sacerdotal Duties.

From what has been said, it appears, that the Widows and Children of the inferior Clergy, are, of all others, most the Objects of Compassion; and that it is Want of common Humanity, in the Public, to neglect making any Provision for them.

But farther; not only Pity towards the Distrest, but a Regard to Religion, exacts such a Provision of us. Not only the Man of Piety; but even he who professes a decent Regard to Religion, as to a wholesome, civil Institution, must agree in the Necessity of preserving the Priesthood from the Contempt of the People. How inseparable Contempt is from Poverty, in a Nation where Riches are held in such Estimation as with us, requires, I think, no Reasoning nor Evidence to prove. Nor will it, I believe, be deny'd, that much of the Contempt attracted by these poor Wretches, will fix on the Order to which their Husbands and Fathers belonged. I do not affirm there is either Reason or Justice in this; nay, on the contrary, to despise Poverty itself, is surely very unjust and unreasonable; and so it is in Vice, which is the proper Object of Contempt and Abhorrence, to carry our Contempt and Abhorrence beyond the guilty Person. But will any Man deny that this is the constant Practice? Who hath not seen and heard Instances of this? What else is meant by the Phrase so common in every Mouth—That he is a Scandal to his Family, or a Scandal to his Profession? If Poverty reflected no Contempt beyond the poor Object himself, why are Men, as is observed above, who are apparently void of all Humanity on every other Occasion, so generally careful of preserving their Relations, and sometimes their very Name, from this Imputation? Or why are Monarchies, in which the Honour of the Nobility is zealously maintained, so watchful that none of that Order shall be subjected to Want or Beggary? I have often thought this was one Reason of that Policy in the Church of *Rome*, by which Marriage is inhibited to their Priests. And perhaps the Distresses which I would now propose to relieve, have brought more Contempt on our own Clergy, than hath been cast upon them by the utmost Malice of Infidels or Libertines. What more invidious Reflection can be invented on the whole Order, or what more wickedly calculated to degrade and debase it in the Minds of the People, than that vulgar (I hope false) Assertion, that the greatest Part of the *London* Prostitutes are the Daughters of Parsons.[1]

Upon the whole then I conclude, there never was any Charity more reasonable, nor, indeed, more necessary than this. It is, indeed, suggested to us by every Motive which can most forcibly operate on a humane, or a pious Mind, and must be heartily espoused by all those who have any sincere Regard for true Religion, or any Share of that benevolent and beneficent Disposition which our excellent Religion inspires, and of which it enjoins the Practice.

In promoting this Charity, I do not think the superior Clergy are, in truth, more concerned than the Laity. Every good Man hath an equal Interest in serving the Cause of his Religion, and in relieving the Distresses of his Fellow-Creatures; yet, in the Opinion of the World, it is thought to be more especially incumbent on every Order of Men, to promote the Good of that Order; and if they neglect this Duty, others will think themselves very easily excusable for not performing it. I doubt not, therefore, there will be found, among the higher Clergy, some who will

---

[1] Cf. *CGJ* no. 57 of 1 August 1752: 'whence are our Prostitutes themselves to be supplied? Most of these are Daughters of Parents, whom they have made miserable by their Infamy. Some of them are of good Families, and many, to the great Scandal of the Nation, the Offspring of the Clergy'. See also *JJ* no. 31, above, p. 330 and note 1 there.

patronize and adopt one or other of the Schemes which have been mentioned in this Paper; or invent some more effectual Scheme for the Purpose. Surely he is a very bad Man, of whatever Denomination he may be, who would oppose it: Nor can he be a very good one, who is not ready to set his Hands, and his Shoulders too, to so good a Work.

After which the Court was adjourned to *Thursday, July* 14.

SATURDAY, JULY 16, 1748.   NUMB. 33.

To JOHN TROTT-PLAID, *Esq;*

Sir,

> ——*What tho' the Field be lost?*
> *All is not lost; the unconquerable Will,*
> *And Study of Revenge, immortal Hate,*
> *And Courage never to submit or yield:*
> *(And what is else not to be overcome)*
> *That Glory never shall his Wrath or Might*
> *Extort from me.——*   Milton, *Book I.*[1]

The Lines I have chosen for my Motto, are a Part of Satan's Speech to the fallen Angels, after their final Overthrow and Exclusion from Heaven; and the Sentiments they contain are extremely suitable to the Character of that wicked Being who is supposed to utter them. 'Twas the Pride of his Heart, the Discontent of his Mind, and the Corruption of his Nature, joined to the vilest Ingratitude, that first prompted him to Rebellion against his Almighty Benefactor; and the terrible Destruction that overtook him, was so far from awakening his Mind to a Sense of his Crime, and Acknowledgment of his Sin, that he takes Occasion from thence to confirm himself and his Comrades in Wickedness; seems to gather Hope even from Despair, and adds to the Guilt he had already incurred, by a Resolution to practise greater.——A Degree of Folly and Madness beyond this it is impossible to conceive, and needless it is to enlarge on what is already the Subject of universal Detestation.

With Grief I am obliged to own that a recent Example, like in Kind, though different in Degree, as it recalled this Passage to my

---

[1] *Paradise Lost,* i. 105-11.

Mind, so it furnished me with Matter for the ensuing Speculation.

I wish, for the Honour of my native Country, I was not obliged to say, that there is a Party yet subsisting in this Land, who seem to have been actuated by the same diabolical Spirit: I wish that daily Experience did not too sadly convince us, that the same Study of Revenge, the same implacable Hatred, and a like Degree of Madness, did not still continue to terrify and distract us: But, alas, it is too notorious to be denied, that we have Men among us so degenerate, as openly to plead for Slavery; Men, who professing themselves Protestants, contribute all in their Power to introduce Popery: Who, sharing in common with their fellow Subjects the invaluable Blessings of Peace and Security, are so exceeding mad, as to attempt to destroy the one, and to render the other precarious, by reducing us to a State of Civil War, and by subjecting us and our Property to the lawless Will of an arbitrary Monarch, and to the relentless Cruelty of a bigotted Papist.

'Tis by this Time (I doubt not) obvious to every Reader, that in the foregoing Account I meant to describe their and their Country's avowed Enemies, the *Jacobites*; of whom, if they would not be thought to act from the Motives imputed to the evil Spirit in my Motto, I expect an Answer to the following Questions.——Are we not in the full Enjoyment of the most extensive Liberty, both Civil and Religious, that we ever could boast? Has any Encroachment been made on the Constitution— any Man's Property invaded—any known Law of the Land perverted—any new Tax laid—any Imposition imposed—unless by the free Consent and Approbation of the Representatives of the People? In a Word, is there any Grievance, or any Hardship, (except what our own Sins and the Malice of the *Jacobites* themselves have brought upon us) that might be, and yet is not, either redressed or removed?——Is not the Life, the Conscience, the Property of every Man secure?—Exempt from the Restraints to which, under arbitrary Governments, all these are subjected, either through the Caprice of their Monarchs, or the Imposition of their Priests?——Is it not the peculiar Happiness of our Times, that we may "Entertain what Sentiments we please, and freely declare the Sentiments we entertain?"[1]——May not every

---

[1] Cf. Tacitus, *Historiae*, I. i: *rara temporum felicitate ubi sentire quae velis et quae sentias dicere licet.*

Man (in the figurative Language of the Prophet) at this Day, *sit securely under his own Vine, and his own fig-tree, and none dare make him afraid?*[1]——If our Taxes have been multiplied, and our Burdens increased, hath not this been with our own free Consent, nay, at our unanimous Request, to prevent the most terrible of all Evils; and if not occasioned, have they not been heightened, by the restless Attempts and wicked Designs of the very Men I have been describing? Will the *Jacobites* fly openly in the Face of Truth, and deny all this? If not, to what can we impute the late Rebellion, or all their Murmurs and outragious Proceeding since, but to the Discontent and Wickedness, the implacable Hatred and revengeful Spirit, of these *Jacobites?*

Now, what might have been reasonably expected from the Men, who had so lately experienced the Folly and Rashness of their Undertaking, and afterwards had tasted, in so peculiar a Manner, the unexampled Clemency of their Sovereign?[2]—— Certainly the largest Returns of Gratitude, the deepest Sorrow for their former Misbehaviour, and a fixed Resolution to attone, by the Goodness of their future Demeanor, for the Wickedness of their past Conduct. How far this hath been the Case with a few, more immediately concerned, and what Influence Mercy hath had upon them, I know not; 'tis certain, as to the Party in general, it hath had no such due Effect on their Minds, or wrought any Alteration in their Conduct. It is evident, that they notwithstanding continue to embarrass and oppose the Government, with more Violence than ever; and dare even to depreciate that Clemency to which so many of their Associates owe their Lives. Indeed their present Behaviour too evidently discovers, that as no Defeat, however signal, can deter, so no Clemency, however unmerited and extensive, can reclaim them:—That they do in Truth too nearly resemble the Character of the evil Being abovementioned, whose principal and distinguishing Crimes were Revenge and Ingratitude. Instigated by this Spirit, they spare no

---

[1] Micah iv: 4: 'But they shall sit every man under his vine and under his fig tree; and none shall make *them* afraid.'

[2] The 'Act for the King's most gracious, general, and free Pardon', which received the royal assent on 17 June 1747; *Journals of . . . Commons*, xxv. 408. In his speech at the close of the session on 17 June the King implied that his clemency was intended to palliate the rigour of the trials and the corrective legislation which followed the putting down of the Jacobite rebellion; Hansard, xiv. 65. For the provisions of the Act (21 Geo. II, c. 52) see *Statutes at Large*, xix. 170–84.

Pains, and neglect no Means, to weaken and traduce that Government which they know they cannot subvert: To this End, by the vilest Misrepresentations, they calumniate the Ministry; by wicked Insinuations, nay, by the grossest and most manifest Lyes, they endeavour to raise the Jealousies, and to foment the Divisions and Discontents of the People; to seduce the Unwary, to impose on the Ignorant, and to allure and gain over Men of profligate Principles and desperate Circumstances; and 'tis with Grief I own that these Arts have hitherto been too successful.

Of numberless Instances to the present Purpose, which will occur to every one who has any Communication or Conversation with this Party, or who has read a few only of the many flagitious News-Papers and Pamphlets which have been of late so industriously spread over this Kingdom, and which, as they contain neither Wit nor Humour, Learning nor Sense, can only be encouraged and propagated from these wicked Purposes abovementioned, I shall here point out one only, which, for its Impudence as well as Malice, can hardly, I believe, be parallelled in all History. And here I cannot help observing (highly to the Honour of our Government) how destitute this Party must be of any real Matter for Censure or Abuse, when they are driven to the hard Necessity of inventing a Falshood in which they must be sure to be detected by every Man living. The Reader must already conceive that I am going to mention the many wicked Suggestions which have been for a Year last past spread abroad against the Government concerning an Attack on the Liberty of the Press.[1] To omit many malicious Invectives scattered up and down in the *Jacobitical* Papers, and even in Pamphlets,[2] the scurrilous Author of *Old England* entertained his Readers, for two Months together, on this single Article.[3] Such, indeed, was the Stile in which these invidious Suggestions were communicated, so inveterate was the Spirit in which this Rumour was propagated, that the Writers

[1] See *JJ* no. 18, above, pp. 218–20, and General Introduction, above, pp. lxix–lxxi.

[2] For example, in the second edition of Horace Walpole's *Letter to the Whigs* (15 April 1748), his *A Second and Third Letter to the Whigs* (26 March 1748), and the combination of these, entitled *Three Letters to the Whigs* (27 May 1748); see A. T. Hazen, *A Bibliography of Horace Walpole* (New Haven, Conn., 1948), pp. 32–6. It was to defend Lyttelton from attacks like these that Edward Moore published (26 May 1748) his poem *The Trial of Selim the Persian*; see below, p. 345, n. 2.

[3] The series of six essays on the freedom of the press appeared first in *OE* of 28 November, 12 and 19 December 1747, and 2, 9, and 16 January 1748. They were gathered together and published in a pamphlet, by M. Cooper in March 1748.

appeared plainly to insinuate that such an Attack was absolutely resolved on; that this Measure was already on the Carpet, and immediately to be executed; and many, I doubt not, who live remote from the Scenes of publick Business, were persuaded that the Attack was absolutely begun; and some, very probably, believe at this Day, that the Ministry did really make the Attempt, and miscarried in it.

Now I can with great Assurance say, that this Design, so far from being resolved on, and much less attempted, was never once publickly mentioned, or, I firmly believe, ever thought of, by any Persons now in Power.

The Truth of the Fact is this. The Liberty of the Press is one of the many, and perhaps one of the most valuable Privileges which we enjoy under the present mild Administration. It is a Privilege unknown to former Ages under the Tyranny of the *Stuarts*, and is secured to us by the glorious Revolution, and by that Establishment which the *Jacobites* are so desirous to overturn. I may surely add, that this is a Privilege never enjoyed in so free and unrestrained a Manner, indeed with such absolute Impunity as at present. The People of this Nation know the Value of this Liberty, and have experienced such Advantages resulting from it, that they would be very unwilling to part with such a Blessing; and no less jealous of any Attempt to restrain or destroy it. But according to that trite Maxim, *The Corruption of the best Things produces the worst,*[1] so hath this Liberty produced many Evils, and hath by bad Men been perverted to the most pernicious Purposes. To scatter Falshoods among the People; to asperse the best Administrations; to inflame the turbulent Passions of the Multitude; to increase the Discontent, and to rouse the Jealousies, Fears and Suspicions of the Public; and by such Means to create Disaffection, Faction, Sedition, and even Rebellion itself, against a Government which hath never ONCE exceeded the Limits of our Laws, nor hath any other Object in View, but the Happiness and Prosperity of this Nation.

In such Hands this truly *English* Privilege, this Bulwark of our Liberty, hath become the dirty Instrument of private Scandal, the Advocate of lawless Tyranny, and hath been often forced to plead the Cause of Slavery itself, and to endeavour its own Ruin.

---

[1] *Corruptio optimi pessima,* apparently derived from Aristotle, *Ethics,* VIII. x (1160^b9).

These Consequences, I believe, the Men in Power have lamented, and so hath every other good Man in this Kingdom; but have lamented them as unhappily, and perhaps inseparably, incident to a Liberty too invaluable to be abolished.

What an Instance, therefore, have the *Jacobites* given of the Weakness, as well as Baseness of their Cause? How excellent must that Government be which its Adversaries cannot abuse but by such glaring Falshoods as this? Is not this highly sufficient to defeat all their Designs upon other Men; nay, we could almost think to reclaim,[1] many, at least, among themselves?

But this last can hardly be hoped from any Reasoning or Experience. For by what Arguments can we hope to persuade the Men, who manifestly laugh at all Argument? What Reasons of publick Utility can sway those who are Enemies to the Community? What Motives, however powerful, will influence the Men, whom even Oaths cannot bind?[2] What Considerations of Religion, will reclaim such as are indifferent to all Religion? What Arguments, in Favour of Liberty can convince the avowed Advocates of Slavery? What Ties of Friendship or Society can restrain the Men, who would destroy all Society? In short, what Argument, of any Sort, can awaken those, who are already blind to their own Interest, and their Country's Welfare? To him, therefore, and to him alone, who hath Ears to hear, would I address the remaining Part of this Paper.——If, therefore, the *Jacobites*, are so mad and so wicked, as to persist in the Pursuit of a bad Cause, in order to introduce the most terrible of all Evils, shall not this strongly excite us to exert our utmost Efforts, in Maintenance of the Best Cause, in order to perpetuate the greatest of all Blessings?——If they strive, by all possible Means, to weaken, divide, and oppress us; let this prevail upon us to strengthen and support each other's mutual Interest, by a more firm and cordial Union among ourselves.——Lastly, if to this End they scruple not to make Use of the base Means of Scandal and Defamation; it will be our Wisdom and our Prudence, heartily to despise and detest such low and wicked Artifices.—— By such Means we shall baffle all their Attempts, confound their Devices, and defeat their Designs.——By such Means, we shall effectually, perhaps, put a Stop to the ill Effects of those Practices,

---

[1] Cf. *JJ* no. 32, above, pp. 335-6.
[2] Cf. *JJ* no. 21, above, p. 246 and note 2 there.

which, though evidently productive of the most fatal Consequences, it is not in the Power of our Laws, or, perhaps, even of the Legislature itself, entirely to suppress or prevent.

I am, Sir,

Your most humble Servant,

An ENGLISHMAN.

Proceedings at the Court of Criticism, Thursday July 14.

M. *Cooper,* late at the *Globe* in *Pater-Noster-Row,* was indicted upon the Statute of TAKING IN,[1] for having lately published a Poem called *The Trial of* Selim *the* Persian;[2] by which Title his Majesty's good Subjects were induced to believe, that a certain great Character was notoriously and scurrilously abused; and many of them were deceived into buying the said Poem, from the same worthy Motive, which leads them to encourage the Works of other modern Authors: But to their great Surprize, as well as Concern, they found no Satire contained in the said Poem; and so they were TAKEN IN, to their great Deceit and Prejudice, contrary to the Form of the said Statute, *&c.*

Thomas Scandal, Esq; (sworn.) I bought the Poem of the Defendant, imagining it to have been a Satire against an honourable Gentleman; whereas it is one of the genteelest Panegyrics I ever read.

Prisoner's Council. You shou'd say Abuse; for no Satire can be writ on that Gentleman.

Scandal. I know what I say.

Prisoner's Council. Sir, I question whether you do or no— What is the Difference, pray, between Satire and Abuse?

Scandal. I won't answer you.

Mrs. *Grace,* (sworn.) I likewise bought the Poem of the Defendant, expecting to have read some pretty Things in it, such as one reads in other Authors; something to make one laugh at

---

1 See *JJ* no. 26, above, p. 294 and note 2 there.

2 The anonymous *Trial of Selim the Persian for divers High Crimes and Misdemeanours* was advertised as published, in *GA* of 26 May 1748. Written by Edward Moore, author of *The Foundling,* the *Trial* was an ironic defence of Lyttelton against three charges: having accepted a 'place' in the Pelham coalition; having written a 'free-thinking' pamphlet on the conversion of St. Paul; and having ruined the livelihood of the author of *A Second and Third Letter to the Whigs.* See also *JJ* no. 18, above, pp. 217–20, 222–5.

some People. Upon my Word, I never was more deceived in my Life.

Prisoner's Council. So you expected Abuse too, Madam?

Mrs. *Grace.* I cannot help saying, I did.

Prisoner's Council. I am sorry a Lady should have such a Taste.

Mrs. *Grace.* Sir, I am a true *Englishman,* (here was a great Laugh) *Englishwoman,* I mean; and I shall always relish Satire against any of the present Copulation of Ministers. (Here was another great Laugh, but the Lady afterwards explained her Meaning to be Coalition.)

A Point of Law now arose, whether this Fact was within the Statute; which having been very learnedly spoke to on both Sides, the Court delivered their Opinion as follows:

I am clearly of Opinion that this Case is neither within the Meaning, nor within the Words of the Statute.

Within the Meaning it cannot be: For this Statute was made to prevent a Custom which hath prevailed much of late, of TAKING IN the Reader by prefixing a pompous and promising Title Page to Books and Pamphlets which contain nothing at all; according to the Case of the Cyclic Author reported by *Horace* in his Laws of Poetry.[1]

But the Author of the Poem now under Consideration hath been so far from doing this, that he promised nothing, and hath performed very much: For what more unpromising Title could he have prefixed to his Book, than the Trial of a Gentleman, whom all the World knows to have committed nothing for which he can be liable to any Censure. A Gentleman of so unblemish'd and unstain'd a Character, that not only Justice, but even Envy and Malice must be, and have been too, obliged to acquit him.

What then cou'd any Person of Common Sense expect from a Performance, of which he must imagine the Author to have been some wretched *Grub-street* Garreteer? For what Man who had the least Regard to Honour, could abuse such a Character? Nay, who that hath any Regard for Letters, would endeavour falsely to asperse and calumniate almost the only Patron which the Muses at present can boast among the Great?[2]

---

[1] *Ars Poetica,* 136–9.

[2] For Lyttelton's considerable contemporary reputation as a patron of letters see Rose Mary Davis, *The Good Lord Lyttelton,* Chs. II and V; *JJ* no. 27, above, p. 301; and General

Nothing, therefore, could be said to have been promised in such a Title; but surely much may be said to be contained in the Poem itself: Much more, indeed, of true Wit than hath lately come from the Press.

Can any Allegory be finer than the following which I will read you?[1]

> Begin we then (as first 'tis fitting)
> With the Three CHIEFS in Judgment sitting.
> Above the rest, and in the Chair,
> Sat FACTION with dissembled Air;
> Her Tongue was skill'd in specious Lies,
> And Murmurs, whence Dissentions rise;
> A smiling Mask her Features veil'd,
> Her Form the Patriot's Robe conceal'd;
> With study'd Blandishments she bow'd,
> And drew the captivated Croud.
> The next in Place, and on the Right,
> Sat ENVY, hideous to the Sight;
> Her snaky Locks, her hollow Eyes,
> And haggard Form forbad Disguise;
> Pale Discontent, and sullen Hate
> Upon her wrinkled Forehead sat;
> Her Left-hand, clench'd, her Cheek sustain'd,
> Her Right (with many a Murder stain'd)
> A Dagger clutch'd, in Act to strike,
> With Starts of Rage, and Aim oblique.
> Last on the Left was CLAMOUR seen,
> Of Stature vast, and horrid Mien;
> With bloated Cheeks, and frantic Eyes
> She sent her Yellings to the Skies;
> Prepar'd with Trumpet in her Hand,
> To blow Sedition o'er the Land.
> With these, Four more of lesser Fame,
> And humbler Rank, attendant came:
> HYPOCRISY with smiling Grace,
> And IMPUDENCE with brazen Face,

Introduction, above, p. lxi. *OE* of 27 May 1749 refers to Lyttelton's great efforts to 'push' *Tom Jones*, and the issue of 26 August 1749 alludes to 'the fam'd Dedication' of the novel, in which Fielding credits Lyttelton with having assisted at the conception of the work.

1 Fielding here reprints lines 11-60 of the *Trial*, pp. 2-4. In its May number *GM*, xviii (1748), 199-200, had reprinted virtually the same passage.

CONTENTION bold, with Iron Lungs,
And SLANDER with her hundred Tongues.
The Walls in sculptur'd Tale were rich,
And Statues proud (in many a Nich)
Of Chiefs, who fought in FACTION's Cause,
And perish'd for Contempt of Laws.
The Roof in vary'd Light and Shade,
The Seat of ANARCHY display'd.
Triumphant o'er a falling Throne
(By emblematic Figures known)
CONFUSION rag'd, and LUST obscene,
And RIOT with distemper'd Mein,[1]
And OUTRAGE bold, and MISCHIEF dire,
And DEVASTATION clad in Fire.
Prone on the Ground, a martial Maid
Expiring lay, and groan'd for Aid;
Her Shield with many a Stab was pierc'd,
Her Laurel torn, her Spear revers'd;
And near her, crouch'd amidst the Spoils,
A Lion panted in the Toils.

But if I would read you every Beauty of it, I must go through the whole Poem.

Within the Meaning therefore of the Statute the Prisoner certainly cannot be brought; nor is the Case more within the Words, though I should not, indeed, abide by these with the Rigour of other Courts.

I admit, notwithstanding what I have said, that Satire is promised in the Title-page, and the Witnesses have sworn that they bought it from that Apprehension.

But will any Man say there is no Satire in this Poem? Surely it contains some of the finest and justest that ever was written. Satire on those who, of all others, at present, most deserve it; on the scandalous, flagitious, anonymous Writers of the Age; Wretches, who are the Scandal of the Press, and Pest of Society. Against these, here is as fine and as keen Satire, as can flow from the most spirited Pen.

Upon the whole, I order that the Prisoner be discharged, and I do most earnestly recommend the Poem to the Public, as I do the

---

[1] An acceptable eighteenth-century spelling of 'mien'.

Author likewise, if ever he should be known, since I am convinced, that the Goodness of his Heart is, at least, equal to that of
his Head.[1]
(*Adjourned.*)

SATURDAY, JULY 23, 1748. NUMB. 34

——*Talem se læta ferebat*
Per medios, instans operi, regnisque futuris.
Virgil.[2]

To the Author of the Jacobite Journal.

Sir,

The serious Truths contained in this Letter, will, I hope, make
an Apology unnecessary. You are to know, that I am of that high
Order of Beings, which the World calls a married Man; that to
render my State of Life happy, as well as honourable, I have, in
every Thing, submitted to the Will of my Wife: And this, I can
truly say, not more from a Conviction of the great Duty of
Obedience, than to avoid Contention, and to promote Family
Peace, and Good-humour in my House. It is now eleven Years
since the kindest and the loveliest of her Sex honoured me with
the Possession of her Sweetness: In all which Time, 'till within a
little more than a Twelvemonth,[3] she has condescended to make
my Servitude my Delight, abridging me only where my Wishes
were strongest, and consequently leading to Excess; and in-
dulging me in every Thing indifferent in my own Opinion, or

---

[1] Cf. Fielding to Lyttelton, 29 August 1749: 'I never wished for Power more than a few
Days ago for the Sake of a Man whom I love, and that more perhaps from the Esteem I
know he bears towards you than from any other Reason. . . . The Name of this Man is
Moore'; as quoted by Cross, ii. 246. Cf. Walpole to Bentley, 18 May 1754, in *Letters*, ed.
Paget Toynbee, iii (Oxford, 1903), 234: 'You will laugh when I tell you, that I am
employed to reconcile Sir George [Lyttelton] and Moore; the latter has been very flippant,
nay impertinent, on the former's giving a little place [the office of the Clerk of the Buck-
Warrants] to Bower in preference to him.—Think of my being the mediator!'

[2] *Aeneid*, i. 503–4: 'so moved she [Dido] joyously through their midst, pressing on the
work of her rising kingdom' (Loeb). Murphy reprints this *JJ* leader in his edition (1762)
of the *Works*.

[3] Apparently referring to the period of the June 1747 elections. The curiously precise
nature of this dating and of the preceding one ('now eleven Years since'), which seems to
allude to some adjustment in the structure of the covert Opposition formed around the
Prince of Wales (c. 1737) after his marriage, suggests that the entire *JJ* leader may have
had greater topical significance for politically acute contemporaries than has yet been
disclosed.

desirable in hers. This uniformity of Conduct had rendered us the Admiration and Envy of all our Acquaintance; there was hardly a married Woman who visited us, but proposed me as an Example to her Husband, and treasured up the Maxims of my Wife, as so many Lessons for her own Conduct. We were, in short, a Couple who left not Happiness to Chance; one plann'd what the other executed, and both enjoyed the Fruits of our Care. Alas! Mr. *Trott-Plaid*, I wish the Business of this Letter was only to tell you of my Happiness; but that (however well secured as you may think) has known its Period, and I am at present the most miserable of all Beings.

It is now about a Year since a grave Clergyman from *Oxford* came to board with us. To this Gentleman (though no Seducer of what my Wife calls her Virtue) I owe all my Misfortunes. He had not been a Month in the Family, before I observed that my Wife's Head had taken a political Turn; the Affairs of her Family began to be neglected; and notwithstanding we owed our entire Support to a genteel Post I enjoyed under the Government,[1] I was compelled every Day at Table to hear that Government abused. At every Glass after Dinner, a Laugh and a whisper'd Toast between my Wife and her Friend, gave me fresh Cause of Uneasiness. My eldest Boy made his Appearance in a Plaid Waistcoat, and my Girl's Petticoat and Doll were of the same Stuff. I was pleased, indeed, at first, to hear the Child checked by her Mamma, for drinking *the King over the Water*;[2] but was as much displeased at the Reason of that Check, which was, that *James* was a plain Name, and would save the Trouble of such unnecessary Distinctions.

Upon this Occasion it was, that I took upon me, for the first Time, to make a Remonstrance, in private, to my Wife: Which tho' I did with all the Submission of a Husband, I found, to my Cost, that I had done wrong. Instead of the Compliance I in some measure expected, I was upbraided by her as a mean-spirited

---

[1] As an office-holder he would have taken an oath abjuring the Pretender. See *JJ* no. 16, above, p. 202, n. 1.

[2] A favourite Jacobite oath. See *JJ* no. 1, above, p. 92 and note 2 there. On the wearing of plaid at this time cf. Walpole to Mann, 11 March 1748 (*Yale Walpole*, xix. 471): '. . . besides having dressed her husband in Scotch plaid, which just now is one of the things in the world that is reckoned most offensive'. By the terms of the 'Act for the more effectual disarming the highlands in Scotland . . . and for restraining the use of the highland dress' (1746), the wearing of plaid material was prohibited for inhabitants of Scotland; see 19 Geo. II, cap. 39 (*Statutes at Large*, xviii. 526–7).

Wretch; one who was willing to subsist by Shame, and to acknowledge Favours from a Set of Men, whose Friendship was a Disgrace to me; and that if I expected the Continuance of her Regard, I must think of some other Means of supporting my Family, than by an infamous Place, given me by those, who derived their Power of bestowing it from one who wanted Right to confer that Power. You will judge of my Concern, Mr. *Trott-Plaid*, at these Words.——I was sorry to differ in Opinion from my Wife, and yet was almost apt to imagine that Opinion a little unreasonable. To think of giving up my Post was an impracticable Thing, and to live under the Displeasure of my Wife, an impossible one. I intreated her to proceed with the utmost Caution in this Affair; and telling her I would ask her Friend's Advice in it, I left her to consult him.

I had the Pleasure of finding this honest Clergyman of a contrary Opinion. He saw no Objection, he said, to my holding a Place under the worst of Governments, provided I endeavoured, as much as in me lay, to act in Opposition to those who had obliged me. That neither Religion nor Conscience required me to refuse Favours from the Hands of those whom it was my Duty to detest. That an Opposition of this Kind was the more meritorious, as it was the more disinterested; and the Hazard of Property would be the best Proof I could give of the Sincerity of my Zeal. That all Men were under an Obligation to provide for their Families in the best Manner they were able: But tho' Necessity compelled me to eat the Bread of Shame, yet Conscience forbad me to live a Life of it. It was no Sin, he said, in War, to plunder the Enemy that we have first killed: And, by a Similitude of Reasoning, he conceived it was as innocent to plunder the Friend we intended afterwards to kill. That Measures, more than Men, wanted a Change; and that Power was the surest Means to ruin those who raised us to it. That for his own Part, he had Hopes of Preferment himself from the Government, which he intended to accept of without Scruple, as it might furnish him with the Means of doing Good, and of keeping weaker Men from Power, whose mistaken Gratitude for Obligations might tempt them to make unsuitable Returns. For these Reasons, he said, he begged Leave to differ from the good Lady of the House, and advised me to continue in my Post, as it served me in a double Capacity, both for private Support, and national Advantage.

I cannot conceal the Satisfaction of my Mind at the Reasoning of this worthy Gentleman. I submitted entirely to his Opinion; my Wife who is the best of Women, was easily brought over by her Friend, and domestick Harmony was again restored. The Groans of our bleeding Country[1] indeed were too often in our Ears, and somewhat disturbed the Tranquility of our Minds; but the Hope that *every one would have his own at last*,[2] set all things right, and we lived in Expectation of the happy Change.[3]

It was about this Time that my Wife, who had very much improv'd her Spelling under the Tuition of her Friend, commenced Writer in the Cause. A Pamphlet, called *The State of the Nation*,[4] and *Three Letters to the Whigs*,[5] are the Product of her Invention. In these she so well succeeded, that many were of Opinion they wanted nothing but Truth to be finish'd Performances. Indeed that noble and free Spirit of Scandal, which is the Characteristic of those Pamphlets, is sufficient Evidence that their Author could be no other than a Woman.

We had the Pleasure, soon after this, to learn from the Clergyman, that a Friend of his in the Administration had presented him to a considerable Benefice in the Country. The good Man received our Congratulations upon the Occasion with Tears; and taking a most affectionate Leave, he retired to his Living. The Satisfaction we received in our Friend's Promotion would hardly have made us amends for the Pains of parting with him, if an unfortunate Accident, and some Information that followed it, had not opened our Eyes to see that worthy Gentleman in his proper Character.

My Wife was busied in her political Studies one Day, with her

---

[1] A cant phrase of Opposition parties. In this and the preceding paragraph the 'grave Clergyman from *Oxford*' is made to express exaggerated versions of arguments popular in Opposition propaganda. For the relation of such arguments to Oxford see *JJ* no. 17, above, p. 212, n. 3, and no. 24, above, p. 279 and note 4 there.

[2] Cf. the Jacobite toast, ' 'till the king enjoy his own again', derived from the refrain of the popular seventeenth-century ballad, 'Upon Defacing of White-Hall' (*c.* 1643–6), which Augustan Jacobites appropriated to apply to the Old Pretender; John Doran, *London in the Jacobite Times* (Boston, [n.d.]), i. 68–9. Fielding uses it similarly in *TP* no. 24 of 8–15 April 1746. For text and tune see *The Loyal Garland*, ed. J. O. Halliwell (Percy Society, no. lxxxix, London, 1850), pp. 16–18, and *Roxburghe Ballads*, vol. vii., ed. J. Woodfall Ebsworth (Hertford, 1893), 633–4, 680–4.

[3] Cf. the Jacobite oath, 'the Royal Exchange', *JJ* no. 1, above, p. 92.

[4] See *JJ* no. 10, above, p. 150. Of the several pamphlets with this or a similar title, *The State of the Nation for the Year 1747, and respecting 1748* best fits the date implied by the association with Walpole's *Three Letters to the Whigs*.

[5] By Horace Walpole. See *JJ* no. 18, above, pp. 217–20, 222–5.

Bayley's Dictionary¹ before her, when I received a Message from above, that my Employment was taken from me.———I enquired into the Meaning of such Procedure, and I was answered, that I was an infamous, ungrateful Fellow; one that deserved hanging; and if I did not mend my Manners and my Wife, the Government might possibly take a severer Notice of me. With these Words the Messenger left me; and I retired to my Wife's Apartment for Comfort and Advice. That heroic Woman, instead of calling my Dissimulation² a Misfortune, gloried in the Occasion. ———It was now, she said, she would apply to the People for that Emolument the Enemies of their Country had dispossessed me of. That she had long been solicited by the Proprietors of certain News-Papers to lend her Abilities. That she had desired Time to consider of their Proposals, but was now determined; that she had indeed, for some Weeks past, administred Helps to *Old England*, and the *London Evening-Post*,³ and had occasionally furnished a few Papers upon Naval Affairs in the *Fool*; but that the Writers of those Papers were so incorrigibly dull, that her bare Intervention was of little Use; she therefore declared, as the Ministry had provoked her to plan their utter Ruin, she would hesitate no longer to undertake the sole Direction of them. That the Advantages arising from such Papers would treble those of the Post I had lost; and that I ought to look upon myself as the happiest of Men, in having a Head to my Family, who knew how to secure the Emoluments of a Husband by the very Means that must save her dearer Country from Destruction.

My Heart was overflowing with Comfort at these Assurances, when the Visit of a Friend interrupted the Discourse.———He condoled with me in the kindest manner for the Loss of my Place; but how, Mr. *Trott-plaid*, shall I express my Astonishment, when he assured me, upon his own Knowledge, that my Friend the Clergyman, that Friend I so dearly loved, was the Person to whom I was indebted for this Obligation! He told me, that the Business of this Viper, during the Time of his stay with us, was to

¹ In view of Mrs. Supple's attention to orthography, probably Nathaniel Bailey's *Universal Etymological English Dictionary* (1721), not the English translation of Pierre Bayle's *Dictionnaire historique et critique*, is meant.

² Perhaps glancing at his wife's original objection to his dissembling while in office, but an emendation to 'Dismission' would improve the sense.

³ On p. 4, col. 1, of the original issue of *JJ* no. 34 Fielding reprints some items from *LEP* under the heading 'W——t and P———ks, or rather Italicks, by Mrs. Anna Maria Supple'.

pay his Court to the Administration, in which he so well succeeded as to obtain a Promise of Preferment. That to perfect this Promise, and to remove any Suspicions they might possibly entertain of his Principles, he had made a voluntary Sacrifice of my Wife and me; concluding, that I was an avowed Jacobite, and my Wife the Writer of every scurrilous Pamphlet that had infested the Public. I own to you, Mr. *Trott-plaid*, upon this Discovery I began to be ashamed of the Part I had acted.——It occurred to me, that the Principles of this Man might possibly be as false as his Friendship; but my Wife conceived a different Opinion.——Bad Practices, she said, were no Proof of bad Principles; hers she knew were right; and however ill her Friend might have treated her, his Name and Memory deserved Respect, as by his Means she was become a Pillar of Support to a falling Nation.

I will not tire you, Mr. *Trotplaid*, with my Wife's Arguments, or my own Submissions.——The News-Papers abovementioned have been ever since under her Direction; but, whether from a Want of Taste in the Public, or from a Knowledge that they are the Writings of a Woman, the proposed Advantages have fallen short, even of common Subsistance.——It is impossible to represent to you the Distresses we have struggled with; but what is the worst of all, I have the Concern to see my Children taught Treason as soon as they can speak; and my little Boy, just eight Years old, the Hopes of my Family, is turn'd Poet, and writes the *Varses*, as he calls them, in the *London Evening-Post*: He has just sent some Lines on the Eclipse* to the Press.[1] Dear Sir, advise me what to do; for tho' my Wife hates you, and has often abused you in Print, I am

Your affectionate Friend,

and most humble Servant,

SIMON SUPPLE.[2]

Note. *As all the Grub-street Authors are now going into the Country to Harvest-Work, the Court of Criticism is adjourned till their Return to Town.*

* *Note.* These were printed in the *London Evening-Post,* of *Saturday* last, and are well enough for such a Child.

---

[1] *LEP* of 14–16 July 1748 printed a poem entitled 'The National Eclipse', which drew a parallel between the eclipse of the sun on 14 July and the supposed eclipse of British glory owing to the imminent peace of Aix-la-Chapelle.

[2] The surname is that of the curate of Mr. Allworthy's parish; see *Tom Jones,* IV. x.

Simplex Munditiis.

Horace.[1]

There are few Passages in any of the antient Authors that have more puzzled the Generality of Readers than those two Words which I have placed at the Head of this Paper. It is, I believe, the common Opinion, that this Place cannot possibly be translated, which is a sly Method of insinuating that it cannot be understood; for I shrewdly suspect that we often lay the Blame on the wrong Language, and complain of the Barrenness of our own Tongue, when we ought rather to lament the Obscurity of another. To say Truth, the Translator often generously consents to bear the Disgrace of not being able to convey certain Ideas to his Reader, when, in Reality, the original Author hath never communicated any such Ideas to him.

Milton renders *Simplex Munditiis* by, *Plain in thy Neatness.*[2] An Expression, perhaps, less happy than that of *Horace*, who hath in two Words drawn us the Picture of a beautiful Girl, dressed in the plainest, and at the same Time the most elegant Manner; such as hath been often remarked in the young female Quakers, the Simplicity of whose Dress doth really set off great Beauty more than is in the Power of the richest Fineries.

Simplicity of Language is the same Ornament to our Thoughts, as Simplicity of Dress to our Persons. In this, however, as in the other Instance, there is a certain Degree of Elegance necessary; for though we need not be courtly in our Phrase, we must not be rude.

And here again the Quaker shall serve me for a Model. In the Conversation of the more sensible and better Sort of these People, there is no less elegant Simplicity, than *Horace* would describe in the external Ornaments of his *Pyrrha*.[3] The Goodwill and Sincerity which appear in their Discourse, make abundant

---

[1] *Odes*, I. v. 5. For a translation, see the first sentence, second paragraph, of this leader.

[2] 'The Fifth Ode of Horace, Lib. I', first printed in 1673, with the subtitle '*Quis multa gracilis te puer in Rosa*, Rendred almost word for word without Rhyme according to the Latin Measure, as near as the Language will permit'. Milton's Latin text, which he subjoined to his translation, reads *Simplex munditie*. See *Poetical Works of John Milton*, ed. Helen Darbishire (Oxford, 1955), ii. 158, 328–9.

[3] The 'addressee' of Horace's ode quoted in the motto above, she is a 'type' of the coquette or flirt.

Amends for their Bluntness, and have indeed more Charms for me, than the forced unnatural Flowers of courtly Complaisance.

I am therefore well pleased with the honest and plain Sentiments which appear in the following Speech. This I shall make no Apology for publishing now, though it was spoken so long ago as while the late detestable Rebellion was actually on foot. Indeed I wish with all my Heart I may live to see the Day when it shall be no longer necessary to obviate those hellish Doctrines, and that infatuated Spirit, which gave Birth to that calamitous Season; this Day, at least, I am well assured, is not yet come.

The Gentleman who furnished me with this Dialogue, and to whom indeed it was spoken, is a very hearty Well-wisher to the true Interest of his Country; but was formerly in his Inclination too severe against those Protestants who differ from the established Church. He is an honest Man, and yet hath been too apt, in the Impetuosity of his Zeal, to forget that no Establishment can take away the natural Freedom of Conscience; and that all Men have as much Right to differ from him, as he can have to differ from them.

This Gentleman, therefore, meeting an honest Quaker soon after the unfortunate Affair at *Preston-Pans*, began to rally him on what the several Sectaries must expect, if the *Pretender's* Arms should prove finally successful. "I fancy, Friend, (cry'd he) all the People of thy Persuasion are very much alarmed at this surprizing Progress of the Rebels; for should they succeed, you must hope for no Quarter. We are alarmed, Friend, (answer'd the Quaker) and so must thou be, and all of thy Persuasion, if thou art a Protestant. The *Scarlet Whore*[1] hath no more Friendship for the Church of *England* than she hath for us; nay, the less thou differest from her, if thou dost differ at all, the more she hates thee: For which Reason, the Man they call the *Pope* is a better Friend to the Man they call the *Great Turk*,[2] than he is to any

---

[1] A term of opprobrium for the Roman Church. Cf. Revelation xvii. 1–6. On 12 May 1746 the General Assembly of Quakers, meeting in London, addressed the King in part as follows: 'As none among all thy protestant subjects exceed us in an aversion to the tyranny, idolatry and superstition of the church of *Rome*; so none lie under more just apprehensions of immediate danger from their destructive consequences. . . .' See *GM*, xvi (1746), 306.

[2] The Ottoman Sultan, also known to eighteenth-century Englishmen as the Grand Signor. The incumbent, Mahmud I (*r.* 1730–54), had in fact entered into a number of treaties with Christian countries.

Protestant Prince. I am afraid, indeed, there are some Protestants who wish well to the Cause of their Enemies; but if there are any such, they must be Fools or Madmen: For thou mayst as wisely put thy Sheepfold under the Protection of a Wolf, as a Protestant Congregation under the Protection of a Popish Prince. It is but t'other Day that we turned away this Man's Father for endeavouring to force the Nation into Popery: Can the Son, or the Grandson, make more solemn Promises to protect the Protestant Religion, than the Father, or Grandfather did, and why should we believe that these would be better kept? Or why should we run so dangerous a Risque? The Truth, I am afraid, is, we are a fickle Nation. I remember when *William* came over, though I was then but a little Boy; he had no sooner delivered us from Popery, than we wished to be delivered from him.[1] The same wicked, inconstant Spirit, I am afraid, still reigns among us; maketh us weary of Happiness itself, and willing to exchange for worse, rather than not to exchange at all. This, it must be owned, is a very extraordinary Degree of Folly, and yet we see it happens every Day in many Instances where Men must have their Eyes open. Thus they frequently exchange the most comely Women, the richest and finest Houses, and most sumptuous Dainties, for others of an inferior Degree. Those Things, indeed, I regard as mere Vanities; but so do not they. It is not that with a true Christian Spirit they despise the outward Pomps of this World; but with a true luxurious Spirit, they are soon sated with the Possession of what at once seemed so lovely in their Eyes. In the same Manner they are surfeited with that best of all outward Gifts, Liberty, and are desirous to espouse Slavery in its Stead: For what but Slavery can they expect from the Exchange? I am persuaded, Friend, thou hast too much of inward Light to require me to prove a Matter so plain, and which hath been so often proved. Popery and Slavery are, indeed, so inseparable from the Cause of this Man, whom they call the Pretender, that nothing less but an utter Darkness of the Spirit, can avoid seeing the Connection. If Men do not desire those Abominations, wherefore are they uneasy? Can any of them produce one just Cause of Complaint against our present Rulers? It is true we labour under the Miseries of War, and thou well knowest how odious War is to those of my Persuasion. But should those Men complain of these

---

[1] See *Proper Answer*, above, p. 72 and note 3 there.

Miseries, who first forced the Nation into them; and who, not contented with the Calamities which we have suffered abroad, have brought this War home into their own Country? For my own Part, Friend, I live at a vast Distance from the Great City, and have no Communication with the Men they call the Ministry; yet, in all the Discourses which I have heard from others, I do not remember to have once heard the Beginning of the War charged on these Men. Why then should they be supposed to be desirous of continuing it?* On the contrary, I have heard, that these Men are very heartily disposed to Peace; but we cannot expect Impossibilities of them; and how can we hope, that the *French* Ruler should accord us any tolerable Terms of Peace, while he is so greatly encouraged to continue the War? Believe me, Friend, the Murmurs of these discontented People do not arise from the Calamities, how great soever they may be, which this War hath brought on the Nation; for then would they charge them to the Account of those who forced us into it. No, my Friend, they have other Sources. The Malice and Envy, the Ambition and Avarice of a few of the great Ones in the Land, who desire themselves to be called the Ministry, give the first Rise to these Clamours; and that fickle, restless Spirit, which I have already mentioned, opens the Ears of the Multitude to receive them. Of this, peradventure, thou mayst live to see a mighty Example. For what wouldst thou say, Friend, if the present Rulers should be able to procure us a much better, and more advantageous Peace, than we can even reasonably desire our Enemies should accord us; I say, if after that, the same People should still be as clamorous as ever: If those who before called aloud for Peace, should then as loudly call for a Continuance of the War?——Believe me, all these Things may happen, and the Spirit within whispers me they will happen.†
Indeed nothing can prevent it but the final Success of these wicked Rebels, which would end in the utter Destruction of this Nation, and of the Protestant Name; but this Ruin the Spirit tells me will not overtake us, how much soever our Ingratitude, our Heart-burnings, our Discontents, our Murmurs, our Slanders, and our Rebellions may deserve it."

Here the Quaker ended his Speech; and the Gentleman, who,

---

* See the Pamphlets and News-papers of 1744-5-6-7, if they can be found.

† For the fulfilling of this Prophecy, see the Pamphlets and News-papers of 1748. Some of which are yet, I believe, in Being.

as the Reader will easily believe from the Character I at first gave of him, was not a little inclined to Superstition, declares he much doubts whether the honest Friend was not, as he said, inspired with the Spirit of Prophecy; and hence the Gentleman hath lately spoken so favourably of these Quakers, that some have suspected an Inclination in him to embrace their Opinions.

SATURDAY, AUGUST 6, 1748.   NUMB. 36.

The following excellent Paper, taken from Mr. *Addison's* FREEHOLDER,[1] is so truly applicable to the present Times, that I doubt not its being acceptable to the Public.

————*Incendia lumen*
Præbebant; aliquisque malo fuit usus in illo.
Ovid, *Metamorphoses*, Book 2, verse 331.[2]

Sir *Francis Bacon*, in the Dedication before his History of *Henry* the Seventh, observes, that peaceable Times are the best to live in, though not so proper to furnish Materials for a Writer: As hilly Countries afford the most entertaining Prospects, though a Man would choose to travel through a plain one.[3] To this we may add, That the Times, which are full of Disorders and Tumults, are likewise the fullest of Instruction. History indeed furnishes us with very distinct Accounts of Factions, Conspiracies, Civil Wars and Rebellions, with the fatal Consequences that attend them: But they do not make such deep and lasting Impressions on our Minds, as Events of the same nature, to which we have ourselves been Witnesses, and in which we or our Friends and Acquaintance have been Sufferers. As Adversity makes a Man Wise in his private Affairs, civil Calamities give him Prudence and Circumspection in his publick Conduct.

[1] No. 28 of 26 March 1716.
[2] *Metamorphoses*, ii. 331–2: 'But the burning world gave light, and so even in that disaster was there some service' (Loeb).
[3] 'To the Most Illustrious and Most Excellent Prince, Charles, Prince of *Wales*, Duke of *Cornwall*, Earl of *Chester*, &c.' Bacon's text reads: 'And it is with Times, as it is with Wayes. Some are more *Up-hill* and *Down-hill*, and some are more *Flat* and *Plain*; and the *One* is better for the *Liver*, and the *Other* for the *Writer*'; *Historie of the Raigne of King Henry the Seventh* (London, 1622), [A2]ᵛ.

The Miseries of the Civil War under the Reign of King *Charles* the First, and the Consequences which ensued upon them, did, for many Years, deter the Inhabitants of our Island from the Thoughts of engaging anew in such desperate Undertakings; and convinced them by fatal Experience, that nothing could be so pernicious to the *English*, and so opposite to the Genius of the People, as the Subversion of Monarchy. In the like Manner we may hope that the great Expences brought upon the Nation by the present Rebellion; the Sufferings of innocent People, who have lived in that Place which was the Scene of it; with that dreadful Prospect of Ruin and Confusion which must have followed its Success; will secure us from the like Attempts for the future, and fix His Majesty upon the Throne of *Great-Britain*; especially when those who are prompted to such wicked Practices reflect upon the Punishments to which the Criminals have exposed themselves, and the Miseries in which they have involved their Relations, Friends, and Families.

It will be likewise worth their while to consider, how such Tumults and Riots, as have been encouraged by many, who, we may hope, did not propose to themselves such fatal Consequences, lead to a Civil War: and how naturally that seditious kind of Conversation, which many seem to think consistent with their Religion and Morality, ends in an open Rebellion. I question not but the more virtuous and considerate Part of our Malecontents are now stung with a very just Remorse for this their Manner of Proceeding, which has so visibly tended to the Destruction of their Friends, and the Sufferings of their Country. This may, at the same time, prove an instructive Lesson to the Boldest and Bravest among the Disaffected, not to build any Hopes upon the talkative Zealots of their Party; who have shewn by their whole Behaviour, that their Hearts are equally filled with Treason and Cowardise. An Army of Trumpeters would give as great Strength to a Cause, as the Confederacy of Tongue-Warriors; who, like those military Musicians, content themselves with animating their Friends to Battle, and run out of the Engagement upon the first Onset.

But one of the most useful Maxims we can learn from the present Rebellion, is, That nothing can be more contemptible and insignificant, than the Scum of a People, when they are instigated against a King, who is supported by the Two Branches of the Legislature. A Mob may pull down a Meeting-house, but will never be able to overturn a Government, which has a couragious and wise Prince at the Head of it, and one who is zealously assisted by the great Council of the Nation, that best know the Value of him. The Authority of the Lords and Commons of *Great-Britain*, in conjunction with that of their Sovereign, is not to be controul'd by a tumultuary Rabble. It is big with Fleets and Armies, can fortify itself with what Laws it shall judge proper for its own Defence, can command the Wealth of the Kingdom for the Security of the People, and engage the whole Protestant Interest of *Europe* in so good and just a Cause. A disorderly Multitude, contending with the Body of the Legislature, is like a Man in a Fit under the Conduct of one in the Fulness of his Health and Strength. Such a one is sure to be over-ruled in a little time, though he deals about his Blows, and exerts himself in the most furious Convulsions while the Distemper is upon him.

We may farther learn from the Course of the present Rebellion, who among the Foreign States in our Neighbourhood are the true and natural Friends of *Great-Britain*, if we observe which of them gave us their Assistance in reducing our Country to a State of Peace and Tranquillity, and which of them used their Endeavours to heighten our Confusions, and plunge us into all the Evils of a Civil War. I shall only take Notice under this Head, that in former Ages it was the constant Policy of *France* to raise and cherish intestine Feuds and Discords in the Isle of *Great-Britain*, that we might either fall a Prey into their Hands, or that they might prosecute their Designs upon the Continent with less Interruption. Innumerable Instances of this Nature occur in History. The most remarkable one was that in the Reign of King *Charles* the First. Though that Prince was married to a Daughter of *France*, and was personally beloved and esteemed in the *French* Court, it is well known that they abetted both Parties in the Civil War, and always furnished Supplies to the weaker Side, lest there should be an end put to those fatal Divisions.

We might also observe, that this Rebellion has been a means of discovering to His Majesty, how much he may depend upon the Professions and Principles of the several Parties among his own Subjects; who are those Persons that have espoused his Interests with Zeal or Indifference; and who among them are influenced to their Allegiance by Places, Duty, or Affection. But as these, and several other Considerations, are obvious to the Thoughts of every Reader, I shall conclude, with observing how naturally many of those, who distinguish themselves by the Name of the *High-Church*, unite themselves to the Cause of *Popery*; since it is manifest that all the Protestants concerned in the Rebellion were such as gloried in this Distinction.

It would be very unjust, to charge all who have ranged themselves under this new Denomination, as if they had done it with a Design to favour the Interests of Popery. But it is certain that many of them, who at their first setting out were most averse to the Doctrines of the Church of *Rome*, have by the Cunning of our Adversaries been inspired with such an unreasonable Aversion to their Protestant Brethren, and taught to think so favourably of the *Roman Catholick* Principles, (not to mention the Endeavours that have been used to reconcile the Doctrines of the two Churches, which are in themselves as opposite as Light and Darkness) that they have been drawn over insensibly into its Interests. It is no wonder therefore, that so many of these deluded Zealots have been engaged in a Cause which they at first abhorr'd, and have wished or acted for the Success of an Enterprize, that might have ended in the Extirpation of the Protestant Religion in this Kingdom, and in all *Europe*. In short, they are like the *Syrians*, who were first smitten with Blindness, and unknowingly led out of their Way into the Capital of their Enemy's Country; insomuch that the Text tells us, *When they opened their Eyes, they found themselves in the midst of* Samaria.[1]

SATURDAY, AUGUST 13, 1748.   NUMB. 37.

Rarus enim ferme sensus communis in illa
Fortuna.———

Juvenal.[2]

Ulysses, in the 8th *Odyssey*, being about to retort the Affront of *Euryalus*,[3] begins with a very high Compliment on his Beauty.

---

[1] 2 Kings vi. 20: 'Elisha said, Lord, open the eyes of these *men*, that they may see. And the Lord opened their eyes, and they saw; and, behold, *they were* in the midst of Samaria.'

[2] *Satires*, viii. 73–4: 'for in those high places regard for others is rarely to be found' (Loeb).

[3] Foremost among the hecklers of Odysseus at the Phaeacian games, Euryalus was, according to the *Odyssey*, viii. 115–17, 'the peer of man-destroying Ares, the son of Naubolus, who in comeliness and form was the best of all the Phaeacians after Laodamos' (Loeb).

"Thy Form (says he) is so extremely beautiful, that a Deity could not fashion any thing beyond it.——But (adds he) as to Understanding, thou art an errant Simpleton."[1] The same Conduct is preserved by this Hero in his Contention with *Ajax*, in the 13th Book of the *Metamorphoses*: He calls his Antagonist a *Blockhead*, and endeavours to prove him one, but at the same Time allows him a great Degree of Bravery.

> ——*Tibi dextera bello*
> *Utilis; ingenium est, quod eget moderamine nostri.*
> *Tu vires sine mente geris: Mihi cura futuri est.*
> *Tu pugnare potes; pugnandi tempora Mecum*
> *Eligit Atrides. Tu tantum Corpore prodes;*
> *Nos animo.*[2]

In all which Instances, *Ovid* as well as *Homer* hath placed the Commendation before the Censure. And it is well known that this Character of *Ulysses* was by the Antients considered as a perfect Model of Wisdom. How unlike to this wise and moderate Temper is that political Spirit, which not only overlooks the most eminent Virtues of one of a contrary Party; but, in Defiance of Truth, Modesty, and even Common Sense, arraigns him for the opposite Vices. Abuse may indeed be called the *Nostrum* of the present Set of Jacobitical Writers, which they apply as indiscriminately, as Quacks do their Physick, without having any more Regard to the different Diseases of the Mind than the Quack hath to the several Distempers of the Body. But as nothing can be more base and infamous than this, so no Conduct can be more foolish; since, as we have formerly observed,[3] to fly in the Face of public Notoriety, is to give the Lye to, and to combat with the general Opinion of Mankind.

As we chuse, however, rather to form ourselves on the great Models of Antiquity, than on our Cotemporaries, we shall continue to preserve the former Rule in our Writings; and this is indeed highly agreeable to our Disposition, which is much more inclined to Panegyric than to Satire. We shall proceed, therefore,

---

[1] viii. 176–7.

[2] Ovid, *Metamorphoses*, xiii. 361–6: 'Your good right arm is useful in the battle; but when it comes to thinking, you need my guidance. You have force without intelligence; while mine is the care for tomorrow. You are a good fighter; but it is I who help Atrides select the time of fighting' (Loeb), emending to *nostro* and omitting *est* of line 3.

[3] See *JJ* no. 31, above, p. 322.

in this Paper to animadvert on the many Virtues which adorn the *Jacobites* of this Nation; nay, and to carry our Good-nature still farther, shall from these very Virtues derive to them the highest political Advantages.

It may, perhaps, seem strange, that so polite and candid a Writer as Mr. *Addison* should have avoided the same Opportunity of paying a Compliment to that Party, in his *Freeholder* which we transcribed last Week;[1] nor can I account for this any otherwise, than by considering that the *Jacobites* of his Days were not so conspicuous either for Virtue or Wisdom, as their Successors of these Times.

For this Reason, I suppose, among the many useful Maxims which he derived from the happy Conclusion of that Rebellion in 1715, he omitted any Mention of the great Mercy shewn to the conquered Rebels;[2] which was then scarce to be equalled in all History: For it is manifest that he could not have drawn a useful Maxim from hence, without paying a high Compliment to those whom he had supposed capable of drawing any such Maxim. Examples of a different Kind, and which are intended to convey Terror, are the properest to operate by raising Fear in bad Minds; whereas Mercy hath an Effect only on good and generous Souls, in whom it creates Admiration, Gratitude and Love.

Now, as I am sensible that the *Jacobites* of this Age are Men of a noble and generous Way of Thinking, I do earnestly recommend to their Consideration the Lenity shewn by the present Government to such Numbers who had forfeited their Lives to Justice by that most atrocious Attempt to subvert the Religion and Liberties of their Country;[3] a Lenity which these good *Jacobites* may see in the fairest Light, by comparing it with the

---

[1] The lead essay of *JJ* no. 36 is in effect a transcription of *Freeholder* no. 28 (26 March 1716).

[2] Modern estimates generally support the view that treatment of the rebels of 1715 was merciful: 26 of the captured rebel officers suffered the death penalty; approximately 700 of the rank and file were tried and sentenced to be indentured for 7 years in the West Indian plantations; after being sentenced to death, 4 of the 7 captured English and Scottish lords had their sentences commuted to imprisonment; and in 1717 the Act of Grace released the three lords still confined to the Tower, as well as some 100 other rebels either under sentence of death or confined in English or Scottish prisons. See Basil Williams, *The Whig Supremacy*, 2nd ed. (Oxford, 1962), p. 163; Alistair and Henrietta Tayler, *1715: the Story of the Rising*, pp. 172–7.

[3] See *JJ* no. 33, above, p. 341 and note 2 there. *GM*, xviii (1748), 370, reprints this paragraph and condensations of the next two paragraphs.

Behaviour of King *James* and his bloody Ministers to those poor Wretches who had embraced the Cause of the Duke of *Monmouth*.[1] This Comparison will do more Honour to the present Government, and will paint forth its Lenity in more lively Colours than is within the Power of the most rhetorical Pen. This alone, we should imagine, might be a sufficient Motive to such good and worthy Men as the present Race of *Jacobites* are, to lay aside all future Thoughts of rebelling against a Prince whose Throne is established in Mercy.

But generous and noble as these Gentlemen are, since they plead the Principle of Loyalty for Disloyalty to a Prince who hath every Title which Nature and Law can give him, and would, by the Pretence of Conscience, justify those Crimes which Conscience most abhors, it may not be safe entirely to rely on their Virtue; I shall therefore apply to their Wisdom, a Quality which they are known to have in no less eminent a Degree.

This Wisdom will teach them to deduce every Maxim from the Suppression of the Rebellion in 1746, which Mr. *Addison* formerly deduced from that in 1715;[2] and most of these indeed will be much stronger and more evincing in the present, than they could have been in the former Case.

For, besides that a second Experiment adds a double Force to that Maxim which it is brought to establish, there are many Particulars which make the Extirpation of the late Rebellion more exemplary and more conclusive against any future Undertaking of the like Nature, than any thing which could be justly predicated of that in 1715.

First, it was begun in the most favourable Season which could ever possibly offer; when we were engaged in an unequal, successless War, with two very powerful Princes on the Continent; at the Close of an unhappy Campaign, in which our Army

---

[1] Notably the so-called 'Bloody Assizes' presided over by Chief Justice Jeffreys on the Western Circuit in the summer of 1685. Conservative modern estimates put the number of executions at 150 and the number of deportations at 800; see Sir George Clark, *The Later Stuarts*, 2nd ed. (Oxford, 1955), p. 120; but cf. Ogg, *England in the Reigns of James II and William III*, pp. 149–54. The view of Hume, *History of England*, Ch. LXX, *sub* 1685, may be taken as roughly that of Fielding's contemporaries: 'The whole country was strewed with the heads and limbs of traitors; every village almost beheld the dead carcass of a wretched inhabitant; and all the rigours of justice, unabated by any appearance of clemency, were fully displayed to the people by the inhuman Jefferies.'

[2] In *Freeholder* no. 28; see *JJ* no. 36, above, pp. 359–62.

had extremely suffered;[1] when even that Army was abroad, and the Kingdom almost left defenceless;[2] and when we had just Reason to fear that the same Wind which must waft over our own Troops, would likewise being a Reinforcement from the Enemy to the Rebels.

Again, this wicked Attempt was, from some fatal Accidents, at its beginning successful: Nay, so far did this Success proceed, that after having twice attacked, and once (at least) defeated the King's Troops,[3] a Body of the Rebels marched into the very Heart of the Kingdom,[4] and became a surprizing Object of Terror to the Metropolis.

This, surely, was a Day which the most sanguine *Jacobite* could hardly have promised to himself; a Day far more terrible to all the Lovers of Liberty and the Protestant Religion, than this Age had ever seen before, or is, I hope, in any Danger of seeing again.

And if such a Day as this so soon vanished; if this great Object of Terror disappeared, as it were, like a Meteor: If all these astonishing Successes produced nothing in the End but the Ruin and Confusion of those who had obtained and contributed to them; what Hopes can Reflection afford the warmest *Jacobite*, of any future Success, when he considers how fatal a Turn the Affairs of his pretended Prince have since taken, and how morally impossible it is, that he should ever again be in that

[1] After the sanguine ambiguities of Fontenoy in April 1745, the Flanders campaign, under the direction of Cumberland, deteriorated further with the losses of Ghent and Ostend; see Fortescue, *History of the British Army*, ii. 108–23.

[2] At the beginning of the 1745 campaign British troops allotted for service in Flanders were raised to a strength of 25,000, with a consequent reduction of the garrison in Great Britain to 15,000; Fortescue, ii. 108. By July 1745, however, Walpole estimated 'not five thousand men in the island', a figure which agrees with the projections of French intelligence; Walpole to Mann, 26 July 1745 (*Yale Walpole*, xix. 79); and d'Aulnay to d'Argenson, 24 May 1745 N.S., cited by H. W. Richmond, *The Navy in the War of 1739–48*, ii. 161.

[3] The rebels attacked and defeated the 'King's Troops' at Prestonpans (Gladsmuir) on 21 September 1745. The only other 'attack', at least in the conventional sense, prior to their penetration into England, occurred on 30 August 1745, when a small force attacked the royal garrison at Ruthven and was driven off; see Walpole to Mann, 13 September 1745 (*Yale Walpole*, xix. 105), and Walter Biggar Blaikie, *Itinerary of Prince Charles Edward Stuart*, p. 10. Contemporaries acknowledged Jacobite initiative at the siege of Carlisle (10–15 November 1745).

[4] They reached Derby at night on 4 December 1745. The news came to the London public on 6 December, and 'the consternation was so great as to occasion that day being named *Black Friday*'; see *Yale Walpole*, xix. 178 n.; *Dialogue*, above, p. 7 and note 3 there; and for another contemporary account, possibly by Fielding, *TP* no. 6 (10 December 1745), p. 2, col. 2.

Situation (however desperate that was) in which he saw himself at *Derby?*

And yet, admitting that this was possible, what Comfort could it bestow? since one Conclusion, I think, must inevitably be drawn from the late Rebellion, *viz.* That not only Arms, Discipline, and Property, are on the Side of the Government, but that Numbers, likewise, are, in the highest Degree, on the same Side.

This last, I believe, was much less the Case in the Year 1715, than at present. The Populace had then been inflamed by a High-Church Clergy;[1] had been alarmed with the Danger of the Church, and frighten'd with many bug-bear Stories of the present Royal Family;[2] the Falshood of all which Time hath, at length, sufficiently discovered.

The Cause is, indeed, at present, so desperate, that the good Understanding of our *Jacobites* must certainly give it up. It is one Thing to be able to see the Absurdity of a Moral or Religious Principle, and another not to be able to discern a manifest, physical Impossibility. For Instance, if I am told, by my Father, or by my Tutor,[3] That I ought to believe that Kings have a Divine Right: That this is indefeasible: That they may, consequently, use their Subjects as they please: And that a Prince who believes this, and who claims this Right, will, when in Possession of what he claims, protect a Religion which he firmly believes he shall be damned for protecting: When I am bid believe all this, because the Person who tells it me hath heard it

---

[1] For example, by Dr. Sacheverell at Sutton, near Birmingham, in Warwickshire, where he preached on the Sunday before the coronation of George I in October 1714: 'and above two hundred of the Birmingham people came so far to attend upon him, and the consequence of it appeared a day or two after. Several of the principal inhabitants of Birmingham having resolved in a suitable manner to express their joy on the day of coronation, an entertainment was prepared for them at the Castle-Tavern. When the night came on, a tumultuous rabble got together, broke the windows of the house, and forced the company to remove: all the cry was Sacheverell for ever; and down with the whigs. If any one in the street cried, God bless king George, he was in danger of his life' (N. Tindall, *History of England . . . by M. Rapin de Thoyras . . . continued from the Revolution to the Accession of King George II*, Bk. XXVII, sect. i, *sub* 1714, note *t*).

[2] In particular, stories about the supposed ill effects of the House of Hanover's divided allegiance between the Electorate and England, and the threat of this to the 'Church'; Wolfgang Michael, *England under George I: The Beginnings of the Hanoverian Dynasty*, i (London, 1936), 88–9. Michael, i. 131, estimates that by the summer of 1715 two-thirds of the nation were hostile to the new dynasty, in particular those people most influenced by High-Church assertions that the 'Church was in danger'.

[3] Cf. *JJ* no. 21, above, pp. 246–8, and *TP* no. 24 of 8–15 April 1746.

from some other, it is most certain I shall see the Absurdity, and reject it, if I have that Portion of natural Capacity or Genius, which Mr. *Lock* requires to embrace certain sublime Truths,[1] such as that two and two are equal to four, *&c.* and which is vulgarly called Common Sense. But this, alas! is not the Lot of every one. Whereas to attempt to overturn St. *Paul's* Church by running your Head against it, is a Degree of Folly which it may be reasonable to expect no human Creature should be incapable of discerning, since it is more than probable that some of the higher Order of Animals, an Ass for instance, would not undertake the same; and this Degree of Understanding, I do very strongly contend, is possess'd by all the *Jacobites* in this Kingdom.

Here I am aware a Matter of Fact may be urged against me, and I may be asked, What then is meant by all those Tokens of Disaffection which we have lately heard of;[2] and, particularly, by all those Outrages and Riots which have been so scandalously committed in more Parts than one of this Kingdom?[3] To this I fairly answer, It must proceed merely from Want of thinking at all; a Misfortune which is very apt to attend that Kind of Good Sense which I have asserted to be the Property of all this Party: For surely no Man is so in Love with the Reputation of Folly, that he would expose himself not only to a just Exclusion from all Pretensions to every Post of either Honour or Profit in the Community, but to very severe legal Censures and Punish-

---

[1] Probably Locke's *intuitive knowledge*, whereby the mind 'perceives the agreement or disagreement of two *ideas* immediately by themselves . . . and is at no pains of proving or examining but perceives the truth, as the eye doth light, only by being directed toward it'; *Essay concerning Human Understanding*, IV. ii.

[2] For example, the original issue of *JJ* no. 29, p. 4, col. 1, reprints an item about the celebration at Lichfield of the anniversary of the Old Pretender's birthday (10 June 1688): 'We hear from L—f—d, that Friday last, being the 10th of June, was concluded with a Bonfire, Ringing of Bells, Fireworks, Rockets, and other Demonstrations of Joy. Diligent Enquiry having been made for *white Roses*, a Number of People went about the Town singing, *The King shall enjoy his own again*, and other such-like Songs; while others met in large Companies to drink Healths *suitable to the Occasion*, and distinguish themselves from the Friends of Gower and Anson.' The *JJ* commentary reads: 'Who will, for the future, have the Impudence to deny the Existence of Jacobitism in this Nation?'

[3] The newspapers of the spring and summer do not seem to record any such 'Outrages and Riots'. Possibly Fielding is referring once more to the Oxford disturbances of February 1748, or even to the Staffordshire election riots and the Lichfield race-meeting difficulties in June and September 1747, respectively. Perhaps by purest coincidence, the trials of the defendants in the latter two cases came on at the Stafford assizes on 13 August 1748, the date of this issue of the *JJ*; see *GM*, xviii (1748), 378.

ments, only for the Sake of being called a Fool: And that this will be his only Reward, he must on the slightest Consideration be convinced; since, to conclude with a serious and solemn Truth, it is a Question with me, Whether the Principles of *Jacobitism* be at present more demonstrably absurd, or the Success of its Schemes be more apparently impossible.

SATURDAY, AUGUST 20, 1748.   NUMB. 38.

Mirror tot Millia virorum tam pueriliter idemtidem cupere currentes equos, insistentes Curribus Homines videre. Si tamen aut velocitate Equorum; aut hominum arte traherentur, esset Ratio nonnulla. At nunc FAVENT PANNO, PANNUM AMANT; *et si in ipso Cursu medioque certamine hic Color illuc, ille huc transferatur, studium favorque transibit, et repente agitatores illos, equos illos quos procul noscitant, quorum clamitant nomina, relinquent.* TANTA GRATIA, TANTA AUCTORITAS IN UNA VILISSIMA TUNICA.

Pliny, Book 9, Epistle 6.[1]

Dear COUSIN,   *Litchfield, Aug.* 16, 1748.

Whatever may be your Opinion of the desperate Situation of our Cause, I promise you we shall not give it up yet; of this you will be convinced, if you dare shew your Face at our ensuing Horse-Races,[2] when we intend to march a very large Body of Forces into the Field, all drest in Plaid, which is, you know, the Regimentals of our Dearly Beloved. For this Purpose all the Taylors in this Country are very busily employed in making up Plaid Waistcoats and Breeches; nay, one Troop of us intend to appear in Plaid Boots. The Women's Taylors are likewise hard at work, and we are to be reinforced with a considerable Body of Amazons in Plaid Jackets, every one of whom is able to fight, ay, and to drink too, with any He-Whig in the Kingdom. I am your affectionate Cousin, and humble Servant, though an Enemy to your Party,

Humphrey Trottplaid.

[1] Pliny, *Letters*, ix. 6 ('To Calvisius'), translated below in the penultimate paragraph of this leader. The capitalization for emphasis in the Latin text is Fielding's.

[2] During the summer months the press carried a number of advertisements and notices, some of them politically pointed, of the race meetings to be held at Lichfield in August and September. Hence the satirical dateline of this letter. The 'Jacobite' meeting here referred to was publicly advertised as beginning on 30 August; see *Whitehall Evening Post* of 2–5 July 1748.

As the Honour arising to any Country from the Cultivation of what is useful, manlike, great and noble, is highly encreased when that Country can claim the original Discovery or Invention to itself; so the Disgrace which results to a whole People from any worthless, childish, mean or base Customs that have generally prevailed among them, should be in some Measure alleviated by a Consideration that they were not the first Inventors of this Vice or Folly, especially if such bad Customs have been imported from the greatest and most renowned of Nations.

For this Reason I am not a little pleased to find that it is no new thing for Gentlemen to dress themselves up like Fools, on certain public Occasions; nor had this Custom its first Beginning (as was supposed by many) no longer ago than last Year, and in this Kingdom:[1] For on the contrary, I find that in the Chariot Races exercised in the *Circus* at *Rome*, it was usual for the Men of the first Fashion to divide into Factions, and to distinguish themselves by certain antic Dresses.

Amongst these the *Prasina Factio*,[2] or the Green Coats, was far the most eminent, as appears from *Juvenal*, who, when he lashes these ridiculous Factions, mentions only the Green, and insinuates that this (as it was probably the most ridiculous) was principally favoured by the *Romans*.

> *Totam hodie Romam Circus capit: et fragor aurem*
> *Percutit; Eventum viridis quo colligo Panni.*
> *Nam si deficeret, mœstam attonitamque videres*
> *Hanc Urbem, veluti Cannarum in Pulvere victis*
> *Consulibus.*[3]

Suetonius, in the Life of *Caligula*, tells us that worthy Gentleman was so addicted to the Green Coats, that he used to sup in his Stable with a Green-coat Jockey, named *Cythicus*, on whom he

---

[1] For example, at Lichfield during the race meetings of 1747; see *JJ* no. 1, above, p. 93 and note 2 there.

[2] Literally the 'green faction'. Before Domitian's abortive attempt to add two, there were four factions in the Roman Circus, consisting of supporters of the four charioteering colours or 'stables': white, red, blue, and green. The latter seems to have been the favourite of emperors; see Suetonius, *De Vita Caesarum*, IV. lv. 2 ('Life of Gaius Caligula'); also Gibbon, *Decline and Fall of the Roman Empire*, XL. ii.

[3] *Satires*, xi. 197–201: 'all Rome today is in the Circus. A roar strikes my ear which tells me the Green has won; for had it lost, Rome would be as sad and dismayed as when the Consuls were vanquished in the dust of Cannae' (Loeb). Copy-text reads *deficerat* and *attonitemque*.

bestowed a vast Sum of Money.[1] The same Author likewise numbers up the many extraordinary Presents he conferred on a favourite Horse, and ends with, *Consulatum quoque traditur destinasse, He is reported to have designed him for the Consulship.*[2] In short, *Caligula* here is represented as a true *Jacobite* Squire, who would most probably rather give his Vote for his Horse at an Election, than for a Man of proper Capacity to serve his Country.

But why should *Caligula* be censured, as he is by *Suetonius,* for favouring these Green Coats? Or why should *Juvenal* fall more severely on this Colour than on the Red, or the White, or the Blue? In short, the Word *Prasina* is ill rendered. It is not here derived from Πράσον, a Leek;[3] but from Πρᾶσις and ὄνος;[4] *i.e.* of the same Value with an Ass; or perhaps the true Reading is *Prasona, a Faction that behave themselves like Asses.* Thus the Censures of both the Satyrist and the Historian are vindicated; and a very satisfactory Reason is given for the Favour of that wanton and absurd Tyrant, which would be sure to have been bestowed on the most ridiculous and absurd.

Again; can it be conceived that so elegant a Writer as Pliny should give the name of *Vilissima, the vilest,*[5] to a coat, merely because it was of a green Colour; whereas, if we can suppose that this prasinian, or prasonian Faction, were drest up in Patch-work, or in Cloth which resembled Patch-work,[6] nothing can be juster than that Epithet; for nothing, surely, can be viler than a Fool's Coat.

Had I an Opportunity of resorting to the Antiquities of *Grævius,*[7] or could consult *Ferrarius,*[8] I make no doubt, I should find direct Instances of this *Prasonum Vestimentum,* or Fool's

---

[1] *De Vita Caesarum,* IV. lv. 2, where in modern texts the driver's name is Eutychus, not Cythicus. According to Baker, item no. 263, Fielding's library contained *Caji Suetonii Tranquilli Opera,* ed. Samuel Pitiscus (Leovardiae, 1714–15), in which the latter name is given (ii. 617).

[2] IV. lv. 3. Caligula's generosity to his horse is also alluded to in *The Champion* of 22 March 1740.

[3] *Prasina* does in fact derive from πράσινος, meaning 'leek-green' or light green.

[4] πρᾶσις means a 'sale' or 'contract'; ὄνος means an 'ass'.

[5] See the last line of the motto for this leader.

[6] That is, in the plaid.

[7] Johann Georg Graevius (1632–73), Saxon philologue, student of Heinsius, protégé of Gronovius, and professor at Utrecht, published his 12-volume *Thesaurus antiquitatum romanarum* at Utrecht in 1694–9.

[8] Ottaviano Ferrari (1518–86), Italian antiquarian and philosopher, whose posthumous *De Origine Romanorum* (Milan, 1607) was later reprinted by Graevius.

Coat; since *Livy*, I remember, mentions, the Words *vestimentum versicolor*;[1] and there is a Passage in *Cicero de Oratore*, which must be understood of such a Dress: I mean, where *Cicero*, speaking of a Buffoon or Merry-Andrew, says, "Quid potest esse tam ridiculum? Ore, vultu, *denique corpore ridetur toto*;"[2] *His whole Body is the Object of Laughter*: Which can arise from no other Circumstance than his being drest like a Fool.

A learned Friend of mine contends, that the Dress lately abolished in the Highlands,[3] and which will, probably, be soon taken up in *England*, is the very Habit worn formerly by the *Prasinean* or *Prasonian* Faction; for which he urges the Authority of *Casaubon*, who, in his Notes upon *Suetonius*, *Aug. cap.* 82. says, "That the great Difference between the *Roman* and the modern Dress, consists in the Article of Breeches."[4] Now the Highlanders are, I believe, allowed to be the only *civilized* Nation which are *unbreeched*; or, at least, were so, till *breeched* by Act of Parliament.

Another very learned Man will have it, that the *Romans* themselves first borrowed the *Prasonian* Habit from the Inhabitants of this Island. "This, (says he) it is probable, was formerly the Vestment of the *Picts*, who are possibly fabled to have painted their Bodies of various Colours, only from their Custom of wearing a Party-coloured Garment."[5] Thus we may arrive at the true reading and understanding of those excellent Lines,

> *A painted Vest Prince* Voltiger *had on,*
> *Which from a* naked Pict *his Grandsire won.*[6]

---

[1] More accurately, *vestimento versicolori* ('parti-colored garment'); *Ab Urbe Condita*, XXXIV. i. 3, where the context refers to the Oppian Law of 215 B.C., prohibiting women from wearing particoloured garments.

[2] *De Oratore*, II. lxi. The accepted text reads: *Quid enim potest esse tam ridiculum . . . sed ore, vultu, imitandis moribus, voce, denique corpore ridetur ipso.*

[3] By the terms of 19 Geo. II, cap. 39 (1746); see *JJ* no. 34, above, p. 350 and note 2 there. The 'learned Friend' has not been identified.

[4] Casaubon's gloss of *et feminalibus et tibialibus muniebatur*, in *Caii Suetonii Tranquilli de XII Caesaribus*, ed. of 1611, pp. 283–4, reads: *In vestitu veterum Iudaeorum, Graecorum & Romanorum, nihil tam alienum fuit a nostris moribus, quam quod eorum usum ignoraverint quae hodie appellamus femoralia & tibialia . . . Nostras braccas non fuisse Graecis Latinisque in usu . . . Non igitur braccas antiqui noverunt.*

[5] Not identified.

[6] Quoted from *Spectator* no. 43 of 19 April 1711, where they are attributed to Edward Howard's *The British Princes* (1669), 'that Celebrated Poem, which was . . . deservedly called by the Wits of that Age *Incomparable*'. Howard's text, II. i. 87–8, reads: 'A Vest as Admir'd *Vortiger* had on,/Which from this Islands foes his Grandsire won.' *Spectator* no. 43 prints 'Voltager'.

Here Mr. *Addison*[1] well observes, That neither Prince *Voltiger*, nor his Grandfather, could strip a naked Man of his Clothes; whereas, if we restore bare-ars'd instead of naked, which I am convinced (says he) is the true reading, the Verses will remain a fine Monument of Antiquity.[2]

However this was originally, certain it is that this *Prasinian*, Party-coloured, or Fool's Coat, hath long been naturalized in this Kingdom, and appropriated to those merry Wags, whose Business it is to divert the Public at Fairs, and other public Meetings. Of these Wags, as Mr. *Addison* observes, we are so fond, that we have given them the Name of our favourite Dish, a Pudding; by which we seem to imply, that we love them well enough to eat them.[3] Had that learned Gentleman been now alive, he would have seen, likewise, the Etymology of the former Part of their Appellation of Jack-Pudding;[4] for *Jack* is the Abbreviation of *Jacobite*; and is a *diminutivum blandiendi*,[5] which they are often fond of applying to themselves.

But whether these Jack-Puddings were at first chosen out of the Jacobite Party, as the properest Objects of Ridicule; or whether the Name was, with a kind of prophetical Spirit, meant to denote the whole Party, I will not determine; but the Dress was formerly confin'd only to those of the lower Kind; nor did any Jacobite, of the Rank of a Gentleman, put on the Fool's Coat, and appear publickly as a Jack-Pudding, till the latter End of the Year 1747; when a great Number of Country Gentlemen were resolved, as *Congreve* says of a Lawyer dress'd in black, to wear their Conscience on their Outsides,[6] and to suit their Dress to their Patch-work Principles.

I hoped, indeed, that these Gentlemen had been long since ashamed of so childish a Frolick, and that *that* Ass which we

[1] *Spectator* no. 43 was written by Steele.

[2] The *Spectator* gloss reads: 'Here if the Poet had not been Vivacious, as well as Stupid, he could not in the Warmth and Hurry of Nonsense, have been capable of forgetting that neither Prince *Voltager*, nor his Grandfather, could strip a Naked Man of his Doublet; but a Fool of a colder Constitution, would have stay'd to have Flea'd the *Pict*, and made Buff of his Skin, for the Wearing of the Conqueror.'

[3] Both the term and the implication would appear to derive from *Spectator* no. 47 of 24 April 1711, which is by Addison.

[4] See *JJ* no. 13, above, p. 178 and note 2 there.

[5] More commonly *deminutivum blandiendi*, a 'flattering diminutive'.

[6] *All for Love*, IV. ii: 'Why does that lawyer wear black ?—does he carry his conscience withoutside ?'

exhibited so many Weeks in his Plaid, at the Head of this Paper, would have been the *last* in *England*, who would have been seen in this Dress.

But it appears from my Cousin's Letter, that this is not the Case, and that we are shortly to have another Rendezvous of the *Prasona Factio*, in plain *English*, a Meeting of Jack-Puddings.

However, out of Respect to my Name, I yet hope Mr. *Trott-plaid* will not make one of the Number. I wou'd advise him, in the first Place, to decline this Absurdity from respect to his own Party. *Cicero*, (says *Plutarch*) observing something ridiculous and finical in the Dress of *Cæsar*, cried out, *Who could imagine it should enter into the Head of such a Man to subvert the* Roman *Common-wealth?*[1] With how much more Justice may it be said of a Set of Jack-Puddings, Who would imagine it should enter into the Heads of such Men to be the Pillars of the Public? Or who will take them either for Patriots or Politicians?

Again, the Honour of our Country is at stake. Nations have been often characterized for their Dress. *Augustus*, says *Suetonius*, seeing the public Assembly crowded by a Multitude in shabby Apparel, cried out with Indignation, burlesquing a Line of *Virgil's* Æneid, *En*,

> *Romanos rerum dominos, gentemque togatam.*[2]

> The Subject-World shall *Rome's* Dominion own,
> And prostrate shall adore the Nation of the Gown.
>   DRYDEN.[3]

After which he commanded the Ædiles never to admit any one into the Forum, or the Circus, who was not decently drest, and in his Gown. What would that wise Prince have said, or what must any sensible Foreigner say of a Nation of Jack-Puddings!

Lastly, I hope my Cousin will consider the Digniture of Human Nature itself; for a Jacobite Country Squire, in his Plaid Waist-coat, is, in reality, a Disgrace to his very Species.

Now as few Gentlemen in Plaid Waistcoats understand *Latin*, I will conclude my Paper with the Translation of my Motto, as I find it excellently rendered by Mr. *Melmoth*, the late ingenious Translator of *Pliny*. "It is the more surprizing, therefore, that so

---

[1] 'Life of Caesar', iv. 4.
[2] *De Vita Caesarum*, II. xl. 5. The Virgil allusion is to the *Aeneid*, i. 282.
[3] 'Virgil's *Aeneis*. The First Book', 384–5.

many Thousand People should be possessed with the childish Passion of desiring often to see Horses gallop, and Men standing upright in their Chariots. If, indeed, it were the Swiftness of the Horses, or the Skill of the Men, that attracted them, there might be some little Pretence of Reason on their Side. But it is THE DRESS THEY FAVOUR; it is THE DRESS THAT CAPTIVATES THEM. And if in the Midst of the Course the different Parties were to change Habits, their different Favourers would change Sides, and instantly desert the very same Men and Horses whom they just before were eagerly following with their Eyes as far as they could see, and hallowing out their Names with all the Warmth of Exclamation. SUCH MIGHTY CHARMS, SUCH WONDROUS POWER IS THERE IN A VILE TUNIC."[1]

So far my Author; and here I cannot help adding a Note of his Translator's, which I seriously recommend to the Consideration of all the Plaid-Waistcoat Gentry: "*In the Reign* (says he) *of Justinian, a Tumult arose in Constantinople, occasioned merely by a Contention among the Partizans of those several colours,* (viz. the Green, Red, White, and Blue) *wherein no less than* 30,000 *Men lost their lives.*"[2]

SATURDAY, AUGUST 27, 1748.   NUMB. 39.

Quam non Ingenio Nomina digna meo!

Ovid, *de Tristibus.*[3]

To Mr. TROTT-PLAID.

Sir,

I am a Widow of about Sixty, with a good Two hundred and fifty Pounds in my Pocket. My Husband was by Trade a Bookseller, and a very warm Man in what they call the *Country Interest.* With such a Profession and such Principles, and keeping

---

[1] 'Letter VI' ('To Calvisius'), *Letters of Pliny the Consul*, trans. William Melmoth (London, 1747), ii. 138–9. Baker, item no. 220, lists this edition among Fielding's books. William Melmoth the younger (1710–99) abandoned a career in law (*c.* 1739) for a career in writing and translating. Sometime antagonist of Dr. Johnson and acquaintance of Fielding's friend Edward Moore, Melmoth first established himself with his pseudonymous *Letters of Sir Thomas Fitzosborne on Several Subjects* (1742).

[2] A portion of Melmoth's note on 'it is the *dress* they favour'; ed. cit., ii. 139. The parenthetical matter has been added by Fielding.

[3] *Tristia*, x. 6: 'names how unworthy of my talent' (Loeb).

a Table besides, you will easily believe he was not unacquainted with political Writers. Among these Gentlemen, I will freely confess, there was one of so intrepid and adventurous a Spirit, that my Heart has never been at Ease since I first knew him. If the Writer of a Paper called *Old England*[1] should enter your Head, you will have a good Guess.———In short, as I have now had it in my Power for above these three Weeks to reward his Passion, he has pursued me with such Diligence as would certainly have carried me, if it was not for one Circumstance: The Matter is, that the unfortunate Swain above-mentioned happens at present to be almost reduced to a Condition of starving. This deplorable Misfortune is owing to that very Mrs. *Supple*, whose Husband furnished out a Paper sometime ago in your *Journal*;[2] for before that Lady undertook the writing of *Old England*, my Lover was in the full Possession of Half a Guinea a Week, which enabled him to eat and drink, and dress and live as well as the best of them. Now, though it appears to him, and every Body else, that Mrs. *Supple's* Papers have not common Sense, or common *English* to recommend them, yet his Bread, it seems, is to be taken from him.———But why, you'll say, do I apply to you in such an Affair?—To you who have been so frequently and scurrilously abused by him? I'll tell you, Mr. *Trottplaid*.——— You have the Character of a mild and charitable Man; one that can forget Injuries, or rather, that can repay ill Offices with good ones. Now you must know that the Favour we have to desire of you is this; that you will admit my Lover to his Half-Guinea a Week, and make use of him in your own Paper.——— He assures me in the Sincerity of his Heart, that he has always had an Inclination to write on your Side, if he could have gotten the smallest Pittance imaginable; and now, indeed, it will be impossible for him to subsist, unless you are kind enough to receive him. He would have written to you himself and told you so, but that it is not his Talent to write civilly and like a Gentleman, even where he asks a Favour; for Abuse, he says, is what he has been always used to, and he finds it impossible to turn his Hand to any thing else.———For this Reason he has commis-

---

[1] On the question of his identity see *JJ* no. 13, above, p. 181 and note 3 there. Cf. also *JJ* no. 40, below, p. 380, where the failure to identify Opposition journalists is made a corollary of their wretchedness as writers.

[2] *JJ* no. 34, above, pp. 353-4, in which it is asserted that Mrs. Supple had taken over the administration of *OE*.

sioned me to be his Advocate, and has given me Instructions in what I am going to propose.

He has desired me to repeat to you, that he is utterly undone, unless you receive him into pay. Your own Understanding, he says, will lead you to believe him, even though he were to be re-admitted as a Patriot-Writer:[1] For as Reason and Argument were never his Talent, any more than Wit or Humour, he has apply'd himself wholly to Scurrility; but as every Thing must have an End, he finds his Genius to be driven to a Stand, and that it is impossible for him to carry Abuse one Step farther against the same Set of People. Indeed, he is apt to wonder at himself that he has been able to hold out so long; and that in Spite of Talents and Inclination, he could so wind up his Bottom[2] as he has done. From this uniform Behaviour to the very last, he begs you to consider how true he can be to the Party that engages him; and as Abuse seems, at present, to be the one Thing needful, in all political Controversies, he is entirely at your Service for any Dirt you have a Mind to throw. His Knowledge of the Party he has so long served under, will furnish him with some entire new Strokes, besides the old Abuse, which he shall be very ready to write over again, if he be allowed the Honour of changing Sides. Besides these, he says, he has many entertaining Stories in private Life, relating to his former Employers, which are absolute Secrets to all the World but the Parties concerned and himself; in which it will appear, that three Parts in four of them deserve to be whipt at the Cart's Tail. He hopes that a Discovery of this Kind will not be called a Breach of Trust; for he humbly presumes, that where Friendship is once broken, every Man has a Right to communicate all he knows; and for this Opinion he begs Leave to appeal to the universal Practice of Mankind. He also desires me to tell you, that if you agree to his Proposals, there is no Office whatsoever that he shall think too mean for him.

[1] That is, readmitted as an Opposition writer for *OE* or some other anti-ministerial paper. At this time the Opposition often went by the name of the 'Patriot' or 'Country' party, as Fielding himself had done when editing *The Champion* (1739–41). One of his aims as editor of the *TP* and, to a lesser degree, of the *JJ* was to redefine the concept of 'Patriot' so as to embrace support of the Government.

[2] To gather up the points of an argument in a compact statement, to sum up, to conclude (*OED*). A 'bottom' is a clew or nucleus on which weavers wind thread, and just possibly this use of a weaving term is intended to glance at John Banks, one of the 'candidates' proposed as chief writer of *OE*, and a sometime weaver himself. See *JJ* no. 17, above, p. 214, n. 1.

He can be very handy, he says, about a Gentleman's Person, having lived in several Services; and tho' his natural Talents rather lead him to throw Dirt than to remove it, he can, however, handle a Brush with Discretion, and has a new Receipt for the best kind of Blacking.

I have troubled you thus far, Sir, with my Lover's Proposals, at his own Desire. If I trespass still farther upon your Patience in Behalf of myself, I hope your Goodness will forgive me. I am (as I told you before) a Woman of Sixty, an Age that is seldom known to invite many Admirers, and which should make me cautious of neglecting the first good Offer. Add to this, that the Man is distractedly in Love with me, is many Years younger than myself, and will, in all Probability, make a faithful Husband; especially as the Necessities of his Life have hitherto secured him from the Acquaintance of lewd Women. From these Considerations, I most earnestly beg your Concurrence with the above Proposals. The Interest of my own Fortune, added to my Lover's weekly half Guinea, and a Shirt now and then from your Bounty, will afford a comfortable Maintenance to a Couple, whose first Consideration is Love, and who only covet the Necessaries of Life, as they contribute to the Gratification of that Passion. Your Answer and Compliance will greatly oblige,

Sir,

Your most faithful humble Servant,

Thursday, Aug. 18.

1748.   MARY REYNHOLDS.[1]

To Mrs. REYNHOLDS.

Madam,

I am unable to answer your Letter in the Manner you would wish, having lately received some Proposals from the *Fool*, and the *London Evening-Post*, of the like kind with yours. The Talent of throwing Dirt, which all these Gentlemen so much glory in, is, I own, very necessary for their own Papers, and, indeed, their

---

[1] Presumably a pun on holding the 'reins', that is, the power. Plomer, *Dictionary*, p. 209, lists only a T. Reynolds, bookseller in the Strand over against Fountain Tavern, 1731–3. Perhaps coincidentally, the dateline of August 18 happens also to be the date of the anniversary meeting of the Tory gentry of Oxfordshire, who gathered then 'for their High Borlace, to elect a pretty toast and damn the Duke of Brunswick'; see R. J. Robson, *The Oxfordshire Election of 1754* (London, 1949), p. 11.

only Recommendation; but at present I cannot see the Use of it in mine. If I should ever entertain a Thought of engaging one or more of these Gentlemen, it can be only to collect the News Articles of this Paper; and even these I should like to see drawn up in a new Manner; I mean, so as they may be understood. The *Fool* has sent me a Specimen of his Talents this Way; but there is a Science called Grammar that I could wish him to be a little acquainted with. The Writer of the *London Evening* may be said to abound in this Want equal to his Brother; but as *Breaks* and *Dashes* are no Parts of Speech, this Gentleman will be liable to fewer Mistakes. Upon the Whole, there is no one of these Gentlemen that I can absolutely determine upon, unless some previous Service be first done me; and there happens at present to be a fair Opportunity for this Service. I have received lately a Letter from the Isle of *Wight*,[1] written in so very bad a Hand, that I am unable to guess at what the Writer means. He seems to hint at a certain Set of grave Gentlemen that make their Appearance there in Plaid Waistcoats; but who they are, or what they are doing, I cannot possibly make out. Now if the Writer of *Old England* will give himself the Trouble of visiting the Isle of *Wight*, and will send me from thence the Particulars of this Affair, it shall recommend him effectually to the Consideration of, *Madam*,

Your most humble Servant,

JOHN TROTT-PLAID.[2]

[1] Apposite for two reasons: its remoteness and inaccessibility to one so impecunious as the supposed writer for *OE*; and its traditional Stuart and Scottish associations. In 1647, for example, Charles I escaped from Hampton Court to the Isle of Wight, where he treated with the Scottish commissioners for support against Parliament; see Clarendon, *History of the Rebellion*, Book x, *sub* 1647.

[2] This leader elicited a reply in *OE* of 3 September 1748, in which a letter signed 'Primonides' urged the latter paper to 'renew the Lash' on 'Trott-Plaid' because of his inability to get over the notion that 'there is no Difference between a poor contemptible Wretch, that *wrote Dissertations at a Crown a-piece for a late* DAMN'D *Paper called the* CHAMPION, and an Author who writes for the public Good'.

SATURDAY, SEPTEMBER 3, 1748.   NUMB. 40.

Hæc neque sunt usquam, neque possunt esse profecto.

Lucretius.[1]

Several good Writers have either through Fear or Modesty endeavoured to conceal their Names from the Public, and have sent the Children of their Brain abroad into the World, as it were to seek their Fortune, without owning them.

In this, however, they have always found it very difficult to succeed, at least for any Time; the Curiosity of their Readers, which operates on such Occasions in Proportion to the Merit of the Performance, hath seldom failed of tracing out the Author; and the Names of very few, I believe, if any, have remained unknown, if they were at all worth the knowing. Indeed this Enquiry is generally very easy; for the Number of good Writers hath been in all Ages so small, that the Search must be confined within a narrow Compass: Seldom more than four or five, and often not half so many, having been known to flourish at one and the same Time.

It may seem, therefore, somewhat extraordinary, that certain Authors should for several Years last past have been constantly pouring their Works in upon us, without any Person being able even to guess from whom these wondrous Works have proceeded. It may be, perhaps, needless to say, that the Writers here meant are those political Scribes who under fictitious Names, such as *Argos Centoculi*, *Caleb Danvers*,[2] &c. have weekly retailed their Lucubrations to the People.

Here I am aware it may be answered, either that no one hath ever thought it worth his while to enquire to whom such Productions belong; or that the Authors themselves are so low, that no Gentleman can possibly know their Names. Now neither of these Answers are true: For with respect to the first, as by the Assistance of the Party they generally find Means to lie on the Table of a Coffee-House, nothing, I believe, is more common than to hear Men express a Curiosity to know who can possibly be the Author of such d——n'd Stuff; and as to the second, it is im-

---

[1] *De Rerum Natura*, iii. 1013: 'these neither exist anywhere nor in truth can exist' (adapted from Loeb). The more commonly accepted text reads: *qui neque sunt usquam nec possunt esse profecto.*

[2] The editorial *personae*, respectively, of *OE* and *The Craftsman*.

possible the Authors should be lower than some Fellows whom
I have heard suspected, and whom I therefore acquit, as I can
hardly believe that such Persons should have the Assurance to
pretend to dictate to, or to libel any Administration.

In fact, I have long had a Suspicion that no such Persons as
these Authors are to be found among the Living; for that in
Reality they are nothing more than Ghosts or Apparitions. And
this Conceit I have entertained for the following Reasons.

First, it is the avowed Privilege of a Ghost to assume what
Shape he pleases, and to vary these as often as he pleases. Now
there is scarce a great Name, either antient or modern, under
which some of these Ghosts have not ventured to appear.

Again, what is our Idea of a Ghost, but that it is the Shadow
only, or Appearance of something which hath once existed, but
at present is no more. Now what are these Writings, but the
Shadow and Resemblance of that Wit and Humour which formerly existed in the Works of *Swift*, *Addison*, *Steele*, and others?
And doth not all this Appearance, on a closer Examination,
dissipate itself into nothing, and vanish away?

Mr. *Locke* hath very well refuted the Opinion that Ghosts
appear only in the dark;[1] but indeed that great Logician did not
perceive this idle Notion was first taken from misunderstanding
the Word Darkness, which should be here metaphorically and
not literally taken. And surely Darkness, in every metaphorical
Sense, may most properly be applied to the Works here intended.

But I wonder what Reason that Philosopher could assign for
the Appearance of a Ghost in a Sheet; which the Vulgar have
always imagined to be his proper Habit; but I defy the wisest
Man alive to mention a probable Cause why a Ghost should
rather appear in a Sheet, than in a Blanket, or, indeed, under any
other Covering. What other Solution, therefore, can there be of
this, than that a Sheet of Paper is here meant? Which is the
very Manner in which the Ghosts abovementioned make their
weekly Visits.

I shall only add one Observation more, which is a known
Fact, and is of itself sufficient to prove what I have above contended for, namely, that these, like other Ghosts, appear no
longer than 'till they are properly spoken to by the Person whom

[1] 'Of the Association of Ideas', *Essay concerning Human Understanding*, II. xxxiii. 10:
'The *ideas* of *goblins* and *sprites* have really no more to do with darkness than with light.'

they haunt: Some of them, after having made much Noise in the World, have been formerly laid for ever by a few mysterious Lines; and others have been confined in a certain *Place*,[1] from which they have never afterwards desired to be set at Liberty.

But for the Comfort of the present Set of Ghosts, I believe I may venture to assure them, that no such Methods will be taken. The noble Person whom they haunt at present,[2] hath too great a Contempt for them ever to ask the usual Question, *In the Name of G–d what do you want?* And they may sing on the same weekly Tune for ever, without any Danger of being laid—unless possibly by the Heels. A Fate which they would have undergone long ago under any other than the present mild Administration.

That these Ghosts should always chuse to haunt the First Commissioner of the Treasury, seems, I own, somewhat difficult to account for. Indeed the Treasury itself is a Place, from that long, dark Passage, divided into so many Caverns, very proper for the Residence of such Beings, and which, if it stood in any distant County of *England*, would certainly be haunted by them; but this will afford no Cause why the first Commissioner only should be the obnoxious Person.

The only Method of giving a satisfactory Answer to this, must be, I apprehend, by endeavouring to ascertain the Persons whose Phantoms these weekly Appearances really are.

Now by conceiving (and why should we not?) that these present Writers are no other than the Ghosts of some former very low Clerks of the Treasury, who, from Want of the smallest Degree of Literature, missed their regular Course of Preferment, every Difficulty will be solved. The Place of their Appearance, their Animosity to the first Commissioner, &c. Nor can I help adding how excellently well this Conjecture agrees with the Parts and Learning of these Authors, and with the Merits of their Performances.

Notwithstanding all which hath been here said, I know there are many so incredulous to the Doctrine of Apparitions, that they will not believe a single Syllable of what I have advanced. These Papers, say they, are not Writings, nor ever called so, but

---

[1] A pun on Limbo and the practice of silencing political writers by buying them off with 'places' or pensions.

[2] Henry Pelham, First Commissioner of the Treasury. He is more clearly identified in the next paragraph.

public Prints, and the Printer of the Paper is the only material and permanent Person.[1] He truly still continues one and the same, while the poor wretched Hacks whom he employs to compose these Libels, have, perhaps, been successively hanged or transported, to the Number of a Dozen, since the first Establishment of this Paper.

I cannot conclude this Subject better than by some Abstracts from what may, I think, be called the Ghost of a political Essay, as it hath only the Appearance of any Meaning. It was printed in the *London Evening* of *Aug.* 25,[2] into which it was transcrib'd from a curious Paper called the *Daily Gazetteer*, and is intituled *Fool.* N° 302.

"The Genius and Dispositions of Mankind, (says the *Fool*) however formed by Nature, or fashioned by Faction, must be necessarily regarded by all Politicians, who intend at the same Time, to be great and generally approved. *Maxims suited hereto were formerly comprized in a very narrow Compass; but are now so dilated, as scarcely to be within any Bounds. The want of Skill in Government rais'd the Taxes; and the rising of Taxes has multiplied the Maxims for governing; so that with less Understanding, more Art is required, and more Judgment, where less Skill seems to exist.*"

And a little lower, after a bombast Compliment upon Queen *Elizabeth*, he goes on thus:

"From the Time of that illustrious Woman's *being destin'd to wear an immortal Crown*, the Face of public Affairs began gradually to alter; Taxes daily gain'd Ground, and *Confusion thereupon began her impious Reign*; SKILL LESSEN'D, MATTER MULTIPLIED; a steady Attention to the Interest of the People was changed into the idolizing of Pimps, Buffoons, and Pun-makers; and true Reverence was metamorphiz'd into senseless and unmeaning Adulation; but Time, that matures all Things, could only ripen this Kind of Folly into Perfection. Political Idol Worship had, by the Year 1640, almost attain'd the Summit; but Contempt of the public Welfare had not acquir'd so bare a

---

[1] In eighteenth-century libel proceedings most commonly 'the printer and publisher, whose imprint is on the offending newspaper, are alone mentioned in the warrant, and only after their examination are further warrants issued for the arrest of those whom they incriminate'; Laurence Hanson, *Government and the Press*, p. 47; and, for the printing trade's loyalty towards the anonymity of its writers, ibid., Ch. III, *passim*.

[2] More exactly, of 23–5 August 1748.

Face, as UNTIL ABOUT THAT TIME, any Man dare openly own, that he preferred his private Interest to the Utility of the Community; a Point now so universally agreed in, that he would be deem'd as mere a Jack-Ass as the Writer of the *Jacobite Journal*, if he did not give himself the Preference; and for this a grave Senator has given us a very eminent Example, having dared openly to say, *Damn the Public, it's our Business to get Estates.*

"All great Changes in the Principles of a Nation, from stedfast Virtue to confirm'd Vice, have their Source in the Degeneracy of Government, *continued on from Reign to Reign, improving with Taxes and the burthening of Commerce, to give Splendor to the Retainers of a Court, and to make the People wretched.* A single Reign, though bad as Nero's, is not sufficient to effect an entire Alteration in good constituted Habits, nor has that been the Case here.

"The Restoration brought us a Prince who had seen too much of the Nonsense of Sects and Parties in Religion and Politics, not to make his *seeming temporary Interest the sole* Rule to his Conduct, *&c.*"[1]

That a Fool might write such Stuff as this, may easily be believed; but that there should be any one Fool enough to transcribe it, is a more extraordinary Fact; unless he had done it, as I have done, with a View of proving, that it is possible to write (or rather print) without any Meaning at all, of which I do not remember to have ever met with so pregnant an Instance. The second Edition of this Nonsense in the *London Evening-Post*, confirms likewise a very common Observation, "That there is no Fool capable of writing so ill, but that he will find other Fools capable of being his Admirers."

SATURDAY, SEPTEMBER 10, 1748.   NUMB. 41.

———*Defensoribus istis*
Tempus eget.———
                              Virgil.[2]

The following Letter, which I received last Week, appears to be written with so much Sincerity, that I cannot help giving it to the

---

[1] Substantively accurate, the *JJ* quotation adds certain typographical emphases to the *LEP* reprint.

[2] *Aeneid*, ii. 521–2: '[nor] these the defenders the hour craves' (Loeb).

Public: Tho' I own the Writer differs from me in Opinion, if he really believes the Authors he mentions to be of any Consequence at all, or to be capable of doing either Good or Harm to any Administration.

To Mr. JOHN TROTT-PLAID.

Sir,

I am a plain spoken Man, and of no Party whatsoever. If this Character (which is a true one) will recommend me to a Place in your Paper, you will act like the honest man you would be thought. The Motive to my Writing is this: In your Journal of *Saturday* last,[1] you have made a Discovery of something like an Intention of taking into your Pay, one or more of the three celebrated Writers in the Opposition; I mean *Old England*, the *London Evening-Post*, and the *Fool*. If this Letter should unfortunately come too late to prevent such an Agreement, it will be some Satisfaction to me to have done my Duty; if otherwise, it may possibly be the Means of preventing much Mischief to these Realms.

You must know, it hath always been a Part of my political Creed, that an Opposition is necessary.[2] By an Opposition I would be understood to mean just such a one as the Gentlemen above-mentioned are engaged in; and I have no Doubt, that the present Ministry have been hitherto kept within their proper Bounds, from no other Reason, than their Fears of exasperating these three great Writers. To speak my opinion truly, I believe no Opposition hath done less Harm, or more Good than theirs; especially in the Manner they have thought fit to manage it. Can any Thing be more artful or insinuating than the Irony of *Old England*, in perpetually censuring the only Measures, which ought to be pursued, and in seeming to recommend others, which would bring inevitable Shame upon us? Or again, Can any one be more delicate than the *Fool*, who has so finely instructed the Lords of the Admiralty,[3] by advancing a System of Absurdities, which ought carefully to be avoided? And lastly, Can

---

[1] *JJ* no. 39, above, pp. 378–9.

[2] An anti-ministerial commonplace. See, for example, *Craftsman* of 7 May and 14 May 1748, reprinted in part by *GM*, xviii (1748), 212–13.

[3] Presumably the 'few Papers upon Naval Affairs' alluded to by 'Simon Supple' in *JJ* no. 34, above, p. 353.

any Thing be prettier than the *London Evening-Post*, who seems every Week to be abusing People in *Breaks* and *Dashes* for doing what they never did, and for leaving undone what they ought not to do? Can any Thing be clearer, than that our present happy Prospect of Peace, is entirely owing to the Clamours of these Gentlemen against an unsuccessful War? Or will any one deny, that their sudden Dislike of this very Peace, is meant only as an Argument for War, whenever the Nation shall be justly provoked to it? Upon the whole, I look upon these seeming Opposers, to be the best negative Instructors that any Ministry can possibly have; and while the latter are careful to avoid whatever Measures the former are pleased to advise, we cannot fail of a just Administration.

If these Arguments are rightly considered, I believe, Mr. *Trott-Plaid*, that you will readily acknowledge such an Opposition ought not to be bought off; especially as it may admit of an Opening to others, who possibly may oppose good Measures in Earnest, and mislead the Ignorant. If the Gentlemen are in want, it will be nobler in you to relieve them, or to propose some Scheme whereby their Writings may enable them to live. For my own Part, I should be pleased to hear that the Government had agreed to take off a Thousand of their Papers weekly, or that the few which are now sold, might be suffered to pass free of the Stamps.[1] In short, something should be done to encourage these generous Opposers in their laudable Undertakings; the Manner of doing it must be left to yourself; and if the Arguments I have here made Use of should have their proper Effect, I make no Doubt but you will exert yourself in their Behalf, and that instead of employing them in the *Jacobite's Journal*, you will secure Bread to their own Papers.

I am,

Sir,

Your most humble Servant,

T. B.

Sept. 4*th*,
1748.

---

[1] By an Act of 1712 (10 Anne, cap. 19) a stamp duty of $\frac{1}{2}d$. had been imposed on every newspaper printed on a half-sheet or less, and a stamp duty of 1*d*. on every newspaper larger than a half-sheet but not exceeding one full sheet; *Statutes at Large*, xii. 369–70. This basic Act had been tightened by Acts of 1725 (11 Geo. I, cap. 8) and 1743 (16 Geo. II, cap. 26); see F. Knight Hunt, *The Fourth Estate* (London, 1850), i. 188–9, 204–5, and Laurence Hanson, *Government and the Press*, pp. 11–13.

In Answer to this Correspondent, I am sorry to say that his Letter came too late to prevent me from entering into an Agreement with *Old England*. According to my Proposal of *Saturday* was se'nnight,[1] that Gentleman set out on Foot for the Isle of *Wight*, and sent me from thence a particular Account of the Gentlemen in Plaid. But tho' I found his Intelligence too abusive to be made public, yet as I had given him a conditional Promise, I could not in Honour recede from it: Accordingly I have appointed him to be the Writer of the News in this Paper.[2]——— How I have proceeded with the others, their own Letters upon the Occasion will shew; and these I shall lay before my Readers, together with one written by *Old England*, exactly as I received them.

To the Scribler of the Jacobite Journal.

Mr. *Ass*,

I would have you to know that I am above any Services you can do me; and so since you have refused me the first Favour I ever asked you, you shall find that until when I am about to think of determining to lay down my own Paper, I shall never desire to undertake yours. I would have you to know I can write Grammar as well as any of you; and so the Writer of the *London Evening-Post* knows, or he would not coat[3] me as often as he does. I would have you also for to know that I am no *Fool*, tho' I call myself so; perhaps other Folks may be more so, who think themselves wise. I understand Naval Affairs too; and so you and your Friends shall know. Therefore declaring that I both despise and detest you,

I am,

Your Friend and Servant,

The FOOL!

To Mr. TROTT-PLAID, *the J–ck A–s.*

Sir,

You are a Sc—n—l, and a R———l, and a V–ll—n to refuse me. The M———y are a Pack of ———s, and I'll treat them as they

[1] On Saturday, 27 August 1748, in *JJ* no. 39, above, p. 379. 'was' means in effect 'ago'; in this case, seven days prior to the Saturday (3 September) preceding the date (4 September) of the letter signed 'T.B.'

[2] That is, the compiler of the news items to be reprinted from other papers. See below, p. 388, n. 2. [3] 'quote'.

deserve. If you had taken me into your Paper the Mischief might have been stopt; but now 'tis all over, and I shall speak my Mind. The Pr–l–m—ry A–t–cles for the G–n—l Peace shall be treated in a new Manner in my next; and you shall find that I can go near to prove, that the D—e of ————, and the E—l of ————, and Mr. ————, and a certain Person that shall be nameless, are no better than S——ls, and that they deserve a G–b—t.[1] All this might have been prevented, I say; and now you shall find me as much above your dirty Business as I am above yourself; and so

Your Servant,

The LONDON EVENING-POST.

To JOHN TROTT-PLAID, *Esq*;

If I knew how to write civilly, and to make my Thanks acceptable for the Favour you have done me, I should set no Bounds to my Acknowledgments. But the Time is come, I hope, that I shall be able to shew my Zeal in a properer Manner, *viz.* by abusing your Enemies. As this will be my principal Pleasure, I entreat to be set at Work as soon as possible; and no one shall be readier to acquit himself than,

Honoured Sir,

Your Obliged and most Abusive Servant,

OLD ENGLAND.[2]

SATURDAY, SEPTEMBER 17, 1748.   NUMB. 42.

Duceris, ut Nervis alienis mobile Lignum.

Horace.[3]

Tho' it seems to be pretty generally agreed, that Man is greatly superior to all the animal Inhabitants of the Globe; there hath

---

[1] Gibbet. The preceding 'disemvowelled' words are, in order of their appearance: Scoundrel, Rascal, Villain, Ministry, Asses, Preliminary Articles, General, Duke, Earl.

[2] On p. 4, col. 1, of the original issue of *JJ* no. 42 (17 September 1748) the department of news items entitled 'Gallimatia' is said to be 'By *Morgan* Scrub, Grubstreet-Solicitor, whileom Author of *Old-England*'. This satirical attribution is repeated in *JJ* no. 43; see Appendix VI below, pp. 480, 482. For a conjectural identification of *Morgan*, see *JJ* no. 13, above p. 181, n. 3 and no. 15, p. 200, n. 1.

[3] *Satires*, II. vii. 82: 'you are moved like a wooden puppet by wires that others pull' (Loeb).

been, I think, some Variety of Opinions concerning the particular Excellence in which this Superiority consists. *Cicero* in his Book of Invention, ascribes the Pre-eminence of Man over all other Animals, to the Power of Speech. His Words are these: *Mihi quidem videntur Homines cum multis Rebus humiliores, et infirmiores sint, hac Re maxime Bestiis præstare quod loqui possint.*[1] "Men, who in many Particulars are below the Beasts of the Field, seem to me in the Article of Speech, principally to excell them." *Juvenal* in his Fifteenth Satyr will have this to consist in Tears.

> ———*Mollissima Corda*
> *Humano Generi dare se Natura fatetur,*
> *Quæ Lachrymas dedit*———
> ———*Separat hoc*
> *Nos a Grege Mutorum.*[2]

Again, one of our Writers considers a Smile as that which constitutes our chief Pretence to such Superiority.

Smiles not allow'd to Beasts from Reason move, &c.[3]

This Dissention, of which many more Instances might be produced, may perhaps give a Latitude to some evil disposed Persons, and who are by no Means Friends of their own Species, to doubt, whether the Fact itself of our Pre-eminence hath not been too hastily taken for granted; nay the Words of *Cicero* above cited, acknowledge that this Superiority hath by some warm Heads been carried much too far, and too universally challenged: "For Men (says he, if literally translated) are in many Things lower, and weaker than the Beasts."

In Reality, this Claim of Precedence is not only to be confined to some particular Instances, but to some individual Persons.

Man differs more from Man, than Man from Beast,[4]

says the Poet, and he says truly; for as I think it must be granted

---

[1] *De Inventione*, I. iv. 5. The source of the translation which follows has not been identified.

[2] *Satires*, xv. 131–3, 142–3: 'When Nature gave tears to man, she proclaimed he was tender-hearted . . . it is this that separated us from the dumb herd' (Loeb).

[3] Cf. *Paradise Lost*, ix. 239–40: '. . . for smiles from reason flow, / To brute denied'.

[4] *Satyr against Mankind*, 224, in *Poems by John Wilmot, Earl of Rochester*, ed. Vivian de Sola Pinto (London, 1953), p. 124. The last line of the longer or 'extended' text of the 1680 editions, it is also cited in *The Champion* of 15 December 1739, and in the *Miscellanies* (1743), i. 153.

that there are Individuals of the human Species, who are of superior Dignity to the highest Order of Animals; so may it, I believe, be proved, that there are others inferior to the lowest.

Divines and Moralists have perhaps been guilty of an Error, in arguing this Inferiority from the many deplorable Vices that have corrupted human Nature. These, 'tis true, do often level Man with the Beasts, but cannot be fairly said to degrade him below them: Forasmuch as there are, I believe, no such Vices of which the Animal doth not pertake[1] in Common, with the human Species. Thus a Bear will be guilty of Drunkenness, a Hog of Gluttony; and in Wantonness, in Cruelty, indeed, in every vicious Habit, it is very easy to find a Match for the most atrocious human Examples among their fellow Savages.

The same may perhaps be said of most Kinds of Folly, for possibly there is no fine Gentleman or fine Lady in the World, who is capable of exceeding the Absurdities of a Monkey or Baboon.

To say the Truth, I know but one Instance in which Mankind can be said to be really inferior to the Brute Creation, who are perhaps tainted with every other bad Quality, but must be allowed to be perfectly clear from this which I am now about to mention. In a Word then, I do not remember to have ever observed in any four-footed Animal, the least Traces of what we call Party: A Word by which I would be understood to mean, a certain blind Instinct, that without any Foundation of Reason, or any Temptation of Interest, impells Men to act and to talk in the most absurd and unaccountable Manner; with the greatest Zeal and Fury to pursue their own Destruction, and with the utmost Inveteracy to fly in the Faces of all who would preserve them from it.

This is an Instinct far below that which was ever supposed to govern the Beasts of the Field. Those Writers who have been too proud to allow the Use of Reason to the Brutes, have, however, given them a Power so very like Reason, that it seems, indeed, little more than a Dispute about Words, whether it be that or no. The famous Case put by the Schoolmen, of an Ass between two Bundles of Hay,[2] is an Argument of this; for what can the

---

[1] Perhaps a slip for 'partake', of which, however, it was an acceptable form in the 16th and 17th centuries.

[2] The philosophical dilemma known as 'Buridan's Ass', from its association with the work of Jean Buridan (d. 1358), nominalist philosopher and follower of William of Occam, on the theory of will and the problem of indifferent choice. It hypothesizes an ass between

highest Degree of Reason do more, than direct us to the Pursuit of our greatest Good; and when two Objects are offered to our Choice, in which the Proportion of Good is exactly ballanced, our Reason consequently must balance on which to fix our Election. The same Trial might be made, I believe, with equal Success, of an Epicure placed between two favourite Dishes of the same Kind; or of a Miser between two equal Heaps of Gold: Unless, perhaps, that in the last Instance, the Miser would extend both his Hands different Ways, and at once would draw both Heaps towards him.

But was ever Man absurd enough to intimate that if a hungry Ass was placed between a Bundle of Hay and a Bundle of Faggot-sticks, he would reject the former and eagerly turn towards the latter? Do we suppose there is any Beast of Burthen so silly, that, if after having been long accustomed to heavy Loads and severe Lashes, he should by a happy Exchange of Masters, arrive at the Enjoyment of Ease and Liberty, he would yet languish after his former Yoke and Whip, and long to return to all his Drudgery again?[1] This, I say, cannot be alledged to the Disgrace of any Animal that hath the Honour to walk on four Feet, for I may call it an Honour to be, on any Account, excepted from the Number of those whom I am just going to mention.

Now, is it not certain, that there are Men so misled by a very perverse Instinct, that if you should offer Happiness or Misery, Freedom or Slavery to their Choice, they would disdain the former, and greedily swallow down the latter? Men, who if they have not groaned under the Yoke, and smarted themselves with the Lash, have at least *heard it with their Ears, and their Fathers have declared it unto them*,[2] who yet murmur and repine, because they are not as cursed as their Fathers were: And detest and vilifie all those who are instrumental in keeping such Curses from them. And all this I may here fairly affirm of a certain Party among us, as all this hath been often already, as well by myself as by others, proved to clearest Demonstration.

As this is a Character far below the Capacity or Dignity of any

---

two essentially identical bundles of hay, with no reason for preferring one to the other, and suggests that reasonable choice must somehow be possible in the absence of true preference. Cf. *Spectator* no. 191 of 9 October 1711.

[1] Cf. *The Opposition. A Vision* (1741), reprinted in Henley, xiv. 324–31.

[2] Cf. Psalm xliv. 1: 'We have heard with our ears, O God, our fathers have told us.'

of the Species of the Brutes, so it justly renders a Man liable to be considered in that Light, in which some whimsical People have unjustly placed those Brutes, I mean in that of a mere Machine; namely, a Body moved by a certain Impulse from without, and which hath not the least Guidance by any rational, or thinking Faculty within itself. A Jacobite is, indeed, as errant a Machine as a Wheelbarrow; or if that should offend by being too low and vulgar, I will say as a Clock; and goes all its Days exactly as it is set and wound up by the Hands of such who possess it. If you should ask either Clock or Jacobite, why they point such a particular Way; or why, at certain Times they send forth certain particular Sounds, they would both render an Account equally satisfactory: Both will go on in one and the same Method, or they will not go on at all. You may to as good Purpose reason with the one, as with the other. The Course of either is only to be prevented by downright Violence; and that Violence is, indeed, no less than what will be sufficient to put an entire Period to their Motion. In fact, there is only this Difference between them; the one is wound up dry, the other wet: The Clock goes by the Weight of Lead; the Jacobite generally goes by the Weight of Liquor.

If there had been any Truth in the old Fable of *Prometheus*, who is reported to have stolen Fire from Heaven, in order to animate his Men of Clay,[1] I should have imagined he had left some of his Statues without any such etherial Rays; and from these had descended the Race of Jacobites: For those who have considered the Beasts as Machines have allowed them the Power of Generation. The having formed such a Set of miserable Tools for the Use of Tyrants, and for the Plague of Society, would have been a better Reason for the Punishment he is feigned to suffer, than any Theft he could possibly have committed.

As I have here considered these People in the Nature of Machines, I shall conclude with likening them to one, which they do, in the strictest Sense, resemble. Surely I may venture to say, there never was a juster Comparison than what I am about to make, *viz.* of a Set of Jacobites to a Ring of Bells. What are the Uses of both these but to alarm the Mob, and to call them

---

[1] A conflation of two customarily separate legends: Prometheus' theft of heavenly fire, and his creation of mankind out of clay and water. For the latter, see Pausanias, *Description of Greece*, x ('Phocis, Ozolion, Locri'), iv. 5; and Horace, *Odes*, I. xvi. 13–16.

together on particular Occasions, and often for no Purpose but to get drunk? With equal Pleasure and Harmony would they summon a Popish as a Protestant Congregation; nor do they ever ring so melodiously as when they ring *the Changes*. Both alike, from their Emptiness, produce Sound; nor can they ever be pulled up to the Top without *turning* ALL *topsy-turvy*: For which, and some other good Reasons, *a Ring of Jacobites*, no more than a Ring of Bells, should ever be pulled up but by a Rope. And here I cannot forbear giving them one good-natured Wish, that the Jacobites may (as the Bells certainly will) remain for the future Quiet without any such pulling; and that as they resemble a mere Machine in so many Instances, so may they likewise resemble it in this, *viz.* never to be put in Motion unless by an adequate Cause from without.

SATURDAY, SEPTEMBER 24, 1748.   NUMB. 43.

διαβολαί δεινόν ἀνθρώποις κακόν.

Euripides, *Alexandros.*[1]

To JOHN TROTT-PLAID, *Esq;*

Sir,

I very readily agree with the Sentiment contained in your Motto from *Ovid de Tristibus*,[2] that the Names, or rather the No-Names of your very, very mean Antagonists, are greatly unworthy of the Honour of the least Notice from a Man of your Genius. And yet though it is impossible for any one to see these Persons in a lower Light than myself, I cannot so easily grant that they are incapable of doing any Mischief. On the contrary, I believe they have done a great deal; and, probably, will yet do much more in this Kingdom. I cannot, indeed, reflect, without great Indignation, that however mean and contemptible the Source may appear, yet these very Writings are, in reality, the principal Source of

---

[1] 'Slanders are a terrible mischief to men'; 'Alexandros', Fragment 56. 1, *Tragicorum Graecorum Fragmenta*, ed. Augustus Nauck (Leipzig, 1889), p. 377. See also Bruno Snell, 'Euripides' Alexandros', *Hermes Zeitschrift für klassische Philologie*, Heft 5 (Berlin, 1937), p. 13.

[2] The motto of *JJ* no. 39, above, p. 375.

that malignant Spirit which hath lately appeared in some Parts of this Nation.

It is well observed by my Lord *Clarendon*, That *we are not to conclude, when we see Men of too base and despicable Parts to enable them to do any Good, that they are therefore incapable of doing any Harm. The worst Qualities*, says he, *do often supply the weakest of Men with the Power of making an incredible Progress in Mischief.*[1] To poison the Minds of Men, as it is the vilest of all Offices, so it requires only the lowest Talents: And as we see Nature infuses that Venom, which destroys our Bodies, into the meanest of Reptiles and of Vegetables; in the same manner hath she equipped the most worthless Part of the Human Species, with the execrable Power of poisoning our Minds.

Among all the Talents which furnish out a Poisoner of this kind, the most mischievous, and, consequently, the most necessary, is that of Lying. If this Character is so detestable and dangerous in private Life, how much more so must it be in public. If a lying Tongue be so dreadful a Weapon as the wisest of Men seems to think it is,[2] in what Light shall we see a lying Pen, which can circulate a Falshood over the whole Kingdom in a Day, and may be said to be telling Lies in several thousand different Places at one and the same Time?

Whoever will be pleased to reflect a little seriously on the Consequences of this, will, perhaps, be induced to think, that a News-Paper is a Matter of more Importance than it may at first Sight appear. Books and Pamphlets make their Way more slowly into the World, if they ever make it at all. The worst of these are often buried in Oblivion before they have contracted any Acquaintance; and the best have sometimes very narrowly escaped this Fate, and have lived (if I may venture at the Expression) to an extreme old Age, in great Obscurity, and have, in a Manner, become only known to Posterity.

This is not the Case with a News-Paper, which is sure of being sent abroad into the World the Moment it is first produced. True is it, indeed, that its Life is very short, no longer, generally, than that of the *Ephemeron* mentioned by *Aristotle*;[3] the Duration

---

[1] Somewhat inexactly quoted from Book III (*sub* 1640) of Clarendon's *History of the Rebellion and Civil Wars in England* (Oxford, 1732), p. 65. Baker, item no. 501, lists this edition among Fielding's books.

[2] For example, Proverbs vi. 17, or xxvi. 28.

[3] 'The insect . . . dies at sunset having lived just one day, from which circumstance it is

of which, as its Name imports, is no longer than that of a Day. But the Mischiefs that such Papers do, and the Lies which, in this short Time, they spread, endure often much longer. For scandalous Authors, of all Kinds, may be compared to an infectious Corpse, which spreads a Contagion, and doth Execution even after Death.

To drop the Metaphor, what more expeditious, what more pernicious Method of propagating Falshood can be invented than this? Are not these Papers spread regularly at certain fixed Days in the Week, through the whole Island, where they are served up to Men as the ordinary Meals of that very hungry Passion Curiosity, which is known to swallow down any Kind of Food with the most voracious Indifference?

And here give me leave to make one Observation, which, however refined it may appear, is, I am persuaded, most strictly true, That these Papers are, of all Writings, the best calculated to do Mischief; because, as the Generality of Readers consider them only as the Relaters of mere Matters of Fact, they are apt to give almost an implicit Faith to what they read. The Mind is, as it were, put upon its Guard against the Impressions of Argument or Ridicule. But an Author (if we must debase the Name by so applying it) who professes only to tell you the Occurrences which happen from such a Day to such a Day, is sure to be read without any Diffidence or Caution. And we no more doubt him, when he assures us, that

"*It appears to be *literally* true, by authentic Accounts from H——r and Got——n,¹ that the *Foreign Adm——n of Br——h Affairs*, is, at present, in the Hands of a *High-German Doctor*"²

* *London Evening-Post*, Thursday, Aug. 11.³

called the ephemeron'; *Historia Animalium*, trans. D. W. Thompson, *Works of Aristotle*, ed. J. A. Smith and W. D. Ross, iv (Oxford, 1910), 490ᵇ1.

¹ *Hanover*, the popular name for George II's electorate of Brunswick-Lüneburg; *Göttingen*, the principal city of the princedom of that name, which had become attached to the electorate. George II had left England for Hanover on 13 May 1748, the day Parliament was prorogued, and Newcastle followed his sovereign a month later; *GM*, xviii (1748), 234, and *London Magazine*, xvii (1748), 282.

² Newcastle, Secretary of State for the Northern department and primarily responsible for Pelhamite foreign policy. *LEP* of 9–11 August derived his title of 'High-German Doctor' from a political paper 'published under that Title against the last Ministry of Queen *Anne*, and the Peace of *Utrecht*'. As part of its general attack on the pacific inclinations of English foreign policy in 1748 the Opposition press charged that by operating

Notes 2 and 3 continued on next page

than when he tells us, in the same Paper, That seven Asses started for the Purse at *Newcastle*.

In the preceding Paragraph it is most plain, there is neither Truth, nor Wit, and yet I am convinced, it hath passed for both with great Numbers. What can be the Reason of this, but that ready Assent, which, as I have said, we are too apt to afford to these diurnal Historians, who profess only to inform us of Matters of Fact, and whose Works we disdain to read with any Spirit of Criticism? If such a Paragraph should occur in an Author who pretended to reasoning, we should expect a very strong Proof of so bold an Assertion. If we were to read the like in Writings where we hoped to find either Wit or Humour, we should reject it with the utmost Scorn and Contempt: Whereas, in the hasty and cursory reading of these Papers, every Article goes down alike, and the Wit and the Truth are taken for granted.

Without transcribing any more Ribbaldry from the worst News-Paper that I believe was ever published, must not this Writer himself, if he has even Common Sense, rely entirely on such a credulous, unexamining Disposition, as I have just mentioned in his Readers; or would he have so often rung the Changes, for these several Months past, on *Cape Breton*?[1] One Day, telling us how useful this Place is to the Fishing Trade. Again, that it is all, or, at least, the most valuable Acquisition which we have acquired by the War. And then, charging the Ministry with having made a Present of this important Fortress to *France*. Now can there be a Man so weak, or so ignorant, as not to be able, on the least Reflection, to answer all these Clamours and Invectives? Who doth not see that the Question is not whether *Cape Breton* be, or be not of Importance; but whether it be of greater Importance to us than the Terms upon which we are to surrender it? And if we can, in our present Situation, conclude a Peace on no other Footing, whether it be more our Interest

---

from Hanover Newcastle was better able to prefer his sovereign's Electoral interests to those of England. During July and August 1748 George II in fact did intrude upon the peace negotiations purely Hanoverian demands that the bishopric of Osnabrück should be made into a hereditary principality suitable as an endowment for his favourite son, the Duke of Cumberland; see Lodge, *Studies*, pp. 370–4.

3 More exactly, the issue of 9–11 August 1748. *LEP* of 24–7 September asserted that this *JJ* leader was occasioned by *LEP* of 17–20 September, which was abusive of Fielding.

1 For example, in the issues of 17–19 May, 11–13 August, 8–10 and 22–4 September 1748.

to restore this Fortress, than to continue a War for its Preservation? A War which we can never hope to put any End to on any other Terms, without reducing *France* to the lowest Extremity.

And if this Island be almost our whole Acquisition, is it not, on that very Account, the more reasonable that we should surrender it, when *France*, at the same Time, agrees to restore her numerous and extensive Conquests?

Can then a Ministry be, with Fairness and Propriety, said to make a Present of that which is thus bartered for almost as good a Consideration, as was obtained by that long, expensive, and successful War, which was carried on during the greatest Part of the Reign of the late Queen *Anne*;[1] and in order to obtain a Peace, which no Nation ever more wanted, more desired, or hath, indeed, more loudly called out for.

But I am here led, unawares, into arguing with a Writer, who is, indeed, more worthy of the Lash which your New Journeyman, Mr. *Morgan Scrub*, hath begun to lay upon him,[2] than of any serious Answer from the Pen of a Reasoner.

And yet however contemptible the Abilities of this Newswriter appear to be, I am very sensible that the Effects of his Writing do, by no Means, deserve our Contempt. To spread Libels three Times a Week over the whole Island, representing the Ministry as a Set of Persons who are Enemies to the Public, and who are engaged in a Conspiracy to betray the Interest of their Country, and, indeed, their Country itself, into the Hands of its Enemies, must produce, in Time, very mischievous Consequences. There is nothing, it is true, so absurd, so nonsensical, and so glaringly false, as this Supposition. It is, indeed, as clear as the Sun, that we never had a more extensive Administration

---

[1] For the terms of the Treaty of Utrecht (1713), which terminated the latterly un successful 'Marlborough's War', see G. Chalmers, *Collection of Treaties between Great Britain and other Powers* (London, 1790), i. 340–86. Most notably, the treaty secured French assent to the Protestant succession as determined by the Act of Settlement (1701), destruction of the Dunkirk fortifications, restoration of the Hudson Bay territory, and clear title to Newfoundland, Nova Scotia, and the island of St. Christopher.

[2] See *JJ* no. 41, above, p. 388, n. 2. 'Morgan Scrub' assumed titular responsibility for 'Gallimatia' in *JJ* nos. 42 and 43; for his abuse of *LEP* in those issues see Appendix VI, below, pp. 480–3. The intensification of Fielding's attacks on *LEP* may be owing to a similar intensification of the abuse of him in that paper. *LEP* of 13–15 September 1748 intimates that Fielding's patrons are dissatisfied with his journal and are contemplating withdrawal of his salary and their support. See also *LEP* of 17–20, 24–7, 27–9 September; 4–6, 8–11, 13–15, 22–5 October; and 5–8 November 1748.

than at present. That in the Circle of this Administration are contained Men of the most known Abilities, of the longest Experience in Business, of the largest Property, and of the most confirmed Integrity that are to be found in the whole Kingdom.[1] I might add, what I firmly believe, that the Honourable Gentleman,[2] who is generally suppos'd to have the Lead, as he is known to possess the most solid Parts, and most thorough Experience in public Affairs, so he is one of the best and worthiest Men in this Nation.

And yet whoever knows the Nature of Mankind must know, that even such Characters are not entirely Proof against Slander, much less against a constant Repetition of the same Slanders. *Stillicidii casus lapidem cavat,* says the Poet.[3] In the same Manner will the almost daily Repetition of Abuse make some Impression on the least credulous Ear, for a Man may hear, as well as tell a Lie, 'till he believes it.

Go on, therefore, Sir, in the noble Task you have undertaken, and apply the only Remedy which can be, I think, applied to this Evil: By ridiculing and exposing these Scribblers, 'till every Man of Common Sense, or Common Honesty, shall be ashamed to own he reads their Writings, which are, upon all Accounts, a Disgrace to the Age.

I am, Sir,

Your Sincere Admirer and Wellwisher,

An ENGLISHMAN.

SATURDAY, OCTOBER 1, 1748.   NUMB. 44.

Nihil est profecto stultius, neque stolidius,
Neque mendaciloquius, neque argutum magis
Neque confidentiloquius, neque perjurius.

Plautus, *in Trinummo.*[4]

To JOHN TROTT-PLAID, *Esq;*

Sir,

I have lately seen a Pamphlet entitled, *Manchester Politics,* in a Dialogue between Mr. *True-Blew,* or Mr. *True-Tory,* and Mr. *Whiglove.*[5]

---

[1] Cf. *Dialogue,* above, p. 46.   [2] Henry Pelham.
[3] Lucretius, *De Rerum Natura,* i. 313: 'the fall of drippings hollows a stone' (Loeb).
[4] *Trinumnus,* i. 199–201: 'There's certainly nothing more silly and stupid, more subdolous and voluble, more brassymouthed and perjured' (Loeb).
[5] *Manchester Politicks. A Dialogue between Mr. True-blue and Mr. Whiglove* (London,

In this Dialogue the Principles of our present Tories are so justly delineated, that I cannot think it unworthy of the excellent Design of your Paper to assist in the Publication by the following Extract from it.[1]

I am, Sir,

Your sincere Well-wisher,

Manchester, Sept. 24.

1748. *An* ENGLISHMAN.

Mr. *W.* Your humble Servant. Sir, Pray where do you come from?

Mr. *T.* MANCHESTER.

Mr. *W.* What are you?

Mr. *T.* A TORY.

Mr. *W.* You may speak out; I assure you, I shall not report it to your Prejudice.

Mr. *T.* I am a *Manchester* Tory.

Mr. *W.* Pray speak out, be free.

Mr. *T.* Sir, all I can say, is, I am a Tory, and a *Manchester* Tory; and if that won't satisfy you, I know not what to say to you.

Mr. *W.* Well, Sir, since you do not chuse to give an Account what you are, or are not able, be pleas'd to answer me a few Questions.

Mr. *T.* Yes Sir, as well as I can.

Mr. *W.* Pray, where was you educated?

Mr. *T.* Sir, I went to St. C—r—n's School in *Manchester*, afterwards to the honestest College in ——

Mr. *W.* Very well, what might you learn there pray?

Mr. *T.* I learned to cry Down with the Rump manfully; to drink Church and King as oft as I dined; to hate all Whigs and Presbyterians cordially; and to believe all Clergy, but Whig Parsons, God's Vicars upon Earth.

Mr. *W.* You speak well, but pray, Sir, what do you mean by down with the Rump?

Mr. *T.* When I explain my Meaning to a Church of *England* Whig, I say, I mean no more than Down with the Presbyterians; to a Presbyterian, I say I mean only Down with the Republicans.

1748) was published anonymously for J. Robinson at 6*d*. *GM*, xviii (1748), 432, lists it among the September books.

[1] The 'Extract' is from pp. 3–11 of the original pamphlet. In the speech assignments '*T*' stands for *True-Blew*, '*W*' for *Whiglove*.

Mr. *W*. But what is your real Meaning?

Mr. *T*. Sir, it is not safe to tell what I really mean 'till Times change.

Mr. *W*. I assure you, Sir, you may safely tell me; I will not betray you.

Mr. *T*. Sir, I must own then, I mean Down with the Government.

Mr. *W*. I am glad to hear you so free: I desire to know what you mean by Church and King.

Mr. *T*. I mean a certain King that shall be nameless, and that the Clergy may both govern him and all *England*.

Mr. *W*. And why do you drink it as oft as you dine?

Mr. *T*. Because should a Whig be in Company he would shew himself, for he would either refuse the Health, or sneakingly drink King and Church, and that would put me and my Friends on our Guard.

Mr. *W*. And pray, Sir, how do you explain this to a Whig?

Mr. *T*. I tell him, by Church, I mean the Church of *England*, and as for the King, there can be but one.

Mr. *W*. Well turned; and now tell me why you hate the Whigs and Presbyterians so cordially.

Mr. *T*. Because I believe if they had Power, they would pull down the Church of *England*, and murder every honest Tory in the Kingdom.

Mr. *W*. What Reason have you to believe so?

Mr. *T*. Sir, in *Manchester* they would have taken Part of the Old Church to have made a Presbyterian Meeting, and would you believe it, Sir, a certain Dignitary in the Church joined them in it.

Mr. *W*. Surely, Sir, you must mistake.

Mr. *T*. Sir, 'tis impossible; I dare appeal to any Man in *Manchester* for the Truth of it, except the Whigs and Presbyterians themselves; besides I saw the Brick Wall built up myself, but the Dogs were obliged to pull it down again.

Mr. *W*. Why do you think they would murder you all?

Mr. *T*. Why, Sir, do you dispute it; did they not prosecute one of our Constables and another Tradesman, nay even one of our Clergy too, for treasonable Practices: If this be not Proof, I never knew what Proof was; besides they have pillory'd one Man for nothing but cursing the Elector of *H———r*; sure these

Things are not to be borne in a Christian Country, nor we can't bear them. I must own they do not meddle with us when we let them alone, but what then, they prevent us from doing what we would do.

Mr. *W.* Pray what would you do?

Mr. *T.* Hang them every Soul, like a Pack of Heretic, King-killing, rebellious Scoundrels as they are, and give their Estates to the poor abused Clergy.

Mr. *W.* You seem to be in a Passion, pray compose yourself.

Mr. *T.* I can scarcely do it, my Blood rises so at the Villains.

Mr. *W.* I desire to know why you believe all Clergy, but Whig Clergy, God's Vicars on Earth.

Mr. *T.* Believe, Sir, why I believe the Clergy, Sir, and I have heard Numbers of *our Clergy* say so in the Pulpit; in the Pulpit, Sir, where they always speak Truth; and, Sir, the Whig Clergy themselves do not pretend to be possessed of any such Right; now, Sir, does it not follow that our Clergy have a Right the Whigs have not; whoever will not allow this as a full Proof is an Atheist, a Deist, or a Presbyterian, which is no Christian I am sure.

Mr. *W.* How, Sir, no Christian?

Mr. *T.* No, Sir, no Presbyterian can be a Christian; for, Sir, their Clergy have no Episcopal Ordination, and consequently have no legal Right to baptize, and if not legally baptized, they cannot be Christians.

Mr. *W.* Excellently said, you have made the Case quite plain; but pray, Sir, is this the Opinion of your Friends?

Mr. *T.* Yes, Sir, it is both of the Clergy and Laity, nay, I have heard much the same Thing said in a Pulpit.

Mr. *W.* Well, but the Whig Clergy are episcopally ordained.

Mr. *T.* Very true, but then, when they turn Whigs they forsake the Church, and those who forsake the Church are Hereticks, and Hereticks forfeit all Right to administer Sacraments, and even *all Right to the Privileges of Christian Communion*, as Dr. *Deacon* learnedly says in his *Catechism*.[1]

---

[1] Thomas Deacon (1697–1753), non-juring Bishop and founder of a Manchester congregation called 'The True British Catholic Church', active in the Jacobite attempts of 1715 and 1745, published *A Full, True and Comprehensive View of Christianity . . . fully laid down in two Catechisms* in 1747. For charges of Jacobitism made against him during and, for a time, after the Forty-Five, see *Manchester Vindicated: Being a Compleat Collection of Papers lately published in Defence of that Town* (Chester, 1749), *passim*.

Mr. *W*. Methinks you should first prove they forsake the Church, before you condemn them as Heretics.

Mr. *T*. There is no Occasion, as the said *Doctor* in Page 408 of his said *Catechism* says; for by his third Proof, viz. *Notoriety of the Fact, they stand liable to Excommunication, Ipso Facto, without any farther Process, or formal Denunciation.* He also says further, *They stood excommunicated, Ipso Facto.*

Mr. *W*. Well, what do you argue from this?

Mr. *T*. Sir, I say the Whigs forsake the Church; this is notoriously known to all true Churchmen; therefore they are, *Ipso Facto*, liable to Excommunication; and as they are liable to Excommunication they are, *Ipso Facto*, excommunicated, and have forfeited all Right to the Privileges of the Christian Communion; consequently no Whig is, or can be, a true Bishop, Priest, or even a Christian.

Mr. *W*. But pray, Sir, have not some of your own Clergy been ordained by Whig Bishops? how are they legally ordained; as you say those Bishops are, *Ipso Facto*, excommunicated?

Mr. *T*. Why really, Sir, I am concerned to see you raise such trifling Objections. The *Doctor* says in his *Catechism*, Page 431, "The Case of heretical, schismatical, episcopal Ordinations, is a Point of Discipline which the Church has Power to relax, or extend discretionally, as she judges most expedient and beneficial to her Service; so that she may either reverse, and disanul the Ordination of episcopal Heretics and Schismatics, for Discipline's Sake, and to shew her Resentment of their Errors, or allow them to stand good, and confirm them for her own Sake, to prevent greater Scandals, and to encourage the Unity of the Catholic Faith." Thus you see our Clergy can either allow the Ordination to be good, or no, as is *for the Church's Service*; so if he that is ordained by a Whig Bishop be a Tory, his Ordination is good, but if a Whig, it is invalid per se.

Mr. *W*. What then is your Opinion of those baptized by Whig Parsons?

Mr. *T*. I beg, Sir, you would not trouble me with such trifling Questions. Sir, the *Doctor* gives the self-same Argument in Cases of heretical, episcopal Baptism, as I gave in my last Quotation, the Word Baptism being transposed for Ordination. See *Catechism*, Page 226.

Mr. *W.* Really, Sir, I perceive you have the Whigs at a very great Advantage.

Mr. *T.* Yes, Sir, the Clergy have the spiritual Power in their own Hands: They can either christian or unchristian, save or damn them, just as they please; and we would soon shew them as much, but that the Rascals have the Temporal Power in their Hands, which prevents us treating them as they deserve, *&c.*

SATURDAY, OCTOBER 8, 1748.   NUMB. 45.

————*Sed quid*
Turba Remi? Sequitur fortunam, ut semper————.
Juvenal.[1]

Whoever reads and observes the Passages in Commonwealths, (says *Machiavel*) *will find a Touch of Ingratitude towards their Citizens in them all.*[2]

These are the Words of that great Politician in his Discourses upon *Livy,* and as they seem to contain the severest Invective which can possibly be cast on Mankind; so I am sorry to acknowledge their Truth seems too much justified and confirmed by History.

Here many moral Writers would content themselves with turning Satyrists, and would think they had very well accounted for the Justness of the above Observation, by laying a heavy Charge upon Human Nature in general, and by supposing, that the odious Vice of Ingratitude is one of the common Ingredients in the Composition of Man.

This is, as I remember, the Sentiment of some modern *French Theophrastus;*[3] but it is no less repugnant to Truth, than to the wise Opinion of the antient Philosophers, and particularly

---

[1] *Satires,* x. 73–4: 'And what does the mob of Remus say? It follows fortune, as it always does' (Loeb).

[2] 'Discourse of Nicholas Machiavel . . . upon the First Decade of Titus Livius', I. xxviii, in *Works of the Famous Nicholas Machiavel,* 3rd ed. (London, 1720), p. 297. Baker, item no. 447, lists this edition among Fielding's books.

[3] Jean de La Bruyère (1645–96) published his *Caractères de Théophraste traduits du grec, avec les caractères ou les mœurs de ce siècle* in 1688. The reference here seems to be to the essay 'Of Man' in 'The Characters or, Manners of the Present Age', *Works of Monsieur De La Bruyère,* trans. N. Rowe, 6th ed. (London, 1713), ii. 210: 'Let us not be angry with Men, when we see them Cruel, Ungrateful, Unjust, Proud, Lovers of themselves and forgetful of others; they are made so.' See also *JJ* no. 29, above, p. 312, n. 2.

404 *The Jacobite's Journal*

those of the *Platonic* Sect, who have taught us to think much higher of our Species, and to consider the ungrateful Man as a Monster, or, indeed, as a Wolf disguised in a Human Shape.

In reality, we must dive much deeper into Nature, if we would reconcile the Words of the Politician to Truth: For I am much deceived if, upon due Examination, we do not find that, tho' this Behaviour, which *Machiavel* remarks in Commonwealths, may have the same Appearance, and the same Consequence with Ingratitude, it arises from very different Motives. All Countries have, indeed, made the basest and most ungenerous Returns to those great Men who have exerted the highest Virtues and Abilities in their Service; but this hath happened through their Blindness and Ignorance, and not from any ungrateful Spirit of the People. They have, I confess, often punished those Virtues which they should have endeavoured to reward; but then they have at the same Time mistaken them for Vices. Thus they have frequently destroyed their Deliverers; but never when they have considered them in that Light.

Taking, therefore, this ungrateful Behaviour of the People for granted, as we have the Authority of the greatest of Politicians, and, indeed, the concurrent Testimony of all the Histories of Free Countries, and particularly of the *Grecian* Commonwealths, to support the Fact; we may, I think, very well account for it by a much better Method, than by making the blackest of all Vices the Characteristic of Human Nature.

First, then, tho' I have a better Opinion of the Understanding of the Multitude than many Writers have profess'd; tho' I do not compare them, with *Polybius*, to the Waves of the Sea;[1] nor with one of the Fathers, to the Clouds which are driven at Pleasure by any Wind that blows;[2] tho' I do not liken them, as *Erasmus* doth, to a Flock of Sheep implicitly following their Leader,[3] and, in another Place, to a much more savage Animal, (*indomitæ bellæ.*)[4] Lastly, tho' I do not, with *Tacitus*, take from them all Judgment as well as Truth;[5] nor agree with him* in *Laertius*,

* *Antisthenes.*

---

[1] *Histories,* XI. xxix. 9–11; cf. also VI. xliv. 3–4 and lvi. 11.
[2] Not identified; but cf. Jude 12: 'clouds *they are* without water, carried about of winds'.
[3] Not certainly identified. But cf. 'Adagiorum', Chil. II, Cent. VII, Prov. xxvi (*Ovium nullus usus*), in *Opera Omnia* (Lugduni Batavorum, 1703), ed. Joannes Clericus, ii. 620.
[4] *Apothegmata,* VI, 'Diversorum Græcorum Apothegmata', xcii, in *Opera Omnia,* iv. 303.
[5] Cf. *Annals,* VI. xxii; *Histories,* II, xxix and xc, and v. xiii.

who boasted, that it was the great Rule of his Life to dissent from, and to oppose the Opinion of the People.[1] Tho' I am inclined, I say, to entertain much more favourable Sentiments of the Multitude than those which I have here cited, I cannot, however, on the other Side, run up my Admiration of them to Enthusiasm; nor can I persuade myself that they are gifted with Infallibility. To speak plainly, I am a little inclined to doubt whether Politics (tho' it seems at present to be thought the universal Science, and within the Reach of every Capacity) be, indeed, the proper Study of the Multitude; since Experience, I am afraid, if not Reason, must convince us, that they are herein liable to commit rather grosser Errors than their Superiors. I acknowledge, that they are generally right in the End proposed; but they are sometimes defective in a right Application of the Means. Thus, for Instance, I am well convinced, that if our Government was, at present, in the Hands of our Country Fellows, or of our Country Gentlemen, which is much the same Thing, the first Resolution they would take would be, as we were advised last Winter in a Pamphlet, *to seize the whole Trade of* France *to our own proper Use.*[2] Again, a second political Measure would be, to make an immediate Peace with that Power (for War is attended with Taxes, which are odious to the People) but this Peace would have been on the same Conditions as if we had had an Army at the Gates of *Paris*, viz. *That France should restore all which she had taken, and we should retain our single Purchase.*[3]

Now could *Machiavel*, or any Politician upon Earth, have invented more salutary Schemes than these? And yet, when we come to consider the Means by which these are to be accomplished, all the Wisdom vanishes in a Moment, and Don *Quixote's* Project of conquering Armies by the Valour of half a Dozen Knight-Errants,[4] presently occurs to our Memory.

---

[1] See the life of Antisthenes, *Lives of Eminent Philosophers*, vi. 1–19. However, Laertius does not record any boast by Antisthenes in precisely these terms. Pupil and friend of Socrates, Antisthenes (*c.* 455–360 B.C.) was a founder of the Cynic school of philosophers.

[2] *The State of the Nation for the Year 1747, and respecting 1748* (London, 1748), esp. pp. 30–2. See *JJ* no. 10, above, p. 150 and note 3 there.

[3] An Opposition commonplace; cf. *State of the Nation*, p. 61.

[4] Perhaps an inexact recollection of *Don Quixote*, part ii, Ch. i, where the Don asserts that from among only half a dozen knights-errant in Spain one could be found to overthrow the invading Turkish armies. But cf. *JJ* no. 10, above, p. 150, where *The State of the Nation* and *Don Quixote* are similarly juxtaposed and the allusion to the latter seems much more general.

Here then lies the Deficiency of the Multitude's Judgment in Politics; and to this Want of duly considering the Means, and proportioning them to the End, is to be imputed all that which *Machiavel* attributes to Ingratitude in Commonwealths; for no Country which I have read of, have ever hanged a Conqueror with his Laurels on his Brow: Then it is *Marlborough* for ever; the Duke for ever;[1] an *Anson* and *Warren* for ever.[2] Even the *Athenians*, the most ungrateful of all Nations to their Deliverers, received their victorious Generals with Acclamations. It was not for doing the great Things they had done; but for not doing the great Things which they could not do, that the greatest of Men have fallen Sacrifices to the Folly of the People.

Why should I seek remote Instances? Let us cast our Eyes only a Year or two backwards, when an Army of Savages had advanced into the Heart of this Kingdom, to the Terror, as it appeared, even of those *Jacobites* themselves, who had any Property to secure. When Numbers were packing up their Goods and their Plate, in order to retire even from the Metropolis, they knew not whither, for Safety. When, at that Time, public Credit stood tottering, as it were on a Pinnacle, whence it was every Moment expected to fall for ever, it is well known to have been principally supported by the Virtues, by the Abilities, and by the Character of that Gentleman whose Name was supposed to stand first in Power.[3] Did not all Men then agree in his Applause? Did any Miscreant then dare to send forth a Whisper to his Disadvantage? With what Glory did he soon after experience the universal Love of his Country, in an Instance which History can scarce equal, when the short Eclipse of his Power[4] was lamented by all Ranks of People, with no less Bitterness than the *Indians* lament the Eclipse of their Sun?

Many other Examples might be produced in Favour of the Gratitude of the Public towards their Benefactors. In Truth when they act otherwise, it is not from an ungrateful Principle, but from their Weakness and Ignorance; and in all such Cases their Heads and Hands are guilty, but their Hearts are free.

Nor can it be wondered at, that they have given frequent Instances of this Weakness, when we add to that Deficiency in their

---

[1] Alluding to the Duke of Cumberland as conqueror of the Jacobite rebels in 1746.
[2] See *Dialogue*, above, p. 45, n. 2.   [3] See *Dialogue*, above, pp. 47–9.
[4] During the 'forty-eight-hour ministry'; see *Dialogue*, above, p. 19 and note 1 there.

Politics abovementioned, another Circumstance, which is ever ready to contribute its Assistance to the Destruction of the best of Men, and without the Intervention of which, scarce any of those black Facts which gave Occasion to the Politician's Remark in the Beginning of this Paper would have happened.

Now as the Multitude are not of themselves, as I have hinted, very adequate Judges of Politics, they must be liable to be misled by others; and such Misleaders they never fail to find in every free Country. These are indeed a Sort of Human Vermin, which are ever certain to generate in the rich Soil of Liberty, and their infectious Breath doth often corrupt, poison and destroy, that very Liberty to which they owe their Being.

These Misleaders of the Public, in one Particular especially, (indeed in many others) do greatly resemble that wicked Tribe of Men who make it their Business to mislead our Youth. Their principal Aim is to inflame the Minds of the People against their best and truest Friends; for before they can hope to accomplish their Ends, it is first necessary to draw them out of the Hands and Protection of an able and faithful Guardian. In this the Miscreant generally succeeds with great Facility: For what the Law tenderly says of the Church, *Ecclesia est infra Ætatem et fungitur Vice Minoris*,[1] may most aptly be applied to the Body of the People, who like Children are always jealous of their Governors, and fearful of their Power, tho' never so honestly exerted for their own Good. A Sentiment which the Annals of every free Nation will confirm, and which hath scarce escaped the Observation of one good Historical or Political Writer. Instead therefore of filling my Paper with Common Place, I shall content myself with transcribing only the Words of *Machiavel*, which are very express on this Head. "Men (says he) of excellent Qualifications in corrupted States (especially in Times of Peace) by Reason of the Envy or Ambition of other People, are subject to be hated; therefore such Councils are generally followed as the deluded Commons think best; *or such as are recommended by those who are more solicitous of the Favour than of the Benefit of the People!*"*

* *Discors Sopr. Liv. l. 2. c. 22.*[2]

---

[1] 'The Church is under age and stands in the position of a minor.' For the legal precedents of this gloss see Edward Coke, *The Second Part of the Institutes*, 6th ed. (London, 1681), p. 3.

[2] II. xxii, ed. cit., p. 361.

There are certain Seasons which these *Solicitors of Favour*, these Demagogues, well know are best suited to their Machinations, and which they are commonly very sure to lay hold of. In the happy Times of Success and public Prosperity, they are obliged to lie dormant and conceal that Venom, which Seasons of Danger, Difficulty and Distress never fail to call forth; for the People, as we have said, consider Ends only and not Means. When the Event, therefore, which *Livy* calls the Master of Fools,[1] is prosperous and agreeable to their Wishes, they never concern themselves about the Means; however accidental, ill-advised, hazardous or even ruinous these may have been. On the contrary, if the End they desire is not wholly obtained, the most regular Plans, and the most prudent, safe, and advantagious Councils lose all Merit in their Eyes, and their Ears are immediately open to the Slanders of the Demagogue.

I will conclude with an Example of this Temper of the People, which I hope no future Age will ever equal. This is the Case of the Dictator *Fabius Maximus*, and of his Master of the Horse *Minucius Rufus*.[2] The former, by delaying and avoiding every Engagement with *Hannibal*, had for a long Time preserved his Country and had almost reduced the Enemy to the last Extremity. The latter, taking Advantage of the Dictator's Absence, had rashly left his strong Camp upon the Hills, and marched into the Plain. The Consequence of which was a Battle, or rather a Skirmish, in which *Minucius* had the good Fortune, merely owing to *Hannibal's* Apprehension of the Approach of *Fabius*, to gain some little Advantage, having killed 6000 of the Enemy, with the Loss of 5000 of his own Forces. Upon this Skirmish, where the Loss (says *Livy*) was almost equal, the News of a mighty Victory, with the vain Letters of the Conqueror, was brought to *Rome*. This threw the City into a Tumult of Joy, and when *Fabius*, being there present, expressed his Doubts and Apprehensions, *Metilius* the Tribune of the People fell most bitterly upon him, accused him of having obstructed the public Service, of detracting from the Glory of him who had effected it, of protracting the War, in order to continue his dictatorial Power, *&c.*

---

[1] *Ab Urbe Condita*, XII. xxxix. 10, where the saying is quoted as part of a speech by Quintus Fabius Maximus, the 'Cunctator'.

[2] For this and succeeding details from the episode in the Punic wars Fielding is drawing upon *Ab Urbe Condita*, XXII. xvi–xxix.

Which Speech had such an Effect on the *Romans,* that *Fabius* thought proper to leave the City by Night and to return to the Army, and the next Day the Master of the Horse was made equal to him in Power. A Promotion, says my Author, which every Individual, either at *Rome* or in the Army, except himself only, considered as an intended Affront to the Dictator, who bore this Insult of the outragious People (*Injuriam Populi in se Sævientis*)[1] with the same Greatness of Mind with which he had borne the Accusations of his Enemies, and with which he afterwards revenged himself in shewing them their Error, by rescuing his insolent Rival, and one Half of the *Roman* Army from the Hands of their Enemies.

SATURDAY, OCTOBER 15, 1748.   NUMB. 46.

Quæris quando iterum paveas, iterumque perire
Possis. O toties servus! Quae bellua ruptis
Cum semel effugit, reddit se prava Catenis?

Horace.[2]

To the two Causes of popular Ingratitude, which I assigned in my last, there may, perhaps, be added a Third, of which, though it should have so much the Air of a Paradox, that the very mention of it might, at first Sight, offend an over-hasty Reader, I doubt not to evince the Truth, from an irresistible Weight of Evidence.

From this Confidence I shall boldly venture to assert, in Contempt of all preconceived Opinions, and vulgar, erroneous Notions, that Man is to be considered as *ZΩON ΦIΛOΔOYΛO-ΣYNON,* in plain *English,* an Animal that delights in Slavery.

This will absolutely acquit us of all Charge of Ingratitude; since, if this Position can be proved, we shall, at once, remove all the Obligation, which the Deliverers of Countries have been hitherto thought to have laid on their Fellow Citizens: For from what have they delivered us, but from our Idol, our Darling, and our Delight? And may we not justly cry out with him in *Horace*;

[1] The generally accepted text, from XXII. xxvi. 7, reads: *populi in se saevientis iniuriam.*

[2] *Satires,* II. vii. 69–71: 'you will seek occasion so as again to be in terror, again to face ruin, O you slave many times over! But what beast, having once burst its bonds and escaped, perversely returns to them again ?' (Loeb), reading *quæres* for *quæris.*

————*Pol me occidistis*, &c.[1]

"My Friends, 'twere better you had stopp'd my Breath;
Your Love was Rancour, and your Cure was Death.
To rob me thus of Pleasure so refin'd,
The dear Delusion of a raptur'd Mind."

Mr. FRANCIS.[2]

To begin, then, with two of the greatest Authorities in all Antiquity. Doth not *Aristotle* most excellently well prove, in the first Book of his *Politicks*, that all Mankind, except the *Grecians*, are by Nature Slaves?[3] And doth not *Cicero* assert pretty much the same of every Nation, except the *Romans? Aliæ nationes servitutem pati possunt. P. R. propria est libertas.* "*Other Nations can endure Slavery; but Liberty is the peculiar Property of a* Roman."[4] It is true, he only says, *can endure it*; but we are to consider the Delicacy, as well as Country of a Writer: Nay, indeed, to endure it, and to love it, is much the same Thing: For, as we shall prove by and by, no Nation ever endured it long, without being enamoured of its Charms.

And here, without observing that the Sentiments of these two great Men, while they concur in proving our general Point, do no less contradict each other's Exception: If we admit both these Exceptions, on a single Authority only, what Argument can they afford against the Position we have above laid down? For besides, that the Numbers excepted will be very inconsiderable when opposed to the whole Race of Mankind, a very good Reason may be assigned, why the *Greeks* and *Romans* should have deviated (I will not say degenerated) from the rest of Mankind in this Instance: Since they are known to have been bred up in an utter Abhorrence of Slavery; nay, may have been said to have sucked in this Abhorrence with their very Milk; as their Mothers were no less likely to teach it them than their Fathers: And what the Force of an early and uniform Education is, need not be here declared. It was to this they entirely owed that Love

[1] *Epistles*, II. ii. 138 ff. The cry is that of an unnamed man in Argos, who used to fancy he was listening to wonderful tragic actors when in fact he sat happily applauding in an otherwise empty theatre. Through the good offices of friends he was cured of his delusions, and this cry shows his profound regret.

[2] *A Poetical Translation of the Works of Horace*, trans. Philip Francis (London, 1747), iv. 235, 237. Baker, item no. 558, lists this edition among Fielding's books.

[3] I. vi. 29–37 (1255A). This is an overstatement of Aristotle's position.

[4] *Philippics*, VI. vii. 19. The accepted text reads: *populi Romani est propria libertas.*

of Liberty, by which they were so distinguished from all other People; and when this once ceased among them, they soon followed the Dictates of unadulterated Nature; and from that Day, these Lands of ancient Freedom have produced as good Slaves, as you would wish to buy in a Market.

We find then, in Opposition to the Vulgar Opinion, these two great Philosophers asserting, that Mankind are, in general, naturally disposed to Slavery. A Truth which the History of all Nations abundantly evinces.

The *Jews* are well known to have been so extravagantly fond of Slavery, that they were not contented with the unspeakable Happiness and Honour of being under the immediate Care and Dispensation of God himself, while they were obliged to purchase these Blessings at the Rate of retaining that Liberty, under which they groaned; and which was so intollerable a Burthen to them, that they cry'd out, with one Voice, *Give us a King, that we may be like unto other Nations*; in other Words, *that we may be Slaves*:[1] For so were all the Nations, which, at that Time, were under Kingly Government.

That the Inhabitants of that vast Empire, which descended from the *Babylonians* to the *Assyrians*, *Medes*, *Persians*, and *Macedonians*, were all Slaves, no Man, who is at all acquainted with Antiquity, will doubt. That they delighted in being so is no less certain. Indeed, that they submitted to be so for such a Succession of Ages is Proof sufficient. In all which Time, there is not one Instance of any Stand made, or even any Attempt in Favour of Liberty. All their Struggles were only to change Masters; and often, if we may judge from the Event, to rivet their Chains on the faster.

I have not Room in this Paper, to run through the Annals of all Countries; in which the Behaviour of the People hath testified that Love of Slavery, which we have above asserted to be inherent in Human Nature; of which modern History furnishes us with no less pregnant Proofs than the antient, with Examples of Nations, whose chief Glory it hath been to be Slaves themselves, and to make others so.

Let us pass at once to our own Country, and come down to an

---

[1] 1 Samuel viii. 19–20: 'Nay; but we will have a king over us; That we also may be like all the nations.' Cf. 1 Samuel viii. 5: 'now make us a king to judge us like all the nations'; and see also *JJ* no. 25, above, p. 285.

Age very little removed from the present; so little, that the Panegyric of Mr. *Carte* hath not yet reached it.[1] Is it possible to give a more undeniable Instance of the general Affection of any People for Slavery, than may be found in the Behaviour of this Nation, during the Reigns of four Princes of the *Stewart* Family? Whence could arise that visible and violent Attachment to all these Princes, and more especially to the worst of all, which hath been remarked by our best Historians, unless from our ardent Love and Desire of that Slavery, which every one of them so plainly endeavoured to entail upon us? It is true, indeed, these Endeavours were fatal to two of these Princes; and the one lost his Throne, and the other his Head, in their Pursuit. But both these tragical Events were accomplished by the Hands of a desperate Party, who were inspired with the enthusiastic Spirit of Liberty, and (as Lady *Fairfax* is reported to have cried out at the Trial of *Charles* I.) not with the Consent of the hundredth Part of the People.[2] Have not Sons, Grandsons, and Great Grandsons, fasted and prayed, and howled almost these hundred Years, to propitiate the tragical Death of the one? And have we not as bitterly (if not quite as publickly) lamented the tragical Expulsion (or rather running away) of the other? As for that facetious Monarch, who dy'd with his Crown on his Head, after many numberless Attempts to put a Chain on our Necks, who, not trusting to our natural Love for Slavery, sacrificed not only the Interest of *England*, but of all *Europe*, to *France*; in order to make himself a mediate Tyrant by that Assistance, and under the Imperial Influence of that Crown. How we loved, how we adored this Monarch, can only be illustrated by the Instance of a poor Lamb, which licks the Hand of the Butcher, while he is preparing to cut its Throat.[3]

---

[1] By this date only the first volume of Thomas Carte's *General History of England* (1747-) had appeared. The *terminus ad quem* of the volume was announced as the death of King John (1216). See also *JJ* nos. 9, 12, and 13, above, pp. 145, 168, 177.

[2] According to Clarendon's *History of the Rebellion* (Oxford, 1732), Bk. XI, p. 562, Lady Fairfax's words were: 'No, nor the hundreth part of them.' Baker, item no. 501, lists this edition among Fielding's books. Wife of Thomas Fairfax (1612–71), 3rd Baron Fairfax of Cameron and commander-in-chief of the parliamentary army, Lady Fairfax is reported by Clarendon to have done her best to prevent her husband, who was one of the judges at the trial, 'from acting any part in it'.

[3] Cf. Pope, *Essay on Man*, i. 81–4: 'The lamb thy riot dooms to bleed to-day, / Had he thy Reason, would he skip and play? / Pleas'd to the last, he crops the flow'ry food, / And licks the hand just rais'd to shed his blood.' Maynard Mack, *An Essay on Man*, Twicken-

Lastly, as our Attachment to such Administrations can be only deduced from that natural Love of Slavery which is in us; so is it, I apprehend, as difficult to derive any Disaffection to the present Government, from any other Cause. This, indeed, will abundantly account for the highest Murmurs at this Season. For it is not only a plain Fact, that no Country under the Sun ever enjoyed a more pure and absolute Freedom than we now possess; but it is surely demonstrable from Reason, that to enlarge our present Liberty, is not in the Power of our Governors themselves; unless, instead of being duly governed by the known Laws of our Country, which is the Idea that hath hitherto been assigned to the highest State of Liberty, we mean, by that Word, an utter Abolition of all Law and Rule whatsoever.

But, in Truth, the Redundance of Liberty is the Evil under which we groan. And this, indeed, is sufficiently apparent, by the Exchange which we are desirous to make, by entailing certain, incurable Slavery on ourselves and our Posterity.

As many will be yet inclined to doubt, notwithstanding all that I have here advanced, whether there be really any Principle in Human Nature, so much below what is to be found among the Brutes, as *Horace* says in my Motto; as I introduced this Essay with the Authority of *Aristotle*, I will conclude it with that of *Plato*; who tells us, in his *Laws*, *That the Excess of Liberty is no less an Evil than that of Slavery.* His Words are, Δουλεία γὰρ καὶ ἐλευθερία ὑπερβάλλουσα μὲν ἑκατέρα κακόν.[1] If this Sentiment be true, I must own the Liberty of this Country is, at present, in Danger;——for sure it is in Danger of running to Excess.

SATURDAY, OCTOBER 22, 1748.   NUMB. 47.

Periculosæ plenum opus aleæ.

       Horace.[2]

My Recollection doth not furnish me with an Example, from History, of any one political Æra, in any Nation, when the

ham Edition of the *Poems of Alexander Pope*, III. i (London, 1950), p. 24, records analogues in Ovid (*Metamorphoses*, xv. 96–142) and Phaedrus (*Fables*, v. i. 4–5).

[1] In fact, the statement is from *Epistles*, viii. 354E, where the accepted text prints πάγκακον for κακόν. A similar statement can be found in *Laws*, iii. 701E.

[2] *Odes*, II. i. 6: 'a task full of dangerous hazard' (Loeb).

Management of Public Affairs hath required that great Delicacy, which hath been so absolutely necessary to, and so admirably preserved by the glorious Saviours of this Kingdom, at this Time.

The dreadful Cloud that, a Year or two ago, hung over our Hemisphere, and which hourly threatened to break upon us, and overwhelm us with inevitable Destruction, was visible to every Eye, and lamented almost by every Voice. But though we all saw too much, very few of us, I believe, saw all. The gathering Storm appeared, but all the black Materials of which it was composed, were known only to the best political Astronomers. And though every Man agreed in the exceeding great Difficulty there was in dispersing this Storm, scarce any knew where the Difficulty principally lay; or what were the Dangers to which we must expose ourselves in the dispersing it.

The Public, to say the Truth, may lately have been compared to a natural Body, afflicted with a Complication of Distempers. In the Case of a single Disease, however violently it may rage, no great Skill is required in the Physician. He hath the Experience of Ages to direct him in his Application; and if his Medicines cannot cure his Patient, it is almost impossible they should injure him: But when we are attacked by contrariant Distempers; when the same Methods which lessen and relieve the one, will inflame and aggravate the other; then it is, that the utmost Sagacity, the utmost Nicety, become requisite to restore us to Health, or to preserve us from Dissolution.

Nor is this Illustration, though it represents our Condition in so wretched a Light, anywise adequate to paint it in its full Extent of Horror. There was one Difficulty, especially, with which our Administration were obliged to struggle, that can be matched by none, which ever occurs to the Physician. This, however, I must be contented to refer, with many other Particulars, to the Knowledge and Admiration of Posterity; if, indeed, they will be able to believe what we are not able, at present, even to mention.[1]

In such a Situation as this, how delicate ought to be the Pen of that public Writer, who should take upon him the Support of

---

[1] Fielding's affectation of forbearance with respect to the 'one Difficulty' facing the Pelhams suggests that he is referring to the divisiveness represented by George II's hostility, Granville's threatening presence in the royal favour, and the Prince of Wales's Opposition tactics. By late 1748, of course, the first two conditions were no longer in effect.

such an Administration? How strictly ought he to follow their great Example, in concealing those dangerous Wounds of the Public, which they are endeavouring to heal? How cautiously must he pursue their Steps, through all the Obstructions and Embarrassments, through which they have so resolutely, and, at the same Time, so prudently waded?

And this Caution I may, with Justice, I hope, say, I have inviolably preserved, in Defiance of those many Provocations, which have been purposely thrown in my Way; though, in this Forbearance, I have sometimes, I confess, done no small Violence to myself: For nothing, perhaps, is so difficult to be attained by an Advocate, especially when his Heart is warm in his Cause, as that Moderation, which, from prudential Reasons, and foreseen Consequences, restrains him from fully defending his Client, when he hath it in his Power.

To this Moderation it hath been wholly owing, that we have often suffered many of those atrocious Falshoods, with which the present Administration hath been aspersed in public News-Papers, to pass entirely unregarded. And this is one Instance, in which we have set before us the Example of those Great Men, in whose Cause it is our Glory to be embarked. For to what do these Scribblers imagine they owe their Impunity, but to the Nature of their Scandal; which, like the Matter of a Contagion, ought not even to be stirred, or meddled with. Thus it is the singular Fortune of these Wretches, to be safe from the very Weight of their Crimes; as their Writings are, in reality, too profligate, and too impudent either to be punished or answered.

It is easy for a Man of any Reflection and Impartiality, to see the Advantage which this Circumstance hath lately given to our public Incendiaries. It is here, indeed, lies their only Strength: For as to Abilities, none ever presumed to handle a Pen with less. These are, indeed, every Way so mean, that in asserting our Superiority to them, we can no more be arraigned of Vanity, than a Man can be said to boast of his high Stature, who avers himself to be taller than a Dwarf; or than a Gentleman ought to be charged with assuming State or Dignity, when he ranks himself above the lowest Labourer who plies in the Streets.

But though, in general, the Difficulties are sufficiently apparent, which a Writer, of any Delicacy, lies under, while he engages with a Set of profligate Scribblers, who have no more

Regard to Decency than to Truth, and who shelter their Deficiency in the latter, by entirely abandoning the former: And though some of the most opprobrious Instances, tho' I dare not even mention them, will, doubtless, here occur to any Reader of the least Knowledge and Sagacity, I shall, however, draw out one Particular at full Length; by which, every Individual, who will divest himself of Partiality, must be forced to acknowledge, how extremely arduous a Task it may sometimes be, to do Justice to the most deserving Ministry, without sacrificing the Good of the Public in their Defence.

It is a notorious Fact, that from the Time of our signing those Preliminaries of Peace,[1] which filled every Countenance with Joy, and, in a few Days raised our Public Funds,[2] from as low a State as they were in even in the Heighth of the late Rebellion,[3] to be almost at a Par with their Situation in Times of the greatest Security: From this Time, I say, it is notorious, that our public Incendiaries, who had (by the by) been engaged, for some Years, in declaiming against the War, and the Continuance of it, began, all at once, to roar forth as loudly against the ensuing Peace. So eagerly were they hurried, by their Malice, to this Topic, that they even traduced the Preliminaries, before they were known; and afterwards upon the most random and uncertain Informations. In the Course of these Scurrilities they were not ashamed to insinuate, or rather to declare, that our Ministers had accepted the most dishonourable, and most disadvantageous Terms of the Enemy. That they had been bubbled and bullied into the Acceptance of these Terms by the Address and Threats of *France*, at a Time when we were more capable than ever of continuing the War and *France* less so. And that besides several

---

[1] The Earl of Sandwich signed for England on 30 April N.S. 1748, and on 24 April O.S. Newcastle received the signed preliminaries, 'the Separate and Secret Article', and the Act for the suspension of arms; see Coxe, *Pelham*, i. 416, 497; *Yale Walpole*, xix. 479 n.; and *GM*, xviii (1748), 186.

[2] In its 'Historical Chronicle' *sub* 24 April 1748, the date the signed preliminaries reached Newcastle, *GM*, xviii (1748), 186, called attention to the 'rise of stocks'. In fact, however, according to the tables printed monthly in *GM*, stocks had been rising since 5 April 1748, the day Newcastle wrote Sandwich that he would soon receive final instructions, and continued to rise until 4 July 1748; see *GM*, xviii (1748), 191, 239, 287, 335; and *Yale Walpole*, xix. 483 n.

[3] In December 1745, the month of greatest crisis during the rebellion, the Bank of England stocks were listed at 127 (*GM*, xv [1745], 669). They went lower and by April 1746 were at 124¼ (*GM*, xvi [1746], 223). With certain brief exceptions, the general drift during 1746, 1747, and early 1748 had been slowly downward.

Compliments paid and Points of Honour given up to that Crown, we had basely and wickedly surrendered *Cape Breton*, a Fortress of the utmost Consequence to the Trade and Navigation of *Great Britain*, without asking any Equivalent on Return.[1]

These I think are the principal Clamours which our Incendiaries have attempted to spread over this Kingdom for almost Six Months last past: The Charge indeed is not very copious, as the Invention of the Gentlemen is by no Means fertile, any more than the Matter on which it is to work; and yet here is Charge enough if it was true, to raise sufficient Animosity against all those who are at present in Power, and who can have been supposed to have contributed towards this Measure.

Now as to every particular Article of this Peace I must own myself a Stranger, and so are I presume all the Gentlemen who have hitherto writ against it.[2] But in the present obscure State of Things, and 'till the Peace itself is actually laid before the Public, doth not every Man see where the Stress of the Argument lies, and consequently how the Ministry must be defended against the above malicious Insinuations.

In the first Place it is most certain, that the Terms of Accommodation between Kingdoms, as well as between private Parties, are, in general, to be considered as dishonourable, with reference to the Situation in which the Parties stand at the Time of Accommodation. To ask your Life of an Enemy, who, when you are disarmed, holds a Sword to your Throat, though some Madmen have refused it, hath never been held dishonourable; and yet, surely, it is a very great Submission. Between Kingdoms, where real Interest ought always to sway more, and Punctilio less than it often doth between private Persons, he must be the weakest of Ministers, or the worst of Men, who would not relieve his Country from Danger, at the Expence of an honorary Concession.

And surely the disadvantageous Part is to be decided in the same Manner. In Contests between Individuals, the more powerful and successful are never called ungenerous, in insisting on advantageous Terms of Accommodation: Nor are their

---

[1] *GM*, xviii (1748), 467, annotates its reprinting of this paragraph by reference to the first item in the 'Gallimatia' of *JJ* no. 42, a mock attack on the *LEP* by 'Morgan Scrub', its supposed former editorial writer. See Appendix VI, below, p. 481.

[2] The definitive treaty was signed at Aix-la-Chapelle on 18 October N.s. by England, France, and the Dutch. A summary of the 24 articles appears in the *DA* of 24 October, that is, two days later than this issue of the *JJ*.

unfortunate Adversaries ever thought deficient in either Understanding or Spirit, when they submit to such Terms: In a Word, when they give up Part to save the rest.

In Politics, and in the Contests between Kingdoms, this prudent Rule holds much stronger, and may be extended much farther. For here, such humane Passions as Generosity or Compassion never (or very rarely, at least) operate upon the Conqueror. Neither do the Laws of Nations restrain him from improving his Power, or his Fortune, to the utmost: And as to the Christian Law, this, I suppose, is held to be confined only to our Conduct in private Life. I do not know, that either Popish or Protestant Divines have extended it to Politics. If they have, I am sure no Politicians have ever yet carried any such Doctrine into Practice. Here, therefore, if the Winner will grant only the worst Conditions he can, it is certainly the Part of the Loser, to accept the best he can obtain. *Pacem adfero ad vos magis necessariam quam æquam;* "The Peace I bring you is rather agreeable to your Necessities, than to Equity;" said the good *Alorcus* to the *Saguntines,* when *Hannibal* was at their Gates.[1] This was spoken like a Man of Sense; and like one who was really and sincerely their Friend; and yet the Terms were such, that *Alcon,* the *Saguntine,* did not dare carry them back to his own Countrymen; *moriturum affirmans,* says *Livy, qui sub conditionibus his de pace ageret;*[2] "affirming, that he would be put to Death, who should dare to treat of Peace on such Conditions."

And if there be any who like more modern Examples, let them remember the Behaviour of the *Dutch* to *Charles* the Second in the Year 1672, when they thought proper to supplicate a Peace in vain, and again in the Year 1673, when by granting almost every Thing demanded, they obtained it.[3] These are a People

---

[1] Livy, *Ab Urbe Condita,* XXI. xiii. 4. Alorcus is identified by Livy as a Spaniard who served with Hannibal and yet was also officially recognized by the Saguntines; see XXI. xii. 4–8.

[2] XXI. xii. 4.

[3] During the third Dutch war, which England entered formally in March 1672, in accordance with provisions of the clandestine Treaty of Dover (1670). In the summer of 1672 Prince William of Orange, the newly elected Stadtholder, proposed that in return for England's detaching herself from France the Dutch would salute the British flag in 'British' waters; would pay both an indemnity for war reparations and an annual sum for the right to fish for herring off British coasts; would pledge the 'cautionary' town of Sluys; would recognize English demands with respect to Surinam and regulation of the East India trade; and would make Prince William sovereign of the United Provinces. Charles II rejected

whose Policy was never questioned; and whose Magnanimity at the Time referred to, is hardly to be paralelled in all History.

It appears then that to know whether the Terms of a Peace be or be not dishonourable and disadvantageous, we are to examine the Circumstances of the contracting Parties. When due Regard is had to these, it is very possible in true Policy, that a Peace may be advantageous to that Party which makes very large Concessions, and disadvantageous to the other which receives them.

The true Question therefore is this, Was this Peace necessary or convenient to us or no, and were we or were we not in a Condition of hoping to beat *France* into a better?[1]

This will resolve the whole Case; since if the Peace was necessary for us, and the Terms the best which could be obtained, our Ministry cannot possibly be subject to Censure; but they will more or less deserve our Applause, as the Terms obtained are more or less equal to our reasonable Expectations and Desires.

[*The Remainder of this Essay will be in our next.*]

SATURDAY, OCTOBER 29, 1748.   NUMB. 48.

Periculosæ plenum opus aleæ.

Horace.[2]

In our last we endeavoured to shew, that in order to determine whether the Conditions of a Peace be or be not disadvantageous to any Country, it is necessary to take an exact View of the Situation of public Affairs in that Country, at the Time when the Peace is made. Whether such Country be capable of longer continuing the War; and whether, by so doing, it may reasonably hope hereafter, to force its Enemies into more desirable Terms of Accommodation, than those which they at present offer.

Here it must be obvious, that in Proportion to the public Distress and Weakness of any Nation, the Persons in Power will

these terms. In 1673, after relatively successful campaigns, the Dutch renewed peace overtures in terms which, though less abject than those offered in 1672, satisfied the grievances contained in the English declaration of war of March 1672, and concluded in the Treaty of Westminster (1674).

1 This paragraph and the next are reprinted in *GM*, xviii (1748), 467.
2 *Odes*, II. i. 6. See *JJ* no. 47, above, p. 413, where the same motto is used.

be more or less justifiable, in accepting such Terms of Accommodation, as may, generally speaking, be thought either dishonourable, or disadvantageous; and more or less laudable, in having procured a Peace on those Conditions, which must, at all Times, be allowed to be both honourable and desirable by any People.

What then? Shall we assert that we are in a Situation as deplorable as was that of *Saguntum*, when within a few Hours of that Destruction with which *Hannibal* overwhelmed it;[1] or as the States of *Holland* were, when Providence itself seems to have declared on their Side, and almost to have worked a Miracle for their Preservation?[2]

This would most certainly aggravate our Case. A Measure which we are so determined to avoid, that we shall not, in Defence of any Man whatever, attempt even to lay open the Wounds of our Country, if, in reality, she have any. Nor will we give Foreigners an Opportunity of shewing, under the Hands of any Writer of Authority, a direct Confession that we are a weak or a miserable People. Here is an Instance of that Delicacy, which we have mentioned to be so necessary to every public Advocate for Power;[3] and of those Hardships to which the Defence of Power is often subject; since it is most obvious, that whatever we shall advance on this Head, in Favour of the Ministry, must be at the Expence of the Nation; and must betray those Secrets to our Enemies, which it highly behoves us to conceal from them.

Let us, however, (for Argument Sake only) put those Sentiments into the Mouth of a *Frenchman*, which do not well become the Mouth of an *Englishman*; and here, perhaps, it will appear, that the weak Defence which we have sometimes made for the

---

[1] See *JJ* no. 47, above, p. 418.

[2] Referring to the Dutch distresses of 1672 when, after political revolution and the loss of Utrecht, Gelderland, and Overijssel to French control, the Dutch were driven to a policy of strategic inundations to keep the invaders from overrunning the key province of Holland. See *JJ* no. 47, above, p. 418, and Mary Caroline Trevelyan, *William the Third and the Defence of Holland, 1672–4* (London, 1930), Chs. VII–XIV. In particular, the hand of Providence was thought to have operated at sea by assisting de Ruyter's fleet to prevent an Allied landing on the Hook during the summer of 1672: 'it is thought that the *English* would have landed near the *Texel*, waiting only for the flood to carry their soldiers ashore in boats, but that the ebb that day, by a kind of miraculous deviation from the common course, having lasted twelve hours, deprived them of the opportunity'; from '*The* Life *of* Michael de Ruyter . . . Written originally* in Dutch *by* Gerard Brandt', as reprinted in *GM*, xviii (1748), 490.

[3] See *JJ* no. 47, above, pp. 413–14.

greatest of Men, hath been truly owing to the abovementioned Delicacy, and to that alone.

Let us then, for a Moment, suppose, that the same Liberty of the Press existed in *France*, which, at present, flourishes here, (happy, perhaps, for us that it doth not) and then we may easily imagine some *French* News-Writer thus addressing himself to the Public.

"At length the two B—thers* may be said to have brought their H—gs to a fair Market. After we have been amused with the Hopes of seeing *Holland* reduced in a single Campaign, which must have been a Matter of greater Ease than what our Arms have actually atchieved in the two last, and which must have opened to us so inevitable a Road to the Conquest of *England*, what has the Mountain produced?——Why, truly, a little P—ce: A P—ce on as good and adv—nt—geous Terms to our Enemies as they could have expected, or even demanded three Years ago, when their Armies were in the Heart of *Flanders*, and the *Dutch* Barrier remained entire.[1]

"If ever Nation may have been said to fight for Gl—ry only, it is ours. For what but Gl—ry have we got by all our Conquests! Double Gl—ry I allow: the Gl—ry of Heroes in taking Towns, and of Chr—stians in restoring th—m.

"For what other Equivalent, besides Glory, have these Br—thers obtained for us? Let that Block-head, Monsieur *Jean de Trottyplad*, or any other Advocate for th—m, tell us if he can. He will answer, perhaps, *Cape Breton*. One single Fortress in *America*, for all *Flanders*, *Brabant*, *Zealand*, I may say *Holland*;[2]

* The two Brother Generals.[3]

---

[1] At the beginning of the 1745 campaign the Allied position in Flanders seemed such that there was talk of penetrating the French frontier along the Sambre; see Fortescue, *History of the British Army*, ii. 108–9. However, after Fontenoy (April 1745) the fortress towns which formed the Barrier began to fall, and by autumn, when the threat of Jacobite invasion at home forced the recall of British troops, the Allies had lost Tournai, Ghent, and Ostend; see Fortescue, ii. 121–3, 149–64; Charteris, *William Augustus, Duke of Cumberland*, pp. 166–7, 201–3; and *JJ* no. 37, above, pp. 365–6.

[2] Cited here as a lost 'opportunity'. In fact, the province of Holland was not taken by the French. However, after the fall of Bergen-op-Zoom in September 1747, and after the capture of most of the fortified places in northern Brabant, British observers were pessimistic. See *Proper Answer*, above, p. 75 and note 1 there.

[3] Marshal Saxe and Marshal Löwendahl, the generals responsible for French military interests in the Dutch theatre. See *JJ* no. 4, above, p. 111, n. 3. By analogy, the satirical reference is to Pelham and Newcastle, whom the anti-ministerial press frequently denominated as 'the two Brothers'.

nay, I may say, *England* itself: For what but our own P——ce-mak—rs could have obstructed the Progress of our Arms?

"Had not our Enemies made their last and greatest Effort against us? And could they, with every Ally whom they could persuade, frighten, or buy to their Assistance, produce an Army in the Field, capable of looking us in the Face?[1] In this Situation, we have made a P——ce upon fair and even Terms. This may be Gl—rious; this may be Chr—stian; but let me ask, is this Politic?

Oh! Policy! O my Country!

"How unworthy are we to be called the Posterity of those glorious *Frenchmen*, who have so often made Fools and Bubbles of these *English*? And who have so often repaired in the Cabinet, the adverse Fortune which we have met with in the Field.

"*Horace* tells us, that *Augustus Cæsar* was weary of Conquest.[2] Surely our Br—thers were so, or they would not have made any P——ce; much less such a Peace, with the *English*, at a Season when their Affairs were so embarrassed as at the signing the c—rsed Preliminaries; when they are involved in a Debt of 30 Millions,[3] of which they are scarce able to pay the Interest, much less to bear the Expences of a War, that must add Millions every Year to their present Incumbrance. Their Public Credit was at a Stand.[4] Their People really under grievous Burthens, and

---

[1] For the discrepancy between the number of troops the Allies promised to supply, according to the terms of the Convention at The Hague in January 1748, and the number actually put in the field, under Cumberland, see *JJ* no. 4, above, p. 111, n. 2, and no. 24, p. 274, n. 4.

[2] *Odes*, III. iv. 37–9. In the original Latin the phrase here translated as 'weary of Conquest' (*militia . . . fessas*) qualifies Caesar's cohorts, not Caesar himself. But see Francis's translation: 'When Caesar, by your forming Arts inspir'd, / Chearful disbands his Troops, of Conquest tir'd'; and his note on l. 38: 'It is a noble Encomium of Augustus, that he was fatigued with Conquest'; *A Poetical Translation of the Works of Horace*, ii. 8, 9. Baker, item no. 558, lists Francis's translation among Fielding's books.

[3] Either a misprint—for 80 millions—or a calculation of that debt which was solely owing to the war with Spain (since 1739) and with France (since 1744). *The State of the Nation for the Year 1747* (London, 1748), p. xv, estimates the debt for 1748 at 'near 80,000,000' pounds and states, p. 57, that since the war with Spain 'we have, including Deficiencies, &c. ran near thirty Millions in Debt.' A modern estimate puts the total National Debt, both funded and unfunded, for 1748 at £76.1 millions; *Abstract of British Historical Statistics*, ed. B. R. Mitchell, p. 401. An Exchequer Office calculation of the debt as of Christmas 1747 (i.e. roughly four months prior to the signing of the preliminaries) puts the total at £64.6 millions, with an interest of £2.5 millions; *Journals of . . . Commons*, xxv. 567. For comparable figures see *Proper Answer*, above, p. 76, n. 4, and p. 77, n. 1.

[4] See *JJ* no. 24, above, p. 274 and note 3 there.

aggravating even those with Factious Complaints: Divided into Parties; jealous of their best Friends; eager after Change; and many of them wishing well to our Cause, hoping to arrive at the Change they desire by our Assistance."

I will pursue so odious a Theme no farther. What hath been said, will abundantly suffice to convey all the Hints for which it was intended. For my own Part, I am so far from being desirous to advance such Facts as Truths, that I should be sincerely sorry if they were true. I have, therefore, put them into the Mouth of a *Frenchman*, a Nation famous for representing themselves, and all which belongs to them, in the most advantageous Light. And so far have I been from attempting to set forth the disagreeable Particulars with any Force of Eloquence, that I have imitated, as well as I am able, the Stile of the worst of all *English* Writers.[1]

Upon the whole, I cannot help observing, that it is one of the unhappy Consequences which too often attends the Liberty of writing in free Countries, to have their Weakness exposed, and their Secrets divulged to the whole World. And this, perhaps, may be one Reason of the disadvantageous Light, in which the Politics of such Countries may have sometimes appeared, when compared to those of more absolute Governments. No Man, I hope, will be either Fool or Villain enough to misrepresent me here, as pleading against the Cause of Liberty. On the contrary, I solemnly declare, that neither this, nor any other Evil, with which the Blessings of Freedom may be embittered, can at all balance the Good which we enjoy from it, or should persuade us to listen to the least Diminution of those Blessings. Human Affairs are so tempered, that there is, perhaps, no one Happiness, however great and solid, entirely and perfectly pure. Health itself may, as Physicians tell us, grow too luxuriant, and be attended with dangerous Consequences; and yet no Man was ever weak enough to advise us to prefer a State of Sickness and Infirmity. No less weak must be all the Arguments drawn from the Inconveniencies attending an exuberant Degree of Liberty, against the invaluable Possession of that Liberty which is the Health of the Body Politic: And yet weak as these Arguments are, cursed be the Pens of those from whose Writings they arise.

[1] Presumably the writer of *LEP*, with his habit of 'disemvowelling' supposedly crucial words. Cf. *JJ* no. 1, above, p. 96 and note 4 there.

But with Regard to our present Race of Scribblers, besides the Protection of the sacred Word Liberty, I will farther observe in their Favour, that however profligate they may be in their Intentions, they are, in reality, incapable of doing much Injury to their Country, by betraying any improper Knowledge to Foreigners. At Home, indeed, the very meanest of them all is able to spread Sedition, and to foment the ill Humours of the Multitude; for the darkest Hints, and most obscure Slanders, are often effectual; nay, most effectual for these Purposes; but to convey Intelligence, it is certainly necessary to be understood. Now there are few Foreigners who understand our Language so well as, with the Assistance of Grammar and Method, to be able to read our very best and purest Authors; much less can they be supposed capable of understanding a Jargon, from which we ourselves can scarce collect any Idea: And as for the Danger of being translated, these Scribblers must be entirely free from it, since what is not originally writ in Language, can never be translated into any.

SATURDAY, NOVEMBER 5, 1748.   NUMB. 49.

A strange Spirit of Jacobitism, indeed of Infatuation, discovered itself at the latter End of the Year 1747,[1] in many Parts of this Kingdom, which was at the same Time engaged in a dangerous and successless War. A Spirit which gave the highest Encouragement to our Enemies, not only as such intestine Divisions must greatly weaken our political Strength; but as it afforded them a reasonable Hope, that if an Invasion of this Island was but coloured over with the specious Pretence of supporting the Pretender's Cause, a considerable Party among ourselves, would be found ready to join and assist the then avowed and declared Enemies of their Country.

As it seemed necessary to apply some Remedy, in order to stop the Progress of this dangerous, epidemical Madness at so critical a Season; so none seemed more proper, or likely to be more effectual than Ridicule: For as to the Means of Force, the Nature of Liberty itself, (if I may be allowed the Expression) doth not abhor it more than the mild Temper of our present Administration. And serious Arguments (besides that they are

---

[1] See General Introduction, above, pp. lv–lvi, lxiii–lxviii.

much slower in their Operation) have been often already essayed to no Purpose.

Here then we see the Design with which the *Jacobite Journal* was first instituted. How far it hath answered that Design, I am not able to say. If it hath not cured, it may at least be said, I think, to have palliated the Distemper; which, surely, rages not at present so openly and violently as it did a Year ago. To eradicate it entirely, is, perhaps, not within the Power of Art, and that for two Reasons: Because it is commonly hereditary; and because it is so complicated with Folly, that the one cannot be removed without the other. Now who ever heard of a Receipt to cure Fools!

Indeed there is one Reason which will abundantly account for the little Effect which any Writings have had, or ever can have, on this Party; and this is, their constant Practice of confining their Reading only to their own Side of the Question. This is so known a Usage with them, that my Vanity is not in the least hurt, by the Neglect they have, for the most Part, shewn to this Paper. Perhaps I am somewhat flattered by the many Assurances I have received, of the great Care and Industry with which some of them have endeavoured to keep my Writings out of the Hands of others. Public Houses, both in Town and Country, have, as I have been credibly informed, been inhibited from taking in my Journal;[1] and where it hath found Admission, it hath been often condemned, on its first Arrival, to that dreadful Hole,[2] which common News-papers have sometimes had the good Fortune to escape for a whole Week together.

As I may reasonably, therefore, despair of making Converts where I can gain no Disciples, I shall here put an End to my Labours;[3] and the rather, as I am well convinced, that however

---

[1] A common charge. Cf. *TP* no. 17 of 18–25 February 1746: 'Whereas we have been informed by several Persons, that they have not been able to procure the TRUE PATRIOT at any Rate: And we have great Reason to believe that many malicious and base Endeavours have been used to suppress the Sale of this Paper, by some who are concerned in imposing on the Public, by propagating Lies and Nonsense, which we have endeavoured to detect and expose.' Cf. the 'Apocrypha' of *TP* no. 11 (14 January 1746): 'We hear several Masters of Coffee-houses have lost some of their best Customers, because they have refused to take in the TRUE PATRIOT.' *LEP* of 13–15 September 1748 claimed that 'Even the *Country Innkeepers* who receive them [copies of the *JJ*] *gratis*, complain that their Customers *will not read them.*'

[2] That is, in the privy, with the other 'relics of the bum'.

[3] Fielding had been appointed to the Commission of the Peace for Westminster on or about 30 July 1748, and had begun signing recognizances as a Justice of the Peace at least

dangerous the Spirit of this Party might have been at that Season, when this Paper was first begun, it is now become the Object only of Derision and Contempt; since by that happy Peace which the present glorious Administration have, so much to their own Honour and the public Good, secured to this Nation, the Hopes of this Party are, in a Manner, plucked up by the very Root: And their Projects are as much the Contempt of every honest and sensible *Briton*, as their Principles were before.

Of this, indeed, they themselves seem sufficiently apprized; for the Proof of which we need only appeal to that universal Dejection, which, from the first signing the Preliminaries, began so visibly to discover itself;[1] and since the compleating the definitive Treaty,[2] hath so totally overspread the whole Party. And surely we must own they have sufficient Reason to be dejected at a Measure which so strongly threatens to frustrate all their Views; nay, I may add, I believe, the only Measure that, in all Human Probability, could have frustrated them.

Here then, I take my final Farewel of these Gentlemen; not with that Air of Triumph which a bad Spirit exerts over a weak or a fallen Enemy; but with that compassionate Hope which is dictated by a more humane Temper of Mind. I hope then, that Despair may have the same Effect on them, which it hath often had in other Cases; and may succeed, where the most solid Arguments have failed to convince. In short, if Reason, Honour, Liberty, Duty, and every worldly Interest, nay, the express Commands of Scripture, cannot engage their Fidelity *to the Powers that be*;[3] I hope they will, at least, become faithful and good Subjects, from a perfect Assurance that *these Powers* will most certainly *continue to be*, in Defiance of all which the Courts of *Rome* or Hell can devise against them.

as early as 2 November 1748, that is, three days prior to the appearance of this, the concluding leader of his journal. During September and October the Opposition press made a number of disparaging references to his imminent translation 'from *Grubstreet* into the Verge of Court' (*OE* of 24 September), and often linked the 'low' nature of the appointment to Lyttelton's supposed dissatisfaction with the *JJ* (*LEP* of 22–5 October and *OE* of 12 November.)

1 England signed them on 19 April 1748; see *JJ* no. 47, above, p. 416.
2 On 18 October N.S.; see *JJ* no. 47, above, p. 417, n. 2.
3 Cf. Romans xiii. 1: 'the powers that be are ordained of God.'

APPENDICES

Title-page statements to the contrary, of the material in the present volume there are, bibliographically speaking, no authoritative *editions* other than the first or copy-text editions. In the case of the two pamphlets, however, there are distinct *states* or *impressions*. The appendixes will designate these by letters of the alphabet, not by numbers, so as to distinguish them from what numbers conventionally refer to, namely, true editions.

Other designations are as follows: W stands for the present Wesleyan edition; M for the Murphy edition of the 1762 *Works*; JJ for the original text of *The Jacobite's Journal*; BM for the British Museum copy; CtY for the Yale copy.

APPENDIX I

List of Substantive Emendations

DIALOGUE

half-title. 4 from] *e*; of *a–d*

title page. 4 from] *e*; of *a–d*

3. 14 had made] *e*; made *a–d*

4. 25 all Civil] *e*; Civil *a–d*

4. 25 Military] *e*; all Military *a–d*

7. 4 to amuse] *e*; amuse *a–d*

12. 29 to the Constitution] *e*; Constitution *a–d*

12. 32 he] *e*; *om. a–d*

13. 6 of] *e*; *om. a–d*

13. 9 this] *e*; the *a–d*

13. 26 of Felony] *e*; Felony *a–d*

14. 2 now] *e*; *om. a–d*

14. 20 to an] *e*; an *a–d*

14. 25 indeed at] *e*; indeed *a–d*

15. 5 this Word] *e*; it *a–d*

15. 18 of the] *e*; the *a–d*

15. 20 been disturbed] *e*; disturbed *a–d*

15. 23 writ in] *e*; writ in in *a–d*

15. 30 have any] *e*; hath any *a–d*

16. 1 for the Justice] *e*; the Justice *a–d*

16. 1–2 for the Candour] *e*; the Candour *a–d*

16. 21 into] *e*; as *a–d*

20. 7 in Counties] *e*; Counties *a–d*

22. 5 unpopular] *b*; popular *a*

22. 22 If (*no* ¶)] W; Gentleman. (*cw*) | ¶ If *a* +

22. 22 Pensioners also] *e*; these two *a*; Pensioners too *b–d*

22. 30 to the] *e*; the *a–d*

23. 10 to explain] *e*; explain *a–d*

24. 26 Gentleman] *e*; Gentlemen *a–d*

25. 3 him] *e*; himself *a–d*

25. 28 that] *e*; the *a–d*

26. 28 if chosen] *e*; chosen *a–d*

27. 23 those] *e*; these *a–d*

28. 26 to] *e*; *om. a–d*

40. 4 greatest Powers] *c*; greatest, I own, *a–b*, *e*

42. 22 by the honest] *e*; the honest *a–d*

43. 24 to a good] *e*; a good *a–d*

44. 8 would] *e*; *om. a–d*

44. 19–20 by the Valour] *e*; the Valour *a–d*

44. 20 by the Care] *e*; the Care *a–d*

44. 32 to resist] *e*; resist *a–d*

46. 28 The Part . . . to] *e*; All the Administration have done hath been to *a–d*

48. 3 State] *c*; Scale *a–b*

49. 10 to be] *e*; *om. a–d*

49. 11 to be] *e*; *om. a–d*

53. 21–2 would not give] *e*; give *a–d*

55. 21 are] *e*; is *a–d*

57. 16 *his*] *c*; *the a–b*

58. 31–2 *See . . . Pamphlet.] *e*; *om. a–d*

60. 30 to the furious] *e*; the furious *a–d*

PROPER ANSWER

66. 5 *Stuart*] W; *Stuarts a–b*

73. 9 standing Corps] W; stand- | Corps *a–b*

JACOBITE'S JOURNAL

90. 1 December 5] BM; December 6 CtY

116. 1 1748] W; 1747 JJ

126. 13 to be] W; be JJ

130. 10 a] W; an JJ

139. 22 on with] W; on the with JJ

174. 24 *Metamorphoses*] W; *Metamorphosis* JJ

175. 1 *Laus*] W; *Lacus* JJ

225. 30 *mock*] W; *make* JJ

232. 16 of] W; *om.* JJ

234. 11 not] W; not not JJ

248. 20 Noblemen's] W; Noblemen JJ

249. 13 what] W; in what JJ

270. 1 *Poscente*] W; *Prosecute* JJ

273. 22 Apprehension] W; Apprehensions JJ

335. 4 *victus*] W; *visitus* JJ

338. 18 than] W; then JJ

352. 24 parting] W; partaking JJ

358. 6 Ministry] W; Minister JJ

362. 15 the Doctrines] W; the the Doctrines JJ

363. 5 *Metamorphoses*] W; *Metamorphosis* JJ

364. 13 in] W; *om.* JJ

367. 23 who claims] W; who who claims JJ

385. 27 in] W; in in JJ

414. 23 the other] W; other JJ

417. 8 Gentlemen] W; Gentleman JJ

APPENDIX II
List of Accidentals Emendations

124. 19 *Metamorphoses*,] W; ~ₐ JJ
125. 17 Performance] W; performance JJ
126. 16 all] W; l JJ
126. 33–127. 1 *India* (says he)] W;
India, says he, JJ
132. 36 inviolate.ₐ]W; ~." JJ
132. 37 Perambulations] W; Pream-
bulations JJ
133. 1ₐThese] W; "~ JJ
136. 30 Intention?] W; ~! JJ
138. 1 Genius,] W; ~ₐ JJ
138. 8 *Offendar*] W; *Offendor* [?] JJ
(penultimate letter broken and
uncertain)
138. 8 *Maculis* ——.] W; ~——ₐ JJ
146. 4 Abbé] W; Abbe JJ
147. 4 (*Adjourned*.)] W; ₐAdjourned.ₐ
JJ
149. 18 us!] W; ~. JJ
151. 12 it?] W; ~. JJ
151. 30 *Bedlam*] W; Bedlam JJ
154. 15 *Horse-piss*] W; ~ₐ~ JJ
154. 15 Fooʟ] W; Fool JJ
154. 19 (*Adjourned*.)] W; ₐAd-
journed.ₐ JJ
156. 2 What,] W; ~ₐ JJ
156. 6 *English*?] W; ~. JJ
156. 17 thof] W; *thof* JJ
158. 23 Non-Resistance] W; ~ₐ~ JJ
159. 24 *Billingsgate*]W; *Billinsgate* JJ
160. 9 *Billingsgate*] W; *Billinsgate* JJ
160. 26 Power,] W; ~ₐ JJ
160. 27 *Grub-street*] W; *Grubstreet* JJ
160. 29 *Billingsgate . . . Billingsgate*]
W; *Billinsgate . . . Billingsgate* JJ
160. 33 *The*] W; the JJ
162. 11 *Grub-street*] W; *Grubstreet* JJ
162. 15 *Grub-street*] W; *Grubstreet* JJ
162. 20 (*Adjourned*.)] W; ₐ~.ₐ JJ
164. 4 Abbé] W; Abbe JJ
164. 27 Abbé] W; Abbè JJ
165. 6 Custom (says *Bannier*)] W;
Custom, says *Bannier*, JJ
165. 14–15 absurd (says he)] W;
absurd, says he, JJ
166. 10 Perversion] W; Pervertion JJ

166. 23 Abbé] W; Abbe JJ
168. 9 The] W; *the* JJ
172. 20 Thing] W; thing JJ
173. 10 Republicanism;] BM; ~, CtY
173. 31 News-Papers] W; ~ₐ~ JJ
175. 13 *frænis*.] W; ~ₐ JJ
179. 6 *Andrew . . . Merry*] W;
Andrew . . . Merry JJ
179. 21 Coffee-house] W; ~ₐ~ JJ
179. 21 *Hounsditch*]W; HounsditchJJ
181. 11 For] W; for JJ
181. 19 *The*] W; the JJ
182. 6 Lucubrations] W; Lucruba-
tions JJ
182. 18 manner?] W; ~. JJ
184. 15 Power?] W; ~. JJ
184. 18 about?] W; ~. JJ
187. 30 purposely] W; purposey JJ
188. 8 *Jacobite Journal*] W; Jacobite
Journal JJ
190. 8 *ok* *ippen*] W; ok* *ippen
JJ
193. 27 Jacobite Journal] W; *Jacobite
Journal* JJ
194. 11 Character begot] W; Character begat JJ
194. 21 Patriotism begot] W; Patriotism begat JJ
194. 26 Jacobite Journal] W; *Jacobite Journal* JJ
195. 6 King'sₐ Evil] W; ~-~ JJ
196. 15 Sea-girt] W; ~ₐ~ JJ
196. 25 *deficiunt*——.] W; ~——ₐ JJ
199. 4 Destruction] W; Destrustion JJ
200. 5 For] W; for JJ
200. 23 *Billingsgate*] W; *Billinsgate* JJ
201. 6 *Adjourned*.] W; ~ₐ JJ
205. 30 Non-Resistance] W; ~ₐ~ JJ
207. 31 outrés] W; outres JJ
209. 15 *Comædia*] W; *Comædia* JJ
209. 26 *Evening-Post*] W; ~ₐ~ JJ
210. 13 *Evening-Post*] W; ~ₐ~ JJ
210. 18 *Adjourned*.] W; ~ₐ JJ
212. 28 Incendiaries] W; Incendaries
JJ
217. 6 contrary] W; conrrary JJ
217. 15 *Adjourned*.] W; ~ₐ JJ

218. 4 *Letter to the Tories*] W; Letter to the Tories JJ

219. 10–11 *Letter to the Tories*] W; Letter to the Tories JJ

219. 24 *Letter to the Tories*] W; Letter to the Tories JJ

222. 34 *Letter to the*] W; Letter to the JJ

223. 16 Page 6ₐ] W; Page 6. JJ

223. 21 Page 8ₐ] W; Page 8. JJ

224. 16 Page 11,] W; Page 11. JJ

225. 20 *Third Letter*] W; Third Letter JJ

229. 3–4 Summerₐ Assizes] W; ~-~ JJ

229. 20 Summerₐ Assizes] W; ~-~ JJ

230. 35 *Aylesbury*] W; *Alesbury* JJ

230. 37 Northamptonshire] W; North-|hamptonshire JJ

231. 30 *Aylesbury*] W; *Alesbury* JJ

235. 4 *mendosum*] W; *mendsoum* JJ

237. 15 *Throne.*] W; ~? JJ

237. 18 *Grub-street*] W; *Grubstreet* JJ

237. 18 *Billingsgate*] W; *Billinsgate* JJ

238. 16 *Letter to the Whigs*] W; Letter to the Whigs JJ

240. 3 *melius"*—] BM, W; ~ₐ—— CtY

240. 6 *Reason*] W; Reason JJ

240. 11 *immedicabile vulnus*] W; *immedica Bilevulnus* JJ

245. 1 *Court of*] W; Court of JJ

246. 20 Common.] W; ~ₐ JJ

246. 29 It's] W; Its JJ

247. 9 World?] W; ~. JJ

248. 20 Gentlemen's] W; Gentlemens JJ

251. 29 imitate] W; imi ate JJ

255. 7 For] W; for JJ

256. 15 Proclaim (said *Diogenes*)] W; Proclaim, said *Diogenes*, JJ

258. 12 of *Cicero*] W; *of Cicero* JJ

258. 15 *Institutions*] W; Institutions JJ

259. 12 Falshood] W; False-|hood JJ

259. 34 Education?] W; ~. JJ

261. 1 agree (says he)] W; agree, says he, JJ

263. 21 That] W; that JJ

270. 2 *Verberibus*] W; *Verboribus* JJ

270. 8 Besides, (says he)] W; Besides, says he, JJ

270. 28 Argumentₐ] W; ~, JJ

281. 3 *Letter'dₐWorld*] W; ~-~ JJ

281. 19 *Menæchmi*] W; *Menoech.* JJ

283. 35 *Jacobites*] W; Jacobites JJ

285. 12 *Jacobites*] W; Jacobites JJ

285. 18 This (saith *Samuel*)] W; This, saith *Samuel*, JJ

285. 19 ₐHe] W; "~ JJ

290. 9 News-Papers] W; ~ₐ~ JJ

291. 17 *Pall-mall*] W; ~ₐ~ JJ

293. 6 Author of] W; *Author of* JJ

293. 14 Booksellers] W; Boooksellers JJ

294. 10 *Grub-street*] W; *Grubstreet* JJ

294. 17 *An*] W; *an* JJ

296. 14 *Letter'd*] W; *letter'd* JJ

297. 21 *July*,] W; ~ₐ JJ

304. 32 Falshood] W; False-|hood JJ

306. 26 Falshood] W; False-|hood JJ

308. 11 Detraction (says he)] W; Detraction, says he, JJ

309. 38 καθεστῶτες] W; καθεσῶτες JJ

310. 1 Anglicé] W; Anglice JJ

310. 8 *Evening-Post*] W; ~ₐ~ JJ

311. 31 it?] W; ~. JJ

314. 18–19 Multitude] W; Mul-|tude JJ

315. 32 Poors-Rates] W; ~ₐ~ JJ

316. 4 *Aristotle*] W; *Aristole* JJ

318. 13 Child, (says he)] W; Child, says he, JJ

319. 20 Madam, (says . . . Creature)] W; Madam, says . . . Creature, JJ

319. 23 Country.] W; ~ₐ JJ

324. 19 *Evening-Post*] W; ~ₐ~ JJ

324. 20 *Saturday*,] W; ~ₐ JJ

325. 4 *W–lp—e*] W; *W–l–pe* JJ

325. 23 *King's-Bench*] W; ~ₐ~ JJ

327. 9 Satire?] W; ~. JJ

328. 2 *Billingsgate*] W; *Billinsgate* JJ

328. 14 ₐThere] W; "~ JJ

328. 17 misguided,] W;   ~; JJ
329. 33–4 deplorable.] W;   ~ₐ JJ
332. 11 Destruction.] W;   ~ₐ JJ
334. 8 Heaven.] W;   ~ₐ JJ
334. 21 or] W;   *or* JJ
338. 10 Beggary?] W;   ~. JJ
342. 19 History.] W;   ~ₐ JJ
346. 32 *Grub-street*] W;   *Grubstreet* JJ
347. 6 you?] W;   ~. JJ
352. 11 *The*] W;   *the* JJ
353. 2 me.] W;   ~ₐ JJ
353. 15–16 *Old*ₐ*England*] W;   ~-~ JJ
353. 16 *Evening-Post*] W;   ~ₐ~ JJ
354. 1 Administration] W;   Adminis-tation JJ
354. 25 *Evening-Post*] W;   ~ₐ~ JJ
354. 34 *Evening-Post*] W;   ~ₐ~ JJ
356. 24 Friend, (cry'd he)] W;   Friend, cry'd he, JJ
356. 27 Friend, (answer'd the Quaker)] W;   Friend, answer'd the Quaker, JJ
357. 1 Protestant] W;   protestant JJ
359. 17 Materials] W;   Ma erials JJ
362. 28 *ferme*] W;   *firme* JJ
363. 2 any] W;   a-|any JJ
363. 2 Thing . . . it.] W;   thing . . . ~ₐ JJ
365. 14 Virtue;] W;   ~, JJ
367. 2 *Derby?*] W;   ~. JJ
369. 10 *arte*] W;   *aret* JJ
370. 25 *deficeret . . . attonitamque*] W;   *deficerat . . . attonitemque* JJ
372. 19 This, (says he)] W;   This, says he, JJ
377. 6 re-admitted] W;   re-admit-|ed JJ
378. 31 *Evening-Post*] W;   ~ₐ~ JJ
378. 33 own,] W;   ~ₐ JJ
383. 11 *Gazetteer*] W;   *Gazeteer* JJ
383. 13 says the] W;   *says the* JJ
384. 25 *Evening-Post*] W;   ~ₐ~ JJ
385. 6 ₐ*Sir*] W;   "~ JJ
385. 13 *Old*ₐ*England*] W;   ~-~ JJ
385. 19 ₐYou] W;   "~ JJ
385. 29 *Old*ₐ*England*] W;   ~-~ JJ
385. 30 recommendₐothers,] W;   ~, ~ₐ JJ

386. 1 *London*ₐ*Evening*] W;   ~-~ JJ
386. 4 Thing] W;   thing JJ
386. 14 ₐIf] W;   "~ JJ
386. 33 *Servant,*] W;   ~. JJ
387. 12 *Old*ₐ*England*] W;   ~-~ JJ
387. 15 ₐ*Mr.*] W;   "~. JJ
387. 21–2 *Evening-Post*] W;   ~ₐ~ JJ
387. 31 ₐSir] W;   "~ JJ
388. 12 EVENING-POST] W;   ~ₐ~ JJ
388. 14 ₐIf] W;   "~ JJ
388. 23 OLDₐENGLAND] W;   ~-~ JJ
389. 25 Menₐ . . . ₐare] W;   ~" . . . "~ JJ
389. 28 Instances, . . . Persons.] W;   ~; . . . ~, JJ
389. 29 *Man,* . . . *Beast,*] W;   ~; . . . ~. JJ
391. 26 latter?] W;   ~. JJ
392. 34 *Sense,*] W;   ~ₐ JJ
393. 2 drunk?] W;   ~. JJ
393. 11 pulling] W;   pul-|ing JJ
395. 28 *High-German Doctor*ₐ] W;   ~ₐ~ ~. JJ
397. 25 Country,] W;   ~; JJ
401. 27 Friends? W;   ~. JJ
406. 1 Multitude's] W;   Multitudes JJ
407. 30 Men (says he) of] W;   Men" says he, "of JJ
408. 4 Times] W;   times JJ
408. 22 latter,] W;   ~ₐJJ
408. 28 Forces] W;   Fores JJ
408. 30 Conqueror,] W;   ~ₐ JJ
408. 32 present,] W;   ~ₐ JJ
409. 16 *Catenis?*] W;   ~. JJ
410. 9 *Politicks*] W;   Politicks JJ
410. 21 Exception:] W;   ~. JJ
412. 21 other?] W;   ~. JJ
413. 23 *Laws*] W;   Laws JJ
413. 25 κακόν] W;   κάκον JJ
415. 6 waded?] W;   ~. JJ
416. 2 former:] W;   ~. JJ
416. 16 Security:] W;   ~. JJ
418. 17 agreeable] W;   agree-|ble JJ
419. 15 cannot] W;   can|not JJ
421. 25 *Cape*] W;   Cape JJ
422. 9 ₐOh] W;   "~ JJ

APPENDIX III

Word-Division

1. *End-of-the-Line Hyphenation in the Wesleyan Edition*

[NOTE. No hyphenation of a possible compound at the end of a line in the Wesleyan edition is present in the copy-text except for the following readings, which are hyphenated within the line in copy-text. Hyphenated compounds in which both elements are capitalized are excluded.]

DIALOGUE

30. 36 hot-brain'd

PROPER ANSWER

85. 21 re-establishing

JACOBITE'S JOURNAL

90. 8 News-papers
102. 36 pre-suppose
120. 24 best-humoured
131. 18 Land-holders
139. 6 Horse-races
139. 26 hempen-Girdle
173. 26 Fox-chace

190. 16 blood-thirsty
193. 9 out-|-of-place
194. 19 Non-resistance
231. 15 any-body
237. 12 Letter-writer
246. 12 School-fellow
254. 13 good-humour'd
274. 2 PEACE-MAKERS
279. 14 joint-tenancy
318. 30 Great-| grand-father
334. 1, 341. 31, 342. 16 above-mentioned
391. 12 Faggot-sticks
397. 19 News-writer

2. *End-of-the-Line Hyphenation in the Copy-Text*

[NOTE. The following compounds, or possible compounds, are hyphenated at the end of the line in the copy-text. The form in which they have been given in the Wesleyan edition, as listed below, represents the usual practice of the copy-text in so far as it may be ascertained from other appearances.]

DIALOGUE

5. 31 Placemen

JACOBITE'S JOURNAL

90. 13 Countrymen
93. 2 Waistcoat
109. 11 new-fangled
130. 27 best-laid
135. 23 ill-natured
139. 18 *Turn-coats*
140. 13 Forestroke
140. 17 Backstroke

145. 17 Band-boxes
151. 29 *Grub-street*
154. 15 *Horse-lie*
157. 28 Lan-tax
157. 29 twopence
160. 32 nonsensi-unintelligi
164. 1 nonsensical
164. 29 Grandmothers
175. 31 Countryman
176. 19 Countryman
185. 11 a-vire
188. 16 Ill-nature

192. 6 Sportsman
194. 3 Well-wisher
204. 30 all-merciful
214. 7 Madman
225. 7 Nonsense
238. 4 -T—dman
240. 18 Utile-dulce
251. 2 downright
252. 30 Archbishop
255. 8 Head-foremost
262. 8 -halfpence
264. 13 over-ruled
269. 17 Schoolmaster
274. 23 Gunpowder

311. 8 Scandal-mongers
318. 31 -grand-father
322. 32 preconceived
324. 14 beforementioned
328. 1 *Grub-street*
335. 1 red-hot
351. 15 Clergyman
355. 31 Good-will
371. 23 Patch-work
383. 29 Pun-makers
390. 36 Schoolmen
394. 20 Falshood
395. 8 Falshood
421. 23 Block-head

3. Special Cases

[NOTE. The following compounds or possible compounds are hyphenated at the end of the line both in copy-text and in the Wesleyan edition.]

PROPER ANSWER

85. 14 Church-men

JACOBITE'S JOURNAL

112. 6 Common-wealth
211. 35 down-right
275. 19 under-taken
292. 20 Law-giver

294. 10 Off-spring
319. 23 un-encumbred
334. 4 in-determinate
337. 11 Gentle-man
365. 25 Under-taking
374. 12 Common-wealth
383. 26 there-upon
386. 11 what-ever
415. 13 fore-seen

APPENDIX IV

Bibliographical Descriptions

A DIALOGUE

(1) THE FIRST PRINTING

State *a*

Title-page: A facsimile of the title-page is found on page [1].

Collation: 8⁰: A² B–M⁴ N²; $2 (—N2) signed (missigning F2 as E2); 48 leaves, pp. i–iv, 1–91 *92*

Press Figures: (sig.-page-fig.) B-7-1, C-10-3, D-20-2, E-30-2, F-36-1, G-45-3, H-56-3, I-63-2, K-66-1, L-77-2, M-86-3

Contents: A1: half-title '[line of type-orn.] | A | DIALOGUE | Between A | GENTLEMAN of *LONDON*, | Agent for two Court Candidates, | and an | Honest ALDERMAN | Of the Country Party. | [line of type-orn.] | (Price One Shilling and Six-pence.)'; A1ᵛ: blank; A2: title (verso blank); B1: HT 'A | DIALOGUE | Between | A Gentleman from *London* | and | An Elector in the Country.' and text (cap.³) ending on N2ʳ with '*FINIS*.'; N2ᵛ: blank

Note: (1) Copies observed: British Museum (8026. c. 51 [3]), William Andrews Clark Memorial Library (*PR3454/D51), Huntington Library (305667), Yale (College Pamphlets 1039), Bodley (G. Pamphlets 1170). Bodley (G. Pamphlets 1918) and Harvard (*EC. F460. 747d) lack A1.

State *b*

As in state *a* except: A1 (half-title [?]) lacking; N2ʳ prints 2-line errata list below '*FINIS*.'

Note: (1) Copy observed: Harvard (*EC7. F460. 747da).

State *c¹*

As in state *a* except: N2ᵛ prints 5-line errata list by transfer of 2-line errata list from state *b* and subtending three additional lines of errata in identical letterpress.

Note: (1) Copy observed: Newberry Library (J 54555.7021), in microfilm.

State *c²*

As in state *c¹* except: preserves A1 (half-title); A2 (title-page) replaces printer's ornament with 'By the Author of the *True Patriot*, and | *A ſerious Addreſs to the People of Great-Britain*. | The SECOND EDITION.' A facsimile of this title-page is found on page [2].

Note: (1) Copies observed: British Museum (102. c. 43), New York Public Library (*C pv. 145 [no. 8]).

State *d*

As in state *b* except: preserves A1 (half-title); N2^v prints 5-line errata list as in state *c*^{1}.

Notes: (1) Copies observed: Yale (Fielding Collection 747d).

(2) William B. Todd, "Three Notes on Fielding", *PBSA*, xlvii (1953), 71–2, demonstrates how the printing of the first impression generated at least four separate states as a result of half-sheet imposition of the final sheet (A^2+N^2) and of adjustments made to accommodate the insertion of two separate lists of errata. When the first or 2-line list (errata for pp. 32 and 33) was received, printing was halted, a slug of type entered in the inner section of the forme at the bottom of N2 (p. 91), and the remainder of the impression run off in this 'corrected' state. At some time during the perfecting (*before* perfection of the 'corrected' sheets) a second list of errata was received, the printing once more interrupted, the slug of type transferred from N2^r to N2^v in the outer section of the forme, letterpress for three additional lines of errata (for pp. 60, 72, and 86) subtended to it, and the printing resumed. All 'uncorrected' sheets perfected before the second adjustment would bisect to produce pairs of copies in states *a* and *b*; those perfected after the second adjustment would produce pairs in *a* and *c*; the originally 'corrected' sheets which were perfected after these, would produce pairs in *a* and *d*.

(3) Todd did not note state *c*^{2}. No evidence is known for determining whether the change in A2 (title-page) was made when the forme was unlocked so as to remove the 2-line errata list from N2^r and to subtend to it the three additional lines of errata on N2^v, or at a later stage during perfecting. On the general assumption that the change in A2 occurred at some point during perfecting, it can be argued that a relatively few copies of a state *d*^{2} (state *d* with the same A2 as state *c*^{2}) would have been registered. None has been observed by the present editor.

(4) One further possibility should be considered, namely, that the variant A2 of state *c*^{2} may be a cancel. Inasmuch as only two copies of state *c*^{2} have been observed, and inasmuch as both of these lack A1 (half-title [?]), the possibility of cancellation seems less attractive. Were it acceptable, however, there would be no way, in view of the fact that both observed copies lack A1, of telling whether the variant A2 is a single-leaf cancel or part of a quarter-sheet cancel.

(2) THE SECOND PRINTING (REVISED)

State *e*

Collation: As in state *a*

Press Figures: (sig.-page-fig.) B-2-1, C-10-3, D-20-2, F-34-1, F-36-1, G-46-1, H-56-3, I-63-2, K-66-1, L-74-2, M-86-3

Contents: As in state *a* except: A1 prints 'from *LONDON*' instead of 'of *LONDON*'; A2 as in state *c*² except for 'of *LONDON*' read 'from *LONDON*' and for 'and | *A ſerious Address . . . Great-Britain.*' read 'and of the | *Serious Address . . . Great-Britain*; | Both published at the Time of the late *Rebellion.*'

Notes: (1) Copies observed: Rylands (R67092). Bodley (Vet. A4 e. 1010) lacks A1.

(2) This printing is the first to bring both A1 and A2 into conformity with the HT reading 'from *London*', which presumably lies closer to MS. authority. This printing is also the first to incorporate (with two exceptions) the errata into the text. The incorporation of the errata and the introduction of a number of substantive variants, as well as the existence of a partly differing set of press figures, indicate that resetting has occurred. It appears to have been limited, however, to single lines and in such a way as to preserve the lineation of the copy-text. In view of the fact that much of the text seems to have been impressed from standing type, this printing has been classified as a *state* and not as a true second *edition*. Todd, loc. cit., does not appear to have known of this state.

A PROPER ANSWER

(1) THE FIRST IMPRESSION

State *a*

Title-page: A facsimile of the title-page is found on page [61].

Collation: *A*⁴ B–F⁴; $2 signed; 24 leaves, pp. *i–iv* v–vi *vii–viii* 5–44 (misnumbering v–vi as iii–iv)

Press Figures: (sig.-page-fig.) C-14-1, D-26-2, E-32-1, F-42-1

Contents: A1: half-title 'A PROPER | ANSWER | To A late | Scurrilous Libel, | Entitled, | *An Apology for the Conduct of a late* | *celebrated Second-rate Minister.*'; A1ᵛ: blank; A2: title (verso blank); A3: 'Advertisement'; A4ʳ⁻ᵛ: blank; B1: HT as A1 except for '*Minister.*' read '*Minister*, &c.' and text (cap.³) ending on F4ᵛ with '*FINIS.*' and, below, printer's ornament.

Note: (1) Copies observed: Yale (College Pamphlets 1040). Harvard (*EC7. F460. 747p) lacks A4. British Museum (T. 1632 [5]) lacks A1 and A4 and misnumbers 12 as 21. British Museum (T. 1791 [3] and 1093 e. 20), William Andrews Clark Memorial Library (*PR3454/p.81), Huntington Library (328825), and Bodley (G. Pamphlets 1918) all lack A1 and A4.

(2) THE SECOND IMPRESSION

State *b*

Title-page: A facsimile of the title-page is found on page [62].

Collation: As in state *a*

Press Figures: (sig.-page-fig.) D-26-2, E-32-2, F-42-2

Contents: As in state *a* except: A1 adds 'The SECOND EDITION.' between line 9 (motto) and the printer's ornament, and alters 'MDCCXLVII.' to 'MDCCXLVIII.'

Notes: (1) Copies observed: Bodley (22863 e. 131), National Library of Scotland (Grindlay 222 [5]). Yale (British Tracts 1748), Boston Athenaeum (Tracts B 698) lack A1 and A4. Yale (NZ/748 Fi) lacks A1 and A4 and pp. 37–44.

(2) The differing press figures of state *b* indicate that it was not made up of remainders from state *a* with an emended title-page. Rather state *b* is a reimpression from standing type. The title-page (A2) seems not to have been reset in its entirety but emended by the insertion of a single line of type ['The SECOND EDITION.'] between the motto and the printer's ornament, and by adding, with visible clumsiness, the necessary roman numeral to the date of state *a*.

APPENDIX V

The Murphy Editions

IN April 1762 *The Works of Henry Fielding, Esq; With the Life of the Author* by Arthur Murphy was published by Andrew Millar in two editions, apparently simultaneously—a quarto in four and an octavo in eight volumes respectively. Although the so-called 'Murphy editions' have always enjoyed a certain *cachet* as the only editions supervised by a person who knew Fielding personally and might therefore have had access to marked or corrected copies, the fact is, as regards the items which make up the present volume, these editions seem to possess no authority whatsoever. Of course, Murphy did not include either of the two political pamphlets and, for reasons which may have been simply reasons of taste, chose to reprint parts of only two numbers of *The Jacobite's Journal*. Collation of these two with the originals strongly suggests that Murphy did not print from texts marked or in any way revised by Fielding himself. One possible exception to this statement—and it is an outside possibility at best—may be found in Number 34, where both M4° and M8° emend the 'partaking' of the original to 'parting', an emendation which has been accepted by the present editor although it has no clear authority. Otherwise, the variants appear to be of the kind that originate in the printing house. Murphy was no very careful editor.

The question of priority as between quarto and octavo is a complicated one, which happens in the case of the materials of the present volume to have very little textual bearing. In view of this fact and in the absence of a technical analysis of the printing of the 1762 *Works*, the editor had best limit himself to remarking the unusual bibliographical features of the *Works* and to suggesting what his own particular texts indicate about the priority of editions. It is well known, of course, that Millar assigned the job of printing the *Works* to more than one printer. Unfortunately, only William Strahan's record of his own assignments is known to have survived. We do not even know for sure who the other printers were, to say nothing of what they printed. In the trade the quarto seems to have been regarded as the first edition. That is to say, no copies of it indicate otherwise, whereas some copies of the octavo (but by no means all) bear the legend 'The Second Edition' on the title page. As the Wesleyan editor has shown, in the case of *Joseph Andrews* at least there is evidence that the quarto was printed from the rearranged standing type of the octavo, which would give priority to the latter as standing closer to Murphy's copy-text. On the other hand, in working on Fielding's plays for the Wesleyan edition, Charles B. Woods concluded that for the volumes printed by Strahan (Volume I of the quarto, Volumes I–II of the octavo) the quarto is prior. As far as the two numbers of *The Jacobite's Journal* are concerned, what little evidence there is suggests that the octavo has, if not authority, at least priority.

The list of variants given below is complete in that it covers everything Murphy printed of both numbers of the journal. The list makes no distinction between substantives and accidentals. Differences in spelling are recorded; purely typographical modernizations (e.g. non-capitalization of nouns) are not. To the left of the bracket the reading is that of the copy-text original (JJ), which in all cases but one (352.24) is that of the Wesleyan edition; to the right of the bracket the reading is that of both 'Murphy editions', unless they are explicitly distinguished.

JACOBITE'S JOURNAL

NUMBER 15

189. 17 sent] sent sent
190. 2 *Bigottry*] bigotry
190. 9 *or*] and M4°; or M8°
190. 11 enough,] ~ₐ M4°
191. 17 and,] ~ₐ
191. 19 Anachronism] achronism
191. 20 Anachronism] achronism
191. 30 Conjurer] conjuror
192. 13 Kennington-Common] Kennington Common
193. 1 Foxhunters] fox-hunters
193. 13 publick] public
193. 16 *William*ₐ] William,
193. 26 Here,] ~ₐ
193. 26 Anchor,] ~ₐ

NUMBER 34

350. 24 pleased,] ~ₐ
350. 30 private,] ~ₐ
350. 31 tho'] though
350. 31 found,] ~ₐ

351. 2 Men,] ~ₐ
351. 25 tho'] though M4°
351. 27 Sin, he said,] ~ₐ~ ~ₐ
351. 33 Government,] ~ₐ
352. 3 Wife,ₐ] ~,
352. 6 Tranquility] tranquillity
352. 14 finish'd] finished
352. 16 Characteristic] haracteristic M8°
352. 24 partaking] parting
353. 1 *Bayley's*] Bailey's
353. 12 solicited] sollicited
353. 30 but,ₐ] ~,
354. 1 Administation] administration
354. 8 me,] ~ₐ
354. 11 Practices,] ~ₐ
354. 15 *Trotplaid*] Trott-Plaid
354. 16 abovementioned] above mentioned
354. 26 Sir,] sir; M4°
354. 34 *Note*. These] Note, these
354. 34 *Post*,] ~ₐ

APPENDIX VI

Doubtful Attributions from *The Jacobite's Journal*

Notes: (1) The material reprinted in this appendix consists almost entirely of two kinds: items which the *JJ* chose to reprint from other papers so as to comment on them, and the *JJ* commentary itself. In bulk this material constitutes a social and political commentary which is consistent with (and in some cases amplificatory of) Fielding's views as they are expressed in his pamphlets and leading essays. It also constitutes a critique of the journalistic practices of his time, a critique which Fielding began with his own earliest journalism and continued throughout his journalistic career. For these reasons, and because the Wesleyan editor wished to make available all material which might possibly have originated with Fielding or under his direct personal supervision, this material has been reprinted in the Wesleyan Edition. Its relegation to a separate appendix is a reflection both of editorial uncertainty as to its authorship and of the larger editorial policy to be rigorous about admissions to the canon. Although there are frequent (if intermittent) signs of Fielding's hand in this material, firm attribution seems impermissible without more evidence than is known to exist.

(2) No attempt has been made either to preserve or normalize the typographical idiosyncrasies of the original. Mis-spellings, dropped and turned letters, wrong fount—these have been silently corrected. Nor has the material of this appendix been accorded the same bibliographical analysis as that accorded the texts unequivocally assigned to Fielding. For the convenience of the reader the items (or excerpts of items) which the *JJ* reprinted from the other papers for comment are here enclosed in editorial bold-faced brackets. Where their length requires and relevance permits, such items have been reduced in length, with the conventional indication. The *JJ* commentary itself is placed in contrasting italic fount, with the usual exceptions for names and for emphasis, as it is in copy-text. *JJ* material which in the original was not directly dependent on reprinted items is here placed in roman, as it is in copy-text. The reader may take it that any unbracketed material originated with the *JJ*. Identifying initials have been substituted for the Latin abbreviation of copy-text (for example, 'D.G.' for 'ibid.') when such substitution is necessary for identification of the source. Particularly in its later issues the *JJ* reprinted many items from other papers without commenting on them. These have not been reprinted here. The material which is original with the *JJ* is covered by the index, but the editor has not attempted to provide explanatory notes.

(3) The following abbreviations of the names of contemporary news-papers cited in the commentary are taken from copy-text:

C.	*The Craftsman*
D. A.	*The Daily Advertiser*
D. G.	*The Daily Gazetteer*
G. A.	*The General Advertiser*
G. E.	*The General Evening Post*
L. C.	*The London Courant*
L. E.	*The London Evening Post*
L. G.	*The London Gazette*
O. E.	*Old England*
S. J. E.	*The St. James's Evening Post*
W. E.	*The Whitehall Evening Post*
W. J.	*The Westminster Journal*

THE JACOBITE'S JOURNAL, No. 1, Saturday, December 5, 1747.

from FOREIGN AFFAIRS.

[By a Letter from Switzerland there is an Account, that one of the most considerable of the Romish Cantons are going to embrace the Protestant Religion. D. A.]—*The* Catholic *Cause is so united with the* Jacobite, *that I look upon this as bad News, as well as the following.*

from DOMESTIC NEWS.

[The last Day of Term Mr. Lucas, of Farnham, who has many Years declined Business, moved the Court of Common Pleas to be struck off the Roll as an Attorney, being in Commission of the Peace for the County of Norfolk. D. A.]—*It is Pity but some Attornies, who decline no Business would follow his Example.*

[The Scholars of Westminster School have *the Ignoramus of Terence* in Rehearsal, which will be play'd one Day this Week, at the Dormitory near the said School. D. A.]—*Happy it is for the Age, that the* Ignoramus *of this and other News-Papers, will be weekly in Rehearsal at our Vigilatory.*

[According to the last Advices from Dorsetshire, Things are very far from being absolutely settled at Shaftsbury, notwithstanding the late Reports of a Compromise, and if we may depend upon some very good Intelligence, Peter Walter, Esq; Grandson to the late Peter Walter, Esq; of Palace-Yard, Westminster, so much *celebrated* in the Writings of Mr. Pope, will *appear* as a Candidate for that Borough at the next Election. D. C.]—*It doth not* appear, *in this Paragraph, whether the News Writer intends to* celebrate *the Grandfather or Grandson.*

[A few Days since came on before the Lord Chief Justice of the King's-Bench, a remarkable Trial against a Clergyman, for Subornation of Perjury, which lasted several Hours. D. G.]—*If this Man was convicted, it would have been more decent to have mentioned his Name at length than his Order; which it is too usual to condemn, for the sake of Individuals.*

CREDENDA.

Being certain Articles of Jacobite-Faith, *consisting of Argument, Wit, Humour, Stories, &c. Calculated to amuse the Party, and serve the Cause.*

Argument. In O. E. an Attaint on the Ministry, *supposing* that they aim at destroying the Liberty of the Press; because somebody hath writ, and somebody hath said something, from which something may be inferred.

In W. J. another Attack on ditto Ministry, *supposing* that they are desirous to make a Peace, and shewing that we should carry on the War without Troops, or withdraw them from the Continent, in order to let the French become more powerful there, because they are already too powerful.

In the C. another Attack on said Ministry, *supposing* that they intend to tax the Lands in Ireland; and, if they do, advising the Parliament there to oppose it.

Wit. [I am debarr'd from making the Encomium I meant on our present most *excellent*, most *able*, most *learned*, and most *disinterested* Ministers. O. E.]

[We cannot expect always to find a Ministry free from Ambition, Rapaciousness, Cruelty, and Corruption, tho' our present Ministry are so happily distinguish'd by the contrary Characteristics. Idem.]

By these two Paragraphs our Party are to understand, that the present Ministry are neither excellent, nor able, nor learned, nor disinterested; but that they are ambitious, rapacious, cruel, and corrupt.

[We hear that the *Two Brothers*, finding themselves secure of their *Numbers* by the first Trial, begin to speak with great *Contempt* of all *future P——ns.*—But may there not be some *Ch–pp—h–m* yet in Reserve? L. E.]—*This Paragraph hath two Properties of true Jacobite Wit; for it is imp–d–nt, and a L–e.*

[*A* STAVE *of* INSTRUCTION.
Ye *New Elect*, attend the *Lord*,
And he will teach you *Truth*:
Ye must be all of one *Accord*,
From *Antients* down to *Youth.*

Then, as the *Tr——re Records* say,
Favour ye shall inherit:
To *Honour*, lo! this is the Way;
For this is *modern Merit.* L. E.]

And this is MODERN POETRY, *and true sterling Jacobite Wit; as is the following from the same Paper:*

[The *Art of Design* is a Thing much talk'd of by *Painters,* and it is humbly presum'd to be no less necessary to *Politicians.* To plan *particular* Schemes, either of Peace or War, and have the *present Moment* always influenced by the *last Event,* without taking in a WHOLE; a *general System* cannot be called acting by the *Art of Design.*—By what Art then do *some Men* act? L. E.]—*This is pure Mystery, and what Dr. Balsora himself cannot explain. But it is sufficient for our Party to be told, that all Words gutted of their Vowels, and printed in Italick, are to be taken for Wit.*

N.B. We would not be supposed to imagine, that every Person who joins in the Designs of our Party is a true Jacobite; but as they contribute all in their Power to distress the Government, so we shall own them at present; and it will be time enough to pay them *their proper Wages* when they have done all our Work.

THE JACOBITE'S JOURNAL, No. 2, Saturday, December 12, 1747.

from DOMESTIC NEWS.

[. . . I must not omit one Circumstance, because it was *a little diverting*: A Woman at Seaford, whose Husband being dead at the Wreck, hir'd a Cart and Horses to fetch him, in order to bury him, but the Carter not knowing him, brought her another Man instead of her Husband, upon which the Woman refus'd to pay the Carter, and he left her the Man. L. E.]—*A story big with the utmost Iniquity, as well as Misery, of human Nature, is a very proper Subject of Diversion.—If this Writer was not of our Party, we should think his Heart as bad as his Head.*

CREDENDA.

Or Articles of Jacobite-Faith, *consisting of a curious Collection of Wit, Humour, Argument, Stories, Healths,* &c.

[. . . IV. Whether the *British Quarrel* with the House of *Bourbon,* cannot be more *easily decided,* with much more Appearance of *Success* on the *British Side,* and of more real and lasting *Injury* to the *Enemy,* by exerting the *whole Naval Force* we can put to Sea in *Europe* and the *Indies,* than by making the *utmost Efforts* we are able, with such *needy Allies* on the *Continent?* L. E.]—*These Jacobitical Queries are rightly put, and in the true Spirit of our Party, which having rallied a Project as improbable for a long while, when it can be denied no longer, begins to censure it. In short, our Business is to censure the Administration every Way: To oppose their making*

Peace. To oppose their continuing the War. To abuse them for the Want of Allies they cannot have. To abuse them for taking those they can. To object to them the Weakness of our Friends, the Strength of our Enemies. To call out at the same Time for War and against Taxes. And lastly, To insinuate that to have been omitted which is manifestly done; as are the Fourth of these excellent Queries. Hae tibi erunt Artes—*my Boy,*—Huzza.

ARTICULI VENTOSI. *Anglicé,* PUFFS or F–RTS.

[No. 41802, a Prize of 100*l.* drawn Yesterday, was sold in Shares at Hazard's Office in Ludgate-street; and we can with Truth assure the Publick, that No. 22529, drawn on Thursday last a Prize of 500*l.* was sold at his Office at the Royal Exchange the 19th of November last, and register'd, to a Gentleman in Kent. D. A.]—*This Broker need not puff so hard in every Paper, since his Name alone is sufficient Recommendation to the Superstitious.*

THE JACOBITE'S JOURNAL, No. 3, Saturday, December 19, 1747.

from DOMESTIC NEWS.

[Duncan Forbes, Esq; Lord President of the Session, died lately at Edinburgh; a Gentleman of great Merit, and of an universal good Character. He discharged all the Social Offices of Life with the highest Virtue; and his Conduct in the late Rebellion was full of Honour, of Duty to his King, and Love to his Country.]—*Note, We shall always praise great Merit, even in a Whig.*

[Yesterday a Post-Chaise, coming from Windsor, was lost in the Waters near Belfond, and a Gentleman drowned. The Boy who drove the Chaise saved himself by Swimming. D. G.]—*As Belfond is not the Road to Windsor, nor near any Waters in which a Chaise can be lost, we hope this is not true.*

from DEATHS.

[Mr. Curle, formerly a noted Bookseller. *His Character may be seen at large in the Works of Swift and Pope.* D. C.]—*rather I believe* in Miniature.

CREDENDA.

Being a curious Collection of Jacobite Wit, *&c.*

Grub-street, Dec. 17.

[ALL HONEST ALIKE.

When WENTWORTH the *Patriot* grew STRAFFORD the *Peer,*
Himself, not his *Country,* he valu'd, 'tis clear:

His Enemy PYM dy'd a *Patriot* indeed;
He *pull'd down the Earl*, but *liv'd not to succeed.*
TONY COOPER, by Turns, was a *Courtier* and *Whig*:
(JOHN DRYDEN had *lash'd him* with PHŒBUS' *own Twig,*)
CHARLES, JAMES, WILLIAM, ANNE, all saw the *same Face,*
Which *all Patriots* assum'd when they came *into Place.*
In Times *more remember'd* how *like* is the Plan?
Once WALPOLE'S *Defection* discover'd *the Man*:
From *G—e* he *retreated* with Rancour and Grief,
And wou'd be *no Servant,*—unless he were *Chief.*
Since Him can St. *J—s's* its *Proselytes* count?
Above *my Arithmetick* far they amount.
Sir ROBERT said wisely, *his Foes* now must own;
'*All Men* may be *bought,* if their *Prices are known.*'

LOND. EVEN.]

The above imitated.

What is the Price of *this great* POET?
HALF A CROWN: full well I *know* it.
Then *why not* bought? *The* Case *is* clear
P——m thinks him *much too* dear.

We have receiv'd a Letter from *Truth itself*, alias *Nonsense itself*. In answer to which, we advise the ORATOR to conceal his Stile better for the future, or he will be gibbetted in this Paper, in a Manner that shall make *even him* ashamed.

We are desired to return the Thanks of all the Jacobites, as well in England as abroad, to Father Paul Maskwell *of the Society of Jesus*, for his excellent Treatise, called an Apology for a late celebrated Second-rate Minister, &c.

THE JACOBITE'S JOURNAL, No. 4, Saturday, December 26, 1747.

from FOREIGN AFFAIRS.

[... Marshal Lowendahl is at present at Namur; it is said he has obtained his Master's Leave to make an Attempt upon Zealand, and in case he succeeds therein Marshal Saxe is immediately to invest Maestricht; but we look upon these Reports as calculated to promote a pacifick Spirit at the Conferences, which we believe to be nearer at hand than either of these Expeditions. L. C.]—*I am sorry to see any thing in the* London Courant *which makes against our Party, as the Author of that Paper is certainly the best of all the public Writers of News. For which Reason, I like not the fore-going Article, and much less the two subsequent ones, all taken from that Paper.*

from DOMESTIC NEWS.

[Last Week was held a General Quarterly Communication of the Free and Accepted Masons, at the Devil Tavern near Temple-Bar, when the Masters and Wardens of the several Lodges of this Metropolis paid in a large Sum of Money for their poor and indigent Brethren. S. J. E.]—*To wit, we suppose, the Scald Miserable Masons.*

[Last Tuesday a Person was arrested in Long-Lane, Southwark, for Fourteen-pence, but the Populace being apprized of the Affair, came in a Posse, and rescued the Man out of the Hands of the Bailiffs, and carried him off in Triumph. Id.]—*Bailiffs are no more in Fault than Bull-Dogs. Those alone are to blame who set such Vermin on their Fellow Creatures.*

[On Saturday Night an uninhabited House in Grub-Street fell down, and a Woman passing by was so miserably bruised, that her Life is despaired of. D. A.]—*Tho' the Daily Advertiser be not a very authentic Paper, we may trust him for a Fact of which he was probably an Eye-Witness, as it happened in his Neighbourhood.*

[. . . Several poor Widows and distressed Orphans are at this present Time starving, some who bravely fought and ventured their Lives now lying in Prison and several daily threatened to be sent there, for want of their Money being paid them. D. A.]—*Tho' this Paragraph be Nonsense and unintelligible, as well as are all the Writings of this Author, yet it seems to point at some Transactions which we wish were enquired into by one capable of explaining them.*

[According to our Accounts from Stockholm, the Paper War is still carried on between the two Parties in Sweden, distinguished by the Names of *Hats* and *Caps*; the former being at the Head of Affairs, and the other in the Opposition. D. G.]—*These Names, since our Party have worn the Highland Dress, will serve very well to distinguish the two Parties here.*

from MISCELLANEA CURIOSA.

Containing Hanging, Drowning, Robbing, Burying, Preferring, Committing, &c. &c. taken from all the Papers.

Several Persons, who never will be heard of any more,
Are chose Common-Council, in the room of those never heard of before.

ARTICULI JACOBITICI.

Verses by the Bellman of Grub-street, in Imitation of the Ode in the London Evening of Tuesday last.

All you that in your Beds do lie and snore,
Get up for Shame, and make a loud Uproar·
For hard it is, that you should sleep so well,
While I must walk the Streets, and ring the Bell.

                    Good-morrow, my Masters all.

A Satyrical Article in the true Style.

As C—m–s is *now coming*, it is well to be wished, that s–me of th–se
who have pl—d–d the P–b—c, by receiving the *Salaries* of their respective
P—ces, which s——l oth–rs would be glad to have from them, would
bestow great Part of their M–ney upon the P—r, in Imitation of good old
E–glish H–sp–t–l–ty, *instead of providing for* th–ms–lves and their F–milies.
This would make some Amends to their C—ntry *for their having accepted*
those Empl—ments, which we desire *to see only* in the Hands of J–c–bites.

The Toast for the next Week is, *No Russian Bears.*

                    JOHN TROTT-PLAID.

THE JACOBITE'S JOURNAL, No. 5, Saturday, January 2, 1748.

from DOMESTIC NEWS.

[Advices from the Hague say, that it has been resolved to establish there a
Military School, in Imitation of those at Paris *and London,* to instruct young
Officers in the true Knowledge of their Profession, as well as of Natural
Philosophy, Geography, and the Languages of most general Use. W. E.]—
We do not know where that at London *is held; but we suppose it to be some-
where* in Covent Garden.

[A Proclamation is published for a general Fast to be held throughout
England, &c. on Wednesday the 17th of February next. D. C.]—*N.B.
Our Party need not fast unless they please; or if they do, they may fast on what
Account they think fit.*

from ARTICULI JACOBITICI.

                                        Grub-street, Dec. 26.

[*No more* GAMBOLS.

'Twas *merry* at *Christmas,* when Money was Plenty,
And *Taxes* took off not above *Five* in *Twenty:*
But how is it possible *Mirth* should arise
Now *all* that can *make it* is under *Excise?*
When *Light* is *not free* in the worst of *dull Weather;*

Wheels pay, if we *ride*; if we *foot it, Shoe-Leather*. L. E.]

IMITATED.

By this *worst of dull Writing*, it is very clear,
The Poet this Christmas drinks only Small-Beer.

[—*We should be glad to hear*, that early Preparations were making for an Attempt to *drive the French entirely out of the North Part of America*, and also for a powerful Expedition against their *West-India Islands*, the present great *Source* of their Trade. *England* hath certainly *large Men of War* enough to undertake *both* these important Enterprizes, and at the same Time, in Conjunction with the *Dutch*, to cover the *narrow Seas*, and block up, occasionally, the *principal Ports* of the Enemy in *Europe*. L. E.]—*If you write the Word* Admiralty *at Length (as there is no Reason for doing otherwise) and put the several Words printed in Italicks into* Roman *Characters, these two Paragraphs, which advise us to do what we are doing, would lose all their Wit, and smell of that Cellar in Grub-street, whence they came.*

ADVERTISEMENT.

Whereas Readers are apt to be tired with the frequent Repetition of the same Thing, and whereas the several Writers of our Party have been long reduced to their Wit's-End, these are therefore to give Notice, that if any Person can invent some new Aspersions to be cast on the Ministry, they will meet with all proper Encouragement, by enquiring for Argos Centiculi in Red-Lion-Court in Fleet-street; Caleb D'Anvers, Esq; in Gray's-Inn; Thomas Touchit in Spring-Gardens; or, lastly, at an Alehouse near the Little Old Bailey for the Porter of the House, who is so universally known by the Name of THE FOOL. Note, It will not be insisted on that the said Aspersions should contain even the least Colour of Truth.

THE JACOBITE'S JOURNAL, No. 6, Saturday, January 9, 1748.

from MISCELLANEA CURIOSA.

[Last Week a Gang of Villains broke open and robbed several Out-houses and Sheds belonging to the Inhabitants of Angel Alley, Maiden-head Court, and other adjacent Places in Little Moorfields; to prevent which for the future, the Officers of Cripplegate-Ward, have ordered some Watchmen to patrole about those Places in the Night, *without crying the Hour, or carrying of Lanthorns*, in order to the detecting such Rogues, and bringing them to condign Punishment. W. E.]—*These Watchmen will, I dare swear, effectually answer the cunning Purpose of the Inhabitants, and will take Care never to be seen by the Thieves.*

[*Extract of a Letter from Helmingham in Suffolk, December* 18.

'The Distemper among the Cattle having lately broke out here, and it appearing that it spread in many Places by Dogs, Orders were given for *tying up* those Creatures; which being complied with, did much Service. But near this Parish lives a Man who keeps Hounds, and tho' the Neighbourhood desired he would not hunt, yet every Day, both wet and dry, he is over their Grounds with his Dogs, and has spread the Distemper into many Dairy Farms. As his Majesty has not given any immediate Directions in his Order of Council concerning them, I question whether he will leave hunting till the Country rise up and kill his Dogs, which I expect will be the Consequence, if not his Desert.' S. J. E.]—*If this Story be true, there is* one very sad Dog, *who deserves to be* ty'd up *more than all the rest.*

[We are well assured, that on Christmas-Day, a Lady living near Cavendish Square, thinking to fulfil the Gospel, invited all the Poor she met with to dine with her on that Day: She had provided a large Buttock of Beef, Plumb-Puddings, and other substantial English Dishes, to entertain them with; and a Lady of her Acquaintance sending a Message, that she would dine with her that Day, her Ladyship desired to be excused seeing her, because she had a select Company to dine with her, but should be glad of her Company another Time. Ib.]—*This Lady may be thought to have kept* (for one Day at least) very bad Company; *but she seems to take a proper Method to introduce herself into the* best Company *in the next World.*

[Last Monday two *well-dressed Women* went into a Hosier's Shop in Little-Britain, under pretence of buying Stockings, and took an Opportunity to carry off several Pair, which being soon missed, they were closely pursued and taken in Aldersgate-street, and carried to the Compter for further Examination. G. E.]—*These are not the first well-dressed Women who have in a hurry packed up Goods in a Shop without paying for them.*

[A Travelling Pedlar, supposed to have lost his Way on Salisbury Plain, and have perished through the Inclemency of the Weather, was found dead early on Friday Morning, near Stonehenge. His Dog lay by him almost frozen to Death. L. C.]—*The Fidelity of this Dog is a fresh Instance what Injustice we do to the Canine Species by giving some Men the Appellation of Dogs.*

THE JACOBITE'S JOURNAL, No. 7, Saturday, January 16, 1748.

from DOMESTIC NEWS.

[It is said, that the Admirals Warren, Hawke, Chambers and Osborne, will shortly put to Sea with strong Squadrons of Ships of War, to protect our

Trade, and annoy our Enemies. S. J. E.]—*Our Party will be nevertheless at Liberty to abuse the Administration for neglecting the Marine. Therefore I say, why don't we pr–s–c–te the W–r at Sea?*

[We hear, that in all the Ports in the Channel there has been a smart Press for Seamen, in order to man a Fleet of Ships which are to put to Sea early this Spring Ib.].—*I say again, why don't we pr–s–c–te the W–r at Sea?*

from MISCELLANEA CURIOSA.

[—The same Day the Wife of a Porter in Dirty-Lane was safely deliver'd of three Boys, all likely to live.]—*My Peggy says it is Pity this Porter should live in Dirty-Lane.*

[We hear that some Fortune-Tellers have found Means to defraud several Female Servants in the Liberties of Westminster of considerable Sums of Money, and from one in Stretton-street only they got 20*l.* D. A.]—*By the Largeness of this Sum the Puffing Lottery-Mongers seem to be the Fortune-tellers here meant.*

[We have an Account from Hereford, that the Person who keeps the Catherine-Wheel in that City has been so fortunate in the last Lottery, that out of five Tickets he has had a 100*l.* a 2000*l.* and a 5000*l.* L. C.]—*This Catharine-Wheel may be henceforth called the Wheel of Fortune.*

[*Dublin, Jan.* 5. Last Thursday Night died Mr. John Winstanley, A. M. L. D. F. S. T. C. D. in the 71st Year of his Age. He had a very polite Poetical Genius, and publish'd a Volume of his Works about six Years ago with great Success. He was a Gentleman well beloved by all who had the Pleasure of his Acquaintance, for his good Humour and facetious Conversation, which makes his Loss the more to be regretted. D. G.]— *As to this Gentleman's poetical Abilities, his Works will speak for him; but as to his Dignity, Post, Place, or Employment, we must refer you to the Decypherers.*

THE JACOBITE'S JOURNAL, No. 8, Saturday, January 23, 1748.

from FOREIGN AFFAIRS.

[*Paris, Jan.* 19. . . . and they write from Brussels, that no Convoy can get safe to Bergen-op-Zoom, the Light Troops of the Enemy being continually in Ambush to intercept them. In the Escorte of the great Convoy, which they lately took, 'tis said we had 500 Men killed or wounded. *There is a Talk of* curing these Attempts for the future, by sending a Parcel of covered Waggons full of Soldiers, as if it was a Convoy of Provisions; and we flatter ourselves that this Feint will succeed. G. A.]—*This Stratagem is manifestly taken from the famous Wooden Horse which the Greeks employed against Troy; but if the French have any such Design, it seems strange there should be a Talk of it.*

from DOMESTIC NEWS.

[Saturday Samuel Childers, of Long Stratton, Norfolk, Labourer, and Robert Scot, of Yarmouth, Mariner, were tried at the Old Bailey for Smuggling, and Capitally convicted. They are two of the Persons who got into a Barn, and fir'd upon a Party of General Huske's Regiment. G. A.]— *See many Abuses on the Government, and particularly in a late Pamphlet, called* The State of the Nation, *for conniving at smuggling.*

from MISCELLANEA CURIOSA.

[On Friday Night John Morgan was committed to the Gatehouse by James Fraser, Esq; for defrauding one James Wallington, at an unlawful Game call'd All-Fours, of *thirteen* Guineas and a half, and one Guinea besides, his Property. D. A.]—*I fancy the Author hath had bad Luck at the Game of All-Fours, and hath lost at least thirteen Pence and a half, and one Penny besides, his Property. Or doth he think this Game of All-Fours unlawful, because Mr. H—— hath not yet prescribed the Laws for playing at it?*

[About a Fortnight ago one Richard Manser, Ostler at the Talbot-Inn, Southwark, was beat by a Servant belonging to a Man who keeps a Livery-stable in the said Yard, in so terrible a manner, that he died in the utmost Agonies at St. Thomas's-Hospital last Friday, and has left a Wife and three Children. This Affair was occasioned by the Deceas'd *not recommending a Person (who wanted to hire a Horse)* to the aforesaid Man; which so provoked him, that he ordered his Servant to beat him, and he would justify his Proceeding. L. C.]—*I recommend to both the Master and Man an excellent Horse, which stands a little beyond the Turnpike in the Oxford-Road, and which will carry them both very well to the End of their Journey.*

[. . . And we hear that Lady Theresa, his Excellency's eldest Daughter, is past all Hopes of Recovery, being attended by Dr. Mead, and several other eminent Physicians. D. A.]—*This is a very impudent Insinuation, that a Person who is attended by several eminent Physicians must be past all Hopes of Recovery.*

from ARTICULI JACOBITICI.

[We hear there are actually about eighty Ships laden with Corn lying in the River, all entered for Exportation to Holland; but it's hoped they will not be suffered to sail without Convoy, lest some of them should be taken, *wilfully*, or otherwise, by the French. L. E.]—*Such Insinuations are greatly laudable when they are to serve our Party; otherwise I confess the Author of them would deserve to be h—g—d.*

THE JACOBITE'S JOURNAL, No. 9, Saturday, January 30, 1748.

from DOMESTIC NEWS.

[*Dublin, Jan.* 16. Yesterday Morning the Right Hon. Countess of Kildare was safely delivered of a Son at his Lordship's House in Suffolk-street, to the inexpressible Joy of that antient and noble Family, and the whole Kingdom . . . W. E.]—*This beautiful young Lady is the Daughter of his Grace the Duke of Richmond, a Nobleman so greatly beloved by all who have the Honour of his Acquaintance, that this Circumstance must give as much Pleasure to many in England as it can in Ireland, where have been the most universal Rejoicings ever known on such an Occasion.*

[By a Cartel Vessel arrived at Dover from Calais, there is Advice that the French take all the Dutch Vessels they meet with and imprison their Crews, as if at open War. S. J. E.]—*This Author is I believe, the only Person to whom the War between France and Holland is a Secret.*

[We hear that the Report of the Distemper among the Cattle being got into Herefordshire, is intirely false; and are assured that there is no Part of that County in which the Cattle are infected. D. A.]—*We are assured that the Distemper of raising false Reports rages, among some very black Cattle, more violently than ever.*

[Within these few Days past upwards of 50,000 Quarters of Wheat have been entered for Exportation to Foreign Parts. D. G.]—*To the great Joy of our poor Farmers, whose Corn lies rotting upon their Hands.*

from MISCELLANEA CURIOSA.

[Letters from Poland mention the great Taste for Literature, which has lately appeared in that Kingdom, and discover'd itself particularly by the Numbers of Books that are translated from other Languages. G. A.]—*Letters from Grub-street mention the little Taste for Literature which hath lately appeared in this Kingdom, and which hath discovered itself particularly by the Number of Books, Pamphlets, and News-Papers which daily issue from the said Grub-street.*

ARTICULI JACOBITICI.

[We hear a Bill will be brought into Parliament, for the more speedy Payment of Prize-Money to the Sailors on board his Majesty's Ships of War. L. E.]—*As the detaining this Money is a national Abuse, why should we not lay it on the Gov—m—nt, as well as other Corruptions for which they are equally accountable.* I shall therefore correct the above Paragraph in the following Manner.

It is hoped a B–ll will *soon* be brought into Parl———nt for the *more speedy*

P—ment of Prize-Money, which it is thought, hath lately stuck too long to the d—ty Fing—rs of SOME PERSONS.

[Daily Gazetteer, Monday, Jan. 25.
To the Author of the DAILY GAZETTEER.

SIR,

We have Advice by the Countess of Leicester Packet, that a Fleet of near Thirty Sail of Merchant Ships, having long waited for Convoy at Jamaica, are now coming home without any; and as there are now many French Privateers of Force out, the said Ships are in no little Danger of being intercepted; which is, I hope, a sufficient Intimation to the Lords of the Admiralty of the Necessity of sending some Men of War to meet them. I am,

SIR,

Your very Humble Servant,

MERCATOR.]

Can any Thing resound more to the Scandal of this Nation, than that a daily, paultry News Writer should dare to censure the Conduct of a Board composed, among other Gentlemen, of two of our greatest Admirals, and presided over by a Noble Duke of the highest Rank, the most extensive Property, and the most unblemished Honour, and whose Labours have ever since he hath presided there, been indefatigable for the Service of his Country, and crowned with most eminent Success. I am,

SIR, *yours.*

THE JACOBITE'S JOURNAL, No. 10, Saturday, February 6, 1748.

from DOMESTIC NEWS.

[Capt. Webb has also taken a French Merchantman, bound to the West Indies; and also retaken an English Snow, bound home from the West Indies. S. J. E.]—*This Gentleman hath very notably distinguished himself by many signal Services in this War.*

[We hear that the Propositions made by France, &c. to his Majesty for a General Peace, will soon be laid before both Houses of Parliament. D. A.]—*I heard an impudent Whig, on reading this Paragraph, wish the glorious Ministry, who signed the Peace of Utrecht, had been as honest as the present.*

from MISCELLANEA CURIOSA.

[A Monument is erecting at the North End of Westminster Abbey, to the Memory of the late Dr. Hugh Boulter, Archbishop of Armagh, and Primate of all Ireland. D. A.]—*Mr. Scheemaker makes good Monuments; but the best are those which Men make for themselves.*

[We hear that a Bill will be speedily brought in to prevent riotous Proceedings at Elections, and for the better preserving that Decency and Decorum which is due to a Matter of such Importance, as the Choice of Representatives to sit in Parliament, and to discourage the scandalous Practice of mobbing before, at, or after Elections, in Counties, Cities, and Boroughs, a Thing that would be highly satisfactory to the true Friends of the Constitution, who will always distinguish between a laudable Zeal for Liberty, and a rash and headstrong Spirit of Licentiousness. D. C.]—*I hope our Party will oppose this Bill; for I like it not. It may infringe the Liberty of Drinking.*

[Last Week a Publican of Bath, coming to London, was met by two Footpads on Marlborough Downs, who stopt him, and bid him deliver his Money; which upon his refusing to do, one of them struck at him, which he returned, though he had nothing in his Hand but a Whip, with which he knock'd one of them down; the other, who was behind him, made a Blow at him; upon which he quitted his Horse, and fought them both for a considerable Time, till a Gentleman and his Servant came up, who knew him; as soon as they appear'd, the Villains made off, pretty much damaged, they having left much Blood upon the Spot; but the Victualler received no Hurt, except one Blow between his Shoulders. The Gentleman made him a Present for his good Behaviour. D. A.]—*The Bravery of this Publican so pleased Fortune (who always favours the Brave) that she encreased his Stores at the very Moment when she threaten'd to lessen them. Quære, however, how these two Footpads happened to escape? since the Gentleman and his Servant might at least have been as useful as the Horse are in an Army, who serve to take those Prisoners whom the Foot have defeated.*

DEAD. A Merchant, a Timber-merchant, two Coal-merchants, a Cabinet-maker, two Distillers, two Esqrs. three Gentlemen, a Widow, a Parson, and a Performer on the Violin. All eminent. Some had large Fortunes, others handsome Fortunes, one reckon'd worth 20000*l*. another 30000*l*. and one had great Learning, but no Benefice. *Who may, we doubt not, be matched by some who have great Benefices, but no &c.*

ARTICULI JACOBITICI.

[To *Fast* and pray, that Heav'n our Arms may bless,
Is wise and pious—we can do no less.
Yet least we should those Blessings hop'd undo,
Says Human Wisdom, Let the *French* fast too. D. G.]

The same a little worse (i.e. better) exprest.

[To Fast and Pray, that Heav'n our Arms may bless,
Is wise and pious—we can do no less:
We might howe'er, methinks, something more do;
What's that, pray? Why, Sir, make the *French fast too.* G. A.]

Imitated.

Sell the *French* Bread! O monstrous! in these times
We Poets hardly get it by our Rhimes.

THE JACOBITE'S JOURNAL, No. 11, Saturday, February 13, 1748.

from DOMESTIC NEWS.

[One hundred thousand Quarters of Wheat are entered in the Custom-House for Exportation; which has raised the Price of that Commodity five Shillings a Load. S. J. E.]—*To the great Joy of the poor Farmers, whom some of their worthy Countrymen wished to have deprived of this Providential Benefit, which I doubt not but they will remember on all proper Occasions.*

from MISCELLANEA CURIOSA.

[Wednesday pursuant to the Will of the Rev. Dr. Trapp, his Poems on Death, Judgment, Heaven, and Hell, were delivered by the Clerk of the Parish to every Parishioner in Christ Church, Newgate-street; the same he has likewise appointed to be given to the Parishioners of Harlington in Middlesex. L. C.]—*This is perhaps the first Time that Poetry hath been devised to charitable Uses.*

[We hear that Mr. Johnson, who fought on Wednesday last Week at Broughton's Amphitheatre in Oxford-Road, is dead of the Wounds he that Day received. L. C.]—*Persons who live in a Country where Christianity is really practised, (if there be any such) will stare at the Encouragement of these Diversions.*

1. Quære, *Whether any thing so malicious, so false, so villanous, and so impudent was ever published in any Nation, as the Queries in the* London Evening-Post *on* Thursday?
2. Qu. *Whether such Licentiousness is not a manifest Abuse of the Liberty of the Press; and whether the scandalous Writer may not be justly suspected of being employed by some, who are Enemies to that Liberty?*
3. Qu. *Whether the Booksellers who employ such a Fellow to write two or three treasonable Libels in every Paper, as Articles of News, do not deserve to be mark'd out, and severely punished?*

4. Qu. *What Appellation do those deserve who encourage the worst and vilest of all News-Papers, for the Sake of such Articles, which are always as dull and insipid as false and scandalous?*

5. Qu. *Whether in the Reign of* James *the Second, or under any other than the present too mild Administration, all concerned in publishing such Libels, would not have been flead at the Cart's Tail?*

THE JACOBITE'S JOURNAL, No. 12, Saturday, February 20, 1748.

from FOREIGN AFFAIRS.

[*Rome, Feb.* 3. As a great many Persons have died here suddenly, the Physicians have opened some of them, to discover the Cause of it. G. A.]— *The Physicians should rather be opened, since the Cause is most probably in them.*

from DOMESTIC NEWS.

[His Majesty hath been graciously pleased to appoint his Grace the Duke of Bedford to be one of his Majesty's Principal Secretaries of State; and the Seals of the Southern Provinces have been accordingly delivered to his Grace. G. E.]—*To the great Joy of all who wish well to the true Interest of their Country.*

from *Comical* OCCURRENCES.

[Letters by the last Mail mention, that Mr. George Archinson, an Irish Gentleman, who went to Rome in the Year 1724 to convert the Pope, died in a Madhouse in that City. S. J. E.]—*Nothing could be more probable than this End of his Journey.*

[Mr. James Ellis hath been presented to the Royal Society, with a new invented Piece of Ordnance, where he had the Honour of Thanks from the Society, and a handsome Present.—This Piece of Ordnance will charge and discharge both at one Time, and twenty times in one Minute. Ib.]—*It is hoped that in a few Years Gunpowder and Gunnery will be so improved, that a few Minutes will be sufficient to destroy a whole Army.*

from *Tragical* OCCURRENCES.

[*Newcastle, Feb.* 13. We hear from Easington, that, after eight Months Deliberation, the Treaty of Marriage betwixt Mr. Ralph Firry, aged 90, and Mrs. Brandling, of the same Place and Age, was *happily consummated,* and the Settlement for the Issue of this Marriage amicably adjusted, after having twice been at Church in that Time, and returned without completing the Ceremony, on Account of *some lesser Incidents occurring, not properly fix'd* for their former or future Offspring, but at last settled to entire

Satisfaction. D. A. L. C. G. A.]—*Qu. Whether the Word* happily *should not be read* hardly; *and whether some* lesser Incidents occurring, not properly fixed, &c. *may not yet retard the completing all Ceremonies necessary for their future Offspring eight Months longer.*

THE JACOBITE'S JOURNAL, No. 13, Saturday, February 27, 1748.

from FOREIGN AFFAIRS.

[The Reports that the Pretender's eldest Son had withdrawn from this Kingdom, are prov'd false by his Arrival in this City last Week with a numerous Retinue: He goes now and then to the Opera and the Playhouse, but never without many Attendants. L. E.]—*We heartily wish all his Friends on this Side of the Water were among the Number of his Attendants on the other.*

from *Comical* OCCURRENCES.

[Last Wednesday Afternoon a Jew, eminent for his great Knowledge of the Hebrew and Chaldee Languages, was, after a proper Confession of his Faith, publickly baptized at the Meeting-House in *Paul's-Alley,* Barbican. D. A.]—*We wish some Jews in* Change-Alley *would turn Christians.*

[Tuesday a large Press-Gang beset the Quarters of the Upper Moorfields, and carried several Vagrants, who had assembled there in order to throw at Cocks, on board the Tenders in the River. D. G.]—*As Gallus is Latin for both a Cock and a Frenchman, it is supposed that this barbarous Custom took its Rise from the Animosity of our Ancestors to that Nation. We hope these Vagrants in their Behaviour against the French, will shew this to be true.*

from *Tragical* OCCURRENCES.

[The Act of Parliament for preventing frivolous and vexatious Arrests, took Place the 15th Instant, and is made perpetual. G. A.]—*Some may think this no Tragical Article; but it is truly so to those worthy Members of the Society, the Pettyfogging Attornies, Bailiffs, and their Followers.*

from ARTICULI JACOBITICI.

Down with the M———y.

An ODE.

I.

To purchase Wine of *France* was thought,
Once, Want of Common Sense.

For why, the gen'rous Juice was bought
With gen'rous *British* Pence.

II.

But now our Patriot Scribes with Scorn
The Min——y attack,
Because they send abroad our Corn,
And bring *French* Money back.

III.

What would you have our Statesmen do?
What mean these scribbling Elves?
Why, fetch their Wine and Money too,
And keep our Corn ourselves.

John Trott-Plaid.

THE JACOBITE'S JOURNAL, No. 14, Saturday,
March 5, 1748.

from FOREIGN AFFAIRS.

[Extract of a Letter from Lausanne in Switzerland.
Feb. 20, 1748. N. S.

'The Levies for the new Regiment of Graffenriedt, lately granted to the
Dutch go on with uncommon Briskness, which give us Hopes that it will
be compleated much sooner than was expected at first, and no wonder, since
Father and Children all enlist together, an Instance of which I myself saw
yesterday. But what is still more surprizing, I have it from very good Hands
at Bern, that a young Woman in Man's Cloaths has likewise entered herself
a Soldier in the same Corps, and upon the Discovery of her Sex refused to
return the Enlisting Money, but insisted on serving the High Allies as a
Soldier. The Case has been laid before the Commissioners of the Board of
Recruits, and we wait impatiently to know what will become of our Heroine.'
G. E.]—*It is hoped this fair Warrior will do as much Injury to the* French,
as the famous Joan *of* Orleans *formerly did Service.*

from *Comical* OCCURRENCES.

[Tuesday Morning died at his House in the King's Mews, Mr. Laws,
Bridle-Bit-maker to his Majesty. S. J. E.]—*He could be called no more than a*
Bit of a Bridle-maker.

from *Tragical* OCCURRENCES.

[On Saturday William Pring was committed to New Prison, by John

Poulson, Esq; being charged on the Oath of Henry Sourmers, Gent. for privately stealing a Handkerchief, his Property. G. A.]—*Mr. Pring will be acquitted, if the Handkerchief appears at the Trial, (as it doth here) to be his Property.*

[On Sunday Night the Jews Synagogue, in Duke's Place, was broke open and robbed of Effects to the Value of three hundred Pounds. L. C.]—*This Robbery was not committed by a good Christian.*

THE JACOBITE'S JOURNAL, No. 15, Saturday, March 12, 1748.

from *Comical* OCCURRENCES.

[We hear, that the Town will shortly be entertained with *a Puppet Show after the Antient Manner*; in which the true Humour of that most diverting Entertainment will be restored. G. A.]—*We are glad to hear this, as the true Humour of the Stage is almost lost.*

[The following Passage in the *Foundling*, spoke by *Faddle*, is supposed to be levelled at the *Hero* of a very curious Poem just published, called *Adollizing*, or a lively Picture of *Adoll-Worship*; and 'tis said was the true Reason why such Endeavours were used to interrupt the Run of the Play.

> *May Grace renounce me, and Darkness seal my Eye-Lids,*
> *If I wou'd not as soon make love to a Milliner's Doll.*

L. C.]—*How this Hero should stop the Run of the Play, I know not, but Decency, I think, should stop the Run of the Poem.*

from *Tragical* OCCURRENCES.

[Last Week died Mr. Butler, Master of the White Swan, a noted public House in Fetter-lane.

Early Yesterday Morning died suddenly, Mrs. Wildshaw, Mistress of Batson's Coffee-house in Cornhill. D. G.]—*By the Death of these two eminent Persons, the above Ale-house and Coffee-house are probably become vacant.*

Clauderum Clumsy is an ingenious Writer; but his Satire is too local to please in general. The Jest in Ephemeridius *is worn out. The Writer who signs G. will excuse us from inserting so dirty a Comparison to ourselves, and which, as we perceive he is a Man of Wit, we hope he will himself think unjust. We have received several other Letters, some of which will have a Place hereafter.*

THE JACOBITE'S JOURNAL, No. 16, Saturday, March 19, 1748.

from DOMESTIC NEWS.

[Monday died the Right Hon. George Wade, Esq; Field Marshal of his Majesty's Forces, Lieutenant General of the Ordnance, &c. who with great Ability and Integrity had long served his King and Country in the most eminent Stations. G. E.]—*He was besides, in private Life, a Gentleman of the highest Honour, Humanity and Generosity, and hath done more good and benevolent Actions than this whole Paper can contain.*

from *Comical* OCCURRENCES.

[Whereas Application hath been lately made to the Worshipful Company of Mercers, for the Vicarage of Repham in the County of Lincoln, as if it was become vacant by the Death of the Rev. Mr. Benet; we are well assured that the said Incumbent is not only alive, but recover'd from his late Illness. D. A.]—*To the great Joy, doubtless, of the Person who made the Application, since it is so plain he desired Mr. Benet's* LIVING.

[We hear from the King's Theatre in the Hay-market, that as the celebrated Opera of Dido, wrote by Abbate Metastasio, and set to Musick by Signor Hasse, cannot be got ready for Representation till within about a Fortnight, the Opera of Lucius Verus (consisting of chosen Airs from the Compositions of Mr. Handel) will be perform'd next Saturday. Ib.]—*The Lovers of Musick will forgive the postponing Signior Hasse's Compositions, provided they are entertained with those of Mr. Handel in the mean time.*

[Last Monday was rang at Croyden in Surrey, by the Society of Croyden Youths, a complete Peal of 5040 *Bob-Majors*, which was the longest Peal rung in that Town for several Years. D. G.]—*Would not some of the Bob-Majors be a pretty Addition to the Opera of Dido?*

from *Tragical* OCCURRENCES.

[It is reported that there are Letters by the Dutch Mails, which mention the Death of the Pretender at Rome. W. E.]—*Hung be the Heavens with Black,* &c.

[Whereas it has been reported in the Daily Papers from Time to Time, that the Pretender's Son was at Paris, and several other Parts of France; yet it is the general Opinion of the People in the North, that he was kill'd soon after the Defeat of the Rebel Army at Culloden, and was very safe under Ground in the Highlands of Scotland; and whatever may be affirmed to the contrary, it is only to support the dejected Spirits of his abject Party in Great Britain. L. C.]—*Many of our Friends know better Things.*

THE JACOBITE'S JOURNAL, No. 17, Saturday, March 26, 1748.

from DOMESTIC NEWS.

[By a Letter from Oxford we have an Account, that the 25th of May is fixed for opening Dr. Ratcliffe's fine Library, when there will be *Disputations and Exercises*, as at a Publick Act, which happens but every twentieth Year. G. A.]—*We hear there have been some very pretty Disputations and Exercises there lately.*

[Last Week the Right Hon. the Lord Anson was married to the Hon. Miss York, Daughter of the Lord High Chancellor of Great Britain. Ib.]—*A young Lady really possess'd of all the Qualifications which can adorn her Sex.*

from *Jacobite Wit in the London Evening Post.*

Nil oriturum alias, nil ortum tale.

Anglicé.

You ne'er shall see, nor have from the Beginning,
Seen such a Paper as THE LONDON EVENING.

Nothing COMICAL *or* TRAGICAL *hath been represented this Week in the News-Papers.*

The Author of two Letters concerning a certain Writer, must excuse us from meddling with any thing so much below our Notice.

THE JACOBITE'S JOURNAL, No. 18, Saturday, April 2, 1748.

from DOMESTIC NEWS.

[It is confidently asserted, that a very strict Enquiry will be made into a Disturbance that lately happened at Oxford, in order to prevent the Seats of the Muses from becoming Theatres of factious Disputes, by which the Students are diverted from their proper Business, and rendered less fit for discharging, in their riper Years, the Duties of civil Life, though certainly the qualifying them for these, ought to be the great End of Education. W. E.]— *To poison the Seminaries of Education with false Doctrine, may in some Sense be compared to the poisoning a Fountain; and indeed it is in Youth only that such monstrous and nonsensical Principles as those of Jacobitism can possibly be imbibed.*

from *Jacobite Wit in the London Evening Post.*

[The ADVICE; or, An *Extempore Address* to the *Freeholders* of the County of *Northampton.*

> Britons, awake! your Country's Cause
>   Retrieve with Resolution;
> Vote for its Freedom, and its Laws,
>   And save the Constitution.
>
> Curst Bribery may destroy the State,
>   And empty the Exchequer;
> Then Ways and Means to fill up that
>   Will ruin us the quicker.
>
> Therefore, to get our Taxes lower,
>   And make us live more sprightly,
> Is to reject bad Men in Power,
>   And choose right honest KNIGHTLEY.

> *From a* Well-Wisher *to his Cause.*
>
> *London Evening Post, Saturday.*]

And surely every one must be a Well-wisher to the Cause of this Great Man, who is to RETRIEVE OUR COUNTRY, *to* SAVE THE CONSTITUTION, *and to make us* live more sprightly. *I am sorry therefore that the same Printer, who hath here set forth his Hero in the Light of Don Quixote, should in his Paper of Tuesday, disgrace him by a Comparison with a common Prize-fighter, in the following Paragraphs.*

THE JACOBITE'S JOURNAL, No. 19, Saturday, April 9, 1748.

from DOMEST   NEWS.

[A few Days since died the Hon. and Rev. Mr. Wandesford, (Brother to the Right Hon. the Lord Castlecomer) Rector of Kirklington and Catterick, and one of his Majesty's Justices of the Peace for Yorkshire. He has left 12000*l.* to be divided between the Rev. Mr. Du Pont, Vicar of Aisgarth, and two of his Curates; also 1500*l.* to a near Relation at Westminster. G. A.]—*The above two Sums seem to be transposed into each other's Places.*

[Yesterday Sophia Fitsammons, Anne Saunders, and Margaret Hill, were committed to Newgate by Thomas Burdus, Esq; for assaulting Mr. Edward Worman, in a House in *Drum-Alley*, Drury-Lane, putting him in Fear of his Life, and robbing him of a Silver Watch, and other Things, his

Property. Ib.]—*I suppose, by the Name of this Alley, all the Ladies there keep* DRUMS.

[Divers Bakers were convicted last Week, before the said Gentleman, for selling short Weight. Ib.]—*It is to be hoped they will receive full Weight from the Hands of Justice.*

[It is said a Bill will be brought into one of the Houses of Parliament, for the better Observation of the Lord's Day, by obliging all Manner of Persons to repair either to Church or Meeting, and attend Divine Service once at least on that Day, except kept away by apparent Necessity. The Ministers, Church-Wardens, and other Officers of each Parish; and in large Parishes, some few of the substantial Inhabitants, besides also the Teachers, and Elders or Heads of each separate Congregation, will be empowered, and even compelled, to be instrumental in carrying this Law into Execution. The Forfeits to be paid by House-keepers for themselves and those in Family; when Servants offend, their Masters to reimburse themselves out of their Wages. When Pension Poor offend, the Overseers to do the same out of their Pensions. W. E.]—*It is to be hoped, that such a Bill may have some Tendency to restore the Christian Religion.*

[Last Saturday Night there was near 2000*l.* contributed towards the Loss sustained by the Sufferers at the late Fire in Cornhill; which is so far from being wholly extinguished, that Engines are obliged to play continually on the Ruins, for the Preservation of the Houses adjoining. Ib.]—*No Nation ever abounded more with Charity, in this Sense, than the English; and that we have so little of Charity in the Sense of* CANDOUR, *is owing to the many malevolent Writings with which the Press swarms.*

THE JACOBITE'S JOURNAL, No. 20, Saturday, April 16, 1748.

from DOMESTIC NEWS.

[—A Petition was read, signed by several Carpenters and Joiners, Freemen of the City, setting forth the Hardships they apprehended they were likely to lie under, by the late Order of Court for employing Foreigners in re-building the Houses consumed by the late Fire in Cornhill; and a Paper was presented at the same Time in the Nature of a Petition, in Favour of the Bricklayers and Tylers, which the Court did not think fit to read, it not being a regular Petition; but at the same Time all the Petitioners were called in, and acquainted by Mr. Recorder, that the late Order was no ways intended to prejudice the honest, industrious Freemen, but only to prevent any unlawful Combinations that might be entered into, in order to distress the unhappy Sufferers. W. E.]—*The Court by their Resolution in the first Paragraph appear to be good Englishmen and Critics; and by their Order in the last, to be good Christians.*

[Last Week the Right Hon. Lady Betty Jermayn paid to Mess. Ironside and Belchier Fifty Pounds, for the Relief of the unhappy Sufferers by the late Fire. Ib.]—*I have heard more Instances of the Charity of this one Lady, than all the rest of her Sex can equal.*

[Last Saturday a Rider to a Distiller in Holborn was attacked on Hounslow Heath by two Highwaymen, and robbed of Money and Notes to the Value of 300*l.* G. A.]—*These Highwaymen, I believe, likewise rode for the Distiller.*

[We hear that the Corpse of Dr. Holmes, late President of St. John's College, Oxford, will be interr'd in the Chapel there with great Funeral Pomp, he having bequeath'd 14,000*l.* towards the Augmentation of Fellowships, and other Donations in the said College. Ib.]—*His Corpse deserves much Funeral Pomp at their Hands.*

On a late Scurrilous Libel.

At *Selim's* Breast tho' Slander aim'd her Dart,
　The Shield of Virtue kept him safe from Wound;
'Twas This, This only, touch'd *His* generous Heart,
　'That so much Malice should in Man be found.'

THE JACOBITE'S JOURNAL, No. 22, Saturday, April 30, 1748.

from DOMESTIC NEWS.

[Private Letters from some Parts of France say, that the greatest Part of that wide Kingdom is in much Distress on Account of the Heaviness of the Taxes, and the Scarcity of Provisions, which are so dear as hardly to be purchased with any Money: We are assured these Advices are authentic. W. E.]—*It is Pity but all those who are disaffected to the best of Governments, were for a while to experience some of these Distresses.*

As there seems at first Sight to be but little Difference between taking a Purse upon the Highway, and soliciting Subscriptions for Books, which are never intended to be published; some of our Correspondents express their Desire of having this Matter cleared up, by a certain D. D. in one of the Universities, who raised a very large Sum of Money, by a Subscription, four Years ago, for two Volumes of Sermons, promised to the Public the following Winter; but which have never yet made their Appearance, though Half the Price was paid down at the Time of subscribing. But—

Auri sacra Fames, quid non mortalia pectora cogis!

Horace *advises an Author* (I suppose those who publish by Subscription are not excepted) *to suppress his Work till the* 9th *Year. So that the Doctor hath* 5 *Years more good.*

THE JACOBITE'S JOURNAL, No. 23, Saturday, May 7, 1748.

from FOREIGN AFFAIRS.

[*Liege, May* 1. *N. S.* The *Pontoons* sent from hence Yesterday to the French are not yet arrived, seven Carts being broke down in the Roads, and the rest so fast stuck, that they must send to their Camp for the Artillery Horses, to draw them out. In this Situation they have sent an Express to demand thirty Carpenters to work on their Boats, without which they cannot repair their Bridge. L. G.]—*As the French are no longer in Want of* PONTOONS. Q. *Whether we should not read* PANTINS?

from DOMESTIC NEWS.

[On Thursday Night there was a most magnificent Masquerade at the Opera-House in the Hay-market; it being done by a Number of Nobility and Gentry by a private Subscription, who all endeavoured to emulate each other in the Grandeur of their Dresses, which were exceeding valuable in Diamonds and Jewels. W. E.]—*Half the Expence which contributed that Night to make others uneasy, might, if it had been charitably disposed, have made many greatly happy.*

[Yesterday, at a Court at Bridewell, was a Nomination of 100 Persons, some of which were of Quality and Distinction, as proper Persons to be Governors of that Hospital and Bethlem. L. E.]—*If proper Officers were to attend every Morning at Mr. Foot's Scandal-shop, they might take up more than* 100 *Persons, some of which are of Quality and Distinction, all proper to be the* Governed *at those Hospitals.*

[Yesterday Evening the Entertainment of the Spring-Garden at Vaux-Hall open'd for the Summer-Season. G. A.]—*But when the Summer-Season will open seems not so apparent.*

[Last Sunday died, at his House in Bow-street, Covent-Garden, Tho. Burdus, Esq; one of his Majesty's Justices of the Peace for the County of Middlesex, and City and Liberty of Westminster, and Chairman to the Justices for the said City and Liberty. Ib.]—*We hear Mr. Foote will speedily sell his Remains by Auction, of which timely Notice will be given in the Papers.*

[We hear, that the Opera of La Semiramide Riconosciuta (in which Signora Casarini is to act the Part of a King) will be perform'd but twice.

Ib.]—*We see no Reason for this, since the Signoras can perform all the Parts of a King as often and as well as the Signors.*

[Sunday, being the first in Term, the Right Hon. the Lord Mayor, Aldermen, Judges, Sheriffs, &c. went to St. Paul's Cathedral, where an excellent Sermon was preached by Mr. Buxton; after which they were elegantly entertained by Crispe Gascoigne, Esq; one of the Sheriffs, at Brewer's-Hall in Aldersgate-street, near Wood-street. W. E.]—*Where, we hope, an excellent Dinner was eat by the said Mr. Buxton.*

[On Saturday three of his Majesty's Messengers were dispatched with the Preliminary Articles of Peace, seal'd up in Silver Boxes, to several Foreign Courts. Ib.]—*If we had sent it in Gold Boxes, it had been worth our while.*

[We hear that the Sale of all Cambricks and French Lawns is prohibited, after Midsummer next.

And that the Wearing of them are forbid after Lady-Day 1749. G. A.]— *The Sale of Cambricks may be prohibited, but Qu. of the Wear! For those who wear them are above the Law.*

THE JACOBITE'S JOURNAL, No. 24, Saturday, May 14, 1748.

from DOMESTIC NEWS.

[By Letters which came by Yesterday's Mail we have Advice, that positive Orders are come over from France and Holland, to their Agents in this Kingdom, to buy up all the Corn they can possibly for fifteen Market-Days successively, in order to supply the immediate Wants of those Places. W. E.]—*This will supply the immediate Wants of our Farmers in the Country, which is drained to supply the immoderate Wants of their luxurious racking Landlords in London.*

[Last Monday Night, as a Servant belonging to James Moore, Esq; of Esher in Surry, was going to Bed, he found a Fellow concealed under the Bed; on which he alarmed the Family, who secured him; and on searching him they found two Pistols upon him loaded; and being examined, he confessed an Intent, with some others, to rob the House. He was kept in Custody there all Night, and the next Day committed to Kingston Goal. He says his Name is Russel, a Blacksmith by Trade. Ib.]—*So faulty are our Laws, that unless this Fellow can be proved to have broken into the House, he will be only guilty of a Misdemeanor.*

From GRUBSTREET.

[*On the Surrender of* Maestricht *to* SAVE THE HONOUR OF FRANCE.

Must SAXE's *Credit* then from *Stain* be clear,
Tho' NASSAU's *Arms* and CUMBERLAND's are near?
The *Baron bold**, who *first* defended well;
Must he *relinquish*—what he *scorn'd* to sell?
Oh *Shame! Reproach!*—Yet RUSSIA's *Troops* advance,
And ENGLAND's *Naval Force* still *humbles* FRANCE.
Can BRITAIN's *Honour* this Affront survive?
Ah! No; *That* cannot *live*, and GALLIA's *thrive*.
How strangely *retrograde* this *Honour* runs!
Our *Fathers conquer'd*—to *disgrace* their *Sons*.

*D'AYLVA.   Lond. Evening.]

So strangely this malicious Nonsense runs,
It would disgrace the Vandals or the Huns.

[The Play of Hamlet intended to be perform'd on Wednesday next, May 11, at the Theatre-Royal in Covent-Garden, for the Benefit of a Publick Charity is deferr'd 'till next Season, on Account of the warm Weather. Ib.]—*If our Public Charity be no warmer than the Weather, it would have been acted to very little Purpose.*

[Thursday Night the Norwich Company of Comedians performed a Play there for the Benefit of the Sufferers by the late Fire in Cornhill; and next Day paid 20*l.* into the Hands of the Right Worshipful their Mayor; Part of which they raised among themselves, besides all the Expences of the Night given in. W. E.]—*How charitable is it in these poor People, who cannot be supposed to have any Houses of their own, to contribute towards the building Houses for other People?*

THE JACOBITE'S JOURNAL, No. 25, Saturday, May 21, 1748.

from DOMESTIC NEWS.

[Last Tuesday Evening a remarkable Discovery was made on board his Majesty's Ship Prince Edward in Kingroad at Bristol.—A Person who went by the Name of John Davidson, having drank freely, became passionately fond of his Mess-mate, which gave him Occasion to suspect something extraordinary; and having inform'd the Officers therewith, on due Examination by Mr. Watson the Surgeon, the Person was discover'd to be of the Female Sex; and has confess'd having been three Years in the Privateer Service, in which she was so successful as to be now intitled to 150*l.* Prize

Money. She has belonged to the Prince Edward upwards of 11 Months; during which Time she has behaved with great Courage, and perform'd her Duty as well as any Seaman on board. G. A.]—*I fancy this Person whom Mr. Watson, on due Examination, found to be of the Female Sex, was almost as good a Man as the Fellow who first informed against her, for having been passionately fond of him.*

THE JACOBITE'S JOURNAL, No. 26, Saturday, May 28, 1748.

from DOMESTIC NEWS.

[We hear for certain, that the above Ships laden with Corn for Exportation are all stopt, and that some particular Affairs must be settled before they can be allowed to depart. W. E.]—*It may perhaps be as good a Way to make Peace with Corn in Hand as with Sword in Hand.*

[We learn from Ireland, that last Thursday the following Præmiums were determined by the Dublin Society at the Parliament-House, when a great Number of Ladies were present.

The Præmium of 10*l.* for the best Imitation of Brussels Lace by the Needle, was adjudged to Mrs. Mihill, for a fine Border for a Handkerchief.

The Præmium of 5*l.* for the second best ditto, was adjudged to Miss King, for a Pair of Lappets.

The Society gave 4*l.* to Miss Wibrants, for a Lappet.

And a Præmium of 5*l.* to Miss Anne Curren, for the best Dresden Work.

And a Præmium of 4*l.* to Miss Mary Woods, for the second best ditto, &c. Ib.]—*This sounds better than it would that Mr. H——le had adjudged the first Præmium to Mrs. Mihill, for playing the best Game at Whist; the 2d to Miss King, for playing the 2d best Game; and so on.*

[Yesterday died, reputed very rich, Mr. Abraham Banks a Cow-keeper, at his House in Castle-street, Shoreditch. G. A.]—*We are assured that Mr. Thomas Banks, the Hog-keeper, remains in perfect Health.*

[*Ipswich, May* 20. Last Monday William York, a Boy something less than ten Years and five Months old, was committed to the County Goal in this Town, by John Cornelius, Esq; for the Murder of Susan Mayhew, a Child about five Years of Age, who was his Bedfellow in the Town-House belonging to the Parish of Eyke. . . . Ib.]—*Lord Chief Justice Hale, in his History of the Pleas of the Crown, mentions a Boy of about the same Age, whom he ordered to be executed for burning a Child in its Cradle in the House of his Benefactor.*

[Yesterday Morning, about Two o'Clock, Mr. Roper, a Tidesman, was attack'd on Tower-Hill by two Fellows, who robb'd him of his Watch and two Guineas, and made off undiscover'd. One of the Fellows was dress'd in a Morning Gown, a Laced Waistcoat, a white Wigg, and a Jockey's Cap. Ib.]—*This is not the first Merry Andrew who hath been a Thief.*

THE JACOBITE'S JOURNAL, No. 27, Saturday, June 4, 1748.

from FOREIGN AFFAIRS.

[M. de Macanus was arrested at St. Vittoria, in his Way to Madrid, by Order of his Catholic Majesty. As this Minister is in his 85th Year, and has always been thought a sincere Friend to his Country, his Arrest gives Occasion to many Speculations. G. A.]—*Those Ministers who are the best Friends to their Country, are often the worst rewarded.*

[According to Letters from Rome, the Pretender has had a long Conference with the Pope, who communicated to him the Preliminary Articles, upon the Subject of the 11th of these Articles, which regards the Recognition of his Britannick Majesty, and his Descendants, of both Sexes, in the Throne of Great Britain for ever. Ib.]—*Qu. Whether he was more shocked at this News than his Jacobite Friends in England have shewn themselves?*

from DOMESTIC NEWS.

[On Wednesday Evening a great Match that had been long depending, between a Horse belonging to an Inn-keeper and the Mare of a Brewer, was decided: They both trotted from the White Hart at Tottenham to the Stones-End at Shoreditch, which is five Miles; the former performed it in nineteen Minutes and a half, and the latter in twenty Minutes. W. E.]— *Trotting is a Sport truly adapted to the English Genius.*

[On Thursday Morning a Gentleman walked up and down the Mall twenty times *for twenty Guineas,* being twenty Miles: He had four Hours and a half to do it in, and performed it in four Hours and ten Minutes. Ib.]—*Many a Man would have walk'd twenty times as far* for less.

[Yesterday Morning a Man was taken up in Piccadilly, for selling Watches with Pewter Cases double wash'd *for Silver.*]—*If he sold them only* for Silver, *it was hard to take him up.*

[On Tuesday last a Cause was tried before the Lord Chief Justice Lee, at the Sittings in the Court of King's Bench at Westminster, between a Gentleman of Chatham in Kent, Plaintiff, and an Officer in the Horse-Guards, Defendant, for criminal Conversation with the Plaintiff's Wife, when the Jury gave a Verdict for the Plaintiff; and the Defendant appearing to have been for some time past a Prisoner in the King's Bench Prison, and in bad Circumstances, they gave the Plaintiff ONLY a thousand Pounds

Damages. Ib.]—*This News Writer should be excepted against by the Defendant, if he should ever be impannel'd to try a Cause of Cuckoldom.*

From the London Evening.

[To Arms, ye *British* Youth! to Arms return;
Resume the Sword, and with fresh Ardour burn! *&c.*]

By this beating to Arms, it appears that the Printer of this Paper hath not yet acceded to the Preliminaries.

[Yesterday being the Anniversary of the Restoration of King Charles the Second, the Morning was usher'd in with Ringing of Bells. At One o'Clock the Park and Tower Guns were fired, and there was a splendid Court at St. James's, when her Royal Highness the Princess Amelia received the Compliments of the Nobility and Gentry on the Occasion. G. A.

The same Day the Right Hon. the Lord Mayor went in State to St. Paul's, and was accompanied by a great many of the Aldermen, *with their Ladies.* Ib.]—*This is the first Time I remember to have heard of the Ladies on a State Occasion; but they never could attend more properly than to celebrate the Restoration of that merry Monarch, who created many Aldermen by means of their Ladies.*

THE JACOBITE'S JOURNAL, No. 28, Saturday, June 11, 1748.

from DOMESTIC NEWS.

Jacobitical nonsensical Poetry, from the London Evening Post.

[*The* Sailor's Consolation *upon the Prospect of a* Peace.

Tho' *Peace* may *discharge* all our Hands at a Jerk,
And *Trade* may be *wanting* to set us to work,
Two Chances, my Lads, we shall have *in Reserve*;—
As *Pyrates*, to *hang*;—or, as *honest Men, starve.*]

The Factious Jacobitical Scribbler's Consolation *on ditto Prospect.*

Tho' Peace should hereafter deprive us of News,
We shall still have our Betters, my Lads, to abuse.
This Choice we shall have in all Times,—to deserve
For Slander to hang, or for Dulness to starve.

[Yesterday the Fellow who was detected in stealing Goods at the late dreadful Fire in Cornhill, was whipp'd from the Mansion-house to the upper End of Cornhill, and back again, pursuant to his Sentence at the Old Baily; which was executed in a very severe manner, and yet no one seem'd to *pity* him; so great a Detestation all Sorts of People had for his Crime.

G. A.]—*It is rather* Pity *that the Law did not extend to have sent him to the upper End of Tyburn Road.*

[On Saturday last the Crew of his Majesty's Ship the Jersey waited on the Lords of the Admiralty with a Petition, praying for an Order for the speedy Payment of their Prize Money, arising from the Captures of the St. George and St. Jago, two Spanish Galleons, taken up the Streights about a Year ago, which was granted. Each Foremast Man's Share is said to amount to 120*l.* sterl. While the above Ship's Crew attended the Admiralty, they met with one of their inferior Officers, who had used several of them exceeding ill while on board, in return for which they gave him a sound Drubbing, as the Sailors term it.]—*This Drubbing, perhaps, came nearer up to the Severity of Justice than the beforementioned Whipping.*

[We hear by a Clause made for the prohibiting the Wearing of French Cambricks, a Penalty of Five Pounds *is levied* on all Persons who shall sell, offer, or expose to Sale any French Cambricks, or Lawns, after Midsummer Day next. G. A.]—*This is the first Clause that ever* levied *a Penalty.*

[Yesterday Afternoon a Boy was detected in picking a Gentleman's Pocket of his Handkerchief, at the Door of the Sign of the Parrot, opposite Bow Church in Cheapside, *whom he* chastised with a Whip; after which *he* was surrounded by the Populace, by whom he was severely duck'd before he got his Liberty. Ib.]—*It is certain from this Author, that it was the Gentleman who was whipt; nor is it at all certain whether it was not the same Gentleman who was afterwards surrounded and duck'd by the Populace.*

[On Sunday Night a Man well dressed was taken up in St. James's Park, and carried to *the Hole* at Whitehall, for Sodomitical Practices. Ib.]—*This Fellow could not possibly be carried to too nasty a Hole.*

[Last Sunday a Nobleman in his Coach and Six, going through Kensington, met with a Post-Chaise, which not giving Way, one of his Servants rode up and knocked the Post-Boy off his Horse; by which he was taken up for dead, and carried into a House, and it is thought he cannot recover. Ib.]—*I suppose the Nobleman will turn this Servant off, if the Boy lives; but if he dies, I am sure Jack Ketch ought to turn him off.*

[A few Days ago two Men were secured by the Guard at Kensington Palace, for stripping and going into the Canal in the Garden, and committing several Indecencies whilst the Ladies were walking there. Ib.]—*These Fellows will, I hope, be decently stript in another Place.*

Jacobitical Prosaic Nonsense, from the London Evening Post.

[We hear that all the *Reports* which were spread, ten or fifteen Days ago, concerning *a new Prohibition* of sending Corn out of the Kingdom, and the laying an *Embargo* on Ships, had no other Foundation than the Impossibility the L—— of the R—— were under of *granting P——ts,* 'till the News of his M————'s Arrival in *H——d* empower'd them to *open their C——n,* &c.]—*The Wit of a Writer is sometimes said to lie in the Expression, so that it can't be translated; this Wit lies in the Printing, and can't be read; for if the Writer (as he safely might) had inserted all the Words at Length, there would have been no Appearance of either Wit or Satire in the Paragraph.*

THE JACOBITE'S JOURNAL, No. 29, Saturday, June 18, 1748.

from DOMESTIC NEWS.

[Several Persons likewise took the Oaths in the Court of King's Bench, in order to qualify themselves for divers Places under the Government. G. A.]—*We hope for the future, that no Persons who are recorded to have taken the Oaths to the Government in the King's Bench, will afterwards be recorded there for having broken them.*

[Tuesday a Farmer's Servant at Bromley in Kent was detected by two Gentlemen in the abominable Sin of Sodomy with his Fellow Servant, who had them both secured and committed to the County Jail. W. E.]—*The Writer I apprehend doth not mean, tho' he hath so expressed himself, that the Fellow-servant had the two Gentlemen secured.*

[Last Saturday se'nnight one Tinnant, a Sailor, who lived in Sun-yard, Nightingale-Lane, committed a Rape on the Body of an Infant of seven Years of Age, Daughter of a Carpenter in Norris's Court in that Neighbourhood, for which Action he is since gone off. The Crime was committed under a Gateway in Bur-street, and was first known by a Daughter of Tinnant's, a Girl of nine Years of Age, *who was with him at the Time,* and has since told the whole Affair. Ib.]—*If this Story be true, the Girl of nine Years old seems to have been almost an Accessary to the Rape.*

[There being not the least Settlement to the sinking Pier of Westminster-Bridge, since the Weight of 12000 Ton of Lead and Iron were laid on it, it is ordered to be finished with all Expedition. Ib.]—*We may then hope, at last, to see this noble Work perfected; and it may be now said of this Bridge, that a Tun of Gold could not raise it, nor could 12000 Tun of Lead and Iron sink it.*

[We hear from L—f——d, that Friday last, being the 10th of June, was concluded with a Bonfire, Ringing of Bells, Fireworks, Rockets, and other Demonstrations of Joy. Diligent Enquiry having been made for *white Roses,* a Number of People went about the Town singing, *The King shall enjoy his own again,* and other such-like Songs; while others met in large Companies to drink Healths *suitable to the Occasion,* and distinguish themselves from the Friends of Gower and Anson.]—*Who will, for the future, have the Impudence to deny the Existence of Jacobitism in this Nation?*

THE JACOBITE'S JOURNAL, No. 30, Saturday, June 25, 1748.

from DOMESTIC NEWS.

[Last Sunday Morning a Salmon was catched in one of the Bucks belonging to Mr. Wills of Caversham-Mill, near Reading, upwards of *four Feet long, and weighed about forty Pounds.* It is the largest Fish that has been taken in those Parts for several Years. W. E.]—*Fishermen and Travellers are remarkable for a certain Quality.*

[On Wednesday last a Gentleman and Lady in a single Horse-Chaise, were overset by a Hackney-coach at Turnham Green: The Gentleman received no Hurt, but the Lady was very much bruised, and now lies dangerously ill. The Coachman drove on towards London, swearing he would do the same by all the Chaises he should meet with. Ib.]—*If this Coachman be not preferr'd to ride in a Cart to Tyburn, we hope, at least, he will be well drove behind that Vehicle.*

[We are assured, that Covent Garden is not to be removed and formed into a Square, as mentioned in some other Papers; but the Lease being expired, there will be more commodious Shops built round it; and a great Number of People who used to *sit about there with Things that were a Nuisance,* will be prevented for the future. Ib.]—*I suppose the Writer means certain Ladies, who walk about there with Things that are a Nuisance.*

[Yesterday in the Afternoon it was currently reported, that Peace would be proclaimed with France and Spain with great Solemnity, at the usual Places, on Monday the 25th of next Month. W. E.]—DICITE IO PÆAN, ET IO BIS DICITE P———M.

[Last Week came on at the Court of Common Pleas in Westminster-Hall, before the Lord Chief Justice Willes, a Cause wherein a Drawer at a Tavern in Kensington was Plaintiff, and a Captain of Marines was Defendant: The Action was laid for the Defendant's Beating, &c. the Plaintiff, in such a Manner that his Life was in great Danger. The Jury gave a Verdict of 40*l.* Damages to the Plaintiff. Ib.]—*I am afraid the Verdict will rather be of 40l. Damages to the* Defendant.

[We are assured, that Yesterday a very considerable Dealer *in Stocks* gained 12,000*l.* by purchasing all he could, on getting early Intelligence of the Preliminaries of Peace being signed with Spain. Ib.]—*This Broker may be said to have fought very cunningly with the Public; but such Dealers in Plato's Commonwealth would have been* put in the Stocks *without purchasing.*

THE JACOBITE'S JOURNAL, No. 32, Saturday, July 9, 1748.

from DOMESTIC NEWS.

[We hear that a General C——l of Calves-Heads, Sheeps-Heads, Rams-Heads, and Round-Heads, will be held at the King's-Head at Wandsworth in the County of Surrey, and adjourn to the Prince's Head and Duke's-Head at Battersea in the same County (a Place remarkable for cutting for the Simples) to undergo the necessary Operation of that Place, and then to take into Consideration the P—— A—— of A——. L. E. P.] —*The Meaning of this Wit, no Head, I believe, but that of the Author can unfold. In the same Paper you have a curious Essay on true Honour, extracted from the* Fool, *which brings to my Mind Mr.* Hogarth's *Poet, who in the most extreme Poverty is writing an Essay upon Riches.*

[It is positively said, that a General Peace is in so great Forwardness, that the Proclamation of it will happen much sooner than is expected. W. E.]— *It cannot be sooner than wished by every true* Englishman.

[Yesterday an Express was dispatched to the Court of Madrid, by the Spanish Agent here, which we doubt not will prove agreeable to all who wish well to the Trade of Great-Britain. Ib.]—*To every other Trade except that of sending abroad weekly Libels against the Government, which is at present in a very flourishing Condition.*

[A Petition of the Watermen who work over the Thames on Sundays to maintain their Poor, has been presented to the Commissioners of Westminster-Bridge, to desire that no Persons may have Liberty to walk over the said Bridge on a Sunday, it being a great Hindrance to the Petitioners. Ib.]—*We expect shortly to see a Petition from the Chairmen, Hackney-Coachmen, &c. that Persons may not be suffered to walk the Streets, which is likewise a great Hindrance to these Petitioners.*

[Doctor Lilly, M. D. lately chosen Chairman to the Bench of Justices, for the City and Liberty of Westminster, gave a grand Entertainment at the Horn-Tavern last Friday, to the Gentlemen in the Commission of the Peace, that attended the Sessions. G. A.]—*We hear the Bench happened that Day to be very remarkably full.*

[On Saturday Morning last Mrs. Baker of Lloyd's Coffee-House was safely delivered of a Son, and is in good Health; which has given great Pleasure to all the Friends of her late worthy Husband. Ib.]—*So it will be to all my good-natur'd Readers, though they had not the Happiness to know the late worthy Gentleman.*

[A magnificent Silver Punch-Bowl, which weighs 250 Ounces, has been finished some Time, and will this Day be sent to Bristol. The following Inscription is engraven on it, under the Arms of the City of London, viz. "The Gift of the Merchants and Insurers of the City of London, to Capt. JAMES SIEX, for his gallant Behaviour, in taking three Privateers from the Enemy." Ib.]—*How much more real Honour doth this Bowl bring to the Captain, than a Bowl won at a Horse-Race brings to a Country Squire?*

THE JACOBITE'S JOURNAL, No. 33, Saturday, July 16, 1748.

from DOMESTIC NEWS.

[Those who object to the Preliminaries lately signed might see, by the Extract in our Paper of the 18th ult. that the Preliminaries to the Peace of Ryswick were less in Number, and altogether as simple in Form, as those agreed to at Aix-la-Chapelle, and also that they did not contain one single Stipulation in favour of Great Britain particularly, except the verbal separate Article concerning the Acknowledgment of King William. The Preliminaries to the Peace of Utrecht, as the French King was driven through absolute Necessity to offer them, notwithstanding what is said in the Preamble, and we had been all along victorious through ten Campaigns, were indeed more expressly to our Advantage: But it will appear, by consulting these also, that next to a Security for our Trade, for which Purpose only we held a few of our Conquests, the procuring a Barrier for our Allies against the House of Bourbon was the chief Point considered by our Ministers. Now if this be done at present, and we have also Security for our Trade, and a Renewal of the Contract, must we not call it a good Peace, that puts an End to a War, which by Land has been in every Circumstance unhappy? G. A.]—*In judging the Wisdom with which Nations or private Men accept any Terms of Accommodation with an Enemy, we must always have Respect to their own Circumstances and those of their Enemies, at the Time when such Terms were accepted. If this Rule be observed in forming our Opinion of the Preliminaries lately signed at* Aix-la-Chapelle, *every* Englishman *must acknowledge, and rejoice in, the Wisdom of our present Administration. But if Envy or Malice should awhile prevent their Praise from being universal, Posterity will not fail to give them that Honour which is so apparently their Due; and will express their Gratitude, as well as Admiration, upon this Occasion.*

[A few Days ago, one Mr. William Allen, aged 86 Years, and an Inn-Pensioner of Chelsea-College, who had a little Time entered into the State of Matrimony, hanged himself at his Apartment in the College. Ib.]—*If he had been admitted, as he ought to have been on his Marriage, an Inn Pensioner of the College of New-Bethlehem, this tragical End had been prevented.*

[The Right Hon. the Lords of the Admiralty have appointed several Guard Ships to lye at divers Ports of this Kingdom and Ireland, for the Security of the Trade, and to prevent the Privateers from continuing at Sea, after they are ordered home. G. A.]—*There is so near a Connection between Privateering and Pirateering, that the one Trade often ends in the other.*

[Mrs. Anger, who died sometime since, as lately mentioned, has left 50*l.* to the Grey-Coat Hospital in Tothill-fields, Westminster: Also 50*l.* to the Blue-Coat Hospital, Westminster; and 50*l.* to the Poor of the Parish. Likewise a Sum to be distributed to 50 poor Widows who have been House-keepers. Ib.]—*This last is much the noblest Charity.*

[Yesterday a Drayman carelessly riding on his Dray through Mount-street, Grosvenor-square, the Wheel went over two Children, belonging to Mr. Glover, a Master Taylor, one of whom was so terribly bruised, that he was carried to the Hospital, where there are little Hopes of his Recovery; and the other lies dangerously ill at home. G. A.]—*If one or two of those Draymen were driven to Tyburn, it would be of great Service to the Public.*

THE JACOBITE'S JOURNAL, No. 34, Saturday, July 23, 1748.

GALLIMATIA *from the Papers.*

[Thursday Morning the Markets at Covent Garden, St. James's, &c. were almost without any Gardeners in them, they being terrified from coming on Account of the Eclipse, and for fear they should be obliged to go home in the Dark. W. E.]—*I believe it will not soon be in the Power of the Astronomers to frighten them so again.*

[Friday the Company of Apothecaries held their grand Annual *Herbarizing* Feast at Putney Bowling-Green, where, after a very learned Lecture on a Number of curious Plants collected in Kent and Surry, a very elegant Entertainment was provided for them. Ib.]—*We hear the Company was much better pleased with the* elegant Entertainment, *than with the* herbarizing Lecture.

[Monday a private Centinel of the Second Regiment of Foot Guards received the last Part of 500 Lashes in St. James's Park, for robbing the Hospital, and divers other offences, and was afterwards drummed out of the Regiment with a Halter about his Neck. Ib.]—*It was kind to give him what is likely to be of so much use to him.*

[On Saturday Morning one Lurkin, a Higgler, was robbed near the Trees called the Seven Sisters, in Tottenham Road, by two Fellows dressed like Sailors, who took from him 10[?] and one Halfpenny. Ib.]—*If this*

Paragraph be, as most probably it is, Invention, LURKIN *should have been the Name of one of the Thieves.*

[In a short Time a *Group* of the most eminent Painters of London and Westminster set out for Paris, to make their Brethren of that Metropolis a visit on the approaching Prospect of Peace, and see their curious Performances during the Separation by War. Ib.]—*The Meeting between these two Groups will probably make a good Picture.*

THE JACOBITE'S JOURNAL, No. 37, Saturday, August 13, 1748.

GALLIMATIA.

[Last Wednesday Mr. Boland, an eminent Apothecary, was married to Miss Rebecca Sumner, of Dame's-Street, a Lady endowed with every Accomplishment necessary to render that State happy with a handsome Fortune. G. A.]—*Small Accomplishments are necessary to render that State happy with a handsome Fortune.*

[They write from Rome, that the Harvest having been very abundant this Year in the Ecclesiastical State, the Pope has ordered three Days of Prayers, and one of Fasting, to return Thanks to Heaven for so great a Benefit, which is, at present, the more inestimable, as that Country has of late suffered very much by a Scarcity of Provisions. W. E.]—*Had not the Harvest been so abundant, I suppose the Pope would have ordered three Days of Fasting and one of Prayer.*

[Thursday George Mackenzie, Esq; late Earl of Cromartie, and his Lady and Family, set out from their Lodgings in Pall-Mall for Devonshire, to the Place he is banished to for Life, near Exeter. Ib.]—*If Ovid had been obliged to have exchanged Scotland for Devonshire, he had never written his* Tristia.

[Thursday the Board of Works surveyed the Roof of Westminster-Hall, and found it to be very ruinous and decay'd; whereupon they ordered several new Spars to be made and affixed to the Roof, and large Iron Bolts to be drove into the Arches, and rivetted for the better Support of the said Roof. Ib.]—*Some will have it that the Floor of Westminster-Hall hath been long more* ruinous *than the Roof.*

THE JACOBITE'S JOURNAL, No. 38, Saturday, August 20, 1748.

from DOMESTIC NEWS.

[They write from Bridgwater in Somersetshire, that Henry Gould, Esq;

of the Inner-Temple, died there as he was going the Circuit. W. E.]—
This young Gentleman (who was of the Middle-Temple) had great Parts,
and had with great Diligence applied them to the Study of his Profession; in
which he was arrived at a very extensive Knowledge, and had very early in
Life acquired much Reputation.

THE JACOBITE'S JOURNAL, No. 42, Saturday,
September 17, 1748.

from DOMESTIC NEWS.

[*Litchfield, Sept.* 9. On Tuesday the 6th of September the Races began
for this City, when his Majesty's Plate of a Hundred Guineas, was won by
the Duke of Ancaster. W. E.]

[There was a very numerous Appearance of Nobility and Gentry at this
Meeting; upwards of 200 Gentlemen dined each Day at the first Ordinary;
among whom were 10 Ladies, and above 100 Gentlemen of good Estates
in the County of Stafford. The Company were entertained each Night with
a Ball, and in the Morning with a Concert. Seventeen Ladies of Quality,
and above 100 Ladies of Distinction, were at a Ball, which was conducted
with the greatest Order and Regularity. A very large Subscription was made
for the next Year's Plates, and the Hon. Richard Leveson Gower and Sir
William Wolseley, Bart. was nominated Stewards. Ib.]—*We begin to*
hope that our Ridicule on the PLAIDS *hath produced some good Effects.*

GALLIMATIA.

By *Morgan* Scrub, Grubstreet-Solicitor, whileom Author of *Old-England.*

That infernal Blockhead, the Grubstreet, Billingsgate, Hackney, Jack-
ass, Scribbler called the *London Evening Post,* in his Braggings of Saturday
last, charges the Ministry with making a Present of Cape Breton. Such a
Fool is best answered by a silly Story. An Irishman, who, as the Committee
says, is above being of a Trade, was asked to sell a Horse: *Upon my Shoule,*
says he, I scorn to sell my Horse; but I will make you a Preshent of him, if you
will make me a Preshent of something more than the Value.

[Yesterday a *well-dressed* Man was taken up in the Green Park, St.
James's, for attempting to commit Sodomy with a Corporal, and carried to
the Guard Room at St. James's. W. E.]—*Had he been delivered to the Popu-*
lace, he would have been much better dressed; *and in a manner more becoming*
him.

[Yesterday Mr. Hynd, a Fellmonger at Deptford, was robbed by three
Fellows in Lock-Fields, of Four Pounds, and his Watch. It is remarkable,

this Robbery was committed during the Execution on Kennington Common. Ib.]—*It was prudent to take the Opportunity while the Hangman was otherwise engaged.*

[Thursday Night a Gentleman and Lady were robbed of their Money, Watches, and Rings, in Ham Walks near Richmond, by two Men in Sailor's Habits. Ib.]—*This is nothing more than privateering at Land.*

[Saturday Morning a Woman who sells Herbs in Newgate-Market, going thro' St. Paul's Church-yard, had her Pocket cut off, in which were six Guineas, besides some other Things of Value. G. A.]—*I suppose she must have had a Hoop on.*

[*Dublin.* The *Honour* of Duelling is at present carried so high in this Kingdom, that last Week at Dungannan, a Journeyman Taylor challenged a Journeyman Wig-Maker to fight him at Sword and Pistol in a Saw-pit. The Seconds were a Journeyman Barber and a Journeyman Baker; but, by the timely Interposition of an old Chelsea Out-Pensioner, the Effusion of Blood was prevented, by his Threats upon the first Aggressor. Ib.]— *The soldier, I suppose, disdained to see the noble Trade of killing Men usurped by Fellows whose Profession it is to kill lice.*

[On Wednesday last died, after four Days Illness, Mr. Atherton, Master of the Valiant Trooper, at Paddington; his Wife was so much affected at his Death, that she immediately fell into Fits, and died on Friday last. They were Yesterday carried to St. Albans to be interr'd together in one Grave. W. E.]—*Over which her Sex ought to erect a Tomb-stone for the Wife, as she hath done them more honour than all the fine Ladies of the Age put together.*

[Yesterday Morning died, at his House in Basing-Lane, Mr. George Druce, a Painter, a Man of *True Natural Humour* as a Companion, of great Integrity in his Business, and very much esteemed by all that knew him. G. A.]—*All of whom, I suppose, very well knew what is meant by* True Natural Humour as a Companion. *Perhaps this True Natural Humour may resemble that True Natural Eloquence printed in the silly* London Evening-Post, *of* Tuesday, *from the Mouth of an* Indian Orator. ['We put a *great deal of Fire* under our Kettle, and the *Kettle boil'd high*, and so it does still, that the *Frenchmen's Heads might soon be boiled.* But when we look'd about us, to see how it was with the *English Kettle*, we saw the Fire was *almost out*, and that it *hardly* boiled at all; and that *no Frenchmen's Heads* were like to be *in it.*']—*It is strange that such a Writer should have any Thing in his Kettle, and consequently any need of more Fire under it, than there is in his Noddle.*

THE JACOBITE'S JOURNAL, No. 43, Saturday, September 24, 1748.

GALLIMATIA.

By *Morgan* Scrub, Grubstreet-Solicitor, whileom Author of *Old-England*.

That sorry Stick of Wood, the London Evening POST, who is as dull as any POST in the Kingdom, after having for near half a Year abused the Ministry, for making Peace with France on Terms too advantagious to her; gives us last Saturday a Balderdash Satire on the French for delaying to sign this very Peace; nay indicates that they will not sign it at all. And not contented with this Absurdity, acquaints us *in the same Paper, that they have signed it a Fortnight ago.*

The Verses are these.

[PROCRASTINATION.

Peace should be sign'd, the *French* did say,
Upon their *Patron* LOUIS' Day.
St. LOUIS past, *five Months* remov'd,
They shew their LOWIS* *well belov'd.*
Still should they *new Illusions* forge;
And give the *happy Day* to GEORGE;
The Diff'rence is a *Double Quarter*,
'Twixt George *the King*† and George *the Martyr.*‖
Thus ring eternally the *Changes*,
Some *Saint* or *Prince* in order ranges;
And *France* from End to End may *lurch*
The *Calendars* of *Court* and *Church*:
For, since our *Sinews* now are slack,
Our *Fleets* recall'd, our *Friends* sent back,
What hinders but She still may *sham Us*,
And put off Peace 'till *Latter Lammas?*‡

* Feb. 15.   † Oct. 30.   ‖ April 23.

‡ A Festival which, like the Greek Calends, never comes.]

GOOD MORROW, MY MASTERS AND MISTRESSES ALL.

If this be Poetry we can write Poetry as well as he, of which we will give him a Specimen by versifying all his domestic News of Tuesday last. A Method which we advise him to follow for the future.

The London Evening-Post, Sept. 20.

On my good Master Trott-plaid the usual Abuse.
The Essex Freeholders consider whom to chuse.
Solicitor to the Foundlings Frank Plumptree has carried.

Tim Markham to an agreeable young Lady is married.
Near his Father-in-law is interr'd Dr. Dry.
Off Genoa and Spain six Ships are to lie.
Three Admirals hold themselves ready to troop.
Captain Hanlinson's Captain of the Badger Sloop.
Mr. Cleveland the River of Thames will inspect.
John Masters Esquire, is of Pool, Mayor elect.
A Lady is safe brought to bed of a Son.
Lord Portmore's grey Horse at Lincoln has won.
On four other Days, four other Plates
Were won by those Horses which won the most Heats.
Mr. Jones his bay Horse, won the Plate at Northampton.
Sir Robert Rich his Cook by grim Death is stampt on.
Sam Archer who once was a Merchant is dead.
Some Tickets have in the Lottery sped.
Justice Hassel hath committed three Men drest like Sailors.
Edward Hammond is likewise in Ward with the Goalers.
Three Fellows, Charles Freeman a Brazier did rob.
On Monday Physicians may hear Dr. Lobb.

Thus we have reduced his Work to a Nut shell, which is at any time capable of containing all his Matter: For this is not only the vilest Scribler who ever strained at Wit, Poetry, or Politics; but his POST, is the worst Informer in even common Matters, which was ever erected, and his Paper hath much less News in it, than any other Evening Paper now published.

THE JACOBITE'S JOURNAL, No. 45, Saturday, October 8, 1748.

GALLIMATIA.

['As the Charge of *abandoning our Allies* in the Treaty of Utrecht has been greatly exaggerated by those who have *since been in Power*, Mr. TROTTPLAID, or any other *M———l Advocate* (for we would not fix on this *egregious Writer* a Task for which he seems so very unfit) is desired to inform the Publick in *what Sense* we are to understand the SECRET ARTICLE, lately *crept* into Light, by which *two Parties* of the Alliance contract with the *Common Enemy* to *compel their other Friends to Reason*, or *leave them to shift for themselves;* which is the Interpretation that *vulgar Readers*, 'till better instructed, put upon this notable Article.

'*N. B.* To prevent Mistakes: The Question is not, Whether it was *right*, in our present Circumstances, to *get rid of burdensome Friends*, who neglected *their Part* in the general *Confederacy?*—But, Whether they are

now got rid of, by the present *upright M———y*, in a more honourable
Manner than they were *before* by the *wicked Ministry* of Queen ANNE?'

LONDON-EVENING-POST.]

> The Question is not whether right or wise,
> It was to force to Reason our Allies;
> But whether to abandon and to bring
> To reason, be in Sense the self-same Thing.
> So holds the Writer for his private Ends,
> Sure ne'er to be abandon'd by his Friends.

If the above Nonsense deserved a serious Answer, the Writer of it hath,
in the same Paper, given us the following; in which he complains, no less
pathetically, of a worse Conduct to us in our Allies.

['Letters from Bois-le-duc, of the 8th Instant, N. S. say, that considerable
Repairs are making at the House occupied by the Duke of Cumberland at
Eyndhoven; from whence they would infer, that his Royal Highness may
probably pass the Winter there. They also tell us, that the Orders given to
the Troops in that Neighbourhood to march have been countermanded. In
the mean Time the fifth and last Column of the Austrian Army, under
Field Marshal Bathiani, is marched away for the Empire; but his Excellency
is yet at Ruremond, with some other Generals.—Will all our Endeavours
for a *general Peace* produce at last a *separate* one between *France* and
———?'

THE SAME LONDON EVENING POST.]

> *Hic est quem quæris; ille quem requiris,*
> *Tota lectus in Anglia,* POSTIS.

INDEX OF NAMES, PLACES, AND TOPICS

In Introduction, Text, Appendices, and Notes
(Coverage of topics is necessarily selective. In addition to the main listing the reader should consult the 'Fielding' entry, where will be found content analyses of the works reprinted in this volume, as well as of the editorial matter. Appendix VI is covered only in respect of the names and places to which the *JJ* commentator, not his source, alludes. In this index Fielding's own notes are designated by an asterisk in front of the number.)